Mastering

Hyper-V™ Deployment

Mastering
Hyper-V™ Deployment

Aidan Finn

Patrick Lownds

WILEY

Wiley Publishing, Inc.

Acquisitions Editor: Agatha Kim
Development Editor: Sara Barry
Technical Editor: Hans Vredevoort
Production Editor: Rachel Gigliotti
Copy Editor: Kim Wimpsett
Editorial Manager: Pete Gaughan
Production Manager: Tim Tate
Vice President and Executive Group Publisher: Richard Swadley
Vice President and Publisher: Neil Edde
Book Designers: Maureen Forys and Judy Fung
Proofreader: Nancy Bell
Indexer: Ted Laux
Project Coordinator, Cover: Lynsey Stanford
Cover Designer: Ryan Sneed
Cover Image: © Pete Gardner/DigitalVision/Getty Images

ISBN: 978-0-470-87653-4

Library of Congress Cataloging-in-Publication Data

Finn, Aidan, 1974-
Mastering Hyper-V deployment / Aidan Finn, Patrick Lownds.
p. cm.
ISBN 978-0-470-87653-4 (pbk.)
ISBN 978-1-118-00313-8 (ebk.)
ISBN 978-1-118-00315-2 (ebk.)
ISBN 978-1-118-00314-5 (ebk.)
1. Microsoft Windows server Hyper-V. 2. Virtual computer systems. I. Lownds, Patrick, 1970- II. Title.
QA76.9.V5F56 2011
005.4'476—dc22

2010037960

10 9 8 7 6 5 4 3 2 1

Dear Reader,

Thank you for choosing *Mastering Hyper-V Deployment*. This book is part of a family of premium-quality Sybex books, all of which are written by outstanding authors who combine practical experience with a gift for teaching.

Sybex was founded in 1976. More than 30 years later, we're still committed to producing consistently exceptional books. With each of our titles, we're working hard to set a new standard for the industry. From the paper we print on to the authors we work with, our goal is to bring you the best books available.

I hope you see all that reflected in these pages. I'd be very interested to hear your comments and get your feedback on how we're doing. Feel free to let me know what you think about this or any other Sybex book by sending me an email at `nedde@wiley.com`. If you think you've found a technical error in this book, please visit `http://sybex.custhelp.com`. Customer feedback is critical to our efforts at Sybex.

Best regards,

Neil Edde
Vice President and Publisher
Sybex, an Imprint of Wiley

To my family who made this possible.

Acknowledgments

So many people have helped with this book — many more people than I can thank here; after all, I have to think of the rain forests.

I knew that I would need help with writing this book. The deadlines would be tight, and the book needed to include some topics I haven't had much experience with. I asked fellow virtualization Microsoft Valuable Professional (MVP) Patrick Lownds to help with some of the chapters. Patrick is a detail-oriented person, and I knew he would provide you with complete knowledge in subjects that I have not dealt with. I could not have completed this book without his help. This book is a better product because of Patrick's knowledge and his willingness to share.

I was asked if I had a preference for the person who would be the technical reviewer for the book. This person had to ensure that everything we wrote was valid. I wanted someone with that expertise but also a person who would question me and raise alternative points of view. Hans Vredevoort was my first and ideal choice. Hans, a respected clustering MVP and virtualization expert, is a consultant in the Netherlands who works with all the technologies in this book. Hans didn't let me down; he corrected many mistakes and made me think, and I thank him for his efforts.

There are many people at Sybex who made this book possible. Rachel Gigliotti and Kim Wimpsett corrected my many grammatical mistakes, made it more understandable, and improved the quality of this book. Sara Barry managed the project and was always a joy to work with. Sara is the person who kept us on schedule and juggled all the pieces when the inevitable problems would occur. I also have to thank Agatha Kim. I approached Agatha with a very raw concept, and she helped me mold the idea into this book. I could not have done this without her faith in this project and the chance that she took with me, a first-time lead author.

Fellow MVPs, my friends on the Internet (especially those on the Minasi Forum), and colleagues I know in the Irish IT community have taught me so much and helped and encouraged me over the years. Ben Armstrong (aka the Virtual PC Guy) in Redmond and Dave Northey, Wilbour Craddock, and Enda Flynn in Microsoft Ireland have helped and given me opportunities that have changed my life.

Mark Minasi is a friend, mentor, and inspiration for me. Not only have I learned a considerable amount from Mark over the years, but he gave me my first opportunity as an author. I will be forever grateful for his belief in me and his endless encouragement. Mark is the rare person who enjoys helping and seeing others succeed.

Finally, I have to thank my family and friends. My mother and father brought me up to always seek further education, to investigate why things work, and to think independently. They, and my sister, have been supporters without whom I would never have reached this point.

—Aidan Finn

About the Author

Aidan Finn (B.Sc., MCSE, MVP) has been working in IT since 1996. He has worked as a consultant, contractor, and systems administrator for various companies in Ireland and with clients around Europe. In recent years, Aidan has worked with VMware ESX, Hyper-V, and Microsoft System Center. Currently, Aidan is working as a senior infrastructure consultant in Dublin, Ireland.

Aidan is the leader of the Windows User Group in Ireland. He regularly speaks at user group events and conferences about Windows Server, desktop management, virtualization, and System Center. Aidan was also a Microsoft Most Valuable Professional (MVP) on System Center Configuration Manager in 2008. He was awarded MVP status with virtual machine expertise in 2009. He is a member of the Microsoft Springboard STEP program and is one of the Microsoft System Center Influencers. Aidan has worked closely with Microsoft, including online interviews, launch events, and road shows, and has worked as a technical reviewer for the Microsoft Official Curriculum course on Windows Server 2008 R2 virtualization.

Aidan wrote four chapters of *Mastering Windows Server 2008 R2.*

About the Contributing Author

Patrick Lownds (MCSE, MCTS, and MVP) has been working in the IT industry since 1988. He has worked as a junior IT analyst, systems engineer, consultant, and solution architect for various companies within the United Kingdom, working across a number of industry verticals for clients in the United Kingdom and Europe. In recent years, Patrick has worked with Citrix XenServer, VMware ESX, Microsoft Hyper-V, and a number of Microsoft System Center products. Currently, Patrick is working as a solution architect with Hewlett Packard and is based in Wood Street, London.

Patrick is the co-founder and co-contributor of the Microsoft Virtualization User Group in the United Kingdom. He regularly speaks at user group events and conferences about Windows Server, virtualization and System Center and is a member of the Microsoft System Center Influencers program. Patrick is a Microsoft Most Valuable Professional (MVP) and was awarded MVP status with the virtual machine expertise in 2009.

Patrick has worked closely with Microsoft for a number of years, including technology adoption programs, events, and road shows, and was a technical reviewer for *Microsoft Hyper-V Security Guide.*

Contents at a Glance

Contents

Foreword

After many years and many missteps, Microsoft has given us a top-quality server virtualization tool, Hyper-V Server. It's about time, then, for us Windows types to understand it. After all, if you already have Windows Server 2008 or 2008 R2, then Hyper-V is essentially free and in the box, so why not take it through its paces and see what it can do for you?

In my life as a technologist, I've been lucky enough to have seen great changes in the computer business. The 1970s brought us personal computers, and the 1980s brought us operating systems and useful applications for those computers. The 1990s brought an explosion of networking and *inter*networking, which led to another explosion: a massive increase in the number of computers needed to *run* that Internet. Fortunately, the 21st century's first decade brought virtualization, the technology that's gone furthest in reducing the number of computers needed to run the world. Virtualization is a technology that can save money, make IT greener, and ease the task of keeping our computers running reliably. Virtualization can do those things, however, only if we take the time to truly understand virtualization technology or, alternatively, if we're smart enough to find someone with the knowledge, tenacity, and hard-earned battle scars to handle that virtualization stuff for us, and to do it well.

In my life as an employer, a colleague, or a friend to techies of all stripes, I've been lucky to have worked with many folks in the IT community. Rarely, however, do I meet someone who doesn't just learn the minimum necessary to get by in some IT-related task. Of course, we *all* want to understand things "down to the bare metal," but as a rule, time pressures on and off the job often conspire to keep that from happening. My friend Aidan Finn is an exception to that rule, though. Once he gets interested in a subject, he refuses to leave it alone until he has mastered it as fully as is possible—and that quality is why I'm pleased that this book has found its way out of his cranium and onto the printed page.

Server virtualization can deliver much, but it's not all wine and roses, and newcomers to Microsoft Hyper-V shouldn't expect that a few wizards will be sufficient to get them up and running. Which servers are appropriate to virtualize, and which are not? How can you back up and, more important, *restore* virtual machines? Can you uproot and transplant an existing physical server into a virtual machine, and how best might you do that? Is it dangerous to run domain controllers as virtual machines? Will you find securing a virtual system harder than securing a physical one? Those are questions that I hear on my online forum—a forum that Aidan has been an active member for years—nearly every day. And nearly every day, Aidan is the guy (or *one* of the guys—it's a smart and feisty lot) with the answer, so if you're looking for Hyper-V help, you've come to the right place.

With that said, I think it's time for me to grab a seat, dig into a bucket of popcorn, and let Aidan take the stage. Come join me; there's an empty chair over here! The show is about to begin, and you don't want to miss any of it!

—Mark Minasi

Author of *Mastering Microsoft Windows Server* series

Introduction

I have been working with Hyper-V since the beta release of it for Windows Server 2008. There was a lot to learn with the brand new product. It quickly became evident that Hyper-V was just a tiny piece of the entire puzzle. A Hyper-V project is much more than just a virtualization project. It is a project that will change how your server and application infrastructure works and is managed. Microsoft's promise of dynamic IT and optimized infrastructure was finally possible thanks to Hyper-V and System Center. Many first-time Hyper-V users will be encountering Microsoft's System Center family of products for the first time. They will see how tightly the products work together to provide an agile and highly managed environment.

I started blogging (`www.aidanfinn.com`) about Hyper-V not long after I started to work with it. I also talked about it at conferences in Ireland, Europe, and the United States. It became clear that although there were many fine publications on the individual products, there was little to help those engineers, consultants, or administrators who wanted to install a complete Hyper-V infrastructure. The same questions, requests for help, and Internet searches kept recurring. It seemed to me that a lot of valuable information was distributed across many sources. Some essential pieces were falling through the cracks and were receiving no coverage at all. We were missing a consolidated guide for deploying the complete enterprise Hyper-V solution, from start to finish.

That is what led me to the idea of writing this book. I wanted to combine everything I knew into one reference that would guide a person through a Windows Server 2008 R2 Hyper-V project. I wanted to give you help to get from the start of the project when you need to ask the right questions to the end of the project when you are implementing those last pieces of the infrastructure that are the difference between a good solution and an excellent solution.

The timing of this book worked out rather nicely. Hyper-V is more than just a feature in Windows Server 2008 R2. It's a collection of products and accelerators that encompasses many product groups in Microsoft, each with their own release schedules. We would have been unable to produce this book last year because many of the components that we have included have become available only in the last few months. Some of the products included were released as we developed the book, and some were still just beta releases! You will never be bored as a Hyper-V expert.

I hope you find value in this book. Many months of work, investigation, troubleshooting, late nights, and long weekends have gone into this project. It is my wish that you find the guidance and knowledge that will help you master your Hyper-V deployment.

Who Should Buy This Book

This book aims to give information for the complete life cycle of a Hyper-V deployment project. It covers the initial proposal, planning of the project, gathering information, designing the solution, implementing Hyper-V, installing the systems management solutions, and implementing backup and disaster recovery solutions.

This book is aimed at engineers, administrators, and consultants who will be working on a project to deploy Hyper-V or who will manage the resulting infrastructure. The following are the technologies covered in this book:

- Microsoft Assessment and Planning Toolkit
- Windows Server 2008 R2 Hyper-V and Windows Server 2008 R2 with Service Pack 1 Hyper-V
- System Center Virtual Machine Manager 2008 R2
- Virtual Machine Servicing Tool 3.0
- System Center Operations Manager 2007/2007 R2
- System Center Data Protection Manager 2010
- System Center Essentials 2010

The Mastering Series

The Mastering series from Sybex provides outstanding instruction for readers with intermediate and advanced skills, in the form of top-notch training and development for those already working in their field, and provides clear, serious education for those aspiring to become pros. Every Mastering book includes the following:

- Real-World Scenarios, ranging from case studies to interviews, that show how the tool, technique, or knowledge presented is applied in actual practice
- Skill-based instruction, with chapters organized around real tasks rather than abstract concepts or subjects
- Self-review test questions, so you can be certain you're equipped to do the job right

What Is Covered in This Book

Here is a glance at what's in each chapter.

Chapter 1: Proposing Virtualization talks about the typical start of a Hyper-V project: the proposal. This chapter discusses the technical merits of a virtualization project that is based on Hyper-V and the many real improvements and meaningful cost savings to a business.

Chapter 2: The Architecture of Hyper-V introduces you to the features of Hyper-V and how things work under the hood. This information is crucial for designing or implementing a solution. This chapter includes the new features of Windows Server 2008 R2 and a discussion of Dynamic Memory, a new feature that was introduced with Service Pack 1 for Windows Server 2008 R2.

Chapter 3: The Project Plan looks at how to create a successful project plan. No one plan will be suitable for everyone, but we give you information about what to think about so that you can design a plan that is suitable for your project.

Chapter 4: Assessing the Existing Infrastructure works from the assumption that organizations will have some existing server infrastructure that will be migrated onto the new Hyper-V infrastructure. The chapter helps you assess the hardware, the operating systems, the applications, and their resource requirements so you can size a new Hyper-V infrastructure.

Chapter 5: Planning the Hardware Deployment covers designing the Hyper-V infrastructure using the information that is created from the assessment. There are many options, and you'll need guidance from the decision makers in your organization.

Chapter 6: Deploying Hyper-V deals with the implementation of the Hyper-V host servers including installation options and implementing the features of Hyper-V. This is where you should look if you want to read about implementing a Hyper-V cluster.

Chapter 7: Virtual Machine Manager 2008 R2 provides a step-by-step guide through the implementation of Virtual Machine Manager (VMM) 2008 R2.

Chapter 8: Virtualization Scenarios focuses on how to design virtual machines to suit the applications that are installed in them. This chapter helps you avoid the common pitfalls of unacceptable performance issues caused by virtual machines not designed appropriately for the applications that were installed in them.

Chapter 9: Operations Manager 2007 focuses on System Center Operations Manager (OpsMgr) 2007. OpsMgr will monitor the health and performance of your entire network, including Hyper-V.

Chapter 10: Data Protection and Recovery explains how you can use System Center Data Protection Manager (DPM) 2010 to back up your Hyper-V systems, the virtual machines, and their data.

Chapter 11: The Small and Medium Business covers Hyper-V for the small and medium business category. We discuss running Small Business Server (SBS) 2008 as a virtual machine and look at System Center Essentials (SCE) 2010, which includes some of the added features of VMM for managing Hyper-V and virtual machines.

Chapter 12: Security is where we talk about the thorny issue of antivirus software on your Hyper-V host servers and how to patch your Hyper-V infrastructure using Virtual Machine Servicing Tool 3.0.

Chapter 13: Business Continuity deals with implementing solutions for disaster recovery, or business continuity. Virtualization makes it easier to implement a disaster recovery site because most of what we deal with is stored as files or is stored on a centralized storage system.

Appendix A: The Bottom Line gathers together all the Master It problems from the chapters and provides a solution for each.

Appendix B: New and Upcoming Products for Hyper-V introduces you to some of the emerging virtualization solutions from Microsoft. Unfortunately, they appeared too late or are still in development, and we could not include them in this book.

How to Contact the Authors

We welcome feedback from you about this book or about books you'd like to see from us in the future. You can reach us by writing to aidanfinn@hotmail.com or patrick_lownds@hotmail.com.

You can find my (Aidan's) blog, where I talk about ongoing developments with Windows Server, desktop management, System Center, and Hyper-V at www.aidanfinn.com. You can also follow me on Twitter @joe_elway.

Part 1

Overview

Chapter 1

Proposing Virtualization

The first phase of any project, whether you're an internal consultant or an external consultant, is to develop a proposal for that project so that you can gain executive commitment. The best way to secure acceptance is to cater to both the technical requirements and the often overlooked business case requirements.

The technical solution should be a business-focused solution and be understandable by both technical and nontechnical staff. It should answer the typical questions. What does this project mean for my company? What are the implications for my company? How can we successfully move forward based on our current environment?

The results should be a vision for the project, executive consensus, and a defined set of clear next steps. The proposal should model areas of business value and map technology against that business value. Case studies, reference sites, white papers, and ROI analysis have a part to play when developing both your business case and your technical case.

Interestingly, it appears that Hyper-V is being implemented not for the expected "virtualization project" but as a component of some other solution required by the business.

In this chapter, you will learn what the elements are for both the technical case and the business case when proposing virtualization.

The Business Case

Virtualization enables you to pool and share IT resources to better serve your business and create a business-ready dynamic infrastructure. From a business perspective, the pooling and sharing of IT resources allows IT supply to keep pace with the ever-changeable business demand.

From a cost perspective, the pooling and sharing of resources helps you increase the utilization of IT assets and thus reduce your total cost of ownership (TCO), in terms of both capital expense (CAPEX) and operating expense (OPEX) costs. This is achieved in part by enabling greater use of your physical resources.

Line-of-Business Application Continuity

Customers are turning to virtualization to enhance their existing business continuity strategies (BCSs) and to provide a simplified form of business continuity for existing x86 platforms as they adopt virtualization. Hyper-V provides a robust, reliable, and secure platform that isolates applications and operating systems from their underlying hardware, dramatically reducing the complexity of implementing and testing business continuity service.

In its most simplistic form, this involves the implementation of replicated storage to support the constituent parts of the virtual machine. Storage vendors for the most part provide either in-box or add-on replication capabilities, which are easily enabled. Replicating the storage presented to the virtualized infrastructure, even without storage array–based replication techniques leveraging software vendors, provides the basis for a business continuity service.

As long as there is sufficient capacity at the designated business continuity site, the virtual machines being protected — independent of the underlying servers, storage infrastructure, and networking — allow for the quantity of servers at the business continuity site to be different. This is in contrast to a traditional x86 business continuity solution, which typically involved maintaining a direct one-to-one relationship between the production and the business continuity site, in terms of servers, storage infrastructure, management infrastructure, and networking hardware.

Storage replication is a simple, yet powerful, approach. However, there are a number of considerations to be made to implement this type of solution in an effective manner. Building a generic business continuity solution can be extremely complex and most physical and virtual implementations, while often automated, are often heavily customized to meet both business and technical requirements.

Centralized Computing

Virtualization offers new methods of implementing centralized computing. Take the concept of a Virtual Desktop Infrastructure (VDI). VDI introduces a new way of managing end-user computing environments. VDI allows IT administrators to host and administer end-user desktops on a virtualized infrastructure running in the datacenter.

Users access their desktop using a remote desktop protocol and often a thin client device. While sharing similarities with other computing models, VDI offers many new and compelling benefits for increasing the manageability, performance, and security of end-user devices. Although VDI is not the panacea today, it is an architecture that is leveraging a centralized computing model.

Centralized computing, however, is not limited to virtualization. Centralized computing through physical consolidation is where servers, storage, and networking from many locations, typically datacenters, are physically relocated to fewer locations. The IT infrastructure is brought under a common operational framework, which has the following advantages:

- Consistent level of service
- Improved level of security
- Reduced operational costs
- Standardized management approach
- Clearer understanding of maintenance, power, and cooling costs

Conversely, centralized computing through virtualization is where the hardware remains in the same location but the number of underutilized servers is reduced, or consolidated, using a consistent methodology to map physical assets to virtual ones. The advantages of this type of centralized computing model are similar to physical consolidation:

- Consistent level of service
- Reduced operational costs
- Standardized management approach

Lower Costs

Virtualization helps drive down both CAPEX and OPEX costs. CAPEX cost savings can come in the form of reduced expenses for the acquisition of hardware and the potential savings for data-center real estate. OPEX costs stem from the reduction in power and cooling costs, management costs, and the costs associated with server downtime or outage costs.

To assist you with developing your business case, Microsoft has made available a return on investment (ROI) calculator that was developed independently by leading TCO/ROI experts at Alinean (`www.alinean.com`). The ROI calculator exists as a sales enablement tool and was designed to help quantify the TCO/ROI savings and competitive advantage of Microsoft's integrated virtualization solution. For more details on the Microsoft Integrated Virtualization ROI Calculator, take a look at Chapter 4.

Server Hardware

Moving to a virtual environment can help you cut costs by reducing the number of physical servers necessary to support your infrastructure. By consolidating your server hardware, you will achieve higher utilization levels and thus reduce your overall hardware requirements.

Power and Cooling

Virtualization can help you take control of rapidly rising power and cooling costs. The savings typically stem from reductions in the number of physical servers in your environment. Advances in both modern hardware and operating systems have parts to play. Microsoft introduced the concept of core parking in Windows 2008 R2; core parking is the ability for the operating system to put cores of processors and entire processors into a low power state when not in use.

Hyper-V R2 supports core parking by allowing virtual machine threads to be moved between cores to enable core parking to happen.

Server Provisioning Costs

Virtualization allows you to rapidly provision virtual machines in less time, which in turn leads to reduced infrastructure management costs. Through the use of System Center Virtual Machine Manager (SCVMM), the act of creating a new virtual machine can occur in one of three ways:

- Creating virtual machines from a template
- Using an existing virtual machine (cloning)
- Using a blank virtual hard disk

In addition, SCVMM supports various different options for provisioning virtual machines. By leveraging its built-in PowerShell script library, you can automate the entire provisioning process.

Green Computing

Energy consumption is a critical issue for IT organizations today, whether the goal is to reduce your costs, save the planet, or keep your datacenter running. One of the easiest ways to reduce the energy demands of your datacenter is through server consolidation and dynamic systems management of your server assets.

Virtualization is a fundamental component of a green computing initiative. Consolidating physical servers into one or more virtual servers is a more efficient use of resources, which in turn means less hardware is deployed, and thus less power is consumed. Less hardware and a reduction on overall power consumption means cost savings and a smaller carbon footprint.

However, green computing is not just about consolidating physical servers and what consolidation ratios you achieve. It is as much about the design and manufacture of that hardware, including any peripherals and the entire life cycle of that hardware, from initial purchase to final disposal.

There are a number of industry initiatives. The Green Grid is a global consortium of IT companies seeking to improve energy efficiency within datacenters and business computing environments around the world. Its website (`www.thegreengrid.org`) has a number of useful resources and tools that may assist with the further development of your green computing strategy.

To calculate your potential green savings, Microsoft has developed a sustainability calculator to estimate your company's carbon footprint and see the potential savings that are achievable through consolidation. For a preview of this tool and to see how it could benefit your organization, visit this site:

`http://www.microsoft.com/environment/greenit/Preview.aspx?type=server`

Self-Provisioning

SCVMM provides a web-based portal where authorized users can provision new virtual machines without directly involving IT staff. This capability especially targets software test and development teams, which often set up and tear down temporary virtual machines for application development purposes.

SCVMM administrators grant users permissions to create and operate their own virtual machines within a controlled environment and on a limited set of Hyper-V hosts. This limited set of Hyper-V hosts is typically organized within a Host Group, which is a logical container within SCVMM. The SCVMM administrator is required to create self-service user roles, which determine the scope of the user's actions on their designated virtual machines.

To create, operate, and manage their virtual machines, self-service users use the SCVMM Self-Service Portal. This website provides a controlled environment for users in the self-service user role. The administrator determines which host groups the self-service users can create virtual machines on. When a self-service user creates a virtual machine, the virtual machine is automatically placed on the most suitable host in the host group.

Active Directory users or groups can be added to self-service user roles. The permissions granted to the user role apply to all members of the user group whether they are individuals or groups.

Virtual machine owners can be individual users or groups. Under individual ownership, an individual owns, operates, and manages its own virtual machines. Under group ownership, virtual machines are owned, operated, and managed by the group.

You can set a virtual machine quota in a self-service user role to limit the number of virtual machines that a user or group can deploy. Quota points are assigned to the virtual machine template or templates that self-service users use to create their virtual machines.

Quota points apply only to virtual machines on a host. If a self-service user is allowed to store virtual machines, the quota does not apply to virtual machines stored in the SCVMM library. When the self-service user's quota is reached, the user cannot create any new virtual machines until an existing virtual machine is removed or stored.

Business Continuity Planning

Business continuity planning (BCP) is the ability to minimize scheduled and unscheduled downtime, using the host-based failover features of the virtualization platform and guest-based clustering.

Windows 2008 R2 and Hyper-V includes support for host-based clustering of virtual machines. This allows an organization to meet the availability thresholds previously reserved only for cluster-aware applications. Because virtualization clustering allows a guest machine to be transferred across physical nodes with zero downtime, the number of machines that can be targeted for virtualization dramatically increases. This is particularly compelling for applications that grow into mission-critical status but were never designed with high availability in mind.

In addition to the benefits of failover clustering, virtualization of target machines can greatly enhance the business continuity and recovery processes. Because each virtual machine is a collection of files on a physical host, the files (VHDs, AVHDs, and so on) can be moved to a new location, including alternate datacenters, and be brought back online without requiring a complete rebuild. Alternate datacenters can consist of far fewer physical machines, specifically designed to provide an emergency level of service. Windows 2008 R2 and Hyper-V also introduces the feature of Live Migration, where running virtual machines can transfer from one clustered host node to another with zero downtime. There are two options for using Live Migration:

- Planned
- Unplanned

Unplanned migrations occur when the active node (Hyper-V host) running the guests becomes unexpectedly unavailable. In this case, the other nodes in the cluster recognize the failure, cluster resources are moved, and the guest machines are brought back up on available cluster nodes, reducing the overall downtime. Note that in an unplanned migration, the guest machine state is lost and is restarted, just as if the "power cord" were pulled.

In a planned Live Migration, guests are transferred between nodes while they are running. This process is carried out automatically by either the Failover Cluster Management tool, a PowerShell script, or SCVMM. In the BCP scenario, the flexibility of moving machines between locations supports the business driver for functionality in the event of a disaster. Windows 2008 R2 and Hyper-V provides an organization with the following benefits:

- Ensures continuity or uninterrupted provisioning of operations, servers, and services
- Reduces service interruptions with failover clustering on the host
- Allows almost immediate rebalancing of resources to guest machines to meet growing or changing business requirements
- Improves disaster response and business recovery requirements by minimizing the infrastructure necessary to run all mission-critical applications under a recovery scenario

The Technical Case

A virtualized environment increases IT flexibility because a varied range of resources can be added, changed, or moved as needed to meet the changes in business demand. Resources can be scaled to either increase or decrease based on changing workloads and patterns. As a by-product, virtualization also improves IT's level of resiliency by simplifying backup, failover, disaster recovery, and business continuity solutions.

Test and Development

Virtualization can maximize test hardware, reducing costs, improving life-cycle management, and improving test coverage. Nearly all test and development machines are good candidates for virtualization, unless you are performing specific production workload tests.

Virtualization of the test and development environment allows you to do the following:

- Consolidate hardware resources and better utilize hardware with consolidated workloads.
- Improve and maximize hardware utilization, especially for machines with short lives or involved in destructive life cycles.
- Reduce TCO for hardware, electrical, cooling, power, and rack space footprint.
- Greatly reduce time to provision new servers (on virtual hardware) to developers as fully imaged servers.
- Reduce time to migrate new software from development to test to production.
- Increase business agility by moving to a dynamic platform.
- Streamline test and development efforts with multiple iterations of the same basic image, differencing hard drives, and undo disks.
- Rapidly duplicate a production environment.
- Access operating system and software CD image from virtual media libraries.
- Schedule test environment provisioning.
- Utilize templates to deploy multiple virtual machines at any given time in a single operation.

Standardization

Hardware and operating system standardization has been considered a best practice for many years. IT administrators running datacenters with standardized server hardware and operating system images typically have fewer headaches than those working in mixed environments. This best practice evolved in the physical world and is more significant now when it comes to virtualization and Cloud-based computing.

Standardizing with two or three types of server hardware and one or two operating system images has the advantages of reusable common components and a flexible and adaptable environment, providing a higher level of technical awareness, simplifying upgrade, and easing ongoing management.

Standardization within a virtualized environment is achieved slightly differently. Although the same standards as mentioned earlier apply to the Hyper-V host, now we are dealing with virtual hardware, and this is where virtual machine templates come in.

With templates, you can avoid many repetitive installation and configuration tasks. The result is a fully installed, ready-to-operate virtual machine in less time than a manual installation could ever achieve. Templates are also used to help enforce consistency and standards. Deploying from templates helps enforce corporate standards for such things as hotfixes/patches, hardening, antivirus, and management software in any machine connected to the corporate network.

A virtual machine template is a library resource consisting of the following parts:

- Virtual hard disk
- Hardware profile
- Guest operating system profile

Rapid Deployment

Rapid deployment allows administrators to take advantage of SAN provider technologies to clone a LUN containing a virtual hard disk and present it to the host while still utilizing the SCVMM template so the operating system customization and Integration Services installation can still be applied. This occurs in near real time and removes the need for the virtual hard disk component of a new virtual machine to be copied slowly over the network. This allows and supports a number of differing scenarios:

- Automated and rapid deployment of large virtualized environments
- Automated and rapid deployment of grouped virtual machines concurrently
- Reduced workload for the deployment of similar virtual machines, such as in a VDI scenario
- Provisioning of an environment for disaster recovery and business continuity planning purposes

Greater Flexibility

Virtualization increases an organization's level of flexibility. It removes the dependency between the operating system and the hardware and allows you to grow, shrink, or move your virtual machines, without having to modify the underlying hardware used.

Virtualization allows you to manage your production environment more flexibly, from anywhere, at lower costs and with a reduced level of risk. By leveraging virtualization, you can provide small-scale environments that are cost effective and that scale up very easily.

Hyper-V R2 increases this level of flexibility by introducing a new processor compatibility feature. Processor compatibility allows you to move a running virtual machine to a physical computer with different set of processor features, without having to restart the virtual machine.

This setting may reduce the overall performance of the application in the virtual machine on nodes that would otherwise support advanced virtualization hardware techniques. However, it will allow virtual machines to be live or quick migrated between nodes of differing processor capabilities.

High Availability

Leveraging virtualization for high availability purposes provides businesses with a vast array of high availability solutions from both Microsoft and third parties. These solutions provide high availability for applications that need to recover from failures to complete fault-tolerant solutions for those critical applications that must run continuously without service interruption.

Virtual machines that do not have cluster-aware software can leverage the high availability features in Windows 2008 R2 to implement high availability through host-based clustering. The level of availability that a host-based clustering provides is not as high as with application-specific clustering or guest-based clustering, because the operating systems or applications deployed within the virtual machines are not necessarily cluster-aware.

With Hyper-V R2, a configuration with host-based clustering provides support for both planned and unplanned downtime. During unplanned downtime, the virtual machines will be restarted on a node within the cluster, and during planned downtime, the virtual machines will be transferred, either via Live or Quick Migration, from one node to another.

Conversely, guest-based clustering enables high availability of services and applications at the virtual layer.

The Private Cloud

The private Cloud is an internal service-oriented infrastructure, optimized for both performance and cost, which is deployed inside your datacenter. You can think of the private Cloud as IT-as-a-service, where virtual machines are provisioned to meet business demand. Virtualization effectively unlocks Cloud computing and is a fundamental building block of Cloud computing. The private Cloud in Microsoft's terms is powered by a number of different server products, including Windows 2008 R2, Hyper-V R2, and the System Center family of products. The private Cloud offers a number of benefits:

- A flexible and familiar infrastructure with a common platform to build and deploy applications between clouds and reduce development and deployment time on new services
- Integrated resource access that enables federated services between clouds, helping ensure capacity and resources needed to achieve the business requirements
- The agility to develop applications and services once and then deploy them in and across any cloud environment, enabling rapid response to changing business needs

Chapter 2

The Architecture of Hyper-V

You cannot successfully design, manage, and troubleshoot a product if you do not understand how it works. Understanding the architecture of Hyper-V requires a little bit of work, but it isn't too difficult. Having an appreciation for the architecture brings many advantages. Consultants can sell and assist with virtualization solutions in an informed and accurate manner. Engineers can design solutions that make the most of the features. Administrators can manage and troubleshoot the product more easily.

You might have already worked with a previous version of Hyper-V. We still recommend that you read this chapter. IT professionals work with many technologies in the course of their jobs, and it is easy to forget little facts that you may have once been able to recite. This chapter will provide you with a refresher, keeping you on your feet when those difficult questions or scenarios eventually arise. Those who have worked with VMware or XenServer will also find this chapter useful. A lot of the ideas are the same. You'll find that you will reuse a lot of knowledge; you just need to understand how things are named and implemented in Hyper-V and System Center.

This chapter will start off by looking at the various kinds of virtualization technologies and how they fit together. We will introduce those who are new to Hyper-V to its features. We will also be looking at the new features that are included in Windows Server 2008 R2 and with Service Pack 1 for Windows Server 2008 R2. Some of those features are game changers, altering how you will design or size a Hyper-V architecture. You will see, as the chapter progresses, how the features of Hyper-V can be used to improve the performance and abilities of the other virtualization technologies.

No enterprise IT infrastructure is complete without a management system. In fact, even the most basic IT infrastructure needs solutions such as a backup and recovery system. Hyper-V is unique because there is an integrated management system for it that spans the physical and virtual network. We will wrap up the chapter by briefly introducing the management systems that are available from Microsoft for managing Hyper-V.

In this chapter, you will learn to

- Understand the architecture of Hyper-V
- List and describe the features of Hyper-V
- Understand the management options of Hyper-V

The Many Kinds of Virtualization

Hyper-V is Microsoft's newest virtualization product. Yes, Microsoft does have more than one. An enterprise may have many virtualization solutions, some of which may be purchased from Microsoft. There are solutions where many of these solutions will work together to provide business services. Understanding what these technologies are and how they can work together can provide you with a distinct advantage when proposing or designing a solution. Our focus in this book is on Hyper-V, but it is a good idea to introduce you to some of those other solutions.

Profile Virtualization

This is a technology that almost all engineers, administrators, and consultants have worked with, but they probably have never thought of it as a virtualization solution. We're going to explain what it is and why it really is a virtualization solution.

When a user logs into a Windows computer, they are provided with a folder containing data. This folder, called the *profile*, is usually unique to the user. By default, the user is provided with a local profile. The local profile contains all the settings for the user. These can be stored as files but also in HKEY_CURRENT_USER in the registry. This is saved as the `USER.DAT` file in the profile. The profile also provides folders for the user to save their data. By default, documents are stored in My Documents. Internet Explorer favorites are stored in the Favorites folder. Music is stored in My Music.

Not only is the local profile unique to the user, but it is unique to the user and the computer. If a user logs into another computer, then they get a different local profile. This means that their settings need to be re-created, and their files need to be copied. This is rather troublesome in an enterprise environment. Administrators prefer computers to be treated like burnable appliances. If a problem takes too long to repair, then administrators like to rebuild the computer. Local profiles cause a delay and a complication issue here because the administrator needs to copy the profile to somewhere safe and restore it. This also needs to be done when computers are being rebuilt with a new operating system image, causing time delays and additional engineering, not to mention the risk of an irate user calling the help desk should something go wrong (and you know it will on occasion).

The solution we got was roaming profiles. This separated the user data from the computer. In other words, it was virtualized. The profile folders are stored on a file share. A user's roaming profile (only the changes) is downloaded to the computer whenever they log in. The changes to the profile are saved to the file share when the user logs out. Now the user can log into any permitted Windows computer in the Active Directory forest and get their settings and files.

There are some concerns with roaming profiles. A user can log into many computers, each with different software installed. Software settings will be saved into their profile, and this can eventually lead to clutter and even profile corruption. There are problems when users log into different types of computers, such as desktops or servers (Terminal Servers or Remote Desktop Services Session Hosts). Windows Vista introduced the version 2 (V2) profile, meaning that a user who logged into Windows XP and Windows Vista (and later) would be back to having two discrete profiles with different files and settings.

The release of Windows 2000 introduced a new term and some new ideas to those working with user profiles. IntelliMirror, the idea of giving the same user experience wherever they logged in, gives you folder redirection. This has evolved over time. Windows Vista and Windows Server 2008 brought folder redirection to a point where you can consider it instead of roaming profiles. The idea is that you can use Active Directory Group Policy to change the location of specified folders in the profile. You can configure the profile, for example, to move My Documents to a user's home directory in a network file share. The user will really be browsing and saving to a folder in their home directory instead of using My Documents in the profile. Now data is isolated from the profile, making it available on mixed operating systems and platforms.

There are some other scenarios where additional, third-party products and solutions are required. It is not unusual to find third-party solutions in use when session virtualization systems are in place.

So, there you have it — you've been working with virtualization for all these years, and you never knew it. Profile virtualization has been with us for many years, isolating user data from the computer and making it mobile across the network.

How is this relevant to Hyper-V? It just so happens that you will probably use profile virtualization on other virtualization technologies such as Virtual Desktop Infrastructure or session virtualization, each of which can be built on Hyper-V.

Session Virtualization

Like profile virtualization, session virtualization will be a new term to many, even though they may have been working with the technology since the early 1990s.

Citrix WinFrame was a leader in session virtualization. Using code that was licensed from Microsoft, Citrix WinFrame used earlier versions of Windows Server to provide organizations with a way to centralize the end user computing environment. Users would work with terminals or stripped and locked-down computers on their desk. The terminal allowed them to log into a session on a specialist server. Many users could log into one server, sharing the processor, memory, and storage abilities. The arguments in favor of this technology were that you could centralize and secure data and applications, simplify the desktop computing environment, and make branch-office and distributed collaboration easier. In short, the total cost of ownership (TCO) would be much lower.

Microsoft added this technology in Windows NT 4.0 Terminal Server Edition. Microsoft formed a tight partnership with Citrix, and each company developed its solutions over the years. Windows Server 2008 R2 saw Terminal Services be renamed to Remote Desktop Services (but we'll come back to that later). Third parties competed with Citrix in developing solutions that would sit on Terminal Services to extend its native functionality and provide additional management solutions.

Microsoft often responded by adding features to match those from independent solutions. Windows Server 2008 saw the addition of three of those features. RemoteApp allowed Microsoft to offer more than just a desktop that was presented on the end user's screen. Now, an individual application could be presented in a seamless window. This allows users to access remote applications that are running on a server without any need to install it locally. The application runs on the centralized server and can access resources local to the server at LAN speeds. This has proved to be an excellent solution for remote application access issues such as cross-WAN data transfer or deployment complications.

Microsoft also gave us a Gateway. This allows SSL-encrypted and encapsulated Remote Desktop sessions. This allows easy access to RemoteApp applications or published desktops from the Internet. This can be seen as a way to replace complicated VPN solutions that often prove confusing for end users.

We also got a solution from Microsoft for the problem of printing. Prior to Windows Server 2008, printing was a nightmare for Terminal Services administrators. Drivers for every possible end user printer needed to be installed on terminal servers. Even if you had a management solution for that, you had to deal with the massive network requirements for print traffic. The terminal server (or a server local to it) was usually the print server. A stream of print data would travel from the print server to the physical printer. A 2 MB PDF document could lead to a LAN or WAN transfer of 20 MB of print data. That's when end users would call the help desk to complain about a print job taking an hour or that the WAN link was congested. Third-party solutions (which cost money) offered to resolve this using, ironically enough, PDF documents. A PDF would be created by the Terminal Server, be transferred to the Terminal Server client, and then be translated into a print job. This kept the large amount of print stream data between the Terminal Services client and the printer. That is, the print data stream stayed on a LAN link or on a USB/serial cable, where it normally would be in a normal desktop computing environment.

Microsoft offered EasyPrint with Windows Server 2008. It works similarly to the PDF solutions, but it uses Microsoft's XPS document standard. The print job is converted into an XPS document, and this small file is transferred to the Remote Desktop client where it is decompressed. Another benefit is that it is printer independent. Administrators do not need to install any printer drivers on the Terminal Servers. The user's printer appears in the session and is processed on their client when the XPS document arrives. The user can simply connect to a Terminal Server, print, and go. The real-world experience is excellent for the end user, not to mention the Terminal Server administrator, whose job suddenly becomes much easier.

Some organizations completely swapped their desktops for session virtualization solutions. Some organizations did partial deployments. They saw it as a way to provide an alternative to VPN. It was also used where there were difficult-to-deploy applications or where applications wanted to transfer lots of data across the WAN (the data and the application can be in the same LAN with Terminal Services).

But many did not deploy Terminal Services at all. One has to ask why this was the case. Costs did not necessarily reduce. Application distribution still had to be managed in larger Terminal Services deployments. Antivirus solutions, which are often licensed per user, still had to be installed and paid for. Desktop computers became cheaper, and terminals often are not more economic. Terminal software also needs to be maintained, adding another management system to the network. Basic tasks such as repairing an installation of Microsoft Office became an operation that came under the management of change control. With a desktop, a help-desk engineer could get a call and fix it in a few minutes. However, a Terminal Server is a mission-critical computing environment that could be used by dozens or even hundreds of users at once. Changes to it must be tightly controlled and are done by a server engineer rather than a help-desk staff member. That means IT becomes less responsive. Some applications just do not support or work well on session virtualization solutions. We have a potential solution for that, which we'll look at soon. The real killer could be licensing. The user requires a Windows Server CAL, a Terminal Services (Remote Desktop Services) CAL, and licensing for any third-party solution that sits on top of Terminal Services (such as Citrix). Don't be fooled into thinking application licensing would be cheaper; you still have to license for 100 copies of Microsoft Office (or anything else) if 100 users can use it.

That sounds like a negative, but session virtualization does have a place in the enterprise computing environment. Sometimes the negatives are far outweighed by the positives.

Profile virtualization works well with session virtualization. An end user may work with many session virtualization silos (a *silo* consists of Terminal Servers with a common application configuration) and desktop computers while maintaining one copy of their common settings and personal data. In other words, their data is always available no matter how they access business applications.

So, how does session virtualization fit in with Hyper-V? Many have found that running Windows Server 2008 R2 Remote Desktop Services session hosts (Terminal Servers as we used to call them) on Windows Server 2008 R2 with modern processors provides excellent performance with reduced hardware, licensing, implementation, ownership, and operational costs. This can mean that you could have many Remote Desktop Services session hosts running on a single Hyper-V Server, with each session host running many end user sessions. Those session hosts can be made highly available by placing them onto a Hyper-V cluster, reducing the impact of downtime caused by hardware maintenance or problems.

Application Virtualization

One of the pain points in providing new IT solutions to the business is the business application. Some applications won't work with others. Some applications are unstable, and this is accentuated on a terminal server. Some businesses need to be able to use different versions of the same application for third-party compatibility reasons.

The problems of application compatibility have become more apparent than ever in recent years with the release of Windows Vista and, subsequently, with the release of Windows 7. Even a medium-sized organization could have hundreds of desktop applications that need to be tested with each other when a new desktop build is being developed. This means there will be countless hours of deployment. Microsoft might expect you to deploy a new desktop operating system every two years, but you'll be lucky to do it every four years because of the time and expense required.

A little help came our way a few years ago. A number of vendors came up with application compatibility solutions. Microsoft acquired one of these and rebranded it as App-V. Application virtualization allows an application to be executed in a contained bubble that is isolated from the operating system and other applications. It can be streamed from a server to reduce the desktop footprint, and it can offer alternative user-centric request-deployment mechanisms (rather than the usual administrator push mechanism).

A computer can now run Office XP, Office 2003, and Office 2010. This is because the applications are not actually installed. A packaging process creates the bubble, and this bubble is executed on the computer. This allows for some interesting scenarios where application virtualization is used with other types of virtualization.

Session virtualization is vulnerable to a design concept called an *application silo*. It may be found that some application is unstable or incompatible with others. For this reason, a number of Remote Desktop Services (RDS) session hosts will be created just for this application. This is an application silo. A medium to large organization may have several of these applications and thus have several of these application silos. They waste hardware, licensing, and administrative effort. These could be eliminated if application virtualization was employed. Each incompatible or unstable application would be isolated and unable to affect other applications or the session host.

Application virtualization also plays an indirect role with Hyper-V virtualization. Obviously an RDS session host can be virtualized. But there is another form of machine virtualization that is called Virtual Desktop Infrastructure. We'll talk about that in a little while.

Server Virtualization

Server or hardware virtualization is a way of using a piece of software (usually a hypervisor such as Microsoft's Hyper-V, Citrix XenServer, or VMware ESX) to allow a number of machines to run on a single piece of hardware.

Each of the virtual machines on the host server runs an operating system of its own and has its own network presence and security boundary, just like a physical server would have.

Each virtual machine exists as files. Their hard disks usually are files that simulate hard disks, but some may also use physical hard disk partitions or LUNs for scalability or performance reasons.

This is actually quite a mature type of solution, despite the relative newness of Hyper-V.

Chapter 1, "Proposing Virtualization," talked quite a bit about the reasons to deploy Hyper-V, so you should refer to that chapter to learn more.

Desktop Virtualization

Desktop virtualization is quite similar to server virtualization. Just like with server virtualization, a piece of software (usually an application that is installed on the desktop operating system) allows many machines to run on the computer.

The virtual machines you can create with this technology can be used for a number of reasons. Testers and developers have used this technology for more than a decade to quickly deploy many machines on their desktop. This granted them the control and flexibility that they needed to quickly do their jobs. Those doing self-paced or class-based training have often used virtual machines running on their computer to simulate larger environments. Some organizations mandate that every administrator should have a normal user account for office work and a higher-privileged account for administration. They can log into their computer with the lesser account for online work and log into a virtual machine for administration work.

Application compatibility led to desktop-based virtualization being used in new ways. Microsoft's offering in this market is Microsoft Virtual PC, which is a desktop-based virtualization solution intended for many purposes. However, the version that was released for Windows 7 is intended as an application compatibility solution. Microsoft even provided a free Windows XP virtual machine license for those running the Professional, Enterprise, and Ultimate editions of Windows 7. Noncompatible applications can be installed into the Windows XP virtual machine. They can be started from the normal Start menu, and they will run in seamless Windows in the Windows 7 interface. An enterprise-based and centrally managed solution called MED-V is also available from Microsoft.

It must be remembered that virtual machines running on the desktop are still separate machines that must be managed, secured, patched, and scanned by antivirus software. They have their own operating systems and their own risks. Wouldn't a datacenter-based alternative be easier to manage?

Virtual Desktop Infrastructure

That brings us to Virtual Desktop Infrastructure (VDI), which uses server virtualization to allow many desktop operating systems to run in virtual machines running on a server (or farm of servers) in the datacenter.

This can be used as an alternative to desktop virtualization. However, VDI can also be used as an alternative to the traditional computer and as an alternative to session virtualization.

Just like with session virtualization, the user will log in using a stripped-down computer or terminal. A remote desktop client will connect the user to a virtual machine running on a server virtualization host such as Hyper-V. This is placed in a central datacenter, alongside all the server applications and data that the user will need to access. This offers simple remote or distributed computing without any sacrifice in performance, such as cross-WAN data transfer with traditional computer computing.

The advantage of this technology over session virtualization is that users get their own virtual machine running a desktop operating system such as Windows 7. Every program the user runs is contained within that virtual machine and cannot interfere with other users' virtual machines. The technology is familiar to the user, so little training is required. Any systems or processes that are developed by IT for computer's can be applied to VDI virtual machines. Importantly, a help-desk administrator can easily and quickly fix a problem for a user without any of the constraints one would have with session virtualization.

All of this sounds wonderful, but it does come at a cost. It is often argued that VDI is the way forward for all end users because of the cost savings. One could argue against this. All of the management systems for desktops must still be employed to manage the virtual machines. Operating systems must be secured and managed, applications must be deployed, patches must be downloaded and installed, and so on.

In fact, more management systems are required for controlling VDI. Usually a broker of some kind must be deployed to connect the end user with a virtual machine. The end user might have a dedicated virtual machine, or they could just be logged into whatever is available from a pool of virtual machines, depending on policy. This broker often offers an SSL gateway service for easy remote access without having to use VPN technology.

The costs of software and hardware are also quite high. Licensing for VDI is quite complex and quite expensive compared to that of a traditional computer. A special Virtual Enterprise Centralized Desktop (VECD) license is required for Windows virtual machines in a VDI deployment. You also have to wonder about the cost of the hardware. A terminal or computer is still required at the user's desk. They log into a server where a gigabyte of RAM or disk space costs much more than that of a computer's gigabyte of RAM or disk space.

It is for this reason that VDI, as a whole, is considered by many to be part of the overall solution rather than being a complete replacement for the desktop. There may be organizations where VDI will prevail, but they will remain in the minority. However, many will find that VDI does offer some advantages for certain scenarios such as disaster recovery (instant deployment of an end user computing environment) or secure remote access (via an SSL gateway).

This form of virtualization pulls in a lot of the other virtualization technologies. VDI is completely reliant on server virtualization. Profile virtualization is a necessity to ensure that the user's data is available no matter which virtual machine they log into. Application virtualization can be used to allow end users to quickly self-provision and stream applications. And Microsoft's Remote Desktop Services includes VDI technology and reuses a lot of the architectural features.

So, now you have a greater idea of what virtualization technologies are out there. You can see how Hyper-V fits in with many of them and how important it will be to your organization's current or future plans.

How Hyper-V Works

Just like a plumber, doctor, or mechanic, you should have an understanding of how something works before you work with it. You should be able to visualize how the features interact so that not only can you plan a suitable design to meet your organization's requirements but also so that you can fix it when something doesn't behave as expected. Many of the requests for help on support forums usually have a cause that is rooted in a lack of understanding.

If you are new to Hyper-V, then with a little work, you will soon come to grips with how Microsoft's enterprise virtualization platform works. Stick around if you are a Hyper-V veteran; doing a refresher once in a while isn't a bad thing. Many of the new and exciting features of Windows Server 2008 R2 and Windows Server 2008 R2 Service Pack 1 are based on what we are about to discuss.

The System Requirements

The requirements for Hyper-V are easy to remember. Understanding them will let you choose your hardware correctly, let you troubleshoot issues more easily, and help you understand the architecture of Hyper-V a bit more.

The requirements for Windows Server 2008 R2 Hyper-V (beyond the requirements of Windows Server 2008 R2) are as follows:

64-bit Processor with CPU Assisted Virtualization Windows Server 2008 R2 requires 64-bit processors because it is a 64-bit operating system. CPU assisted virtualization (Intel VT or AMD-V) must be a feature of the processor and must be turned on in the BIOS of the host machine.

Data Execution Prevention (DEP) DEP is a hardware feature that is used to protect operating systems and software from buffer overflow attacks. This style of attack places executable code into parts of memory that are supposed to be used for data. Eventually the code makes its way to a processor and is executed. A machine can be protected from this when DEP is enabled and the software is aware. This feature must also be turned on in the BIOS of the host machine.

Real World Scenario

HARDWARE MANUFACTURER GUIDANCE

Hardware vendors will typically rebadge a lot of common terms. CPU assisted virtualization and DEP could be called a number of things depending on the hardware you are using. Refer to your manufacturer's documentation for guidance.

You can find information about configuring IBM servers for Hyper-V here:

`http://www.redbooks.ibm.com/abstracts/redp4481.html`

Fujitsu has documentation here:

`http://ts.fujitsu.com/products/standard_servers/server_solutions/microsoft_hyper_v.html`

Dell has guidance here:

`http://content.dell.com/us/en/enterprise/d/virtualization/Dell-and-Microsoft-Simplify-IT-with-Dynamic-IT.aspx`

And HP provides information here:

`http://h18000.www1.hp.com/products/servers/software/microsoft/virtualization/`

Be careful if you are purchasing computers or laptops to run a lab at home or at the workplace. A number of processors have been released in the past few years that have (rather confusingly) included the required features only in some shipments. And rather more annoyingly, some hardware manufacturers have shipped feature-complete computers and laptops but have not included the ability to turn on the features in the BIOS. In some cases, it has been found that a faulty BIOS prevented the feature from working. An upgrade fixed those cases. In others, the manufacturer felt that a user would not need the feature, so it was not included in the BIOS at all. Be very sure that your lab hardware will include the features and the ability to turn them on in the BIOS before you commit to a purchase. An Internet search will often help with your purchasing decision.

Speaking of lab machines, a few people who have deployed Hyper-V in a lab using computers have complained about blue screens of death. Almost always, this was caused by a bad hardware manufacturer driver. Make sure you use the latest drivers so you don't have the same bad experience.

You should watch out for situations where a motherboard is replaced or a firmware upgrade proves to be difficult. These can undo the changes to turn on DEP or CPU assisted virtualization. You will find your virtual machines will not power up because the hypervisor could not start. You simply need to reenable the BIOS features and reboot the host.

The Architecture

An essential thing that we need to do is dispel a myth that has been spread by cynics who have not read genuine information about Hyper-V. Hyper-V is a true type 1 hypervisor. It is not some virtualization software like Virtual Server 2005 R2 SP1 or VMware Server, which are type 2 hypervisors. It is a thin strip of software that separates the hardware from the operating systems and virtual machines that run above.

Microsoft has taken a little different approach than what has been done by some rivals. Hyper-V is what is referred to as a *microkernelized hypervisor*. This is an approach where a host operating system, correctly referred to as the *parent partition*, provides management features and the drivers for the hardware. This approach has made Hyper-V very flexible and allows it to run on almost any piece of hardware with the required hardware features enabled and with drivers for Windows Server 2008 R2.

The alternative, and previously better known, approach was the monolithic hypervisor that you can see compared in Figure 2.1. This is the approach taken by VMware with its ESXi product line. The manufacturer of the monolithic virtualization product is responsible for all the hardware drivers. This means that they must maintain a very tightly controlled hardware compatibility list.

The marketing message from Microsoft was that this restricted your hardware purchasing options. To a certain extent, this is true. You might find that new hardware won't have instant support from a monolithic virtualization product because the vendor is trying to catch up by writing and testing its drivers. But you will find that any server or storage that a typical organization will use is supported by the likes of VMware.

Where Hyper-V really has an advantage here is the breadth of nonenterprise server hardware that is supported because of the more inclusive approach that they took with drivers. You also can get a quicker response to issues because hardware manufacturers can release driver updates, and you can install them straightaway (pending your testing and change control processes).

FIGURE 2.1
Microkernelized and monolithic virtualization

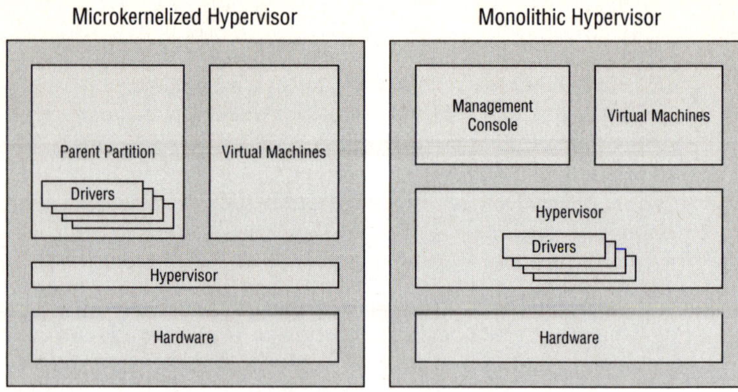

We're going to look at how we get to that final result of a running microkernelized Hyper-V hypervisor. You'll see how the pieces fall into place and work together to produce a highly performing and secure enterprise-level hardware virtualization solution.

The first things that you will do when installing a Hyper-V host is prepare the hardware (for the requirements) and install Windows Server 2008 R2, as shown in Figure 2.2. This operating system is the parent partition. This is where people sometimes get confused. How can this be a hypervisor if you install Windows first? Isn't it just a new version of Virtual Server? You'll soon see that it is not. At this point, all of the drivers are installed, and all of the Windows Server 2008 R2 patches are deployed.

FIGURE 2.2
Installing the parent partition

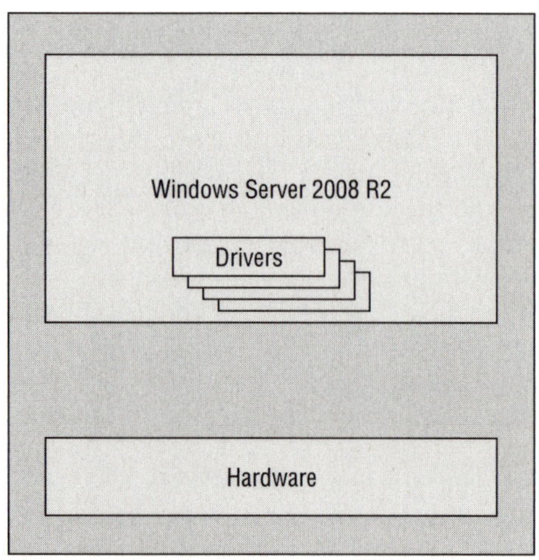

NIC TEAMING DRIVERS

We'll talk more about this subject in Chapter 6, "Deploying Hyper-V." Until then, be sure to read the manufacturer's guidance for NIC teaming and Hyper-V. Read it very carefully.

When you are ready, you can enable the Hyper-V role in Server Manager. After a few reboots, there will be an architectural change to how Windows runs on the server, shown in Figure 2.3.

FIGURE 2.3
Adding the Hyper-V hypervisor

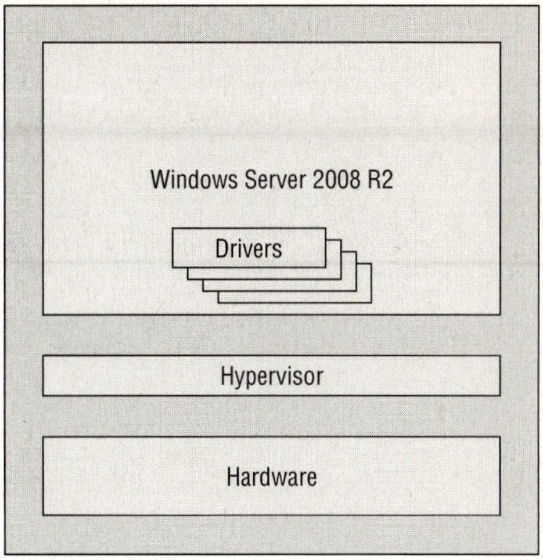

The hypervisor is installed and slips beneath the Windows Server 2008 R2 installation. The parent partition is now a management platform for the hypervisor and hardware. The hypervisor is now underneath the operating system that you originally installed. It is not executing as a process in the operating system.

Now you can add virtual machines to the host server, as you can see in Figure 2.4. The correct architectural term for a virtual machine is *child partition*.

FIGURE 2.4
Virtual machines running on Hyper-Vs

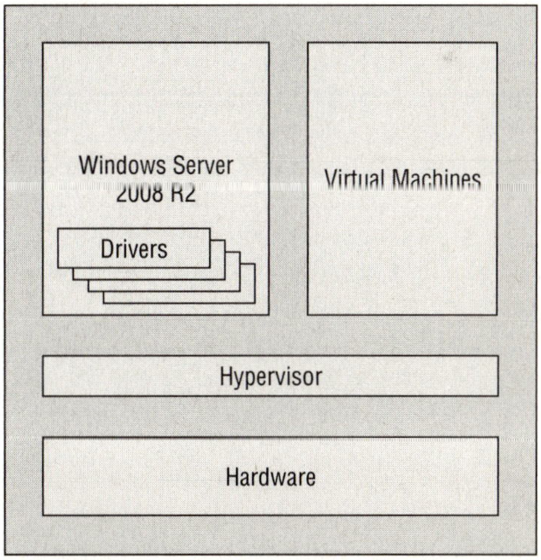

That's a pretty high-level view of what is going on, so we will zoom in a bit next. Figure 2.5 zooms into the detail of what is really going on. Here you see the parent partition (host operating system) on the left and a child partition (virtual machine) on the right.

FIGURE 2.5
An enlightened child partition

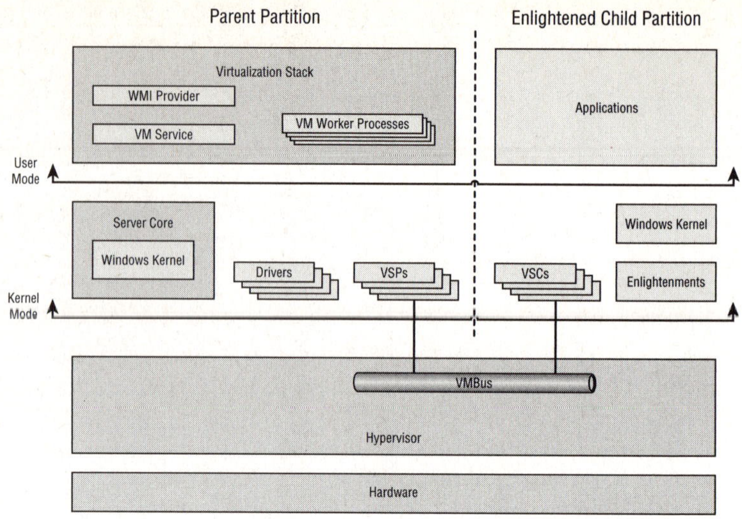

We'll start with the parent partition and work clockwise through it. In kernel mode, you can see Server Core and the kernel of the operating system. In this context, Server Core is not the installation option that doesn't have a GUI. This is the heart of Windows.

In user mode, we can see a VM service and a WMI provider. The WMI provider is particularly interesting because it allows for advanced management of Hyper-V. System Center Virtual Machine Manager 2008 R2 and other solutions take advantage of this management interface, as can you with the required scripting knowledge.

There is one VM worker process for every running child partition on the host.

Back in kernel mode you can see the drivers that were installed in the parent partition. This allows both the parent partition to directly access the hardware and the child partition to indirectly make use of the hardware.

The final pieces are the virtual service providers (VSPs). The VSPs allow virtual machines to indirectly make use of the parent partition device drivers.

Now we delve a little deeper into the hypervisor where we find a VMBus. The VMBus is a direct, one-to-one connection between the parent partition and a single child partition. This allows data to flow between them. For example, if a virtual machine needs to use a network card, then that data must flow across the VMBus.

Interestingly, Microsoft takes advantage of the hardware to run the VM bus and hypervisor at Ring –1, not at the usual Ring 0. This allows the virtual machines' kernel to run at Ring 0, where the kernel also runs in physical machines. The VMBus is also protected by DEP. That means an attacker who has successfully logged into a virtual machine cannot use a buffer overflow attack to attack the parent partition and then other virtual machines. This sort of attack is referred to as a *break out* and is a nightmare scenario in virtualization. This is why Microsoft has rightly made DEP a non-negotiable requirement for Hyper-V.

The VMBus connects the virtual service clients (VSCs) in the child partition to the VSPs in the parent partition. These VSCs are the drivers of the virtual machine.

Enlightenments are the special drivers that provide advanced features and performance for a virtual machine. They are usually referred to as *integration components* or *integration services*. The virtual machine is referred to as *enlightened* once they are installed. The devices that use enlightenments are referred to as *synthetic devices*. Synthetic devices offer the best possible performance in Hyper-V. Most versions of Windows and a few versions of Linux have enlightenments available for them. Your choice of virtual machine specification will be affected by whether the virtual machine is enlightened.

Some operating systems do not have enlightenments available for them. Virtual machines that run these operating systems are referred to as *emulated* virtual machines. They do not have VSCs or enlightenments, so advanced features are not available. They also have lesser performance capabilities compared to enlightened virtual machines.

Why would Microsoft support this possible sort of virtual machine? There are a couple of reasons.

New Operating System Installations Prior to Windows 7 and Windows Server 2008 R2, Windows did not come with integration components already installed. If you installed Windows Server 2003 in a virtual machine, you needed to be able to access emulated devices, such as the virtual CD/DVD drive, in order to be able to install the Hyper-V integration components.

Legacy Operating Systems Microsoft has long since ended development for that legacy operating system, so it will not write integration components for it. However, it has customers with a need to run the operating system. Many organizations are still running critical applications on legacy operating systems such as Windows NT 4.0. Those organizations face great challenges in maintaining and replacing hardware for those machines. They can convert them into virtual machines where that will no longer be an issue. Unfortunately, they must run as emulated virtual machines. However, the applications in those operating systems can now run on modern hardware rather than 10 years old (or older) hardware, and the negatives are far outweighed by the positives.

An emulated device goes through a more complex process, and this explains why the performance is not as good as a synthetic device.

- The emulated devices execute in the virtual machine's worker process.
- The worker process is in user mode in the parent partition.
- Drivers are in kernel mode.
- Changes between user mode and kernel mode require context switches.
- Context switches have an overhead on host processor and virtual machine performance.

The final piece of the puzzle is the Linux virtual machine. You can also run Linux in an emulated virtual machine. It must be said that the performance is not all that impressive. However, that completely changes when you enlighten a Linux virtual machine using integration components. We're going to talk more about the specifics of this in Chapter 6.

Integration Components

Hyper-V's integration components (also known as *enlightenments* or *integration services*) can be thought of as a set of device drivers. When installed, they offer the best possible performance for your virtual machine. They can even allow you to use additional types of virtual devices that are not otherwise available in an emulated virtual machine.

Integration components are more than just drivers. They also provide a set of services that allow the virtual machine to integrate with the Hyper-V host server. For example, you can synchronize the clock of the virtual machine with the physical clock of a Hyper-V host machine. You can configure a virtual machine to automatically start after the host machine starts, specify how long to wait, and also specify what should happen to the virtual machine when the host powers down (shut down or save state).

Microsoft provides integration components for a large set of supported operating systems, which is shown in Table 2.1 later in this chapter (when we discuss virtual processors). You can install integration components using Virtual Machine Manager or the Hyper-V console. Windows 7 and Windows Server 2008 R2 include integration components by default. However, the correct integration components version is dictated by the version of the operating system that is used for the Hyper-V parent partition or host operating system. For example, a Windows Server 2008 R2 host will have older integration components will be older than those on a Windows Server 2008 R2 with Service Pack 1 host. You should always install the latest version in your virtual machines that your host will support.

The one piece of information that is a must to remember is this: always install the integration components in your virtual machine. There have been too many cases where requests for help have been resolved very quickly by installing the absent integration components in the virtual machine's operating system. Virtual Machine Manager 2008 R2 will take care of this for you when you deploy new virtual machines or perform a migration with the virtual machine powered down.

The Design of Hyper-V

There are many pieces in the Hyper-V puzzle. We'll start by looking at how the basic components of Hyper-V fit together. Then we will move on to look at some of the features that were introduced with Windows Server 2008 R2 and then with Service Pack 1 for Windows Server 2008 R2.

The Virtual Machine

We will look at the basics of creating virtual machines and picking and choosing their components. This will give us a good footing to move on to the host machine and then onto the newer features of Hyper-V.

Each virtual machine is its own security boundary. It has its own operating system. Microsoft refers to this as an *operating system environment* (OSE). That's a term you will see quite a lot in its licensing documentation; it will often refer to a virtual machine as an OSE.

Each virtual machine operating system will have its own identity, computer account, domain membership, IP address(es), and access rights to the network and network resources. It will behave on the network just like any regular physical machine.

Virtual Machine Files

The virtual machine consists of a number of files. The number depends on what storage option you choose for the virtual machine and the current status of the virtual machine. The files include the following:

Virtual Machine Configuration (XML) The virtual machine configuration file is an XML file that is located in the virtual machine folder. It contains a description of the virtual machine and links all the files together. This file is critical for the virtual machine to start up. The GUID of the virtual machine is used to name the XML file for that virtual machine.

Symbolic Link Hyper-V knows where to find the virtual machine configuration files of the virtual machines by using symbolic link files. They appear as shortcuts in Windows Explorer and can be found at `C:\ProgramData\Microsoft\Windows\Hyper-V\Virtual Machines`. Note that `C:\ProgramData` is a hidden folder. The GUID of the virtual machine is used to name the symbolic link for that virtual machine.

Virtual Hard Disk (VHD) The most common type of storage for virtual machines is to use a file that simulates a LUN or partition in a computer. This is a VHD file, and there is one for every disk in the virtual machine. There are several types, which we will look at later. A virtual machine can also use physical disks for its storage. This negates the need for a VHD file.

Automatic Virtual Hard Disks (AVHD) These are created whenever a snapshot is made of a computer. This freezes the state of the virtual machine. At this point, the virtual machine creates a single AVHD for every VHD in the virtual machine. All new data is written to and read from the AVHD. The VHD is used only to read data from before the snapshot.

You can have up to 50 snapshots per virtual machine. Removing a snapshot will require a merge to add the AVHD data into the original VHD file(s). The virtual machine must be powered down to allow this to complete. You may see some very odd performance or failure issues occur if you fail to do this after removing the snapshot.

Snapshots are supported by the Microsoft Hyper-V team in production, but most Hyper-V veterans will warn against using them because of the added administration complexity, performance loss, and risk of human error. In fact, some applications, including Microsoft ones (see Chapter 8, "Virtualization Scenarios"), will explicitly state that they will not support snapshots of a virtual machine that is installed with their application.

Saved State Placeholder (BIN) A virtual machine can be placed into a saved state. This freezes the virtual machine as it is. All memory is written to a file on the hard disk. This is like hibernation in a laptop. The virtual machine can be woken from the saved state. It will read the stored memory data and continue processing as if nothing has happened.

The required storage space for the saved state will be no greater than the amount of RAM in the virtual machine. A virtual machine with 8 GB of RAM will require up to 8 GB of disk space to store its saved state. The size of the BIN file will always match the amount of RAM assigned to the virtual machine even if that amount changes automatically, as it would with Dynamic Memory enabled (discussed later in the chapter). Hyper-V will reserve storage space with a `.bin` file.

Saved State (VSV) The saved state of a virtual machine's devices is written into a file with a `.vsv` extension.

Virtual Machine Storage Options

You have a number of ways to create storage for your virtual machines. What you will use may depend on storage space limitations, performance requirements, flexibility, or scalability. You will also find that some options are suitable in lab environments, some are suitable for production environments, and there is even a gray area. We'll start at the best-performing option and work our way down the list from there:

Passthrough Disk This is an option that VMware administrators know as *raw device mapping*. A LUN is presented from the underlying physical storage to the virtual machine. The operating system (or installer) can create a volume (or volumes) and format it. No VHD file is created for the disk.

This option provides the best performance and scalability for virtual machines. It comes with all the characteristics of a physical machine using physical storage. The limitations are that of the operating system and filesystem, not of Hyper-V.

Hyper-V administrators will typically use passthrough disks when they need partitions that are greater than 2040 Gb in size and where they need 100 percent of the potential storage performance.

You should be aware that passthrough disk comes with a price. It does not grant you the mobility (virtual machine storage relocation) and management options (such as snapshot or VHD backup via VSS) that you get with VHD files.

Fixed-Size VHD A fixed-size VHD is the first of the VHD types. It is the preferred option in a production environment. This is because it is a single file where all the potential space of the VHD is allocated at once. A fixed-size VHD of 40 GB in size will create a file that is roughly 40 GB in size on the host's storage system.

Creating a fixed-size VHD can take a little time. This is because Hyper-V secures it by zeroing out the contents of the VHD file. This makes it impossible for anyone who is logged into the new virtual machine to run a disk scan and reveal contents that were previously stored in the physical filesystem. Many administrators who are new to Hyper-V find this to be a bother and switch to dynamic VHDs. They may even use third-party tools that create a fixed-size VHD without performing the security step; this is a definite risk in a production environment.

Fixed-size VHD offers the best performance because there is no additional work for the hypervisor to perform. A virtual machine can simply write to it and read from it as it normally would. There is no dynamic growth process for the file.

Another advantage is of this total allocation with a fixed-size VHD is that it is less vulnerable to fragmentation. This will improve the overall performance of the underlying physical storage, not only for this virtual machine but for all virtual machines.

Dynamic VHD This is the last of the options you will choose in a production environment. You might create a 40 GB dynamic VHD, but it will be only slightly bigger than the amount of data stored in the VHD. For example, if you have 10 GB of data in that 40 GB VHD, the file will be only just a little bigger than 10 GB in size.

The dynamic VHD can be compared to a SQL Server database file in how it behaves. Additional free space will be allocated to the file as it grows. This process was a serious performance limiter in Windows Server 2008. Microsoft improved this in Windows Server 2008 R2 by increasing the amount that the VHD would grow by.

Dynamic VHD's big advantage is that you just consume the amount of physical storage that you require for the data in the virtual machine. This can be very useful when storage space is limited. It is also useful when you are providing some form of elastic computing environment such as a public or private cloud; you will simply bill the customer or cross-charge the department for their data storage, which is based on the size of their dynamic VHDs. The customer will find this very fair, compared to a fixed-size VHD alternative where they will be charged on disk size rather than data size.

Although it is supported in production, there are still concerns that dynamic VHD isn't always suitable for a production environment. I/O-intensive virtual machines do suffer in performance when they use dynamic VHD. You will learn more about this in Chapter 8, when we show how to design virtual machines for different applications and scenarios. Think about it; a write operation to a database file will write data to the database file, extend it, extend the VHD, and do whatever cleanup work needs to be done. That's possibly twice as much than has to be done in a fixed VHD or passthrough disk configuration.

There is also the risk of fragmentation. The file is growing on the fly, over the lifespan of the virtual machine. The same thing is happening to other VHDs in the same virtual machine and in other virtual machines that are probably stored on the same physical LUN or CSV. Fragmentation may eventually lead to performance issues and will require additional maintenance operations.

It is for these reasons that many Microsoft virtualization MVPs and independent experts are recommending that dynamic VHDs should not be used in a production environment.

MONITOR AVAILABLE PHYSICAL DISK SPACE

You should monitor the available disk space on any physical storage that is used to store virtual machines or VHDs. Hyper-V will pause virtual machines if the physical storage they are on runs out of disk space. This is not like a saved state. The virtual machine is simply frozen in time, and nothing is written to disk to preserve its state.

Differencing Disks This is a type of VHD that should never be used in a production environment, but it is very useful when you are working in a lab environment where you need quick results or when you have severe storage space limitations.

A differencing disk behaves like a snapshot. It links back to a master VHD. When you read from the differencing disk, then all old data (prior to the creation of the differencing disk) is read from the master VHD. All new data (after the creation of the differencing disk) is written to and read from the differencing disk. You can have many differencing disks in many virtual machines linked to and referencing a single master VHD file. This is where you get the performance issues and where you can save physical storage space.

The differencing disk also has some of the behavior of a differencing disk. It will start out as a small file and grow as the contents within it increase.

Real World Scenario

QUICKLY CREATE A LAB USING DIFFERENCING DISKS

This is the scenario where differencing disks really shine in an environment with limited hardware and without Virtual Machine Manager (VMM) 2008 R2. You can create and deploy many virtual machines with prepared operating systems and programs by doing just one installation.

Create a temporary master virtual machine. Install the operating system, install the applications, patch them, and perform standard configurations such as enabling Remote Desktop. Now you can run sysprep to generalize the virtual machine. This is being done because the process you are performing is a form of cloning, just without the use of any imaging tools. You can power down the virtual machine move or copy the VHD file to a safe location.

Now you can create many virtual machines. Each one will use a differencing disk and link to the master VHD that you have stored safely. This will configure the virtual machine to use this template as its starting point.

Power up each virtual machine. Each one will run the post-sysprep configuration to generate a unique SID. From this point, everything that is stored by each virtual machine is written into the differencing disk. The original VHD is a read-only file to the virtual machines. Within minutes, you can have many operational virtual machines that are fully configured and patched, with only a single installation of Windows.

Over time, as patches are installed, service packs are deployed, applications are installed, and data is generated, the differencing disks will grow, become fragmented, and increasingly suffer from performance issues. This means that although they might be suitable for short-term lab testing, they are not suitable for long-term deployments.

You should also note that the master VHD should be treated as golden. Replacing it or changing it in any way will cause corruption and is not supported after the differencing disks have been initialized by powering up their virtual machines. Any required change to the master VHD will require deleting the differencing disks and reinitializing the virtual machines.

VHD files can contain up to 2040 GB of data. They are flexible and mobile. They support functions such as snapshots and support VSS backup of the virtual machine at the host or storage level. This is all because they are files.

Our advice is that you should try to use fixed-size VHDs for all your virtual machine storage. There will be times where performance, scalability, and application requirements will force you to use the less flexible passthrough disk option.

You can do a couple of actions to modify the properties of a VHD:

Change Type A VHD can be changed from one type to another. This requires that the virtual machine is powered down. Doing this in the Hyper-V console is a very manual process. You would edit the properties of the disk, convert it to create a new VHD, and manually swap the new VHD for the old VHD. VMM makes this easier by performing all the steps for you as a job.

Extend VHD A VHD can be increased in size. For example, you can increase a 40 GB VHD to an 80 GB VHD. The virtual machine in question must be powered down. You must ensure that available physical storage space is available for the size increase. This process is similar to adding physical disk to a physical machine. Afterward, you will need to run Disk Manager and extend the relevant partition to consume the newly added disk space.

Virtual Storage Controllers

Some of early false statements about Hyper-V were made in relation to the choice and performance of storage controllers in Hyper-V virtual machines. Be aware that this has nothing to do with the storage controllers that are used in the physical host server. Your only requirement there is that you have a suitable Windows Server 2008 R2 driver.

Hyper-V virtual machines may use either IDE or SCSI controllers for attaching their passthrough disks or VHD files. The virtual machine can boot only from an IDE controller. This does sound bad at first. The thing is, you really need to understand that Hyper-V is software, not hardware.

You will get the same performance from a virtual IDE controller as you would from a virtual SCSI controller when you install the integration components in a virtual machine. They are just software so they essentially behave the same way as SCSI controllers, using a VSC in the child partition (virtual machine) to communicate with a VSP in the parent partition (host operating system) via the VMBus.

The IDE controller has the same disk capacity as a SCSI controller, supporting VHDs of up to 2040 GB.

A virtual machine that does not have integration components installed will use an emulated IDE controller. As you learned earlier, this will require context switches from kernel mode into user mode, and it has a longer communication path, requiring execution in the worker process of the virtual machine in the parent partition.

Real-world testing shows that virtual IDE disks with the integration components perform just as well as virtual SCSI disks. There is a difference; an IDE disk has a limit to I/O block sizes of 512 KB or less. A SCSI controller can have block sizes of up to 8 MB. But as we just mentioned, this is not being noticed.

IDE Controller The virtual machine can have up to four devices attached to the virtual IDE controller. This will include the boot disk and usually will include a virtual CD/DVD drive.

SCSI Controller A virtual machine may have up to four virtual SCSI controllers. Each SCSI controller can have up to 64 disks. That gives a potential of 256 SCSI disks per VM.

Windows Server 2008 R2 introduced a new feature for SCSI controllers. You can hot-add a disk to a virtual SCSI controller while the virtual machine is running, depending on the support of the contained operating system, of course. This can be very useful for rapidly adding storage to virtual machines when you can't power them down to extend existing virtual hard disks. It is for this reason that many Hyper-V administrators will build virtual machines with a virtual SCSI controller, even if it is not initially needed. VMM administrators will also create hardware profiles with SCSI controllers.

The advice that we have is this: you must use the IDE controller for your boot disk. Try to use the SCSI controller for any additional disks that the virtual machine may have.

Virtual Processors

A Hyper-V host, clustered or nonclustered, can have up to 384 running virtual processors. A Hyper-V cluster (up to 16 nodes with one of those being idle or redundant) can have up to 1,000 virtual processors. Note that a two-node Hyper-V cluster will support a maximum 384 virtual processors because the single active host's limit is lower than the cluster's limit.

The actual supported limit of virtual processors for a host is calculated by multiplying the number of logical processors (cores) by 8. You can have up to eight virtual CPUs per core. This means an 8-core host, whether it has 2× quad-core processors or a single 8-core processor, can support up to 64 virtual CPUs.

MOORE'S LAW

Microsoft's support statements for virtual processors are based on the tests that they are able to perform in its own test labs. Thus, the support statements are subject to change and increase over time. In fact, the support statement for virtual processors in a Hyper-V cluster changed halfway through the writing of this book, causing a number of edits and reviews for previously completed chapters.

Moore's law tells us that the potential computing power in a processor will double every eighteen months. Microsoft's original test and support figures were created at a time when the quad-core processor was the best available. Since then, we have seen the release of 6-core, 8-core, and even 12-core processors. Microsoft may very well increase its supported number of virtual processors by the time you read this.

These numbers of 384 running virtual CPUs per host are a fantasy outside of a scalability test lab. Supported limitations are not the same as real-world limitations. One virtual machine may require more processing power than another, and this must be reflected in host sizing and virtual machine placement. This is discussed in Chapter 5, "Planning the Hardware Deployment." The Hyper-V support limitations may be overridden by the support for the application that will run in a virtual machine. There is more on that in Chapter 8.

A virtual machine may have up to four virtual processors depending on the operating system installed in it, as shown in Table 2.1.

TABLE 2.1: Supported virtual processor configurations

VIRTUAL MACHINE OPERATING SYSTEM	SUPPORTED NUMBER OF VIRTUAL PROCESSORS
Windows Server 2008 R2	1, 2, or 4
Windows Server 2008 x64	1, 2, or 4
Windows Server 2008 x86	1, 2, or 4
Windows Server 2003 x86	1 or 2
Windows Server 2003 R2 x86	1 or 2
Windows Server 2003 R2 x64	1 or 2
Windows Server 2003 x64	1 or 2
Windows Server 2000	1
Supported Linux distributions (with version 2.1 or newer of the Linux Integration Components)	1, 2, or 4*
Windows 7 x86	1, 2, or 4
Windows 7 x64	1, 2, or 4

TABLE 2.1: Supported virtual processor configurations *(CONTINUED)*

VIRTUAL MACHINE OPERATING SYSTEM	SUPPORTED NUMBER OF VIRTUAL PROCESSORS
Windows Vista x86	1 or 2
Windows XP Professional x86 with Service Pack 3	1 or 2
Windows XP Professional x86 with Service Pack 2	1
Windows XP Professional x64 with Service Pack 2	1 or 2

** Note that Linux virtual machines can have multiple processors (SMP) only if they are installed with version 2.1 or newer of the Linux Integration Components. Versions prior to this will support only a single virtual processor. We will talk much more about Linux virtual machines in Chapter 6.*

VIRTUAL MACHINE MEMORY

The memory that is allocated to a virtual machine is not shared in any way with any other virtual machines. There are no shared paging mechanisms.

By default, a virtual machine will be allocated all the memory in the virtual machine specification. This memory is consumed from the host server. The virtual machine will fail to start if the memory is not available. More often than not, you will find that memory will be your bottleneck in a production environment.

Service Pack 1 for Windows Server 2008 R2 introduces a new feature called Dynamic Memory. Dynamic Memory will allow you to specify a minimum and a maximum amount of RAM that can be assigned to a virtual machine. The virtual machine will boot with the minimum amount of RAM. Additional RAM (up to the virtual machine's assigned maximum) will be hot-added to the virtual machine from the host as required by the virtual machine and returned to the host when no longer required by the virtual machine. The result is that you can get more virtual machines running on a host without oversubscribing the available resources and causing performance issues for the virtual machines. We will dive a little deeper into Dynamic Memory a little later in this chapter.

A Hyper-V host (assuming you are running Hyper-V Server 2008 R2 or the Enterprise or Datacenter edition of Windows Server 2008 R2) can support up to 1 TB of RAM in a single host. Yes, Datacenter can support 2 TB, but Hyper-V has its own support statement.

A single virtual machine can support up to 64 GB of RAM, depending on the support of the operating system running in the virtual machine.

VIRTUAL NETWORK ADAPTERS

There are two types of network adapter. For many organizations, the choice will be pretty simple. However, there are some scenarios where that decision-making process can be a little more interesting.

Synthetic Network Adapter This is a virtual machine network adapter that is made available by the Hyper-V integration components and uses the VSCs in the child partition and the VSPs in the parent partition to access the network. This makes the synthetic network adapter the best performing of the two networking options. Normally you will prepare VMM hardware profiles with a synthetic network adapter to ensure that your virtual machines always have the best networking reasons. Make sure you read about legacy network adapters for a few reasons why you might not always use synthetic network adapters.

Legacy Network Adapter This is an emulated network adapter that requires processing in the virtual machine's worker process in the parent partition's user mode. This means that the performance is lower and resource overhead of the legacy network is higher when compared to a synthetic network adapter. Despite this, there are a few reasons that you might use a legacy network adapter, even in a production environment.

The synthetic network adapter does not support PXE. Many organizations have made a large commitment into building operating system deployment mechanisms that are based on this form of DHCP-based network booting. This can support both virtual and physical operating system deployments. These organizations do not want to invest in another mechanism such as VMM because it will only support virtual deployments and will double the amount of image or template management that must be done. A legacy network adapter will allow PXE boots. Administrators can then choose between temporarily using a PXE network adapter (as a second network adapter in the virtual machine), which would later have to be removed (requiring the virtual machine to be powered down), or permanently configuring the virtual machine with a legacy network adapter.

If an administrator is manually installing a new virtual machine with a legacy operating system, then they will not have any integration components installed. They may need to access the network to install applications or programs. They may temporarily install the legacy network adapter in the virtual machine for network connectivity until the integration components are installed.

Some legacy operating systems, such as Windows NT 4.0, do not have integration component support. Virtual machines with these operating systems must use the legacy network adapter to have any network connectivity.

The advice here is simple. Try to always use a synthetic network adapter. When required, you will switch to permanently or temporarily using a legacy network adapter.

A virtual machine may have up to 8 synthetic network adapters and 4 legacy network adapters, giving a total of 12 virtual network adapters per virtual machine.

The Host

The host provides resources to the virtual machine and can provide network connectivity and use Windows Failover Clustering to make a virtual machine highly available.

Network Connectivity

A lot of requests for architecture information center around how to network a virtual machine. This ranges from being simple to implement basic connectivity to complex when implementing virtual LANs (VLANs) or NIC teaming.

A Hyper-V host server should have at least two physical network adapters. The first one will provide connectivity for the parent partition. This allows access to the host for remote management. You might do this to isolate the parent partition on a secure network or to allow access no matter what is happening to the virtual machines' network connectivity, such as network congestion. The second network adapter will be used to provide connectivity for the virtual machines.

A host may have only one network adapter to share these roles, but this is not recommended. A host may have more than one network adapter. For example, a clustered host should really have three or more network adapters. You may also need to provide more network adapters for your virtual machines to meet bandwidth or redundancy requirements.

The basic mechanism for virtual machine network connectivity is pretty simple. A virtual machine can have between 1 and 12 virtual network adapters. A Hyper-V host can have one or more (technically unlimited maximum) virtual networks. You can think of these as being unmanaged virtual switches.

This Is Where Your Network Administrator Panics

Did we just say switch? Your network administrator is going to panic about spanning tree loops, SNMP, and MIB. Don't worry — these are not like physical switches, and they have absolutely no impact on the physical network. They are simply a means for connecting virtual machines to the network and have no spanning tree or SNMP functionality. Your network administrators will have nothing to do with them.

The virtual machine's network card is connected to a virtual network. The virtual network can be connected to other virtual machines, the parent partition, and/or to a physical network card, depending on the type of virtual network that is created.

You can implement three types of virtual network on a Hyper-V host:

External Network This is the type virtual network that will be most commonly deployed. This virtual network will connect virtual machines to each other and to the physical network. The virtual machines can communicate with physical machines, other virtual machines (via the virtual network or via the physical network), and the parent partition.

Figure 2.6 shows an implementation where an external network connects three virtual machines (via their virtual network adapters) to Physical NIC 2 in the host server. This provides the virtual machines with access to the physical network that the Physical NIC 2 is connected to. The virtual machines will have the same networking constraints as any physical machine. For example, physical firewall rules and routing configurations will apply to them the same as any other physical machine on that network.

Figure 2.6 An external virtual network

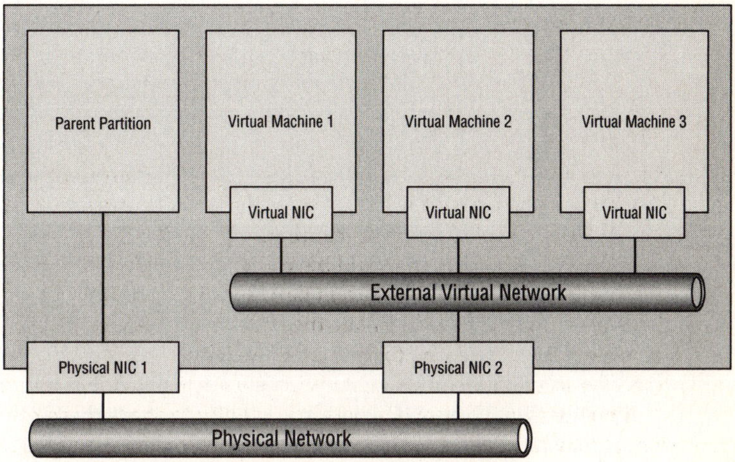

An external network will have a one-to-one binding with a physical network card. This means that you must have two physical network cards for virtual machines if you require two external networks. You can see this Figure 2.7.

FIGURE 2.7
Multiple external virtual networks

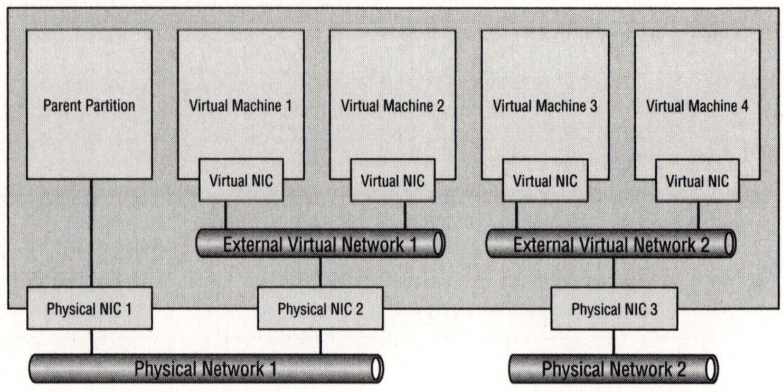

Internal Network An internal network connects virtual machines with other virtual machines on the internal network and the parent partition, assuming that the parent partition is configured to be on the same subnet. There is no direct connectivity to the physical network or to any physical machines. They can also not communicate with any virtual machines on another virtual network. Figure 2.8 shows an implementation of this. The virtual machines will appear to communicate with the parent partition via the parent partition's external network, so there is no need to set up a second network connection for it.

FIGURE 2.8
An internal virtual network

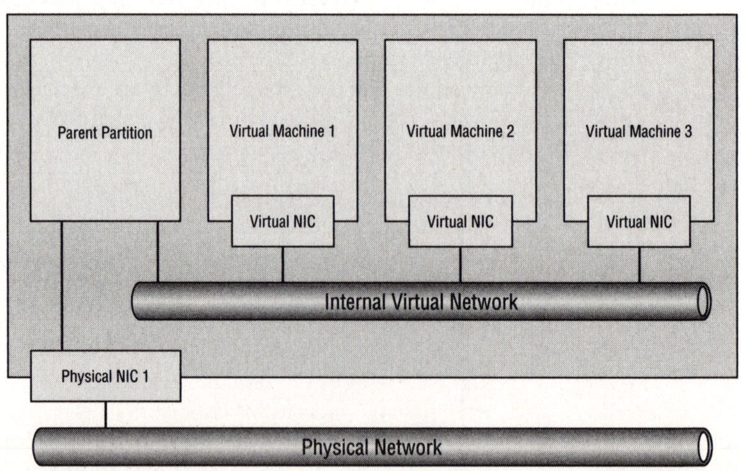

Private Network This takes the isolationism of the virtual machines just one step further. Virtual machines on a private network can communicate with each other but with nothing else. They cannot connect to the parent partition, to any physical machine, or to any virtual machine on another virtual network. Figure 2.9 shows how a private network works.

FIGURE 2.9
A private virtual network

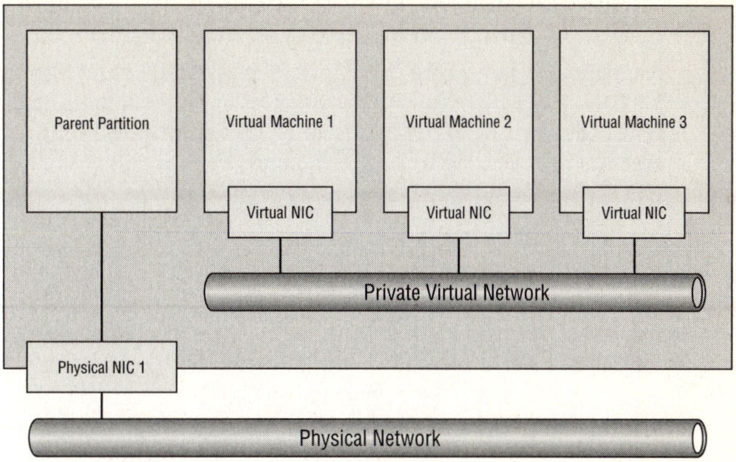

You might consider using a private network in a few scenarios. One might be to run a test lab. Many organizations have a policy of testing backup and recovery. You could recover a server as a virtual machine that is connected to a private network. This will ensure that it does not interfere with the production server on the production network. You may also have a reason to secure and isolate some virtual machines behind a firewall that is running in a virtual machine. You can see this sort of virtual firewall implementation in Figure 2.10. The application virtual machines will route all traffic to the private network adapter of the firewall virtual machine. The firewall virtual machine will filter traffic accordingly and reroute it via its external network adapter. This will protect and isolate the application virtual machines from the physical network.

FIGURE 2.10
A virtual firewall using a private virtual network

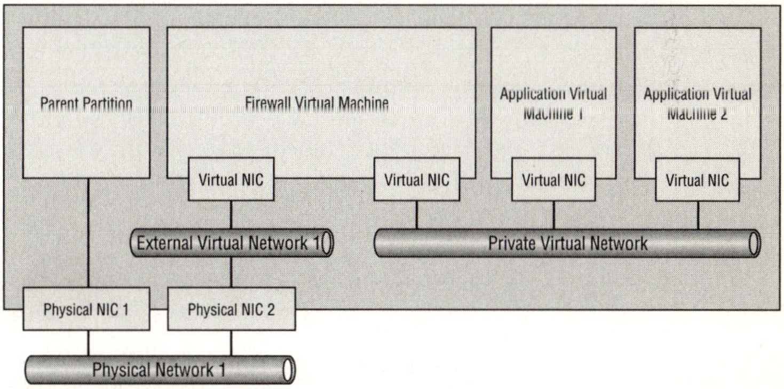

VLAN Support and Firewalls

Only smaller organizations will have a single subnet. Every enterprise network will probably want to have virtual machines running on many subnets or VLANs.

Virtual machines that are on different VLANs will be able to communicate with each other (or physical network nodes) only if the router or firewall rules permit it. This means that you can completely isolate virtual machines from each other and from physical network nodes by using VLANs. This is illustrated in Figure 2.11. In this example, the virtual machines in VLAN 102 can only communicate with the virtual machines in VLAN 103 if the firewall permits it. The virtual machines can be placed on the same host or even on the same Hyper-V virtual network (as you will see soon), and the firewall is still in total control.

FIGURE 2.11 Using VLANs to separate virtual machines via firewalls

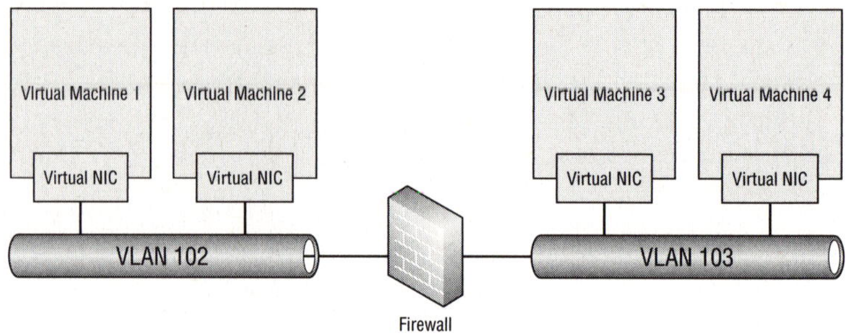

You can place virtual machines on different VLANs using a few different methods. These methods are based on VLAN IDs. Every VLAN has a unique digit ID (or tag) that is configured by the network administrators.

Physical Network VLAN Isolation The first way is to set up a physical NIC in the host for each subnet or VLAN, similar to what was done in Figure 2.7. The network administrators can configure the switch ports for each NIC to be in the appropriate VLAN.

Using Figure 2.7 as an example, the physical switch port for Physical NIC 2 could be in VLAN 102. Any virtual machine virtual network card connected to External Network 1 (and Physical NIC 2) would then be connected to VLAN 102. The physical switch port Physical NIC 3 could be in VLAN 103; hence, all the virtual machine network adapters that are connected to External Network 2 are connected to VLAN 103.

This technique is very simple to set up, but there are a few problems with it. It is very reliant on the network administrator. One of the reasons for virtualization is to facilitate rapid deployment. Involving more people to do physical network administration slows the process down. You also need to have a physical network card for every VLAN. That could get very expensive and complicate host management.

> **NIC TEAMING**
>
> We're going to talk about NIC teaming in Chapter 6. It's interesting to note that it can offer a solution to simulate many physical network cards at the parent partition or host level with just one or a pair. These can each be connected to many external virtual networks.

Virtual Network VLAN Isolation A virtual network can be bound to a specified VLAN using its ID. This means that you can force a virtual network to communicate with a specified VLAN and only that VLAN. Any virtual machine network card that is linked to this virtual network will then be connected to that VLAN. Communications with other VLANs will be controlled by the network appliances such as firewalls and routers.

You can see an example of this technique in Figure 2.12. The network administrator has configured the physical switch ports with VLAN trunking. This pushes many (or all) VLANs down the network cable to the physical network card. It is up to the virtual network (or the physical network card if using the previous technique) to decide which VLAN in the trunk that it will connect to. This is done using the VLAN ID, which you will obtain from the network administrator.

FIGURE 2.12
Virtual network VLAN isolation

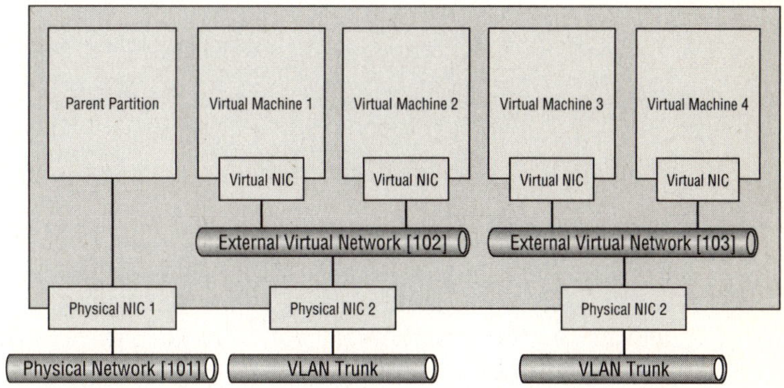

USING BLADES WITH ENCLOSURE SWITCHES?

You may need to implement an ether channel instead of VLAN trunking at the physical switch port to relay the VLANs down to the switches in the blade enclosure.

Figure 2.12 shows that the first virtual network is bound to VLAN 102. That means that its connected virtual machine network cards are going to communicate via VLAN 102. The second external network is bound to VLAN 103; hence, its virtual machine virtual network cards are on VLAN 103.

This VLAN binding is completely in the control of the Hyper-V administrator. The network administrator's only role is to configure the VLAN trunking on the physical switch ports for the virtual machine physical NICs. Users of the virtual machines have no access to the VLAN ID setting in the virtual network properties.

There is a certain amount of trust that will be required by security and network administrators to ensure that Hyper-V administrators do not abuse this power. It is strongly recommended that there only be a few trusted Hyper-V administrators, much like with the Domain Administrators group in Active Directory.

This solution still requires many physical network cards and virtual networks to be set up and managed. There is one per VLAN that there will be virtual machines for. This could become very expensive and very complicated to manage.

Virtual Network Adapter VLAN Isolation With this technique, the VLAN ID is configured as a property of the virtual machine virtual network card. There is no configuration required in the virtual network or in the physical network card. You can see this in Figure 2.13.

FIGURE 2.13
Virtual network adapter VLAN isolation

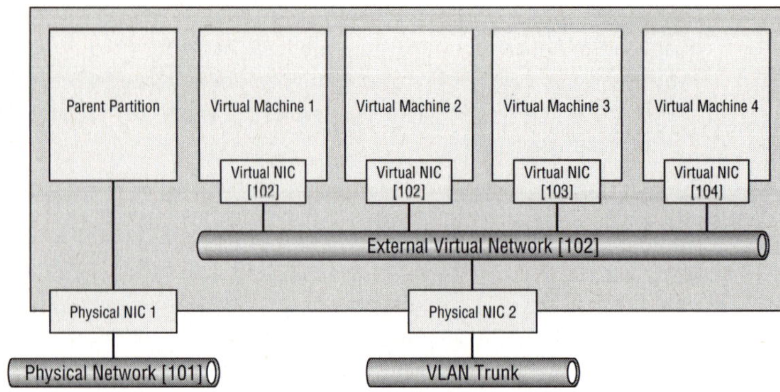

The network administrator has configured a VLAN trunk on the switch port for the single virtual machine physical network adapter (Physical NIC 2). There is no VLAN configuration on this network adapter. There is a single external virtual network bound to the physical network adapter. This passes the VLAN trunk up to each virtual machine network adapter. Each virtual network adapter on each virtual machine must be configured with a VLAN ID.

You can have more than one virtual machine on a single VLAN. You can have many virtual machines on many VLANs. You can even place a virtual machine onto more than one VLAN by providing it with multiple virtual network adapters, each with a different VLAN ID property setting, as shown in Figure 2.14.

FIGURE 2.14
A virtual machine on many VLANs

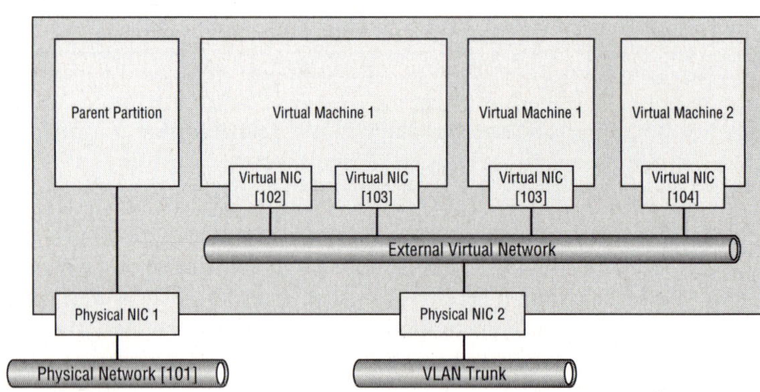

This solution has simplified the infrastructure. Physical network card numbers are minimized; you only need enough of them for fault tolerance or to meet bandwidth requirements. This allows you to minimize the number of virtual networks. Now you just manage the VLAN IDs for the virtual machine network cards. The role of the network administrator has been minimized as well, meaning that you have a flexible and rapid deployment virtualization solution.

There is still a trust issue for the security and network administrators. It is likely that they will want to perform random audits of the Hyper-V network configuration.

> **NIC Teaming and VLANs**
>
> NIC teaming will impact how you can place virtual machines on different VLANs. We'll cover this in Chapter 6.

NIC Teaming

Anyone who has been using VMware ESX up to now is probably familiar with its integrated and very impressive NIC teaming feature. Unfortunately, we have some bad news here. Microsoft does not support NIC teaming in any of its products. This is a long-standing policy that you can read about at `http://support.microsoft.com/kb/968703`.

We Hyper-V consumers have made it clear that we want NIC teaming in Hyper-V, and Microsoft has heard us. We can only hope that a change will be made in future versions.

Until then, you can rely on third-party products that are usually provided by either the network adapter or the server manufacturer.

We're not going to look at the mechanics of NIC teaming here (that will be discussed in Chapter 6), but it is very important to note a few things:

- You must use only versions of the NIC teaming software that explicitly state that they support Hyper-V on Windows Server 2008 R2.
- You must follow the manufacturer's instructions to the letter. Straying from these instructions will probably corrupt the networking stack of the Hyper-V host server and require a total rebuild.
- Microsoft will not support any problems with your NIC teaming. This is the responsibility of the original provider of the solution.

Hyper-V Failover Clusters

When you are reading documentation about Hyper-V solutions, particularly those provided by third parties, it can seem like there isn't a built-in Microsoft way to provide fault tolerance for your Hyper-V host servers. That couldn't be further from the truth.

Microsoft uses Windows Failover Clustering to link Hyper-V hosts together into a single cluster. This allows a farm of host servers to work cooperatively. Virtual machines will be made highly available as a result of this. They can automatically move from one host server to another in the event of a host failure. Administrators and management systems (such as Virtual Machine Manager) can even use migration mechanisms to move virtual machines between host servers in a cluster with no downtime.

Introducing Failover Clustering

Hyper-V fault tolerance is based on the Windows Server Failover Clustering feature. This feature can be enabled in Server Manager. A collection of host servers can be grouped together into a single cluster. A cluster may have up to 16 host servers (also referred to as *nodes*). There should be at least one fault tolerance host in the cluster. A larger and more critical cluster may have two redundant nodes. A cluster with one redundant node is referred to as an *N+1 cluster*. This cluster will have enough spare host capacity to allow one host to fail and still be able to continue running all the virtual machines. A cluster with two redundant nodes is referred to as an *N+2 cluster*. This cluster will be able to suffer two host server failures and still be able to continue running all the virtual machines. A good practice is to allow at least one redundant host in a cluster with up to eight nodes and at least two redundant hosts in a cluster with between 9 and 16 hosts. This will accommodate the greater risk of failure as the cluster size grows.

Failover Clustering is available in the following editions of Windows Server 2008 R2:

- Windows Server 2008 R2 Datacenter
- Windows Server 2008 R2 Enterprise
- Hyper-V Server 2008 R2

Each server must be identical in terms of operating system version and build. The hardware should be as similar as possible. For example, you cannot live migrate (move) a virtual machine from an Intel processor to an AMD processor within a cluster. Windows Server 2008 R2 does allow a virtual machine Live Migration between hosts with different physical processors from the same manufacturer. You can facilitate this by enabling the Migrate To A Physical Computer With A Different Processor Version property of the virtual CPU in the virtual machine. The downside to this is that the newer processors will be brought down to feature the level of the oldest processors. You may need to add additional clusters with newer-only processors if you require the features of the newer processors (for features such as Second Level Address Translation).

How Virtual Machines Will Migrate

There are some common misconceptions about what will happen to virtual machines during different kinds of host failure. Here are the different scenarios:

Nontotal Host Failure This is a situation where there is a problem with the host server that does not prevent the virtual machine from operating. It may be a performance issue or a minor hardware issue where some offline maintenance is required.

Figure 2.15 shows the process of the failure and the recovery. Administrators may manually relocate the virtual machines to another host server using Live Migration. There is no downtime with this move. This will allow them to repair any host issues without introducing downtime to the virtual machines that were previously hosted on the server. Management systems, such as Virtual Machine Manager integrated with Operations Manager, might even perform this Live Migration automatically (see Chapter 9, "Operations Manager 2007"). The result is that the virtual machine stays operational despite the failure on the host server.

Total Host Failure This is a fault where the physical host server or the parent partition suffers a complete failure, such as a motherboard malfunction or a blue screen of death. Everything on the host server fails, including the virtual machines that are effectively powered off without any control.

You can see what will happen in Figure 2.16. The virtual machines on the failed host have stopped. A Failover Cluster knows if other hosts in the cluster are operational by using a heartbeat. This heartbeat is transmitted over the network. A host is considered offline when the heartbeat from that host fails. At this point, the cluster resources, or the virtual machines, are relocated to other hosts with sufficient spare capacity. This is a failover. The virtual machines are relocated, and then they are powered up. They will behave like a physical server that has had the power removed, so they will report unexpected shutdowns. There is a brief outage in this scenario while the virtual machine reboots. Fortunately, a virtual machine can boot up much more quickly than a physical machine can because there is no BIOS to start or physical devices to initialize and test.

FIGURE 2.15
A nontotal clustered host failure

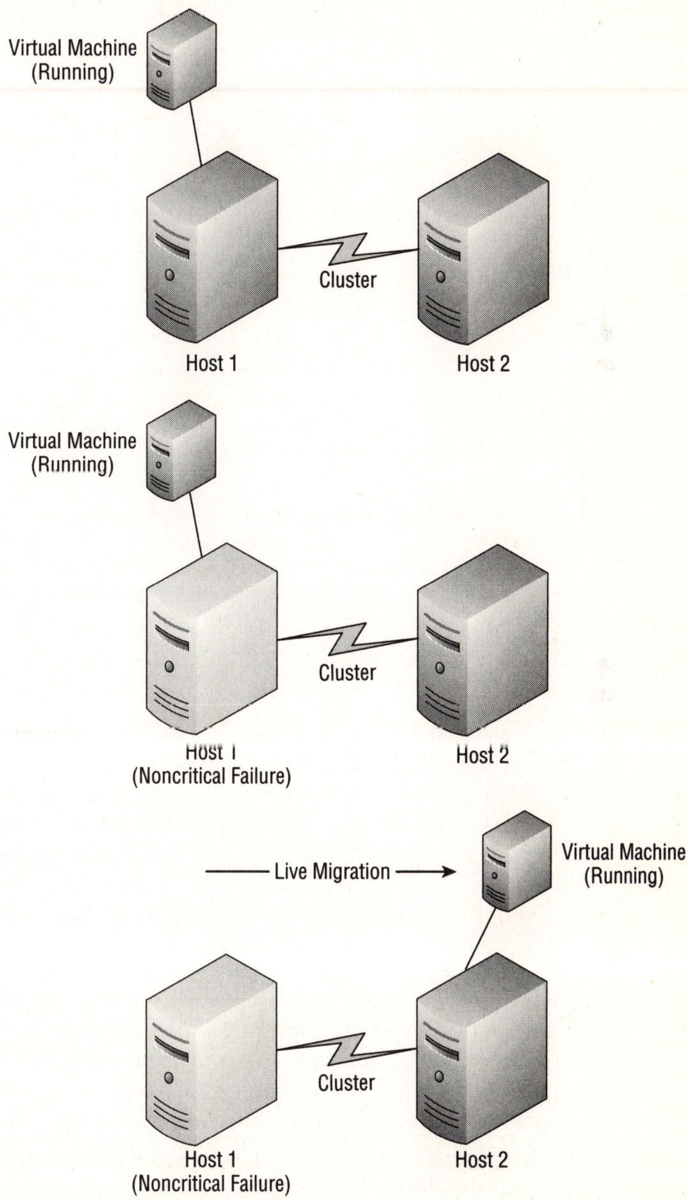

FIGURE 2.16
Total clustered host failure

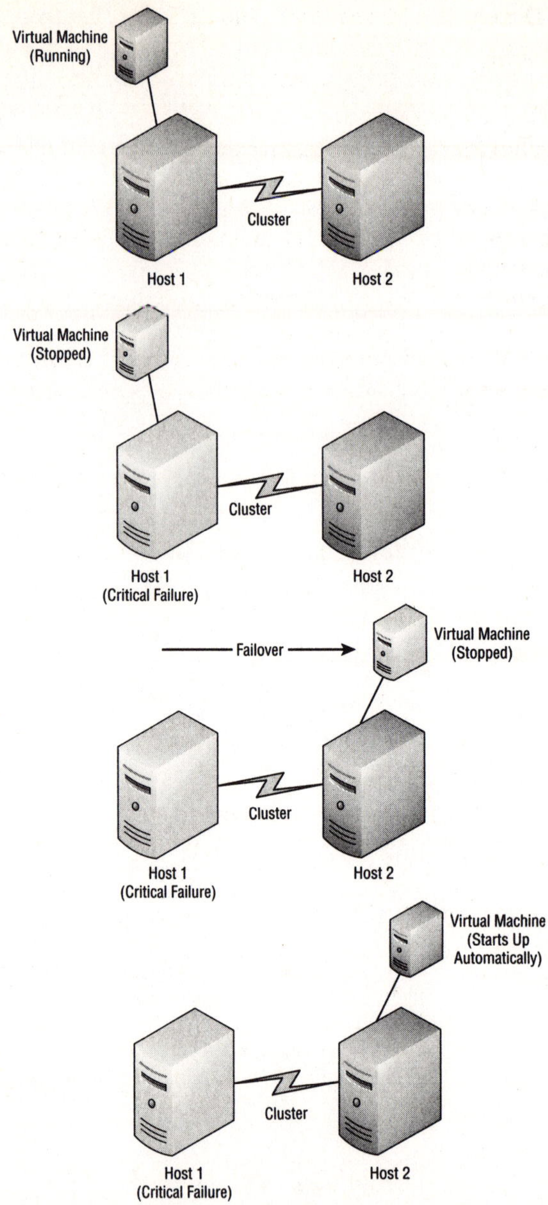

The result of this is that all virtual machines in the cluster become highly available. This gives you better levels of uptime than can be expected with traditional physical servers. The virtual machines are now independent of the hardware and can continue providing services despite hardware failure. The only way to match that with physical servers is to implement a cluster for every physically hosted application, something that would be very expensive and would increase administrative effort.

The Design of a Hyper-V Cluster

This is where veterans of clustering with Windows NT 4.0, Windows 2000, and Windows Server 2003 will shut the book and run out of the building. Please don't; things improved immensely with the release of Windows Server 2008. It used to be the case that building a cluster was something that was done by an expensive consultant over the course of a week, and walking past a production system was banned in case it upset the cluster. Building a cluster became a simple operation that takes only a few minutes in Windows Server 2008, and that continues with Windows Server 2008 R2. The main prerequisite is that you get the hardware design right. This starts with the storage.

A cluster will use a common storage system to store the data for its clustered resources. This common storage is a storage area network (SAN), usually iSCSI or fiber Channel connected. SCSI (SAS) shared storage is also supported. That means that all of the virtual machine files (and any passthrough disks) will be stored on the SAN. The requirements for the SAN are as follows:

- It is certified for Windows Server 2008 R2.
- The SAN supports SCSI-3 persistent reservation. This may require a SAN firmware upgrade.

We mentioned earlier that a nonclustered Hyper-V host server should have at least two physical network adapters — one for the parent partition and one for the virtual network. Microsoft recommends that you have at least four physical network adapters in a clustered Hyper-V host server. Each network adapter should be at least 1 Gb. Figure 2.17 shows the purpose of each network adapter.

- NIC 1: The parent partition.
- NIC 2: The virtual network.
- NIC 3: This is used for network traffic related to Cluster Shared Volumes (CSVs).
- NIC 4: This is used for network traffic caused by Live Migrations.

Figure 2.17
Four NICs in a clustered Hyper-V host server

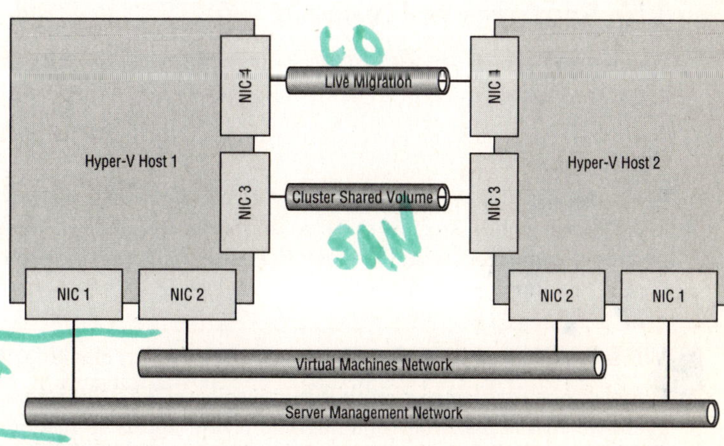

It is supported to merge the roles of NIC 3 and NIC 4 when the Hyper-V deployment will not have much CSV-redirected I/O traffic or too many Live Migrations.

You should allow for two more physical network adapters with MPIO enabled (for storage path fault tolerance) if you are using an iSCSI SAN. This sort of deployment might look like Figure 2.18.

FIGURE 2.18
Clustered Hyper-V host server with iSCSI

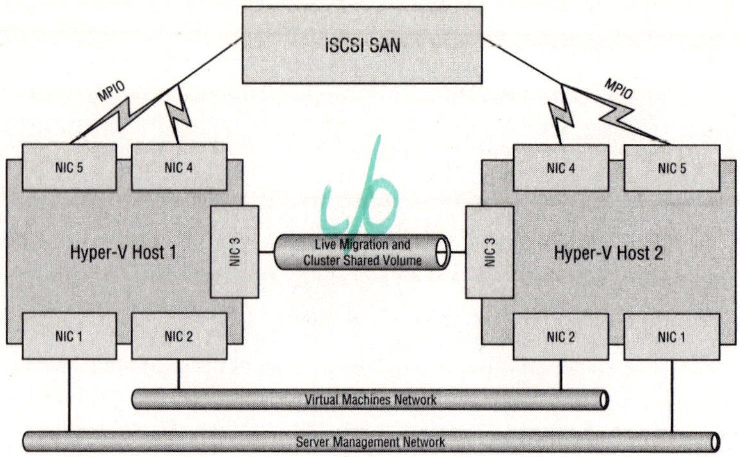

These additional physical network adapters might start to drive up the costs of a clustered Hyper-V deployment, especially if you are using blade servers with enclosure-based switching modules. You should consult with an enterprise-level hardware vendor to discuss alternatives. Some solutions can create physical network connections without purchasing the additional network adapters and blade enclosure switching modules.

Getting the hardware in place is the hard bit. That's where working with a good enterprise-level hardware reseller will help. The easy bit is deploying the cluster. We'll talk more about that in Chapter 6.

The Features of Hyper-V

You can make the most of a product only if you know what it can do. We will now cover a number of the features of Hyper-V and look at how each of them works.

Fault Tolerance

We've discussed how fault tolerance works with a Windows Server 2008 R2 cluster. It is important to know your history in order to understand where you are today. We are going to look at where we came from with Windows Server 2008 Hyper-V clustering and then see how the new features are implemented with a Windows Server 2008 R2 Hyper-V cluster.

WINDOWS SERVER 2008 QUICK MIGRATION

Hyper-V was first released with Windows Server 2008. It provided the ability to have highly available virtual machines that ran on a Hyper-V cluster. It supported automated failover, as was discussed earlier, in the event of a total host failure. We also were given the ability to move virtual machines between hosts using a process called Quick Migration. Quick Migration would move a running virtual machine between different hosts in a Hyper-V cluster using the following mechanism:

1. The virtual machine was usually installed on a dedicated SAN LUN with no other virtual machines on it.
2. The virtual machine was placed into a saved state. Start your stopwatch here.
3. The cluster disk was failed from one host to another host.
4. The virtual machine was woken up from its saved state to return it to where it was prior to the Quick Migration. Stop your stopwatch.

There is downtime with this move, caused by the save state task and the disk failover. The total amount of time was a function of how much memory needed to be written to disk (save state), how fast the SAN connection was, and how long it would take the cluster to failover a clustered disk.

Some tests were done using a Hyper-V cluster, using 15K disks in a SAN, with 4 Gbps Fibre Channel connections. A virtual machine with 1 GB of RAM had at least 8 seconds of downtime during the quick migration. Virtual machines with 4 GB RAM experienced 12 seconds of downtime and a virtual machine with 28 GB of RAM had a massive 70-second outage.

This process received a lot of criticism from Microsoft's competitors. For many virtual machines, this wasn't a big issue. But it certainly was an issue for Microsoft's marketing and for virtual machines that were mission critical.

There were a few problems with Quick Migration:

Shared Nothing Disks No two Windows computers can share a disk. They both can be connected to it, but only one of them can use it at a time. There had to be some form of handover between the host servers of the disk that a virtual machine was stored on.

It was, in theory, possible to store more than one virtual machine on a SAN LUN in a Windows Server 2008 Hyper-V cluster. However, Virtual Machine Manager 2008 did not support this.

Saved State Instead of Live Migration VMware ESX had a feature called VMotion for several years before the release of Windows Server 2008 Hyper-V. This allowed virtual machines to be moved between clustered ESX hosts with zero downtime. It used a mechanism whereby the memory of a running virtual machine was replicated from the original host server to the destination host server. The ownership of the virtual machine files would be swapped when this was complete. Although a VMotion move might have taken some time, there was no perceivable downtime (just a few milliseconds) for the virtual machine, in the eyes of users, network applications, and monitoring systems.

Users and potential customers of ESX or Hyper-V compared Quick Migration, and Microsoft usually came up second best. Those who chose Hyper-V did so knowing that they were also going with Microsoft System Center and with the promise of Live Migration in the not-so-distant future.

This brings us to Windows Server 2008 R2. Microsoft started to release information about what was to come at the end of 2008. Windows Server 2008 R2 was released in mid-2009 with some big improvements that finally met the needs of those who wanted something like VMotion from a Microsoft virtualization solution.

Cluster Shared Volume

CSV was introduced as a feature with Windows Server 2008 R2 Failover Clustering. It is intended to resolve some of the issues with the storage design of Windows Server 2008 clustered Hyper-V host servers:

Simplified Storage It was very likely that you had one SAN LUN for every highly available virtual machine. This complicated the storage design and management. Many LUNs would have to be created. Medium and large organizations often have a dedicated SAN administration team, and this means that another team is involved in the so-called rapid deployment of virtual machines. This negated the possibility of self-service virtual machine deployment for many organizations.

Mistake Prone With so many LUNs, it was a possibility that mistakes would be made, especially when virtual machines were being removed and physical storage was being recycled.

Disk Failover The failover of a virtual machine required the disk that it was stored on to change ownership. This might take a second or several seconds.

> **Warning: CSV Is for Hyper-V Only**
>
> **You will be warned that CSV is intended to be used only for storing Hyper-V virtual machines when you set up this feature. It is not supported for any other function such as file sharing, databases, or Exchange.**

The ideal solution is a single disk. You need to be able to store many virtual machines on it, and you want to be able to allow many Hyper-V host servers to access it at once. This is what CSV is, as shown in Figure 2.19. There are two host servers. Both of the servers are able to access the CSV. Virtual machines are executing on both host servers, and their files are stored on the single CSV.

Figure 2.19
A CSV

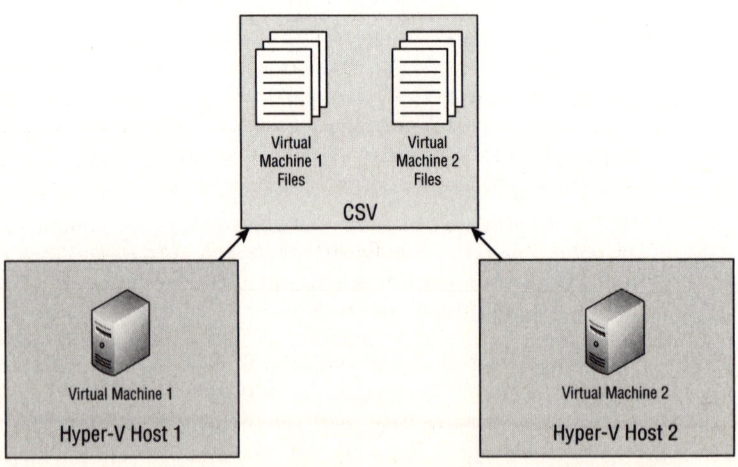

A CSV is a special NTFS filesystem. It still has the concept of shared nothing. There is one coordinator (owner) of the CSV. It delegates access to the virtual machine folders and files to the appropriate host servers. Those servers can then load their virtual machines from the files stored on the CSV. The CSV coordinator role will failover to a different node in the Hyper-V cluster if the original one fails. This role can also be manually failed over.

You can have more than one CSV in a Hyper-V cluster. Each CSV appears as a mounted drive in `C:\ClusterStorage` as a subfolder that is named after the CSV. This occurs on every Hyper-V host in the cluster. For example, if you create CSV1, then it will appear as `C:\ClusterStorage\Volume1` on every Hyper-V host. The virtual machines will be stored in subfolders within the CSV folder. This makes the virtual machine files available on every host server at once.

CSV has a feature that is both useful and troubling. This feature is called Redirected I/O, and it uses the NIC that you installed in the clustered Hyper-V host for CSV networking. The primary purpose of Redirected I/O is to provide storage path fault tolerance. You can see an example of this in Figure 2.20. If a host loses its direct connectivity, then all storage traffic will be redirected to the CSV coordinator via the CSV network (Ethernet network). The CSV coordinator will then relay this traffic to the CSV storage system.

FIGURE 2.20
Redirected I/O in action

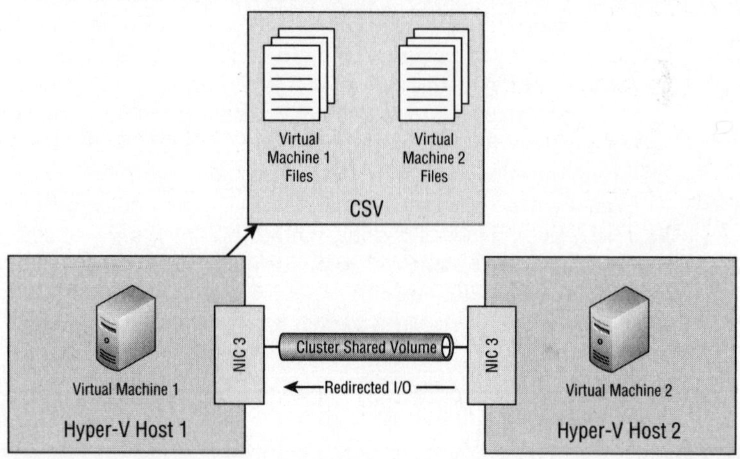

That's the good part of CSV. Yes, there will be a drop in performance, but that is much better than the alternative. Without Redirected I/O, the virtual machines on a host will suddenly stop if there is a storage link failure between the host and the CSV storage. Redirected I/O will allow the virtual machines to continue operating (at a lesser performance capacity) until the storage link is repaired. Ideally you have implemented MPIO for your storage links, and this won't be a situation you have to face.

The other scenario where Redirected I/O is used is less appealing. Some administrative functions on a filesystem require exclusive access to the filesystem. For example, say you wanted to back up your CSV using Data Protection Manager (DPM) 2010 using Volume Shadow Copy at the host level. The CSV coordinator will need exclusive access to the CSV. The only way to get that is to initiate Redirected I/O, forcing all other hosts in the cluster to redirect storage commands via the CSV coordinator. You'll later read in Chapter 10, "Data Protection Manager 2010," about how to implement DPM 2010 and similar backup products with CSV to avoid this issue by backing up at the storage level using a VSS provider rather than at the host level.

This is when you start to ask questions about the sizing of CSVs. How many virtual machines can you place on a CSV? The answer to this question is, it depends. Despite what some have posted on the Internet, the official guidance from Microsoft is that you need to understand both your storage system and the storage performance requirements of your virtual machines.

Your assessment (Chapter 4, "Assessing the Existing Infrastructure") will produce a performance metric, called IOPS, for any physical machines that you will convert into virtual machines. This measures the number of I/O operations per second for the machine.

Your storage system will have an IOPS rating as well. Typically, this is higher when you add more disks into the LUN. For example, if one disk has an IOPS rating of 200, then four disks will have an IOPS rating of 800. Note that this is for RAID-10. A RAID-5 implementation usually gives you just 25 percent of the RAID-10 potential, so our example would have an IOPS rating of 200. This is made much more complicated when you use a high-end SAN that implements a form of virtual disk that is spread across all disks in the SAN rather than just a subset of them. You will need to consult with your storage provider or an expert in the product in question for help on this.

Armed with those figures, you can figure out how many or which virtual machines you can place into a CSV. Eventually you will reach a point where the IOPS performance rating won't allow for any more virtual machines in the CSV, and you will have to add another CSV.

There is also the all-your-eggs-in-one-basket argument. Do you really want to place all your virtual machines in a single CSV? You could have multiple CSVs. Some could be implemented on RAID-5 for larger and slower VHDs. Others might be set up on RAID-10 for faster VHDs. You can even place redundant virtual machines onto different CSVs. If one CSV does experience an outage, then the redundant virtual machine will be unaffected and continue to provide the service to the network.

Even if you do implement multiple CSVs, your implementation and ongoing management will be much easier than was possible with the Windows Server 2008 single VM per disk option. Your need to interact with the SAN administration team is massively reduced, and your ability to provide self-service virtual machine provisioning is enhanced. Most importantly, the disk does not need to be failed over when a virtual machine is moved between hosts in the Hyper-V cluster.

Sanbolic Melio FS

A company called Sanbolic sells a cluster filesystem product called Melio FS. This product can be used to replace CSV. This eliminates the need for a CSV coordinator and the problems that you can have with Redirected I/O mode. Melio FS also provides configuration options for tuning the performance of the filesystem. Sanbolic Melios FS is completely supported by Windows Server 2008 R2 Hyper-V and System Center Virtual Machine Manager 2008 R2.

Live Migration

This is the one feature change in Windows Server 2008 R2 that changed Hyper-V from something that was briefly considered as a solution to something that was seriously considered and then implemented as a production solution in many organizations.

Live Migration is a replacement for Quick Migration. It allows virtual machines to be migrated from one host in a Hyper-V cluster to another with no perceivable downtime to applications, users, or monitoring systems. In fact, Microsoft claims that the time between the virtual machine being on one host and then on another is around two milliseconds.

The process is extremely easy to use as a Hyper-V administrator. You simply select a virtual machine and perform a Live Migration in your preferred administration tool (Failover Clustering or Virtual Machine Manager 2008 R2). The process itself is rather interesting.

Figure 2.21 shows the basis for the Live Migration process. We have shown CSV in our infrastructure. It is not a requirement for Live Migration, but it does make things easier. The key to the process is the Live Migration network. This is why we have a NIC for the role.

FIGURE 2.21
Network and CSV for Live Migration

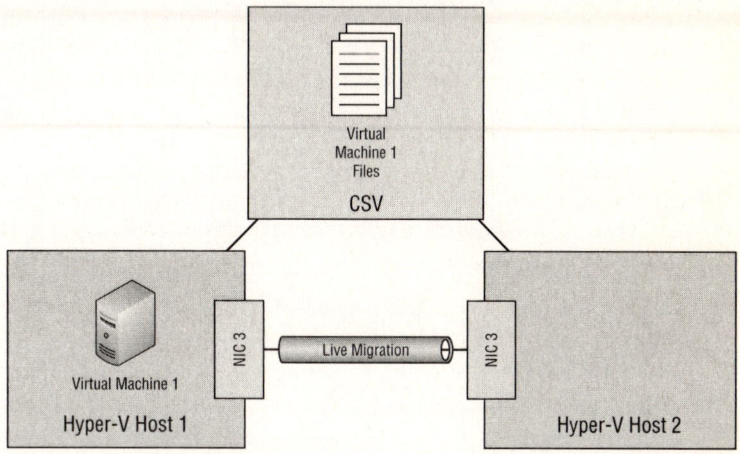

In our example, Virtual Machine 1 will be moved from Host 1 to Host 2 via Live Migration. During the process, the memory of Virtual Machine 1 will be transferred from Host 1 to Host 2. This requires a high-quality network connection. That's why the Live Migration network cards are at least 1 Gb in speed (maybe even 1 0Gb) and are on a private and nonrouted network with only the Hyper-V hosts from the cluster connected.

We would see what is shown in Figure 2.22 if we were to dive a little deeper into the hosts and the virtual machine right before a Live Migration. The virtual machine is running on Host 1. The virtual machine consists of a configuration, RAM, and a state (what is currently happening in devices such as the virtual processors). We will now see how all of this will be moved or copied from Host 1 to Host 2 by Live Migration.

FIGURE 2.22
Before the Live Migration

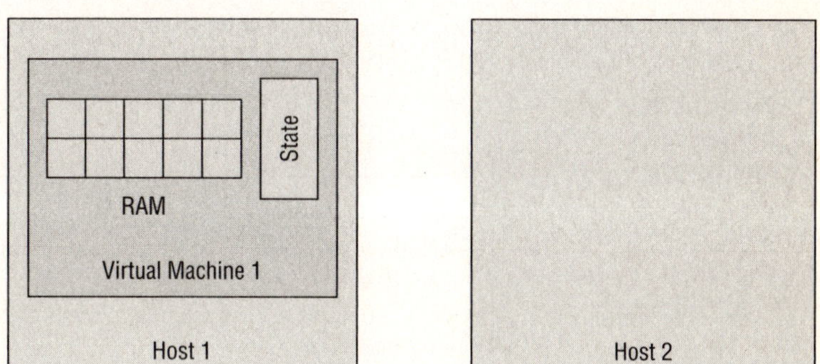

The process starts by copying the virtual machine configuration from Host 1 to Host 2, as depicted in Figure 2.23. The virtual machine exists as an invisible and empty zombie on Host 2 at this point. Remember that the virtual machine is still running on Host 1.

FIGURE 2.23
Copying the virtual machine configuration

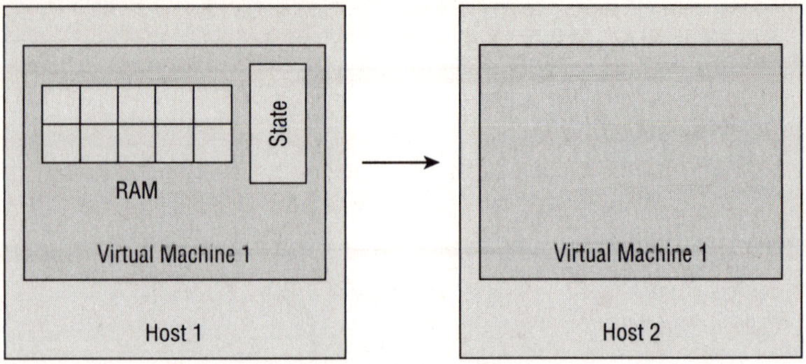

You can see in Figure 2.24 that the memory of the virtual machine is being copied from Host 1 to Host 2 while the virtual machine is still running. The memory is broken up in pages. Each page is copied, over the Live Migration network, from the origin host to the destination host. As a page is copied, it is marked as clean.

FIGURE 2.24
Copying the virtual machine memory

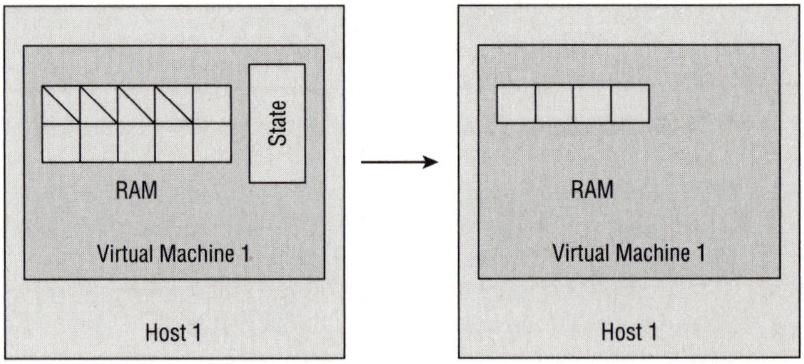

The virtual machine is running on Host 1. This means that the contents of its memory are changing. Pages that have previously been marked as clean may contain objects that have changed. These pages are marked as dirty and must be copied again from the origin host to the destination host. You can see this in Figure 2.25.

FIGURE 2.25
Copying dirty memory pages

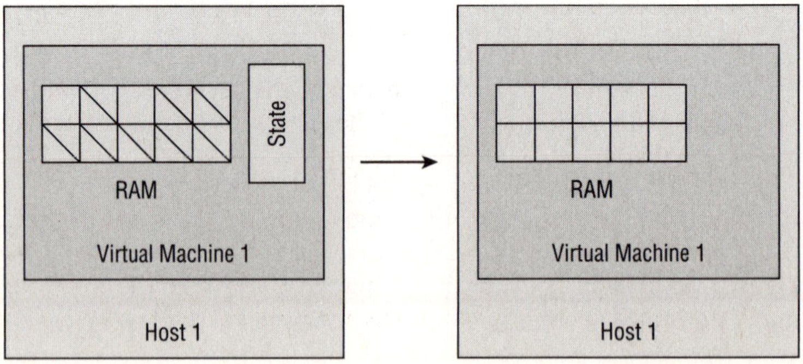

Live Migration will perform this memory copy (over the Live Migration network) a certain number of times. It will complete this stage when the following has happened:

- It has copied everything, and all pages in the virtual machine are marked as clean.
- Almost everything is marked as clean, and there is very little left to copy.
- Live Migration has completed 10 cycles of copying memory.

Now comes the time to measure downtime. The virtual machine is paused on the origin host server. This is done so that the state of the virtual machine (which is very fluid) can be copied in a consistent state. You can see the paused virtual machine in Figure 2.26.

FIGURE 2.26
The virtual machine is paused.

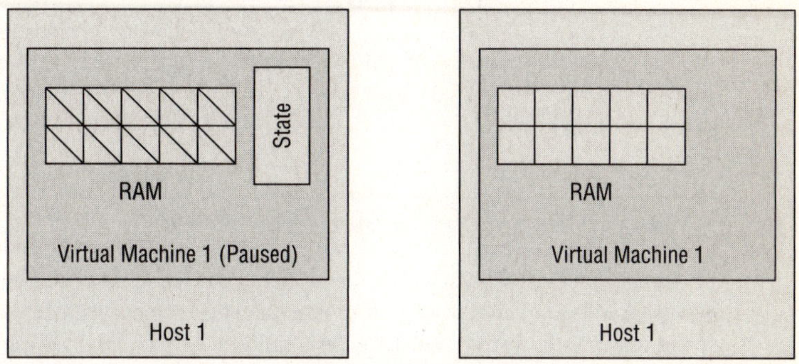

The state of the virtual machine can now be copied (Figure 2.27) from the origin host server to the destination host server. The state is a tiny amount of data, and this is completed extremely quickly.

FIGURE 2.27
The virtual machine state is copied.

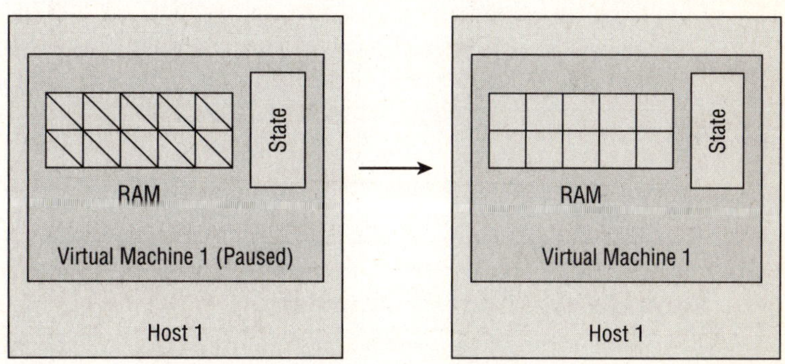

Everything about the virtual machine's dynamic state has been copied from Host 1 to Host 2. Host 2 can safely take control of the virtual machine's storage (VHDs or passthrough disks). The virtual machine is removed from Host 1and started up (from the paused state) on Host 2. The final result is illustrated in Figure 2.28.

According to Microsoft, if you looked at your stopwatch, the virtual machine was in a paused state for about two milliseconds. That is less than any network application will ever notice. You can ping a virtual machine Live Migration on a correctly configured cluster and not drop a single packet. A user who is logged into a virtual machine via Remote Desktop won't notice a thing.

FIGURE 2.28
The Live Migration is completed.

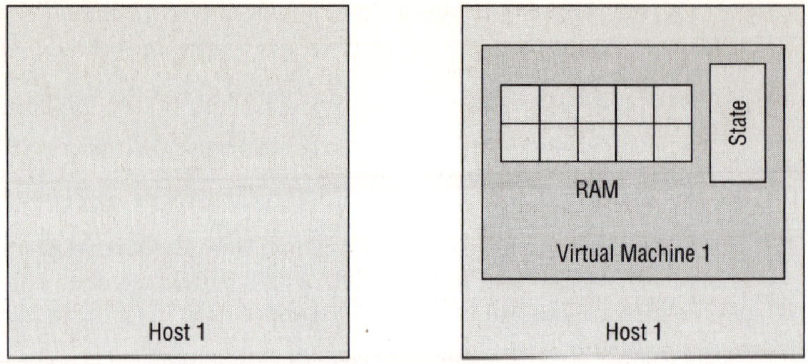

This technology has been out in the wild for some time, and it is proven. It is a very cool process, and you'll impress your boss if you can draw this on a whiteboard during any conversations about Hyper-V.

WHAT TO WATCH OUT FOR IN LIVE MIGRATION

There are a few things to watch out for. Some Linux distributions bind their TCP/IP configuration to a MAC address. The Live Migration process creates a new virtual machine configuration. By default, the new configuration will get a new, random MAC address. This will cause the virtual machine to lose its network connectivity. Set the virtual network adapters in Linux virtual machines to use a static IP address.

Windows Server 2008 R2 allows virtual machines to Live Migrate between different generations of physical processor from the same manufacturer. Make sure that the option to disable advanced processor options is selected in the virtual machine.

Windows Server 2008 R2 also allows virtual machines to use some advanced networking features. There is a check box for this in the virtual network adapter properties. A virtual machine cannot live migrate to a host that does not support these features if this option is enabled in the virtual machine.

With a little preparation work, it is possible to mount an ISO image across the network in a virtual machine. You cannot live migrate a virtual machine if it is currently mounting an ISO image in this fashion. Best practice is to only mount ISO images for as long as you need to do so.

Second-Level Address Translation

A virtual machine believes that it has its own physical memory. This memory actually exists as physical memory in the host server. It is critical that memory from one virtual machine doesn't end up in another virtual machine. Something must provide some sort of mapping process between the physical memory in the Hyper-V host server and the virtual memory in the virtual machine.

With Windows Server 2008 R2, this process was handled by Hyper-V. It sat between the physical and virtual memory. The problem with this is that it consumes CPU cycles and a small amount of memory. The memory overhead for this process is negligible and is really only a concern in huge Hyper-V hosts. However, the impact on the CPU can be noticeable when virtual machines are running a lot of processes that are constantly paging memory. An example of this would be a virtual Terminal Server/Remote Desktop Services session host.

AMD and Intel have both provided new technologies (AMD RVI and Intel EPT) in recently released processors. These technologies allow a new feature in Windows Server 2008 R2, called *Second Level Address Translation* (SLAT), to work. SLAT offloads the labor of maintaining a mapping between physical and virtual memory to dedicated features of the host's physical processors. Using hardware to perform the task is more efficient than using software (Hyper-V) to perform this operation. Figures from Microsoft estimate that using SLAT-enabled processors will save 1 to 2 MB of RAM per virtual machine in the Hyper-V host server. More importantly, there will be less of an impact on the physical processor. That's kind of ironic because the physical processor is now doing the mapping work directly. The effect of this is that virtual machines that were negatively impacted by the pre-SLAT mapping will notice a serious improvement in performance. Many of the recent benchmarks for Windows Server 2008 R2 virtual machines (such as Remote Desktop Services or SQL Server) have been based on host servers with SLAT-enabled physical processors.

Running Windows Server 2008 R2 does not guarantee that SLAT will be running at the host level. You must also have physical processors that support the feature. Figure 2.29 compares hosts that do not support SLAT with those that do.

FIGURE 2.29
Comparing SLAT with non-SLAT hosts

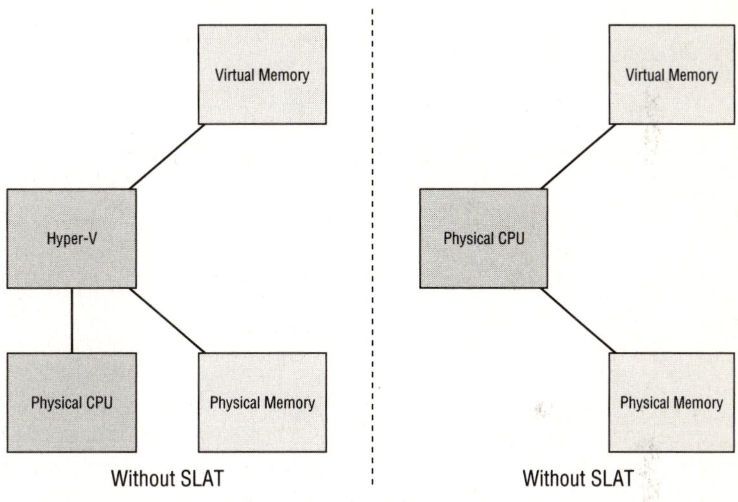

Virtual Machine Queue

Virtual Machine Queue (VMQ) is another new feature to Windows Server 2008 R2 that is intended to optimize how virtual machines perform. VMQ will optimize network traffic processing for virtual machines. Like with SLAT, they depend on new hardware. VMQ has the ability to offload this processing to specialized network adapters with VMQ functionality.

It is not possible to have VMQ in Windows Server 2008 host servers at all or in Windows Server 2008 R2 host servers without the specialized hardware.

Without VMQ, network processing behaves as follows for traffic that is leaving a virtual machine:

- The virtual machine copies the memory containing the traffic to the parent partition.
- A virtual network runs in the parent partition and processes the traffic. It will perform MAC and VLAN ID validation.

- Traffic to other virtual machines on the host will result in a memory copy from the parent partition to the destination virtual machine.
- Traffic to the physical network will be relayed via the physical NIC for the virtual network.

Traffic to the virtual machine (without VMQ) will be processed as follows:

1. The traffic reaches the virtual network and is filtered for MAC addresses and VLAN ID.
2. The network traffic data is copied by the parent partition into the memory of the virtual machine.
3. There is a context switch to the virtual machine so it can process the data.

Figure 2.30 shows the data flow path of Hyper-V virtual machine networking without VMQ-enabled hardware.

FIGURE 2.30
Hyper-V networking without VMQ

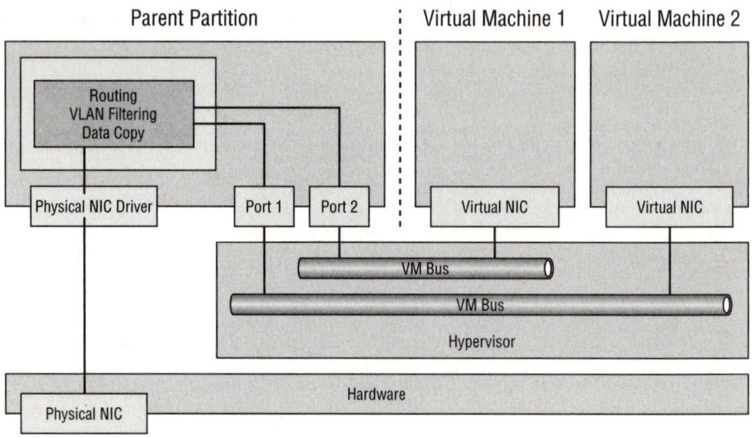

VMQ will offload the process of networking traffic to a VMQ enabled physical network adapter. This modifies the data flow path as shown in Figure 2.31. The changes to the process are as follows:

- A queue is created and managed by the VMQ capable network adapter.
- The network adapter performs VLAN ID validation and MAC address lookup.
- The network adapter places the inbound VM network traffic into the appropriate queue.
- Queues are mapped to a virtual machine's address space so that network traffic data is placed into the virtual machine's memory without a resource wasting copy operation.

You may notice in Figure 2.31 that the pre-VMQ mechanism (marked with a dotted line) is still available. You can use this path by disabling advanced networking features in a virtual machine's virtual network adapter properties. This would be done if you need to be able to Live Migrate a virtual machine from a VMQ-capable Hyper-V host server to another non-VMQ-capable Hyper-V host server in the same cluster.

FIGURE 2.31
Hyper-V networking with VMQ hardware

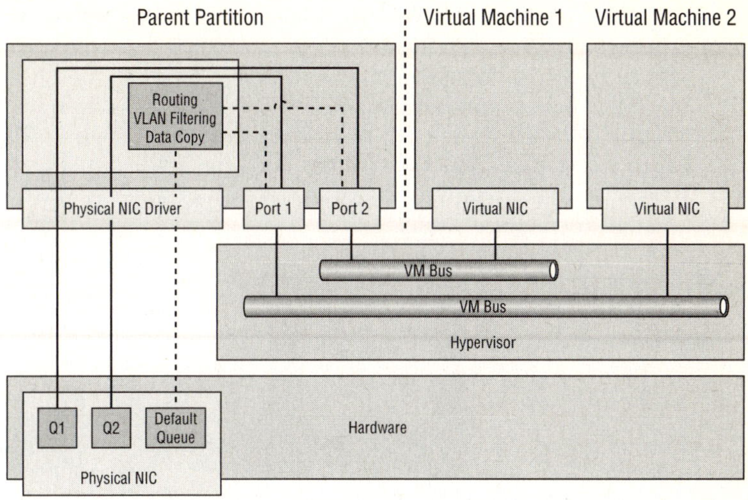

VMQ has the capability of greatly improving virtual machine networking. This might be noticed with a virtual machine that is providing network-intensive services such as streaming media. VMQ will also reduce the CPU overhead of the parent partition.

There is a catch — VMQ can be used only on VMQ capable hardware. At this point, there are very few hardware offerings that provide this capability.

Core Parking

One of the major reasons for deploying a hardware or server virtualization solution is to reduce the cost of powering many physical servers. This allows you to consolidate many physical machines into fewer Hyper-V host servers, each running a number of virtual machines.

Think about your server network. When are your servers busy? Are they always busy, 24 hours a day, 7 days a week? Or are they busy from 8 a.m. until 6 p.m. on weekdays and then just ticking over for the rest of the week? If this is the case, then you are still consuming power. Hyper-V host servers still have to power their CPUs during those quiet periods. If you look at your performance metrics, you might even find that those servers have quiet periods during the day. In fact, there are quiet periods that are too quick for the human eye to even notice, where the CPU is idle but is still drawing power.

What's happening with all this power? The CPU draws in power, even if it is idle. The CPU is a huge generator of heat. Fans in the server must be powered to push that hot air out the back of the server. The computer room or datacenter air conditioning system must then draw that hot air out either for recycling or to eject it from the facility. That means each and every server is consuming power to run and cool idle CPUs.

This applies equally to Hyper-V host servers. They may have periods where the virtual machines are not utilizing the physical processors. Those physical processors are consuming power, and more power is consumed to cool them.

Microsoft came up with a solution called *Core Parking* and included it with Windows 7 and Windows Server 2008 R2. This means that Hyper-V host servers can use this solution.

The aim of the Core Parking is to place idle processor cores into a sleep state. This reduces their power consumption and heat generation. Reducing the heat generation reduces the power consumption to eject and treat that heat.

It will be easier to understand how Core Parking works if we show an example of it working. Figure 2.32 shows the two quad-core processors in a physical Windows Server 2008 R2 machine such as a Hyper-V host server. Both processors are being fully utilized by processes. These processes may be executing tasks for the parent partition or the child partitions (virtual machines) on the host server.

FIGURE 2.32
Two fully utilized processors

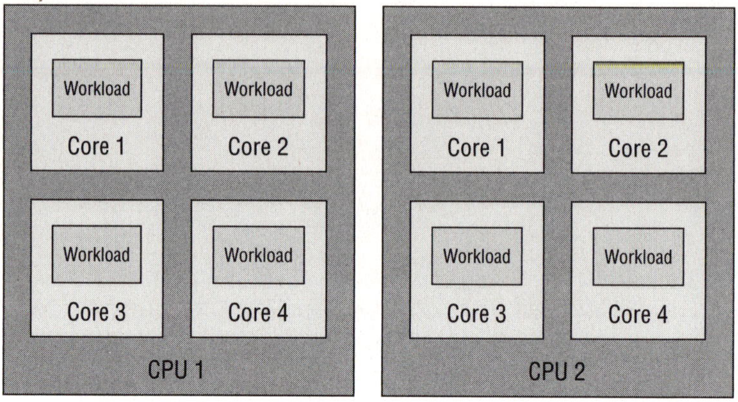

At some point, the processor run queue length (the number of processors waiting to run on the CPUs) may reduce in size. The cores in the processors now may be underutilized. That means there is now more processing power than there are workloads to use it, as shown in Figure 2.33. You can see that CPU 1 is only 50 percent utilized and CPU 2 is only 50 percent utilized. Now those idle processor cores are consuming power and generating heat for no reason.

FIGURE 2.33
CPU cores are underutilized.

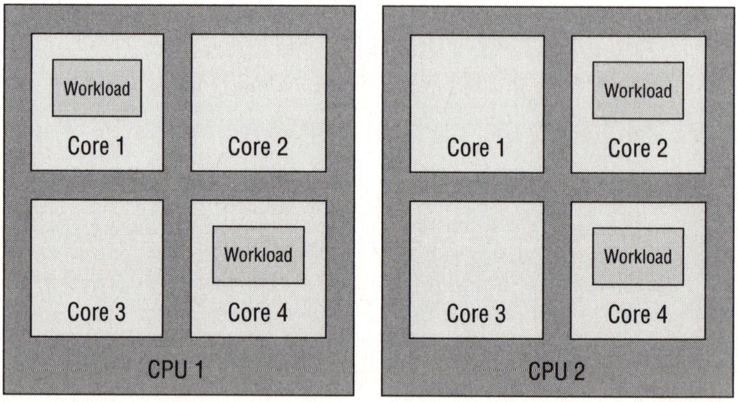

Students of physics and science-fiction fans may know that you cannot observe a subject without impacting that subject. Windows needs to see whether there are enough workloads to justify keeping processor cores operational and powered. If Windows checked utilization rates too frequently, then it would cause a performance issue. However, if the Windows checks were too infrequent, then it would not produce enough power savings. Microsoft found that it got the best results by checking whether cores were being utilized every 100 milliseconds. This was the sweet spot for determining whether power was being wasted or whether processors were being appropriately utilized.

This check will determine that the cores and processors in Figure 2.33 are being underutilized. Windows will now optimize the workloads by placing them onto as few processors as possible (shown in Figure 2.34).

FIGURE 2.34
Workloads are consolidated.

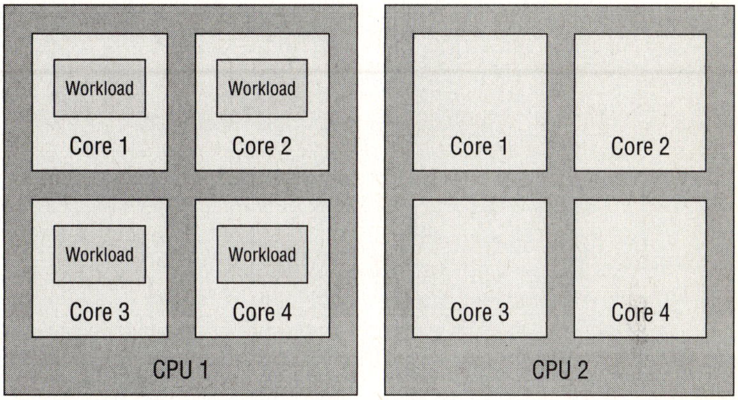

The individual idle cores can be parked, or put to sleep, after the workloads are consolidated. This may result in an entire processor being parked, as in Figure 2.35.

FIGURE 2.35
Idle cores are parked.

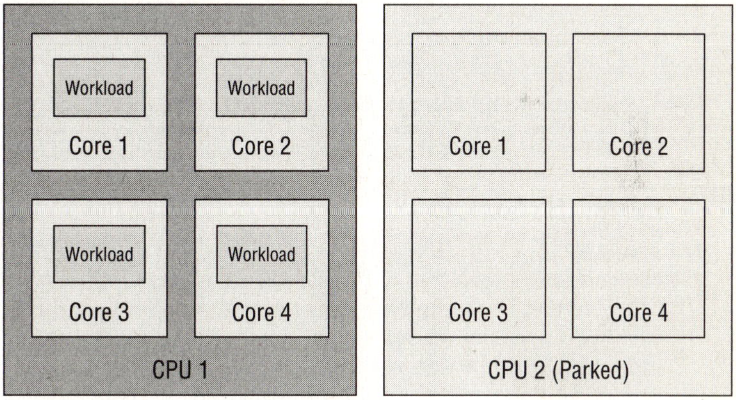

Those parked cores are no longer consuming power. They are no longer producing heat. Your server's fans are no longer working as hard. Your datacenter air conditioning doesn't have to treat as much hot air.

You may be thinking that this saving might only last milliseconds. You're right; an increase in processor capacity may occur very quickly and necessitate that the parked cores are brought back into action, as you'll see in Figure 2.36.

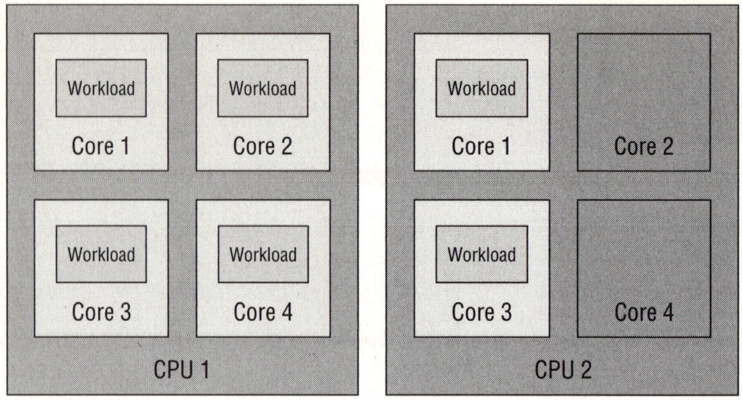

FIGURE 2.36
Increased workloads end core parking.

This brief moment in time might produce an incredibly tiny saving in power costs. Add up all these little moments over a day, a week, or a year, and there will be savings. Late at night when most virtual machines are idle, you may have Hyper-V host servers that are able to save even more money by using Core Parking.

Core Parking is turned on by default. Microsoft says that the default configuration should suit most servers. You can configure Core Parking on your Windows Server 2008 R2 physical servers (if your hardware has specific requirements) using the command prompt:

```
powercfg -setacvalueindex scheme_current sub_processor bc5038f7-23e0-
↪4960-96da-33abaf5935ec <Percentage of Cores to Keep Active>
```

The following example of this command will instruct Windows to keep 25 percent of cores active:

```
powercfg -setacvalueindex scheme_current sub_processor bc5038f7-23e0-
↪4960-96da-33abaf5935ec 25
```

Core Parking in Windows Server 2008 R2 will add to the savings you will make on your power costs after deploying Hyper-V to consolidate your physical server infrastructure.

Dynamic Memory

The lack of Live Migration was the one thing that people complained about with Windows Server 2008 Hyper-V. We've already talked about how Windows Server 2008 R2 fixed that particular problem. The second thing that people usually complained about was the absence of some memory over-commitment features. In other words, they wanted a solution where Hyper-V would provide only whatever memory was being used by the virtual machine, not what it was assigned. For example, your virtual machine might be assigned 4 GB of RAM, but it might only use 2 GB of that allocation. That would mean there was 50 percent waste. Hyper-V in Windows Server 2008 and Windows Server 2008 R2 has no choice but to provide the virtual machine with all of that 4 GB of RAM, despite the wastage.

It's one thing to waste a little bit of memory in an individual virtual machine. It's another thing entirely if you are wasting memory across many virtual machines in your Hyper-V cluster. This can force you to add additional host servers. You'll also find that the cost of a gigabyte of RAM in a typical virtualization host server (be it using VMware, Microsoft, or Citrix software) is usually a lot higher. That's because you are using larger memory sticks. The larger sticks are exponentially more expensive per gigabyte of RAM. You live with this cost because you know that you'll increase your server consolidation, and the savings in power costs will more than override the costs in hardware. However, wasted gigabytes of RAM at these costs should not be tolerated. We really should squeeze every last drop from the RAM that we purchase.

This wouldn't be a problem in a perfect world. Unfortunately, the world isn't perfect:

Memory Sizing Almost every experienced consultant, engineer, and administrator has had the following experience. You are asked to specify a new server for a new application. You get the Windows Server memory requirements and check with the application vendor for the requirements for their application. You might end up with, for example, 8 GB of RAM by the time you add up the operating system, application components, management agents, antivirus, and various add-ons. Eventually the server goes into production, and your monitoring system tells you that you typically have 60 percent utilization. You've just wasted 40 percent of the memory in the server. Unfortunately, it's not always easy to size physical or virtual machines appropriately.

Memory Usage Optimization You might size a virtual machine perfectly but still have times where physical memory is being underutilized. An application server with 4 GB of RAM may have those times of the day where all 4 GB of RAM are required. But it probably spends most of its time using a lot less of that memory. Many have found that they run out of memory in their Hyper-V host servers before they run out of storage or processor resources. What if you had a way to optimize how memory was allocated to virtual machines to meet their actual requirements for that given time? If you had that solution, then maybe you could put a few more virtual machines onto each Hyper-V host server without sacrificing performance.

Meeting Unexpected Peak Demand From time to time, mission-critical application servers may experience a demand in resource requirements. If a virtual machine is configured with a static 8 GB of RAM, then it cannot grow to meet demand. The responsiveness of the application will be reduced, and this may affect your business at a crucial moment. Imagine a brokerage that cannot react quickly to something that is happening in the stock market. A delay of a few minutes could cost millions. There is only one way to increase the memory allocation to the virtual machine. You have to shut it down, change the static memory allocation, and power it back up again. The demand for the application may have subsided by the time you have resolved the issue. That brokerage may have lost many millions even if you reacted as quickly as humanly possible. You've also added memory to a virtual machine to meet peak demand. That peak might be once a month or once a year. This is a waste of host memory.

Virtual Desktop Infrastructure We talked (at the start of the chapter) about how one of the major drawbacks of VDI was the cost of server memory compared to the cost of desktop/laptop memory. You need to reduce those costs by squeezing more virtual desktops onto a single Hyper-V host server without sacrificing performance.

Over-Commitment

Many people talk about over-commitment when they are discussing ways to optimize how memory is allocated to virtual machines. Microsoft spent several months talking about that term and how over-commitment was actually a bad thing to do.

Think about it: over-commitment means that you are sacrificing performance to squeeze out more resources. The goal of Microsoft's Dynamic Memory is to squeeze out more memory resources without sacrificing performance. This should be your goal too.

Windows Server 2008 R2 Service Pack 1 comes to the rescue with a new feature called Dynamic Memory. Dynamic Memory allows Hyper-V administrators to configure selected virtual machines with a minimum and maximum amount of RAM. The virtual machines (that are configured with Dynamic Memory) will boot up with the minimum memory allocation. Additional memory, up to the configured maximum limit, can be added to the virtual machine as it requires it. This uses the ability of Windows to hot-add memory through Plug and Play. Eventually the virtual machine will no longer need all of that memory. A ballooning process will remove the physical memory from the virtual machine and return it to the Hyper-V host server so that it can be reallocated as required.

You should be warned that Service Pack 1 was still a beta release at the time of writing and the functionality of Dynamic Memory is subject to change.

Hyper-V administrators have the choice of whether to use Dynamic Memory or not on a per-virtual machine basis. They have a number of settings that they can configure:

Start Up RAM (MB) This is the amount of memory that will be allocated to the virtual machine when it powers up. This should be enough to start the operating system at the very least. Realistically, it should be enough for normal virtual machine operational levels.

Maximum RAM (MB) This is the maximum amount that Hyper-V should allow the virtual machine memory size to grow to. Memory will be allocated on an as-needed basis up to this limit.

Buffer (5%–95% Slide Control) It takes some time to allocate additional memory to a virtual machine (very little actually). Hyper-V will assign an additional spare amount of RAM to the virtual machine to deal with instant demand. You can control the size of this buffer using this slide control. The amount of RAM assigned will be a percentage of the currently assigned RAM. For example, if the virtual machine currently requires 4 GB RAM and you set the buffer to 25 percent, then the virtual machine will be allocated 5 GB RAM.

Hyper-V does this on a best-effort basis. There will be no buffer allocation if the virtual machine has reached the memory allocation configured in the Maximum RAM setting.

Memory Priority (Low–High Slide Control) Some virtual machines are more important than others. This control will allow you to prioritize virtual machines for memory allocation.

At the time of writing, Dynamic Memory supported a subset of the operating systems that Microsoft supported as guest operating systems on Hyper-V. The operating systems that are supported by Dynamic Memory are as follows:

- Windows Server 2008 R2 Web, Standard, Enterprise, and Datacenter
- Windows Server 2008 Web, Standard, Enterprise, and Datacenter
- Windows Server 2003 R2 Web, Standard, Enterprise, and Datacenter
- Windows Server 2003 Web, Standard, Enterprise, and Datacenter
- Windows 7 Ultimate and Enterprise
- Windows Vista Ultimate and Enterprise

The key to Dynamic Memory is a Dynamic Memory Virtual Service Client (VSC). Go back to the section "The Architecture" earlier in this chapter if you have forgotten what a VSC is. This VSC will be responsible for hot-adding RAM to the virtual machine and removing it when it is no longer needed.

The Dynamic Memory VSC is provided in the Windows Server 2008 R2 with Service Pack 1 integration components. Your virtual machine must have these integration components (or later) to make use of Dynamic Memory.

You'll better understand Dynamic Memory if we work through an example of how it works. Figure 2.37 shows the physical memory in the Hyper-V host server and the virtual machines that are running on it. You can see that each virtual machine has been allocated memory from the RAM in the host server.

FIGURE 2.37
Virtual machine and physical memory

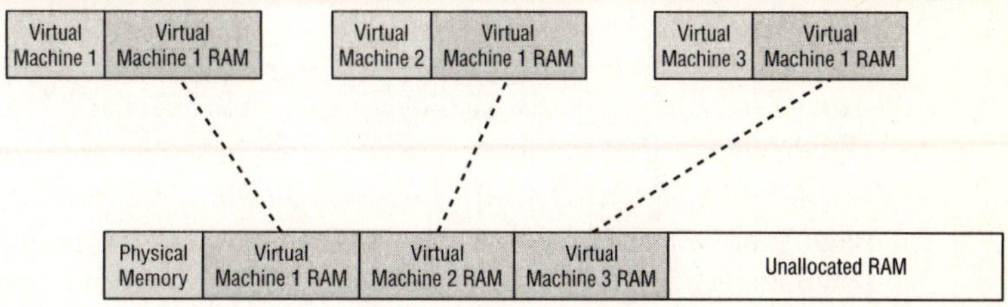

Virtual Machine 3 has been configured to use Dynamic Memory. There is an increase in demand for the services that it provides. Eventually it requires more RAM to meet the increase in demand. The Dynamic Memory VSC in the virtual machine (via the VSP in the parent partition and the VMBus) is able to grow the amount of memory in the virtual machine on an incremental basis. The addition of memory takes advantage of the ability to hot-add via Plug and Play. You can see this in Figure 2.38.

FIGURE 2.38
Dynamic Memory adds memory.

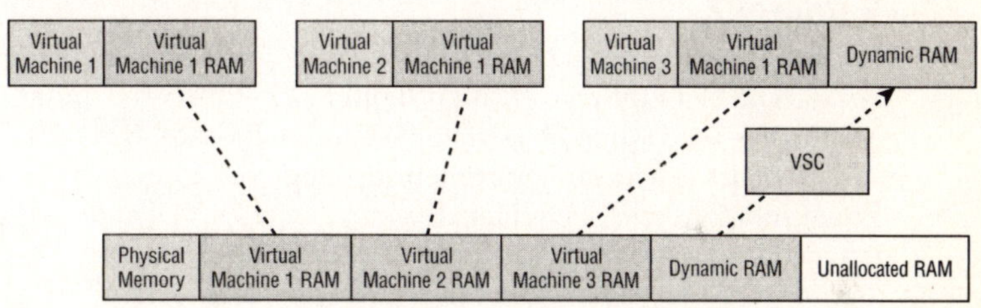

The BIN file, which is a space saver on the physical storage for a saved state, will change in size to match the virtual machine's amount of committed memory. Consider this when sizing the storage for your virtual machines. The paging file of the guest operating system will, if left with the default setting of being managed automatically, expand up to three times the size of the Start Up RAM. This will optimize the performance of the virtual machine. Consider this when sizing the VHD or passthrough disk of the virtual machine.

The need for the additional memory subsides in Virtual Machine 3, and the time arrives to return the memory to the Hyper-V host server. The problem here is that you cannot hot-remove memory from Windows. This is resolved by a ballooning process.

The VSC, which is a driver, reports to the virtual machine that it is using the free memory that is to be return to the Hyper-V host server. This prevents the virtual machine from using the memory. That memory can now be returned to the pool of available memory in the host server. The VSC is effectively inflating itself (like a balloon) in the virtual machine to fill the gap of the returned memory.

This memory is now available to be reassigned to other virtual machines. If Virtual Machine 3 requires more memory, then the VSC will allocate it and deflate the balloon as required (Figure 2.39).

FIGURE 2.39
Dynamic memory VSC balloon

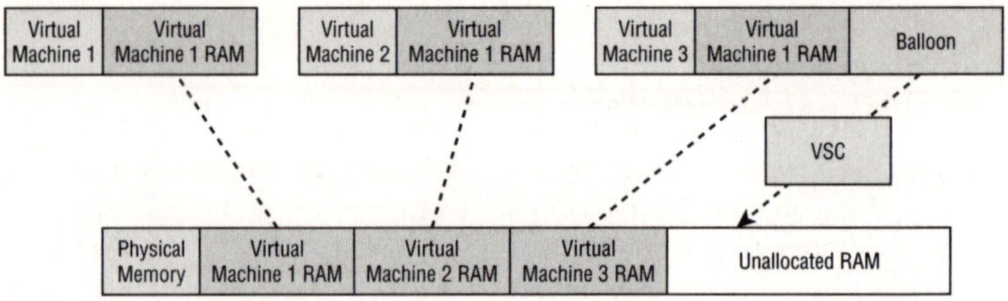

Those of you who are hardware experts are going to be wondering where exactly a virtual machine gets its memory from. Physical memory in a multiprocessor server isn't just one big pool. In fact, it's divided up into Non-Uniform Memory Access (NUMA) nodes. You can have memory performance issues if you give a virtual machine memory from multiple nodes. Dynamic Memory will always try to allocate new memory from the same NUMA node as the existing memory in the virtual machine. It will span NUMA node boundaries only when there is no more available memory in that node. Administrators may decide that spanning NUMA nodes should not be tolerated, and they can disable this from happening at all in the properties of the Hyper-V host server. This means that a virtual machine will only be able to dynamically add memory as long as the current NUMA node has sufficient free space.

RemoteFX

Windows Server 2008 R2 Service Pack (SP) 1 could be called the Hyper-V Service Pack. That's because much of the conversation about SP1 has centered on the two new features it brings to Microsoft's hardware virtualization solution. RemoteFX is the second of those features.

RemoteFX is a technology that brings together a number of virtualization technologies. When solutions such as Remote Desktop Services VDI and session hosts are deployed, there is always a question that you can be sure will be asked: can you put all applications on it? The answer was always no. One of those excluded application types included graphics-intensive applications.

Microsoft acquired a company called Calista Technologies. This gave Microsoft the basis for a new technology called RemoteFX to deal with this problem.

RemoteFX allows graphics-intensive applications to run in a Hyper-V virtual machine. The virtual machine will be either a VDI desktop or a Remote Desktop Services session host. The graphics processing for the application will be offloaded to a graphics processing unit (GPU, or graphics card) in the Hyper-V host server. The high-quality graphics can be transmitted to and displayed on Remote Desktop clients that are logged into these virtual machines.

Management Options

Many people see Hyper-V as more than just virtualization. They see it is an ingredient to a new way of doing IT. Dynamic IT is the ability to provide a very flexible IT infrastructure that can quickly change to add resources and meet the demands of the business. That's what hardware virtualization is all about. Optimized infrastructure gives you the management systems to control all of this flexibility and rapid change. You're going to need management systems to look after your Hyper-V infrastructure, even if you do not buy into the concepts of dynamic IT and optimized infrastructure (yet). We're going to discuss some of the solutions for managing Hyper-V using products from the Microsoft System Center family.

Virtualization Management

An enterprise will have many Hyper-V host servers that they need to manage. You can completely manage all of them using the Failover Clustering console and the Hyper-V console. The problem is that you will be logging in and logging out of a lot of host servers.

Microsoft System Center Virtual Machine Manager (VMM) 2008 R2 is Microsoft's solution for managing Windows Server 2008 R2 Hyper-V. VMM allows you to manage many Hyper-V hosts from a central console. It also allows you to manage Microsoft's older virtualization solution, Virtual Server 2005 R2 SP1, and even the rival product from VMware, ESX.

Most organizations that install Hyper-V will have an existing server infrastructure that they would like to convert into virtual machines that will run on their new virtualization platform. VMM provides the ability to convert physical servers (that are running supported versions of Windows) into virtual machines. It also has the ability to convert virtual machines from the other supported virtualization platforms into Hyper-V virtual machines.

VMM includes the ability to delegate administrative roles and even allow selected end users to provision their own virtual machines from templates in a library using a web-based portal.

As a day-to-day tool, VMM speeds up the administrative process. Everything that it does is based on an included PowerShell module for Hyper-V. This allows you to write your own scripts for automating frequent tasks. Microsoft takes advantage of this ability to combine individual Hyper-V administrative actions into more complex jobs. This can simplify operations such as converting a VHD from one type to another or changing the storage location of a virtual machine.

You can learn much more about VMM 2008 R2 when we talk about it in Chapter 7, "Virtual Machine Manager 2008 R2."

Monitoring

Microsoft provides a monitoring solution for the entire server and application infrastructure. This product is called Microsoft System Center Operations Manager (OpsMgr). This product uses knowledge in the form of management packs to monitor the health and performance of the operating system (Windows, Linux, and Unix) and Microsoft server applications such as SQL Server and Exchange Server. Alerts will be raised, and notifications will be sent out whenever there is a problem.

Using third-party management packs, OpsMgr can also monitor server and storage hardware, as well as server applications such as Tomcat or MySQL. You can even author management packs to monitor bespoke applications. For example, one enterprising person wrote a management pack to monitor a coffee pot.

Operations Manager 2007 and Operations Manager 2007 R2 (with Unix and Linux support) provide support for Windows Server 2008 R2 Hyper-V. This gives you the ability to monitor your entire server and server application infrastructure with the same solution that will monitor your hardware virtualization layer.

You can integrate OpsMgr with VMM 2008 R2. This is called Performance and Resource Optimization (PRO). OpsMgr can detect performance or fault issues on a Hyper-V cluster and inform VMM 2008 R2. VMM 2008 R2 can use Live Migration to move virtual machines onto more suitable host server in the Hyper-V cluster. This will minimize or even eliminate the effect of the issues to any services that are provided by the virtual machines.

OpsMgr provides an optional data warehouse. Reports can be generated from the data that can be retained in it for more than a year. This allows you to report on the performance and health of your Hyper-V host servers, virtual machines, and applications.

Chapter 9 will look at how OpsMgr can be integrated with VMM 2008 R2 and how to use OpsMgr to monitor your Hyper-V infrastructure.

Backup and Recovery

One of the most important tasks that IT can do is back up the business applications and data. A disaster such as the loss of a server can cost a lot of money. Restoring a physical server from scratch can be time-consuming, complex, and very often a frustrating experience. Many administrators have sat nervously, watching the progress bar of a restore job, wondering whether they would still have a job at the end of the day. Virtualization should minimize those risks because the servers in question usually exist merely as a collection of a few files.

Microsoft's backup and recovery solution for Windows Server 2008 R2 is called System Center Data Protection Manager (DPM) 2010. DPM 2010 uses the Volume Shadow Copy Service (VSS) to safely back up servers and compatible application data in a consistent state while they are still operational.

DPM 2010 has been developed to be able to back up Hyper-V virtual machines in a very clever and unique manner. A DPM administrator can configure a backup job to back up a Hyper-V host or the shared storage of a Hyper-V cluster. DPM will initiate VSS to back up the Hyper-V virtual machine files. VSS in the virtual machines will also be initiated. This brings the virtual machine, the services in the virtual machine, and the data in the virtual machine into a state where a DPM agent can back up everything in a consistent and reliable manner.

The data is backed up on a block-level and incremental basis. This means that DPM only backs up the changes within files. A 1 MB change in a 100 GB VHD file will result in a tiny amount of backup data. This allows DPM administrators to run backup jobs as frequently as every 15 minutes with almost no effect on the services being provided or to the network. Gone are the days of the 48-hour weekend full backup and the 8-hour overnight incremental backup job. More frequent backup jobs also minimize the potential for and impact of data loss in the event of a total disaster.

Backup data is stored on a disk storage device. This can be replicated to another DPM server in another site. It can also be streamed to a tape library for offsite archival. It is even possible to replicate the DPM backup store to The Cloud using a partner solution.

Chapter 10 will focus on DPM 2010. There you will learn why many organizations have chosen Hyper-V to change how they do backup and recovery.

Small and Medium Business Management

Smaller organizations may not want to purchase dedicated solutions such as VMM 2008 R2 or OpsMgr 2007 R2. Microsoft provides a solution aimed at organizations with 50 or fewer servers and 500 or fewer desktops. This is called System Center Essentials (SCE) 2010.

SCE 2010 includes much (but not all) of the functionality of Virtual Machine Manager 2008 R2 and Operations Manager 2007 R2 into an integrated, single-console package. It also provides functionality for deploying software and Windows Updates to computers and servers.

The SKU of SCE 2010 is called SCE 2010 Plus and includes DPM 2010 for backing up and recovering your infrastructure.

We will be looking at Hyper-V in the small business in Chapter 11, "The Small and Medium Business." We will also be looking at SCE 2010 in that chapter.

Other Microsoft Solutions

There are some other solutions from Microsoft that you can use to manage your infrastructure. We will not be covering these technologies in this book.

Microsoft System Center Configuration Manager (ConfigMgr) 2007/2007 R2/2007 R3 is a huge systems management product. It provides the ability to deploy operating systems, software, and updates. It also allows you to audit your infrastructure, assess policies, generate reports, and a plethora or other functionality. These solutions can be used for your physical and virtual machine infrastructure.

Microsoft recently acquired a company called Opalis and released its products as part of the System Center family as System Center Opalis. These products are still very new to Microsoft and continue to evolve. Opalis provides the ability to automatically initiate tasks between Microsoft System Center products, Active Directory, and some products from other software companies.

Non-Microsoft Solutions

More and more products are being released by Microsoft partners and third parties to extend the functionality and features of Hyper-V.

Microsoft employee James O'Neill wrote and released a PowerShell module for Hyper-V, which is free to download from `http://pshyperv.codeplex.com/`. Although this is not supported by Microsoft, it has an army of followers who are using it on a daily basis to automate repetitive and complex tasks.

Various other solutions are available including Hyper-V management, storage optimization, backup and recovery, replication, and monitoring. Choosing a viable solution can be a tricky process. The best advice that we can give is that you should do as much research as possible. Do not blindly trust the sales person or the marketing. Seek opinions from others who have used the products. Check to see whether Microsoft has a relationship with the third party and whether the product has been certified to be compatible with Hyper-V (`http://www.windowsservercatalog.com/svvp.aspx`). Some products will support only some Hyper-V features. Look for qualified support statements. For example, will the product work with a Hyper-V CSV?

Some third-party solutions make extraordinary claims. But it must be admitted that many of them do add important and valuable functionality.

The Bottom Line

Understand the architecture of Hyper-V Designing and troubleshooting a Hyper-V infrastructure is much easier if you understand how Hyper-V works.

Master It A virtual machine has been built by a junior Hyper-V administrator on behalf of the business applications department. After a few days, you receive a call from that department. They are reporting that the performance of the virtual machine is unacceptable. The `C:` drive appears to be slow, and network traffic is not as fast as with other virtual machines. What will be the first thing you will check, and why do you suspect that it will be the cause of the problems?

List and describe the features of Hyper-V There are many features in Hyper-V such as the components in the hypervisor or virtual machines, as well as the functions for optimizing or managing those components.

Master It You have been asked to design a Windows Server 2008 R2 with Service Pack 1 Hyper-V cluster that will be used for Remote Desktop Services VDI. The virtual machines will need to run applications with high quality graphics. What hardware features will you need in the Hyper-V hosts for this solution?

Understand the management options of Hyper-V Hyper-V can be managed using a suite of solutions from Microsoft.

Master It What products will you use to manage many Windows Server 2008 R2 Hyper-V host servers, monitor the entire server infrastructure including the Linux virtual machines, and quickly back up the virtualization infrastructure?

Part 2

Planning

- Chapter 3: The Project Plan
- Chapter 4: Assessing the Existing Infrastructure
- Chapter 5: Planning the Hardware Deployment

Chapter 3

The Project Plan

The most important part of any project is the plan. Without any organization, even a modest project is subject to greater risks. It's easy to fall into the trap of thinking that a hardware virtualization deployment project will be a quick and simple one. Even in a green-field site, there are a lot of components to consider. The virtualization engineers and administrators will need to consider servers, storage, networking, security, and future maintenance. Imagine an existing infrastructure being virtualized! There are existing servers to audit, assess, and plan for. Support contracts need to be checked, server and application owners need to be involved, and there may be further complexities with hardware integration.

Planning the virtualization project is critical. There is no one-size-fits-all plan. What we will try to do with this chapter is give you a template of a project plan and things to consider. You can then customize the plan according to the needs of the organization you are dealing with.

In this chapter, you'll learn to

- Understand the need for a virtualization project plan
- Identify the major steps involved in a virtualization project
- Vary the project plan according to the organization's needs

Why You Need a Project Plan

An all-too-common occurrence in IT is that important systems are deployed without a plan. For example, a team requests a server for a trial or demo of a product. Two months later, IT discovers that this server has gone into production without any of the required processes being implemented, such as security hardening, backup, documentation, and so on. This lack of communication and planning probably won't be unusual to too many people. It's a risk not just to IT but, more importantly, to the business.

Hardware virtualization (or virtualization for the purposes of this book) will probably affect all aspects of IT and thus the business. Any risks of failure or of unwanted difficulty must be mitigated. It's too easy to just deploy some virtualization hosts and shout out, "Who wants virtual machines?" That could be referred to as an IT time bomb. Eventually it will explode, probably in your face, and consume all available resources and possibly take your employment status with it.

With some planning, you will be able to identify any risks and deal with them. You'll be able to put in steps to deal with issues that arise as the project progresses and still produce a clean installation at the end, instead of something that is thrown together like in a 1980s TV action show. There may be some objections to this. Managers might have heard stories from colleagues in other organizations where a deployment took no time at all. You should not worry about what other people did; focus on doing your project right. By the end of this chapter, you'll be able to explain why. As a consultant, you might find the customer looking to rush into having a solution. You should be able to explain the complexities of virtualization and the potential positive *and* negative impacts of a project. As a services customer, you should be wary of consultants who promise a rapid deployment. Even a virtualized small-business installation will take some time. A medium or large deployment will take much longer, much of the time being spent gathering information before a single virtualization host is even deployed!

Note that you haven't seen the words *Microsoft* or *Hyper-V* yet in this chapter. These risks come with any virtualization project. This book is specific to Hyper-V, so we will focus on the steps that you will likely encounter in a Hyper-V implementation project.

What risks are we talking about? Take a quick look at the hardware costs. When you are deploying a virtualization platform, you aren't buying those $2,000 servers — far from it, unfortunately. You're buying "big iron" — servers that cost tens of thousands of dollars because they have multiple CPUs, lots of network cards, and really dense amounts of RAM that can be very expensive. You might send your organization down one path with this purchase only to find that you've incorrectly sized it. It's one thing to have to buy more resources. The financial officer might be a little upset, but at least the resources are needed. But what if you purchased too much? The risks don't end there either. It's possible to send your organization down one path with a storage solution only to find the requirements are not what you thought they were. What if the business really wanted a disaster recovery (DR) solution? That $100,000 storage area network (SAN) you requested might be incapable of doing what is really needed.

With great risk comes great reward. If you mess up this project, you will be seeking a career alternative. If you get this right, you will be a hero. You can change how IT works. IT can become more efficient and more agile to respond to change in the business. Your internal customers will perceive you differently as they become empowered and enabled to deploy virtual machines for themselves. The business will have more reliable ways to back up and recover servers and data. Potentially, you also have a much better infrastructure to enable disaster recovery or business continuity implementation and planning.

We are going to present a high-level plan for a Hyper-V virtualization implementation project. We will explore the different parts of that project and map them to the chapters in this book. We will also cover the variations you might encounter in your organization.

A Virtualization Project Plan

The plan contained here might not be correct for your organization or every virtualization project that you may work on. The idea is to make you think about your project and to figure out what the plan should be. We will provide you with a sample project plan and describe it. It will be up to you to either use the provided project plan as is or adjust it to suit your requirements. Maybe the plan is fine as is. Maybe you'll tweak some steps, add some, or even remove some. What is important is that you will think about the plan and use one for your virtualization project.

Figure 3.1 shows the flowchart for a sample project plan. It covers many aspects of a deployment of Microsoft Windows Server 2008 R2 Hyper-V with System Center Virtual Machine Manager 2008 R2, Operations Manager 2007 R2, and Data Protection Manager 2010. This plan could vary. For example, there's no mention of the Virtual Machine Servicing Tool. System Center Configuration Manager 2007 R2 hasn't been included. In fact, some of the included phases of the project could be reordered, as you will see in the alternative project plan that is presented later in this chapter. We will now go through the key steps of the sample project plan presented in Figure 3.1 and discuss some of the variations.

FIGURE 3.1
A sample project plan

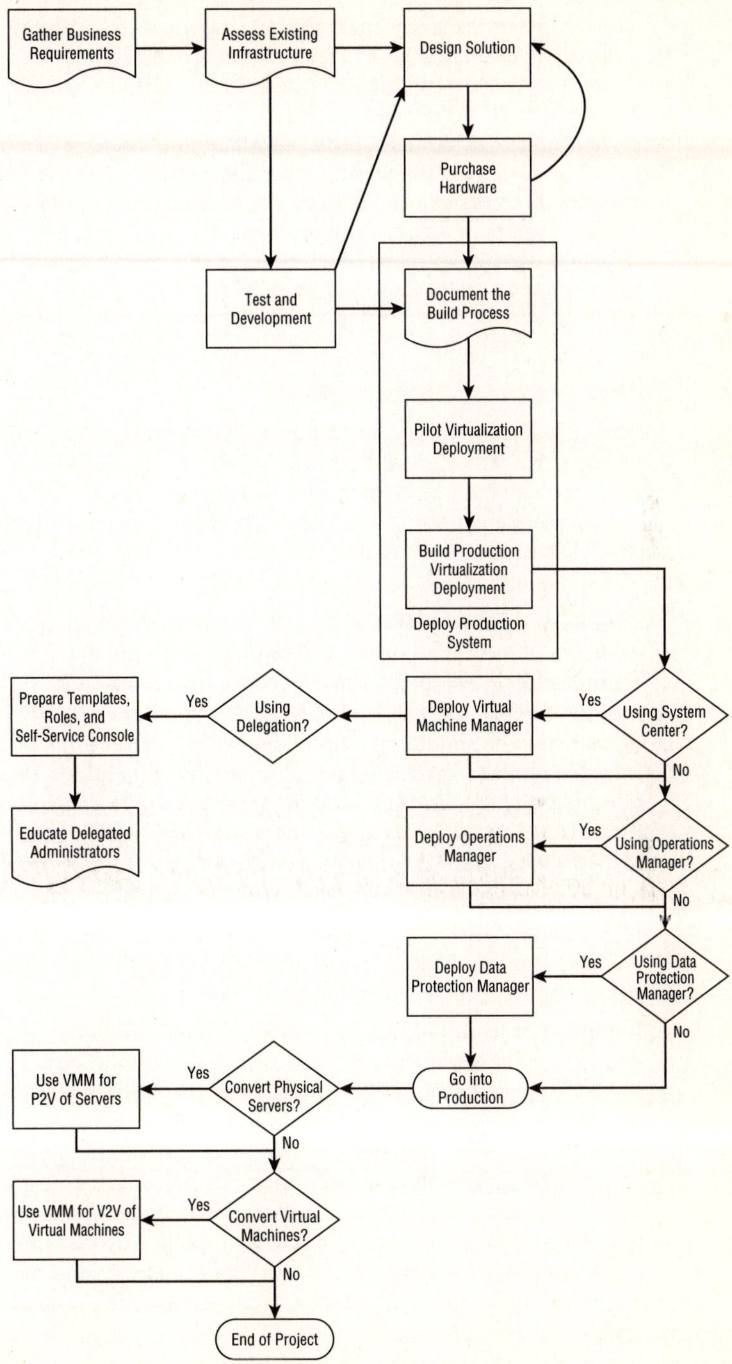

ADDITIONAL MICROSOFT VIRTUALIZATION MANAGEMENT PRODUCTS

Microsoft provides a number of management products, some of which are focused on virtualization and some of which manage the entire IT infrastructure. Virtual Machine Manager (VMM) 2008 R2 is the current release of VMM, and it is used to manage many Hyper-V servers. It can also manage VMware servers and Virtual Server 2005 R2 installations. The Virtual Machine Servicing Tool can be used to patch virtual machines that are stored in the VMM library and are therefore not able to run and update as normal. Operations Manager is Microsoft's health and performance monitoring solution. It integrates with VMM to allow VMM to adapt the deployment of virtual machines according to circumstances. Configuration Manager is Microsoft's biggest System Center product. It is often mistaken as a desktop management solution, but it is much more. It allows you to manage servers, desktops, and mobile devices. It includes operating system deployment, update management, software deployment, auditing of resources, and auditing of configurations.

Gather Business Requirements

Gathering business requirements should be the most critical part of any IT project. How can you know what to design and build if you do not get guidance from those who will be using the system? You need to involve not just IT people but also the decision makers in the business. The list of people you should talk to can be varied. In reality, you should talk to as many people as possible because the virtualization solution can offer new opportunities to a lot of people in the organization:

Business Decision Makers You are making a huge change to the infrastructure of the business. This affects all systems, and those systems are the business enablers. The decision makers in the business, such as the chief executive officer (CEO) or chief information officer (CIO), may have plans that you are unaware of. You might not get direct access to these senior figures, but you should aim high. Ideally you'll land some informed managers who can help steer the project. You might start a project that is right for your organization now, but will it be suitable by the time you are finished? Will that branch office still exist? Will IT functionality still be centrally located or distributed? Will servers be located in just the headquarters or in all locations? Are there going to be new corporate mergers or acquisitions? These questions can be answered only by the people who make those decisions, so you need to include them.

IT Steering Some organizations have a steering committee for directing IT decisions based on input from the board. They usually have a big-picture view of where the organization is going and are a great source for requirements.

Business Continuity Planners Business continuity planning (BCP), usually referred to as disaster recovery (DR), can be made much easier with virtualization. Instead of operating system, application, and data installations that are bound to a piece of hardware, you now can have installations that are contained within a file or a set of files. That makes them much more portable, easier to back up/recover, and easier to replicate from one site to another. This will be appealing to those who are responsible for getting an office back into production should it shut down because of an unforeseen disaster. Those recovery requirements can be a few minutes, a few hours, a day, or a week. Anyone who has done a traditional DR dry run knows how tricky this is. Approaching the BCP team can give them new opportunities and may offer you a new budget. It is much easier to implement a disaster recovery–capable architecture from the start than afterward. For example, a Hyper-V cluster for highly available virtual machines will require some form of SAN. Some SANs allow for easier and more powerful DR deployments than others. And some don't have the ability to take advantage of newer technologies that are included in Windows Server 2008 R2.

IT Security The implementation of any new service or infrastructure will always draw the interest of IT Security. The thoughts of Microsoft hardware virtualization being used to host all systems might raise some eyebrows. The most important thing is that there has been no break-out attack on this platform. That's where an attacker who has access to a virtual machine can get out of the security boundary of that virtual machine and into the host or other virtual machines. Things you'll need to cover with them are patching of hosts, virtual machines and stored virtual machines, administration delegation, and network security.

IT It goes without saying that you should involve the IT professionals you work with. They may have ideas and know of potential risks and threats to the project that you do not know. For example, you'll need to work very closely with your Linux team members. They may have concerns with running their production machines on a Microsoft virtualization platform. Get them involved early on the testing and evaluation process. Don't treat them as outsiders on the project. Treat this as a hardware virtualization project, not as a "Microsoft" project. Network administrators will need to be involved because there may be some level of redesign. Quite often, the traditional network administrator is very confused by the idea of a virtual switch. They worry about spanning tree loops and VLAN tagging. Again, get them involved as early as possible. Soon they'll see how virtualization may make their job a lot easier. An important aspect of their involvement will be the availability of access switch ports. Your Hyper-V hosts are going to be network port hungry compared to normal servers, and you don't want to have your project delayed when you push through an emergency order of some switches.

Developers Who really wants to get the developers involved? But seriously, developers and testers will be very interested in the presence of a virtualization environment. They'll be keen on the idea of the self-service deployment of test and development environments using Virtual Machine Manager. You may not use highly available virtual machines for their needs; maybe they'll have their own host servers, or maybe there will be a pool of stand-alone hosts for less critical machines. Your ability to help and include your colleagues may bring returns in the future. Imagine a day where IT doesn't have to deploy one server after another to meet the frequent needs of the testers and developers. You'll be happier because you will end up doing less work for them, and so will they because they can fulfill their own needs without waiting for IT.

Application Owners Consult the owners of the server-based applications running on the network. This could be the most time-consuming part of this phase of the project, purely based on the numbers of people you end up dealing with. You may need to use several means of communication. For example, deal with owners of more important applications or owners of multiple applications in person; deal with others by email or maybe by survey (a chance to use SharePoint if you have it). You could try to arrange workgroup events, but the chances of getting many people in a room at the same scheduled time could be very difficult. In reality, you'll probably use a few ways to communicate with application owners.

There are a lot of people to talk to! That's probably just a small sample. Your organization may have multiple branch offices, divisions, or a fragmented IT infrastructure. You cannot gather requirements without talking to all of them.

How do you talk to them and get their requirements? Odds are, they know little to nothing about hardware virtualization. Their eyes will glaze over when you ask, "What requirements do you have of a virtualization project?" The answers will vary from "Keep it on budget" to the ever-inspiring "Whatever you think is best." You're going to have to do a little bit of education. The best way to do this is to get a white board and talk through the technology and business benefits. Odds are this has been discussed in a proposal already, but you're generally not dealing with hands-on IT professionals who are concerned with this technology on a day-to-day basis. Much of that will have been forgotten. Go through the available features, how you'll deploy them across the network, and how the business can use them. As you talk, they'll figure out how their plans are impacted, or they'll see possibilities. Those possibilities become requirements.

Eventually you'll have a set of requirements for the project. They become your deliverables. Those deliverables will steer your design. For example, there may be a need to have self-service deployment. In universities, it is not unusual to have many IT departments, one per faculty, with lesser administrative rights. The complication is that each faculty will have its own budgets and be very conservative about relinquishing control. So, each faculty might have its own Hyper-V hosts. You can set up self-service roles in Virtual Machine Manager for each faculty. Because they don't use centrally owned hosts, there won't be a quota model. You'll instead restrict each self-service role to a group of Hyper-V hosts owned by that faculty. You might not have known to do that if you hadn't gathered requirements and used the information to design the administrative model.

Assess Existing Infrastructure

This phase really applies only to organizations with an existing infrastructure that will be converted to run on the new Hyper-V servers. If it doesn't apply to you, then you can skip ahead to the "Design Solution" and "Test and Development" phases. The assessment may include physical servers or virtual machines running on other virtualization platforms such as VMware ESXi or Virtual Server 2005 R2 SP1. The assessment phase of the project will be discussed in detail in Chapter 4.

The goal of this phase is to gather information about those machines. You want to identify which machines are suitable for conversion to run as virtual machines. You're doing this so you can accurately size your hardware platform. This will be an expensive acquisition, and you will want to get this right up front.

Assessment requires gathering performance information about the servers on the network. Using various tools, you will try to find virtualization candidates:

Microsoft Assessment and Planning (MAP) Toolkit You can download this free tool from here:

`http://technet.microsoft.com/solutionaccelerators/dd537570`

This will allow you to gather information about servers without using an agent. This data gathers information about the servers and their resource utilization. Using this, you can generate a specification of required hardware based on real data rather than an estimate.

Microsoft System Center Operations Manager 2007 R2 OpsMgr, by default, will gather performance information about monitored servers. If you have the reporting feature deployed, then more than a year of data will be archived and available to report from. That's a pretty good window into the life of a server, showing the peaks and troughs in resource utilization. Be careful, though — the data is aggregated, and spikes may not be clear in the graphs. Inspect the text detail lower down in the report. The standard deviation reports also give a good insight into the life of the servers. OpsMgr 2007 does have this functionality, but OpsMgr 2007 R2 can also monitor Linux machines, making it a better alternative where you will need to convert them.

Virtual Machine Manager 2008 R2 and OpsMgr 2007 R2 When you deploy and integrate these two products, you will get a series of new reports added to OpsMgr 2007 R2, leveraging the data gathered by OpsMgr. The virtualization candidates report allows you to specify criteria for the number of processors, processor speed, maximum CPU usage, average CPU usage, total RAM, and average RAM usage over a time frame of your choosing — assuming the data is in the reporting database.

Microsoft System Center Configuration Manager 2007 R2 Using the data gathered by ConfigMgr hardware auditing, you can get information about operating systems, service pack levels, disk sizing, memory allocation, and CPU details.

You may now be wondering about all this talk of System Center. How could you use it now if you are deploying it as part of your virtualization project? Here's the great thing. System Center isn't *just* about virtualization. You'll likely end up using products like Operations Manager, Configuration Manager, Data Protection Manager, and Service Manager to manage the physical machines on the network too. There is nothing to stop you from deploying these products earlier than in the project plan shown in Figure 3.1. Earlier deployment would allow you to take advantage of their in-depth data-gathering abilities and also allow other aspects of IT to gain some early benefits from the project. That would change the start of the original project plan to what you see in Figure 3.2.

FIGURE 3.2
Alternative System Center deployment timing

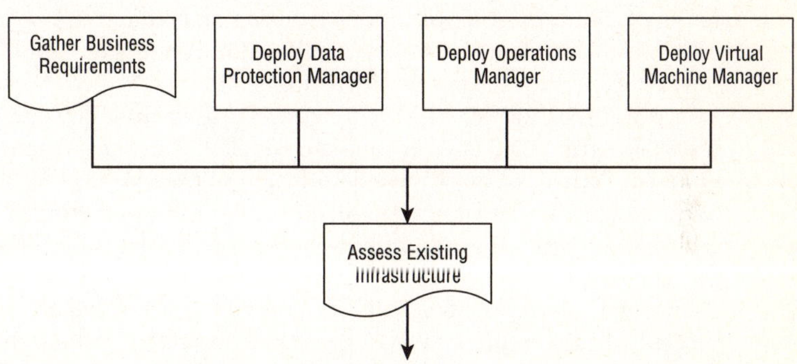

The assessment might reveal something interesting. Larger organizations often have servers that are sitting unused or forgotten about that are still on the network. They probably contain data that must be retained, but the applications might be used only once a year, if at all. It might be decided that some machines can be completely decommissioned. Those rarely used machines might be virtualized and stored in the VMM library, only to be deployed as and when required.

Of the discovered systems that will be virtualized, you will now need to start working with the associated application owners, vendors, and responsible IT staff. Things like support statements, licensing and hardware integration must all be considered when moving applications from a traditional hardware installation to a hardware virtualization installation.

With the assessment complete, you can start working on two concurrent phases in the project. One part of the team might start testing and developing, while another will plan the architecture. One will impact the other. For example, a design will have to be tested, or a test's results may alter the design. This means that open and clear communications will be required.

Test and Development

You can learn only so much by reading blog posts, studying white papers, or attending training courses. Sometimes there is just no beating hands-on experience. And that means getting access to a piece of hardware that you can run Hyper-V on.

This doesn't mean that you ask your boss for a cluster of hosts and a SAN that will resemble your final solution. Maybe you'll get a single 1U server. Maybe you'll be lucky and get a few machines where you can set up a software-based iSCSI SAN with a couple of hosts. The important thing is that you start learning about virtualization, Hyper-V, and System Center.

> **CHEAP ISCSI**
>
> There are a number of ways to get a cheap iSCSI SAN for your test and development system. One is to use a Microsoft storage server as your target. Companies such as StarWind also provide a software solution where you can create an iSCSI target on any Windows computer.

Now is a good time to start getting application owners and developers back involved in the project. You can start to figure out and learn how to design not just the Hyper-V servers but the virtual machines as well. Virtual machine configuration (Chapter 8) can play a huge role in the performance of applications running on Hyper-V. Using application owners' and developers' knowledge and that of any application vendors or support, you can start to figure out the best design for business-critical applications.

VMM is the tool you will use for converting existing physical and virtual machines into Hyper-V virtual machines. It should be deployed on a test machine. You should try to obtain a number of other test machines so that you can practice the process of conversion at this point. Use a variety of hardware, virtualization platforms, operating systems, and applications. You can test both the online and offline conversion processes for physical server conversions. You should be sure to try the different methods of virtual machine conversion too. This will allow you to learn the steps and document the process. It is a bad idea to be still developing the process when you start converting production servers. Although you probably will not damage production servers, you may very well damage confidence in the solution if you are seen to be still figuring out how to complete the task.

There is always a risk with test and development systems. Somehow or another, production applications seem to find their way onto test servers. You'll need to be really strict about this. That's because you'll likely rebuild these machines several times, trying hardware solutions, Server Core vs. the full installation of Windows Server 2008 R2, and so on.

Design Solution

You are ready to design the architecture of your virtualization solution once a complete assessment has been done. This phase, along with the hardware acquisition phase, will be discussed in Chapter 5.

Design requires in-depth knowledge of all the technology components involved:

- Hyper-V
- Networking
- Server hardware
- Storage hardware
- Each of the systems management solutions

You will map the used technologies to each of the requirements and objectives you have gathered from the business at the start of the project.

You'll see that there is input from the parallel testing and development stage as well as the subsequent purchasing stage. This is because of the following:

- You will learn more about the involved technologies, problems, solutions, and opportunities as you try the products.
- Your interactions with hardware vendors might reveal new solutions that are constantly evolving.

The design that you start with might be quite different from the design that you eventually implement. This task is running concurrently with the test and development task. One will impact the other. Possible designs should be tested. The results of these tests might be negative and require an alternative. The tests may even bring up alternatives that were not previously considered. Don't consider this evolution to be a problem. Quite the contrary — it is a good thing. Technology is always changing, so what was possibly the right solution now might be considered old in six months.

Purchase Hardware

Using the information from the assessment of the existing infrastructure combined with your education on your test environment, you should be able to produce an accurate specification of the server, storage, and networking hardware that you will need for your production systems. This will allow you to start working on your pilot and eventually your production builds.

This is the area where most of the cost of the project will be centered. It is critical that the requirements you gathered are steering the design accurately. You will need to understand how your network design will impact virtual machine networking and live migration, how your storage design will impact performance and disaster recovery, and how CPU and RAM will impact scalability and virtual machine/host density. You also need to balance the cost of purchase with the cost of operations over the life span of the hardware. There is a sweet spot where the purchase costs are not too high and you can get as many virtual machines on a host as is possible.

Deploy Production System

You now get to the fun bit of the project, much of which we will discuss in Chapter 6. You'll take delivery of lots of new big-iron toys. Many engineers and administrators have never worked with hardware like this before. Here's where it can get tempting for the business to rush too fast into production. They've potentially spent hundreds of thousands or millions of dollars on hardware and want to see results fast.

You should take your time, build a pilot system, and work out the kinks. There will be mistakes; it's inevitable. Make sure you document the solutions or ways to avert the problems in the future. Eventually you will have procedures for building your Hyper-V hosts and for allocating storage and network to the hosts.

Real World Scenario

A Perfect Production System Build Process

You'll really want to seek perfection when you build your Hyper-V servers. Building a cluster for the first time can be complex. There may be some amount of troubleshooting. That's why you might want to do three builds:

First Build — Document the Build Process Your first attempt at building will likely be a bit messy. You'll be figuring out the hardware, the drivers, things like network card teaming, and failover clustering. Document the troubleshooting process, and learn from your mistakes. This is a good time to learn the PowerShell cmdlets that are built into Windows Server 2008 R2 and in VMM 2008 R2 to automate the installation and configuration steps. You will be able to build scripts for the following rebuilds.

Second Build — Pilot Virtualization Deployment This should be a much cleaner build. There may still be one or two issues, but they will likely be minor. You will be able to use this build for your pilot or proof of concept. This is another good opportunity to involve the owners or developers of business-critical applications to ensure that the production Hyper-V design and implementation are suitable for the needs of the organization.

Third Build — Build Production Virtualization Deployment By now your build process should be perfected and done according to a documented procedure. You will build your Hyper-V cluster according to that procedure and then put it into production.

This might become a four-build procedure if that pilot build doesn't go well. You will repeat the pilot build to ensure that any testing will be as clean as possible. You might ask why you would destroy the pilot to build a clean production system. The key word there is *clean*. You will do a lot of stress testing with the pilot system. You will want a very clean production system that will not inherit any potential flaws you might have created during the pilot.

You can take advantage of automated server installation techniques to speed up the server build process. Chapter 2 in *Mastering Windows Server 2008 R2* includes information for automating server installations. *Mastering Windows 7 Deployment* includes information for advanced operating system deployment techniques that can also be employed for servers. For example, an installation of System Center Configuration Manager could be used to perform rapid automated deployments of Windows Server.

Be careful about rushing into production now. Make sure you have completely tested the new Hyper-V installation and that all of your management systems and procedures are in place before announcing that the new system is ready for the next phases of the project.

Deploying Virtual Machine Manager

There is a possibility you have deployed your production VMM server(s) before now, as mentioned earlier and as covered in Chapter 7. You will want to put it into production as soon as possible to start managing your Hyper-V servers. You can fully manage Hyper-V using the Hyper-V and Failover Clustering consoles, but VMM really does make things immediately easier:

Reduced Complexity Complex tasks that require many manual operations are combined into a single job.

PowerShell It is possible to script and automate actions by using the VMM PowerShell module. Everything that VMM does is done using PowerShell and can be saved as a script in the VMM library, which you can customize and reuse. Imagine a customized response to an OpsMgr application performance alert where VMM automatically deploys a virtual machine to resolve that alert.

Library You can build up a library with virtual machine templates. This automated process is similar to a sysprep solution for traditional operating system deployment. A virtual machine is captured as a VHD. Templates are created for the machine configuration and for running sysprep to configure the operating system in the VHD. This allows you to build up images for all your possible operating system builds such as Windows Server 2003 R2 Enterprise, Windows Server 2008 Enterprise, or Windows Server 2008 R2 Enterprise. These images allow virtualization administrators and delegated administrators to rapidly deploy new virtual machines from these templates in just a matter of minutes.

One of the biggest features of virtualization is facilitated by VMM. It's the ability to enable self-service deployment. That is a facet of your delegation model where you create roles in VMM based on the requirements gathered from the business. You will be enabling delegated administrative rights to subsets of Hyper-V hosts, clusters, and the ability for nonadministrators to deploy VMs without having to involve IT (possibly constrained using a quota). Getting this working early will impress the right people and win over early support from the business and your colleagues in IT who are often overwhelmed by the repetitive task of deploying servers.

Operations Manager

The role of OpsMgr, discussed in Chapter 9, is to detect and alert you about any potential health or performance issues. And that's exactly why you will want to get monitoring agents onto your production build servers as soon as possible. The Microsoft management packs that provide the knowledge of how to monitor your infrastructure are written by the teams that wrote the products or features that they monitor. That means that Hyper-V monitoring was written by the teams that wrote Hyper-V. Who else would be better at identifying any issues?

When combined with VMM integration, you can enable Performance and Resource Optimization Tips (PRO Tips). Microsoft provides default functionality for this. Other vendors such as SAN communications and server manufacturers also provide PRO Tips management packs that extend Microsoft's functionality to provide a more aware Hyper-V cluster, capable of relocating virtual machines according to detected issues.

The best time to test something like PRO Tips is before the cluster goes into production. You can use stress tools to push CPU utilization to their maximum to trigger a reaction by OpsMgr and VMM.

Data Protection Manager

Much of your assessment gathering will or should focus on backup and recovery. This is because you suddenly have a new way to back up servers thanks to the ability to back up virtual machines at the host or storage level. Using DPM 2010 (Chapter 10), you can recover those atomic virtual machines to their original location or to an alternative location. You can even recover individual files from this atomic backup. Volume Shadow Copy Service (VSS)–aware applications such as Exchange Server or SQL Server can be backed up in a safe and supported manner using this technique. Some applications or deployments will mandate the need to install a backup agent within the virtual machine for a more traditional backup.

Your process of learning how DPM 2010 will work with Hyper-V should be introduced in the project as early as possible, ideally during your test and development stage. You may find that backup becomes the driving factor behind your virtualization project.

Go into Production

This is when you are either very excited, very nervous, or possibly both! All those months of hard work will suddenly be judged when you flip the virtual switch and start deploying production virtual machines.

You really need to be sure that everything — including all the management systems — is in place and is tested before you go into production. You do not want to put production systems live on your new Hyper-V servers and suddenly have failures, be they in the form of procedure, design, a crash, or bad performance. You also do not want to put production virtual machines onto your Hyper-V servers without the management systems being there. Would you like to call up a business application owner some Monday morning to tell them that they lost data and no backup was available?

Don't take anything for granted. Get key influencers and power users involved in the earlier pilot and testing phases. They will likely be the ones who will find any issues. They will then become your supporters when you go live because of their personal investment and involvement in the project. They will also become champions who can help in the education process when you do go live.

Convert Physical and Virtual Machines

It is only after your Hyper-V cluster and all the management systems are in place that live virtual machines should be created. Most organizations will have existing physical and virtual machines to convert into Hyper-V virtual machines. Those lucky administrators and engineers in green-field sites won't have to worry about that process.

Physical-to-virtual (P2V) conversions can be particularly difficult. Windows virtual machines should not be too bad as long as you follow the guides for P2V conversions using VMM 2008 R2. Those (ideally) rare circumstances where normal procedures will not work can be circumvented using third-party solutions. Linux P2V can be especially difficult because it does not have a supported solution from Microsoft.

You should really test these procedures as much as possible during your test and development phases. There might even be an opportunity to kill two birds with one stone here! Businesses should really test their server backups every now and then. That means being able to perform a complete server recovery onto test hardware. There is an opportunity here to use those test machines for testing and developing your P2V processes. Try to include a variety of operating systems and applications that give you a representative sample of the systems on your network that have been identified as virtualization candidates. Be sure to include as many variations of Linux as you can. The conversion process will be difficult and will require the involvement of Linux administrators because much of the troubleshooting will require some advanced skills.

It is not unheard of for some key server to not perform up to requirements after it has been converted into a virtual machine. Often this comes down to the VM not being configured according to best practices for its workload. It usually ends up being a server that was predictably going to have some sort of issue because of its criticality. These would be the servers that are ideal to work with during your P2V testing in the testing and development phase.

An Alternative Project Plan

As was stated earlier, there is no right project plan. What you use will depend on your organization. The previous project plan is very much a waterfall approach, being almost sequential. A larger organization that has more staff available for the project may want to adopt a project plan where more progress can be made earlier in the endeavor. You can see an example of this in Figure 3.3.

This plan would be appropriate for organizations that want to deploy the systems management solutions at the start of the project. This allows them to be immediately available to other parts of the infrastructure and systems management teams outside of virtualization. It also allows some time for those who will be responsible for those products to get to learn them before the production virtualization system is in place. Some products do take time to "bed in." A perfect example of this is Operations Manager. Organizations that realize how powerful OpsMgr is will want to take the time for engineering. This could include building bespoke management packs to monitor their internally developed or third-party applications, creating a delegation model that matches their administrative and applications customer/ownership logical organizations, and designing models of IT-provided services for SLA monitoring.

Having System Center Operations Manager 2007 R2 and Virtual Machine Manager 2008 R2 installed as early as possible will allow for more in-depth performance and reporting for the assessment of any existing infrastructure. You will then be able to use this information for identifying virtualization candidates, for designing their deployment, and for sizing the hardware requirements.

With Virtual Machine Manager 2007 R2 in place, you can start developing templates for new virtual machines. Building templates should be easy enough; they'll typically be built according to the process that is already being used to build physical servers. If you already use an automated solution such as Windows Deployment Services, Microsoft Deployment Toolkit, or Configuration Manager, then you can even use those to build your templates. The templates will be sitting in your library when you are ready to start pilot testing.

Having VMM ready early will also allow you to build the administration delegation and self-service models. You might need to be careful about how far you engineer it, though. You will probably learn a lot more from the assessment.

There is a risk with this approach. Deploying products such as Data Protection Manager, Operations Manager, and Configuration Manager for the IT systems outside the scope of a Hyper-V project is a mammoth task. In fact, each one is its own project. You will likely have partner projects running alongside yours. It is imperative that you work closely with the project leaders of each of those implementations to ensure that they are ready for you when you need them. For example, you will need Operations Manager to be deployed and storing performance data in the reporting database for your assessment of the existing IT infrastructure if you want to use it instead of the Microsoft Assessment and Planning Toolkit.

FIGURE 3.3
An alternative project plan

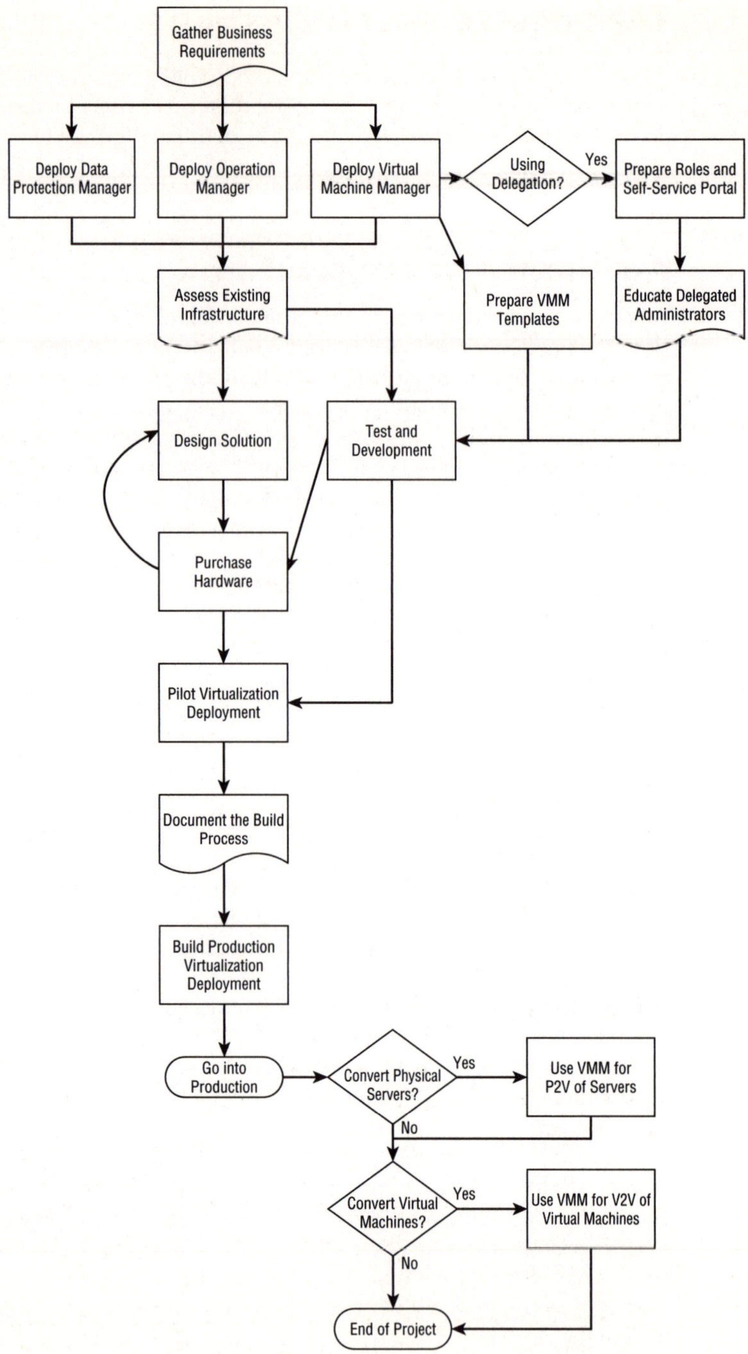

The Project Plan and This Book

You will find that much of this book is based on the plan shown in Figure 3.1 in this chapter. This will give you a framework that you can build upon for your virtualization project. We advise that you read through this chapter and the rest of this book before sitting down with your copy of Visio or Microsoft Project. There is a lot to consider in this type of project. The features of all the involved products may cause you to reconsider the order of implementation. For example, you may be introducing Data Protection Manager 2010 for your virtualization project, but you may also see how it could provide an immediate return for backing up your Exchange 2010 servers. Or you may have access to a large team and have tight deadlines.

The book covers each of the major stages contained within the project plans displayed in this chapter:

Assess Existing Infrastructure Chapter 4, "Assessing the Existing Infrastructure"

Design Solution Chapter 5, "Planning the Hardware Deployment"

Purchase Hardware Chapter 5, "Planning the Hardware Deployment"

Build Production Virtualization Deployment Chapter 6, "Deploying Hyper-V"

Deploy Virtual Machine Manager Chapter 7, "Virtual Machine Manager 2008 R2"

Deploy Operations Manager Chapter 9, "Operations Manager 2007"

Deploy Data Protection Manager Chapter 10, "Data Protection Manager 2010"

Convert Physical Servers Chapter 7, "Virtual Machine Manager 2008 R2"

Convert Virtual Machines Chapter 7, "Virtual Machine Manager 2008 R2"

Additional content that will be used in these phases is also provided. Guidance on configuring virtual machines for specific applications is in Chapter 8, "Virtualization Scenarios." Small or medium-sized organizations might not use OpsMgr or VMM. They might be interested in Chapter 10, which focuses on the small to medium-sized organizations, Small Business Server, and System Center Essentials 2010.

We have tried to order the chapters according to the typical implementation order. However, the final decision on how you design your project plan will be up to you.

The Bottom Line

Understand the need for a virtualization project plan. A project plan will help you organize and schedule the various tasks to be completed during a hardware virtualization project.

> **Master It** You are a consultant, and you have been engaged by a customer to advise on the deployment of Microsoft Windows Server 2008 R2 Hyper-V with various supporting Microsoft System Center products. Upon entering the site, you find that the IT staff is rushing into a deployment. What would you say to them to encourage them to take a more considered approach?

Identify the major steps involved in a virtualization project. There are a number of discrete steps in a Microsoft Windows Server 2008 R2 Hyper-V deployment. Some of them should be conducted in every project, and some are conducted only if the associated products are to be deployed.

> **Master It** You are to deploy Windows Server 2008 R2 Hyper-V and Microsoft System Center in an organization with an existing IT infrastructure. This contains a mix of servers including legacy Window NT 4.0 servers and newer Linux and Windows Server computers, all running a wide variety of business-critical applications. You want to design a suitable architecture. How will you start the project?

Vary the project plan according to the organization's needs. No one project plan is suitable for all organizations. It will be necessary to vary the project plan according to the directions given by the decision makers and to suit the needs of the organization.

> **Master It** Although it was purchased only as part of the Hyper-V project, your organization will be using Microsoft System Center to manage all IT systems. Various managers have expressed a desire to see immediate results and are providing suitable skills for the project. You will need to schedule tasks in the project accordingly. How will you schedule the implementation of Microsoft System Center?

Chapter 4

Assessing the Existing Infrastructure

Few organizations that will deploy Hyper-V will have so-called green-field sites where there is no existing infrastructure. Most will have existing servers that consume power and space. Some may have expiring or expired support contracts. These are the sorts of machines that the planners of a virtualization project would hope to convert to be virtual machines on the new infrastructure. Will the existing physical servers be suitable for virtualization? How will this impact the specification of the virtual host and storage hardware?

In this chapter, you will learn about the need to undergo an assessment. We'll look in detail at the Microsoft Assessment and Planning Toolkit solution, which is free to download and use. You may find an opportunity to leverage an existing installation of Microsoft System Center or even do an early deployment of these management tools. You will also see how to use these tools to perform an assessment of existing infrastructure. Using these solutions, you will be able to identify suitable servers to convert to virtual machines and use this data to accurately size your Hyper-V infrastructure.

In this chapter, you'll learn to

- Understand the need to assess the existing infrastructure
- Use the Microsoft Assessment and Planning Toolkit
- Use System Center for assessment

An Overview of Assessment

Most organizations that are planning a Hyper-V deployment may already have tens, hundreds, or even thousands of servers. They all sit in racks, consuming power for their CPUs, memory, hard disks, and, of course, the fans to cool them. Strangely, the estimated average CPU utilization of physical servers before virtualization was somewhere between 8–12 percent. That means that up to 92 percent of server capacity was wasted. It also implies that a very large percentage of rack space and electricity was wasted.

It therefore makes a lot of technological, financial, and sometimes even marketing sense to consolidate the server infrastructure by converting the existing physical servers into virtual machines. You can even convert existing virtual machines into virtual machines that run on Windows Server 2008 R2 Hyper-V.

Why Do an Assessment?

The desire to use less rack space and consume less power means that you need to get more out of less. Typically Windows engineers deploy one server application per operating system. That means one application per server chassis. Hardware virtualization solutions, such as Hyper-V, allow you to still run one application per operating system. But now you can have one operating system per virtual machine and many virtual machines per server chassis. But now the questions start to arise!

What Are the Best Practices?

Here we do have to warn you that, quite often, there are no hard-and-fast rules that you can always depend on. There are guidelines that are usually good rules of thumb. But sometimes there are exceptions to the rule.

Can I Convert Every Server into a Virtual Machine?

Typically the answer to this question will be a quick no, with responses about the need to consider host utilization by virtual machines and compatibility.

Let's start with resource utilization. People who are new to hardware virtualization have a misconception that you get more processing power or denser storage when you use this technology. Actually, it's probably fair to say that hardware virtualization is a (very) tiny bit less efficient.

Consider a server that uses 75 percent of its 2.8 GHz quad-core processor and uses 200 GB of its 250 GB of storage. If you were to convert this server into a virtual machine, those requirements would not simply vaporize. The processor would be in the host Hyper-V server, and the host would possibly have four of those very same physical processors. Now the virtual machine would require at least 75 percent of one of the 4 × 2.8 GHz quad-core processors in the host. The storage requirements still remain the same. Actually, to be completely honest, the CPU and storage requirements would increase a small bit for this virtual machine. There would be a small amount of overhead for the virtual machine on the processor. This amount is usually negligible. But there also would be overhead on the storage to account for the VM configuration, potential saved states, and copied ISO files for the VM to mount. (There is a way to mount ISO files over the network, saving on this disk space. This will be discussed in Chapter 6 when the implementation of Hyper-V is covered.)

What if the original physical server had two quad-core processors and they were 90 percent utilized? Would you consider converting them to virtual machines now? You might know that Hyper-V supports a maximum of four virtual CPUs in a virtual machine. That's four logical processors on the host that can be used at once. The original machine has eight cores that are nearly fully utilized, so a virtual machine with half of the same computing power will not suffice.

Converting Non-Windows Servers

There is no Microsoft-supported way to perform a physical-to-virtual (P2V) conversion of a non-Windows computer such as Linux. In fact, Windows 2000 Server with Service Pack 4 is the oldest operating system that Microsoft provides a way to convert for production environments. We will deal with this more when we deal with Virtual Machine Manager in Chapter 7.

Therefore, it goes without saying that you will assess every server to measure static resource (such as storage) and dynamic resource (such as CPU, RAM and I/O) utilization to see whether it would be a candidate for virtualization. How you make the decision in the end really depends on understanding the objectives for the project. For example, if your goal for virtualization is to enable easier disaster recovery, then having just a few virtual machines (with greater resource requirements) per host might be appropriate. However, a dense private cloud computing environment might prefer that such servers remain as physical machines.

Can Every Business Application or OS Be Virtualized?

A second consideration is application or operating system compatibility. Some operating systems or applications may not have vendor support for running in virtual machines on Hyper-V. Or there may just be a complete lack of support for virtualization. To determine this, you need to understand what applications you have on your network, what versions they are, and how important they are to your business. Working with the application owners in the business may reveal that some legacy noncompliant applications are neither critical nor required any longer. It is also quite possible that the application owners either decide or are encouraged (by the senior decision makers) to find upgrades or alternatives that are supported on Hyper-V.

> **Do Not Make Assumptions**
>
> The worldwide adoption of virtualization for production servers appears to have been a surprise to many, despite the many headlines, advice, and conferences on the subject in the previous decade. Some very large and well-known business application vendors have tried to be very uncooperative to protect their revenue streams. This can involve going as far as not supporting any virtualization solution. However, it is well known that threats to dump their software and move to their rivals have led to custom support contracts being very quietly introduced.
>
> Be sure to check every application edition and version for support with the vendors. If it seems like they are being difficult, then you should get the application owners to let the vendors know that their product and their support contract could be dumped in favor of products from rival companies who are willing to help. This has been known to help, sometimes even resulting in bespoke support contracts.

How Many Hosts Are Needed?

Only by understanding the actual resource utilization of your existing physical servers will you be able to plan the physical server and storage requirements for your Hyper-V servers. For example, if you find eight servers with 25 percent quad-core utilization and eight servers with 50 percent quad-core utilization, then you would be safe to assume that you need at least six total cores for your Hyper-V hosts for the converted virtual machines to run at the same capacity. You can only know this by measuring your servers' performance requirements over a sustained period. Remember that a typical server's performance statistics don't sit at one level over a year, a month, or even a week. There are usually spikes based on demand by end users or other network applications. Your Hyper-V hosts need to allow for these spikes.

Will Virtualization Cost Much?

It is possible to calculate the costs of running the existing physical and/or virtual server network. This can include a lot of costs that are not immediately obvious. It is also possible to analyze the costs of deploying and operating Hyper-V once the infrastructure is sized.

The resulting figures can make for a very convincing argument for any nontechnical decision maker. It is normal that a hardware virtualization project will save the organization a significant amount of money over three years.

How to Do an Assessment

It's pretty clear now that some form of assessment that looks at static data such as storage requirements, operating systems, and applications, as well as changeable data such as performance statistics averages and spikes, must be done. This will typically require data to be gathered over a period of time to guarantee reliable data rather than some simple snapshot.

An assessment will run over a period of time on all your servers that are supported by the assessment mechanism. Depending on the mechanism, it will be done either using an agent(s) or remotely over the network. Data will be gathered into a central database(s). At the end of the chosen assessment period, you can run a report(s) to see which machines will be candidates for virtualization.

How Long Should the Assessment Run?

This is one of those "how long is a piece of string?" questions. At the very least, an assessment should run for a week. However, that may very well miss out on occasional spikes in utilization that occur in line with monthly, quarterly, or annual operations by the business. A month long assessment is recommended. In an ideal world, you would run an assessment for one entire year. That way, you could account for all spikes in demand. But you do have to be realistic here. It would probably be cheaper to purchase an extra host or two to deal with unexpected spikes rather than delay a major operating costs–saving project such as a virtualization project. For example, the power savings over a month could possibly pay for a host server.

Using MAP

The Microsoft Assessment and Planning (MAP) Toolkit is free to download and use and can be used in many kinds of deployment projects. One of these is Hyper-V deployments where it will enable you to assess your Windows physical servers and VMware virtual machine network over a period of time and then produce a set of reports. This agent-less solution will discover your servers over the network. It will gather performance data and report the requirements of each candidate for virtualization conversion. It can even give you an indication of how many Hyper-V machines will be required to host the assessed servers if they were converted to virtual machines. It should be noted that it does not account for redundant nodes in a Hyper-V cluster. You can then use this for planning your architecture and budgeting for and purchasing your hardware. In this section, we will look at installing the product, running an assessment, and generating reports from the gathered data.

Version 4.0 was the current release of MAP at the time of writing. However, a beta release of version 5.0 was being tested. This includes the ability to assess existing Linux machines as well as Windows ones.

Planning MAP

MAP will be talking to each and every server on your network. It does this using WMI. The requirements for this will be discussed later in this chapter. A larger organization with a wide area network (WAN) will need to plan for this traffic.

This might mean running assessments over the WAN during off-peak hours. If this is done, then you could use Group Policy–enforced Quality of Service (QoS) to manage bandwidth utilization for Windows Server 2008 and Windows Server 2008 R2 servers. Network-based controls would be required for legacy server operating systems.

Alternatively, you could deploy more than one MAP installation in each branch office or region. This would require more work. There would be more installations, and the report data would have to be assembled from the many sources. An option might be to create a virtual machine for MAP. It could be relocated from one site to another over a longer time frame. However, even that virtual machine move would consume bandwidth. You could even store this virtual machine on an encrypted piece of removable storage. Another solution is to install MAP onto a laptop that is encrypted using BitLocker. An engineer or consultant could visit each site with the laptop to perform an assessment, or it could even just be sent by courier.

Using and Installing MAP

You should plan your installation before you start trying to use MAP. The first thing you should know is that Microsoft updates MAP on a pretty frequent basis. Use your favorite search engine to find the latest version when you start your project. Version 4.0 is the current release at the time of writing and can be found here:

```
http://technet.microsoft.com/library/bb977556.aspx
```

Version 5.0 was an early beta release at the time of writing this book.

Installing MAP

MAP will be installed onto a central computer. This can be a server or a workstation. The hardware requirements at the time of writing for the current version are as follows:

CPU 1.6 GHz processor. 1.5 GHz dual core for Windows Vista, Windows 7, Windows Server 2008, and Windows Server 2008 R2.

Storage 1 GB of disk space. Allow for more for the database.

Network A network connection will be required to connect to machines that will be assessed.

Display 1024 × 768 minimum resolution.

You can run MAP on an existing computer that already serves a purpose. Microsoft recommends that the computer be dedicated to MAP if more than 5,000 computers need to be assessed.

The operating system, 32-bit or 64-bit, requirements are as follows:

- Windows 7
- Windows Vista Ultimate, Enterprise, or Business Editions
- Windows XP Professional with Service Pack 2 or newer
- Windows Server 2008 R2
- Windows Server 2008
- Windows Server 2003 R2
- Windows Server 2003 with Service Pack 1 or newer

The software requirements are as follows:

- .NET 3.5 SP1 or newer
- Windows Installer 4.5
- Microsoft Word 2003 SP2 or Word 2007
- Microsoft Excel 2003 SP2 or Excel 2007
- Microsoft Office Primary Interop Assemblies
- Install all Microsoft updates for Windows and Microsoft Office
- SQL Server 2008 Express Edition, SQL Server 2008, or SQL Server 2005

SQL Server 2008 Express Edition is included with and is installed by default with MAP 4.0. You can use another supported version of SQL Server, but you will need to create an instance called MAPS first.

Excel 2007 is recommended if there are more than 2,000 computers to be assessed. Excel 2003 will struggle and possibly fail to handle these loads. Excel 2003 will require all available updates.

For this exercise, we will be using the lab network that is shown in Figure 4.1. There are four computers in this network:

- DC1 is a Windows Server 2008 R2 domain controller.
- Server1 is a Window Server 2003 machine running SQL 2008.
- Server2 is a Windows Server 2003 web server.
- Server3 is a Window Server 2008 computer with Windows SharePoint Services 3.0 SP2 installed.

FIGURE 4.1
The lab network

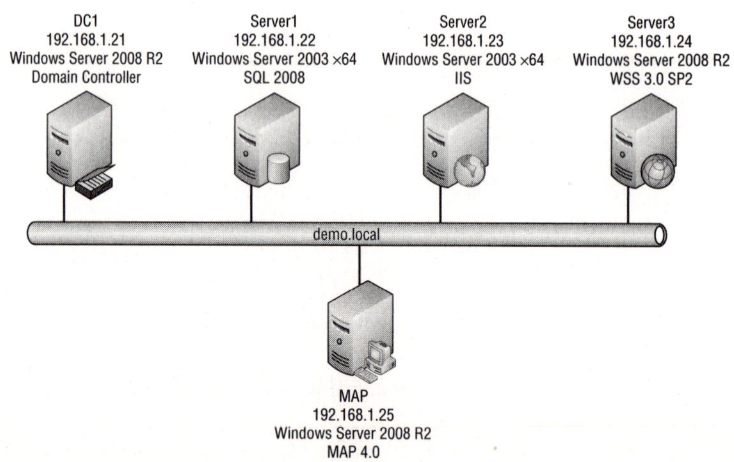

In this exercise, we will add a fifth computer called MAP. We will be installing Microsoft Assessment and Planning Toolkit 4.0 onto this computer. In this lab, MAP is configured with Windows Server 2008 R2, but you can use any of the previously mentioned operating systems that are supported.

All computers in the lab network are members of the `demo.local` domain.

You can build a lab network of your own choosing; the bigger, the better! Try to have as much diversity as possible in your servers. To make things simple, make them all members of the same domain. You'll need to do some configuration changes, which are easier done using Group Policy. You can allow for workgroup members, but that will require manual configuration changes later.

Prepare your MAP computer. Download MAP, and run the installer. It's a pretty simple setup routine. It will only get a little bit more complicated if you choose to use an installation of SQL Server rather than the easier SQL Server Express. As mentioned before, not using the default SQL Server Express installation requires that you configure a SQL Server instance called MAPS.

> **TIME SAVINGS FOR CONSULTANTS**
>
> Here's a handy time saving tip for consultants. You can build a virtual machine that already has MAP installed and ready to run. Then you can save that image. Every time you go into a customer site, you can copy that image and create a virtual machine for that project. You can simply turn up at a customer site, join the machine to the network, and start working. Your customers will be impressed.

Start the installation routine. You can see in Figure 4.2 that there is a warning about Internet connectivity. Access to the Internet will be required by the installer unless you have already downloaded SQL Server Express 2008. That normally won't be an issue, but consultants or those working in limited-access networks should take note of this and be prepared by downloading SQL Server Express 2008 in advance.

FIGURE 4.2
Starting the MAP setup

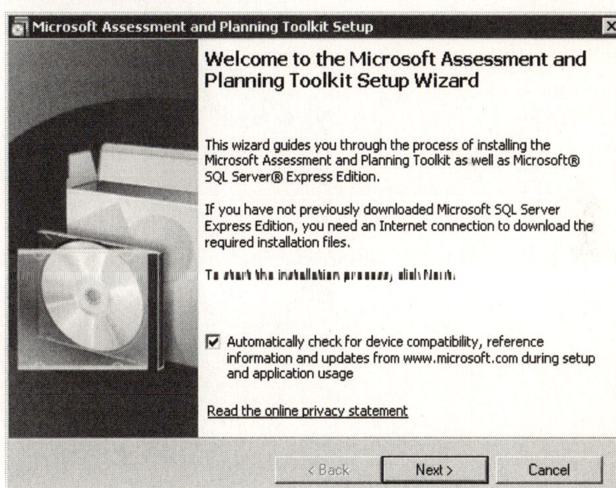

The next steps are to accept the EULA and choose the installation location. The default location is usually OK.

The SQL Server Express screen gives you a choice, as you can see in Figure 4.3. You can download and install SQL Server Express from the Internet. Alternatively, you can install it from previously downloaded files. Choosing the previously downloaded option prompts you to provide a path.

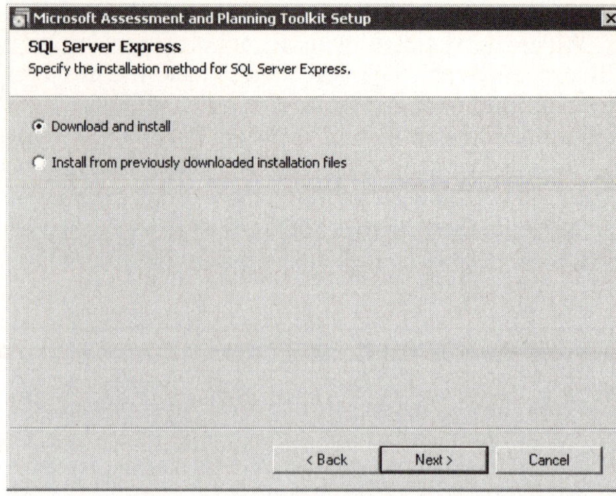

FIGURE 4.3
SQL Server Express installation options

The SQL Server Express screen is skipped if a SQL instance called MAPS is already installed.

In this lab, you will be downloading the installer from the Internet. This will add some time to the total installation. Eventually you get to the end of the setup wizard. Here you are told that SQL Server Express and MAP will be installed if you click the Install button. Click it, and the packages will be ready for you to start using in a little while. Eventually the installation completes, and you'll see the screen in Figure 4.4.

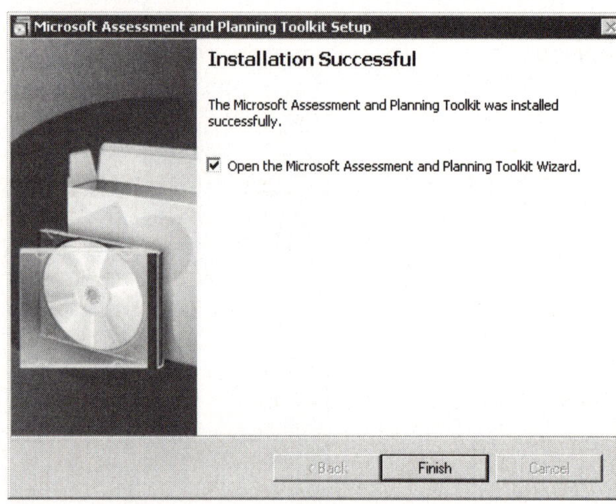

FIGURE 4.4
MAP installation complete

The setup is completed, but don't try to use MAP yet. You need to configure the servers you want to assess, the virtualization candidates, so that MAP can talk to them.

CONFIGURING COMPUTERS FOR ASSESSMENT

MAP does not use an agent to gather data from virtualization candidates. Instead, it uses Windows Management Instrumentation (WMI) to gather data over the network. There are some requirements for this:

Remote Registry Access You must enable this exception if the Windows Firewall is enabled on your candidate computers. This will open TCP port 135. You'll need to be sure that any network devices or firewalls between your MAP server and your candidate computers also allow this traffic.

Enable File and Printer Sharing This must also be enabled on candidate computers if they have the Windows Firewall is enabled. TCP 139 and 445 as well as UDP 137 and 138 are affected. Network appliances and firewalls must allow this traffic.

Remote Registry Service This service is used by MAP to identify which roles are installed and to gather performance information.

Windows Management Instrumentation Service The WMI service must be enabled and running.

Local Administrator Credentials MAP will be using WMI to remotely access each candidate computer. This requires administrator credentials to be provided to get administrative access to each machine.

Each of these can be done manually, by script, or by using Group Policy Objects (GPOs) in an Active Directory domain. We will cover that in action in a few moments. Before we do, we have a few other scenarios to cover. If you suspect that all of those requirements are already in place, then you can do a test run with MAP. You can then very quickly troubleshoot those exceptions that fail to be discovered correctly.

It is possible that you will have servers that are members of workgroups. Each of the previous will have to be achieved either by manual configuration or by using a script. You will also need to change the Network Access: Sharing And Security Model For Local Accounts local policy setting from Guest to Classic. More information on this is available here:

```
http://technet.microsoft.com/library/cc786449(WS.10).aspx
```

Legacy operating systems such as Windows Server 2003 and Windows NT 4.0 require a few additional changes:

Windows Server 2003 The nondefault Windows Installer Provider must be installed on 64-bit installations. You can do this using Add/Remove Programs in Control Panel. The option is available under Management And Monitoring Tools as WMI Windows Installer Provider.

Windows NT 4.0 You will need to install the WMI Core on machines with this operating system. This is available here:

```
www.microsoft.com/downloads/details.aspx?familyid=AFE41F46-
   E213-4CBF-9C5B-FBF236E0E875
```

This sounds like a lot of work. However, there's a good chance you might have already done a lot of this work for any systems management systems that you have in place. And as we mentioned, a lot of the settings configuration work can be done with a little bit of work in Group Policy. That's what we'll cover next.

In this example, you'll be using the Group Policy Management tool to create a GPO that will be linked to the organizational unit (OU) that contains all the computer objects for your servers. That GPO will be configured with a number of settings to make a lot of the previous configurations for you. A solution like this will allow you to configure thousands of servers in just a few hours — the time it takes for GPOs to refresh on each machine.

In this example, create and link a new GPO called Servers, as shown in Figure 4.5. It will contain all the settings you need under Computer Configuration.

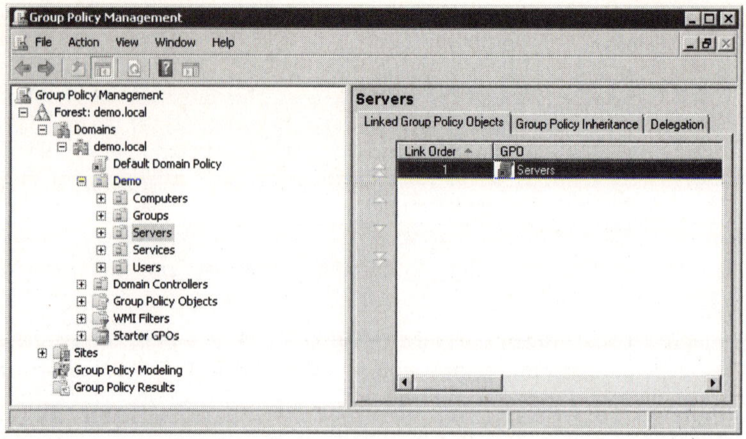

FIGURE 4.5
The Servers Group Policy Object

You will start off by configuring the sharing security model for local user accounts. Go to Computer Configuration ➤ Policies ➤ Windows Settings ➤ Security Settings ➤ Local Policies ➤ Security Options. Configure Network Access: Sharing And Security Model For Local Accounts to use the Classic: Local Users Authenticate As Themselves setting. You can see this in Figure 4.6.

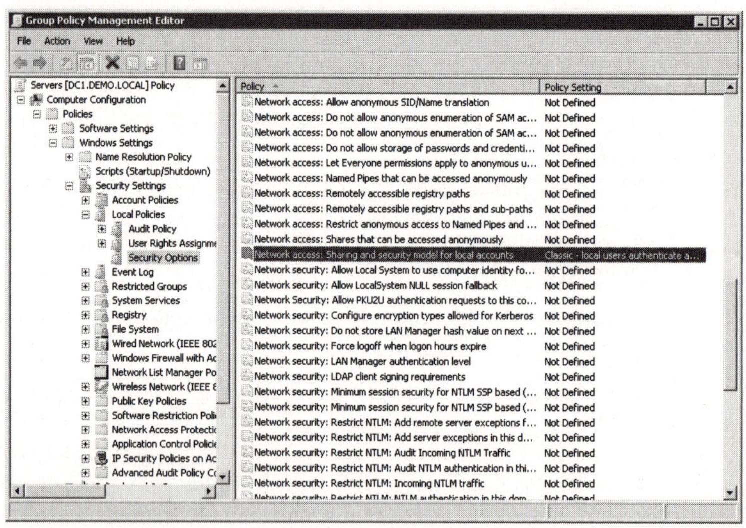

FIGURE 4.6
Network Access Model for Local User Accounts

Next you will need to start working on the firewall. Navigate to Computer Configuration ➤ Policies ➤ Administrative Templates ➤ Network ➤ Network Connections ➤ Windows Firewall ➤ Domain Profile. Here you will configure Windows Firewall: Allow Inbound Remote Administration Exception. You can see in Figure 4.7 that there is a bit more to this setting. You will also need to configure the IP address of the MAP server. In this example, it is 192.168.1.25.

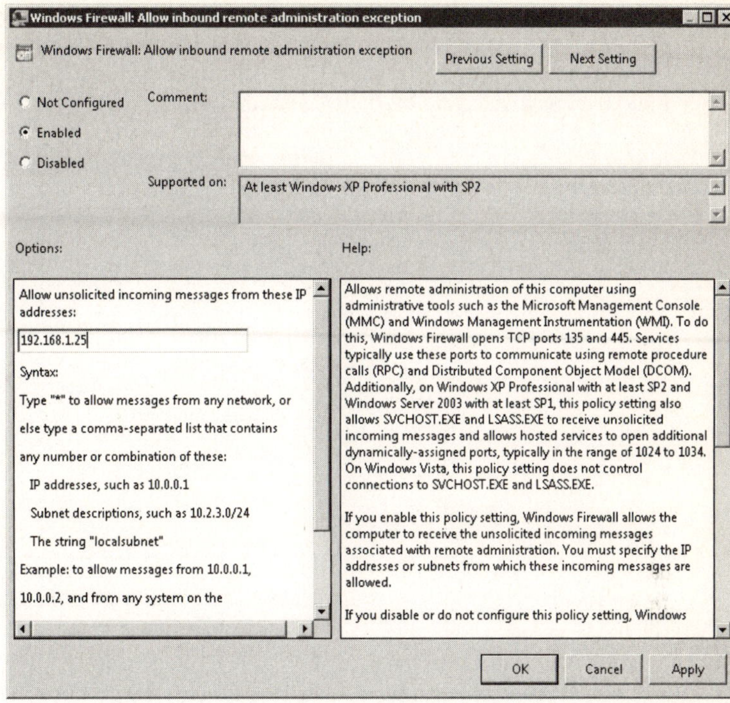

FIGURE 4.7 Allowing inbound remote administration

You will also need to configure the Windows Firewall: Allow Inbound File And Printer Sharing Exception setting. You will enable it and enter the IP address of the MAP server in the same way as you just did to enable remote administration.

You've now taken care of the firewall rule requirements for MAP. If you go take another look at the prerequisites, you'll see that we also need the Remote Registry and the Windows Management Instrumentation services to be running. It is quite possible that services may be stopped. For example, some people will disable Remote Registry as part of a security-hardening process. Enabling it won't be dangerous if you are managing the Windows Firewall as shown earlier. So far, you have allowed access to the service to one IP address, the MAP server. Now you will see how to set these services to run automatically using Group Policy.

You can navigate to Configuration ➢ Policies ➢ Windows Settings ➢ Security Settings ➢ System Services. In the pane on the right, you will see all the services that you can manage using Group Policy. For this example, you will start with the Remote Registry service. Double-click it to manage the settings. In Figure 4.8, you can see that you must select the Define This Policy Setting box and then set the service to Automatic. You can restrict who can manage the service locally by clicking Edit Security and using a traditional Windows permissions dialog box.

You should then repeat this process for the Windows Management Instrumentation service.

The final piece of the puzzle is local administrator access. You could go and create a local user account on every server, but that would take a very long time! You could be lazy and use a domain user account that has domain administrator rights. That's really insecure because it gives more rights than are required. You certainly should not be doing that if any delegated administrators or external nonemployees will be using MAP. Instead, you can create one or more ordinary domain users, specifically for MAP authentication, and grant them local administrator rights on the servers. You can log into every server and add the MAP user account into the Administrators group on each server. Some organizations may already be using Restricted Groups in Group Policy to manage the Administrators group on the servers. That allows automated, manageable, and by-policy control over that local group. We'll now look at that in action.

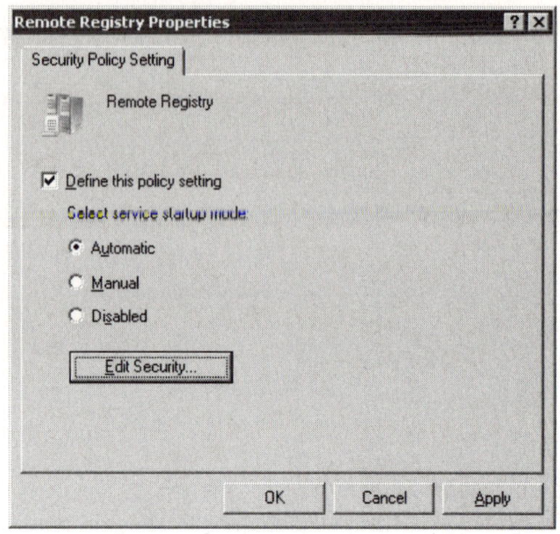

FIGURE 4.8
Configuring the Remote Registry service policy

We'll continue to use the same GPO. Navigate to Configuration ➤ Policies ➤ Windows Settings ➤ Security Settings ➤ Restricted Groups. Right-click in the detail pane, and select Add Group. Type in the name of the local group as it appears in Computer Management on the computers you are managing. Here you want to manage the Administrators group, so type in **Administrators**, as shown in Figure 4.9.

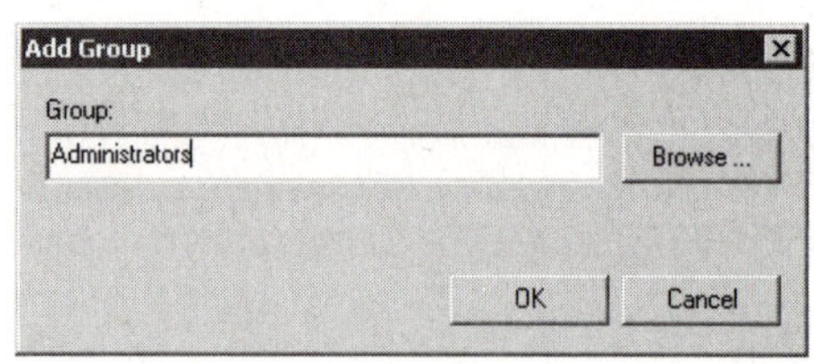

FIGURE 4.9
Managing the Local Administrators group

You need to understand that this policy will replace the membership of the Administrators group. It affects only domain groups and domain users that are members. It does not affect the default local Administrator account. For example, if DEMO\JoeBloggs were a member of the Administrator group on Server1, we would remove that membership by not including him in this policy. The local Administrator group does not need to be listed and will not be removed. You should include Domain Admins in this group because they should always be members of the local Administrators group.

In our example, we are using a domain (`demo.local`) user called MAP (DEMO\MAP). We will add it and Domain Admins (DEMO\Domain Admins) to the Administrators Restricted Groups policy. You can see the end result in Figure 4.10. Make sure you get the domain specification correct. You can see that we have specified DEMO\. Failing to do so will lead the policy to think you are working with a local user account or group. A good tip for avoiding mistakes here is to use the Browse button when you click Add. The Add Member dialog box will allow you to make mistakes. The Browse button will open to the usual Select Users, Service Accounts, Or Groups dialog box and will not allow mistakes.

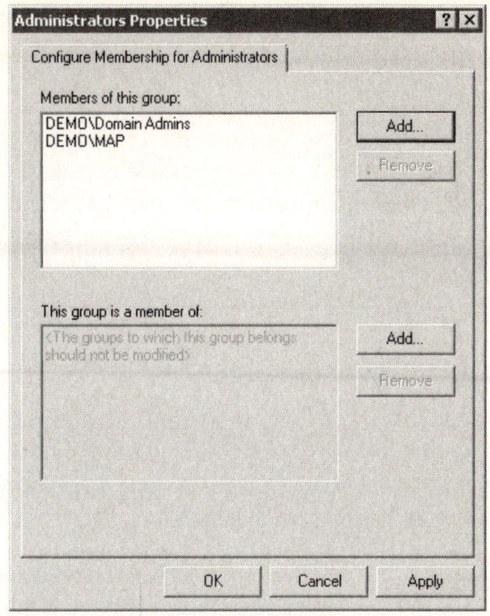

FIGURE 4.10
Configuring the Administrators Restricted Groups policy

Real World Scenario

TESTING GROUP POLICY

You'll be eager to test any new Group Policy settings. Waiting on Group Policy to refresh might take a few hours. You can run `gpupdate /force` to cause a machine to download and apply Group Policy. Use the Group Policy Results feature of Group Policy Management if things don't work out quite as expected. The usual suspects are that the policy link isn't enabled or the policy is not linked to the OU that contains the server objects (or a parent OU). Multisite domains will require time for a GPO to replicate to a remote site before the computers in that site can apply the policy. Multidomain forests and multiple forest or untrusted domain environments will require the GPO to be created in each domain.

Allow time for Group Policy to apply to your candidate computers. They will then be ready to start producing information for MAP. It is time to configure MAP to start gathering that data.

Real World Scenario

TRUSTING CONSULTANTS WITH ADMINISTRATOR ACCESS

The security officer of an organization might have some concerns about granting local server administrative rights to nonemployees. That is quite understandable. Using the approach shown in this book will allow some limitations to be put into place.

The easy approach of using a domain administrator account, which would give total and complete access to everything, has not been used. A domain user account that is granted access on a local server level, as used here, is much more secure.

By using domain user accounts and Group Policy, the local administrator access can be restricted to a number of servers at a time. You can even use different user accounts for different sites, domains, or OUs in the forest.

You can put an expiration date and time on the user account, based on the time allocated for the task. If a consultant has seven days to do the work, then the user account will automatically expire and be disabled at the end. You can easily extend this if the assessment task runs late.

Finally, it is easy to revoke access by disabling the user, deleting it, or removing it from the centrally managed GPO.

DISCOVERING SERVERS WITH MAP

MAP uses SQL Server to store the data that it gathers. When you start MAP for the first time, it will ask you to choose Create An Inventory Database or Use An Existing Database, as you can see in Figure 4.11. You will need to create a database the first time you use the tool. The name of the database in this example is MAP.

FIGURE 4.11
Selecting a MAP database option

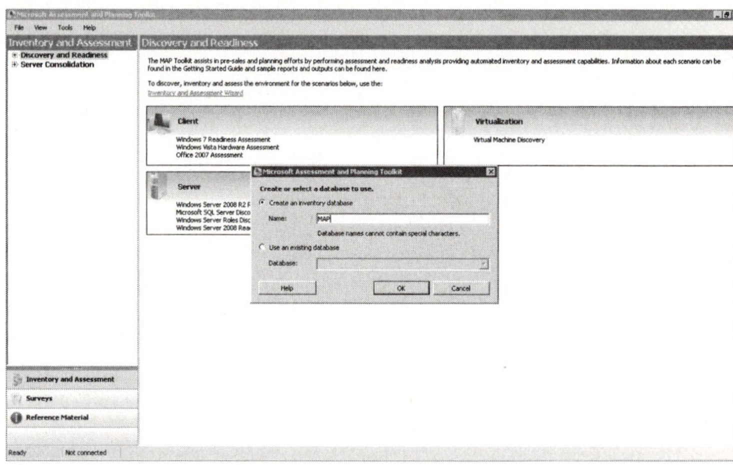

The database is created quite quickly. Now you are free to navigate around and use the tool. You'll soon see that MAP includes the ability to perform assessments for much more than Windows Server 2008 R2 Hyper-V deployments. Windows 7 deployment project managers will be very interested in it, not to mention many others. We're going to focus on the Hyper-V side of things.

The layout has the typical System Center interface that appears to have been inherited from Microsoft Outlook. The bottom left has what are referred to as *wunderbars*:

Inventory and Assessment This is where you will do most of your work.

Surveys MAP can include surveys for gathering more information.

Reference Material Since the release of Windows Vista, Microsoft has learned the importance of making it easy to find information. Here you will find links to useful sources such as utilities and accelerators that can assist with the many kinds of projects that MAP will be used for.

The navigation pane on the left allows you to drill a little deeper into each of the subjects represented by the wunderbars. Under Reference Material, you will find lots of links to virtualization tools and guidance. Under Inventory and Assessment, you will find there is a navigation tree. This provides you with a way to view the collected data in different contexts such as server consolidation, Windows 7 deployments, or a Hyper-V deployment.

The first step in the assessment will be to discover your servers. You will need to run the Inventory And Assessment Wizard to do this. You will find a hyperlink to do this by clicking the Inventory And Assessment wunderbar and navigating to Discovery And Readiness.

Figure 4.12 shows you the first screen where you will specify the methods you want to use to discover computers on your network. You can select from a number of options:

Use Active Directory Domain Services This method is on by default. It will discover computer accounts from your domain and use them in the discovery process. You can limit the scope to a domain, OU, or container. It is limited to 120,000 computer objects per domain. The Active Directory Domain Services method will not discover any additional computer objects beyond 120,000. Microsoft recommends that this method should not be used with the Windows networking protocols method because it will take more time to complete the process.

Use The Windows Networking Protocols This method will query the Computer Browser service using WIN32 LAN Manager APIs. You will use it to discover computers in workgroups and Windows NT 4.0–based domains. Microsoft recommends that this method should not be used with the Active Directory Domain Services method because it will take more time to complete the process.

Import Computer Names From A File You may have a scenario where the Computer Browser service is not enabled or you cannot query Active Directory using LDAP. If so, you can specify computer names, NetBIOS names, or fully qualified domain names in a text file. It is not a CSV; it is a simple text file with one computer per line.

Scan An IP Range This option offers lots of flexibility. You could target a branch office where the logical (OU or container) architecture of Active Directory does not match the physical site structure. You could also use it to discover Windows NT 4.0 domain members or workgroup members where the Computer Browser service isn't functioning.

Manually Enter Computer Names And Credentials Use this method if there are a few known machines that you want to target and the previous methods either are unsuitable or are too much work.

VMware Server Discovery This will use VMware web service to discover ESX, ESXi, and VMware Server installations in your environment. This would be useful if you are considering using the virtual-to-virtual (V2V) functionality of Microsoft System Center Virtual Machine Manager to migrate from VMware to Hyper-V.

In this exercise, you will go with the simple Active Directory Domain Services method to discover your servers.

The next screen in the wizard, which is shown in Figure 4.13, will look for your domain details. It will want to know the name of the domain, the name of the user to use in the discovery process, and the password for that user. This should be a domain user who has rights to read the objects from the part of the domain you will discover. We used DEMO\MAP in this example.

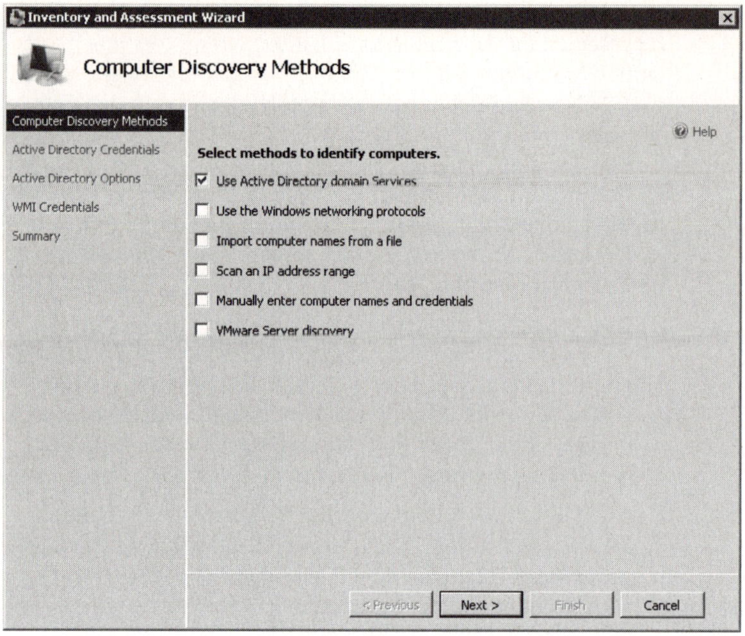

FIGURE 4.12
Computer discovery methods

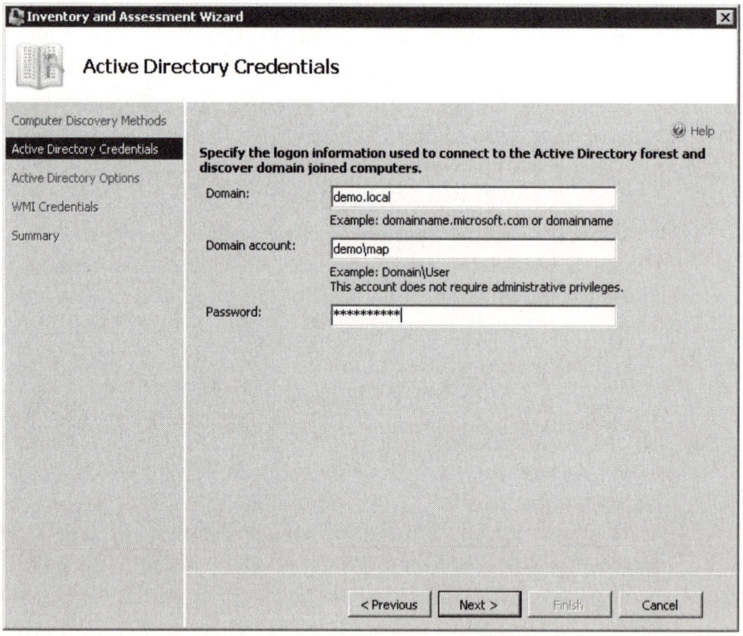

FIGURE 4.13
Active Directory discovery credentials

You have the ability to constrain your discovery to a specified part of your domain. You can discover all machines in the domain or within an OU or container. This would be useful if your OUs did match the physical structure of the organization or if the discovery user account you are using only has rights to servers within certain OUs or containers. Figure 4.14 shows how we have constrained the discovery to the OU that contains all of our candidate servers. We don't want to include domain controllers.

FIGURE 4.14
Active Directory discovery options

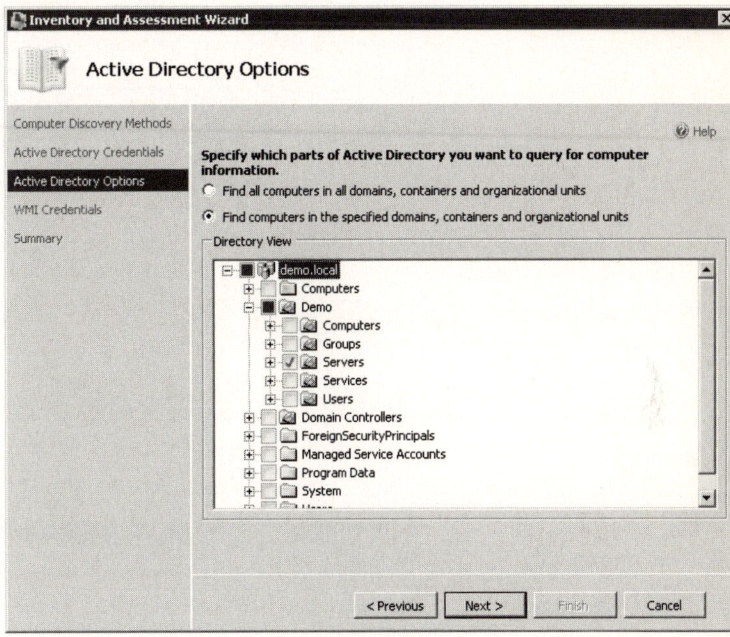

The next step, illustrated in Figure 4.15, allows you to specify the user account(s) that will be used to connect to the servers using WMI. It is a very flexible process, as you will see.

Clicking the New Account button will open a new screen called Inventory Account. As you can see in Figure 4.16, here you can enter the domain, username, and password of a user account to be used in the Active Directory discovery process. By default the discovery method will attempt to use this account on all computers. You might have one or a few machines where you need to use alternative credentials. In that case, you would use the Use Only On The Following Computer option. Note that you are not restricted to domain user accounts. You do not have to specify a domain name. If you do not, then it will assume that the user is a local user account on the server.

You will be returned to the WMI Credentials screen in the wizard when you close the Inventory Account window. Figure 4.17 shows the newly saved WMI credentials. You can edit this to make changes, or you can further WMI credentials if you need to use more than one account for the discovery.

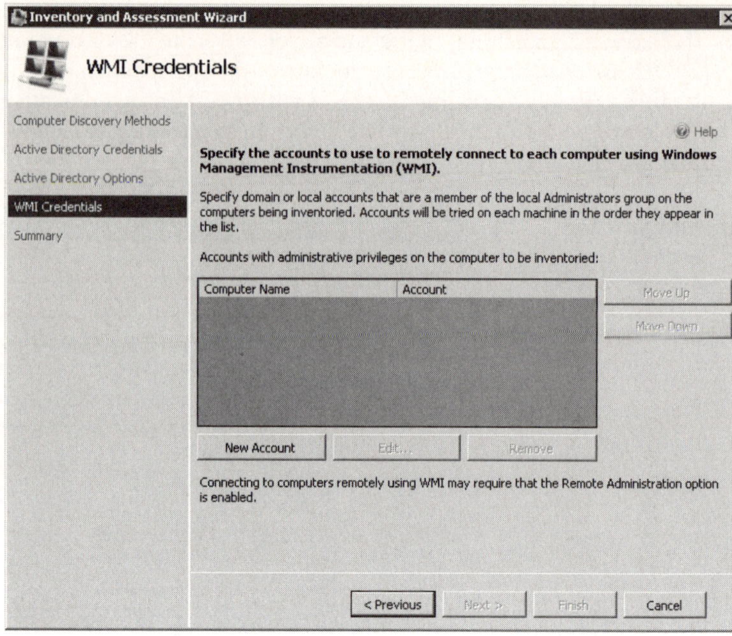

FIGURE 4.15
WMI connection credentials

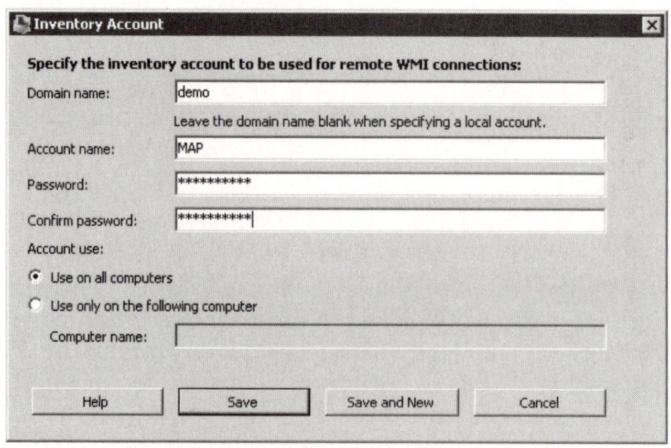

FIGURE 4.16
Inventory Account screen

You will come to a summary screen where you can either cancel the discovery or start the process. The discovery will run and reveal the progress screen shown in Figure 4.18.

You can check the results of the discovery process by browsing through Discovery And Readiness. You can see that our example discovered some web and SQL servers on the network in Figure 4.19.

FIGURE 4.17
Configured WMI connection credentials

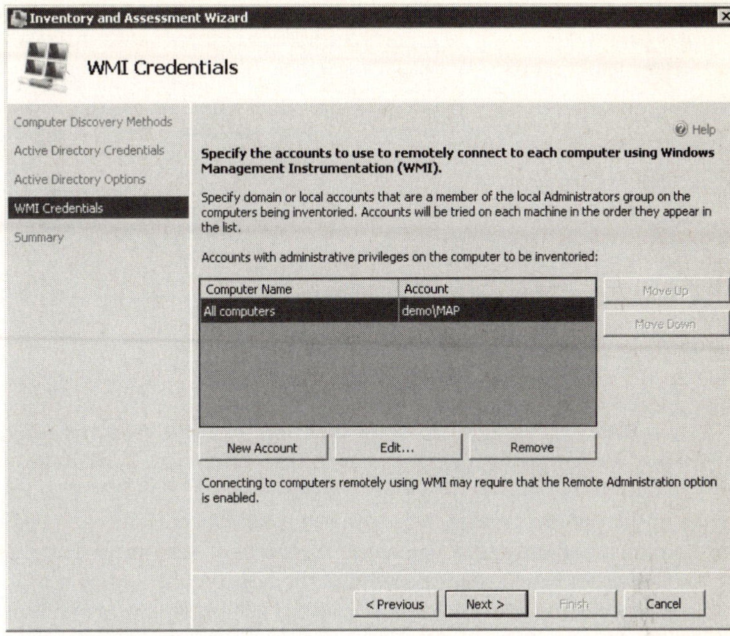

FIGURE 4.18
Active Directory discovery method progress

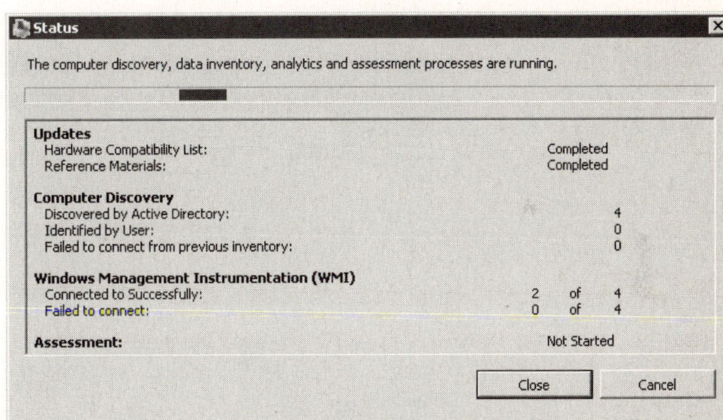

You should note that MAP is capable of distinguishing between physical and virtual machines. So, you will not get the results you might hope for if trying MAP in a virtual lab.

You can generate a number of reports containing a summary of the discovered servers on your network. Each one is appropriate to the type of project you are running in MAP. When you have created a report, you can click the View menu and click Saved Reports And Proposals. This will open a Windows Explorer menu that reveals a folder named after your MAP database name in Documents. Any created reports are generated in here.

FIGURE 4.19
Discovery verification

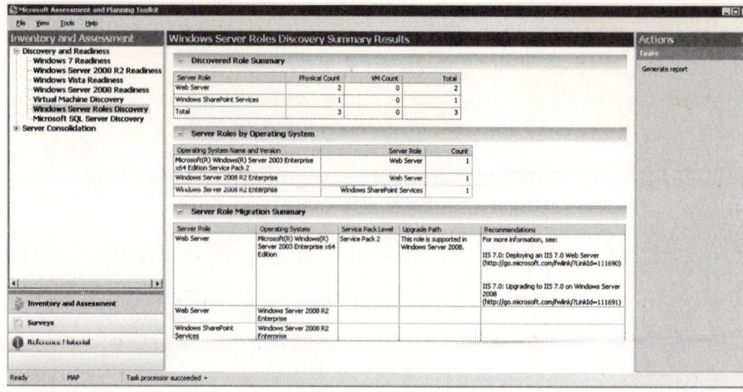

The next step in the process will require a text file containing the names of all the computers you want to gather performance information from. You can get a listing of the MAP-discovered computers by navigating into Windows Server 2008 R2 Readiness and clicking Generate Reports in the Actions pane. After a while, a spreadsheet will be created in My Documents. You can open it and browse to the Server Assessment worksheet. Simply copy the column with the Computer Name column (without the heading) and paste it into a text file. The resulting file will have one line per computer, listing the computer names of all machines to be assessed.

MAP is now aware of the candidate servers, their configuration, and their specifications. As you can see in Figure 4.20, the next step is to gather performance metrics over a period of time to determine their resource utilization.

FIGURE 4.20
Hyper-V assessment progress

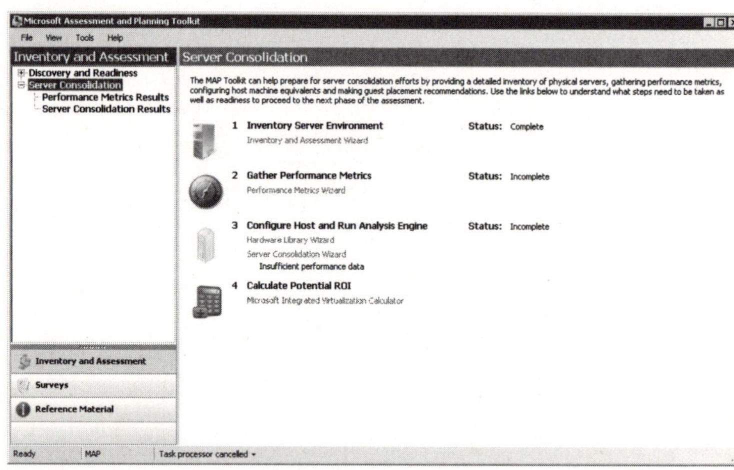

GATHERING PERFORMANCE METRICS

By gathering performance data over a predetermined time window, you can do the following:

- Determine how appropriate it will be to convert a physical server into a virtual machine.
- Compute how many Hyper-V hosts and the storage architecture that will be required to host the complete set of virtual machines.

Before you do this, you will need to decide how long you want to gather performance metrics for. The default setting is for one hour. As you'll see, one hour is the absolute minimum that MAP can use for the later steps. One hour is way too short to get an accurate assessment of the resource requirements of a server in a real-world environment. Even a day is a little short. Realistically, you should consider one week being the minimum. The more data you have, the better the assessment will be. The contradiction to this is that the entire process will take much longer and will delay the project while increasing the costs.

You also will want to consider how many machines you want to assess at once. You will be using the previously generated text file containing the discovered computer names. You can include or exclude server names to control the numbers being processed at once. This text file is also how you can exclude machines that you do not consider as virtualization candidates.

You should browse into Server Consolidation ➤ Performance Metrics Results once you are ready to progress. In here there is a hyperlink called Performance Metrics Wizard. You can initiate a collection of performance data by using this wizard.

Figure 4.21 shows how you can import the names of the computers you want to assess the performance of. The file containing the names of each computer is selected.

FIGURE 4.21
Importing computer names

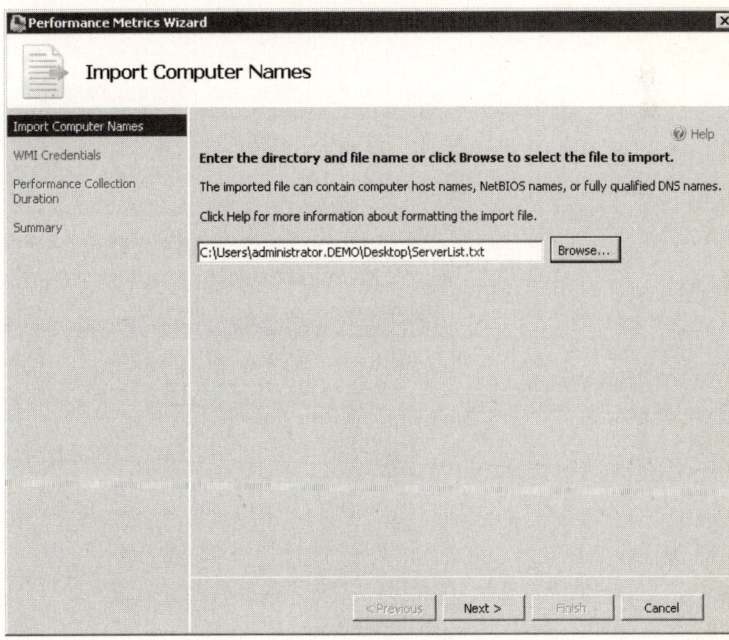

The next screen in the wizard will look for the credentials to remotely access the WMI of each candidate computer. It is identical to the WMI Credentials screen that you used during the discovery. Again, DEMO\MAP is being used in this example.

Before you complete the wizard, you must specify when the performance gathering will terminate. The default is in one hour's time. Configure this as required. The screen is shown in Figure 4.22. Note that at least 12 samples (approximately 1 hour) are required to use the Server Virtualization Planning Wizard. It's easy to just run a 5- or 15-minute job, but it will not contain enough data to be useful.

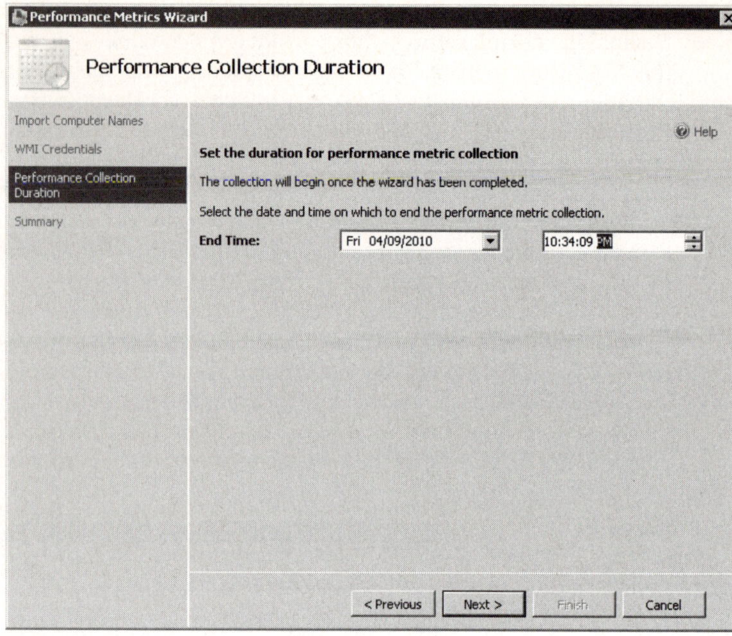

FIGURE 4.22 Performance collection duration

A window will appear showing the progress of the job. You can hide this window, shown in Figure 4.23, by clicking Close. This will not terminate the job. A little pop-up menu is in the bottom of the main MAP window called Performance Metrics Collection. You can use this to cancel the job or reopen the progress window.

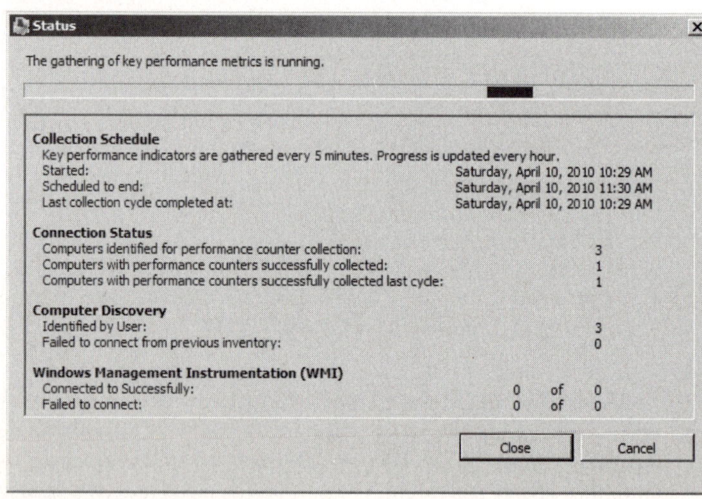

FIGURE 4.23 Performance Metrics progress window

Data will be gathered every five minutes from your servers. Don't panic if all your selected servers do not show up as being successfully collected in the first few minutes. It can take a little while for the statuses for all servers to be updated.

When the job completes, the Performance Metrics Results pane will be updated, illustrated in Figure 4.24. There will be one line per server assessed. The lower part of the screen gives you a bit more detail. If you browse through there, you will find the following:

Summary As the name suggests, this presents a brief summary of the data collected for the selected server. You will also find hyperlinks here to open windows showing information on the discovered services and the installed applications.

Processor The processor model, speed, and numbers installed are displayed along with the performance information.

Network Each discovered NIC is displayed. Details on packets and bytes sent and received are presented here.

Physical Disk This holds information on the disk model, size, and performance information.

Logical Disk Each volume, including those with no letter, is displayed with its performance metrics.

FIGURE 4.24
Performance metrics results

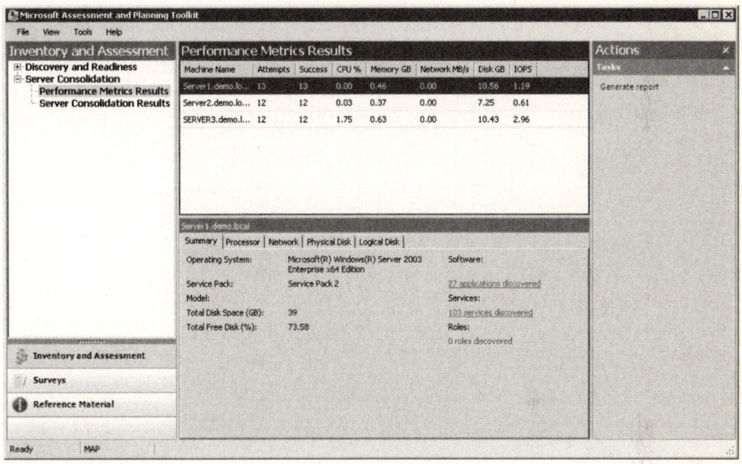

You can use the Generate Report option in the Actions pane to create a report based on the collected information. Instead of breaking the information down by server, the created spreadsheet breaks it down by each of the previous headings first. It also contains more information and metric data. You now want to use this data to size a Hyper-V platform. You need to create a library of hardware before you do that.

Picking Virtualization Candidates

Now you get to the tricky bit. You need to identify which of these servers will be virtualized. MAP has given you the information about the servers. You need to decide whether a server with high amounts of CPU, network, memory, or storage utilization will be converted into a virtual machine.

This will all depend on what the goals of the project are, and the goals will be based on the directives from the business. Do you virtualize a server that will consume 50 percent of a Hyper-V host's capacity? Maybe you don't because it will be expensive. Or maybe you do because you want to free up space or make it easier to replicate the server to a DR site.

Browse through the previously generated PerfMetricResults Excel report, and use the detailed metrics to make your decision.

Copy the name of every server that you decide to virtualize into a text file. You will be importing this file into MAP again later. There should be one computer name per line and a maximum of 120,000 computers.

Unfortunately, this is a manual process because there is no best practice. Some organizations will consider one or two virtual machines per host to be acceptable. And some others will consider 10 virtual machines per host to be the absolute minimum.

HARDWARE LIBRARY WIZARD

MAP is now aware of the candidate servers and their resource utilization. You can see in Figure 4.25 that the next step in the process is to run the Hardware Library Wizard. This will allow you to input a possible hardware specification for the Hyper-V hosts. You will then be able to combine this with the performance metrics to calculate how big the end solution might be.

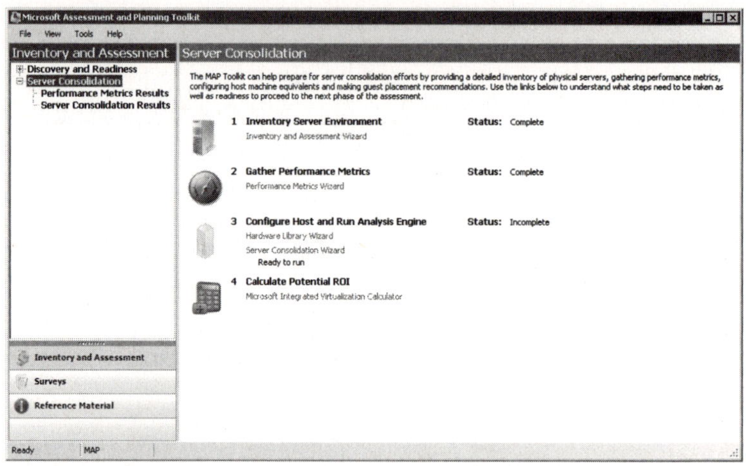

FIGURE 4.25
The Hardware Library Wizard is next.

You should start the Hardware Library Wizard by clicking the hyperlink. The first screen, shown in Figure 4.26, allows you to create a new hardware specification or reuse one that you previously created. Use a description that accurately represents the hardware that is being used as a Hyper-V host in your model.

The next step is one that will require a little research on the Web. You need to enter the specification and numbers of the processors that you want to use in the Hyper-V host. The screen is illustrated in Figure 4.27. The Model list box is a little out-of-date, but that's probably not a problem. The real meat of this screen is below, where you enter the capabilities of the processor. You will probably need to search for each one on the Internet. The manufacturer's website probably will use different terminology or measurements.

The next step is to model your available storage. You can approach this in one of two ways. If the Hyper-V host will use internal disks, then you will probably want to take the approach shown in Figure 4.28. We have selected Calculate Total Available Storage Using The Option Below. That allows us to specify the disk types such as SATA 7.2K disks and the number of them and enter the cache size on the controller. If you are using a SAN, then you might want to choose the lower Define IOPS And Total Available Storage option. Then you simply need to know the available throughput (which you can get from the storage manufacturer) and the size of the SAN you plan to use. When using a SAN, simply plug in the maximum size of the SAN based on the disk chosen.

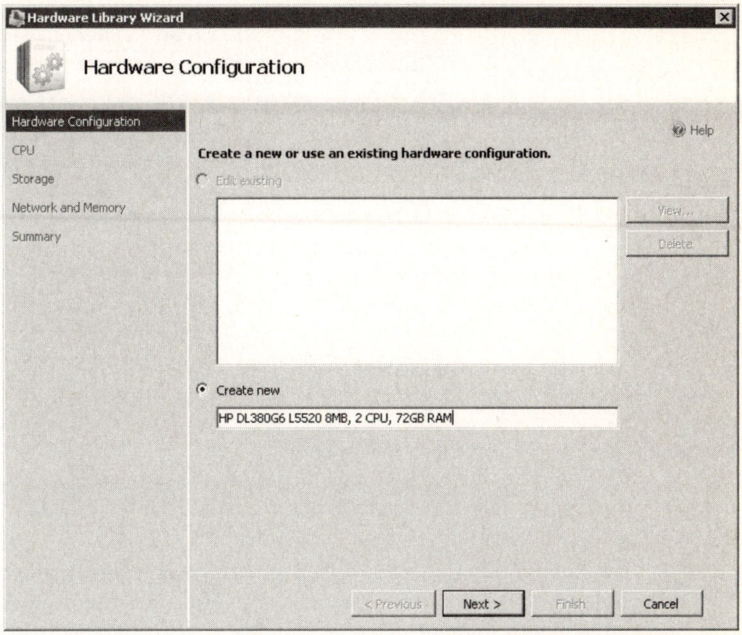

FIGURE 4.26
Describe the Hyper-V host.

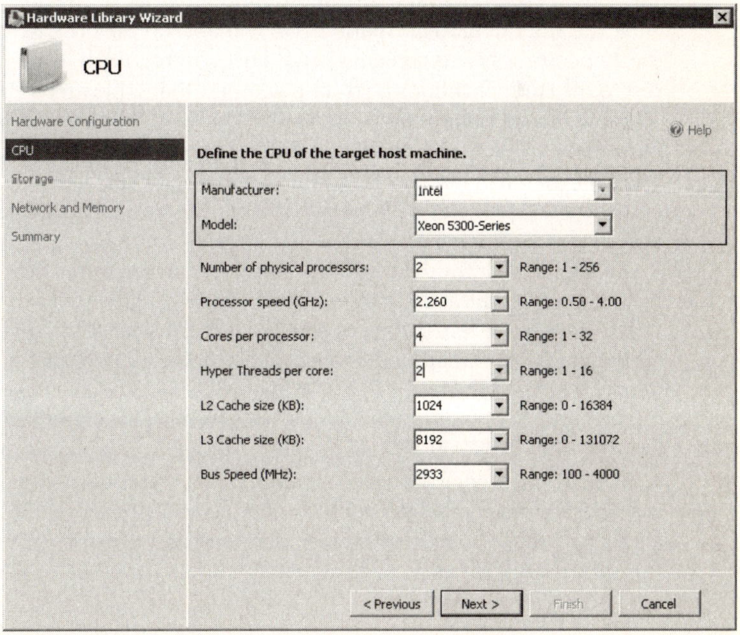

FIGURE 4.27
CPU details

FIGURE 4.28
Storage details

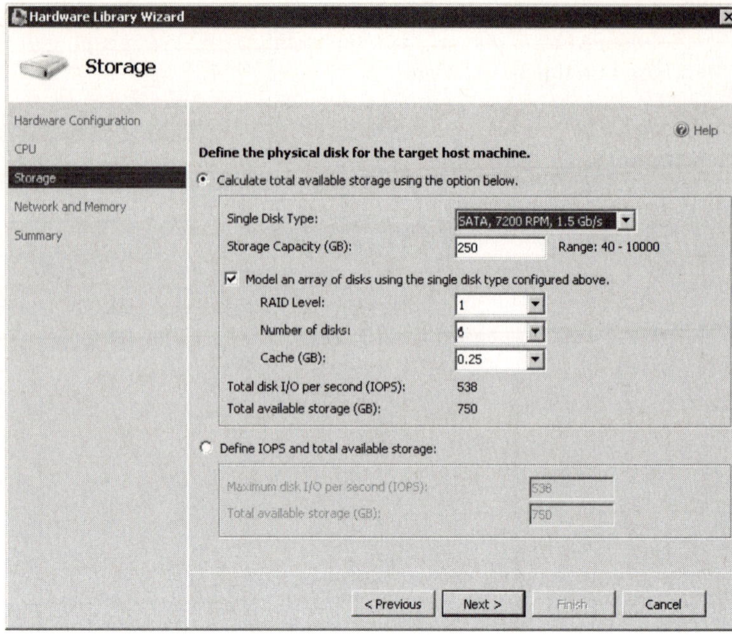

The final step in this wizard is to enter details regarding the network cards in the host and the amount of RAM that will be available. This does require understanding a bit about Hyper-V design and requirements. Don't worry; we cover the subject of Hyper-V host design in Chapter 5 and delve into more detail on Hyper-V in Chapter 6.

Enter the speed and the quantity of NICs that are in the host, as shown in Figure 4.29. Next enter the amount of RAM that will be available on the host. Remember that the parent partition (host operating system) on a Hyper-V host will require a few gigabytes of RAM. That leaves the rest to the child partitions (virtual machines) that will run on the host.

Some installations of Hyper-V include hosts with both 1 GB and 10 GB network cards. 10 GB Ethernet is still rather exclusive, and its usage in a Hyper-V host or cluster is limited to specific roles, for example, the Live Migration private network. This wizard does not allow for this sort of installation. You might want to just enter the slowest speed here, see the preliminary results, and change it afterward.

Check through the details of the summary screen to see whether this matches your Hyper-V host. You can then save the server specification.

MAP does not restrict you to using just one model of server. You can easily return to this wizard and enter other models and specifications of potential hosts. Multiple server specifications are entered in Figure 4.30. It is also possible to edit or delete existing server specifications.

Consultants or engineers who are using a reusable virtual machine for running MAP on multiple sites can take advantage of this wizard to appear even more efficient to their customers. They can preenter all of the commonly used specifications from the different manufacturers into the database before saving the template virtual machine/database.

You can move on to the next step once you are happy. It is finally time to run the Server Consolidation Wizard.

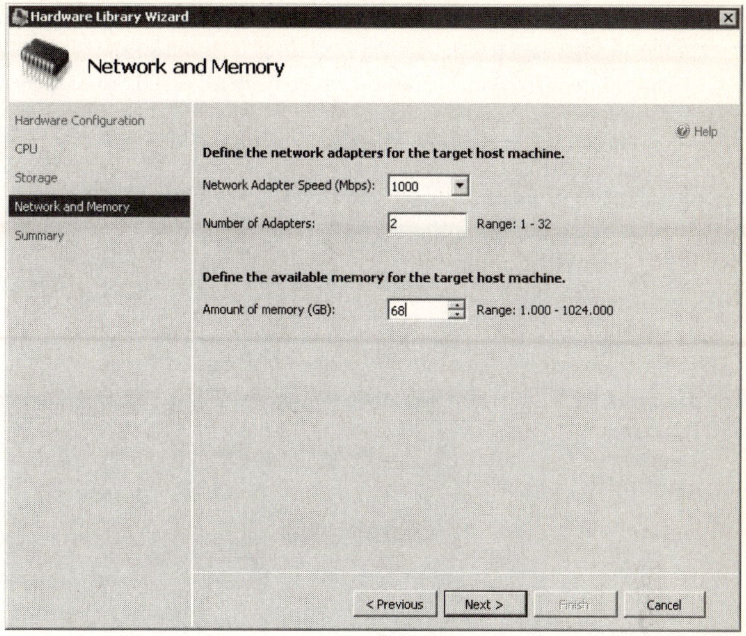

FIGURE 4.29
Network card and available memory details

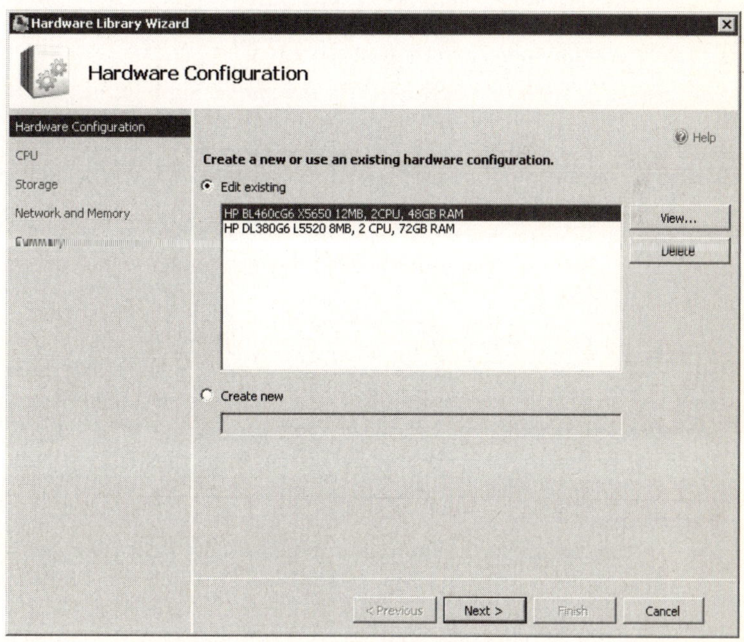

FIGURE 4.30
Add, edit, or delete multiple host specifications.

Server Consolidation Wizard

In this step, MAP will suggest a possible sizing for the Hyper-V deployment based on the candidate virtual machines that have been assessed. You should run the wizard once you've completed the previous steps.

The screen in Figure 4.31 allows you do one of a few things:

- Select an existing hardware specification from the library.
- View the details of a selected specification.
- Use the currently in use specification. If one is not loaded, it will allow you to create one from scratch.

Figure 4.31
Selecting a hardware specification

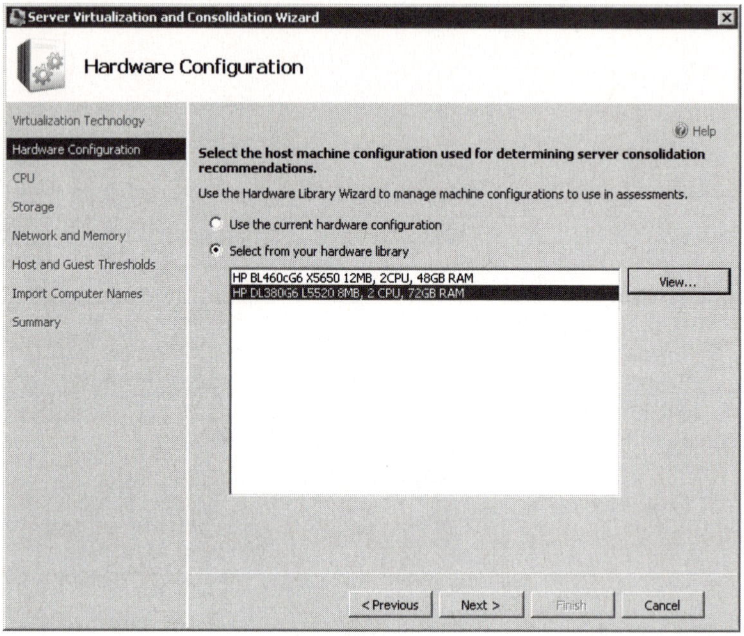

You can select one machine from your library because you have done the preparatory work.

The wizard will allow you to view or edit the details of the selected hardware specification as you browse through the wizard. You then reach a screen where you can determine the host and guest thresholds. You can see this in Figure 4.32.

The first option, Number Of Virtual Machines Per Host, allows you to specify how many virtual machines you want to put on a host. This will rarely be used, and it is grayed out by default.

You can set up the amount of spare memory (in megabytes) and disk space (as a percentage) to allow per virtual machine on the host. This will allow for future expansion of the virtual machine specifications. The free disk space is set at 50 percent. That means the wizard would allow for 200 GB if a virtual machine required 100 GB. A more mature server network probably won't need 50 percent.

FIGURE 4.32
Host and guest thresholds

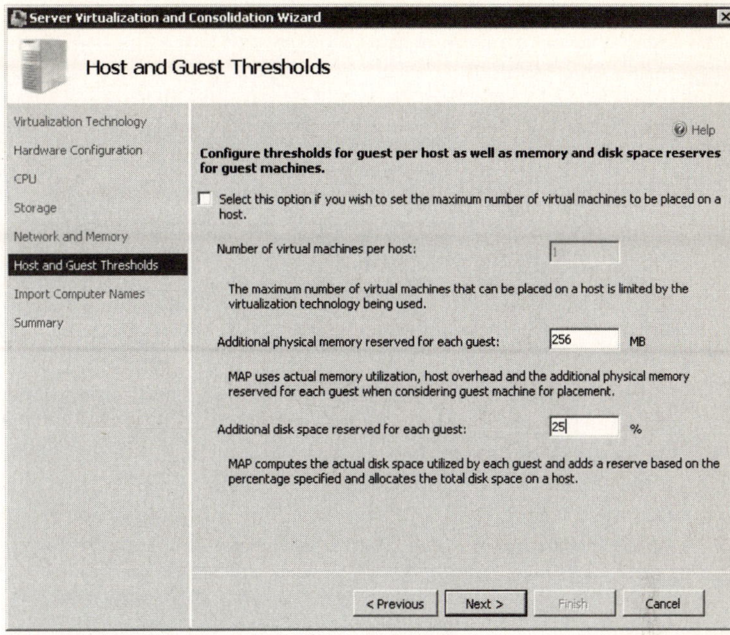

You now need to tell the wizard which servers you want to virtualize and consider in this sizing process. You will be importing the text file that you created while selecting servers to convert. Browse to the file and select it, as shown in Figure 4.33.

FIGURE 4.33
Selecting the file with servers to convert

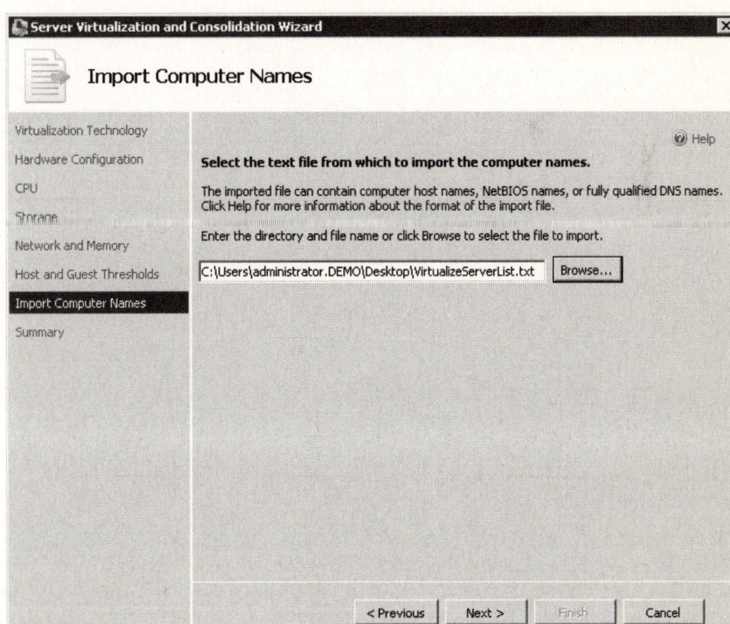

After the summary screen, the window in Figure 4.34 will appear. A job runs to model your final solution. This might take a few seconds for a small environment but will take longer for a larger one.

FIGURE 4.34
Server consolidation job status

Browse to Server Consolidation Results, and you can now see the summary of the results from the Server Consolidation Wizard, shown in Figure 4.35. The one tiny little bit of information you are looking for here is in the first table. The Total Number Of Physical Servers value under After Virtualization is the key to calculating the cost of your Hyper-V project. You can see that the selected physical host with 72 GB of RAM will be more than capable of hosting the three servers in the `demo.local` domain that you want to convert into virtual machines.

FIGURE 4.35
Server consolidation results

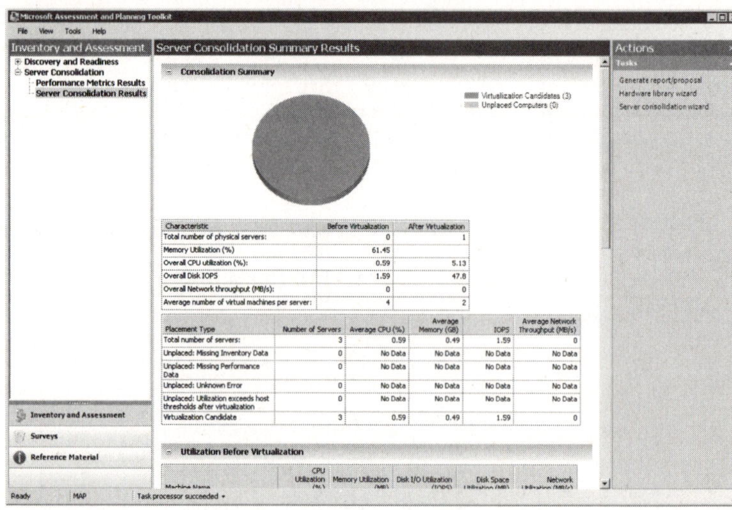

Be careful. The results that are presented show you how many Hyper-V hosts are required to run your virtualized workload. It does not consider clustering or host redundancy. You will need to add an extra host or two for host fault tolerance if you plan to deploy a Hyper-V cluster.

That screen is great, but it isn't very presentable to a manager or executive. Imagine printing it out and handing it over to them. You'll quickly see their eyes glaze over, and you'll spend the following three days responding to lots of emails full of questions. The designers and developers of MAP understand our need to present the results to nontechnical decision makers. And that is exactly why they cater to this need.

Clicking Generate Report/Proposal in the Actions pane will start a job to create a Word document and an Excel spreadsheet. This might take a little time in a larger organization. The files are created in the usual location in My Documents, in a folder named after the MAP database.

The Word document is a superb starting point for a report that you would present to your bosses or customers. It goes through the summary information and explains what a Windows Server 2008 R2 Hyper-V project can offer. It is Microsoft branded, but you can easily rebrand it for your needs.

A spreadsheet is also created for the techies who need a bit more detail on the host configuration, virtual machine placement, host performance based on those placements, and any information on servers that could not be placed.

Return on Investment

Typically, some of the decision makers will have an accountant's point of view. They will decide on the merits of a virtualization project based on the numbers. For example, one of the ways you can pitch a hardware virtualization project is to claim that the purchase of hardware will eventually lead to a major saving in ownership and operational costs. You can bet that someone like a financial controller will hold you to that promise and expect to see how you calculated this before you even proceed!

Microsoft thought of that and has created an online Return on Investment (ROI) utility. It will load an XML document that was created in the usual MAP report location and produce the numbers you will need. We will look at that now.

You can click the Microsoft Integrated Virtualization Calculator hyperlink in Server Consolidation. That will open up your browser and navigate to the Microsoft Integrated Virtualization ROI Calculator website. You can see in Figure 4.36 that you will scroll down a bit and click Integrated Virtualization ROI Calculator.

Figure 4.36 Microsoft Integrated Virtualization ROI Calculator website

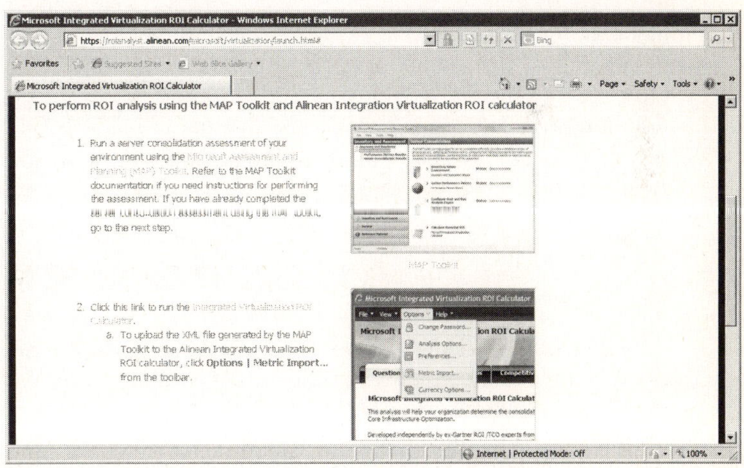

This will open a web application in a new window. This window, which you can see in Figure 4.37, is where you will enter some information and configure how the ROI calculator will work.

FIGURE 4.37
Microsoft Integrated Virtualization ROI Calculator application

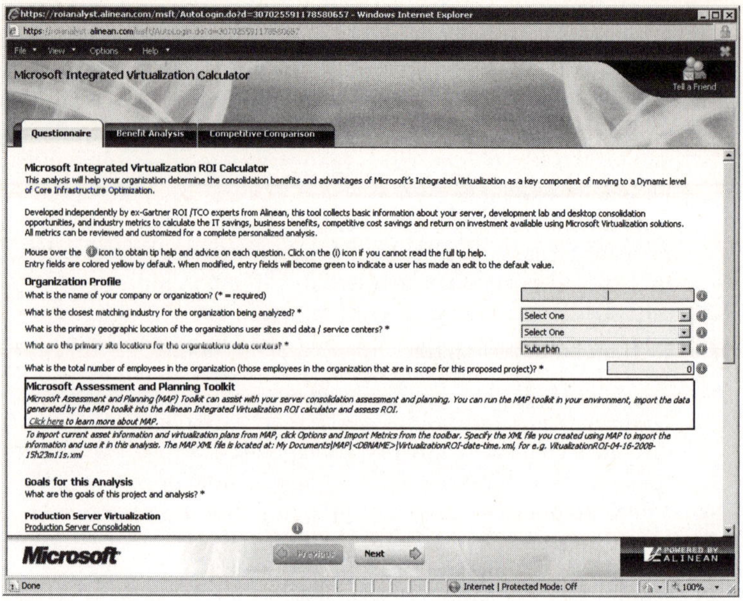

The first thing you need to do is import the performance metrics that you gathered from your virtualization candidates. The XML file is in the usual reports location. Click Options in the web application, and select Metric Import. As you can see in Figure 4.38, you just need to select the XML file that MAP created automatically when the performance metrics were gathered and click the Import Metrics button.

FIGURE 4.38
Metric import

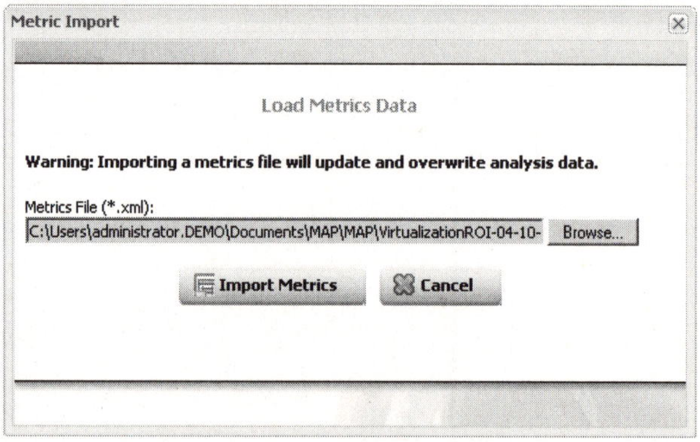

Back in the ROI web application, you can enter lots more information and answer a few questions about the organization you are assessing:

- The name of the company
- The size of the company
- The geographic location of the organization

- The type of area that the data centers or computer rooms are located in
- The total number of employees

You can specify the reasons for considering virtualization. For example, you might select Green IT or Production Server High Availability. You can also include a competitive (alternative virtualization providers) analysis and Microsoft licensing analysis.

That is just a sample of what you can configure here. This is a web application and is therefore likely to be improved over time, making it subject to change. You will find that many of the questions being asked in this application are financial. You will need the assistance of someone who has the current support and operational cost details of IT in the organization to answer them. There are some buttons at the bottom that allow you to go into great detail on environment and licensing configuration and costs that will be specific to the organization that has been assessed.

Back in the Options menu, you have a few more configuration screens that you can use:

Analysis Options You can enter details about the project here, such as the status and the customer details.

Preferences Branding is important when it comes to a report. You can upload a logo to use here.

Currency Options This utility is all about money. The U.S. dollar is the default currency. You can change this and set the current exchange rate.

When you are ready, you can move from the Questionnaire tab to the Benefit Analysis tab to start reviewing the ROI. You can see the results in Figure 4.39.

FIGURE 4.39
ROI benefit analysis

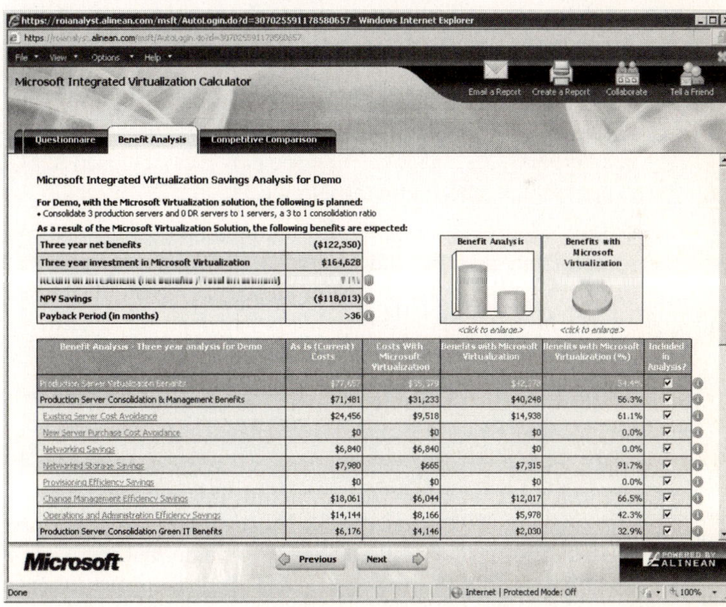

There is summary information presented at the top of the screen. You can see that converting just the three servers in `demo.local` to virtual machines could save $122,350 over three years.

That is a massive 74 percent reduction in operating and ownership cost over the current physical server deployment.

That figure does seem rather incredible. It is easy to fall into the trap of thinking that a server's cost is the purchase price. Clicking each of the hyperlinks associated with the costs gives you an insight into how much your business is really paying to run those servers. It is quite scary, especially when you realize we are looking at a three-server demo lab. Walk into your now full computer room, and think about what the costs could possibly be.

You can clear the check box beside each benefit to exclude it from the analysis should you consider it irrelevant.

You can then move onto the competitive analysis to see how a Microsoft solution will fare against the competition.

All of this is great to look at, but you will need to present a report. You can email a report to yourself or save it. You can even collaborate with someone else on the report by inviting them in. All of these options will require you to register, but the process is rather quick and simple.

Creating or emailing a report gives you the choice of either a PowerPoint presentation or a Word document, either of which you can then customize. These are based on templates that include helpful descriptions of benefits of the technology for the nontechnical audience. They also include the figures that this audience will want to see. Be sure to go in and edit or delete any pieces that require changes.

That's it! You have used the Microsoft and Assessment Planning Toolkit to produce financial and technical information based on the existing server network.

Pros and Cons of MAP

Now we have discussed MAP in depth, we'll cover the positives and negatives of using this solution for an assessment. The positives are as follows:

Free Everyone likes free! And it doesn't suffer by being free either. It is quite a powerful package, capable of doing much more than server virtualization assessments.

Powerful The skills developed and the data gathered by MAP can be used for more than just Hyper-V. Take a look; you'll see how it can be used in SQL Server, Windows 7, application virtualization, and many more projects.

Useful Reports Detailed information on performance is produced in a spreadsheet. A spreadsheet and a Word document are created to show how many hosts you will need (remember to add extra hosts for cluster fault tolerance) for your final solution. You can also satisfy the needs of decision makers who focus on the financials by analyzing the return on the investment in hardware virtualization.

Server Consolidation Wizard Being able to provide an estimate on the Hyper-V requirements out of the box is very impressive.

ROI Calculator The decision makers in any organization like to have the numbers. You can use MAP, a free tool, to assess your infrastructure, give you a good idea of your Hyper-V requirements, and then calculate the return on the investment using the Server Consolidation Wizard results. This could make the decision-making part of the project with the executives much easier for you as an engineer, architect, or consultant.

No Agents Organizations that must tightly control configurations, such as those in the pharmaceutical industry, hate change. It means testing, procedures, and documentation, all at great expense and with an obvious delay to the project. Being able to gather data without the need to deploy an agent will be very attractive to these sorts of organizations.

On the negative side you have the following:

Lots of Preparatory Work To allow agent-less scanning, older operating systems will require some installations. Group Policy must be deployed in domains. Nondomain machines will require manual changes. Yes, you can automate much of this, but there can be a lot of work.

Network Security Changes Some organizations will have application or appliance firewalls installed with very tight controls. Either they will have to make adjustments to allow the required traffic or the MAP server will have to be moved from network to network for many assessments.

WAN Traffic The required MAP traffic might be seen as not being WAN friendly. This will require engineering to resolve.

The Performance Assessment Although the reporting is very impressive, the performance metrics information you are presented with is a little simple. It presents averages, which can be misleading. Spikes and a standard deviation should be considered when trying to calculate how many hosts will be required for a virtualization conversion of existing servers. The length of time that the assessment will run for is relatively short. This means that you may miss out on seasonal spikes in resource consumption. For example, the accounts server may be quiet most of the time, but it probably is pretty busy at the end of every month, quarter, or tax year.

Supported Operating Systems MAP supports Windows platforms only. You might want to include Linux servers, but this will require alternative tools. Note that version 5.0 of MAP will add support for Linux.

Using System Center for Assessment

Why would you even consider System Center? Some organizations may have System Center installed already. The required performance and configuration data is probably already sitting in reporting databases. A lot of Hyper-V deployments will include some or all of the Microsoft System Center products in the project. It could be possible to install System Center before the Hyper-V deployment if a commitment has already been made by the organization.

Using the various products that are in Microsoft System Center could resolve some or all of the issues with MAP.

Here is a high-level view on how System Center can be used in your assessment and sizing process:

Configuration Manager ConfigMgr (pronounced Config Manager) or SCCM (the current release at the time of writing is 2007 R2 with 2007 R3 expected in the near future) will store data on machine specifications, operating systems, and applications installed. Most implementations of ConfigMgr focus only on desktop management, but there are many reasons to also deploy the ConfigMgr client on servers as well. It natively only supports Windows, but third-party solutions exist for non-Microsoft operating systems.

Operations Manager OpsMgr (pronounced Ops Manager), the current release at the time of writing is 2007 R2, automatically gathers performance data from managed computers.

OpsMgr 2007 R2 offers Cross Platform Extensions. This gives you Microsoft-written agents and knowledge for managing Linux (selected RedHat and SUSE versions) distributions. By default, more than a year of data can be stored in the optional reporting database. You can run reports to see the performance of the various parts of each server you are considering converting into virtual machines.

Virtual Machine Manager You will use the latest version, VMM 2008 R2, if you are deploying Windows Server 2008 R2 Hyper-V or Hyper-V Server 2008 R2. The role of VMM in an assessment is very limited; additional reports are added to OpsMgr when you integrate it with VMM 2008 R2. There is one report you can use to quickly identify candidates for conversion based on your OpsMgr reporting database's stored performance data.

System Center Essentials 2010 The latest release of SCE will be used for small to medium-sized organizations (up to 50 servers and 500 clients) that want to get the core elements of Microsoft System Center for managing Hyper-V and other parts of the server infrastructure. It includes features from ConfigMgr, OpsMgr, and VMM. It does not include a reporting database, but you will be able to see current performance information. Realistically, these organizations will probably be better off using MAP for the assessment, so we will focus on the aforementioned three System Center products.

As you can see, there is no host server calculation. There is no ROI analysis. And no management reports are created for you. You will be back to doing that work by hand. However, your virtualization assessment can take advantage of existing data. And that existing data could include more than a year of gathered performance data in scenarios where OpsMgr has been in place for a while. That means you can account for seasonal resource utilization spikes.

Another major advantage is that System Center is designed to think beyond a single-site or single-domain organization. For example, OpsMgr agents are light on the network. Agents are installed, and they don't require the more complicated firewall (Windows and network) configuration associated with the WMI configuration for MAP. Cross Active Directory forest deployments are also possible.

Gathering Configuration Data

Microsoft System Center Configuration Manager can automatically perform hardware audits of machines in a site that have a ConfigMgr client installed. This function, performed by a client agent, is normally enabled to allow the creation of collections, which are groups of managed computers that meet some query criteria. The audit happens on a scheduled basis, reflecting changes to machines over time. Data is returned to the site server (running Configuration Manager) and is made available via a reporting point, which is running IIS.

This audit will include information such as the following:

- Computer name
- Operating system
- Service pack
- The specification of the physical or virtual hardware such as disks, volumes, memory, and CPU
- The details of software that is installed

You can run reports on this data to identify the servers on your network and see their specifications. This is part of the information that will be used to size your Hyper-V host servers and storage.

> **LEARN MORE ABOUT CONFIGURATION MANAGER**
>
> This book will not be covering the in-depth details and architecture of Configuration Manager 2007. You should read *Mastering Configuration Manager 2007 R2*, published by Sybex, if you want to learn more about the product.

HARDWARE AUDITING CONFIGURATION

Configuration Manager deploys a client onto every computer it manages. This client uses agents to perform specific tasks. The Hardware Inventory Client Agent, shown in the Configuration Manager Console in Figure 4.40, is responsible for gathering what is referred to as *hardware data*. As you have already read, that includes more than just the hardware. Usually, this agent is turned on by default because it allows ConfigMgr administrators to use the collected data to create collections. Collections are like groups where the membership is more dynamic, thanks to the membership being based on a query. For example, all machines that have an operating system called Windows 2003 would be in a collection called Windows 2003.

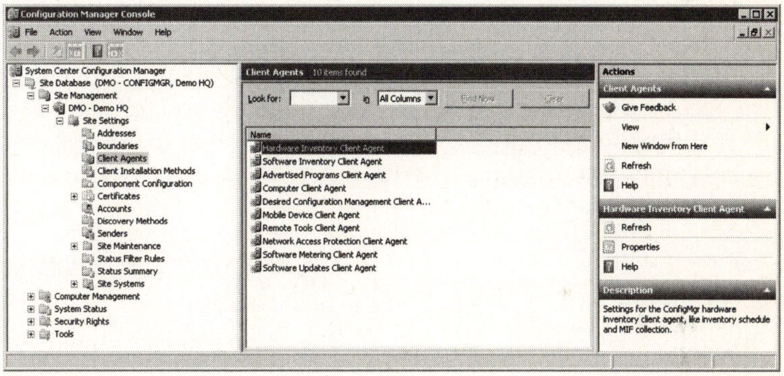

FIGURE 4.40 Configuration Manager Client Agents

You can see how the agent is configured by double-clicking it. Figure 4.41 displays the properties of the agent on the lab server. By default, this agent will audit hardware when the agent is enabled on a client and then every seven days. You might want to increase this frequency in a lab.

> **CONFIGURATION MANAGER AND PATIENCE**
>
> Nothing happens immediately in Configuration Manager. This can be quite frustrating when you first start to use the product and are unaware of how it works underneath the covers. With a little experience, you can tweak the default settings, such as those for the hardware inventory client, to get it to work faster. But even then, you must be patient.

FIGURE 4.41
Hardware Inventory Client Agent Properties dialog box

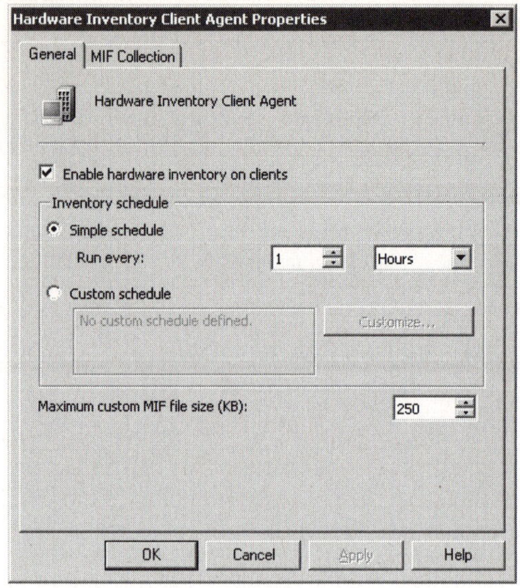

You can manually trigger a hardware inventory on a managed computer. To do this, log into the machine and open Control Panel. Open the Configuration Manager item in Control Panel. Navigate to the Actions tab, as shown in Figure 4.42. Select Hardware Inventory Cycle, and click the Initiate Action button. You can close the dialog box then. There is no easy way to see what is actually happening. Normally you just have to trust that the ConfigMgr client will perform the action and report the result to the site server. The data will then be available for reporting.

FIGURE 4.42
Initiating a hardware inventory cycle

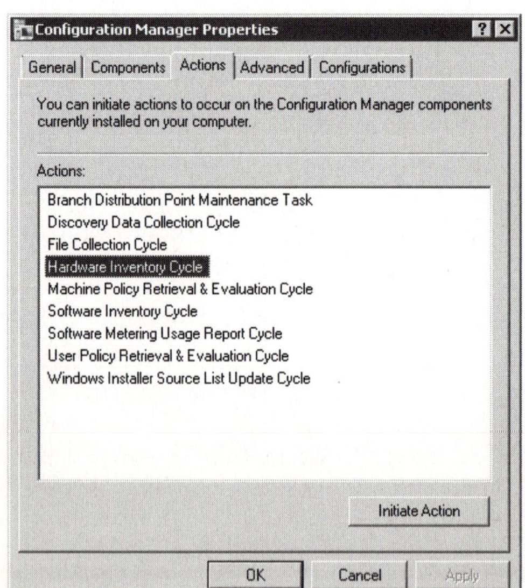

HARDWARE EXTENSIONS

Hardware manufacturers such as HP and Dell have created management packs to extend the functionality of Configuration Manager. This includes the ability to get extremely detailed information on the hardware that they supply.

HARDWARE REPORTING

You can enable an optional Site Server role called the Reporting Point in Configuration Manager. It is not unusual to see this role enabled. This is because it allows you to generate reports based on the vast amount of knowledge that ConfigMgr can gather and allows you to view the status of scheduled tasks.

There are two ways you can run reports. The first, and the one you are least likely to use, is to use the Configuration Manager Console. As you can see in Figure 4.43, this is not necessarily going to be the best way to make this data available. Larger organizations will have delegation of roles enabled within Configuration Manager and will not want everyone to be using this console.

FIGURE 4.43
Reports in the Configuration Manager Console

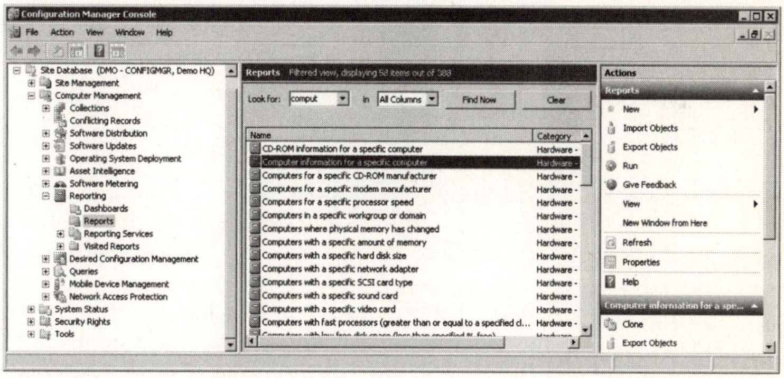

You are more likely to use the Reporting Point than to create reports in the Configuration Manager Console. Figure 4.44 shows the ConfigMgr Report Viewer website. This web interface is much more user friendly and suitable in larger organizations, especially if nonemployees will be performing the assessment.

The navigation pane on the left allows you to browse through the different categories of reports. You are most likely going to be interested in the following:

Hardware – Disk There is a report that you can run to count the discovered different disk configurations. For example, how many machines have 40 GB, 80 GB RAM, or 200 GB of physical storage? You can browse deeper into the report to see which machines have that configuration.

Hardware – Memory Here you can run a report to count the discovered different memory configurations. For example, how many machines have 1 GB RAM, 2 GB RAM, or 4 GB of RAM? You can browse deeper into the report to see which machines have that configuration.

Hardware – General The reports here will allow you to browse through the specification of a particular known computer or find all the managed computers in a workgroup or domain. The latter will be useful for your discovery process.

Operating System The reports here will allow you to identify the servers on the network.

Software – Companies and Products You can use these reports to identify machines that have specific software installed that might complicate the virtualization conversion process. You can just get a listing of discovered software, or you can get a detailed report on each virtualization candidate.

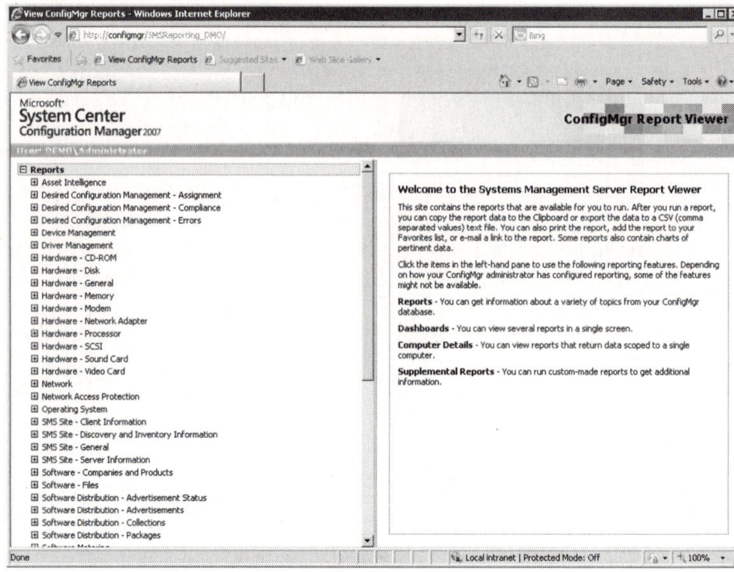

FIGURE 4.44 Configuration Manager Report Viewer website

Hardware manufacturer management packs for ConfigMgr will offer additional reports. For example, you could identify all servers of a specific model.

In this exercise, you will identify all the servers on the network. You then want to get the hardware configuration of those servers.

There is a report in Reports ➤ Operating System called Windows Server Computers. You can see it in Figure 4.45. Most of these reports work in a similar way. They require some sort of input from you to filter the search results. This report wants to know what sort of servers you want to find. You can click the Values button to see the possible filter criteria and select one.

The possible criteria can be generated from the knowledge that was discovered by ConfigMgr on the network, or they can be built in. Figure 4.46 shows the possible criteria in this case. If you want to find all servers on the network, you can click All Windows Server Systems.

That will complete the Collection ID field on the screen shown previously in Figure 4.45. You can then click Display, and the report will be generated from the ConfigMgr database.

You can see the report for the `demo.local` lab network in Figure 4.47. All servers on the network are included. Note that you can click the Export link at the top to save the results of a report into a CSV file. That will allow you to manipulate the data in Excel.

Each row gives you details on the managed servers. This includes information on the operating system and service pack level installed on the machine.

There is a little button with an arrow on the right side. That allows you to delve a little deeper into the known information about each server. You can click that to open a new window. This has been done to create the screenshot depicted in Figure 4.48.

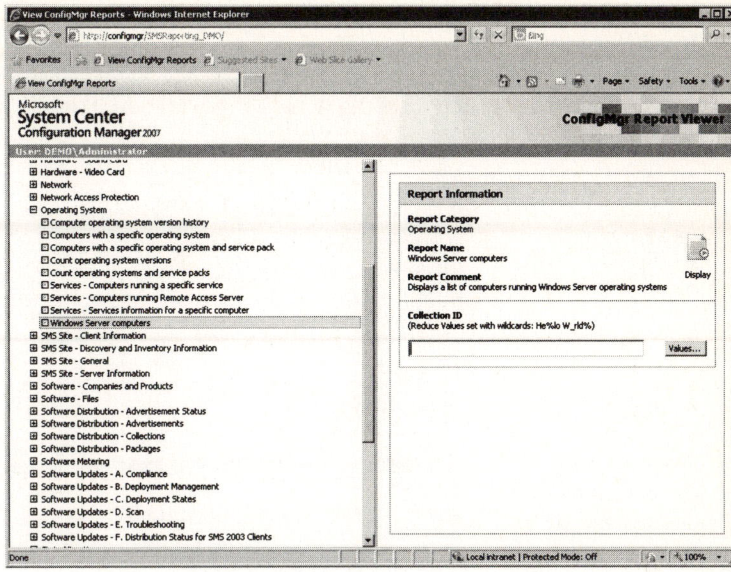

FIGURE 4.45
Generating a Windows Server computer report

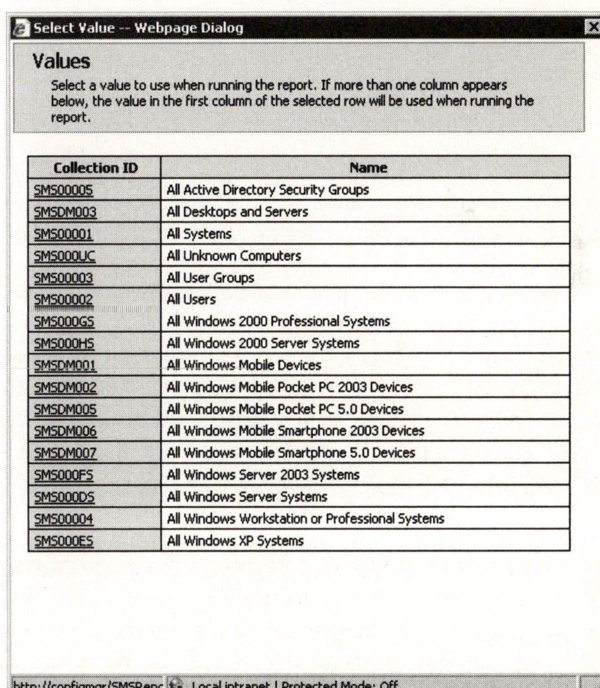

FIGURE 4.46
Possible filter criteria to find servers

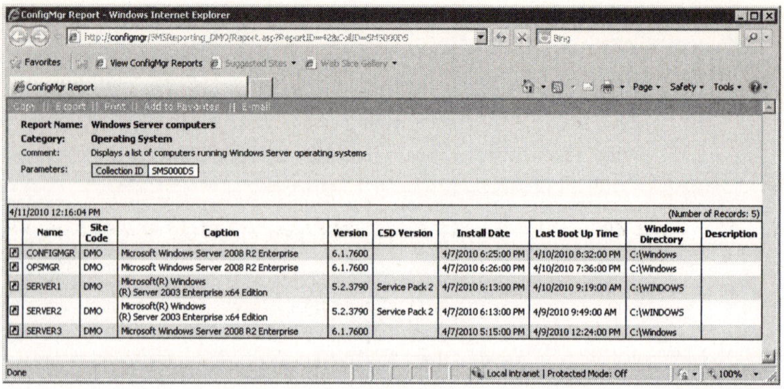

FIGURE 4.47
The All Windows Servers report

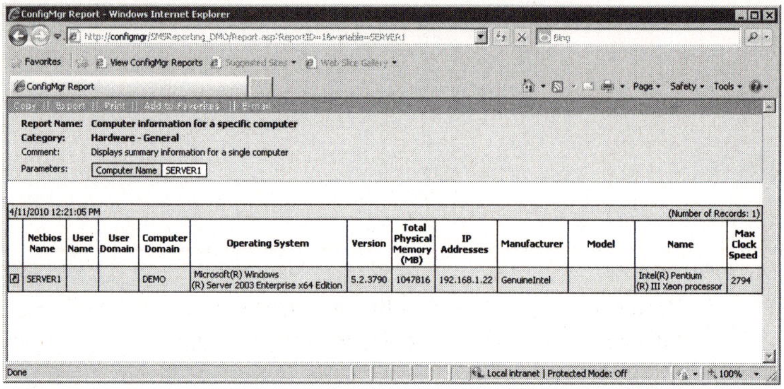

FIGURE 4.48
Computer information for a specific computer

You can see the allocated memory, the CPU model, and the CPU speed of the server. You can drill down deeper again to browse the complete hardware configuration of the server by clicking the little arrow button again.

This will open the Computer Details report, shown in Figure 4.49. This allows you to browse through the complete hardware inventory for that computer. It's a roundabout way to get to this report. You could have easily just run it from the main reporting window, but this approach allows you to discover all servers and then browse the details of each.

You now have enough information to do the following:

- Identify all servers on the network that are managed by Configuration Manager. Note that third-party management packs do allow for non-Windows operating systems to be managed.
- Identify the operating systems, service packs, software installed, and hardware specifications of all those servers.
- Use the gathered information to identify some machines that will be excluded from virtualization conversion or those that will require special attention.
- Size some parts of the Hyper-V architecture. For example, you now know how much disk space is required. You also have an estimate on the memory requirements. It is an estimate because

you really do not know yet either if a server is using the entire allocated RAM or if it really needs more.

- Estimate savings on licensing. Virtualization allows for an alternative way to license your virtual machines using Microsoft products. This is a much cheaper way than the traditional one server = one license approach.

FIGURE 4.49
Hardware inventory of a server

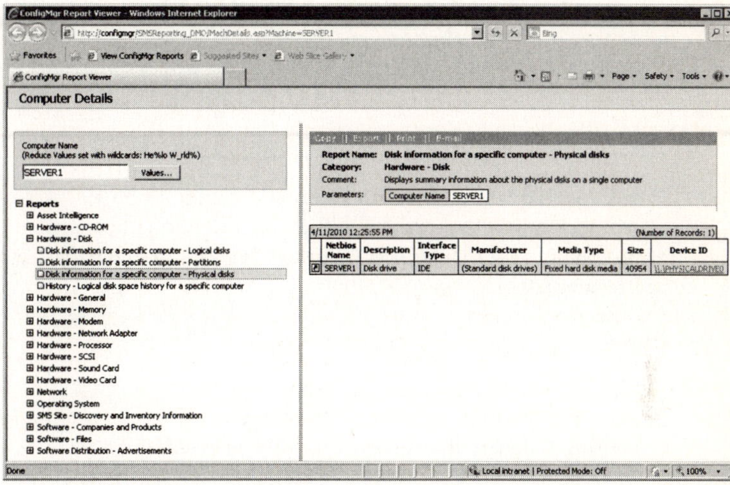

You should be left with a list of machines that you need to gather performance metrics for. That's where we will turn to Operations Manager.

> **CONFIGURATION MANAGER 2007 R3**
>
> At the time of writing this book, the current release of Configuration Manager was 2007 R2. The 2007 R3 release was in a private testing program with few in-depth details being released to the public. The focus of ConfigMgr 2007 R3 is power management. This could be of interest to those who are proposing a virtualization project. It might be possible to use actual power usage data to calculate the pre-virtualization costs, contrast them predicted post-virtualization costs, and then compare the predictions with actual post-virtualization costs.

Reporting on Performance Metrics

System Center Operations Manager is the system you will use to report on performance data. An OpsMgr agent is usually installed on a server that is to be monitored. This agent will gather fault and performance data and report it to the management server. Knowledge about what to monitor and how to process the information is provided in management packs. These are installed on the management server and are automatically deployed to relevant agents using a discovery process. Performance data is gathered and used in alerting. An optional data warehouse can be installed. Data from the management server will be migrated to the data warehouse. Note that over time, the data is consolidated to reduce space. This means that short spikes in resource utilization might not be immediately visible.

You can take advantage of this data warehouse and reporting facility. By default, more than a year of data will be retained in the data warehouse. If OpsMgr is already installed in a site, that gives you a great insight into the life and resource utilization of a server, allowing you to accurately size the Hyper-V architecture.

> **LEARN MORE ABOUT OPERATIONS MANAGER**
>
> You can learn much more about Operations Manager by reading *Mastering Operations Manager 2007*, published by Sybex. Most of what is included will be valid for the 2007 R2 release.

You might encounter a number of versions:

MOM 2005 Microsoft Operations Manager 2005 was the first version of Microsoft's monitoring solution that really grabbed the attention of consultants and engineers. It uses the older architecture of management packs. They might have been simpler and easier to understand, but they were less capable than the 2007 architecture. The focus was on Microsoft systems with third-party support offered by partners. Some third-party management packs are free, and some require a purchased license.

Operations Manager 2007 A new, more complex, architecture was introduced to make the system more intelligent and scalable. The focus was still on Microsoft systems. Third parties continued to provide support for non-Microsoft products.

Operations Manager 2007 R2 This is the current release. It is an evolution of OpsMgr 2007 that introduced Cross Platform Extensions. This provides Microsoft written agents and management packs for specified Linux and Unix operating systems. Third parties continue to provide additional support for non-Microsoft products.

We will be using the current release of Operations Manager 2007 R2 in this example.

There are a few ways that you can access the performance history of a server in OpsMgr. We will cover just two of the methods to access reports.

ACCESS REPORTS USING REPORTING WUNDERBAR

You can click the Reporting wunderbar, as shown in Figure 4.50. This gives you the ability to select a report template and then populate it with all the information that you need.

A handy report for our needs is the Operating System Performance report. It will contain a number of key metrics. You can double-click it to run this report. This will open the report-viewing tool, shown in Figure 4.51. You will need to do a little bit of work with this approach, so be warned!

The first thing you need to decide is what time frame you want data from. The longer the period, the better the data will be; that is the beauty of using OpsMgr for performance metrics gathering and reporting. You will need to watch out for changes in the functionality or demand of servers if you choose a long time window like one year. A server might have had a big demand six months ago, but that demand might be long gone after an application migration. The earlier high demand would affect your analysis if you were not aware of this. You can set the time frame of your choice in the top-left corner of the window.

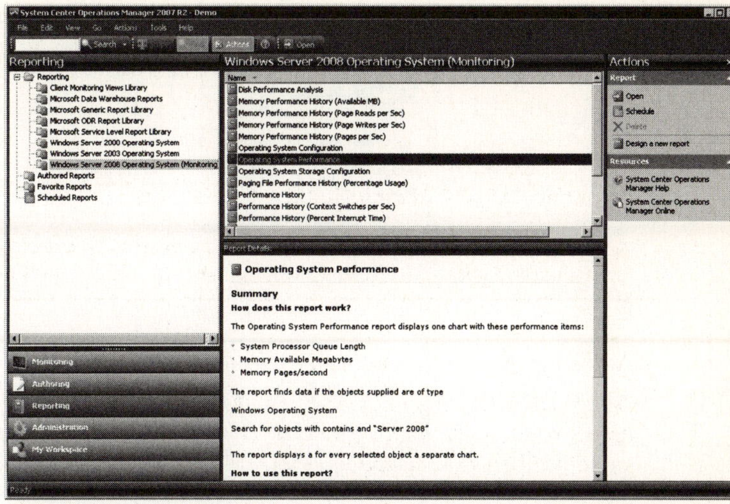

FIGURE 4.50
Reporting wunderbar

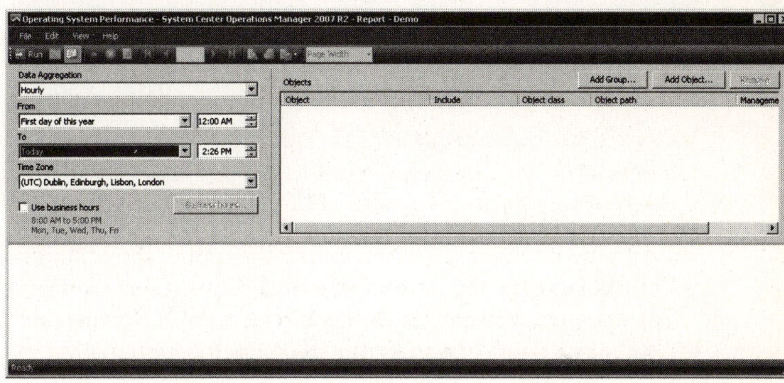

FIGURE 4.51
Configuring the report time window

You can see in the Objects pane at the top right that no objects are selected. You will need to add one. This requires knowing the fully qualified domain name (FQDN) of the server as OpsMgr knows it. You can get this information from your earlier ConfigMgr server identification reports.

Click the Add Object button to start the process. That opens the Add Object window in Figure 4.52. Then click the Options button.

The Options window opens. Click Add to find an object class that will contain the server object you want to report on. You should use a class such as Windows Server Operating System. You can then click the OK button to return to the Add Object screen. Click the Search button, and all objects of that class (Windows servers) will appear. You can see this in Figure 4.53.

You should select only one server here. That will mean you only get a performance report for one server. Selecting more than one will give you an aggregated report, which is not very useful right now. Click the Add button to choose the server you have selected. That gives you the window shown in Figure 4.53.

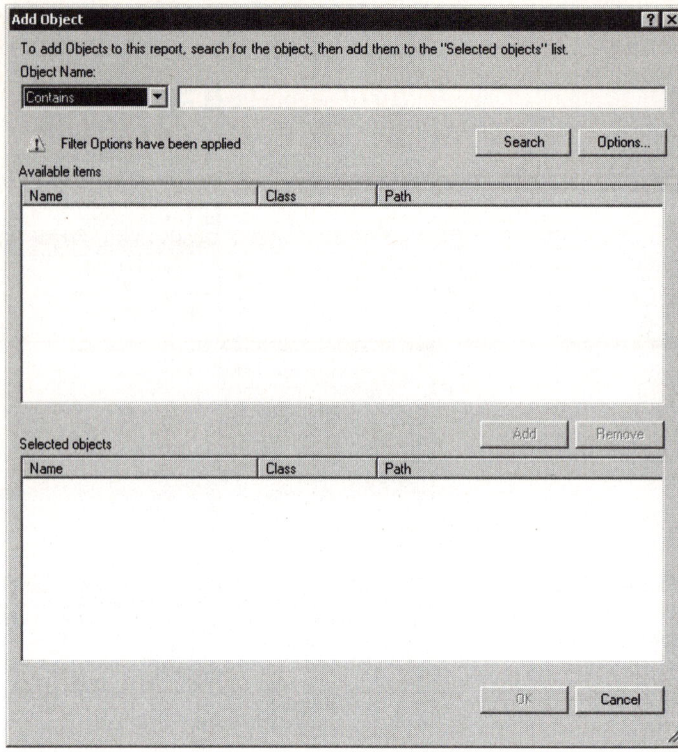

FIGURE 4.52 The unpopulated Add Object window

You are now returned to the reporting window shown in Figure 4.54. You have selected a server object to get a report on and a time frame for the report information. You are now ready to run the report. You can do this by clicking the Run button in the top-left corner.

It can take a few seconds for the database to run the query behind the report. When it does, the report will appear as shown in Figure 4.55. The report contains four metrics:

Process % Processor Total Time This indicates how busy the CPU was.

System Processor Queue Length The length of this queue indicates how many threads were waiting to get access to the processor so they could execute. There should not be more than two times the total number of logical processors (CPU cores) waiting. For example, a server with a single quad-core CPU should not have more than eight queue threads.

Memory Available Megabytes Using this figure, you can tell how much memory a server really needs.

Memory Pages per Second You can tell how busy the paging file was to resolve hard page faults. Figures greater than 1,000 can indicate a memory leak.

The shown report contains just over four months of data. You can see that there are many peaks and valleys in the resource utilization of this server. Imagine if the assessment used only a small time window. It could happen during one of those peaks or valleys and give you a poor analysis of your requirements.

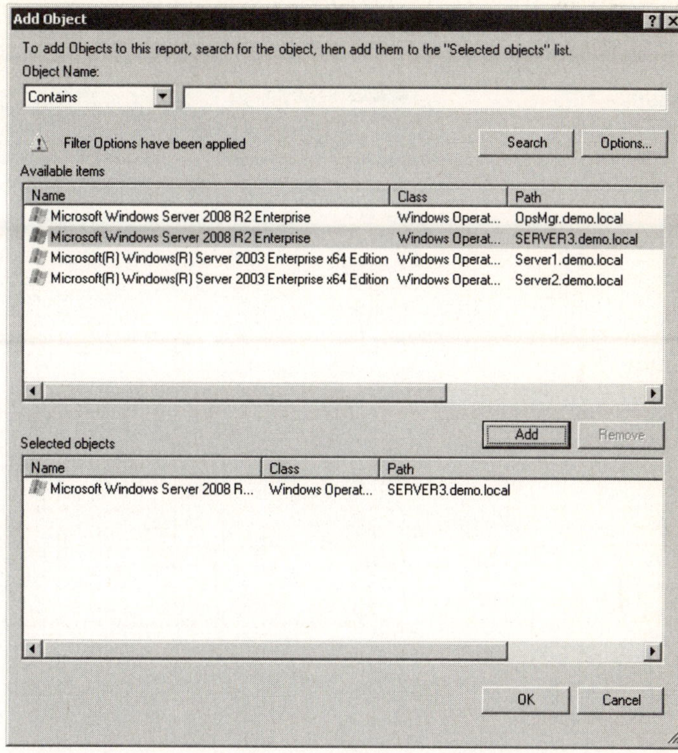

FIGURE 4.53
Populated Add Object window

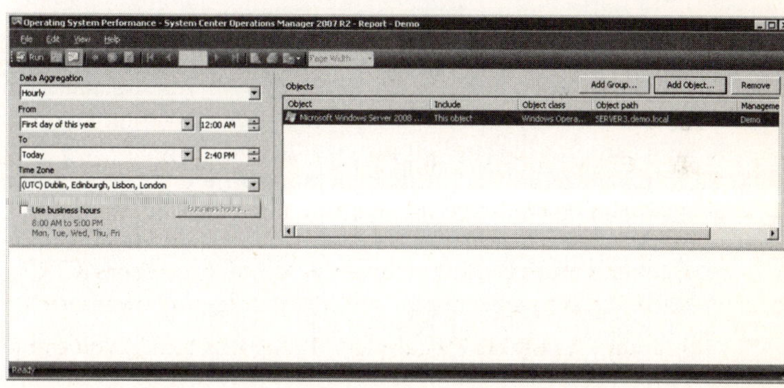

FIGURE 4.54
Ready to run the report

You can click the hyperlink for each of the metrics to get a better and more accurate view of what is going on.

Clicking any of the metrics hyperlinks will cause another report to run. The window refreshes to give you the new report, which you can see an example of in Figure 4.56. This contains much more information on the processor utilization. The graph not only contains the average utilization but also contains the minimum, maximum, and standard deviation (a statistical measure of variability). You can click the + button to expand the detail table. This contains detailed performance metric information for each time interval in the report.

FIGURE 4.55
The Operating System Performance report

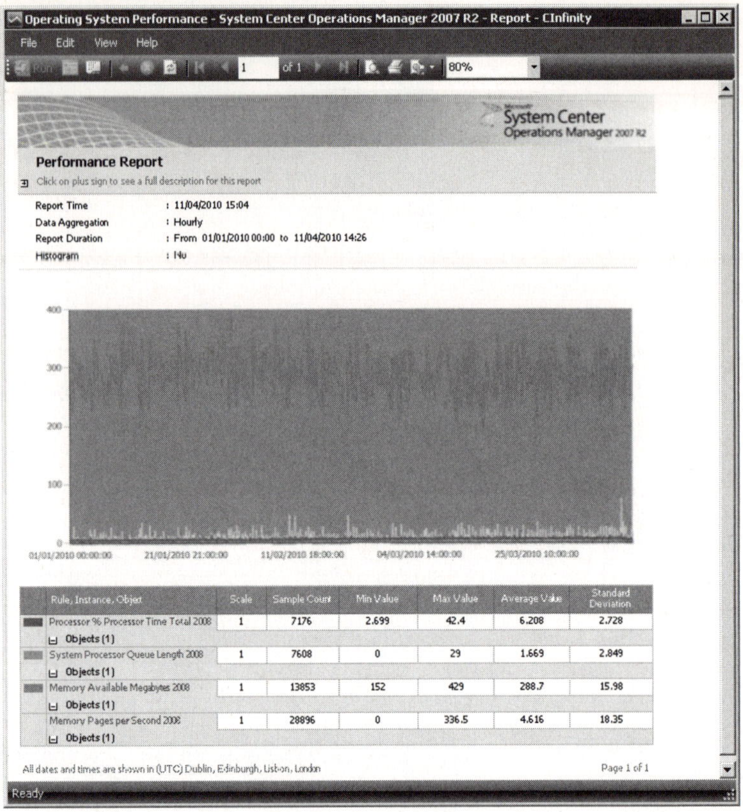

You can click the blue left-arrow button at the top to return to the Operating System Performance report and drill down into a different metric. You can also click the Export button at the top to save the viewed report as any of the following:

- XML file with report data
- Comma-delimited CSV
- TIFF file
- PDF
- Web archive
- Excel spreadsheet

You can continue to use this type of reporting to view the many other metrics that are available such as network card utilization, disk usage, or storage space consumed. OpsMgr 2007 R2 also allows you to do this for Linux virtualization candidates.

FIGURE 4.56
Detailed view of processor performance metrics

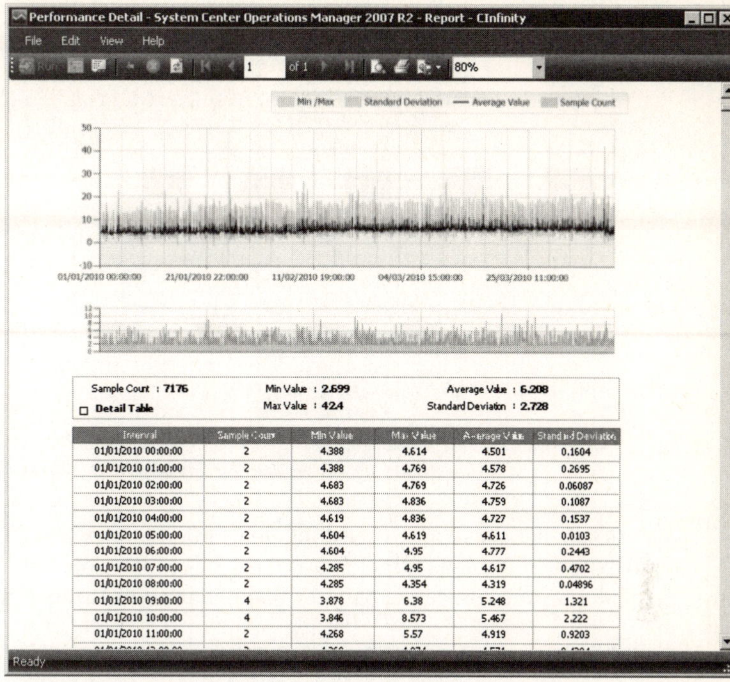

ACCESS REPORTS USING THE MONITORING WUNDERBAR

Another way to access reports is to click the Monitoring wunderbar in the Operations Manager Console and navigate to the server that you are interested in. The Actions pane on the right side is context sensitive. You can scroll down the Actions pane, and a number of reports will be visible, including performance reports, as shown in Figure 4.57. You can select one of those. The now-familiar reporting utility will appear. But this time the object is already loaded. That's because OpsMgr is aware of what server you want to work with. All you need to do is select a time window and run the report.

You can now use the generated reports to identify which servers you want to convert into virtual machines and which you do not. You will also be able to calculate how many host servers you will need using some very accurate performance metrics. You will be using data from over a very large time window if OpsMgr was already being used before the virtualization project started.

We're not quite finished with OpsMgr yet. There is still one more trick up its sleeve thanks to the possible integration with Virtual Machine Manager.

Virtualization Candidate Report

When you install Virtual Machine Manager 2008 R2 and integrate it with Operations Manager 2007 or 2007 R2, you will get a series of new reports. Actually, to be honest, you don't really need to even install VMM. You can access the System Center Catalog and download the management packs for VMM 2008. That will load the reports for VMM.

FIGURE 4.57
Context-sensitive reports

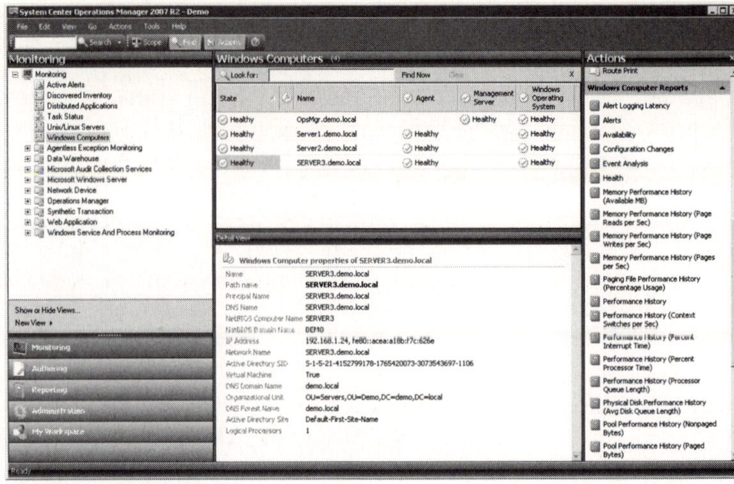

You can find the report by clicking Reporting wunderbar and navigating to Reporting ➤ System Center Virtualization Reports 2008. The report you will be using is called Virtualization Candidates. You can see the window that will open in Figure 4.58.

FIGURE 4.58
The Virtualization Candidates report

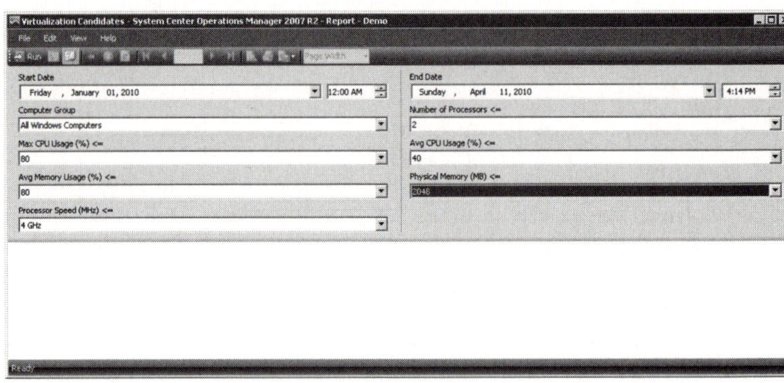

Using this report, you can set some very general criteria for identifying virtualization candidates:

- Number of processors
- Maximum processor speed
- Maximum CPU utilization
- Average CPU usage
- Average memory usage
- Physical memory

Try this report, and you will see that there is a limitation. The Physical Memory (MB) selection box doesn't offer anything greater than 2048 MB. That means physical servers with greater than 2 GB of RAM will not be considered by this report. That's not ideal when you know that Hyper-V can support running many virtual machines with up to 64 GB of RAM each.

This report might be limited in what machines it can offer. But it probably will identify 80 percent of those machines that are obvious virtualization candidates. That's the bulk of the work done with one easy-to-run report. That allows you more time to focus on identifying other candidates and running more detailed reports to confirm their candidacy.

You can use your list of selected virtualization candidates to retrieve the server specifications from the previously generated Configuration Manager reports. You can use this data, combined with the actual resource utilization metrics from OpsMgr, to size your Hyper-V host servers and storage.

Pros and Cons of System Center

The advantages of using System Center for the assessment of virtualization conversion candidates are as follows:

The Data The data is incredibly detailed. You also get instant access to data gathered over a long time if System Center was already installed. Data gathered over a longer period will give you an insight into seasonal spikes in resource utilization.

WAN Friendly Both OpsMgr and ConfigMgr are designed for large organizations and therefore are network-friendly.

Limited Firewall Impact Client devices need little to no configuration. Network devices need very little configuration to allow agents to communicate with the management servers.

Secure There is no need to grant local administrative rights to any servers to anyone. Agents on the computers will gather data and send them back to a central data warehouse. ConfigMgr and OpsMgr administrators can then delegate access to reports to standard Windows domain user accounts.

Supported Operating Systems Windows and Linux physical servers can be assessed. OpsMgr 2007 R2 can gather performance metrics without any additions. ConfigMgr 2007 R2 will require third-party additions to assess the hardware specifications.

Leverage an Investment Making use of existing systems will make management happy. It is also possible to start making instant use of any System Center products that are to be installed as part of the Hyper-V deployment project.

The disadvantages are as follows:

Agents Required If you are introducing System Center during the Hyper-V project, then it might take some time and considerable work to install it. This is especially true in organizations, such as pharmaceuticals, that must have very tight controls on change, procedures, and documentation.

Not as Complete as MAP MAP gives you an end-to-end solution for Windows servers in one free package. It will identify candidates, assess their performance, select the successful candidates, and set the size architecture. You can use the data to perform ROI analysis. System Center can do only some of this.

Lack of Management Reports The reports you get in System Center are aimed at people who understand and appreciate technical data. They are not suitable for presenting to managers and directors. No fancy proposals are generated. You will have to get used to using Microsoft Word and PowerPoint if you take this approach.

Not as Integrated as MAP There is more work required to connect the dots between the different phases of the assessment, compared to how MAP works.

Choosing an Assessment Option

You have two very interesting sets of tools for assessing the physical servers on your network and producing data to start sizing and architecting your Hyper-V architecture.

MAP is free, is quick to get up and running, and is agent-less. It is capable of producing excellent proposals for management and ROI analysis for the accountants. Because of how it collects performance metrics, it is probably best used for relatively short time frames only.

System Center gives incredible technical information. It understands that averages can be misleading. Existing installations can produce information from more than a year of data that reflects the seasonal peaks and valleys in demand for server resources. This allows technical staff to design a very accurate installation.

Which one should you use? It depends — you could decide based on who your audience will be. If you are a consultant selling to a business decision maker, then MAP with the ROI analysis seems to be ideal. If you are an engineer who is tasked with designing and implementing with just high-level oversight from management, then the System Center approach might be the one to use. In the end, you should weigh the pros and cons of each approach and choose the one that is right for each Hyper-V deployment project.

Third-Party Assessment Products

You are not restricted to using products from Microsoft. We have looked at Microsoft products because one was free and the others either are often already installed or are installed during a Hyper-V project. Third-party products are available that will do discovery, inventory, and assessment.

The Bottom Line

Understand the need to assess the existing infrastructure An assessment is a necessary step in any hardware virtualization project where there is an existing physical infrastructure to convert into virtual machines.

Master It You are one of a team of engineers that is designing and deploying a Windows Server 2008 R2 Hyper-V infrastructure in a very large organization. Your objectives from management are to consolidate the infrastructure as much as possible with no negative impact on performance. Overspending on the project will not be tolerated because of economic conditions. One of your colleagues wants to start the installation now without performing an assessment. How will you argue for an assessment?

Use the Microsoft Assessment and Planning Toolkit MAP is free to download and can be used to perform an assessment of a physical and virtual server infrastructure.

Master It You are working as a presales technical consultant. A potential customer has asked your company to perform an assessment. The local IT staff will make all the required preparations on your behalf to facilitate the task. They only run Microsoft Windows on their servers. The goal of the task is to prepare a proposal for the directors of the customer company. They are nontechnical and will be focusing on the cost effectiveness of the project. You do not have budget to purchase software. What will you do to meet the requirements of the potential customer company?

Use System Center for assessment System Center is capable of collecting vast amounts of very detailed information from a large and complex network. You can use the System Center reporting features to use this information for an assessment.

Master It You have just joined a large organization as a senior engineer. You have been placed in charge of designing and implementing a Windows Server 2008 R2 Hyper-V infrastructure. The organization is large and complex. It has many servers in branch offices, and there are some Linux servers. Many systems experience demand only once a month or once a quarter. The organization has made a continued investment in Microsoft systems management software and third-party extensions over the years. How will you perform an assessment of the infrastructure to achieve an accurately sized consolidation?

Chapter 5

Planning the Hardware Deployment

During the assessment, as you saw in Chapter 4, you gathered information about candidate machines for virtualization. That data was used to identify the servers that will be converted into virtual machines and will run on your new infrastructure. The sizing of the new infrastructure will be based on the data you collected during the assessment.

There is a dizzying array of hardware options available to the buyer of a new hardware virtualization infrastructure. It can be an exciting and fun time for the engineer who is a bit of a gadget geek. It can, at the same time, be a worrying time for the owner of the IT budget and the investors of the business. You will need to balance needs and desires with the budget while understanding how hardware decisions impact your design. We will cover the various options and discuss some technologies that you might be unfamiliar with.

We will cover the process of converting that data into a server and storage specification. To do this, you will have to consider whether you want to use highly available virtual machines on a Hyper-V cluster, understand the maximum specifications of Hyper-V, and consider other elements that will be covered in more detail later in this book.

Finally, we will discuss the issue of licensing for host operating systems, guest operating systems, and Microsoft System Center. We were hesitant about including this material because it does age quite quickly. However, the fundamentals stay the same, and you can quickly get an update from an official licensing specialist. Many of the early cost savings come from the licensing story. That's a story worth telling in the Microsoft world!

In this chapter, you will learn to

- Understand the hardware requirements for Hyper-V
- Convert assessment results into a hardware specification
- Be able to discuss Hyper-V licensing

Understanding Hyper-V Hardware Requirements

The basic requirements for Hyper-V are actually quite simple. If you are doing anything other than the most basic of deployments, then you really need to think beyond those basic few requirements. You have to understand the following:

- The business requirements of the project
- The hardware requirements of Hyper-V

- How Hyper-V scales out on a server or on a cluster
- Your hardware purchasing options and how they apply to your organization
- How to get the very best deal you can from your hardware and software vendors

We will now delve deeper into each of these subjects.

The Business Requirements

A recurring theme in this book is the business requirements. You need a list of requirements that are mapped into clearly communicated and understood objectives. It is now that they really count. We will show a few examples that you might encounter and analyze how they steer your decision making process.

"We have previously purchased VMware ESX. We have looked at the comparative costs of Hyper-V and decided that we want to migrate completely to the Microsoft platform."

That's a pretty simple one and will make your local Microsoft office very happy. If you're a consultant working for a Microsoft partner, then you can bet that there's a nice case study in it.

In this project, the key piece is the migration. It will require using VMM 2008 R2 to migrate virtual machines using a virtual-to-virtual (V2V) process. We will talk about this more in Chapter 7. There is an opportunity here where you might be able to recycle servers and storage as they are reused. You will need to verify that they are capable of running Hyper-V, which we will discuss later in this chapter. It is possible that the servers are a little old. If so, you might want to purchase servers that have more life left in their manufacturers' support life cycle. You might also want to compare their power consumption with that of more modern servers. A server from 2007 will consume much more power than one from 2010, even to handle the same workloads.

"We have invested significantly in VMware. It has features that we need that are not present in Windows Server 2008 R2 Hyper-V. However, we accept that Windows Server 2008 R2 Hyper-V can play a part in our virtualization strategy."

It is claimed that VMware has a presence in every Fortune Global 100 company in the world and 95 percent of the Fortune Global 500. The who's who list of VMware's customers is impressive. VMware did have a huge head start, paving the way for hardware virtualization acceptance for production server computing. Many CIOs and CFOs will understandably balk at the idea of throwing away an existing system to introduce Hyper-V. Some will see features in VMware's products that they use and that Hyper-V might not have yet. However, they will also see the cost savings that Hyper-V can bring compared to a VMware solution.

This can be an opportunity to bring in Hyper-V for specific virtualization roles. Not all virtual machines may require the few features of VMware that are not present in Hyper-V. This hybrid solution could allow an organization to make the best of both virtualization platforms, while maintaining their existing investment and minimizing future spending.

"Our corporate goal is to keep our carbon footprint to the absolute minimum."

This is a quote that has become increasingly common in the past few years. It can easily be compared to this:

"We must minimize our spending on electricity."

There are a few things you can take from this:

- You will need to use the latest generation of server, storage, and networking hardware.
- Be very careful in choosing hardware models. Sometimes the slightly more expensive model actually consumes less power. That can lead to a cost saving over time.

- Check the components for options. Sometimes, for example, you will have a choice between standard memory and low-power memory.
- Server chassis types might also be affected. You might find yourself moving toward blade servers instead of traditional rack servers.
- Consider the heat being generated by the equipment and the subsequent impact on your cooling system. Newer data centers are taking alternative approaches to the big concrete freezer that you are used to. Many new data centers run at higher temperatures because they require less power for air conditioning. This requires checking with the manufacturer. Others use a container-based approach where the use of natural cool air in colder climates reduces the need for air conditioning.

WHY USE BLADE SERVERS?

A traditional server is completely self-sufficient, containing all of its power supplies, network, and storage connections. It is racked and connected directly to the power and network systems. A rack will typically allow for 42 × 1U servers. Blade servers are smaller. They slide into a chassis, which is racked. The chassis will have fault-tolerant modules for power, networking, and storage connections. This allows for more servers to be put into a rack. One manufacturer allows for 64 blades (of the same specification as the 1U server they replace) in a 42U rack. They also allow for lower power consumption than traditional rack servers.

"We need fault tolerance and the ability to deal with peaks in demand for various server applications."

This is one of the more common requirements of a hardware virtualization project when the decision makers realize the potential of the technology. They are looking for highly available virtual machines. In other words, you will need to build a Hyper-V cluster.

Highly available virtual machines are capable of moving from one host to another. On Windows Server 2008 R2, this is achieved with the assistance of Live Migration. That means there is an undetectable amount of downtime. We're told that it is around two milliseconds. No network application or human will detect this downtime during Live Migration in a correctly built system. No network packets will be dropped, no Remote Desktop sessions will momentarily freeze, and no processes will crash.

This requirement will drive you toward Windows Server Failover Clustering. For many, this will be the first time to use this technology. It can be a daunting prospect. However, Windows Server 2008 and later are nothing like their ancestors. The feature is pretty easy to implement, as you will learn in Chapter 6.

Your hardware requirements will be more complex now. You need to figure out how many Hyper-V hosts you have. A Windows Server 2008 R2 cluster can have up to 16 hosts. Best practice is that there should be at least 1 redundant host in a cluster with up to 8 hosts. This N+1 cluster can handle the failure of 1 node without losing any virtual machines. A cluster with between 8 and 16 hosts should have 2 redundant hosts. This N+2 cluster can handle the loss of 2 hosts without losing any virtual machines.

The other requirement of a failover cluster is shared storage. You cannot use local disks to store the virtual machines. You must use either an iSCSI, Fibre Channel, or SAS-connected storage area network (SAN) to store your virtual machines. This allows them to be shared between

Hyper-V hosts and therefore to move freely across the hosts. As you can see, the cost of the hardware investment did just increase, but it is still cheaper than traditional servers. Don't worry if you have a smaller deployment; there are more economic and rather interesting hardware options for you.

You will need to watch out for the server applications that will be running in highly available virtual machines. During your assessment, you should have verified their compatibility with Hyper-V. The Windows Server 2008 R2 logo program allows for a special Hyper-V designation:

```
http://msdn.microsoft.com/library/dd744769(VS.85).aspx
```

This means that an application *must* be tested and supported with Hyper-V R2. If a supplier cannot meet this requirement, an explanation must be given for not being able to meet to this rule. You may find a few exceptions. For example, at the time of writing this book, servers that are part of an Exchange 2010 database availability group (DAG) are not supported on any hardware virtualization availability solutions such as Live Migration.

"We want to restrict our spending to the absolute minimum while reducing power and space consumption."

Highly available virtual machines just exited stage left. This sounds like the decision makers will not pay for a SAN. They will probably seek to reuse as much hardware as possible. Instead of having a cluster, you will have individual Hyper-V hosts, each packed with as much memory, CPU, and storage as is required or they are capable of. Each virtual machine will run on just one host. There will be no Live Migration. You will be able to move virtual machines from one host to another with minimum downtime if you use Virtual Machine Manager 2008 R2 thanks to a feature called Quick Storage Migration. This approach may be cheap, but it suffers from having many eggs in one basket. If one virtual machine starts to hog the CPU or storage channel, then it will negatively affect other virtual machines. There is no load balancing. The more daunting prospect of a host server failing and possibly bringing down 10 or (potentially many) more virtual machines with it until a repair can be completed is a scary one.

This approach will also affect the types of processor and storage you might purchase. The new 12-core CPU that you had been dreaming of will remain a thing of your dreams. You might even find that you end up purchasing 7,200 RPM SATA disks instead of 15,000 SAS RPM disks. This will definitely affect how well your virtual machines' storage will perform and will negatively impact the potential density ratio of virtual machines per host.

"Performance is critical. Every virtual machine must have the maximum performance possible."

Ah, the gadget geeks just woke up when they heard this one in an otherwise dull meeting with management. This is a free license to buy the best of everything and lots of it (within reason, of course). It's time to look at maybe having one physical core per virtual CPU in a host. You can now afford those 12 core CPUs, that Fibre Channel SAN, the best storage controllers, and the fastest disks.

You can see that in each of these very simplistic scenarios you have radically changed the hardware design. Unfortunately, the real world tends to be shades of gray instead of being simply black and white. Or maybe that should read as *fortunately*, because it certainly will make the project more interesting with plenty of opportunities to prove yourself during its duration.

"Virtualization will be an enabler for a business continuity or disaster recovery solution."

Your project suddenly brought the WAN engineers and resellers into the scope of the project. Your hardware salesperson is also willing to take you out to a nicer restaurant for lunch.

Now you need to double your hardware requirements. You will have multiple Hyper-V hosts in the production site and identical machines in the secondary site. Your storage will be identical in both sites and will have some form of replication. That might be controller-based synchronous LUN replication of a SAN. It could be storage striping across the WAN. It could even be third-party software performing Hyper-V host internal storage replication.

The Hardware Requirements of Hyper-V

There really are only a few set-in-stone requirements for Hyper-V. Everything else changes with the scenario in question. We'll start off with the basics:

- You must have a 64-bit processor(s) with support for hardware-assisted virtualization.
- Hardware-assisted virtualization must be turned on in the BIOS.
- Data Execution Prevention (DEP), which has various vendor-specific names, must be enabled in the BIOS.

After that, you get into the "if-then" world. For example, if you are deploying a Hyper-V cluster with iSCSI storage, then you might have the following (at least 1 Gb) network cards:

Parent Partition The host operating system, referred to as the *parent partition*, will have one NIC. This will be used for systems management of the host machine.

Virtual Machines This is the NIC that a Hyper-V virtual switch will be bound to. All traffic between virtual machines on the Hyper-V host and the physical network will route via this NIC.

Live Migration This NIC will be connecting to the first private network that contains only the Hyper-V hosts. It will be specified as the preferred network for Live Migration traffic.

Cluster Shared Volume (CSV) A CSV is a special kind of storage volume on the SAN that allows many virtual machines that are stored on it to run on many Hyper-V hosts at once. This NIC will be connecting to the second private network that contains only the Hyper-V hosts. CSV has a mode called Redirected I/O where storage traffic from all Hyper-V nodes routes through the owner of the CSV. This will be the preferred network for that traffic.

iSCSI This is the NIC that will be used to connect the Hyper-V host to an iSCSI SAN. It is recommended that a pair of NICs is used with MPIO enabled for fault tolerance.

A number of variations can be applied to this scenario. Windows Server 2008 R2 has native Multipath I/O (MPIO) support. This allows you to have two NICs for each storage connection. They will automatically failover in the event of a fault. Each connection will usually go to a different switch and then on to a different controller in the SAN. This gives complete storage path fault tolerance. This would be the preferred option.

Some organizations have limited budget for 10 GB Ethernet. It is still a premium networking solution. If they have the option for a limited deployment, then they might install 10 GB NICs for the Live Migration private network. This will speed up the end-to-end process of Live Migration of virtual machines between hosts in the cluster.

Another variation is the introduction of teamed NICs. This is currently not supported by Microsoft in any way. However, there are solutions by hardware manufacturers, such as Intel and Broadcom, and OEMs, such as HP and Dell, which have been designed with Hyper-V in mind. This would allow for NIC and/or network appliance failures without impacting Hyper-V or virtual machine network connectivity. Be aware that NIC teaming does add some other complexities into the mix.

Another interesting subject is the question of storage. The variations start here with the question, are the hosts clustered or not?

If the hosts are not clustered, then you can use simple servers that are capable of storing a lot of disk and RAM. The reality has proven to be that CPU is rarely the constraint in server virtualization. The RAM in the Hyper-V host is usually the first to be fully utilized, followed by the available disk and network slots in the server. This server could be connected to extremely scalable "just a bunch of disks" (JBOD) or to a SAN to alleviate the storage limitation.

Once you decide on that, you have the question of how to arrange the disk. Will one LUN be sufficient for all virtual machines? It might, but maybe you need to have dedicated LUNs per virtual machine or for selected virtual machines to improve I/O rates. Maybe you even need to have one storage channel per virtual machine. This sort of question will be answered by the results you got from your assessment (focusing on IOPS) and compared with the capabilities of your potential hardware.

If you return to the cluster, then you need to decide on SAS vs. iSCSI vs. Fibre Channel. There are questions of speed and features. Oddly enough, some of the mid-tier storage solutions have some features that are as-yet missing (but promised) from the higher-end solutions, such as the ability to support a CSV in a multisite Hyper-V cluster.

As many are figuring out, the hardware best practices for Hyper-V are few in number. Much of the work is figuring out the capabilities of the available hardware and using that. This is an ever-changing subject. An administrator or engineer working on an internal deployment might face learning about this just once. Consultants will find themselves in briefings on a very frequent basis to ensure that their clients get the very best service.

Your goals should be to use the assessment data to size correctly and use your project objectives to steer how you utilize the budget. You will then use hardware that suits the requirements of those objectives.

How Hyper-V Scales Out

You cannot sit down and just draw up a hardware architecture for a Windows Server 2008 R2 Hyper-V deployment without first understanding what the supported scalability limits are. Some of them will sound like theoretical fantasy. And some of them are critically important. It also should be noted that some are changing, even as this book is being written, almost a year after Windows Server 2008 R2 was released to volume licensing customers. Table 5.1 shows the currently supported maximum configurations for a Windows Server 2008 R2 host.

TABLE 5.1: Windows Server 2008 R2 Hyper-V host maximums

ITEM	MAXIMUM SIZE OR QUANTITY
RAM per host	1 TB. Note that Windows Server 2008 R2 Standard edition allows up to 32 GB RAM.
Hosts per cluster	16.

TABLE 5.1: Windows Server 2008 R2 Hyper-V host maximums *(CONTINUED)*

ITEM	MAXIMUM SIZE OR QUANTITY
Physical processors (sockets) per host	8. Note that Windows Server 2008 R2 Standard edition supports only up to four physical processors (sockets).
Physical CPU cores or logical processors per host	64.
Virtual machines per virtual network	Unlimited.

You also need to understand the maximum configurations for virtual machines that will run on a Windows Server 2008 R2 host, a shown in Table 5.2.

TABLE 5.2: Windows Server 2008 R2 Hyper-V host maximums

ITEM	MAXIMUM SIZE OR QUANTITY
Virtual machines per host	384 running with 512 virtual processors on a nonclustered host.
RAM per virtual machine	64 GB. Note that you are still constrained by the virtual machine operating system limitations.
Storage controllers per virtual machine	2 IDE. 4 SCSI.
Disks per virtual machine	4 IDE disks. 256 SCSI disks. The virtual machine must boot from the IDE controller.
VHD size	2040 GB per VHD. Use passthrough disks for greater scalability.
Virtual network cards	4 Emulated. 8 Synthetic.

The maximum number of virtual machines for a Hyper-V cluster is a little complicated. It used to be rather simple: up to 64 virtual machines per clustered host and allowing for at least one redundant host in the cluster.

Microsoft changed this in June 2010. Now, a cluster can support up to 1,000 virtual machines. The cluster must have at least one redundant host. A host can support a maximum of 384 virtual machines.

If you have a three-node cluster, it means that you have two nodes, each with a maximum of 384 virtual machines and one redundant node. That three-node cluster can have up to 768 virtual machines. This is less than the cluster maximum of 1,000, so that is OK. A five-node cluster is a little different. There will be four active nodes and one redundant node (although you may spread the load across all hosts). Four hosts with a maximum of 384 virtual machines give a potential of 1,536. That is beyond the supported cluster maximum of 1,000. So, this means you must take a different approach. Instead, you will divide 1,000 by 4 to calculate the average maximum number of virtual machines per node, giving you 250. A single node in this cluster will still have the ability to support 384 virtual machines. These are pretty fantastic numbers; you would need some incredible hardware to be able to reach this sort of virtual machine density without sacrificing performance.

The last piece you need to know is the list of supported operating systems that can run as child partitions, guests, or virtual machines. These are shown in Table 5.3. Note that an unsupported operating system, for example CentOS Linux, might work perfectly well on Hyper-V, but Microsoft cannot provide technical support for it if something goes wrong.

TABLE 5.3: Windows Server 2008 R2 Hyper-V supported guest operating systems

OPERATING SYSTEM	VIRTUAL PROCESSORS
Windows Server 2008 R2	1, 2, or 4
Windows Server 2008 x86 and x64	1, 2, or 4
Windows Server 2003 R2 x86 and x64	1 or 2
Windows Server 2003 x86 and x64	1 or 2
Windows Server 2000	1
SUSE Linux Enterprise Server 10 SP3 x86 and x64	Up to 4
SUSE Linux Enterprise Server 11 x86 and x64	Up to 4
Red Hat Enterprise Linux 5.2 x86 and x64	Up to 4
Red Hat Enterprise Linux 5.3 x86 and x64	Up to 4
Red Hat Enterprise Linux 5.4 x86 and x64	Up to 4

Note that SUSE Linux Enterprise Server 10 SP2 x86 and x64 was originally supported by Microsoft. Novell terminated support for it on April 12, 2010, and recommended that all machines should be upgraded to SP3.

The figures presented are for the Linux Integration Service V2.1. All prior editions of the Linux Integration Services allowed only one virtual CPU per Linux OS virtual machine.

Hardware Options

The variety of hardware that is available for a project such as this is amazing. It is difficult to filter through just the options available from a single manufacturer, let alone deal with the marketing and sales efforts of each to outdo the other. Always go back to what the core of this project is about, and that will help you steer through the variety of solutions you can choose from.

Hardware Decision-Making Suggestions

We can't just recommend particular manufacturers and device models. We can give you a few tips on what to look for when picking your hardware:

Windows Server 2008 R2 compatibility Look for the logo and check the Microsoft Hardware Compatibility List (HCL) at `www.microsoft.com/whdc/hcl/default.mspx`.

The Sales Contract Make compatibility and suitability for Hyper-V, Failover Clustering, Cluster Shared Volumes, Live Migration, and VDS/VSS hardware providers (for backup of the running virtual machines via the storage) a condition of sale.

System Center One of the big reasons to choose Hyper-V as a hardware virtualization platform is the manageability you get with Microsoft System Center. Make sure that the hardware manufacturer has real (and not just headline) support for products such as Operations Manager for the complete hardware set. This will be critical for health and performance monitoring. It will also be beneficial if the hardware manufacturer provides a Performance and Resource Optimization (PRO) management pack. This will allow further integration between OpsMgr and VMM.

Think Beyond Existing Infrastructure The adoption of virtualization radically changes how server and storage hardware is used in the organization. Don't fall into the trap of automatically just buying from the same old vendor and manufacturer as always. Some vendors will have little implementation experience and can offer poor advice. Some manufacturers will have better-tuned solutions for a Hyper-V architecture.

Ask for Advice Do not be afraid of seeking advice from those who have been there before you. Ask to meet technical people from the hardware vendor. Consult with representatives of the manufacturers and attend trade shows. And make use of the IT community. There are plenty of experts out there who are willing to help; they can answer face-to-face questions at events, offer support through online forums, or maybe even pay a visit.

Hardware options are constantly changing. Whether it be a new processor, a faster network card, or a an alternative form of SAN storage, there is exponential growth in opportunities to add new efficiencies, avail yourself of new opportunities, and resolve business issues that you were previously struggling with.

Sample Hardware Solutions

Sometimes an example that feels familiar will help you understand a concept. In this section, you will look at a number of scenarios and the possible hardware solutions for them.

Scenario 1: A small to medium-sized business wants one Hyper-V host for hardware consolidation reasons. The budget is limited.

This is a budget situation where clustering is not a concern. A single physical server will be used to allow multiple virtual machines to be hosted by it. It might have one or two processors, depending on the need for processing capacity. The probable bottlenecks on growth are RAM and disk.

A potential pitfall is to purchase many small memory kits and fully populate the slots, not allowing new memory to be added without throwing away old. Try to purchase larger memory kits that are within budget but will allow for greater capacity.

As painful as it would be to replace RAM, adding storage capacity to a server with fully utilized disk slots is even harder. A 1U server will have a limited number of slots. You should aim to use two of those for the host operating system installation. This will be a RAID-1 LUN.

Boot from Flash

Hyper-V Server 2008 R2 has the ability to boot from flash. Microsoft is making this available to OEM partners as part of the OEM Preinstallation Kit (OPK). You can learn more about the OPK here:

```
http://oem.microsoft.com/script/contentPage.aspx?pageid=552859
```

It is not supported if you create this solution for yourself. However, Ben Armstrong, a virtualization product manager in Microsoft, did discuss how you could emulate this for your own testing and demonstration (not production) purposes here:

```
http://blogs.msdn.com/virtual_pc_guy/archive/2009/11/18/booting-hyper-v-r2-off-
a-usb-stick.aspx
```

The remaining disk slots would be used for virtual machine storage. That might leave you with as little as 500 GB or 1 TB of storage. That might be fine early on but may cause problems when you need to grow your file or Exchange Server in the future. With no free disk slots, you are left with the choice of purchasing an expensive direct attached storage (DAS) disk tray or disrupting the business by migrating to a new, larger physical server. Maybe a 2U server with larger disk capacity would be a better option.

Scenario 2: A larger organization requires a highly available Hyper-V design that will minimize power and space consumption.

Blade servers appear to be the solution to this installation. Blade servers are smaller machines that slide into an enclosure. That enclosure is what is mounted in a rack. The enclosure is a manageable device, allowing remote management such as KVM over IP. The blade servers do not usually connect directly to the power supplies, the storage, or the network. Instead, switches and power supplies are inserted into the enclosure.

A blade server will typically have only a small number of disk slots, for example two. These can be used to store the Hyper-V operating system. The virtual machines will need to be stored on some form of external storage. This can be DAS or SAN.

Returning to the enclosure, you will remember that the blade servers have no direct connections to the SAN or network. SAN connections require a worldwide name (WWN), and a network connection requires a MAC or Ethernet address. These uniquely identify the server. The switches in the enclosure can mask these physical identities, revealing only the ones that are stored in a profile in the enclosure appliances. That allows the blade servers to become easily replaceable. If one blade server fails, you simply replace it with another. The new one will assume the identities of the old one.

The scenario calls for highly available virtual machines. A SAN, not DAS, will be the required storage solution. Shared storage is a requirement for Windows Failover Cluster. One can choose between iSCSI, Fibre Channel, and SAS connections. There is a premium to using a Fibre Channel SAN. The questions are, which provides the required performance, and which is affordable within your budget?

The concept of a replaceable blade server combined with a SAN offers a new option. You can run the servers with no disks at all. Instead, a LUN will be provided from the SAN for storing the operating system. This LUN will be masked, so only the enclosure profile for the blade server can see its own LUN.

Blade servers have a very expensive entry point. The enclosure and the contained appliances are an expensive investment. You should consider this particular option only if you believe that you will make use of most of an enclosure or even fill it, requiring more enclosures (which can be stacked for easier management).

Scenario 3: A medium organization requires a highly available Hyper-V solution using traditional rack servers. They require a disaster recovery architecture with a secondary site.

This organization has analyzed blade servers and decided that their server requirements are too small to justify the expense of an expensive blade enclosure. Traditional rack servers will be purchased instead.

The servers can boot from internal disks or from the SAN disk. In this scenario, there is no virtualization for the SAN WWN, so server replacement is a difficult task. It will be cheaper to boot the operating system from an internal disk.

All virtual machines in the Hyper-V cluster will be stored on either an iSCSI or Fibre Channel SAN.

The requirement of a disaster recovery or business continuity secondary site means that an identical deployment of host servers and storage is required. Both the primary and secondary site Hyper-V systems must be identical. There are three ways this can be approached:

Controller-Based Replication This is an expensive way to replicate data changes to the storage from a primary SAN to a secondary SAN. It is usually available only on very high-end systems, sometimes as an additional license. It has a very expensive WAN requirement. Dark fibre is required to connect the primary and secondary sites in order to keep up with the replicated SAN operations. At this time, not all vendors can offer support for CSV with this form of replication and require a one LUN per VM approach to SAN storage.

Storage Striping between Sites This is a system that is present, typically in iSCSI solutions. Oddly, this is a more effective form of replication for Hyper-V because it does support CSV. It works by presenting all of the storage nodes (individual machines that can be in one or both sites) as a single block to the servers. Hyper-V cluster nodes in the secondary site simply see it as the same SAN as the nodes in the primary site, making failover clustering deployment nice and easy. Be aware that vendors of these solutions require at least 2 × 1 Gb connections between the sites.

Host-Based Replication Third-party solutions such as those from DoubleTake and Steeleye allow you to replicate files from one host to another. This negates the need for a SAN in the first place, as long as the virtual machines can fit onto server internal storage. There is a cost to this software. It also adds complexity. It is best used in smaller deployments. Medium and larger deployments might want to consider the previous methods.

Scenario 4: A medium-sized organization wants to deploy a Hyper-V solution that is flexible, powerful, and cost effective. It must be power and space efficient.

This probably describes the scenario that most businesses will fit into. Not every business has 50,000+ users and thousands of servers. Most of them are actually small to medium-sized organizations with a relatively small number of servers. There is an ideal solution for them in the form of a compact blade enclosure.

This is a self-contained unit that is intended to be small, portable, run from normal office power supplies, and a cost-effective way for small to medium businesses to take advantage of advanced server computing.

With one of these solutions, a single enclosure can contain a small number of Hyper-V hosts, the systems management solution running on physical servers, an iSCSI SAN, and a tape library backup unit.

This allows a small to medium-sized business to use less power. Less space is required; a very small computer room is all that is needed for an enclosure that is approximately only 5–7U tall. It is very tidy and self-contained, with just connections for power and network connectivity to the switches in the rear. The entire server presence for the organization can reside in this small unit, instead of consuming half of a 42U rack.

Getting a Good Deal on Hardware

The process of getting a good deal and depressing a salesperson is a lot of fun if you know what you are doing. If you are the sort of person who enjoys the process of buying a secondhand car, then you will enjoy this. If you are not, then you should find someone who can do this and substitute for you. You can save a significant sum if you have the right strategy. Just be careful and ensure you comply completely with any purchasing procedures in your organization or country.

Regulated Purchasing

If you operate in an environment with regulated purchasing, then you should completely ignore this section and comply exactly with the procedures you are prescribed to use.

Server virtualization has made a significant dent in the numbers that hardware salespeople had become used to. It should be possible to play a number of vendors against each other to get the best deal. Let them know that they are competing and who they are competing with. Don't be shy about sharing figures, as long as there are no clauses of confidentiality.

Hardware manufacturers have many ways of pricing their products. The regular retail price is usually what is advertised on the Internet. You should rarely be paying this. Ensure that a bid price is requested by the reseller. If you buy directly, then get an account manager to find you a better deal. If you are free to do so (regulations or procedures), then let the various manufacturers know that they have competition. It is interesting to see what happens when HP, IBM, Dell, or Fujitsu all know they are competing for the same deal.

An interesting scenario is when you decide on a manufacturer and ask for quotes from three vendors. Each will get the same purchase price from the manufacturer for your deal. Each vendor will then assign their own profit margin. You can only do so much to get the price down. Bringing in another vendor from another manufacturer will create the reaction you might have hoped for.

You can use other strategies. If your organization has a reputable brand name in your market or industry, then the reseller or manufacturer might be interested in doing a case study or press release. This might bring down the cost a small bit. The same can happen if you know that you will have future hardware requirements and can make a commitment to that.

As any consultant or field engineer will tell you, some salespeople greatly dislike visiting a customer with a techie from their company tagging along. There is something about us techies — we do not like to make promises that we cannot live up to. If we are the ones who will be installing something, then we will not lead the customer off on some fantasy that can never be achieved. Always refuse to meet a salesperson without a qualified technical person being with them. Double-check every claim made by the salesperson with the techie. If a salesperson says, "Our solution can do XYZ," then ask the techie how this is done. Make sure the salesperson knows you are going to do this beforehand. You can then judge by the techie's reaction whether you can trust the salesperson. It is a strategy that has worked many times and avoided some of the traps that some salespeople are willing to set up to make a deal.

The last piece of advice is that you should choose your reseller and implementer carefully, especially if you are deploying a cluster. Even though cluster installation has been significantly improved, it has an amazingly complex set of hardware with interdependencies down to the smallest level; for example, the firmware in different components must be at compatible and identical release levels. Don't just choose an implementer or reseller because you've known them for some time. Choose one that has experience in dealing with enterprise hardware, who can steer you through the many options to find you the right solution, who has the correct manufacturer accreditations, and who can perform a professional installation.

Converting an Assessment into a Hardware Specification

We briefly discussed this subject near the end of the previous chapter. There we discussed the various performance metrics and the server specifications that were gathered during the assessment and allowed you to size the infrastructure. The Microsoft Assessment and Planning Toolkit even predicted how many servers would be required to run the virtual workload, without including any redundancy in a possible cluster.

In this section, we will cover a little deeper the process that you can use to accurately size your Hyper-V infrastructure based on the information that you previously gathered in the assessment. Doing this requires understanding just how Hyper-V will consume some of the key resources. As you move through each resource type, you will see how you can size your host and storage hardware to cater for the requirements.

MAP AND HARDWARE SIZING

If you have used or are planning to use the Microsoft Assessment and Planning Toolkit, then you will have gotten an estimation on how many hosts will be required to run your converted virtual machines and physical servers. It might be easy to turn a few pages and move on to another subject. Please don't; it is important to understand how Hyper-V consumes resources.

How Hyper-V Consumes Resources

A key to understanding Hyper-V hardware sizing and virtual machine placement is in knowing how those resources will be consumed. There is a misconception that virtualization will always lead to using less processor, RAM, and storage. It can but not always. We are going to look at how virtual machines will consume each of the following:

- Processor
- Storage
- RAM

How Virtual Machines Consume Processor

This has been discussed previously in Chapter 4, but it is important enough to cover again.

When you gathered the performance metrics of a server, you could see how much processor was required to run the operating system, the server applications, and the processes to respond to client demands. That amount of processing power will always be required. Table 5.4 shows an example of a few servers.

TABLE 5.4: Processor utilization performance metrics

SERVER NAME	NUMBER OF 2.8 GHZ CORES	PROCESSOR AVERAGE UTILIZATION
Server1	4	25 percent
Server2	2	90 percent
Server3	4	50 percent

If you assume that the destination Hyper-V hosts will have 2.8 GHz processors, then how many cores or logical processors will be needed? Based on the previous information, you can see that you have the following:

```
(4 × .25) + (2 × .9) + (4 × .5)
```

That works out as follows:

```
(1) + (1.8) + (2) = 4.8 cores
```

4.8 cores will require 2× quad-core processors or a single six-core (or more) processor. You can process this quickly using a spreadsheet with a set of formulas (see Table 5.5). The "Total core utilization" column in Table 5.5 shows how many cores will actually be required to run each converted physical server or virtual machine if they are converted.

TABLE 5.5: Hyper-V host core requirements calculation

SERVER NAME	NUMBER OF 2.8 GHZ CORES	PROCESSOR AVERAGE UTILIZATION	TOTAL CORE UTILIZATION
Server1	4	25 percent	1
Server2	2	90 percent	1.8

TABLE 5.5: Hyper-V host core requirements calculation *(CONTINUED)*

SERVER NAME	NUMBER OF 2.8 GHZ CORES	PROCESSOR AVERAGE UTILIZATION	TOTAL CORE UTILIZATION
Server3	4	50 percent	2
Server4	4	33 percent	1.32
Server5	2	40 percent	0.8
Server6	4	10 percent	0.4
Server7	4	18 percent	0.72
Server8	2	75 percent	1.5
Server9	4	20 percent	0.8
Server10	6	8 percent	0.48
Total Cores Required:			10.82

This gives you a total number of cores required in Hyper-V hosts to run the physical servers once they are converted into virtual machines. But that assumes that they always stay at average utilization. Some will be higher, and some will be lower. But some servers will cause their CPU utilization to spike. You need to allow for this. If you are using third-party products or System Center Operations Manager to gather metrics, then you will be able to get data on this to skew the required numbers of cores upward.

It might not be a bad practice to allow one free core per host. This will ensure that the parent partition will have some computing power and allow management.

You might want to allow for at least 12 cores to handle these workloads. In this case, you might consider running 2× six-core processors or 4× quad-core processors in a single host for these virtual machines.

If you required highly available virtual machines in an N+1 Hyper-V cluster, then you could use one of the cluster architectures shown in Table 5.6.

TABLE 5.6: Highly available physical core deployments

CORES/ PROCESSOR	PROCESSORS/ HOST	TOTAL HOSTS	TOTAL CORES DEPLOYED	TOTAL ACTIVE CORES	TOTAL REDUNDANT CORES
6	2	2	24	12	12
4	4	2	32	16	16
4	1	4	16	12	4
6	1	3	18	12	6

One of the things you might want to consider is the total number of physical processors, or sockets, you deploy in the cluster. The more processors you use, the higher your licensing bill will be if you do (and you probably will) use per-processor licensing for your Hyper-V hosts, as is the case with Microsoft Windows Server Datacenter edition.

You might also want to consider those larger processors because it allows you to have fewer host servers. Fewer servers means less electricity being consumed. That in turn reduces the cost of ownership and the environmental impact of your servers.

SERVER ENVIRONMENTAL IMPACT

What is the real impact on the environment of your servers? We have only started to consider the electrical demands and how they create a carbon footprint in recent years. The real impact goes beyond this. It starts while the server is being built. The various chipsets are produced in many locations around the world and are shipped to a central factory for assembly. The server then has to be transported to your region and then into your office. Each shipment has an impact. And every server you order compounds that impact. If you are concerned about this, then you will try to consolidate the numbers of physical servers employed as Hyper-V hosts.

HOW VIRTUAL MACHINES CONSUME STORAGE

You will need to understand this topic because storage is one of the first bottlenecks you will encounter on virtual machine growth. There are two consumers of storage, assuming you ignore System Center for the moment:

The Parent Partition You will size the disk for the Hyper-V host operating system as if it was a normal Windows Server 2008 R2 machine with 2 GB to 4 GB of RAM. The recommended minimum (minimum does not mean it is the size to use) is 40 GB of space. Typically the only things that are installed on this machine are systems management agents, which are usually quite small.

The Virtual Machines Each virtual machine will consume some space. We will cover that in more detail now.

SIZING SYSTEM CENTER

The sizing of System Center will usually involve more than just the Hyper-V project. System Center products such as Operations Manager and Data Protection Manager are capable of managing and protecting physical servers as well as the virtual ones you will concentrate on in this project. You can find storage calculators for DPM 2010 here:

```
www.microsoft.com/downloads/details.aspx?FamilyID=c136c66c-bd4a-4fb1-8088-
f610cd02dc51
```

DPM will usually use slower, larger, and cheaper storage such as SATA disks. A sizing helper for OpsMgr 2007 R2 can be downloaded from here:

```
www.microsoft.com/downloads/details.aspx?FamilyID=b0e059e9-9f19-47b9-8b01-
e864aebf210c
```

The databases for OpsMgr will require faster SAS drives.

Virtual Machine Manager 2008 R2 uses a relatively small SQL database. Most of the space consumed by VMM will be used by the library. The size of the library is determined by how many ISO images, scripts, template VHDs, and virtual machines will be stored in it. This is a tough one to calculate. Often cheaper SATA drives will suffice.

When you create a virtual machine, you have a choice of four types of storage:

Pass-Through Disk An unformatted LUN is presented to the VM. The operating system or its installer can format the disk and use it. Features associated with VHD files cannot be used, but it gives raw disk performance, which is used in extreme scenarios.

Fixed-Sized VHD This type of virtual hard disk is the preferred one in a production system. The VHD file is created on the Hyper-V host's allocated storage and expanded to the size of the simulated hard disk. It gives the best overall performance and requires the least maintenance.

Dynamically Expanding VHD A small virtual hard disk file is created and expanded as required. The performance of this type was greatly improved in Windows Server 2008 R2 over the original Windows Server 2008 release. However, it still requires disk I/O to expand the file, and there is a risk of fragmentation on the underlying physical filesystem. This requires costly maintenance.

Differential VHD A template VHD is used as a starting point. It possibly contains a generalized (sysprep) operating system. A differential virtual hard disk points at this as a starting point. All new data is written to and read from the differential VHD. The differential VHD expands over time. It does save space, but the performance is not suitable for production systems. This approach should be saved for the lab where space is limited.

As you can see, this calculation is starting to get a little difficult. There are two ways to start. You can identify the required starting point for your storage by identifying the following:

Storage Actually Utilized You will use your assessment data to show you how much space actually is used by your physical machines, as well as the virtual machines you want to migrate to Hyper-V. This approach would be useful if you plan to use dynamically expanding VHDs. Be careful to allow free space for the growth of the VHDs. Virtual machines will go into a paused (offline) state if they run out of physical disk space. And allow for expansion of your SAN. If you think you'll need 35 TB to start with, then a SAN that can only expand to 40 TB is probably not a good purchase. SAN controllers can be replaced, but it is not a good idea to plan on expensive upgrades that require downtime only six months after a deployment.

Disk Space Deployed Now you are looking at calculating storage required for passthrough disks and fixed-sized VHDs. Both of these approaches use roughly the same amount of space as the original machines. If a physical server required 100 GB of physical disk, then its virtual version will use around 100 GB of disk space too.

The space calculations do not stop there. Each virtual machine will also require space for a BIN file. This is the size of the RAM in the virtual machine and is used as a placeholder in case the virtual machine is put into a saved state (similar to hibernation but for a virtual machine and handled by the hypervisor). If the virtual machine is placed into a saved state, then the BIN file is replaced by a VSV file (containing the saved state).

The final component for the virtual machine calculation is ISO files. These files, less than 5 GB in size, may be copied to the virtual machine's location so that they can be mounted. Ideally they will be mounted over the network to avoid this.

Any Windows administrator knows that you should not plan on filling a volume too much. That makes for an unhealthy filesystem, and it prevents the usage of tools, such as defragmentation, that require some free space to work. You should leave 10 percent to 20 percent of free space on a volume.

We're looking at a formula like this to calculate the storage space required for each virtual machine, assuming you allow around 10 percent free space on the volume:

```
(<VM Disk> + <VM RAM> + <5 GB>) × 1.1
```

You can return to the example we provided when talking about processor sizing, assuming 10 percent free space and allowing for ISO files to be copied. Table 5.7 shows details of this example.

TABLE 5.7: Storage consumption of virtual machines

SERVER NAME	VIRTUAL STORAGE REQUIRED (GB)	RAM (GB)	HOST STORAGE REQUIRED (GB)
Server1	400	4	449.1
Server2	100	2	117.7
Server3	200	8	234.3
Server4	200	4	229.9
Server5	100	6	122.1
Server6	40	2	51.7
Server7	80	3	96.8
Server8	100	4	119.9
Server9	500	12	568.7
Server10	200	4	229.9
Total GB storage required (5 GB + 10 percent free space included)			2220.9

Now you know how much to leave for the parent partition and how much space to allow for any virtual machines that you will convert from physical. You should still allow for space for future growth. That will require some sort of guidance from IT management and decision makers, as well as your colleagues who look after the business applications.

Unfortunately, you are not quite finished yet. There is one more variable to throw into the mix. Snapshots (a Hyper-V term) or checkpoints (a VMM term) allow you to save a virtual machine's state, data, and configuration as they were at a particular time. This allows you to go on to do work to a virtual machine and then instantly revert to a known point in time by applying a previous snapshot. You can have up to 50 snapshots per virtual machine. Snapshots use an AVHD file for each virtual hard disk that a VM has. An AVHD is a form of differencing disk. All new data created after the snapshot is written to and read from the AVHD file. That impacts performance and can lead to very unpredictable issues happening over time. Removing a snapshot also requires shutting down the virtual machine to initiate a merge of the AVHD into the original VHD file. Hence, it is recommended that snapshots should be used very selectively and only for very short periods of time. It also implies that some production applications that store changing data should not have snapshot functionality used on them. For example, domain controllers and SQL Server instances that are in production should not have snapshots because it can lead to data loss and inconsistencies.

The AVHD file that is used in a snapshot will grow over time and will need disk space. That is a difficult one to calculate. To try, take the total disk space of the largest VM (storage-wise). Add the total storage size of that VM to the previously estimated required storage size. In our example, you would add an additional 500 GB to the 2024 GB to give you 2524 GB. Ideally your usage of snapshots will be limited, and you won't need that much disk space. This is a very cautious method.

Even if you don't plan on using snapshots, the Quick Storage Migration feature of VMM 2008 R2 uses this feature very briefly (and quite safely) to physically relocate virtual machines.

We will now move on to the one piece in the puzzle that confuses everyone when they first encounter it.

Which RAID Level?

Those who are new to virtualization often wonder what RAID level to use for the physical storage that hosts VHD files.

Here's how you should plan for RAID. If a physical server required RAID-1 or RAID-10 for write speed, then it will still need the same as a virtual machine. You can size and deploy many CSVs in a Hyper-V cluster. For example, one CSV can be on RAID-10 physical storage, and the other CSV can be on RAID-5 physical storage. Alternatively, a nonclustered host could have a RAID-10 LUN and a RAID-5 LUN. You now can locate VHDs according to their speed or space efficiency requirements. This will complicate your computations, but it will guarantee the performance that your customers or users were used to before virtualization was introduced.

How Virtual Machines Consume RAM

A Hyper-V host will be configured with a certain amount of RAM. For a small Hyper-V deployment, you will want to know how much RAM to put in a host. The project will probably not reach the hardware limitations of the host machine. A larger project will have a different question. The members of that project will want to know how many Hyper-V hosts they will need. A common anecdote heard in the Hyper-V user community is that RAM is usually a bottleneck on host capacity long before the CPU. The amounts of affordable RAM you can put into a host are long used up before the potential 384 virtual machine CPUs can be created and run.

Planning and sizing your hardware requires you to understand the RAM requirements of the virtual machines. Once again, you will return to the performance metrics of the physical machines and virtual machines that will be converted into Hyper-V virtual machines. It will also be necessary to consult with decision makers and application owners to find out about potential future growth.

Real World Scenario

HOW MUCH RAM TO PUT IN A HYPER-V HOST?

This is a common question. You must return to your objectives and compare them with your budget for hardware investment. There are three ways you can approach this:

Small Deployment In this scenario, you put only as much as you need into the one or two hosts that you will have. You probably will not come close to the limits of the hardware.

Minimize Investment You can obviously greatly increase the virtual machine capacity of a host by using larger memory kits. If only it were that easy! RAM gets exponentially more expensive as you increase each board's capacity. For example, at this time, an 8 GB ECC DDR3 one-piece memory kit is nearly four times more expensive than a 4 GB ECC DDR3 one-piece memory kit. That's nearly four times the price for double the capacity. Some organizations will decide to fully populate a server with more affordable memory kits rather than the more expensive and greater capacity ones. That could mean, for example, using 4 GB memory kits instead of 16 GB memory kits. This would in turn require more host servers and rack space. But the investment in new servers could be cheaper than using fewer servers with larger memory kits.

Minimize Host Footprint This is the opposite approach to the minimize investment one. The up-front investment in more expensive and larger memory kits is accepted, knowing that fewer Hyper-V hosts will be required, less power will be consumed, less space will be used, and less per processor licensing will also be needed. The long-term cost of ownership will be much lower than an installation that uses more physical hosts.

How much RAM will be consumed by your virtual machines? Before you get there (are you enjoying being teased?), you should see how much RAM will be required by the parent partition or host operating system.

The parent partition will usually require no more than 2 GB of RAM. It must have at least 512 MB RAM. Remember that there should be no Windows roles or features enabled other than those required to run Hyper-V and any systems management agents. The parent partition shouldn't be a SQL Server, a domain controller, or a web server. The hypervisor will require an additional 300 MB of RAM. You should allow some RAM for any drivers. Most systems management agents, for example System Center, are small and will easily fit into the allowance of the parent partition. However, if they are large, then you need to allow for them too. That gives you a formula to calculate the total RAM required for the parent partition:

```
<Parent OS> + <Hyper-V> + <Drivers> + <Systems Management>
```

THERE IS ALWAYS AN EXCEPTION

System Center Data Protection Manager (DPM) 2010 has the ability to recover individual files from a virtual machine's VHD file(s). This can be done only if the DPM server is a physical machine and the Hyper-V role has been enabled. This requirement provides DPM with the necessary system tools to mount and access the contents of a VHD file. The DPM server is a Hyper-V server, but it really should not be used as a host.

Anecdotally, 2 GB of RAM seems to be the amount being allowed for the parent partition. But you should try to be a bit more scientific about this.

Now you finally get to looking at how a virtual machine consumes RAM from the host machine. First we need to cover a couple of technical things:

Shared Memory Paging Hyper-V does not have the ability to share memory pages between virtual machines.

Dynamic Memory This is a feature that was added to Windows Server 2008 R2 Hyper-V with Service Pack 1. It will be discussed more in Chapter 6. It allows a host to provide more RAM capacity and allows for flexible RAM sizing in virtual machines. It should be treated with care so as not to oversubscribe the system.

It would be nice to say that if a virtual machine has 4 GB of RAM, then it will only consume 4 GB of RAM from the host. Then you could say that a 48 GB RAM host with a 2 GB allowance for the parent partition could have 46 GB RAM assigned to virtual machines. It is not that easy. This is best explained with that virtual machine that has 4 GB of RAM.

There is an overhead for every gigabyte of RAM assigned to a VM. The first 1 GB of RAM has a potential management overhead of 32 MB. The hypervisor might not consume that full 32 MB, but it could if there is a lot of memory activity. That means that the first 1 GB of RAM in the VM really can consume 1024 MB plus 32 MB or 1056 MB. Each additional 1 GB of RAM in the VM has a potential management overhead of 8 MB. That means each additional 1 GB of RAM in the VM really can consume 1032 MB. For the 4 GB RAM VM, you end up with the following:

```
(1024 + 32) + ((1024 + 8) X 3) = 4152 MB
```

The 4 GB RAM VM can potentially consume up to 4152 MB of RAM or just fewer than 4.05 GB RAM. That might not seem like very much of a difference, but it is enough to ensure that 46 GB of RAM that is free on the host does not give you 46 GB of virtual machine RAM.

WINDOWS SERVER 2008 R2 HYPER-V MEMORY OPTIMIZATIONS

Windows Server 2008 R2 Hyper-V introduced a number of new features such as Virtual Machine Queue (VMQ) and Second Level Address Translation (SLAT) that optimize how resources are consumed. However, the figures presented are still what are provided by Microsoft in the Performance Tuning Guidelines for Windows Server 2008 R2 document under the Correct Memory Sizing for Root Partition heading. You can download this document here:

`www.microsoft.com/whdc/system/sysperf/Perf_tun_srv-R2.mspx`

As you have probably already thought, these calculations are best done in a spreadsheet with a formula. Fortunately, one already exists, and you can download it from `www.aidanfinn.com/?p=10587`. Using the example servers from earlier, you can see in Table 5.8 just how much physical RAM will be required to run them as virtual machines on Hyper-V.

TABLE 5.8: Virtual machine RAM actual RAM consumption

SERVER	VM RAM (GB)	TOTAL (MB) FOR FIRST 1 GB	TOTAL (MB) FOR ADDITIONAL 1 GB	TOTAL (MB) ACTUAL RAM
Server1	4	1056	3096	4152
Server2	2	1056	1032	2088
Server3	8	1056	7224	8280
Server4	4	1056	3096	4152
Server5	6	1056	5160	6216
Server6	2	1056	1032	2088
Server7	3	1056	2064	3120
Server8	4	1056	3096	4152
Server9	12	1056	11352	12408
Server10	4	1056	3096	4152
Total RAM (MB) actually consumed				50808
Total RAM (GB) required (rounded up)				50

Now you have all that you need to manually size a Hyper-V architecture or to understand how an automated process (such as used by MAP) works.

OTHER SIZING CONSIDERATIONS

We've gone into detail on the big three. A lot of the time, basing your design on them will steer you in the right direction. However, when reviewing the metrics, you should look at all of them. You might find one that isn't used here that stands out and warrants attention. The following are two to watch out for:

Network Utilization If you see an assessed machine using a large amount of network, then you need to consider how many hosts you will need for this. You can deploy more than one physical NIC or even switch from using 1 GB networking to 10 GB networking for virtual machines on a Hyper-V host. Be sure to configure them uniformly across a Hyper-V cluster; otherwise, you may find virtual machines losing network connectivity when they failover or live migrate from one host to another.

IOPS The number of input/output per second (IOPS) can play a major role in how you design your disk solution. Higher requirements will require that you use faster disks, such as SAS instead of SATA. Very high requirements may require employing a 1 VM per LUN solution or even the usage of passthrough disks for your virtual machines.

Sizing a Solution

So far, you have seen how many physical logical processors or cores will be required to run 10 virtual machines. You have also seen how much disk space is required and how much RAM will be required. This is summarized here:

- Physical cores: 12
- Disk: 2524 GB
- RAM: 50 GB

The host requirements are as follows:

- RAM: 3 GB
- Disk: 72 GB

It has been decided to deploy an N+1 Hyper-V cluster. This means that if one host can meet all of the requirements for the virtual machines, then an additional one will be deployed for redundancy. This additional node would have sufficient capacity to handle the workload of the first one should it fail. Alternatively, if three hosts were required, then four would be deployed, with one being redundant.

Server hardware has been analyzed, and a model has been chosen. It will allow for up to 48 GB of RAM per host. That is not enough for the existing workload of 50 GB of RAM. However, if a three-node cluster is built, then there will be 96 GB of production RAM and 48 GB of redundant RAM. That will cater to the planned deployment of additional virtual machines to meet demand. Each host will have two 72 GB15K SAS drives for the installation of the parent partition on a RAID1 LUN.

Based on the previously calculated processor options, a single six-core CPU in each host will provide sufficient processing power. That provides 12 production cores and 6 redundant cores. But this will not meet future demands. The allocated RAM will nearly double the VM capacity of the cluster (from 50 GB to 96 GB). With approval from management, it has been decided to purchase servers with a single 12 core processor. This doubles the capacity of the host and keeps per-processor licensing costs to a minimum (one per processor license per host instead of two).

5 TB of storage will be provided in the SAN. This more than meets the immediate storage requirements and will also allow for growth and for a Virtual Machine Manager library to be stored on the SAN. An iSCSI SAN with a storage striping feature will be purchased. The organization is planning on deploying a cross-campus disaster recovery solution.

Each Hyper-V host will have six NICs:

- Parent partition
- Virtual machines
- Private network — CSV
- Private network — Live Migration

- iSCSI with MPIO enabled
- iSCSI with MPIO enabled

Because of a lack of free ports and limited budget for network reengineering, there can only be one 10 GB NIC in each server. The Live Migration private network will utilize this NIC.

During discussions with management and other members of IT, it has been discovered that Exchange 2010 will be deployed in the near future. A DAG member will be present in this site and will run as a virtual machine. You have discovered that this virtual machine cannot be run on the Hyper-V cluster. Another third-party line-of-business application is being purchased with a similar limitation. An additional nonclustered host will be deployed with one CPU and 12 GB RAM. It will store virtual machines on the SAN using a masked LUN. This will allow the virtual machine files to be replicated to the disaster recovery site using the SAN's data striping feature.

Licensing for Hyper-V

At this point, we would expect many readers to start quoting Monty Python: run away, run away! People start to think the very worst when it comes to Microsoft and licensing. Yes, Microsoft doesn't make it very easy. Sometimes there are pitfalls that can be painful. Please believe that there is a reason to continue reading. There is a good news story here — one that can and will save you money. Unfortunately, there is bad news for others. We will start with the bad news and wrap up the chapter with the good news.

LICENSING DEEP DIVE

Microsoft product usage rights policies change on a frequent basis and are therefore not suitable for a book. This book will cover some of the more general details that are less likely to change over time. You should consult a licensing specialist or read the Product Usage Rights document found here:

`www.microsoft.com/LICENSING/ABOUT-LICENSING/PRODUCT-LICENSING.ASPX`

Hosting companies using Services Provider License Agreement (SPLA) should read the Services Provider Usage Rights (SPUR) document found here:

`www.microsoft.com/hosting/en/us/licensing/splabenefits.aspx`

The Bad News: OEM Licensing

Original equipment manufacturer (OEM) licenses have been commonly purchased because they are more economic. This is true not only for desktops but also for servers. There is a reason that these licenses are cheaper. The license is legally tied to the computer it is either supplied with or first installed on. The license is nontransferrable. You cannot move the license to another machine, even if you remove the installation from the original one.

This affects virtualization (not just Hyper-V) in a few ways. The first is that any converted physical server will require a new license for the converted virtual machine. It is also illegal to migrate an OEM-licensed virtual machine from one host to another.

Unfortunately, there will be a relicensing required. That sounds pretty horrendous. You can step back from the ledge. There is a reason you left the good news story until last.

The Good News: Hyper-V Is Better Than Free

To be fair to them, Microsoft has made quite an effort to get this message across, but many have still not gotten the message or they choose to not believe it. And to be fair to Microsoft's competition in the hardware virtualization wars, what we are about to describe applies to all virtualization platforms.

When you license the 2008 R2 version of Hyper-V, you have a number of edition choices, as described in Table 5.9. There are a few things to note first. SPLA licensing for hosting companies has a very different pricing system, but the basic rules apply. Datacenter edition licensing is done on a per physical CPU (or socket, not core) basis rather than the usual per-server model. The amount of RAM shown as supported takes into account the 1 TB limit that is supported by the Hyper-V role, not the operating system edition. (The prices illustrated were obtained from the Microsoft website for the U.S. market and are subject to change.)

TABLE 5.9: 2008 R2 HYPER-V EDITIONS COMPARISON

EDITION	PRICE	FEATURES	FREE ON HOST VIRTUAL MACHINES
Hyper-V Server 2008 R2	Free	1 TB RAM, 8 CPU, clustering, Live Migration	0
Standard	$1,029 per server	32 GB RAM, 4 CPU	1
Enterprise	$3,999 per server	1 TB RAM, 8 CPU, clustering, Live Migration	4
Datacenter	$2,999 per CPU	1 TB RAM, 8 CPU, clustering, Live Migration	Unlimited

The "Free on host virtual machines" column is the interesting one. If you install an Enterprise edition as the parent partition (host operating system) of a Hyper-V server, then it can have four free virtual machine licenses. That means four virtual machines that run on this host do not require a Windows purchase. They can run the Enterprise or lower editions. If you do the sums, then you will see that four copies of the Standard edition ($1,029) will cost a total of $4,116. An Enterprise edition purchase, which gives you four free virtual machine operations system licenses, will cost $3,999, saving you $177. It also simplifies your license purchasing. The news gets better, so keep reading!

The ever-increasing capacities of servers with 6 and 12 core processors, with even larger memory banks, means that you can get 10, 20, or more virtual machines onto a host. Imagine if you had a 10:1 virtualization ratio on a three-node N+1 cluster. That means you would have 20 virtual machines running across 3 nodes. If they all ran the Standard edition, then the total license purchase cost for the virtual machines would be $20,580.

The Datacenter edition of Windows Server allows you to run unlimited free virtual machines on a licensed host. It is licensed per CPU. We will assume that there are 2× six-core CPUs in each of the three hosts in the cluster. That gives you six CPUs, requiring $17,994 to license the hosts with the Datacenter edition. That saves the company $2,586. Look at the specification of those hosts; they have 12 cores each. They could probably run at a 20:1 ratio, which is 40 virtual machines across the three-node N+1 cluster. If they did, then running Hyper-V would save the company $23,166.

There are a few admissions to make here. If you have already purchased volume licenses for your virtual machines, then you won't really save anything on their licensing. You will be able to take advantage of the savings for future virtual machine deployments. For example, you could license your hosts with Software Assurance and allow for a more economic adoption of future releases of Windows Server.

This money savings for the Windows Server scheme is not exclusive to Hyper-V. You can purchase Enterprise edition and Datacenter edition licenses and assign (not install) them to XenServer or VMware hosts to get a similar result for your Windows Server costs. You will get the same savings with the free XenServer and free editions of VMware. However, you still have to purchase the license and support for the nonfree editions from VMware, reducing or even eliminating the license cost savings.

The benefits of using Windows Server 2008 R2 Datacenter edition licenses go beyond the purchasing costs. The concept of Dynamic IT is that you in IT deploy and change as and when the organization requires it. Whether it is manual or automated, you want to be able to quickly deploy virtual machines as and when required. Even with an Enterprise agreement with flexible true-up licensing, the organization should have controls on license deployment for accounting. With Datacenter licensing, there is no additional license cost to a virtual machine. Machines can be deployed more quickly. This isn't to say that you can go crazy with what is called *virtual machine sprawl*. But it does mean that you do not have to wait for days or even weeks to OK a license usage when there isn't one being used.

The free product, Hyper-V Server 2008 R2, has a role. This edition, which has only a Server Core installation option (command line only), offers no free licenses. It might be an option for those who are converting already licensed physical servers where purchases of the Standard, Enterprise, or Datacenter editions make no economic sense. It has a similar specification in features and capacities as the Enterprise edition. It will also play a role in Virtual Desktop Infrastructure (VDI) deployments where the free Server licensing of the paid-for editions offers no benefit.

The odd-one-out in the mix is the Standard edition. Enterprise deployments are extremely unlikely to use it. It offers only one free license for virtual machines. It has limited capacities and has no clustering or Live Migration. Don't completely ignore it; it plays a big role in Small Business Server (SBS) virtualization, which you can read about in Chapter 11.

System Center and SQL

Every machine that System Center is installed on requires a purchase of the server product and a management license or CAL for each machine managed by it. You can purchase a bulk management license for all the System Center products called a System Center Server Management Suite. There are two editions you can purchase (shown in Table 5.10).

TABLE 5.10: System Center Server Management Suite editions

EDITION	DESCRIPTION
Enterprise (SMSE)	Includes licensing for four virtual machines that run on the assigned host. The host operating system is also licensed if it is used only for Hyper-V.
Datacenter (SMSD)	Includes licensing for all virtual machines that run on the assigned host and the host operating system. This is licensed on a per physical processor (socket, not core) basis, and at least two processors must be licensed per host.

This is a very economical way to provide licensing for all virtual machines and hosts for all the management capabilities of System Center including backup, virtualization management, configuration management and auditing, and health and performance monitoring.

SQL 2008 R2 licensing has brought some changes. It is also possible to purchase an Enterprise or Datacenter edition of the SQL license and assign it to the host (shown in Table 5.11).

TABLE 5.11: SQL 2008 R2 per host processor edition comparison

EDITION	DESCRIPTION
Enterprise	You can assign the license to a host and obtain free licensing for up to four instances of SQL Server in virtual machines running on that host.
Datacenter	You can assign the license to a host and obtain free licensing for unlimited instances of SQL Server in virtual machines running on that host.

The per-processor option for installing SQL Server could get expensive if you have multiple processors in a host and have only a few SQL Server virtual machines. You can return to traditional installations of SQL Server. It is strongly recommended that you consult your assigned licensing specialist and/or read the Product Usage Rights document for details.

You now understand how Hyper-V scales, how to combine this with an analysis of your assessment to size and specify your hardware, and how to license your solution. It is time to deploy Hyper-V!

The Bottom Line

Understand the hardware requirements for Hyper-V Understanding the correct maximum limits of Hyper-V is critical in performing a valid hardware sizing and specification that will be supported by Microsoft and be reliable.

Master It You are working as an engineer in a company that is considering options for deploying Windows Server 2008 R2 Hyper-V. A consultancy company has convinced your manager that they should assist. During your first meeting, the lead technical consultant has started talking about being able to use 2 TB RAM per host on Datacenter edition Hyper-V hosts, with more than 500 running virtual CPUs per host. What is wrong with that statement, and what are the correct maximum limits?

Convert assessment results into a hardware specification When you understand the capabilities of Hyper-V, you can use the assessment data to size your host and storage hardware. Performance and size metrics of existing physical and virtual machines will be used to calculate the specifications and numbers of host servers.

Master It You have been asked to size the amount of RAM that will be required for a number of virtual machines. How do virtual machines consume RAM from a Hyper-V host?

Be able to discuss Hyper-V licensing There are potential savings to be made with the licensing of Hyper-V that also simplify the accounting and administration of licensing the virtualized environment.

Master It You are working as a consultant and are preparing a presentation to give to some potential customers who are deploying a completely new IT infrastructure with no existing servers. You need to discuss the potential cost savings of using Windows Server 2008 R2 Hyper-V. What can you talk about?

Part 3

Deploying Core Virtualization Technologies

Chapter 6

Deploying Hyper-V

Let the fun begin! All the preparation work in the project has been completed. You have purchased your servers and storage. They are racked, powered, and waiting for you to get Hyper-V up and running.

We will start this chapter by looking at the installation of the parent partition, also known as the *host operating system*. This is your software prerequisite for enabling the Hyper-V role on Windows Server 2008 R2. You might manually install Windows, the patches, and Hyper-V in a small, one-off deployment. Larger organizations or those who expect constant growth might want to look at automated solutions, which will allow an unattended installation of Windows Server 2008 R2 and include the patches and the Hyper-V role. We'll discuss these topics and some of the options that you have.

Chapter 2, "The Architecture of Hyper-V," introduced you to the theory behind some of the configurations in Hyper-V such as networking. This chapter will cover how to configure Hyper-V. This will include all the subjects that seem to top the search charts such as networking, VLANs, NIC teaming, CIFS delegation, disk configuration, physical storage, and Dynamic Memory. Don't worry; we won't forget about Failover Clustering!

One could be forgiven for thinking that Hyper-V is completely focused on the Microsoft world. This could not be further from the truth. Microsoft has made huge efforts and formed strategic partnerships to ensure that supported Linux distributions and versions are full-rights citizens on the Hyper-V platform. It has been a process that has evolved over time. We will wrap up the chapter by talking about what Linux support means for Microsoft and how you can install Linux virtual machines and install version 2.1 of the Linux Integration components.

In this chapter, you will learn to

- Deploy Hyper-V host servers
- Configure Hyper-V
- Manage Linux virtual machines

Deploying Hyper-V Host Servers

The installation of Hyper-V starts with the installation of Windows Server 2008 R2 onto the physical server. This might sound wrong for a hypervisor. It sounds more like the process for installing a product such as Microsoft's Virtual Server 2005 R2 SP1 or VMware Virtual Server. As we explained in Chapter 2, enabling the Hyper-V role in the operating system will slip the hypervisor beneath it and convert the operating system into the parent partition (or host operating system).

You have two basic ways to install the parent partition. The first is to perform a manual installation. This is time-consuming, requiring you to sit at the server (or remote console), install Windows Server 2008 R2, enable the Hyper-V role, and install the patches and security updates. This is fine if you are installing only a very small number of host servers with little or no growth.

The alternative is to use an automated operating system installation technique. An automated solution may consume a little time at the start of the deployment, but it will return huge time savings if many Hyper-V host servers need to be deployed or there will be frequent and constant growth. An automated solution can install the operating system, install any updates, and potentially script the enablement of the Hyper-V role. We're going to look at both techniques now.

Manually Installing Hyper-V

If you have only one or two host servers to build, you might decide to go with the simpler, fully manual approach of installing a Hyper-V host server.

The Installation Media

You have a number of choices for your installation media. You should start by using the latest media available, such as Windows Server 2008 R2 with Service Pack 1. This will install the server operating system with Service Pack 1 already in place.

You can use physical media and insert that into your server. Many servers won't have a DVD drive. This could be for budget reasons. It could be that they are blade servers and they don't have the capacity for a DVD drive. Your servers might have some form of remote console, which allows you to mount an ISO image of your installation media.

Your next option is to prepare a USB memory stick with the installation media. The USB stick must be at least 4 GB in size. You can use a free tool from Microsoft called the Windows 7 USB/DVD Download Tool to copy the files from the Windows Server media onto the USB memory stick. You can download this tool and get instructions for it at `http://store.microsoft.com/Help/ISO-Tool`. Then insert the USB memory stick into your host server and install Windows Server 2008 R2. Just be sure to remove the USB stick when the first reboot takes place if the server is configured to prioritize booting from USB over booting from the hard disk with the `C:` drive (or the storage controller).

Alternatively, you can replicate the process used by this tool to create an installation USB memory stick by using the following process:

1. Install a utility such as Virtual CloneDrive (`http://www.slysoft.com/en/virtual-clonedrive.html`) to mount the ISO. This gives you a virtual DVD drive that you call the `G:` drive, for example. Make sure there's nothing valuable on your USB memory stick, and insert it into your admin computer. That might be the `I:` drive. Right-click Command Prompt in your Start menu, and select Run As Administrator.
2. Run `diskpart`. Then run the following subcommand:

   ```
   List disk
   ```

3. Identify the disk you want to use, and select it by running the following:

   ```
   Select disk 1
   ```

4. Prepare the USB stick:

```
Clean
Create partition primary
Select partition 1
Active
Format quick fs=fat32
```

5. That gives you a FAT32 filesystem on the USB stick using a quick format. You can make the USB stick bootable by running this command:

```
Assign
Exit
```

6. Copy the contents of the mounted ISO (`G:`) onto the USB stick (`I:`). Do that by running the following `xcopy` command:

```
xcopy g:\*.* /s/e/f i:\
```

The final method we will recommend is to prepare a server with Windows Deployment Services (WDS) or some similar PXE boot and installation service. You can add the boot image (`boot.wim`) and installation image (`install.wim`) from your installation media onto the WDS server, add your host server's network and storage drivers, and then use a PXE boot on the host server to perform a manual installation of Windows Server 2008 R2 over the network.

Installing the Parent Partition

You need to configure the BIOS of the new host server. Consult your hardware manual or manufacturer's support site to turn on the following:

- CPU Assisted Virtualization
- Data Execution Prevention

This is a simple Windows Server 2008 R2 installation. Windows Server 2008 R2 (and Windows Server 2008) will be new to many people who are working with Hyper-V for the first time. The installation is very similar to that of Windows 7. You are asked to select the regionalization for the setup routine and then pick an edition and installation type.

Most installations of Hyper-V will be done on a Windows Server 2008 R2 Datacenter edition installation, because of the licensing benefits that it can provide. The next decision is the installation type.

Server Core Can you imagine Windows without any windows? That's what Microsoft gives you when you select a Server Core installation type. All you get when you log in is a command prompt. A basic menu system (sconfig) is provided with Windows Server 2008 R2 Server Core installations. Everything else must be done from the command prompt or by remote administration. This installation type first appeared with Windows Server 2008. The idea is when you strip away the GUI, you can save on disk space, reduce the number of required patches and security updates, and save memory and CPU resources. Microsoft has been strongly recommending that you use a Server Core installation type for your Hyper-V parent partition.

The problem with Server Core is that there is no GUI. There is an assumption by Microsoft that everything can be configured from the command prompt or PowerShell, that you have the skills to do this, or that you will have the ability to manage all features by remote administration. This is unfortunately not the case. Many early adopters wanted to use the Server Core installation for the benefits we just mentioned. They sadly found that some critical tools were not available. For example, they could not use the OEM hardware management tools or configure NIC teaming. Many inexperienced administrators did not have the necessary skills to do basic administration tasks from the command prompt. And veteran administrators struggled to perform diagnostics on the server when things (as they eventually do) went wrong.

Full Installation This is the traditional installation of Windows Server that you have been used to up to now. All of Windows is present, including the windows. You can manage the computer by using the GUI, by command prompt or PowerShell, or by remote administration. All third-party tools can be installed, used, and configured as normal. The disk requirements for a full installation are a tiny bit greater than a Server Core installation. CPU and RAM differences are negligible. More patches are required for a full installation, but there is a good chance you would have been patching and rebooting on a monthly basis with a Server Core installation as well. Check out Virtual Machine Servicing Tool 3.0 in Chapter 12, and you'll soon see that patching of a Hyper-V cluster will be something you can completely automate with zero downtime for your virtual machines (although patching of virtual machines still requires reboots for them).

Hyper-V Server 2008 R2 It would be foolish of us to forget the free Hyper-V Server 2008 R2, which you can download from `http://www.microsoft.com/hyper-v-server/en/us/how-to-get.aspx`. It can be compared with a Server Core installation of Windows Server 2008 R2 Datacenter edition in terms of features and scalability. This free edition does not come with the licensing perks, and it does not have a GUI. It does have a text-based menu and configuration utility. This launches automatically when you log into the parent partition.

The testing phase of your project should have given you an opportunity to assess which of the installation types is right for your organization.

MASTERING WINDOWS SERVER 2008 R2

You should check out *Mastering Windows Server 2008 R2* (also published by Sybex) if you are new to installing and configuring this version of the Windows Server operating system. Chapter 2 of this book describes the process for installing Windows Server 2008 R2. It walks you through the creation of an unattended answer file for setting up Windows Server automatically. You will also find instructions on using Server Manager to install roles and features, including the Server Manager PowerShell cmdlets.

Pick your installation type, and then you can configure your storage for the parent partition installation. The parent partition will reside on the `C:` drive of the Hyper-V host server. Your virtual machines will normally reside on another set of disks, which are either internally or externally connected. The recommended minimum for the `C:` drive, according to Microsoft, is 40 GB. This is not so big to waste disk space and not so small to cause issues with service pack and patch installation.

What about the paging file? Your host server might have 32 GB of RAM or much more. Shouldn't the paging file be 1.5 times that? Luckily, the answer to that is no. The parent partition might see all the memory in the host server, but it won't really be using it like a normal server. The most common recommendation is to set the paging file to be 4 GB in size. You can set it to be larger, but it won't be of much use in normal scenarios. The only possible use would be to allow complete crash dumps in the event of a blue screen of death, knowing that a huge dump file will take some time to write and a very long time to upload to Microsoft's support services.

The C: Drive

You should always use the default drive letter of *C* for your Windows partition. For example, Cluster Shared Volume requires that it has a folder called `C:\ClusterStorage`.

Your Hyper-V host server will install the operating system and greet you with a request to set the local Administrator password. Do this, and you are logged into the parent partition of the host server.

The Initial Configuration Tasks utility will start up automatically. Here you can do a number of things such as the following:

- Name the computer (parent partition) and reboot.
- Configure IPv4 and/or IPv6.
- Join the computer (parent partition) to a domain. You will need to do this if this host will be a member of a Hyper-V cluster.

Most administrators will usually close the Initial Configuration Tasks utility and perform the subsequent configurations in Server Manager. Server Manager is intended to provide you with a central point for server administration. You can add functionality to your server by adding roles and features. Hyper-V is a role that you can enable. Windows Server 2008 required that you download and install the RTM code before enabling the Hyper-V role. Windows Server 2008 R2 is supplied with the latest version. All you have to do is add the role.

An alternative way to do this is to use the PowerShell cmdlet for Server Manager. The PowerShell cmdlets you would run are as follows:

```
import-module servermanager
add-windowsfeature Hyper-V -restart
```

The first cmdlet will add the Server Manager PowerShell module and allow you to manage the configuration of the server using PowerShell cmdlets. The second cmdlet will add the Hyper-V role and reboot the server.

The server will configure and reboot a couple of times after you add the role. It will eventually return to the login prompt. You now have a Hyper-V host server.

You can return to Server Manager and add the Failover Clustering feature if this Hyper-V host is to be a member of a cluster. This will not add your machine to a cluster or create a cluster. We'll return to look at that a little later.

You will need to install the latest service pack for Windows Server 2008 R2 if your media did not already include it, such as media marked as Windows Server 2008 R2 with Service Pack 1. You can run `winver.exe` from the command prompt to see what the current build level of the operating system is. Be careful to ensure that the build of this new machine will be identical to other hosts if you are planning on adding it to a cluster.

The last step in the process is to patch your new server. You can use Windows Update download updates directly from Microsoft, or you can use any existing automated patching solutions that are on your network such as WSUS or System Center Configuration Manager. Check out Chapter 12 for more on this subject.

There are more patches available independently of those you will get from Windows Update. Microsoft has provided a page listing all of the updates that are available for Hyper-V:

```
http://technet.microsoft.com/library/ff394763(WS.10).aspx
```

These hotfix or bug fix updates are optional. Most, if not all, Hyper-V experts will advise that you should install any of these updates that may have any relevance to your infrastructure. Many problems that are reported on support forums can be avoided by applying these updates. You will have to manually download each update and install it. Configuration Manager administrators can automate the deployment of these updates using the System Center Custom Updates Publisher (SCUP) utility.

There you have it — a new Hyper-V host server, all ready to be configured and used to host virtual machines. We're going to look at how you might automate the deployment of a Hyper-V host server before we get into the details of Hyper-V configuration.

Using an Automated Process to Build a Hyper-V Host Server

Manually building a Hyper-V host server is a time-consuming process. It will probably take most of a day when you consider all the waiting for progress bars, reboots, installing updates, and the guaranteed requests to have a quick look at something. An automated installation process is going to be attractive to people in a few different scenarios:

Consultants Virtualization consultants can spend a large percentage of their time building host servers. Any automated process that can reduce this time will reduce the boredom caused by repetitive work. It will allow them to turn a production system around more quickly, allowing you to get to the more difficult and bespoke engineering tasks. An end-to-end automated build will also impress the customer. There is a very good chance that it's going to be something the on-site techies have not seen before, and it might lead to requests for more work in the future to provide them with the tools and/or the skills for this sort of mechanism.

Large Deployments No consultant, engineer, or administrator will wake up in the morning looking forward to manually installing and configuring a large number of servers. It is a manual process that is repetitive. A project manager should also be concerned with manually building many servers. Humans make mistakes, even with checklists, procedures, and lectures about quality. An automated solution will build many servers with little human interaction, build them consistently, and ensure that you get a quality product. The responsible staff members will be able to work on other parts of the project or do other engineering tasks while the automated builds are running. This is a much better use of their time.

Rapid Growth We promise to restrict the use of the word *Cloud* in this book. Cloud computing, whether it is the private Cloud or the public (Internet hosting company) Cloud, is the current trend in our business. The flexibility and elastic nature of Cloud computing is based on virtualization technologies such as Hyper-V. This requires the ability to rapidly provide new host servers in advance of (or to instantly respond to) consumer demand on a very frequent basis. The host farms can be huge, spanning many clusters. Consistent quality and standardization is a must in this sort of environment. There is no way that a business that runs a Cloud computing infrastructure can successfully depend on a manual build process.

Building an automated build process will require more time and effort than manually building just a few Hyper-V host servers. This investment will provide a return if you have more than just a few servers to build.

AUTOMATED BUILD SOLUTIONS

There is an abundance of potential operating system deployment solutions. Some are well-known cloning solutions that might be already used in your environment. Some are solutions that are included or sold with servers. Make sure that you check for Windows Server 2008 R2 compatibility if using any of those solutions. Microsoft also provides operating system solutions, some of which are free, with the remaining one requiring a purchase.

Windows Automated Installation Kit (WAIK) WAIK for Windows 7 and Windows Server 2008 R2 is a free download from the Microsoft website. It can be used with all the Microsoft operating system deployment solutions to customize how Windows is installed. This is done by creating an XML unattended answer file using a GUI-based tool called Windows System Image Manager (WSIM). This subject is covered in depth (along with a sample answer file) in Chapter 2 of *Mastering Windows Server 2008 R2*.

Using WSIM, you can create an answer file that will be loaded from removable media (usually a USB memory stick) by the usual Windows Server 2008 R2 installer during the initial start-up. The file will be used to customize the installation. For example, you might join the computer to the domain using the answer file and configure the licensing (product key and activation) and networking. One of the features you might use is GUIRunOnce. This allows you to run a command. Your command could, for example, run a PowerShell script (stored on a network share) with the Server Manager cmdlets to enable the Failover Clustering feature and the Hyper-V role.

Now you have a solution where all you have to do to build a server is insert the Windows Server 2008 R2 DVD, insert a USB stick with a WSIM answer file, and wait for 30 to 45 minutes for a newly built Hyper-V host server. You only need to patch the server, and it is ready for configuration.

Windows Deployment Services (WDS) WDS is an imaging solution that has been provided as part of every version of Windows Server since Service Pack 2 for Windows Server 2003. It is a network-based solution, taking advantage of a server's ability to (PXE) boot using a network card. An administrator can import an installation image and a boot image for Windows Server 2008 R2 onto a WDS server. Any additional storage or network drivers for the host server can be added to the WDS server if they are not included as part of Windows Server 2008 R2. The administrator can then log into the server to install any remaining updates.

We're not finished yet! WDS is an imaging solution, meaning you can deploy and create images. A capture boot image can be created from your original boot image. You can generalize the customized server using sysprep and capture an image of it using the capture boot image. The new image can be deployed to many servers, allowing very rapid deployment of new Hyper-V host servers. That image can be associated with a WSIM answer file to add the Hyper-V role.

Real World Scenario

THE HYPER-V ROLE AND SYSPREP

It is possible to sysprep a server that has the Hyper-V role enabled and create an image from it. Any new Hyper-V host that is deployed from this image will have a few things that might not be as you would have expected.

The hypervisor should autostart when you a deploy a new machine, assuming that you are working with a Windows Server 2008 R2 Hyper-V host server. This was not the case with Windows Server 2008 where you had to configure the hypervisor to start by running the following:

```
bcdedit /set hypervisorlaunchtype auto
```

Any Hyper-V external networks that may have been created in the original template machine will be converted into internal networks. You will have to change the type and bind each external network to the appropriate physical network adapter in the Hyper-V host server.

The dynamic MAC address pool will be cleared and recreated. This is to avoid a problem where virtual machines with dynamic MAC addresses are placed onto cloned Hyper-V host servers and end up with identical MAC addresses.

Any passthrough disks that were on the original host server will need to be set up once again.

Be aware that you should not add your template server to a cluster before generalizing the machine using sysprep.

Microsoft Deployment Toolkit (MDT) MDT is another free solution from Microsoft for operating system deployment. The other solutions that we have talked about are simple imaging solutions. MDT uses the concept of a task sequence for operating system deployment. This allows a set of individual tasks to be done in a single automated process. The deployment or capture of an image is just one of the tasks in the sequence. Other steps might include installing updates or adding roles and features. You can see how a solution like this might be a superb solution for combining many configurations in a server deployment.

Configuration Manager 2007 ConfigMgr includes a feature for operating system deployment. The other solutions we have discussed are referred to as *light-touch solutions*. ConfigMgr is referred to as a *zero-touch solution*. Like MDT, ConfigMgr uses task sequences and can combine many operations into a deployment.

Your organization may have already invested in an operating system deployment solution. Some never think of using these solutions for server operating systems. A little bit of work will give you a solution for quickly preparing new Hyper-V hosts with the tiniest amount of effort each time.

Configuring Hyper-V

In this section, we will cover how you can configure your Hyper-V hosts to develop your hardware virtualization infrastructure.

NIC Teaming

Microsoft does not provide any support for NIC teaming in any of its products. This is a bit of an issue with Hyper-V. There may be many virtual machines on a single host server. A NIC, cable, or switch port failure could terminate the network connectivity of all those virtual machines.

All is not lost; Microsoft's hardware partners have updated their NIC teaming solutions to include support for Windows Server 2008 R2 Hyper-V. Each manufacturer has a set of instructions for configuring NIC teaming on a Hyper-V host server. You must follow these instructions precisely. You will have to completely rebuild a host server if you implement the steps in the wrong order.

You should check your hardware manufacturer's support website for the latest downloads and setup instructions. You may find that your manufacturer's NIC teaming solution may change how you implement VLAN tagging (as discussed in Chapter 2). For example, one solution requires that you create a new virtual NIC in the teaming software for each VLAN that is to be supported. This virtual NIC is bound to the VLAN in question. A Hyper-V virtual network is created and bound to this virtual NIC. Each virtual machine is connected to the appropriate virtual network for VLAN connectivity.

We talked about the required network adapters in Chapter 2 for a nonclustered Hyper-V host server. NIC teaming will change things, as shown in Table 6.1.

TABLE 6.1: Nonclustered host with NIC teaming

PHYSICAL NIC	NIC TEAM	PURPOSE
Parent 1	Parent NIC team	All parent partition communications
Parent 2		
Virtual 1	Virtual network NIC team	All virtual machine communications
Virtual 2		

Four physical network adapters will be placed in the nonclustered Hyper-V host server. The first two will be teamed to create one NIC team. This appears as a new network adapter in the parent partition. You will set up the IPv4 and/or IPv6 configuration for the parent partition in this network adapter's properties.

The second pair of physical network adapters will be teamed to create a second NIC team. This team will be the one that you bind the Hyper-V virtual network to. All virtual machine communications will be transmitted by this NIC team.

An engineer who is planning for network fault tolerance will ensure that the network cables connected to each physical network adapter in a team will be plugged into different network switches. Each network switch will be plugged into different power supplies and have an independent path to the next appliance in the network. Figure 6.1 illustrates these connections.

A clustered host with four network connections will require eight physical network adapters, as shown in Table 6.2.

FIGURE 6.1
Nonclustered host network fault tolerance

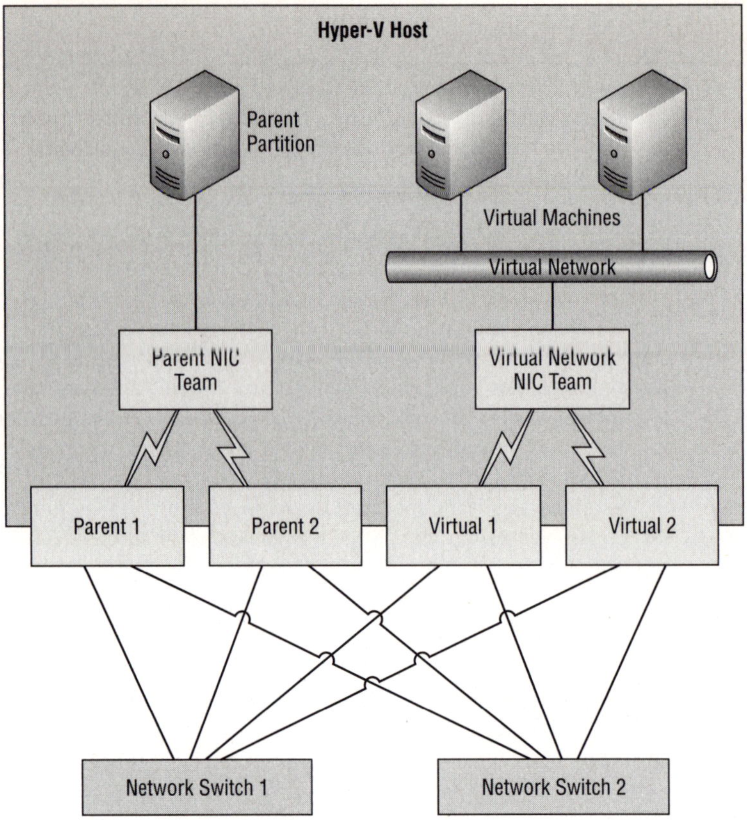

TABLE 6.2: Clustered host with NIC teaming

PHYSICAL NIC	NIC TEAM	PURPOSE
Parent 1	Parent NIC team	All parent partition communications
Parent 2		
Virtual 1	Virtual network NIC team	All virtual machine communications
Virtual 2		
Live Migration 1	Live Migration NIC team	Preferred network for Live Migration traffic
Live Migration 2		
CSV 1	CSV NIC team	Preferred network for CSV Redirected I/O
CSV 2		

It would be pointless if you did not match these efforts with the power supplies in the host server. Each host server should be powered by independent power circuits. This will give you A+B power and networking, allowing 50 percent of your network and/or power to be lost while the host server and its virtual machines stay fully operational.

You could be easily confused by all of network connections if you plug them in all at once. You should label each of the network adapters, in the parent partition, according to the role they play. You can then label a network cable, and plug it into the appropriate adapter. Doing this one at a time will allow you to ensure that everything is correctly connected.

Failover Clustering

Don't get stressed over implementing a cluster for the first time. It really is not difficult, thanks to the improvements that were first introduced in Windows Server 2008. We're going to walk you through the steps of building a Hyper-V cluster. You will have highly available virtual machines up and running in no time.

Preparing the Hosts

You host servers do not have to be 100 percent identical, but they should be configured consistently:

- Install the hardware and shared storage.
- Connect the shared storage, preferably using multipath I/O (MPIO).
- Have all of the servers running the same edition of Windows Server 2008 R2.
- Make sure they are all at the same service pack level and installed with the same security updates and patches.
- Make them all members of the same domain.
- Have administrative rights on each of the host servers.

Failover Clustering will require some network configuration. You will need a computer name and IP address for the new cluster.

The CSV network adapter and the Live Migration network adapter should each be in a private, nonrouted network. Table 6.3 shows a possible IP configuration of Host1 in a new cluster:

Table 6.3: Clustered host IP configuration

Network Adapter	IP Address	Description
Parent	10.1.1.1/255.255.255.0	The server network
Virtual	IPv4 and IPv6 unbound	No connectivity for the parent partition
Live Migration	192.168.1.1/255.255.255.0	A nonrouted network dedicated to Live Migration in this cluster
CSV	192.168.2.1/255.255.255.0	A nonrouted network dedicated to CSV Redirected I/O in this cluster

There are potentially a lot of network adapters to work with. You might want to cable them as they are configured so you can be sure of exactly which network adapter you are working with. The labels that Windows applies, such as Local Network Adapter 2, are random and cannot be relied upon. It is not a bad idea to rename the network adapters to document the role that they serve.

Preparing the Shared Storage

A cluster requires some form of node majority or quorum mechanism to be defined. This is used to failover resources (such as highly available virtual machines) during a host failure. You will typically utilize one of two (from a possible four) options for a Hyper-V cluster that is present in a single site:

- Node Majority
- Node And Disk Witness Majority

The choice is easy. Node Majority is used when there will be an uneven number of hosts in the Hyper-V cluster. Node And Disk Witness Majority is used when there is an even number of hosts in the cluster. Node And Disk Witness Majority is a method that uses a disk from the shared storage to break the vote. You can change the majority mechanism as your cluster grows or shrinks to suit the number of hosts in the Hyper-V cluster with absolutely no downtime.

> **Other Cluster Quorum Configurations**
>
> We have listed the two quorum configurations that you would use in a single site cluster. There are two other quorum configurations that are available to use.
>
> Node And Fileshare Majority is used in special scenarios such as a multisite cluster. This is when cluster nodes are placed into more than one site and the shared storage is replicated in some way between the sites. Typically this is used in a disaster recovery design. The file share is placed in a third site and is used as a witness to help decide which nodes (or which site) should be active.
>
> No Majority: Disk Only is the final quorum configuration and is not recommended by Microsoft. This configuration will continue to be operational with just one cluster node operational. It comes with a risk: the quorum or witness disk is a single point of failure.
>
> You can learn more about the quorum configurations at `http://technet.microsoft.com/library/cc731739.aspx`.

You will need to associate a 50 MB disk (some SANs have a minimum LUN size of 1 GB) from the shared storage with every host in the cluster if you want to use Node And Disk Witness Majority. Use Disk Management to bring the disk online and format it.

Adding the Failover Clustering Feature

You can use Server Manager to add the Failover Clustering feature if doing a manual installation. You will use the Server Manager PowerShell cmdlets to add the feature if doing an automated or scripted installation:

```
import-module servermanager
add-windowsfeature failover-clustering
```

The first cmdlet will import the Server Manager PowerShell module, allowing you to add and remove roles and/or features. The second cmdlet will enable the Failover Clustering feature. No reboot is required.

MANAGING WINDOWS FAILOVER CLUSTERING

You can manage the Failover Clustering feature using the Failover Clustering Manager. You can find this in Administrative tools on your Hyper-V host server. You might find it a bit bothersome to have to log into a server to do day-to-day administrative operations. You can install the Remote Administration Tools for Windows 7 on your computer and fully manage Hyper-V and Failover Clustering on your Hyper-V host servers from the comfort of your desk. This free download is available here:

```
http://www.microsoft.com/downloads/details.aspx?FamilyID=7d2f6a
d7-656b-4313-a005-4e344e43997d
```

Note that this toolkit can be installed only on the Professional, Ultimate, and Enterprise editions of Windows 7.

CREATING THE CLUSTER

We are going to show how to create a three-node cluster. This N+1 cluster will provide the organization with the hosting capacity of two Hyper-V hosts with a third for automatic fault tolerance. This work will be done in the Failover Cluster Manager console, which is shown in Figure 6.2.

FIGURE 6.2
The Failover Cluster Manager

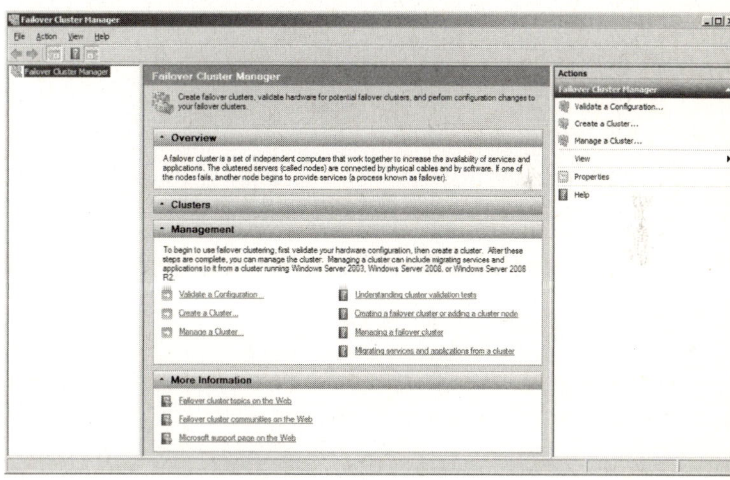

You will start the creation of the new Hyper-V cluster by selecting Failover Cluster Manager in the navigation pane (on the left side) and clicking the Create A Cluster task in the Actions pane (on right side). This will launch the Create Cluster Wizard, illustrated in Figure 6.3.

The Select Servers screen allows you to enter the name of each of the intended cluster members. You can enter them all in one line with each server name being separated by a space. The entered servers will be assessed for suitability when you click Add. Each valid server will appear in the Selected Servers box after it is assessed.

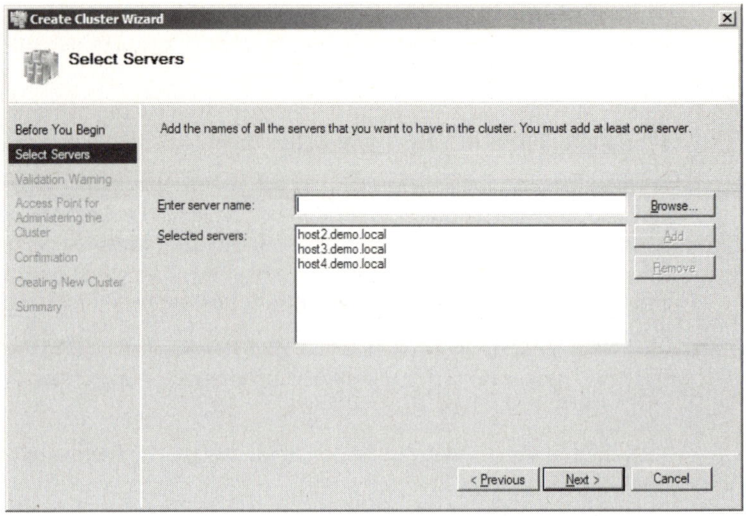

FIGURE 6.3 Create Cluster Wizard

Microsoft used to hold a very tight reign over the supported hardware in a failover cluster before the days of Windows Server 2008. This led to a smaller hardware compatibility list that you could use for clustering. Some could argue that this also led to clustering solutions being more expensive. Microsoft's support statement for Failover Clustering is somewhat different now. The requirements are as follows:

- The hardware must have Windows Server 2008 R2 support.
- Your cluster must pass a validation test.

Figure 6.4 shows the Validation Warning screen where you are reminded of this requirement. You can validate your cluster now by selecting the Yes option. You can select the No option if you do not want support from Microsoft. We recommend that you should do the validation tests no matter how trivial the reason is for building the cluster. They may identify issues that could affect cluster functionality. You will be able to rerun this test as your cluster changes and matures.

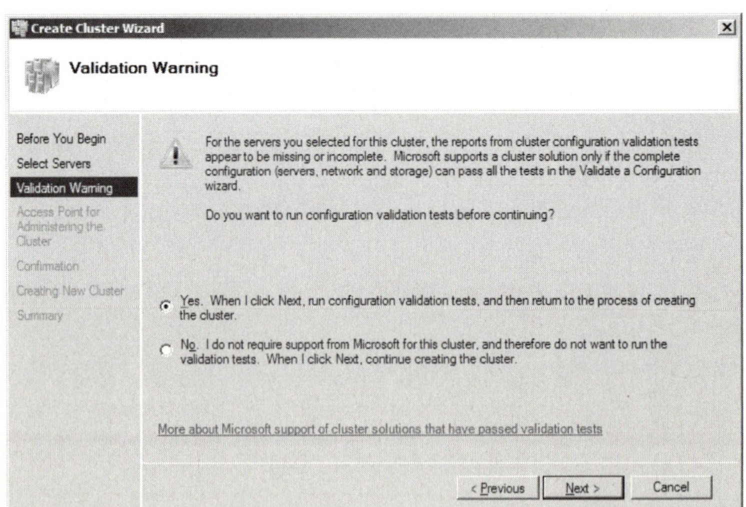

FIGURE 6.4 Validating the cluster warning

This spawns the Validate A Configuration Wizard for testing your cluster configuration. You can see in Figure 6.5 that you have a choice of the tests that will be run during the validation.

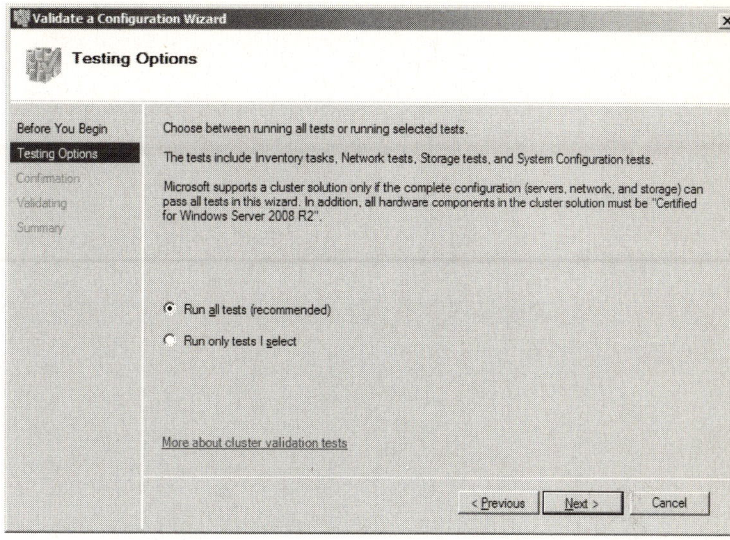

FIGURE 6.5
Cluster validation testing options

You can choose to run all tests. You would choose this option when building a new cluster or maybe when trying to identify the root cause of a problem in a malfunctioning cluster.

You can also choose to run only selected tests. This is the option you will normally use when you want to revalidate an existing cluster that is in production to minimize impact to business systems.

The following Confirmation screen gives you an option to review the tests and make any changes before committing to the cluster validation process. The Validating screen will then appear and show you the overall progress of the cluster validation tests. This will test each of the nodes in the intended cluster, including the networking and the storage solution. The time required for the entire validation will depend on how big the cluster is and how complex your storage is (each shared disk is individually tested).

The Summary screen, shown in Figure 6.6, will present the results of the validation tests. You can scroll through the results of the validation test. The overall result is displayed at the bottom and is an aggregate of the individual test results.

Individual results may be as follows:

Success The tested component is suitable for failover clustering.

Warning The item has an issue, but this does not prevent the cluster from being supported by Microsoft.

Failed The item in question prevents the cluster from being supported by Microsoft.

You can click the View Report button to open a very detailed report in your browser. The report is automatically saved in `C:\Windows\Cluster\Reports` for later reference. It is possible that Microsoft's support services might request a copy of a report if Microsoft is assisting you with a clustering issue.

You are returned to the Create Cluster Wizard to complete the creation of the new cluster. The Access Point For Administering The Cluster screen (Figure 6.7) is where you will configure the identity and network presence of the cluster. Enter the name of the cluster in the Cluster

Name field. This will be used to create an Active Directory object. You will also enter the IP address for the cluster in this screen. These identities can be used to manage the cluster using the Failover Cluster Manager.

FIGURE 6.6
Failover cluster validation summary

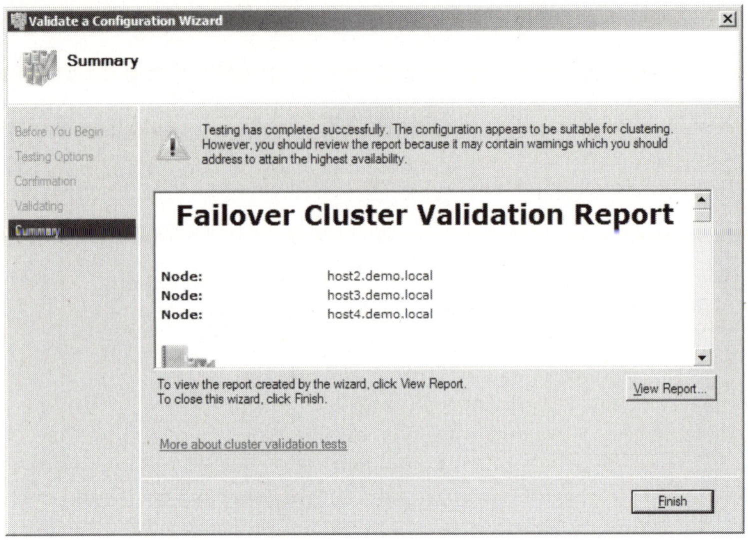

FIGURE 6.7
Access point for administering the cluster

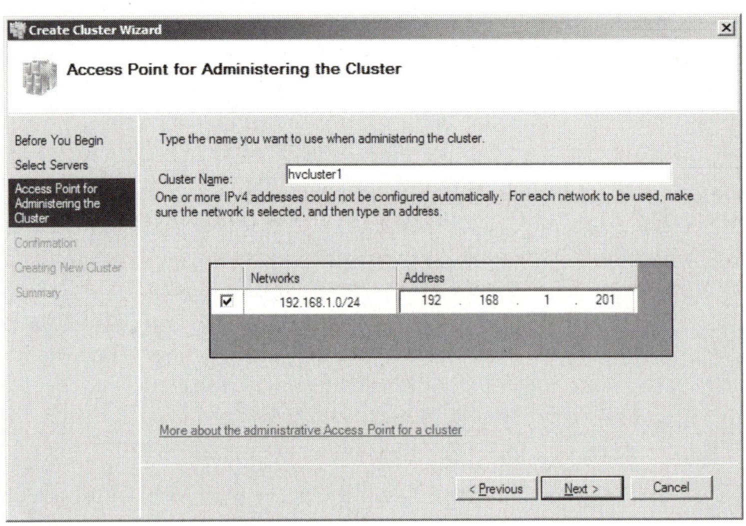

A Confirmation screen will allow you to review the details before committing to the creation of the new cluster. The cluster will be configured if you are OK with the details and continue with the wizard. After a few minutes, the configuration will be completed. You will be able to return to the Failover Cluster Manager and see your new Hyper-V cluster, as shown in Figure 6.8.

FIGURE 6.8
A new Hyper-V cluster

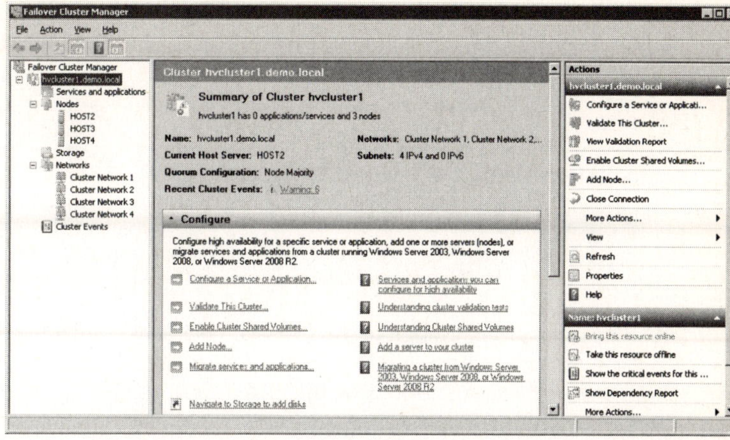

From now on, you should use the Failover Clustering Manager instead of the Hyper-V Manager to do all Hyper-V administration for your clustered Hyper-V host servers. Of course, if you have Virtual Machine Manager 2008 R2, then it should be your preferred administration tool. This is because the Hyper-V Manager does not make Failover Clustering aware of virtual machine configuration changes that you might make. Those changes would disappear after migrating a virtual machine to another host. You can use the Refresh Virtual Machine Configuration action in Failover Clustering to avoid this if you do use the Hyper-V Manager.

You can configure the cluster quorum model by right-clicking the cluster and selecting More Actions ➢ Configure Cluster Quorum Settings. You will need to add a disk to the cluster if you need to implement Node and Disk Majority.

CONTROLLING THE LIVE MIGRATION NETWORK

You can manually control which network is used for Live Migration. For example, you might have purchased 10 Gb physical network adapters just for the Live Migration network. Browse to a virtual machine resource in the Failover Clustering Manager. Right-click it, select Properties, and go into the Network For Live Migration tab. You can order the networks according to your preference. You can also prevent certain networks from being used for Live Migration by clearing the check box associated with them.

CREATING A CLUSTER SHARED VOLUME (CSV)

The steps of creating a CSV are as follows:

Step 1: Add Storage Prepare a LUN on your shared storage, and present it to every Hyper-V host server in the cluster. You should pick a label, such as CSV1, for the LUN in your storage management utility.

Step 2: Format the Disk Launch Disk Management on one of the Hyper-V host servers (by logging in locally or by connecting to the server using Computer Management). Bring the disk online using GPT as the partitioning system. (GPT stands for GUID Partition Table.) This will allow your LUN to grow beyond 2 TB, unlike MBR. Format the disk using the same label for the NTFS volume that you used for the LUN in the storage management system, such as CSV1. Do not assign a drive letter to the disk.

ADD ONE DISK AT A TIME TO THE CLUSTER

It can be very confusing if you try to add many disks at a time to a cluster. Go through the entire process, end to end, with each disk that you want to add.

Step 3: Add the Storage to the Cluster Navigate into Storage in the Failover Cluster Manager, and select Add Storage from the Actions pane. Select and add the new disk that you have just prepared. Open the properties of the disk, and rename it to match the label you have used in the storage management system and to label the NTFS volume, such as CSV1.

Step 4: Enable Cluster Shared Volume in the Cluster The operation to enable CSV in the cluster will only ever have to be done once for the cluster. You can enable CSV by right-clicking the cluster and selecting Enable Cluster Shared Volumes. The subsequent dialog box must be read and taken very seriously. You are warned by Microsoft that CSV functionality and CSV volumes are only ever to be used for Hyper-V. It is a very specialized system. You should not use CSV volumes for clustering other products. You must agree to the terms of the dialog box, shown in Figure 6.9, if you want to enable CSV in your cluster.

FIGURE 6.9
The terms for enabling CSV

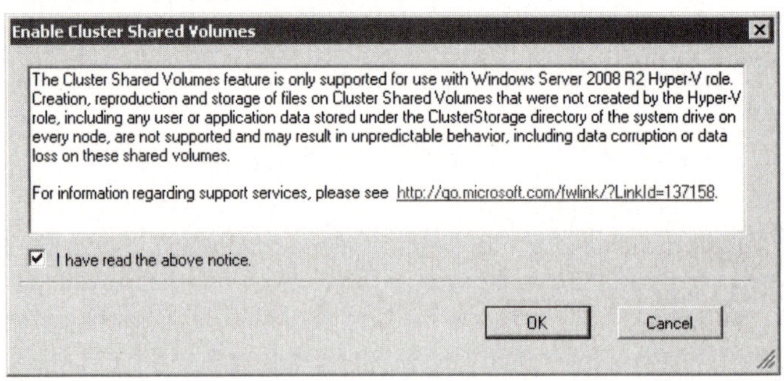

The Failover Clustering Manager will refresh, and a Cluster Shared Volumes will appear in the navigation tree. You can see this in Figure 6.10.

Step 5: Create a CSV You can click the Add Storage action in Cluster Shared Volumes to create a CSV from an existing clustered disk. Make sure the CSV is labeled consistently, such as CSV1.

The CSV will appear on every Hyper-V host server in the cluster as a folder contained within `C:\ClusterStorage`.

You should familiarize yourself with the architecture of CSV to understand how it works. You should pay special attention to Redirected I/O, which is discussed in Chapter 2. Chapter 12 will discuss how `C:\ClusterStorage`, and your CSVs should not be scanned by antivirus, no matter what any security expert might say. Chapter 10 will discuss how the backup can potentially impact CSV by initiating Redirected I/O.

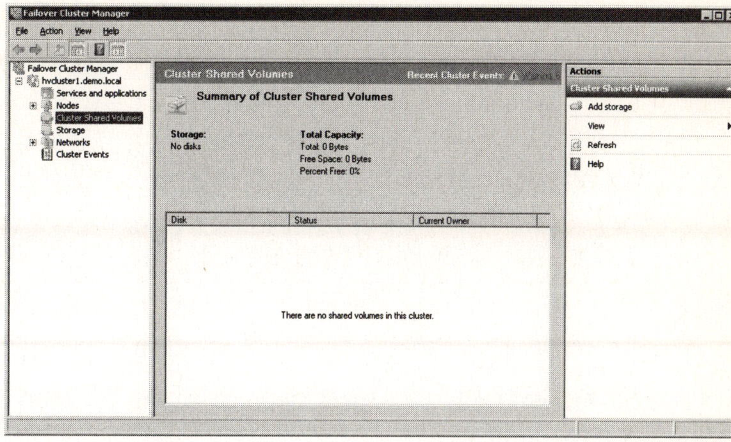

FIGURE 6.10
CSV is enabled in the cluster.

You can use the Failover Clustering Manager to control which Hyper-V host server in the cluster holds the CSV coordinator role. This is the server that will provide the route to the storage when Redirected I/O is initiated. This role will automatically failover during a host failure.

You can also use the Failover Clustering Manager to view how much free space is available in a single CSV for virtual machines. You can automate this operation using some PowerShell scripting. This is discussed on the Microsoft Failover Clustering and Network Load Balancing Team Blog here:

```
http://blogs.msdn.com/b/clustering/archive/2010/06/19/10027366.aspx
```

CONTROLLING THE CSV NETWORK

CSV will automatically prefer a private (nonrouted) network with the lowest metric. The metrics for private networks range from 1,000 to 10,000. The metrics for public (routed) networks start at 10,000.

You can alter the metrics of a host's networks to control this choice. This will be done using PowerShell. Start by loading the Failover Clustering module:

```
Import-Module FailoverClusters
```

Then identify the networks and their metrics:

```
Get-ClusterNetwork | fl*
```

The following example will set the metric of a network connection called CSV to be 1100.

```
( Get-ClusterNetwork "CSV" ).Metric = 1100
```

EXPANDING A CSV

The time will come when your CSV will not be big enough to meet demand. At this point, you have a choice:

Create a New CSV You should monitor the performance of your existing CSV. The demands of the VHDs stored on the CSV should not exceed the potential of the physical storage beneath the CSV. There will come a time when you will decide that you should create a new CSV to meet performance requirements.

Many of us dislike having too many eggs in one basket. You might decide to have more CSVs even if there are not any performance requirements to do so. This will allow you to spread your virtual machines across different storage solutions. For example, you might have a pair of load-balanced virtual machines, each of which is stored on a different CSV. This will allow an application to stay operational even if a CSV is lost in a disaster.

Increase the Size of the CSV The process of expanding a CSV is not much different from that of expanding any other volume.

You can increase the size of a CSV by doing the following:

- Ensure there is sufficient space left in the physical storage.
- Use the storage management to expand the CSV's LUN.
- Use `diskpart` or Disk Management on the CSV Coordinator to expand the NTFS volume.

CSV Engineering

If you sit back and think for a while, you might come up with many reasons to create more than just one CSV to make the most of the available physical storage. These may include the following:

Spreading the Risk As discussed earlier, you might place virtual machines from the same application onto different CSVs. This will limit the risk of a single failure bringing down all components of an application.

Disk Speed and Type A storage solution might consist of fast/expensive (such as SAS) and slow/economic/larger (SATA) disks. You might want to create a CSV that runs on faster and more expensive disks as well as a CSV that runs on slower, larger, and more economic disks. This will allow you to tailor the performance, cost, and size of your VHDs to each solution.

RAID Levels Some people will advise that all virtual machine storage should be RAID-10 at the physical level to provide the best performance. That is a rather simple perspective and does not consider the cost of this. RAID-10 gives just 50 percent of the potential storage. For example, four 1 TB drives in a RAID-10 configuration will provide just under 2 TB of storage.

You should probably create more than one CSV to match your RAID requirements. You could have a RAID-5 CSV and a RAID-10 CSV. The VHDs of your virtual machines could be placed onto a CSV with the appropriate underlying RAID level.

Other reasons to create more than one CSV might include selective storage replication, support or multiple backup/recovery policies, and storage ownership.

With a little bit of practice, you will find yourself being able to build a Hyper-V cluster in no time at all. The days of the clustering consultant naming their price for a five-day cluster project are well and truly over. The focus on building a cluster should be on the servers and storage architecture. And there is still plenty of work left for the Hyper-V and System Center consultant!

Constrained Delegation for ISO Sharing

You will find the need to provide virtual machines access to operating systems and software that normally is installed from a DVD or CD. You could insert a DVD into a host server and provide the virtual machine passthrough access to the drive in question. This assumes that you are physically near the host servers and that your software vendor even provides physical media.

You might be working from an office with a remote datacenter, and your software vendor, such as Microsoft, might not provide any physical media.

There is a good chance that you already have a file share with a collection of ISO files that you have downloaded from various software suppliers. You can create one to contain all the media for your virtualization platform. You will also have a library in Virtual Machine Manager 2008 R2. It is a file share with some metadata in a SQL database.

There are two ways to mount an ISO file in a virtual machine. The first method requires that you copy the ISO file to the Hyper-V host server and mount the image. There are two problems with this technique. A 4 GB DVD ISO file will take some time to copy. The ISO will probably be copied to the virtual machine folder. You might find that these ISO files aren't always (or ever!) cleaned up afterward and are present all over your virtualization storage, needlessly wasting expensive disk space.

The second method is one that causes some confusion to those who are new to Hyper-V. You can configure a virtual machine to mount an ISO file that is located in a file share. You'll argue that this isn't possible if you try it without the necessary preparations. You need to configure constrained delegation in Active Directory. Failing to do so will cause the mounting of an ISO across the network to fail with an access rights error.

This process will need to be done for every Hyper-V host server in your infrastructure. Find the computer object for the Hyper-V host in Active Directory, and open its properties. Figure 6.11 shows the Delegation tab in the properties of the computer object. Select the option for Trust This Computer For Delegation To Specified Services Only. Select the Use Any Authentication Protocol suboption. Click the Add button to select the protocol that you want to use.

FIGURE 6.11
Configuring constrained delegation

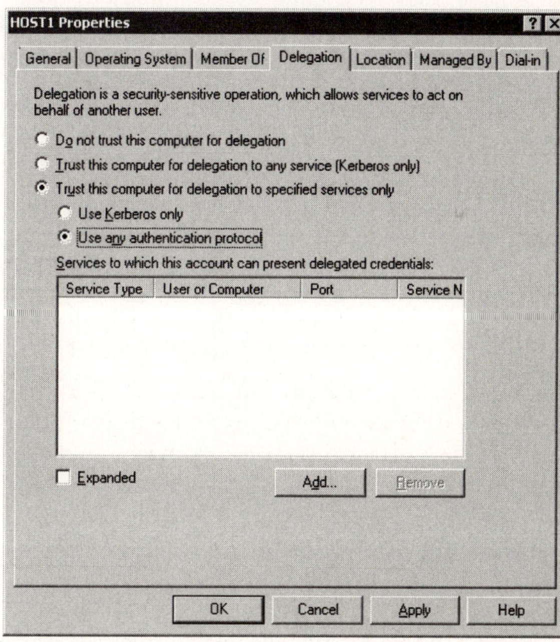

The Add Services dialog box will appear (Figure 6.12). Click the Users Or Computers button to select the file server with the ISO file share.

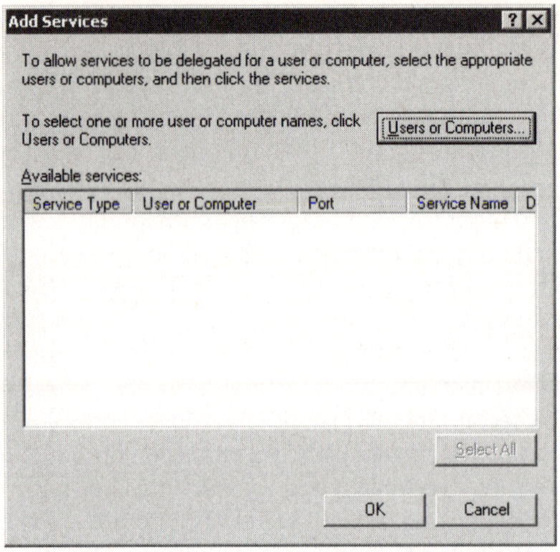

FIGURE 6.12
The Add Services dialog box

Enter the name of the file server that you want to add. This could be the name of the server with the VMM Library, or it could be a file server with the IT file share containing the ISO files. This returns you to the Add Services dialog box. You will see in Figure 6.13 that the list of available services is displayed. Select the CIFS protocol, and click OK. You can close the computer account properties dialog box or repeat the process for any other file servers.

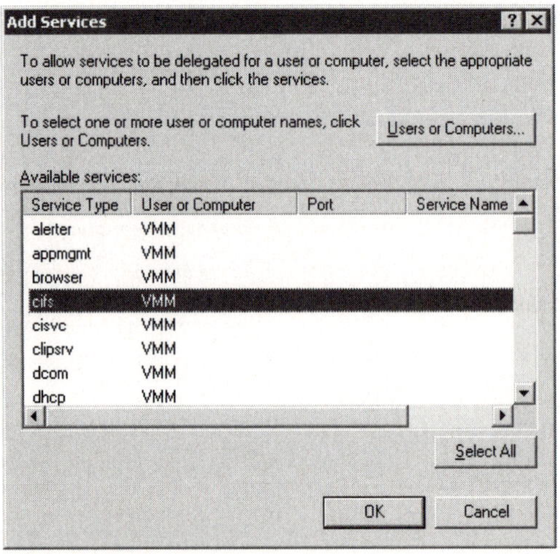

FIGURE 6.13
Selecting the CIFS protocol

You will now be able to configure virtual machines on this host server to mount ISO files from file shares over the network.

Managing Hyper-V

We will now cover some of the steps you will perform to configure your Hyper-V host servers and the day-to-day operations of managing virtual machines.

Hyper-V Management

You can use three possible tools to manage Hyper-V in your environment:

Failover Clustering Manager You will be using this tool for managing Hyper-V clusters. It obviously will be used to manage the cluster, the cluster storage, CSVs, and Live Migration. It can be used to manage Hyper-V virtual machines.

Virtual Machine Manager (VMM) 2008 R2 VMM is one of the Microsoft System Center products. It should be the primary solution for managing Hyper-V if it is installed.

Hyper-V Manager This console is added to the parent partition when you enable the Hyper-V role and allows you to manage the virtual machines on the host server.

System Center Essentials (SCE 2010)

Medium-sized businesses may choose to use SCE 2010 instead of VMM 2008 R2. You can learn more about this in Chapter 11, "The Small and Medium Business."

You can launch the Hyper-V Manager console from Administrative Tools on the Start menu. This launches the console shown in Figure 6.14. The current host server is usually shown. You can connect to other Hyper-V host servers using the console from the current server or from an installation of the console on your desktop (the previously mentioned Remote Administration Tools for Windows 7) by navigating to Hyper-V Manager and clicking the Connect To Server action in the right pane. This will allow many Hyper-V host servers to be visible and controllable using the Hyper-V Manager.

FIGURE 6.14
Connecting to a Hyper-V host server

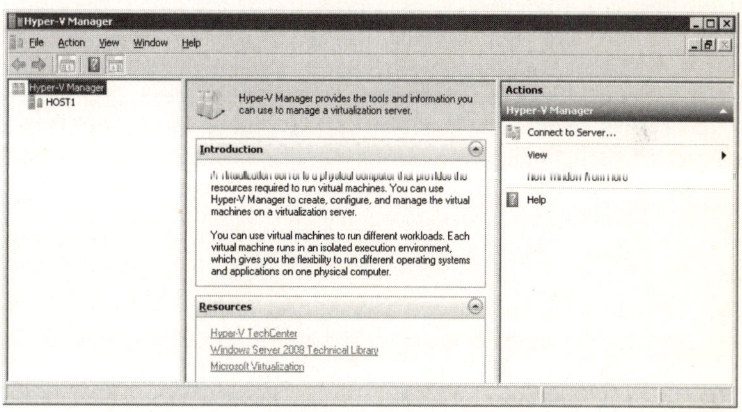

You can select a Hyper-V host server to manage it, as shown in Figure 6.15. The virtual machines that are placed on this host are presented in the top-middle pane, called Virtual Machines. Here you can see the name, state, CPU usage, memory, and uptime of each virtual machine.

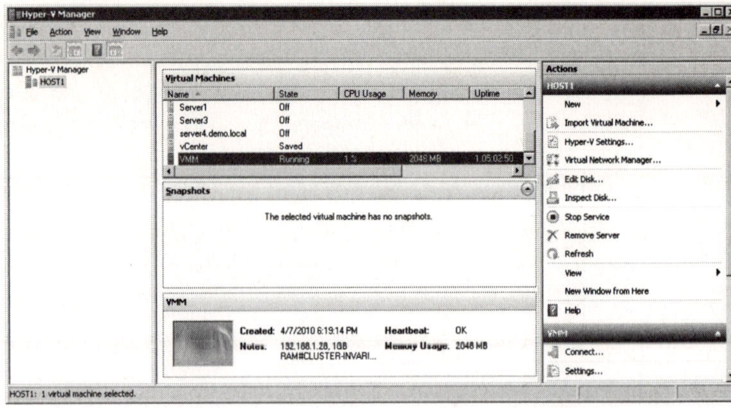

FIGURE 6.15
Managing a Hyper-V host server

Context-sensitive actions will appear in the Actions pane in the right pane of the Hyper-V Manager.

The middle pane of the window presents any snapshots that have been created for the selected virtual machine.

The bottom-middle pane of the window presents you with a thumbnail screenshot of the currently selected virtual machine's console window and some information about it.

Hyper-V Settings

You can configure a number of server settings for a Hyper-V host server. You can open the dialog box for doing this by right-clicking the server and selecting Hyper-V Settings. That will open the dialog box shown in Figure 6.16.

Virtual Hard Disks allows you to configure the default location for creating new virtual hard disks on this Hyper-V host server.

You can view the current location for storing Hyper-V symbolic links to virtual machine files in Virtual Machines. The default location is `C:\ProgramData\Microsoft\Windows\Hyper-V`.

You will be able to connect to virtual machines using a console window. You can control how special keyboard key sequences are captured:

- Use on physical computer
- Use on the virtual machine
- Use on the virtual machine only when running full-screen

The mouse pointer will be captured (and retained) by a console window if the integration components are not installed in the virtual machine. You can change the default key sequence (Control+Alt+Left Arrow) in Mouse Release Key.

A console connection to a virtual machine will use your current credentials to authorize your access. You can enable a prompt for alternative credentials in User Credentials by clearing the Use Default Credentials Automatically check box. Delete Saved Credentials will allow you to remove any saved details.

Reset Check Boxes will return any notification windows back to their default settings if you have chosen not to see them again.

FIGURE 6.16
Hyper-V Settings dialog box

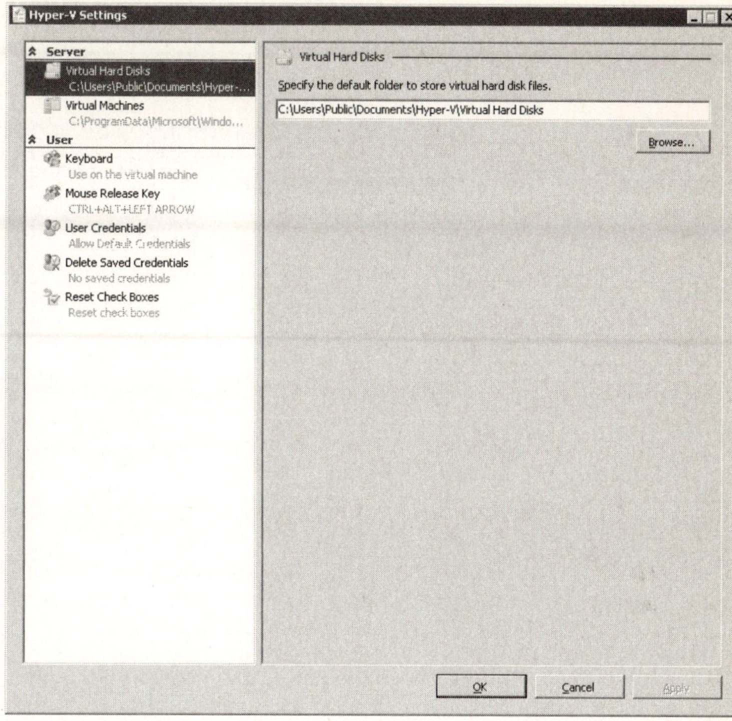

Virtual Network Manager

Chapter 2 looked at each of the different kinds of virtual network that you can have in Hyper-V:

- External
- Internal
- Private

One of your first steps to bring your Hyper-V host servers into an operational state (initially for testing) will be to configure some virtual networks.

VIRTUAL NETWORKS AND VMM

If you are using VMM, then you should use it rather than the Hyper-V Virtual Network Manager console to configure your virtual networking. It provides a centralized console for managing settings across many servers at once. The resulting changes will also be immediately visible to other users of VMM. Changes that are made directly via the Hyper-V Virtual Network Manager will not appear in VMM until the host server is refreshed by the VMM agent.

You will manage the networking in Hyper-V using the Virtual Network Manager. You can launch this from the Actions pane of the Hyper-V Manager console. This opens the window shown in Figure 6.17.

FIGURE 6.17
Hyper-V Network Manager

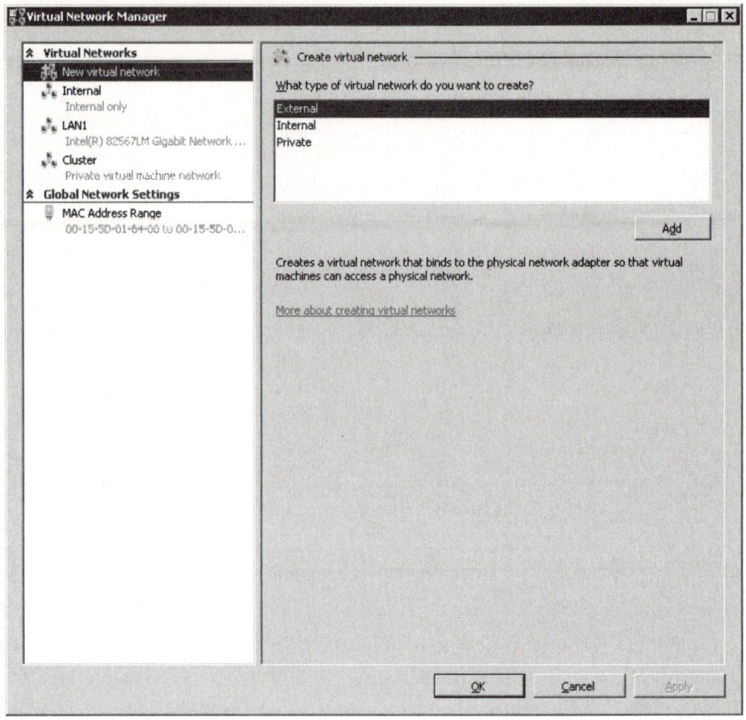

The top left shows the existing virtual networks that are configured on this host server. Note that these virtual networks exist on one host server only. You will have to create identical virtual networks on each host server in a Hyper-V cluster. You can select an existing virtual network to edit its properties.

You can select New Virtual Network in the top left, select a virtual network type from the listed options, and click Add to create a new virtual network on this Hyper-V host server.

The dialog box will change to show the New Virtual Network screen (Figure 6.18). Set the name to a descriptive value. The name is what will be displayed in the various tools that you will use when connecting virtual machines to the network.

You can choose from one of the three virtual network types. An external network will require a one-to-one binding to a physical network adapter in the Hyper-V host server. You cannot bind a physical network adapter to a second virtual network. The drop-down list box allows you to select a physical network adapter. Unfortunately, this dialog box lists physical network adapters that are already bound to external virtual networks. A handy tip is to rename the physical network adapters in the parent partition (Network Connections) to match the Hyper-V virtual networks that they will bind with.

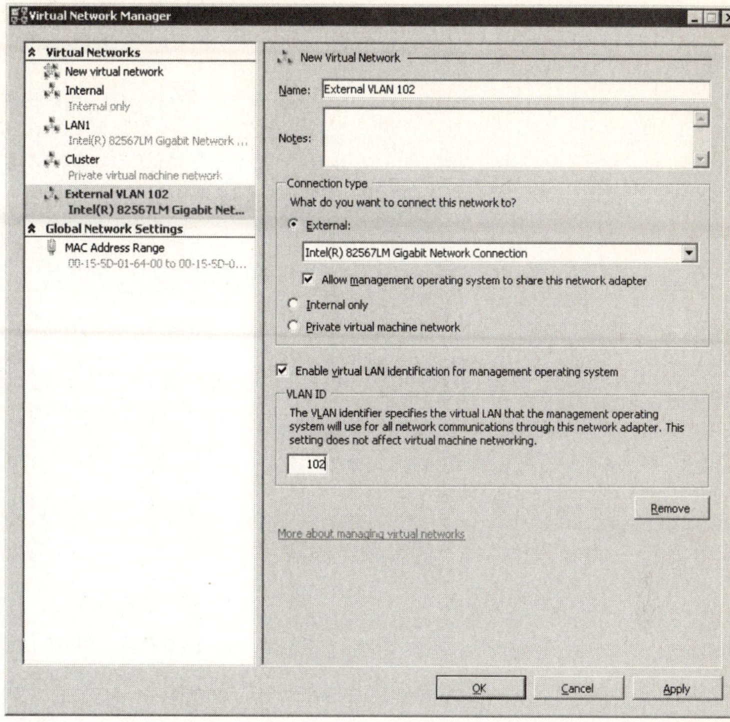

FIGURE 6.18
Creating a new Hyper-V virtual network

There is a check box called Allow Management Operating System To Share This Network Adapter. This option allows the parent partition to share a physical network adapter with a Hyper-V virtual network. This would mean that the parent partition and virtual machines would share a physical network connection. This is not recommended; that's why we recommend at least two physical network adapters in a Hyper-V host server. This option should be used only in lab servers with limited hardware options and budget.

We mentioned in Chapter 2 that you could bind a Hyper-V virtual network to a single VLAN. This is where you can enable this option and specify the VLAN ID (or tag). You can select the Enable Virtual LAN Identification For Management Operating System box and enter the ID of the VLAN. Any virtual machine connected to this Hyper-V virtual network would then be connected to that VLAN.

You can click OK to create the Hyper-V virtual network. Be aware that changing the properties of a virtual network that is shared with the parent partition may cause a brief network outage for the parent partition.

Virtual Machine virtual network adapters will get a dynamic MAC address by default. Figure 6.19 shows the dynamic MAC address range for this Hyper-V host server.

You need to configure the network protocol bindings in the parent partition of any network adapter that is linked to an external virtual network. These adapters should be used only for the Hyper-V virtual networking. This requires unbinding everything except for the Microsoft Virtual Network Switch Protocol, as shown in Figure 6.20.

FIGURE 6.19
MAC address range

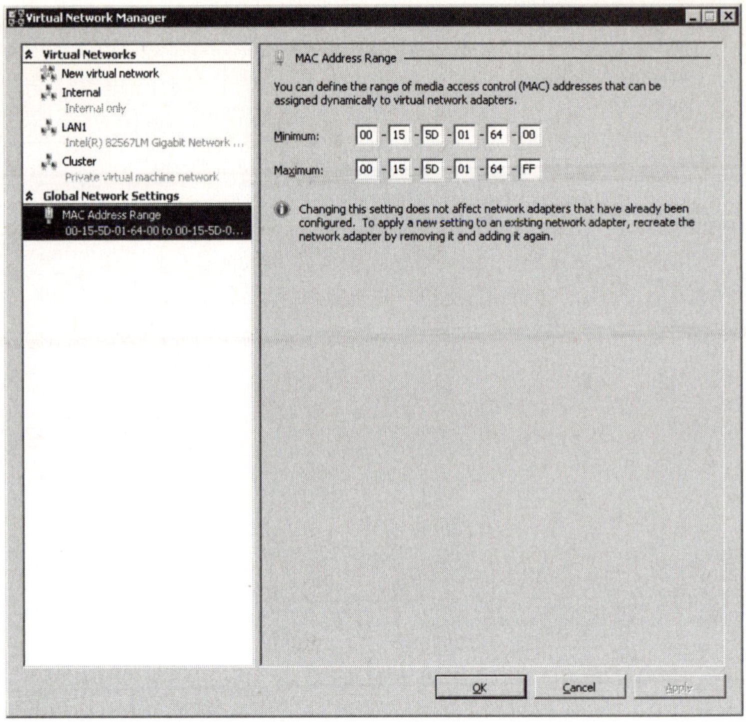

FIGURE 6.20
Optimizing the virtual network physical adapter

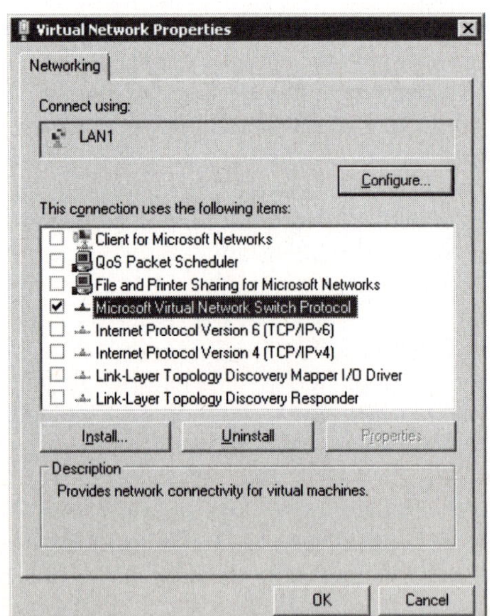

This is being done for a few reasons:

Control This network adapter can end up picking up an IP address (DHCP) on the parent partition network in a flat network. This can cause confusion by giving the parent partition two IP addresses on two physical network adapters. For example, you might need to manage a Hyper-V host that is experiencing virtual machine network congestion. If your Hyper-V virtual network adapter has an IP address on the management network, then you might find that the DNS name will randomly resolve to that address. You would be unable to log into the parent partition in this scenario. You should make every effort to isolate the parent partition for management reasons.

Security The network adapter that is bound to a Hyper-V virtual network can participate in a virtual network if it has the required networking protocols bound to it. For example, the network adapter could pick up a DHCP address from a DHCP server that can communicate on its Hyper-V virtual network. This would be a security issue if the networking protocols were enabled.

Performance Optimization Removing all unnecessary networking protocols from the Hyper-V virtual network adapter will improve the performance it can offer to the connected virtual machines.

Virtual Machine Management

This is what you have been waiting for: now you finally get to create a virtual machine and put Hyper-V to work!

CREATE A VIRTUAL MACHINE

You will click New in the Actions pane and select Virtual Machine. This will open the New Virtual Machine Wizard (Figure 6.21). You should name the virtual machine as it will appear in the Hyper-V Manager. You might have many virtual machines so it might not be a bad idea to use the planned fully qualified domain name of the operating system that will be installed in the virtual machine. This will make the virtual machine easy to identify.

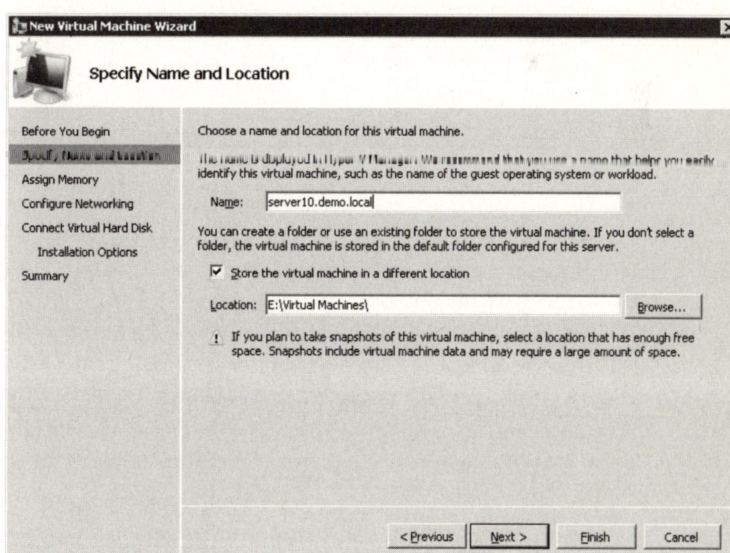

FIGURE 6.21
New Virtual Machine Wizard

You will probably not use the default storage location for your virtual machine, which is on the `C:` drive. Instead, you will probably use another volume (on a nonclustered host) or on a CSV (on a clustered host).

The Assign Memory screen (Figure 6.22) allows you to specify the amount of memory (in megabytes) to assign to the virtual machine.

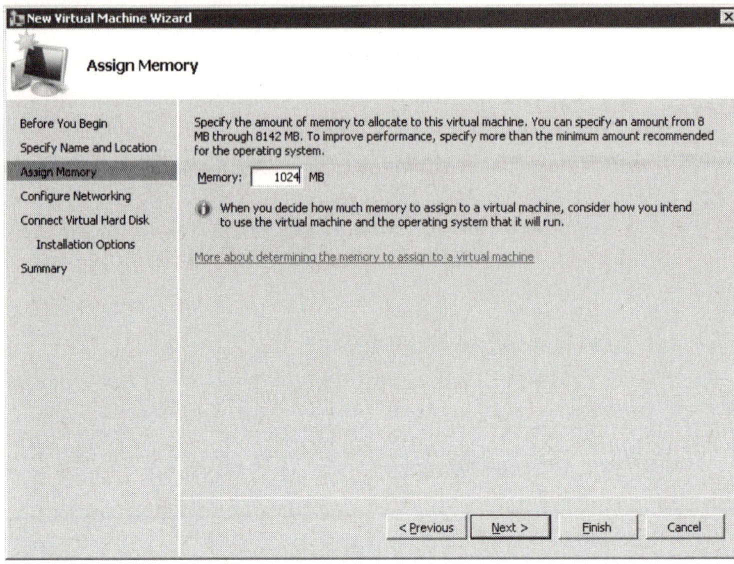

FIGURE 6.22
Assigning memory to the virtual machine

> **DYNAMIC MEMORY**
>
> Service Pack 1 for Windows Server 2008 R2 adds a new feature to virtual machine memory assignment called Dynamic Memory. Service Pack 1 was a beta release at the time of writing this book. The screenshots in this part of the chapter are for the pre–Service Pack 1 release. We will discuss Dynamic Memory later in this chapter.

The virtual machine will have one virtual network adapter by default. You can specify which Hyper-V virtual network that the virtual network adapter will be connected to on the Configure Networking screen, shown in Figure 6.23.

A virtual machine will normally require some sort of hard disk storage. The Connect Virtual Hard Disk screen, shown in Figure 6.24, gives you a number of options to create a boot disk for the virtual machine. The boot disk will be a dynamic VHD.

Create a Virtual Hard Disk This option will create a VHD as part of the virtual machine creation. You can name the VHD and specify a storage location for it. The storage location is usually the same folder as the virtual machine folder. This option allows you to specify the size of the VHD.

Use an Existing Virtual Hard Disk This option allows you to connect the virtual machine to a previously existing VHD file.

FIGURE 6.23
Configuring networking

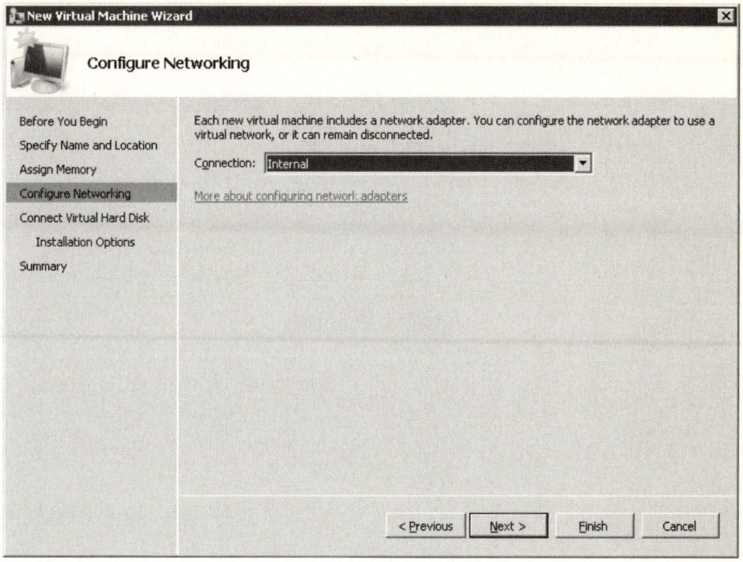

FIGURE 6.24
Connecting a virtual hard disk

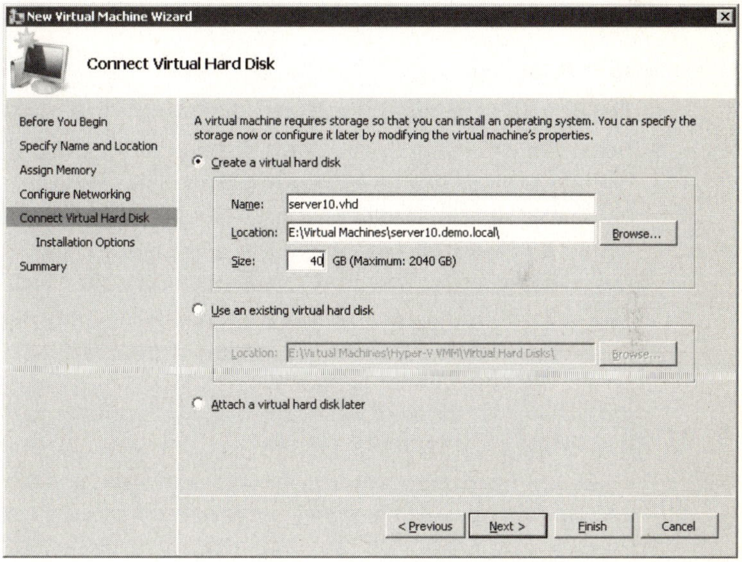

Attach a Virtual Hard Disk Later You can choose this option to not create a VHD now and to provision storage for the virtual machine at a later point.

This is the option you will normally use. This is because we normally do not recommend usage of dynamic VHDs in a production environment. Fixed-size VHDs offer better performance and require less maintenance. Passthrough disks offer the ultimate in performance and scalability, but with the loss of VHD features.

Figure 6.25 shows the Installation Options screen. This allows you to prepare the new virtual machine for the installation of an operating system.

FIGURE 6.25
Installation options

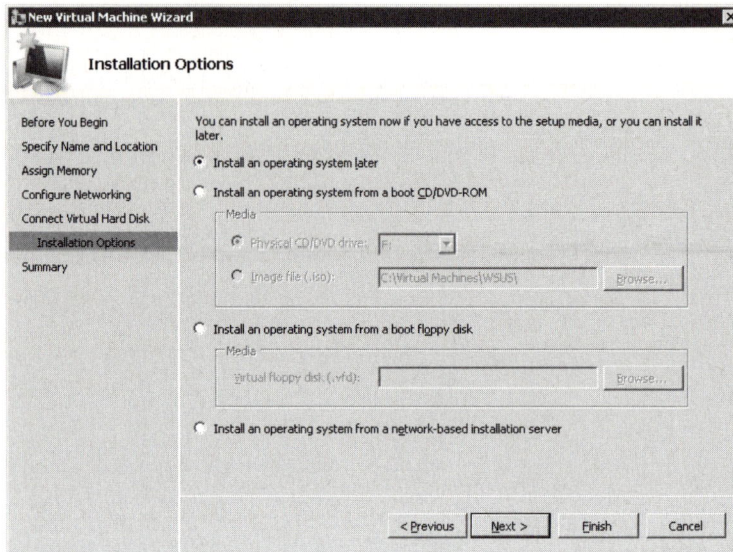

You have four options:

Install An Operating System Later No changes will be made to the virtual machine.

Install An Operating System From A Boot CD/DVD-ROM You can configure the virtual machine to mount the physical optical drive in the Hyper-V host server or to mount an ISO file. You can install an operating system from either of these media types.

Install An Operating System From A Boot Floppy Disk Virtual machines will have a virtual floppy drive. This drive can mount a `.VFD` file, which simulates a floppy disk.

Install An Operating System From A Network-Based Installation Server This is the option you will use if you want to boot the virtual machine using PXE to access an operating system deployment solution such as WDS, MDT, or Configuration Manager. This requires that the virtual machine has a legacy network adapter that is connected to an external network with access to the appropriate services for the operating system deployment solution.

This wizard will create the virtual machine with a synthetic network adapter. You will have to edit the properties of this virtual machine to add a legacy network adapter to use this option.

You can complete the wizard, and the virtual machine will be created on the Hyper-V host server. You might be wondering about many of the virtual machine design options you read about in Chapter 2. The wizard did not ask you for very much information and really did not give you very many options.

EDITING A VIRTUAL MACHINE'S PROPERTIES

You will need to edit a virtual machine to take advantage of all the design options available to you. For example, do you want to use a legacy network adapter to allow installation of an operating system over the network? Do you want to use fixed-size VHDs or passthrough disks? Do you want more than one disk in your virtual machine? You will now see how to edit a virtual machine to configure a virtual machine to meet your exact requirements.

You can open the properties of a virtual machine by right-clicking it and selecting Settings from the menu. This will open the Settings window shown in Figure 6.26.

FIGURE 6.26
Virtual machine settings or properties

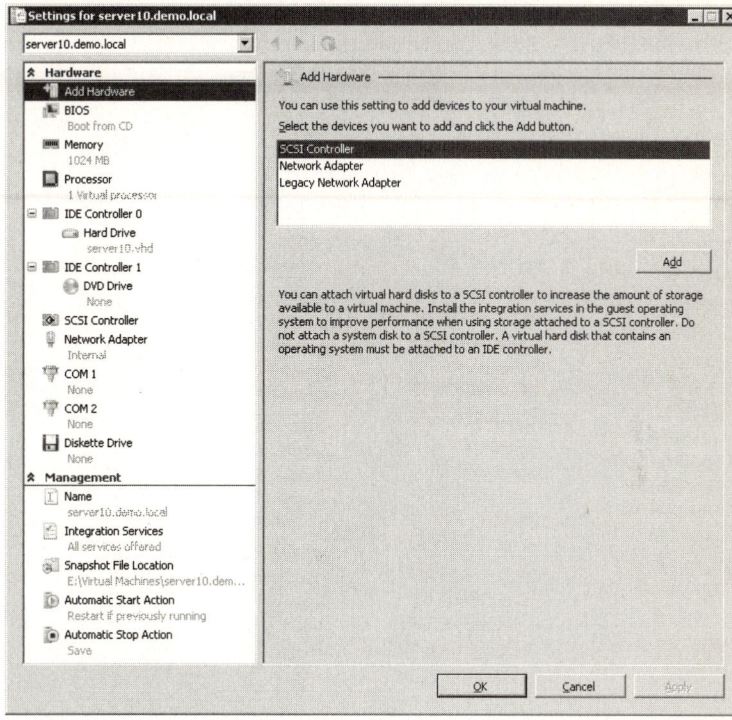

You will be able to navigate directly into any of the screens in this window. Your first option is to use the Add Hardware screen. There are three types of virtual device that you can add to a virtual machine:

SCSI Controller The virtual machine was created with a default SCSI controller. You can add up to four SCSI controllers to a virtual machine.

Network Adapter This is the synthetic network adapter. It will be possible to use this device in the virtual machine only if the guest operating system includes the Hyper-V integration components. It is recommended that you try to use this as your standard type of network adapter because it offers the best possible performance.

Legacy Network Adapter This is the emulated network adapter. You should restrict your usage of the legacy network adapter because it has a performance overhead. You will use this type of network adapter when you need to boot a virtual machine from the network (for operating system installation solutions such as WDS) or when the virtual machine's guest operating system does not have the integration components installed.

Be aware that you can only add or remove devices to or from a virtual machine when it is powered down. The only exception to this is that you can add/remove disks to the SCSI controller while the virtual machine is booted up. The storage will be added/removed using Plug and Play.

A Hyper-V virtual machine doesn't really have a BIOS that you can boot into and configure. You can control a few settings that would normally be controlled in the BIOS of a computer in the BIOS screen (Figure 6.27).

FIGURE 6.27
Configuring the virtual machine BIOS

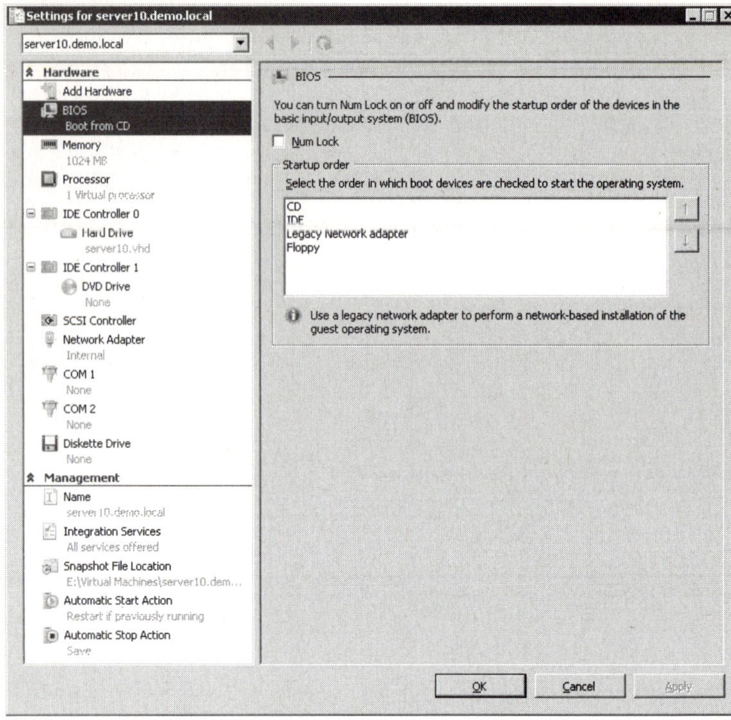

The Num Lock check box allows you to configure whether Num Lock is enabled or not when the virtual machine boots up. You can also control the boot device order of the virtual machine. The default order is as follows:

- CD
- IDE
- Legacy Network Adapter (assuming there is one)
- Floppy

The Memory screen (pre–Service Pack 1) allows you to specify the static amount of memory that is assigned to the virtual machine. The virtual machine will be instantly assigned the entire amount of memory when it boots up. The virtual machine will not be able to boot up if the entirety of the memory is not available on the Hyper-V host server.

We will be returning to this screen later when we cover Dynamic Memory.

By default, a virtual machine is configured with one virtual CPU. This will often be insufficient for the needs of the virtual machine's workload. You can alter the CPU configuration of the virtual machine on the Processor screen, as illustrated in Figure 6.28, where you can see the default settings.

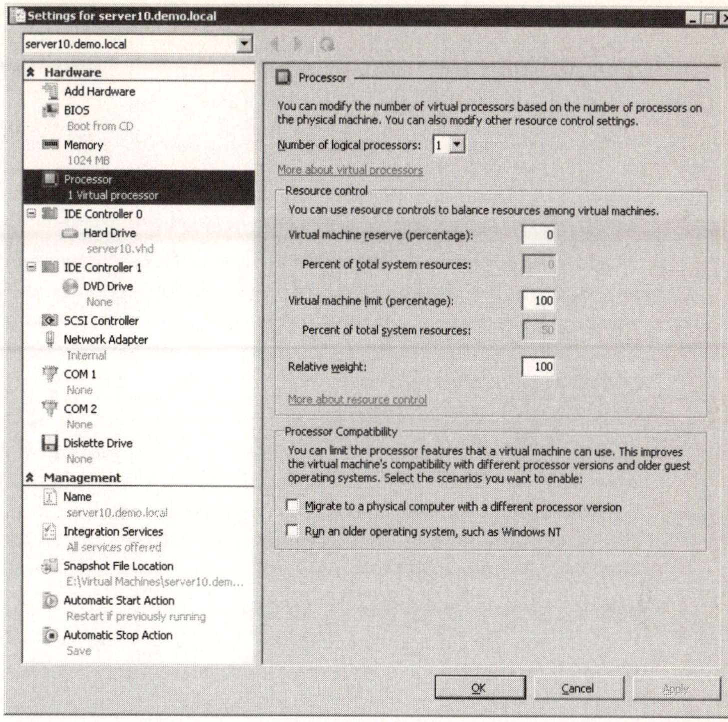

FIGURE 6.28
The virtual machine processor configuration

Number Of Logical Processors allows you to configure a virtual machine with between one and four virtual CPUs (often referred to as vCPUs). You must take into account the maximum number of virtual CPUs that is supported by the guest operating system.

The Resource Control settings allow you to control how physical processor resources are allocated to the virtual machine.

Virtual Machine Reserve This is the amount of physical processor capacity that will be reserved by the Hyper-V host server for this virtual machine and guarantee it a minimum level of performance. This setting should be treated with care. Be careful not to over commit a host server by reserving more than 100 percent of the processor capacity. This could be a very difficult setting to manage in a Hyper-V cluster where virtual machine placement could be very fluid.

For example, you might have two virtual CPUs that are guaranteed 40 percent of physical processor capacity on a host with 16 logical processors or cores. This does not guarantee the virtual machine 40 percent of those 16 cores. The Percent Of Total System Resources display will show how much of the total physical CPU resources in the host server will actually be committed to this virtual machine. Therefore, the actual percentage of physical processor power being reserved is based on the 40 percent of two physical cores in a server with 16 physical cores.

Virtual Machine Limit This is the maximum amount of physical processor power that the virtual CPUs in this virtual machine can consume. Each virtual CPU equates to one physical processor core. By default, a virtual machine with one virtual CPU is allowed to consume up to 100 percent of the capacity of a single physical core.

The Percent Of Total System Resources box shows how much of the total physical processor capacity this virtual machine will be capable of consuming. By default, a virtual machine with one virtual CPU (and a 100 percent virtual machine limit) can consume 25 percent of the total capacity of a quad-core Hyper-V host server.

Relative Weight This setting allows you to instruct Hyper-V how to prioritize virtual machines when there is contention for physical processor resources.

There are two settings that allow you to configure processor compatibility options:

Migrate To A Physical Computer With A Different Processor Version This check box (new to Windows Server 2008 R2 Hyper-V) allows you to enable Live Migration of this virtual machine between hosts in the cluster if they do not have identical processors. You may move the virtual machine as long as the processors are from the same manufacturer. For example, both the origin and destination hosts must be using Intel processors. Otherwise, they must both be using AMD processors.

Without this setting enabled, both hosts must have identical processors from the same manufacturer. This would be rather difficult for most cluster implementations because you will probably purchase host servers on an as-needed basis. For example, your first few hosts might be purchased 18 months before your last few hosts. Although they might have all AMD or all Intel processors, they will most likely be different versions.

There is a downside to this option. You might purchase a set of servers with new CPUs to take advantage of advanced CPU features such as Second Level Address Translation (see Chapter 2). Enabling this option will disable advanced features such as this because they won't be supported on hosts with older CPUs. You might need to consider starting a new Hyper-V cluster if you require a mixture of older hosts and newer hosts where the hardware features of the newer hosts are required.

Run An Older Operating System, Such As Windows NT Older operating systems will need the functionality of the virtual CPU to be pared back a little. You can do this by selecting the box for this setting.

Each virtual machine will have a pair of IDE controllers, IDE Controller 1 and IDE Controller 2. The boot disk is assigned to one of the two IDE Controller 1 channels. A virtual DVD device is assigned to one of the two available IDE Controller 2 channels. You can see the DVD screen in Figure 6.29.

You can change the IDE controller (Controller) and the channel (Location) that is being used by the virtual DVD drive. You have three options when it comes to supplying media to the device:

None This configures the drive to have no inserted or mounted media. You should try to use this setting when a virtual machine is not actively using any media. For example, you cannot use Live Migration on a virtual machine if it has mounted a network-based ISO file. Such a configuration will interfere with automated Live Migration attempts by any management systems, such as VMM responding to a performance or health issue.

Image File You can mount an ISO file using this option. The ISO file can be on the Hyper-V host server, in the same location as the virtual machine, or in a file share (if constrained delegation is configured).

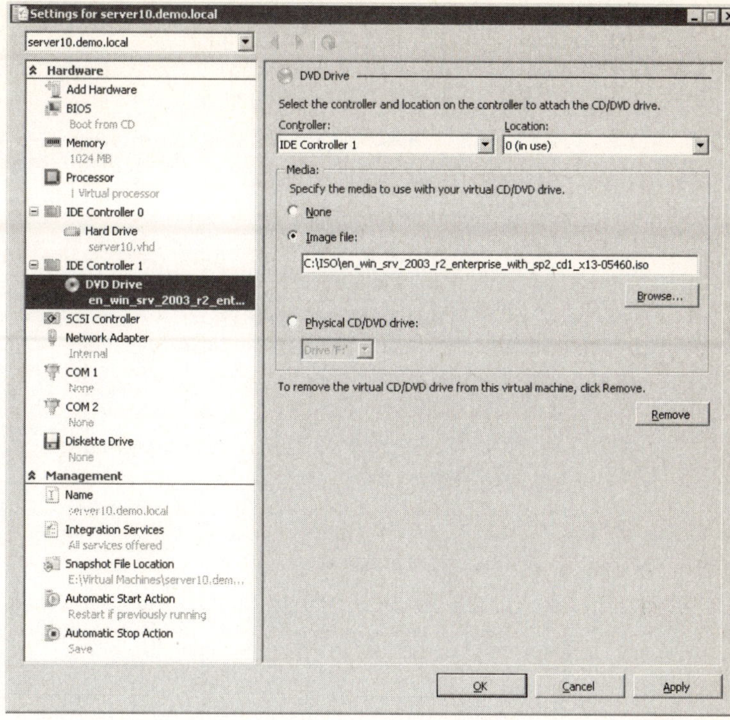

FIGURE 6.29
Configuring the virtual DVD

Physical CD/DVD Drive You can insert a CD or DVD into an optical drive in the Hyper-V host server and grant the virtual machine access to it using this option.

Hyper-V Manager will provide virtual machines with a single SCSI controller by default. This is quite useful because you can hot-add a disk to a running virtual machine, pending guest operating system support. For example, a Windows guest will use Plug and Play to detect the new drive and allow near instant access. You can see the SCSI Controller screen in Figure 6.30.

The process of adding an additional drive is pretty simple. You start off by clicking the Add button. A device is added (Figure 6.31) to the SCSI controller, pending your completion of the Add process.

You can switch this disk to a different controller using the Controller list box and to a different channel using the Location list box.

You can choose between a VHD and a passthrough disk at this point. You can either click New to create a new VHD or click Browse to attach an existing VHD to the virtual machine. A VHD can be attached to a single virtual machine at once.

You can create a passthrough disk using the Physical Hard Disk list box. Any offline disk that is inserted or associated with the Hyper-V host server can be used as a passthrough disk. You can connect to the virtual machine to prepare the disk as you normally would with any disk in a physical server.

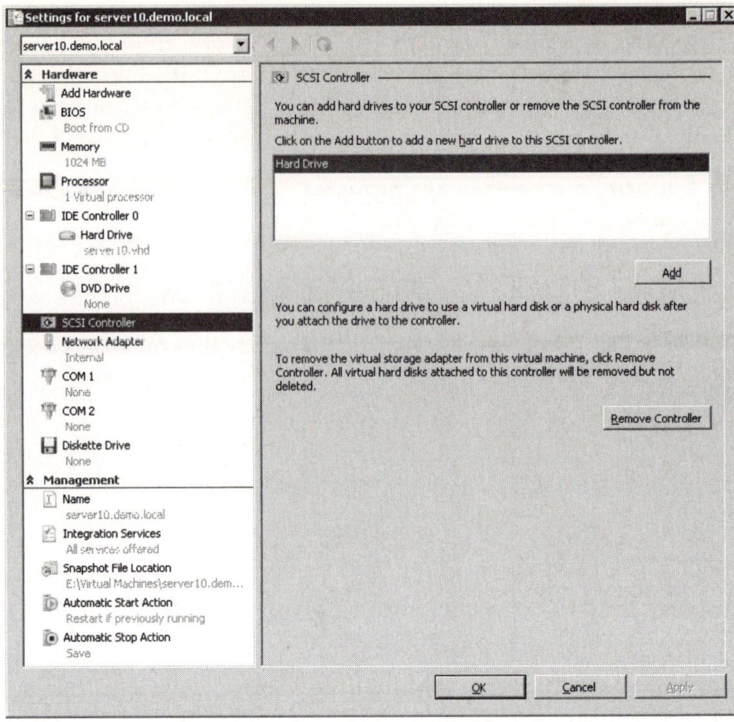

FIGURE 6.30 The SCSI Controller screen

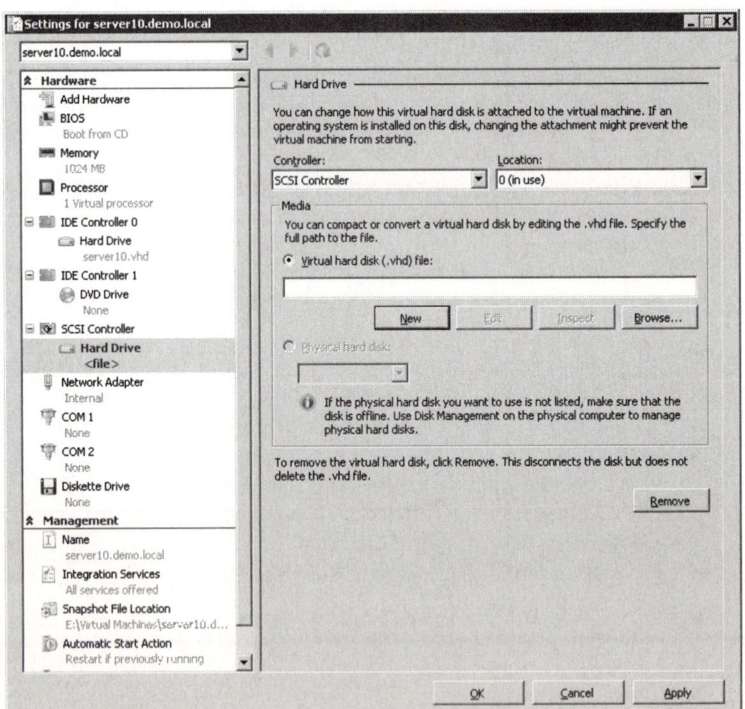

FIGURE 6.31 Adding a new SCSI disk

We have chosen to create a new VHD. You can see the choices in Figure 6.32. You will normally use a fixed-size VHD in a production environment. You can choose to use a dynamic VHD or even a differencing disk. We recommend that dynamic VHDs are not used in production. We strongly urge you to only use differencing disks in lab environments where performance is not a high priority and storage space is scarce.

FIGURE 6.32
Choosing a VHD type

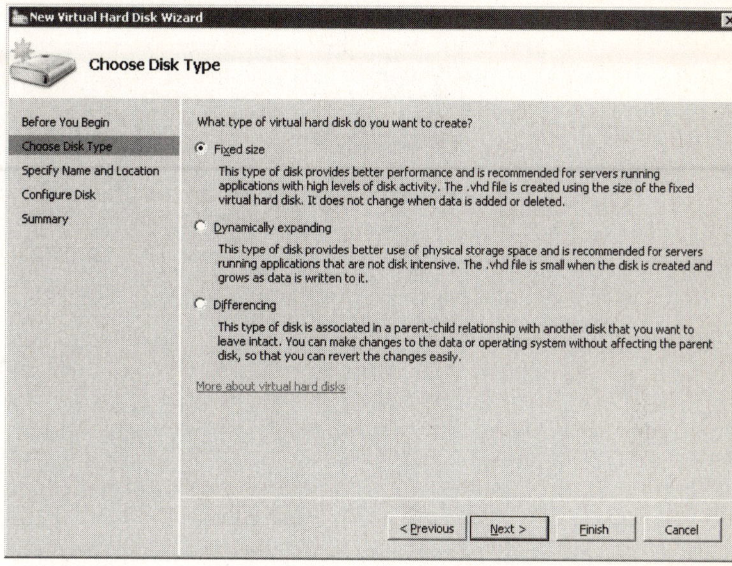

The Specify Name And Location screen (Figure 6.33) allows you to name the VHD file and specify the location of the file. The Hyper-V Manager will probably try to store the file on the C: drive of the parent partition. Be careful and make sure that you store it where you really want it to be, such as the folder where the virtual machine is stored.

FIGURE 6.33
Specifying the VHD name and location

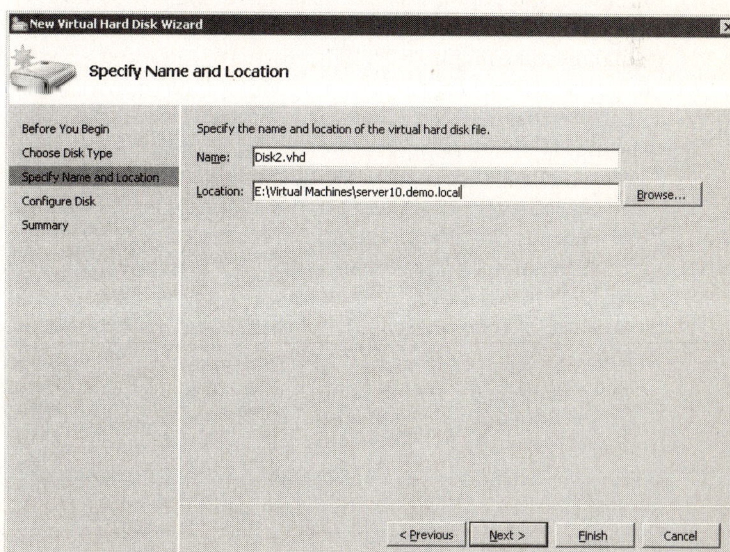

The following Configure Disk screen, in Figure 6.34, allows you to specify the physical characteristics of the VHD. You can specify the size of the VHD (in gigabytes) or instruct the Hyper-V manager to build a VHD from a currently attached physical disk volume.

FIGURE 6.34
Configuring the VHD

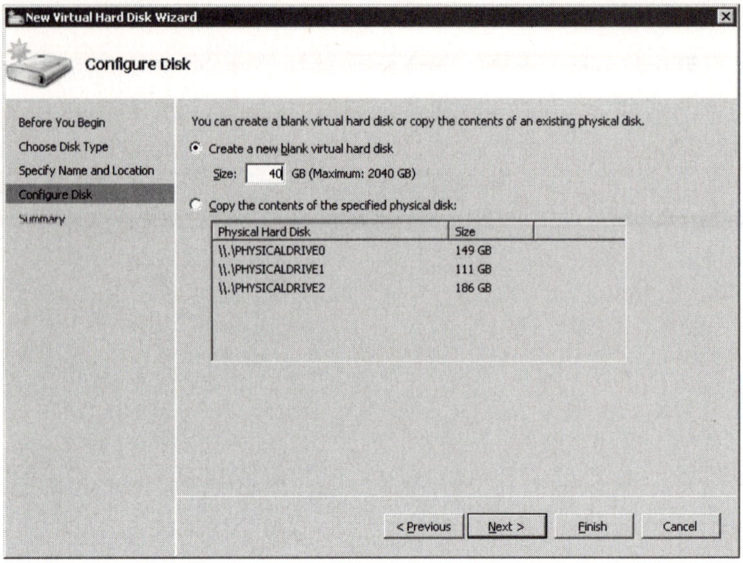

The VHD will be created when you click Finish. A differencing or dynamic VHD will be created in a few seconds. A fixed-size VHD will take some time to create. This is because Hyper-V will zero out the contents of the file to securely wipe the contents of the physical disk that were previously stored there. You can use some third-party tools to quickly provision fixed-size VHDs without this security step, but we recommend against using them on production storage systems because of the risk of data access being compromised.

The resulting VHD is added to the SCSI controller and is immediately available to use by the virtual machine (Figure 6.35). The process for attached a VHD to an IDE controller is the same except that the virtual machine must be powered down.

Each virtual network adapter in a virtual machine will have an associated Network Adapter or Legacy Network Adapter screen (Figure 6.36).

A virtual network adapter can be connected to a single Hyper-V virtual network. You can control the virtual network association by using the Network list box and selecting the desired Hyper-V virtual network.

The virtual network adapter will use a dynamic MAC address by default. This is normally OK for Windows guest operating systems. However, some network deployments and Linux distributions will require a static MAC address. You can force this by selecting Static on this screen.

You may also need to allow MAC address spoofing by selecting the Enable Spoofing Of MAC Addresses. An example of this is when you create a virtualized Network Load Balancing (NLB) cluster.

You can bind a virtual network adapter to a single VLAN. You can do this by selecting the Enable Virtual LAN Identification and by entering the VLAN ID or tag in the following text box.

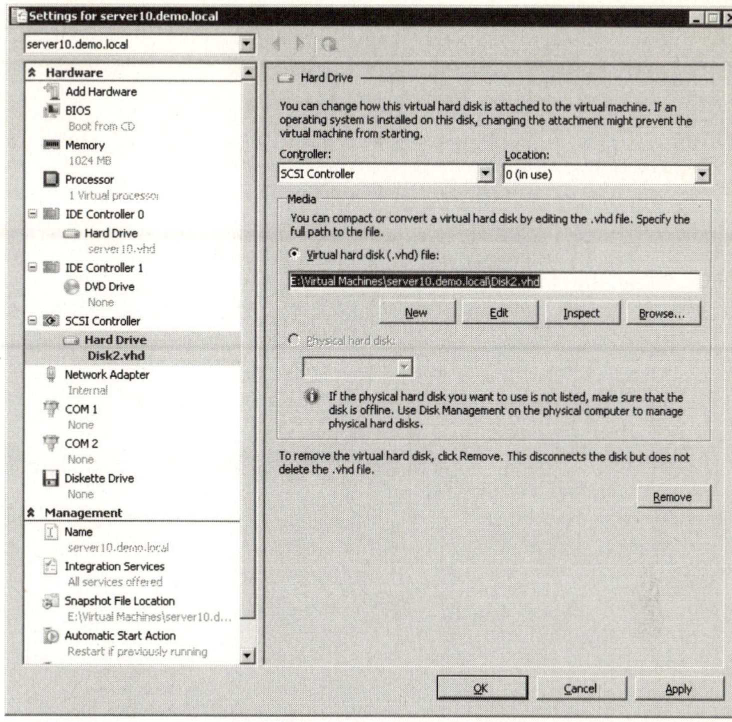

FIGURE 6.35
The new SCSI-attached VHD

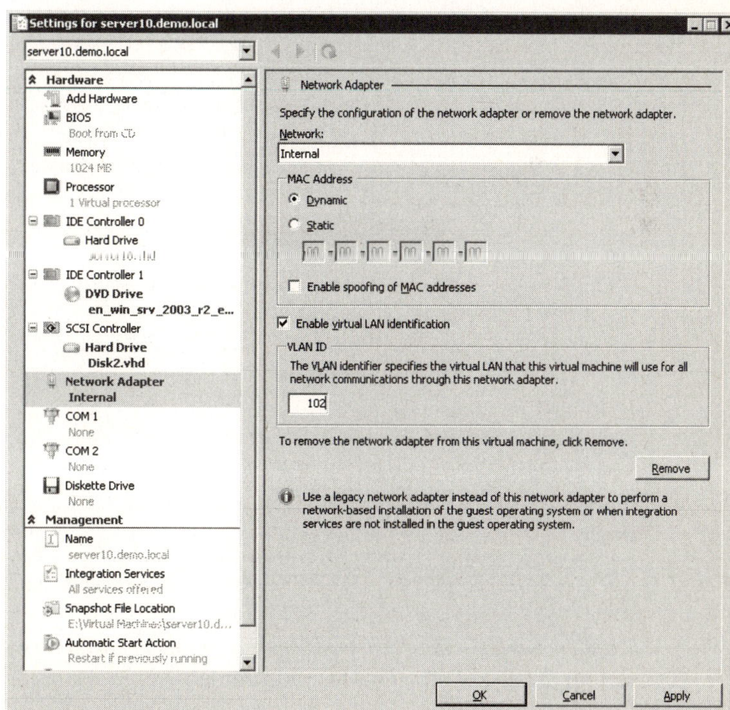

FIGURE 6.36
Configuring the virtual network adapter

This is probably the easiest to manage of the VLAN binding techniques that are available to you as Hyper-V engineers or administrators. You should read Chapter 2 for more information. You will also need to check with your physical network adapter manufacturer for NIC teaming support of this method; it is likely to be unsupported.

The COM1 and COM2 screens provide functionality for simulating COM connectivity. The Diskette Drive screen allows you to mount a `.vfd` file, which will simulate a floppy disk. For our younger readers: floppy disks existed in a time when USB memory sticks did not exist and dinosaurs roamed the land.

The Name screen allows you to control the name of the virtual machine and enter some notes to document its purpose or configuration.

The Integration Services screen (Figure 6.37) gives you the ability to control which of the integration services are provided by Hyper-V to the virtual machine. You might remember from Chapter 2 that integration services can be used to integrate Hyper-V with the virtual machine when the integration components are installed.

FIGURE 6.37
Controlling the integration services in a virtual machine

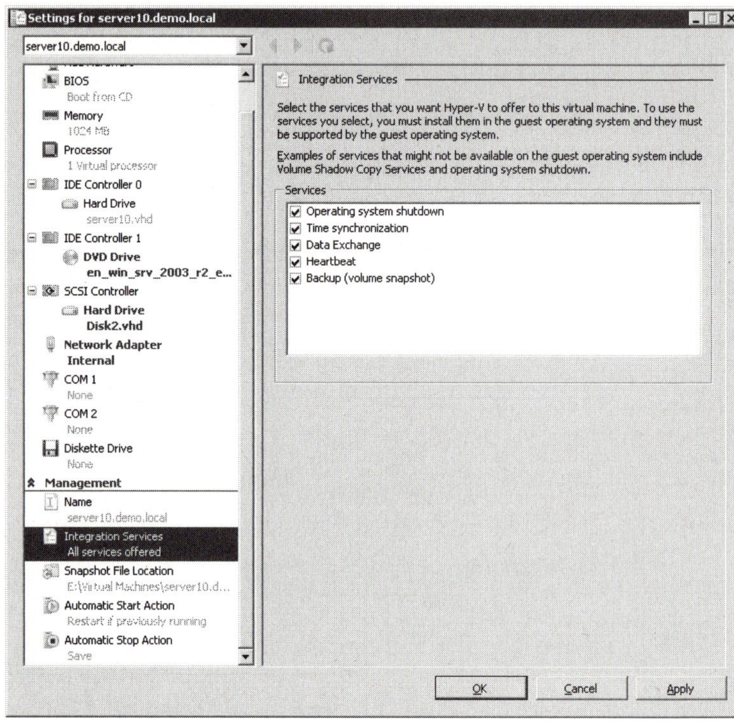

The integration services are as follows:

Operating System Shutdown Enabling this service provides the ability to cleanly shut down a virtual machine when the host server is being shut down.

Time Synchronization This service will synchronize the clock of the virtual machine with that of the host server. This is not always desirable. You'll learn more about that in Chapter 8.

Data Exchange This integration service will securely reveal some information about the virtual machine to the Hyper-V host server.

Heartbeat The Heartbeat integration service is used to keep the hypervisor aware of the running state of the virtual machine.

Backup (Volume Snapshot) The physical storage that the virtual machine is stored on is able to be backed up using Volume Shadow Copy Service (VSS). This option allows the backup of the virtual machine to be safe and consistent by using VSS inside of the virtual machine for its filesystem and VSS-enabled services, such as SQL Server or Exchange.

You can create snapshots of a virtual machine. This uses a form of differencing disk called an AVHD. This subject was discussed in Chapter 2. You can specify the location of the snapshots for this virtual machine on the Snapshot File Location screen (Figure 6.38). The virtual machine's folder is used by default.

FIGURE 6.38 Snapshot File Location screen

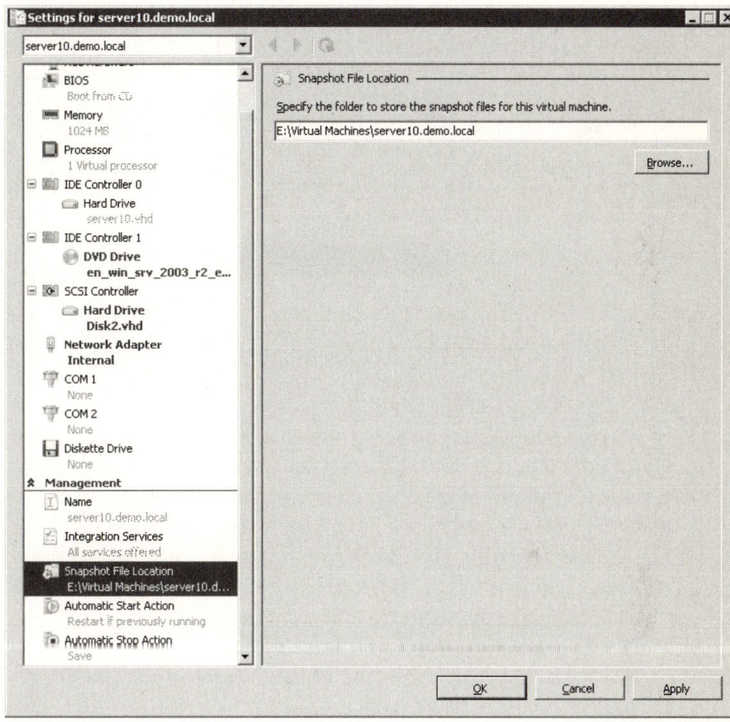

The Automatic Start Action screen (Figure 6.39) is where you tell Hyper-V what to do with the virtual machine when the Hyper-V host server boots up.

You have three options:

Nothing Hyper-V will not boot the virtual machine no matter what its state was when the host server was shut down.

Automatically Start If It Was Running When The Service Stopped This will configure the virtual machine to be started up automatically if it was running when the Hyper-V host server was shut down. You will normally use this default option.

Always Start This Virtual Machine Automatically The virtual machine in question will always start up no matter what its state was when the Hyper-V host server was shut down.

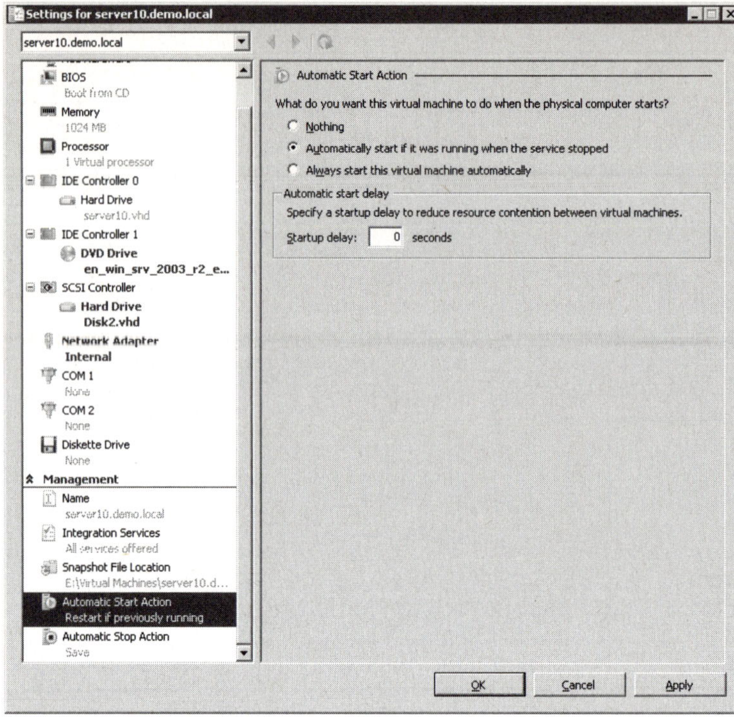

FIGURE 6.39
Automatic Start Action screen

You have the option to delay the automatic start-up of a virtual machine. The default is that the virtual machine will start up automatically when Hyper-V starts (zero seconds). This can cause contention on a highly loaded host server. We recommend that you delay all virtual machines by at least 120 seconds. High-priority virtual machines can start first. Lower-priority virtual machines can start later. For example, you might want domain controllers to be powered up first. Then you might start up SQL Servers. Finally, you might start up application servers that use SQL for the back-end data processing.

The Automatic Stop Action screen (Figure 6.40) allows you to similarly control the behavior of the virtual machine when the Hyper-V host server is shut down.

Your options are as follows:

Save The Virtual Machine State The virtual machine will be placed into a saved state when it is powered down. This default option is rather useful because the virtual machine is effectively placed into a frozen or hibernated state. It will continue uninterrupted when it is restarted.

Turn Off The Virtual Machine This is the option you are least likely to use. It effectively holds down the power button on the virtual machine to stop it in its tracks.

Shut Down The Guest Operating System This is the clean alternative to turning off the virtual machine. The Operating System Shutdown integration service is used to cleanly initiate a shutdown of the virtual machine, assuming that the integration services are installed in the guest operating system.

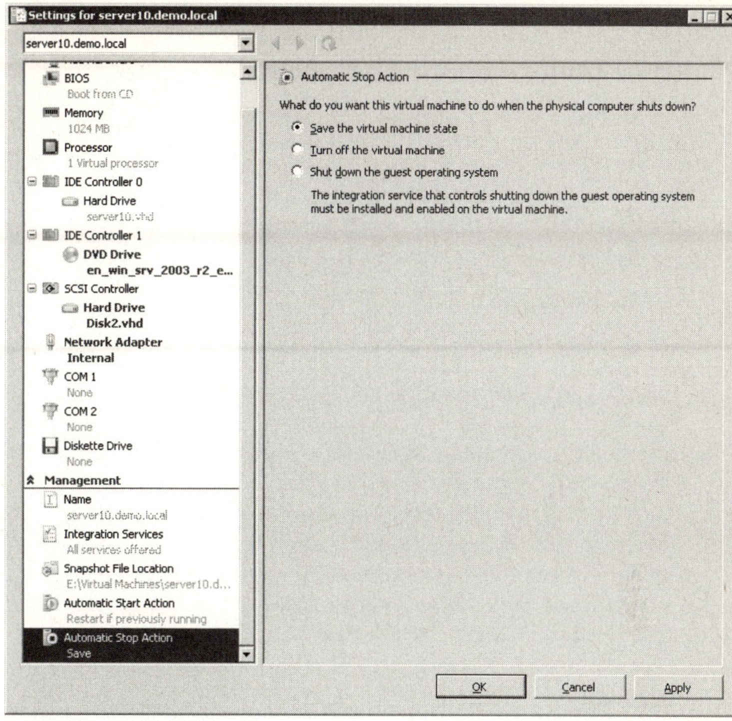

FIGURE 6.40 Automatic Stop Action screen

Unfortunately, operating systems that do not have integration services support will be turned off or powered down.

Ideally you will be using a Hyper-V cluster and will simply be able to Live Migrate the virtual machine to another host in the cluster to avoid any kind of virtual machine shutdown, making this screen irrelevant to any Hyper-V host server maintenance.

> **WHERE IS THE USB DEVICE?**
>
> We have a little bad news for you. Hyper-V virtual machines cannot use USB. There is no passthrough for USB like you get with Microsoft Virtual PC for Windows 7. Many organizations have a need to use USB dongles for software licensing. They use USB over network devices as a solution to this problem.

INSTALLING AN OPERATING SYSTEM AND USING A VIRTUAL MACHINE

There is really nothing different from installing an operating system in a virtual machine compared to a physical machine. You can use the same mechanisms you've always used in the past:

- A completely manual installation
- An unattended answer file using an ISO image mounted in a second virtual DVD drive
- PXE-based network deployment solutions using a legacy network adapter
- Cloning

We will look at a way to clone virtual machines a little later in the chapter.

You can control the power status of a virtual machine in the Hyper-V Console by right-clicking it and selecting options such as the following:

- Start
- Shutdown
- Turn Off
- Save
- Pause
- Reset

You can connect to a virtual machine with console access by right-clicking it and selecting Connect. The Virtual Machine Connection window will appear. This simulates sitting in front of the virtual machine. Mouse access will work correctly only if the integration components are installed in the guest operating system.

You can install the latest version of the integration components by clicking the Virtual Machine Connection Action menu and selecting Insert Integration Services Setup Disk. An ISO image containing the integration components will be mounted. The setup routine will start if autoplay is enabled. You can start the setup from the mounted ISO image if autoplay is disabled. The integration components setup will require a reboot.

SNAPSHOTS

A snapshot allows you to capture the state and configuration of a virtual machine as it was at that moment in time. The virtual machine can change configuration; the operating system, programs, and data can change; and you can return it to exactly how it was when the snapshot was created.

You can have up to 50 snapshots per virtual machine. This allows you to create a test or development environment where you can jump a virtual machine back to previous configurations. This can be pretty valuable when you are dealing with repeatable tasks or need to reset an unclean environment.

We talked in Chapter 2 about how a snapshot works. It uses an AVHD file, which is very similar to a differencing disk. This can cause a loss in virtual machine performance. You also need to shut down the virtual machine to allow Hyper-V to merge the AVHD into the original VHD when you delete the snapshot.

Snapshots are supported by the Hyper-V team in a production environment. But there are risks. Snapshots should not be used with production virtual machines that have changing data. For example, you might take a snapshot of a SQL Server instance. The database contents will be changed over time by user transactions. You might restore the snapshot after some time to restore the virtual machine to a healthier state. The problem is that this also returns everything else in the virtual machine to that point in time, including the database contents. All the user data from after the snapshot is lost. For this reason, many products in a virtualized deployment do not support snapshots in production. You can learn more about that in Chapter 8.

That all sounds rather scary. The reality is that snapshots can be a useful tool if used in the right scenario and managed carefully.

It is easy to create a snapshot of a virtual machine. You just have to right-click the virtual machine in the Hyper-V Manager and select Snapshot. The virtual machine can be running or powered off. The snapshot will start. The progress of the snapshot will be shown in the Status column of the Virtual Machines pane in the Hyper-V Manager. The snapshot will be visible in the Snapshots pane in the middle of the Hyper-V Manager window, as shown in Figure 6.41.

FIGURE 6.41
A new snapshot

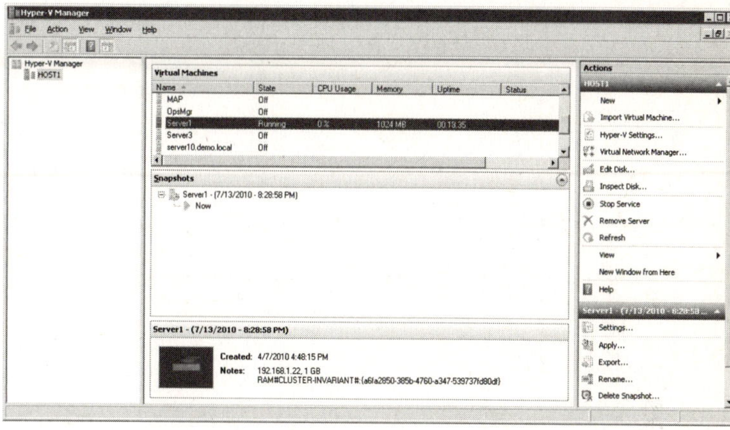

You can apply a snapshot, or restore the virtual machine to that point in time, by right-clicking the snapshot and selecting Apply. This will cause the virtual machine to power off and start back up in the state that the virtual machine was in at the time of the snapshot.

Figure 6.42 shows you how you can have many nested snapshots for a virtual machine. You can apply any one of those snapshots to jump the virtual machine between different states. This can be very powerful when working in a lab environment. The green Now arrow shows you what the current state of the virtual machine is.

FIGURE 6.42
Nested snapshots

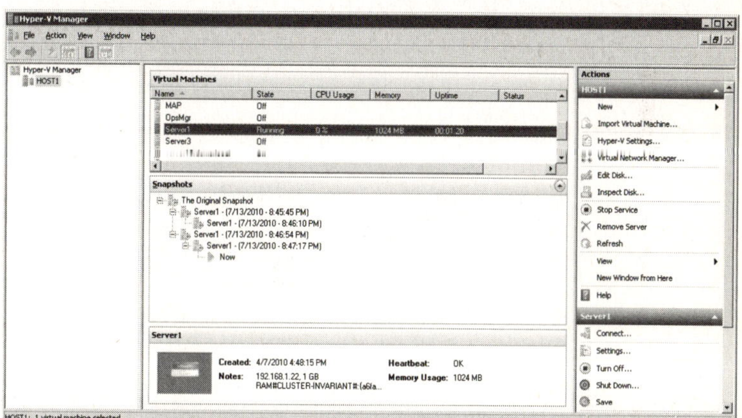

Eventually you will want to delete snapshots. You can delete many nested snapshots in one go by right-clicking one and selecting Delete Snapshot Subtree. You can delete a single snapshot by right-clicking it and selecting Delete Snapshot.

Here is where the nasty problem with snapshots resides. The snapshot might not be visible in the console anymore, but your administration work is not complete. The AVHD for the deleted snapshot must be merged back into the original VHD. This can be done only when the virtual machine is shut down. You can see this happening in Figure 6.43.

FIGURE 6.43
Merging a snapshot

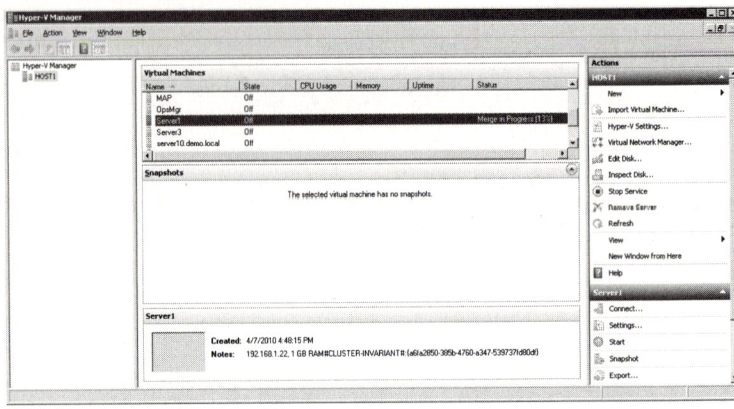

It is very easy to forget this final step. The resulting complications can result in performance issues with strange and unpredictable symptoms. There are no clues in the Hyper-V Manager that a snapshot must still be merged. This is why you must be very careful if you do decide to use snapshots. You can use PowerShell (and WMI) to identify virtual machines with a merge in progress. The cmdlet you will run is as follows:

```
Get-WmiObject -Namespace "root\virtualization" -Query "select * from
↩Msvm_ConcreteJob" | Where {$_.ElementName -eq 'Merge in Progress'}
```

VHD Management

A guaranteed way to get lots of hits on your blog is to write about VHD management in Hyper-V. It seems like people are constantly looking for knowledge about this subject. Look no further; we have what you need right here.

You have two options for editing an existing VHD. You can open the settings of a virtual machine and navigate to the disk you want to manage. Figure 6.44 shows the properties of an IDE-attached VHD in a virtual machine. This screen will be identical if managing a SCSI-attached VHD. You can view information about the VHD by clicking the Inspect button. You can launch the Edit Virtual Hard Disk Wizard by clicking the Edit button. This will actually start the wizard and skip the first screen, which is rather useful.

You can launch the Edit Virtual Hard Disk Wizard directly from the Hyper-V Manager by clicking Edit Disk in the Actions pane. This allows you to edit a VHD even if it is not attached to a virtual machine. You will see in Figure 6.45 that you will have to specify the VHD that you want to edit by using this way to launch the Edit Virtual Hard Disk Wizard.

There are three possible edit tasks that you can perform on a VHD (Figure 6.46). You must shut down the virtual machine to perform these operations if the VHD is being used.

FIGURE 6.44
Editing a VHD in a virtual machine

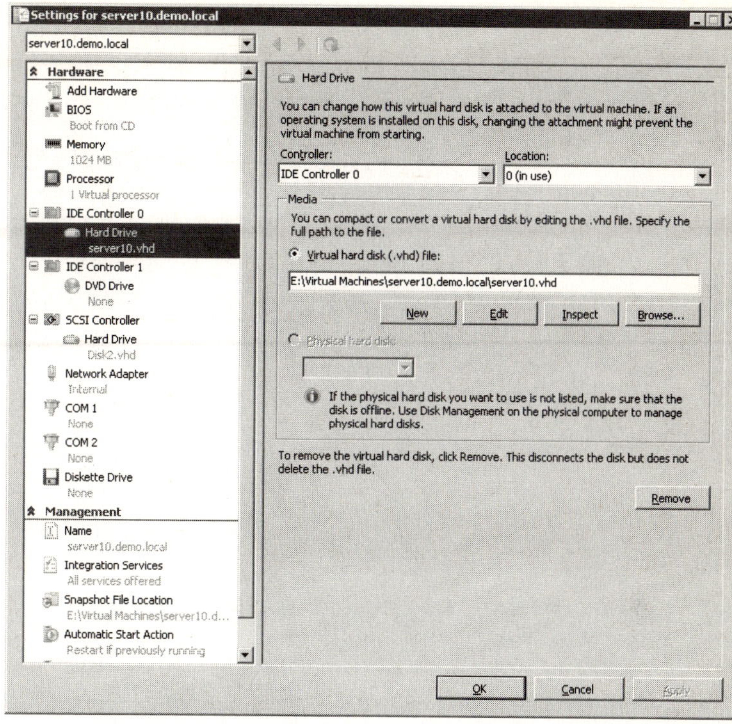

FIGURE 6.45
The Edit Virtual Hard Disk Wizard

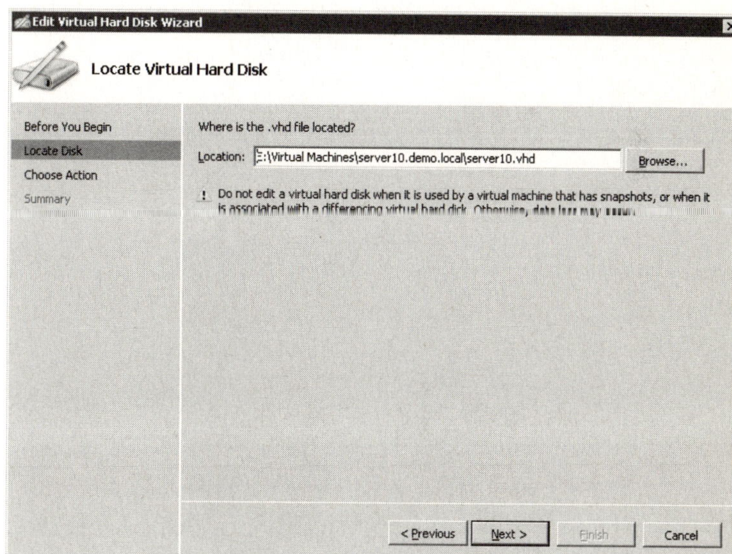

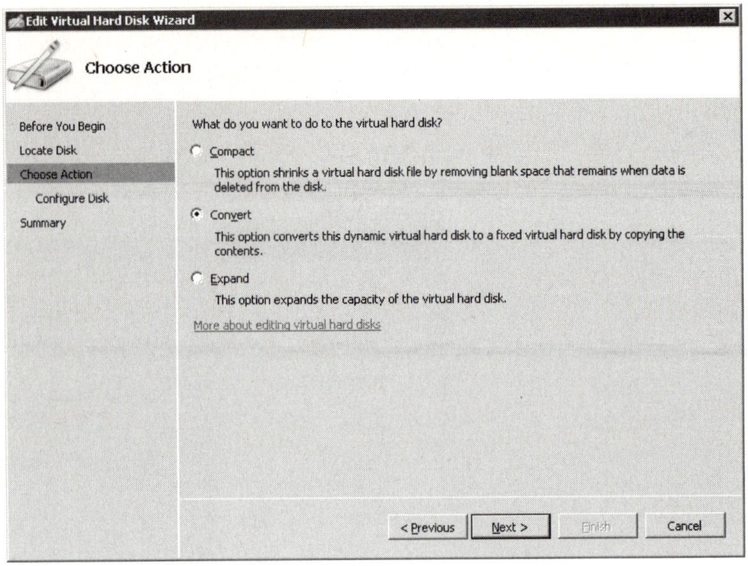

FIGURE 6.46
The possible VHD edit operations

Compact A dynamic VHD will have empty space when you delete a lot of data from the contained filesystem. A compact operation will reduce the size of the dynamic VHD by removing that empty space. This operation is usually not recommended.

Convert This is the operation that you can use to change a dynamic VHD into a fixed-size VHD, and vice versa. The subsequent screen, shown in Figure 6.47, will require you to specify the name of a new VHD. The convert operation will create this new VHD from the original VHD. It will be up to you to configure a virtual machine to use the new VHD and to remove the original one.

This is an example where VMM simplifies administrative tasks. VMM will convert the VHD, change the virtual machine settings, and delete the original VHD as a part of the convert job.

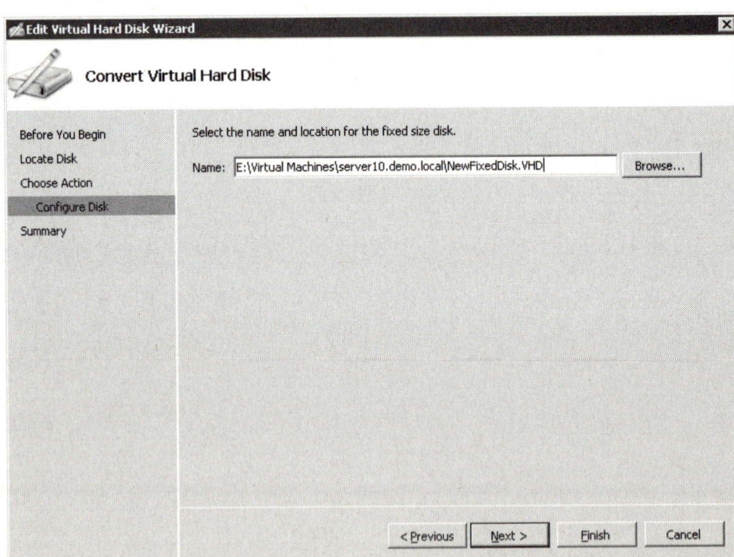

FIGURE 6.47
Creating a new converted VHD

Expand You can increase the size of a VHD to give additional storage space to a virtual machine. Make sure the physical storage has sufficient free space, and then all you have to do is specify the new increased size of the VHD (Figure 6.48).

FIGURE 6.48
Expanding a virtual hard disk

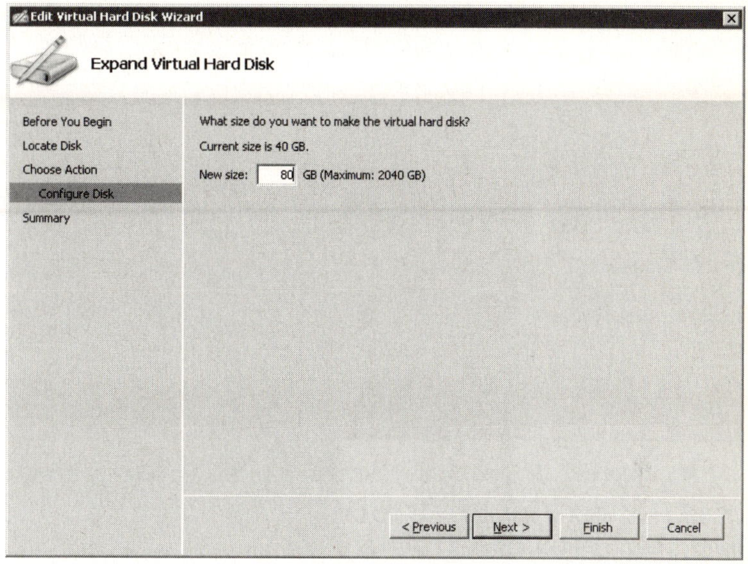

There is not much to this subject because the operations are pretty easy to do.

EXPORT AND IMPORT

You can't just copy a virtual machine's files to create a new virtual machine. Hyper-V requires an import operation of a set of files in a special layout. Hyper-V gives you the ability to export a virtual machine so that you can reuse or move the files. You can then import the virtual machine on the same or another host server.

You can export a virtual machine that is shut down by right-clicking it and selecting Export. This will open a dialog box (Figure 6.49) that asks for a destination location for the files. You can click Export to confirm the operation. A subfolder will be created automatically, and the exported virtual machine files will be placed into it. This includes a file called `config.xml`. This file is required for importing the virtual machine.

FIGURE 6.49
Exporting a virtual machine

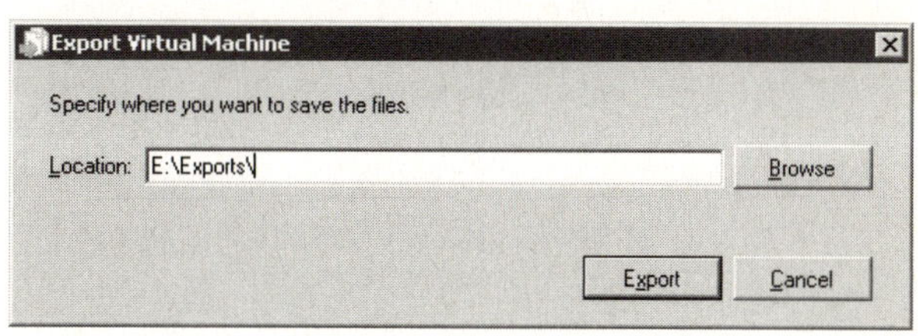

The export operation will not remove the virtual machine from Hyper-V. What you have done is create a copy of the virtual machine. You can delete the original virtual machine by right-clicking it and selecting Delete.

Importing a virtual machine will move the exported files to the location where you want to store the imported virtual machine. You can import that virtual machine by clicking Import Virtual Machine in the Actions pane. This opens the Import Virtual Machine dialog box, which is depicted in Figure 6.50. You can do two kinds of import.

FIGURE 6.50
Importing a virtual machine

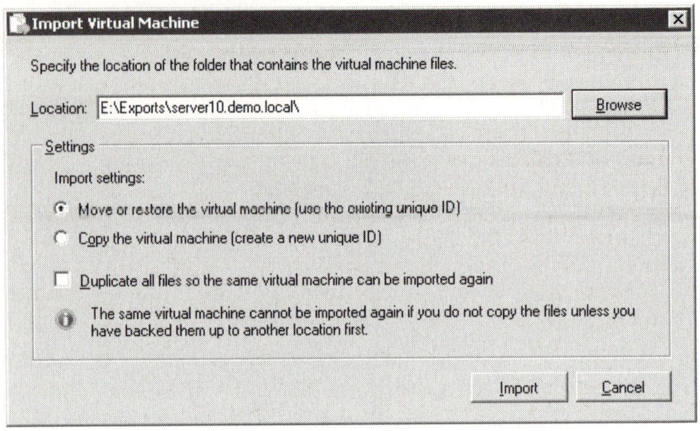

Move Or Restore The Virtual Machine (Use The Existing Unique ID) This will allow you to import the virtual machine and reuse the original ID that was used to identify the virtual machine within Hyper-V.

Copy The Virtual Machine (Create A New Unique ID) This will import the virtual machine into Hyper-V using a unique ID that is new to Hyper-V.

You can select the Duplicate All Files So The Same Virtual Machine Can Be Imported Again box. This will cause a new virtual machine to be created. The export files will be left untouched, allowing you to import the virtual machine again. This is a rather messy option because the VHDs for the new virtual machine will be created in the Virtual Hard Disks folder location defined in the host's Hyper-V settings (Figure 6.16), rather than the usual location with the rest of the virtual machine files.

CLONING VIRTUAL MACHINES

You can quickly build a virtual machine–based test or production environment using the Hyper-V Manager. A possible procedure might be as follows:

Step 1: Build a Template Virtual Machine Prepare a virtual machine, install the desired operating system, configure it as required, install your standard software, and patch it.

Step 2: Generalize the Virtual Machine Use sysprep to generalize the virtual machine's guest operating system and shut down the virtual machine. You can use an unattended answer file to customize the machine when it is deployed.

Step 3: Export the Virtual Machine Create an export of the virtual machine and store the folder somewhere safe.

Step 4: Copy the Exported Virtual Machine Copy the export folder of the template virtual machine to create new virtual machine folders in the desired storage location(s).

Step 5: Import Each of the Copies Import each virtual machine using the Copy The Virtual Machine (Create A New Unique ID) option.

Step 6: Power up the Imported Virtual Machines Each virtual machine will boot up as a unique machine with a unique SID.

This is a rapid method of cloning virtual machines, giving you the ability to create a complete production or lab environment in very little time. However, VMM 2008 R2 can do much of this work for you and provides additional deployment features.

Advanced Networking

All the hype about Hyper-V in Windows Server 2008 R2 focused on Live Migration and Cluster Shared Volumes. It is true that those were the game-changing features that made Hyper-V a viable option for many organizations. But that was only part of the story.

Why do we have servers? They are there to host applications that are accessed by clients over the network. Like just about everything we do in IT infrastructure, networking performance is crucial to virtualization and the applications that we run in the virtual machines. Some of the less heralded improvements of Windows Server 2008 R2 gave us improved or new networking features. Some of these features will improve the performance of a Hyper-V cluster. Some will give end users a better client-server experience. They all have one thing in common: you are not finished working with your networking team.

Jumbo Packets

Any file or network communication that you send will descend through the networking stack in Windows (or any network operating system or appliance). Each layer in the stack has a networking protocol. Each of those protocols will do the following to the transmission:

- Divide it.
- Add management headers to for doing things such as flow, transmission, and routing control.

The stream of data that is transmitted will contain many packets, each containing data and management headers. Using small packets for large amounts of data transmission can be inefficient because the management headers must be repeated.

You can increase the maximum transmission unit (MTU) or maximum size of a packet by enabling the usage of jumbo packets. This requires that the sender, the receiver, and all in-between network devices both support jumbo packets and have the functionality enabled. The result is that each packet can contain more of the data you want to transmit, and fewer packets need to be transmitted.

There are two reasons why jumbo packets are interesting in the Hyper-V world:

Cluster Networking You require one or more private networks between the hosts in a Hyper-V cluster to cater to CSV Redirected I/O and Live Migration. You can increase the speed of these operations by enabling jumbo frame support for the associated physical network adapters in the parent partition of each host server.

The only prerequisite is to ensure that the networking team can support and enable jumbo packets on the networking appliances that reside between the individual cluster nodes.

You then can enable jumbo packets for the required physical network adapters in the parent partition.

Virtual Machine Networking You may have some virtual machines that need to be able to handle massive networking loads. For example, a file server storing web farm content or a virtual machine that is directly connected to an iSCSI target will require the ability to transfer larger than normal data packets. You can enable jumbo frame support on the associated virtual network adapters to improve performance.

Just like with cluster networking, you will have to work with the networking team if your virtual machines will need to transmit jumbo packets on the physical network. You must enable jumbo frame support on the physical network adapter in the parent partition if the virtual machine's network adapter is connected to an external Hyper-V virtual network. You then will enable jumbo frame support on the required virtual network adapter in the virtual machine's guest operating system.

You will not be able to enable jumbo frames on a legacy network adapter because it is not supported.

You can enable jumbo packets in the properties of the network adapter. Browse to it in Network Connections and open the properties. Then click the Configure button and browse to the Advanced tab in the new properties dialog box that will open (Figure 6.51). Select Jumbo Packets, and choose the packet size that you desire. You can choose from Disabled (turn off jumbo packets), 4,088 bytes, and 9,014 bytes. You should choose a size that is supported by all of your networking hardware, including the physical network adapters and networking appliances.

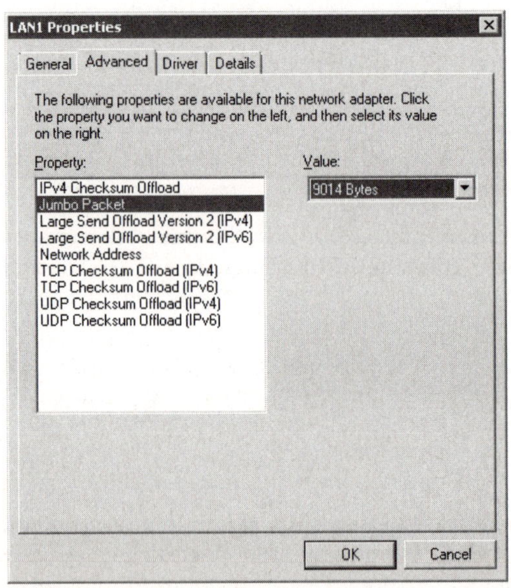

FIGURE 6.51 Enabling jumbo frames

TCP Chimney Offload

The processing of data as it passes through the networking stack requires processor resources. By now you probably are used to the idea of trying to reduce as much unnecessary processor utilization as possible. TCP Chimney or TCP Chimney Offload will allow the processor on the physical network adapter take over some of that processing workload. This can make a significantly positive impact on the performance of machines that are heavy users of the network.

Windows Server 2008 R2 offers support to enable TCP Chimney, not only on the parent partition but also in the virtual machine, by offloading traffic on an external Hyper-V virtual network. The latter is a new feature.

Turning on or configuring TCP Chimney requires a little understanding of how it works, planning, and performance analysis. Before we cover how to configure it, look at the compatibility of TCP Chimney in Table 6.4.

Table 6.4: TCP chimney compatibility

Feature	Compatible?
Windows Firewall	Yes. But some Windows Server 2008 R2 firewall rule changes can cause offloading not to function.
Other firewalls	Check application vendor support.
IPsec policy	TCP Chimney will offload traffic not subject to IPsec.
Network adapter teaming, also known as *load balance* and *failover*	Check manufacturer support.
Hyper-V	Yes.
Network monitoring tools	Check application support. Some monitoring tools will not monitor offloaded traffic.
Network load balancing	No.
Cluster service	Traffic that uses `netft.sys` (network fault-tolerant driver) is not offloaded.
Network Address Translation (NAT) and Internet Connection Sharing (ICS)	No. Traffic is not offloaded if these features are enabled.

The next requirement is that you are using a physical network adapter that supports TCP Chimney Offload. A limited set of hardware offers support for this advanced feature.

Microsoft recommends that you do some performance analysis for the machine in question before configuring TCP Chimney. You should try to identify a trend where network traffic affects CPU utilization. This could be difficult to do because applications and services will obviously muddy the water.

Then they suggest you look at enabling and configuring TCP Chimney. TCP Chimney is enabled on Windows Server 2008 R2 by default in what is referred to as Automatic mode. This means that TCP Chimney will offload traffic only when four conditions have been met:

- The network connection between sender and recipient is at least 10 Gbps.
- The round-trip latency is less than 20 milliseconds between the sender and the recipient.
- At least 130 Kb of data has already been transmitted over the connection.
- TCP Chimney has been enabled on the network adapter.

You can enable TCP Chimney on a physical network adapter by opening its properties in Network Connections. Click the Configure button, and select the Advanced tab. Browse for and enable a setting called TCP Chimney Offload or TCP Connection Offload. Note that TCP Checksum Offload does not refer to TCP Chimney. You might have a TCP Chimney Offload setting for IPv4 and IPv6, so you will have to enable it for the appropriate protocol for your network or server.

You now can enable or configure TCP Chimney. This is done at the command prompt using the `netsh` command:

```
netsh int tcp set global chimney=<setting>
```

You can use a number of settings with this command:

Automatic This setting is available only on Windows Server 2008 R2 and Windows 7. It is the default setting. We mentioned earlier the requirements for Automatic mode to offload processing of traffic to the physical network adapter.

Enabled This mode will attempt to offload all network processing on a first-come, first-served basis.

Default This will return the TCP Chimney setting to the default mode for the operating system.

Disabled This will turn TCP Chimney Offload optimization off.

You can configure the TCP Chimney mode for a particular application:

```
netsh interface tcp add chimneyapplication enabled <Program Path and Name>
```

You can prevent TCP Chimney from offloading traffic for an application:

```
netsh interface tcp delete chimneyapplication <Program Path and Name>
```

It is possible to instruct TCP Chimney to offload all traffic on a particular network port number:

```
netsh interface tcp add chimneyport enabled localport=<Port Number>
```

And it is also possible to instruct TCP Chimney not to offload traffic on a specific port number.

```
netsh interface tcp delete chimneyport localport=<Port Number>
```

You can check the current status of TCP Chimney by running:

```
netsh interface tcp show global
```

You can also check the current statistics of TCP Chimney with this command:

```
netsh interface tcp show chimneystats
```

TCP Chimney works only with virtual machine traffic that passes through a physical network adapter, so it will not offer any improvements to internal or private Hyper-V virtual networks. You should enable TCP Chimney on the physical network adapter that is connected to your external Hyper-V network(s) to offload virtual machine network processing.

There is one situation in which you will probably see performance gains with TCP Chimney in a Hyper-V context. If you use iSCSI with 10 Gbps networking, then you should enable TCP Chimney on the storage network adapters.

A number of performance counters (see Table 6.5) can be used to check on the performance of TCP Chimney on your machine. They are found in Per Processor Network Interface Card Activity ➤ Available Counters.

Table 6.5: TCP Chimney performance counters

Performance Counter	Explanation
TCP Offload Receive Indications/sec	The average incidents per second at which the Windows Network Driver Interface received an offload receive indication call from a network adapter
TCP Offload Send Bytes/sec	The average rate in bytes per second that data was delivered to a network adapter using offload send request call
TCP Offload Send Request Calls/sec	The average incidents per second at which the TCP/IP protocol requested an offload transmission on a network adapter
TCP Offload Receive Bytes/sec	The average rate in bytes per second at which data was delivered by a network adapter using the offload receive indication call

Microsoft recommends that you check CPU utilization once you have set up TCP Chimney and compare the results with those you obtained before the configuration. You should tune your configuration to reach optimal performance.

Virtual Machine Queuing

Virtual Machine Queuing (VMQ) was introduced in Chapter 2. A queue on the physical network adapter optimizes network traffic to and from a virtual machine by offloading the filtering and processing of network traffic from the parent partition. These queues are a limited resource. VMQ will assign them to virtual machines on a first-come, first-served basis. It is for this reason that Microsoft urges you to limit the number of virtual machines that will use VMQ; otherwise, it will offer unpredictable and limited performance benefits.

You must have a physical network adapter that supports VMQ. There are a very limited set of options at this time.

> **Check with the Manufacturer**
>
> The precise ordering of steps for enabling VMQ will depend on the hardware you are using. Please check with the physical network adapter manufacturer's support services for the required implementation steps. You might also have to find out what brand name the manufacturer uses instead of VMQ.

VMQ will have to be enabled on the physical network adapter that is bound to the external Hyper-V virtual network. Open the properties of the physical network adapter, click the Configure button, browse to the Advanced tab, and enable the VMQ setting.

There are two registry keys for enabling VMQ in Windows Server 2008 R2 (Table 6.6).

TABLE 6.6: VMQ registry keys

KEY	TYPE	PURPOSE	VALUES
HKEY_LOCAL_MACHINE\SYSTEM\CurrentControlSet\services\VMSMP\Parameters\TenGigVmqEnabled	Enable or disable VMQ on all 10 Gbps physical network adapters	REG_DWORD	0=System default (disabled for Windows Server 2008 R2) 1=Enabled 2=Explicitly disabled
HKEY_LOCAL_MACHINE\SYSTEM\CurrentControlSet\services\VMSMP\Parameters\BelowTenGigVmqEnabled	Enable or disable VMQ on all physical network adapters less than 10 Gbps	REG_DWORD	0=System default (disabled for Windows Server 2008 R2) 1=Enabled 2=Explicitly disabled

Microsoft warns that you should not enable VMQ on 1 Gbps networks if interrupt coalescing is not enabled. The process for doing this is a little complicated. You must start by finding the physical network adapter in the registry here:

```
HKEY_LOCAL_MACHINE\SYSTEM\CurrentControlSet\Control\
↩Class\{4D36E972-E325-11CE-BFC1-08002BE10318}
```

The network adapter will be a key in this location. It will have a four-digit ID.

You will have to run a pair of commands to edit the registry, substituting this four-digit ID of the physical network adapter where indicated:

```
C:\>reg add HKEY_LOCAL_MACHINE\SYSTEM\CurrentControlSet\Control\Class\{4D36E972-
E325-11CE-BFC1-08002BE10318}\<4 Digit-ID> /v MaxRssProcessors /t REG_DWORD /d 1 /f

C:\>reg add HKEY_LOCAL_MACHINE\SYSTEM\CurrentControlSet\Control\
↩Class\{4D36E972-E325-11CE-BFC1-08002BE10318}\<4 Digit-ID> /v
↩RssBaseProcNumber /t REG_DWORD /d 0 /f
```

Performance Monitoring of Virtual Machines

It is easy to fall into the trap of trying to do performance monitoring of your virtual machines the same way you always have in the past. Running Performance Monitor in a virtual machine gives you only some of the information. The only place where you get all the information, and get it accurately, is in the parent partition. There is a collection of dedicated Hyper-V performance counters. They are easy to find; as you can see in Figure 6.52, they all begin with *Hyper-V*.

Rather than reinvent the wheel, we will refer you to an excellent blog post by a Microsoft staff member, which provides information about useful Hyper-V performance counters. You can find it here:

```
http://blogs.msdn.com/b/tvoellm/archive/2009/04/23/monitoring-hyper-v-performance
.aspx
```

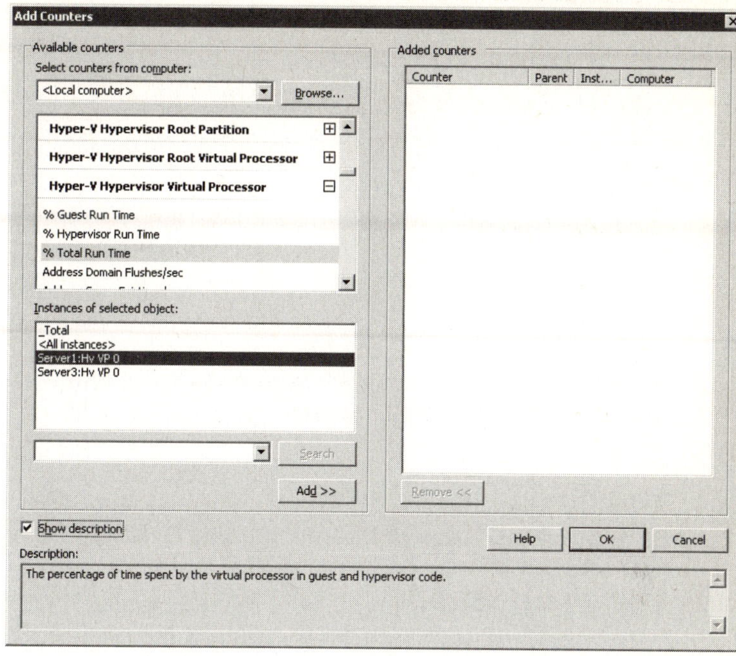

FIGURE 6.52
Using the Hyper-V performance counters

Dynamic Memory

Chapter 2 gave you an insight into how Dynamic Memory works. We're going to look at how you can use Dynamic Memory to get more from your Hyper-V hosts.

Dynamic Memory is a new Hyper-V feature that is provided by Service Pack 1 for Windows Server 2008 R2 and Windows 7. This service pack was still a beta release at the time of writing this book. We normally don't include unfinished software or features in a book such as this, but Dynamic Memory is a very important new feature that will probably be available by the time you read this book. The functionality and configuration of Dynamic Memory is unlikely to change substantially between now and then, but some of the presentation in the user interface might be subject to change. Everything we have covered so far is based on a pre–Service Pack 1 of Hyper-V.

DYNAMIC MEMORY REQUIREMENTS

The requirements for Dynamic Memory are as follows:

Service Pack 1 You should install Service Pack 1 for Windows Server 2008 R2 on your Hyper-V host servers. It should be installed on all hosts in a Hyper-V cluster before you start enabling the feature on virtual machines.

A Supported Operating System The following operating systems are supported:

- Windows Server 2008 R2 Web, Standard, Enterprise, or Datacenter Edition SP1
- Windows Server 2008 Web, Standard, Enterprise, or Datacenter Edition SP2

- Windows Server 2003 R2 Web, Standard, Enterprise, or Datacenter Edition SP2 or newer
- Windows Server 2003 Web, Standard, Enterprise, or Datacenter Edition SP2 or newer
- Windows 7 Ultimate or Enterprise Edition
- Windows Vista Ultimate or Enterprise Edition SP2

Dynamic Memory uses Windows ability to hot-add memory. This is a feature that was previously only available in higher-end editions of the Windows products. An update will probably be required for operating systems prior to Windows Server 2008 R2 and Windows 7.

Current Integration Components Dynamic Memory uses a new integration service to add and balloon memory in the virtual machine. You must install the current integration components on the Hyper-V host server in each of your guest operating systems for which you want to enable this feature. It should be your practice to do this anyway whenever any service pack or update upgrades the integration components.

More Dynamic Memory Theory

We will cover some more of the theory behind Dynamic Memory and expand on it just a little before we show how to use it.

Dynamic Memory Settings We will start with three of the settings that can be configured for each virtual machine. The minimum configured amount of memory is what the virtual machine is going to boot up with. Dynamic Memory can increase the amount of memory assigned to the virtual machine up to the maximum amount. The buffer setting is a percentage that dictates how much additional free memory is allocated to the virtual machine. For example, a virtual machine that currently has 8 GB of committed memory and a 25 percent buffer will actually have up to 10 GB of memory allocated to it, assuming that this doesn't go beyond the maximum amount of memory that the virtual machine can be assigned. This buffer allows for a rapid increase in demand for memory resources in the guest operating system while Dynamic Memory responds. Very often the additional memory provided by the buffer is used for caching by the guest operating system to improve performance.

Pressure In Dynamic Memory, pressure is a measure that is based on committed memory in the virtual machine. It is a ratio of how much memory the virtual machine currently wants vs. how much it has.

Priority A Hyper-V host server has a finite amount of physical memory that it can allocate. It is possible that a number of virtual machines will all request large increases in memory at the same time. The Priority setting is used to weigh the pressure of each virtual machine. Higher-priority virtual machines will be allocated additional memory before others of a lower priority.

Lower-priority virtual machines may even lose memory to provide for the demands of higher-priority virtual machines. This may cause a virtual machine to be allocated less physical memory that it currently requires. That will lead to paging file activity and a drastic reduction in performance.

Note that the Priority setting is used only when there is not enough physical memory in the host server to meet demand. You should be trying to prevent this from happening by sizing your hosts according to your virtual machine requirement and by not allowing over-commitment.

Parent Partition Memory Reserve

Before the arrival of Dynamic Memory, virtual machines had a statically assigned amount of RAM. We could accurately size a Hyper-V host server, knowing the total amount of RAM required by the virtual machines and figure out how to leave the desired amount of RAM for the parent partition to function successfully.

Service Pack 1 for Windows Server 2008 R2 allows you to specify exactly how much RAM should be allocated to the parent partition. All other memory on the Hyper-V host server will be reserved for virtual machines. You can configure the parent partition memory reserve by editing the registry here:

```
HKLM\SOFTWARE\Microsoft\Windows NT\CurrentVersion\Virtualization
```

and adding a REG_DWORD value called MemoryReserve and entering a number to specify the number of megabytes to reserve. This should be followed by a reboot of the Hyper-V host server.

It would be easy to get greedy and set the parent partition to something very small so that there is more memory available for your virtual machines. That might be fine in a test lab with limited resources. However, you should be scientific in your calculation of the real needs of the parent partition when configuring the memory reserve. You should consider factors such as the following:

- Windows Server 2008 R2 requirements
- Drivers
- The memory footprint of any management agents on the parent partition

Enable Dynamic Memory on Virtual Machines

The memory screen in the settings of each virtual machine in Hyper-V Manager will be updated to allow you to optionally enable and configure Dynamic Memory. You still have the choice of statically configuring memory in a virtual machine. You might ask why you would still do this. There are a few reasons, which are mainly cosmetic but could have an implication. Note that the Dynamic Memory settings will only be effective if the latest integration components and any required Windows update have been installed in the virtual machine's guest operating system.

Most of the settings for Dynamic Memory require that the virtual machine is turned off or shut down. You can open the settings of the virtual machine and navigate to the Memory screen, as shown in Figure 6.53.

You now have two ways to configure memory:

- Static
- Dynamic Memory

The first two settings for Dynamic Memory are as follows:

- Startup RAM
- Maximum RAM

FIGURE 6.53
Configuring Dynamic Memory in a virtual machine

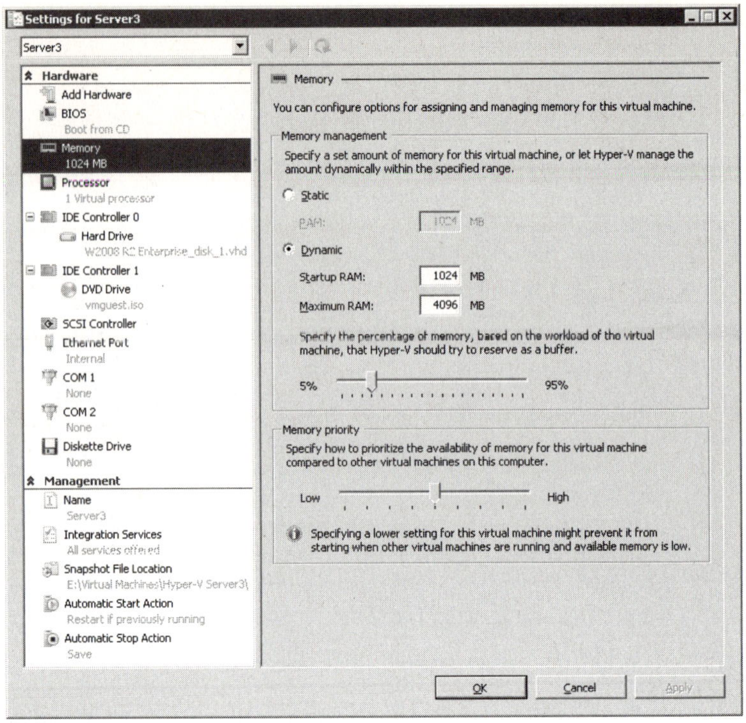

These settings will allow you to define how much memory a virtual machine will boot up with and how much memory the virtual machine can grow up to.

The Startup RAM setting should not be less than the minimum supported requirement of the virtual machine's guest operating system. Realistically, it should be set at an amount that is enough for the normal functions of the virtual machine to operate without needing to expand.

This virtual machine is set up to boot up with 1024 MB of memory. It will be able to expand up to 4096 MB of memory if it needs to do so.

The Buffer slide control allows you to specify how much memory, in addition to the currently committed memory in the virtual machine, should be allocated. This control moves from 5 percent to 95 percent. Providing more will improve the responsiveness to the virtual machine by Dynamic Memory. This memory will probably also improve the virtual machine's performance by being used for caching by the guest operating system. Providing too much of a buffer will cause contention for physical resources. The default is 20 percent.

The Memory Priority slide control moves from Low (1) to High (10,000) with a default of medium (5,000). This is used to weigh the memory pressure of virtual machines for the allocation and deallocation of memory.

Note that the settings for Dynamic Memory might be available for all virtual machines, but it will only function in supported guest operating systems that have the up-to-date integration components installed.

Dynamic Memory in Action

You can start up the virtual machines after you have saved the settings for Dynamic Memory. You will see the virtual machine boots up with the allocated minimum amount of RAM. You should log into the virtual machine if you want to learn more about Dynamic Memory. Launch Task Manager, and look at the Performance tab, paying attention to how much memory is assigned to the virtual machine. Task Manager shows you that this virtual machine (Figure 6.54) has expanded up to 1229 MB of memory out of a possible 4096 MB.

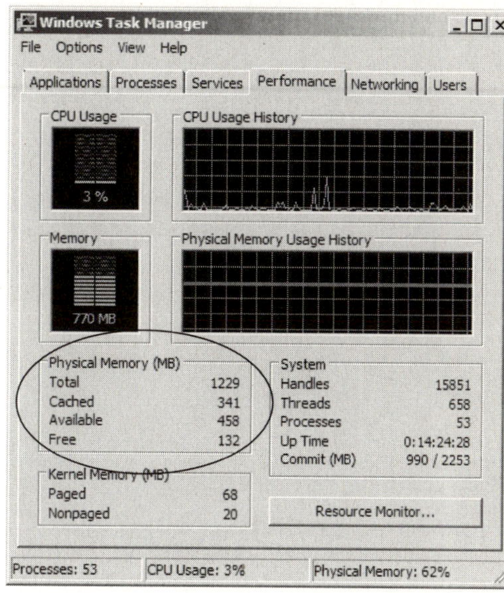

Figure 6.54 Task Manager showing the memory expansion

The Hyper-V Manager shows you the current amount of physical memory that is allocated to the virtual machine (Figure 6.55). You can see that it has reduced from 1229 MB to 1193 MB by means of the Dynamic Memory balloon. The virtual machine still believes that it has 1229 MB of RAM, but only 1193 MB of physical RAM is allocated by the Hyper-V host server.

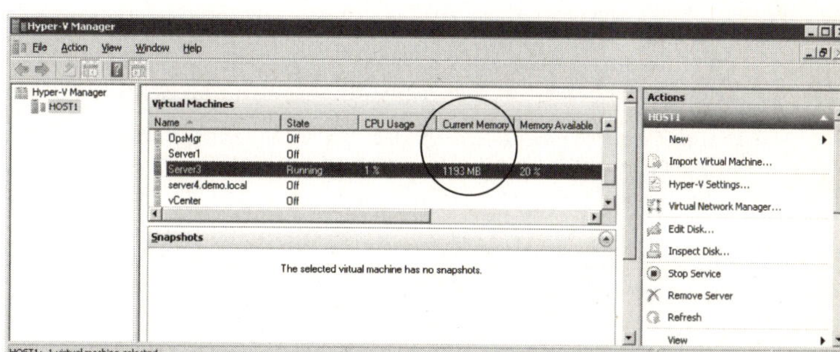

Figure 6.55 Hyper-V Manager and the current physical memory allocation

Run some sort of program or service in the virtual machine that will cause an increased demand in memory resources. Hyper-V will allocate more memory to the virtual machine. You will see the amount of memory in Task Manager in the virtual machine increase. This will be duplicated in the Hyper-V Manager. Now you should terminate the memory demanding program. The Hyper-V Manager will indicate a reduction in assigned physical memory. However, Task Manager will not mirror this. It will continue to show the high point of the memory expansion. This is a result of the ballooning process by the Dynamic Memory VSC running in the child partition (virtual machine). You can learn more about this in Chapter 2.

You can create several virtual machines with mixed priorities and create contention for physical memory. You will see in the Hyper-V Manager how lower-priority virtual machines will lose memory so that higher-priority virtual machines can be allocated memory.

Non-Uniform Memory Architecture

Chapter 2, "The Architecture of Hyper-V," discussed how Non-Uniform Memory Architecture (NUMA) could negatively affect virtual machine performance when Dynamic Memory is disabled. You can disable NUMA being used for virtual machine physical memory allocation in the host server's Hyper-V Settings (Hyper-V Manager) by clearing the Allow Virtual Machines Span NUMA Nodes check box.

Usage of Dynamic Memory

There are many reasons to use Dynamic Memory including the following:

- Virtual Desktop Infrastructure where memory is a big cost
- Assisting with difficult to size virtual machines
- Squeezing the most out of lab machines
- Reducing costs associated with virtual machines that have infrequent resource demand peaks

There are some drawbacks to Dynamic Memory:

Appearances Can Be Misleading Imagine, for a moment, that you are the owner of a virtual machine. You are paying for 8 GB of RAM to be allocated to that virtual machine. You log in one day and run Task Manager, and it informs you that your machine has only 6125 MB of RAM. Would you be upset that your machine is missing approximately 25 percent of the memory that you are paying for?

This angry customer is something that you might have to deal with if you enable Dynamic Memory in an environment where your customers (internal or external) pay for the allocated or available resources.

The virtual machine might well be able to reach the full 8192 MB of RAM. But your customers base their complaints on what they see. You might be able to prevent a few help-desk calls with some communications. Experienced IT professionals will know that their customers don't always read our beautifully crafted communiqués. This is a scenario where you will have to balance the benefits of Dynamic Memory (increase host capacity, easier sizing, and reduced cost of resources for the customer) against the risks (upset customers consuming a lot of time and possibly refusing to renew their business with you).

Misuse or Unplanned Over-Commitment It would be very easy to over-commit a resource such as Dynamic Memory. Care should be taken to not increase memory pressure to a point where the host does not have sufficient capacity to meet the demands of the virtual machines.

You should try to understand the real demands on memory by your virtual machines over the peaks and troughs of a week or month. This might be an opportunity to use the performance monitoring and reporting of Microsoft System Center Operations Manager. You can use the results of this study to configure Dynamic Memory so that you can optimize how memory is allocated without over-committing the host server. For example, you would want to avoid a scenario where a few high-priority virtual machines might permanently prevent many lower-priority virtual machines from expanding their memory to meet end user demand.

VIRTUAL MACHINE MANAGER 2008 R2 AND DYNAMIC MEMORY

VMM 2008 R2 did not have support for managing Dynamic Memory at the time of writing this book. It would be expected that it would have the ability at the time of the release of Service Pack 1 for Windows Server 2008 R2, or not long after. It might also be possible that the Microsoft Performance and Resource Optimization (PRO) management packs for Operations Manager 2007 would also provide a response to a scenario where a clustered Hyper-V host server experiences unserviceable memory pressure and needs to Live Migrate virtual machines to a more suitable host server.

MONITORING DYNAMIC MEMORY

If you enable it, Dynamic Memory will require a lot of care. Left unmonitored and uncontrolled, this powerful feature could become a source of performance issues. Microsoft has provided two sets of performance counters that you can monitor using Performance Monitor.

Table 6.7 shows the counters that are available in the parent partition under Hyper-V Dynamic Memory Balancer.

TABLE 6.7: Hyper-V Dynamic Memory Balancer performance counters

COUNTER	DESCRIPTION
Added Memory	The cumulative amount of memory added to virtual machines
Available Memory	The amount of memory left on the host server
Average Pressure	The average pressure on the balancer host server
Memory Add Operations	The total number of memory add operations
Memory Remove Operations	The total number of memory remove operations
Removed Memory	The cumulative amount of memory removed from virtual machines

Table 6.8 shows the counters that are available in the parent partition under Hyper-V Dynamic Memory VM.

TABLE 6.8: Hyper-V Dynamic Memory VM performance counters

COUNTER	DESCRIPTION
Added Memory	The cumulative amount of memory added to the virtual machine
Average Pressure	The average pressure in the virtual machine
Current Pressure	The current pressure in the virtual machine
Guest Visible Physical Memory	The amount of memory visible in the virtual machine
Maximum Pressure	The maximum pressure band in the virtual machine
Memory Add Operations	The total number of add operations for the virtual machine
Memory Remove Operations	The total number of remove operations for the virtual machine
Minimum Pressure	The minimum pressure band in the virtual machine
Physical Memory	The current amount of memory in the virtual machine
Removed Memory	The cumulative amount of memory removed from the virtual machine
Added Memory	The cumulative amount of memory added to the virtual machine

DYNAMIC MEMORY PERFORMANCE PROBLEM SOLVING

Dynamic Memory usually operates extremely quickly, but extreme situations can occur. Microsoft has identified three scenarios where there may be performance issues and provided the solutions. These are shown in Table 6.9.

TABLE 6.9: Dynamic memory performance problems and solutions

PROBLEM	SOLUTION
The virtual machine performs poorly when too much memory is removed.	Increase the Minimum RAM setting to a suitable level to meet demand.
Dynamic Memory does not allocate memory quickly enough.	Increase the Buffer setting to a higher percentage.
No Dynamic Memory settings improve performance.	Increase the size of the virtual machine paging file. Statically define the size of the file if the guest operating system does not take advantage of it.

Now you know how to use the latest feature in Hyper-V that has had Hyper-V customers chatting for quite some time. Now we're going to move onto a subject that will scare a lot of Windows/Hyper-V administrators.

Linux Virtual Machines

Contrary to rumor, Hyper-V does support Linux guest operating systems. We're going to wrap up this chapter by spending some time on Microsoft's support for running Linux in Hyper-V virtual machines.

The History of Linux on Hyper-V

Microsoft has developed integration components for Linux. There have been three releases over the years. Version 1.0 offered support for SUSE Linux Enterprise Server (SLES). Version 2.0 was released at the same time as Windows Server 2008 R2 and added support for Red Hat Enterprise Linux (RHEL).

Microsoft made some history with the release of the version 2.0 Linux Integration Components. Microsoft took the bold step of releasing the code under GPLv2 licensing and submitted it for inclusion into the Linux kernel. It was approved and included in Linux kernel 2.6.32. That meant any Linux that was based on that kernel (or later) would have built-in integration components for Hyper-V.

The first two versions of the Linux Integration Components had some limitations. The first one was that it provided support only for a single virtual processor. This lack of symmetric multiprocessing (SMP) prevented Hyper-V from running anything but light Linux workloads. The second weakness was that the Linux Integration Components lacked any integration services. An example of this is the lack of an operating system shutdown integration service. A Linux virtual machine must be manually shut down if it is hosted on a nonclustered Hyper-V host server and that host is being powered down. Otherwise, the Linux virtual machine will simply be turned off, possibly causing problems.

Microsoft knows that its customers run a heterogeneous server infrastructure and takes the need to support Linux extremely seriously. Microsoft continued to take feedback from its customers and developed the Linux product support. Version 2.1 of the Linux Integration Components has taken a huge leap forward, ending the days of Linux being a second-class citizen on Microsoft's hardware virtualization platform.

Linux Integration Components 2.1

Version 2.1 of the Linux Integration Components is the latest version of the enlightenments for Linux guest operating systems on Hyper-V.

Supported Operating Systems

Version 2.1 of the Linux Integration Components offers support for the following Linux distributions and versions:

- SUSE Linux Enterprise Server 10 SP3 x86 and x64
- SUSE Linux Enterprise Server 11 x86 and x64
- Red Hat Enterprise Linux 5.2, 5.3, 5.4, and 5.5 x86 and x64

New Features

This release of the Linux Integration Components fixes two of the problems that many had with the previous releases:

SMP Support It is now possible to have up to four virtual CPUs on the supported Linux distributions and versions.

Integration Services Microsoft has added a set of integration services to the Linux Integration Components for the first time:

- Symmetric Multi-Processing (SMP) Support
- Timesync
- Pluggable Time Source
- Integrated Shutdown

The Pluggable Time Source integration service is not supported on Red Hat Enterprise Linux x64.

Installing the Integration Components

The installation process will vary depending on whether your guest operating system is SLES or RHEL. There are even some variations for SLES 11.

Preparing the Virtual Machine

You will start by preparing your virtual machine. There is one special consideration. Linux will often bind a TCP/IP configuration to a MAC address. Hyper-V uses dynamic MAC addresses by default. A Linux virtual machine will lose network connectivity if the virtual network adapter's MAC address changes. This will happen during a Live Migration or if a virtual machine is moved. You should configure the virtual network adapter of any Linux virtual machine to be static.

> **Synthetic Devices Require Integration Components**
>
> Remember that synthetic devices such as the synthetic virtual network adapter or the virtual SCSI device require integration components to work in the virtual machine.

Installing SLES 10 and 11

Install the operating system, making sure to add the C/C++ Compiler And Tools component. You will not be able to configure a network adapter during the installation if you have used a synthetic (not legacy) virtual network adapter. When the installation is completed, follow these steps:

1. Log into the virtual machine as the root user.
2. For SLES 11 only, edit `/etc/modprobe.d/unsupported-modules`, and find the following option:

   ```
   allow_unsupported_modules
   ```

Change this to read as follows:

```
allow_unsupported_modules 1
```

Reboot the virtual machine, and log in as the root user.

3. Now we return to the instructions for SLES 10 and 11. Mount the Linux Integration Components ISO file in the settings of the Linux virtual machine. Run the following commands to instruct the guest operating system to mount the CD-ROM device:

```
mkdir /mnt/cdrom
mount /dev/cdrom /mnt/cdrom
```

4. Run the following commands to copy the installation files to the disk in the Linux virtual machine:

```
mkdir /opt/linux_ic_v21
cp /mnt/cdrom/* /opt/linux_ic_v21 -R
```

5. Use the following commands to install the Linux Integration Components:

```
cd /opt/linux_ic_v21/
make
make install
```

The installation is completed for SLES 10. The next steps should be completed for SLES 11.

6. Edit `/etc/fstab`. Search for all of the `/dev/disk/*` entries. Change them to `/dev/hd*`. For example, `/dev/disk/1` would change to `/dev/hda1`. Save your changes.

7. Edit `/boot/grub/menu.lst` to have the following:

```
root=/dev/hda2 resume=/dev/hda1
8.      Edit /etc/modprobe.d/unsupported-modules and find the following
option: allow_unsupported_modules
```

Change it to the following:

```
allow_unsupported_modules 0
```

9. That is the end of the installation process for SLES 11. Reboot your virtual machine, and log back in as a root user.

Configuring SLES 10 and 11

You can configure the network adapter using YaST in SLES 10. You must not use YaST in SLES 11. Instead, you should edit `/etc/sysconfig/network/ifcfg-seth`*X* where *X* is the number of your virtual machine's network adapter.

You can confirm the functionality of the SCSI driver (requiring the integration components) by running `ls /dev/sd*`.

Once confirmed, you can configure the disk using Partitioner in YaST.

INSTALLING RHEL 5

Install the operating system including the Software Development feature. Mount the integration components ISO file in the virtual machine settings. Log into the virtual machine as a root user, and run the following commands to mount the ISO in the Linux guest operating system:

```
mkdir /mnt/cdrom
mount /dev/cdrom /mnt/cdrom
```

Copy the integration component installation files to the disk in the virtual machine:

```
mkdir /opt/linux_ic_v21
cp /mnt/cdrom/* /opt/linux ic_v21 -R
```

Run the following commands to install the integration components:

```
cd /opt/linux_ic_v21/
make
make install
```

That is the end of the installation process for RHEL x64 virtual machines. You must continue the process for RHEL x86 virtual machines.

With the ISO still mounted, run the following command:

```
rpm -ivh /mnt/cdrom/Server/adjtimex-1.20-2.1.x86_64.rpm
```

Reboot the virtual machine, and log back in as a root user.

CONFIGURING RHEL 5

You can use the Network Configuration Tool to set up the network adapter in the RHEL guest operating system.

Run the following command to verify that the SCSI controller is functioning: `cat /proc/scsi/scsi`.

You can run the next command to check that disks are connected to the SCSI controller: `ls /dev/sd*`.

You can now use `fdisk` to configure the SCSI-attached disks in the virtual machine.

VERIFYING INTEGRATION COMPONENT FUNCTIONALITY

You can run the following command to verify that the integration components are working. It should return information about the VMBus driver.

```
/sbin/modinfo vmbus
```

You can also run the following:

```
/sbin/lsmod | grep vsc
```

It should return information about the following:

- `netvsc`
- `storvsc`

- `blkvsc`
- `vmbus`

Using the Mouse Integration Component

This won't be much of an issue for most Linux administrators because they hardly ever install the GUI. There isn't much use for a mouse in a Telnet session. It is possible that you might need to install the GUI. You'll log in and find that you are lacking a mouse. That's because Microsoft has not added a mouse driver in the Linux Integration Components.

Microsoft and Citrix have cosponsored a project called Satori. Project Satori (`http://www.xen.org/download/satori.html`) has developed and shared a mouse driver for Linux under the GPLv2 license.

You can perform the following steps to install the Project Satori mouse driver:

1. Download the ISO file from the website.
2. Mount the ISO in the Linux virtual machine.
3. Navigate to the CD/DVD drive in the Linux guest operating system.
4. Run `./setup.pl inputdriver` to install the driver.

SUSE Linux Enterprise Server 11 is not supported by the Project Satori mouse driver at this time.

Understanding Other Linux Distributions

A common comment is that Hyper-V allows only a very small number of the many Linux variants to run as a guest operating system. It is true that Microsoft supports only a few distributions and variations. But the key word in that sentence is *support*.

You have to understand what support really means to Microsoft. When Microsoft talks about support for Linux, it means that it has a partner it can work with when a customer has a technical issue. This is pretty hard to do with freeware such as Ubuntu or CentOS. Microsoft might have a limited set of supported distributions, but it does not mean that other distributions won't work (and work well) on Hyper-V. The truth is quite the contrary.

At the very least, you can run an unenlightened Linux virtual machine. This would use just the IDE controller and the legacy network adapter. The performance would not be great. A number of bloggers have documented how to install the Microsoft integration components for Linux on unsupported distributions. They will work, and work well, but Microsoft won't support this.

Microsoft included the Linux Integration Components in version 2.6.32 of the Linux kernel. Any Linux based on this kernel or newer will include those kernels and be able to use the synthetic devices, and the performance would be excellent.

Few of the Linux distributions stay current with the Linux kernel. The Linux Integration Components can be installed on many different Linux distributions. The process of installing them may vary, but all of the distributions are based on the same kernel. A quick search on the Internet will yield step-by-step instructions for the commonly used distributions.

Now you have the knowledge to deploy Hyper-V, configure it, use all the newest features, and deploy Linux or Windows virtual machines.

The Bottom Line

Deploy Hyper-V host servers There are a number of ways to build new Hyper-V host servers, depending on the size of your infrastructure and your need to rapidly expand the infrastructure.

Master It You have created an image of a Windows Server 2008 R2 Hyper-V host server. The original machine was configured with a number of external networks. You have deployed the image and found that new virtual machines cannot communicate on the physical network. What is wrong?

Configure Hyper-V You can configure Hyper-V to match the requirements of your organization.

Master It You are working as a consultant for a hardware manufacturer. A customer has purchased hardware from your company for a new Hyper-V cluster. They need Live Migration to be as quick as possible. They have purchased the equipment for a 10 Gb network for Live Migration. They are complaining that Live Migration is taking too long. You suspect that it is not operating on the 10 Gb network. What will you do to configure it?

Manage Linux virtual machines Hyper-V offers support for running Linux as a guest operating system.

Master It You have created a small virtual machine to run Red Hat Enterprise Linux 5. You configured a synthetic network adapter and a disk on a virtual SCSI controller. You have tried to configure the network adapter and the disk, but you cannot find the devices. What will you do?

Chapter 7

Virtual Machine Manager 2008 R2

Although you can manage Hyper-V using the Hyper-V console and the Failover Clustering console, almost, if not all, enterprises will manage their Hyper-V hosts using Virtual Machine Manager (VMM). VMM is a member of the Microsoft System Center family. It is the tool that most Hyper-V enterprise administrators will use the most.

VMM builds upon the built-in tools. It provides the ability to perform more complex tasks with little effort, it allows repeatable work to be done in a few mouse clicks, and it provides a PowerShell library for managing itself and Hyper-V. We will look at the reasons for using VMM and how it can be licensed. We will then talk about the planning and architecture of the virtualization management solution.

The most powerful features leverage the VMM library. This is where reusable resources such as virtual hard disks, scripts, ISO files, and templates are stored. A VMM administrator can delegate roles to allow restricted virtualization administrators to manage a piece of the infrastructure. But more importantly, a VMM administrator can empower selected staff members to become self-service users. Members of this role type have the ability to deploy virtual machines using the web-based Self-Service Portal without any need for administrative rights in Hyper-V or VMM. IT can control VM sprawl using a quota mechanism. The users can deploy virtual machines as and when needed, making them and the business happier with their newfound agile IT infrastructure. We will look at how you can build up content in the VMM library to simplify future Hyper-V administration. You then will see how that content can be used to enable self-service virtual machine provisioning in a controlled manner.

VMM also provides the ability to manage and migrate from an existing physical and virtual infrastructure. This chapter will describe how you can migrate from physical machines to virtual machines using VMM. We will also cover how VMM not only can manage but also can migrate from Microsoft Virtual Server 2005 R2 SP1 and VMware ESX and ESXi.

In this chapter, you will learn to

- Plan the installation of Virtual Machine Manager 2008 R2
- Use the library for automation and self-service features
- Manage and convert existing physical and virtual machines

Introducing Virtual Machine Manager 2008 R2

Microsoft System Center Virtual Machine Manager 2008 R2 is a product with several names. There is the formal and very long name, but it is also referred to as SCVMM 2008 R2 or VMM 2008 R2. The current version (previous versions were 2007 and 2008) is just referred to as SCVMM or VMM. Microsoft has several aims for VMM:

Centralized Management Most deployments of Hyper-V in a business environment will include a number of host servers. This could be quite a significant number of machines. Hyper-V can be managed with the built-in Hyper-V console and the Failover Clustering console, but these tools alone would not be enough to manage large or complex installations. VMM provides the ability to manage many host servers using a solution that is designed for this task. Policy can be defined using host groups, virtual machines can be deployed from centrally hosted templates, the delegation of administration can be configured, and so on.

Complete Management Solution Some functionality is added to Hyper-V by adding Virtual Machine Manager. Core functionality such as Live Migration is built into the Hyper-V product. However, some extras do come at a cost. The only officially supported method for converting existing physical Windows servers into Hyper-V virtual machines is to use VMM. A feature such as Quick Storage Migration (used to change the physical storage location of a virtual machine) is provided by VMM.

Simplified Administration A library is provided for storing objects that will be reused in the future. The most basic of these is the ISO image. This can be mounted by a virtual machine (either using local storage or over the network to the library share) and used to install an operating system or an application. VMM can be used to create clones of a virtual machine, create a sysprep-prepared virtual hard disk and template, or even move an idle virtual machine into the library. Administrators can use any item in the library. For example, a template and prepared VHD can be used to create new virtual machines in a quick and near-zero-touch manner.

Automation Everything that VMM does is based on PowerShell. Every wizard that you complete will allow you to view the resulting script. You can save that script for reuse in the VMM library for later customization and reuse. An administrator could deploy a large number of virtual machines by running a PowerShell script that is based on the code that is produced by the New Virtual Machine Wizard.

Empowered End User A self-service role and a web-based Self-Service Portal enables the organization to allow selected end users to deploy virtual machines from assigned templates that are stored in the VMM library. Application administrators, developers, and testers can deploy and destroy virtual machines as and when required with little delay or interaction with the IT infrastructure department. One of the concerns with this approach will be virtual machine sprawl. This could impact licensing. It certainly would consume hardware resources. This sprawl can be controlled by assigning quotas to self-service users and by assigning a quota score to each template that can be deployed. This concept is the basis of Visual Studio Lab Management 2010, a feature of Visual Studio 2010 (`http://msdn.microsoft.com/en-us/vstudio/ee712698.aspx`) that allows testers and developers to quickly set up and tear down complex virtual environments.

Cross-Platform Support Microsoft acknowledges that most of its big customers are already customers of VMware. Microsoft wants a piece of that pie because hardware virtualization is now the software foundation of server computing, not to mention Virtual Desktop

Infrastructure (VDI). Many of those organizations have been customers of VMware for some time. Many prefer VMware's ESX/ESXi because of a few features that it may have. Microsoft's approach is to ask how many of those virtual machines really need all the features of VMware's more expensive product. Using VMM, those organizations can manage the VMware infrastructure using Microsoft System Center and migrate those virtual machines to the cheaper Hyper-V. This gives Microsoft an opportunity to bring Hyper-V into that market. It also allows those organizations to centralize their systems management into a single integrated product set. VMM is also capable of managing the older Microsoft virtualization product, Virtual Server 2005 R2 SP1, and converting its virtual machines into Hyper-V ones.

System Center Integration One of the selling features of Hyper-V is the ability to manage the entire server network (including hardware, virtualization, operating system, and applications) with a set of integrated products from a single vendor. System Center's VMM can integrate with Operations Manager 2007/2007 R2 using Performance and Resource Optimization (PRO) management packs. Provided by Microsoft or hardware vendors or custom developed, these packs allow OpsMgr to detect issues, and it instructs VMM how to react. For example, a hardware PRO management pack might detect a server hardware fault, and VMM will react by moving all virtual machines to other hosts in the cluster using Live Migration. This means that the virtual machines will automatically have minimal downtime thanks to the fault.

VMM is a pretty big product. We will explore the core aspects of planning for and using VMM in this chapter. The focus will be on those features that are most critical to a Hyper-V deployment. You should read *Mastering Virtual Machine Manager 2008 R2* (Sybex, 2009) if you want to learn more about this product.

The Components of VMM

VMM uses a number of components to manage hosts and virtual machines. Understanding these components, shown in Figure 7.1, enables you to plan an architecture for your VMM deployment.

Virtual Machine Manager Server This is the server that will run the System Center management product. It is a single server. You can install VMM in a virtual machine. However, there are some considerations. Those who rely on VMM for Hyper-V administration will not want a potential chicken-and-egg scenario. For example, what do you do if the Hyper-V server that hosts the VMM virtual machine has a problem and you can no longer access VMM? This could cause issues where PRO is relied upon to resolve OpsMgr-detected faults automatically. Microsoft does not support performing a Live Migration of a virtual machine from VMM via that installation of VMM.

VMM Database A SQL database, either SQL Express or SQL Server, is used to store data about the configuration of VMM. This can be installed on the VMM server or on a dedicated SQL machine.

SCVMM Admin Console This console can be installed on the VMM server or on the computer of any administrator or delegated administrator. It is the GUI-based tool that will be used to manage VMM.

PowerShell This is a VMM module that is installed as part of VMM. VMM uses this module to perform all management actions on hosts and virtual machines. Administrators can save the scripts for later customization and usage, or they can write completely new scripts.

Library The library is a repository where files including templates, virtual hard disks, scripts, OS deployment answer files, ISO files, virtual floppy disks, and hardware profiles can be stored.

These resources can be deployed over the network to managed host servers. There is at least one library that is installed on the VMM server. Additional library servers can be deployed. A library consists of a file share and some metadata in the SQL database to describe and possibly link the contents. It is for this reason that you cannot use file replication techniques to completely replicate a VMM library. You might be able to replicate the files, but you won't be able to replicate objects, such as a template or hardware profile, that exist only in the SQL Server database.

FIGURE 7.1
The VMM components

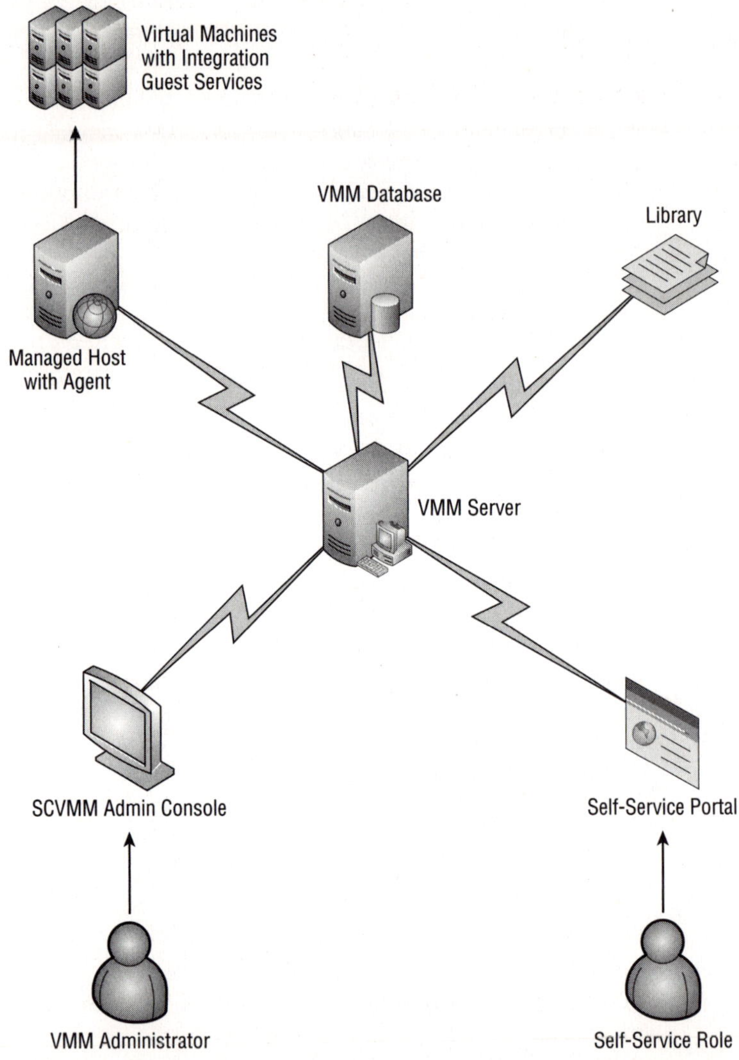

Self-Service Portal This is a web-based interface where members of a self-service role can deploy and manage their virtual machines. It provides them (assuming they have the granular access) with the ability to perform functions such as starting, stopping, and resetting a virtual machine or accessing the remote console.

Agent VMM will deploy an agent to any virtualization host that it will manage. This allows VMM to gather information about the host and the virtual machines on the host, and it allows VMM to control them.

Integration Guest Services These are known as Integration Components to the Hyper-V administrator. They aren't really a feature of VMM. VMM will automatically attempt to install the latest version of the Integration Services in a virtual machine whenever VMM deploys it or changes its physical storage location (not a Live Migration).

Planning for VMM 2008 R2

A smaller organization may be able to deploy VMM on a single server. A larger organization may need to consider deploying VMM across many servers. The one thing both will need to consider is the hardware required and how to size their libraries and databases.

Designing VMM 2008 R2

It is necessary to understand the numbers of your current and future planned hosts in order to decide how to design your VMM 2008 R2 architecture.

If you have 20 or fewer hosts, you can install all the components of VMM on a single server.

If you have between 21 and 150 hosts, then you should install either the library or the database on the VMM server. The remaining component should be installed on a dedicated machine. Microsoft recommends installing the database on this server and the library on another server.

If you have more than 150 hosts, then Microsoft recommends that each component is installed on a dedicated server.

An organization with a branch-office network with Hyper-V hosts in many locations can approach this in a few ways. A single VMM server can be installed in the central office. Administration delegation can provide required access to administrators and self-service role members in the branch offices. A centralized library is not really an option here. Imagine deploying a 40 GB VHD or a 4 GB ISO file from this library across the WAN to host servers in a remote location. The performance would be horrendous, application traffic would be badly affected, and all the speed and flexibility benefits of virtualization would be eradicated. A library can be installed in each site. This would allow files to be copied to hosts from a local library. Remember that there is no supported way to replicate all of the library contents. This means that each library will require content to be added manually. You can see an example of this deployment in Figure 7.2.

Many distributed organizations may require greater local ownership for political, business, or technology reasons. Individual installations of VMM can reside in each required location to suit the needs of the organization. This comes with a greater hardware and licensing cost. It also requires more administration and distributed skills.

Alternatively, a hybrid approach can be adopted where VMM servers are installed in head offices and hub offices. Each of these VMM-installed sites may manage host servers in their own sites and a number of host servers in subsidiary regional offices. The regional sites would be configured with libraries that are managed by the VMM servers in their managing head or hub offices. Figure 7.3 shows an example of this sort of architecture.

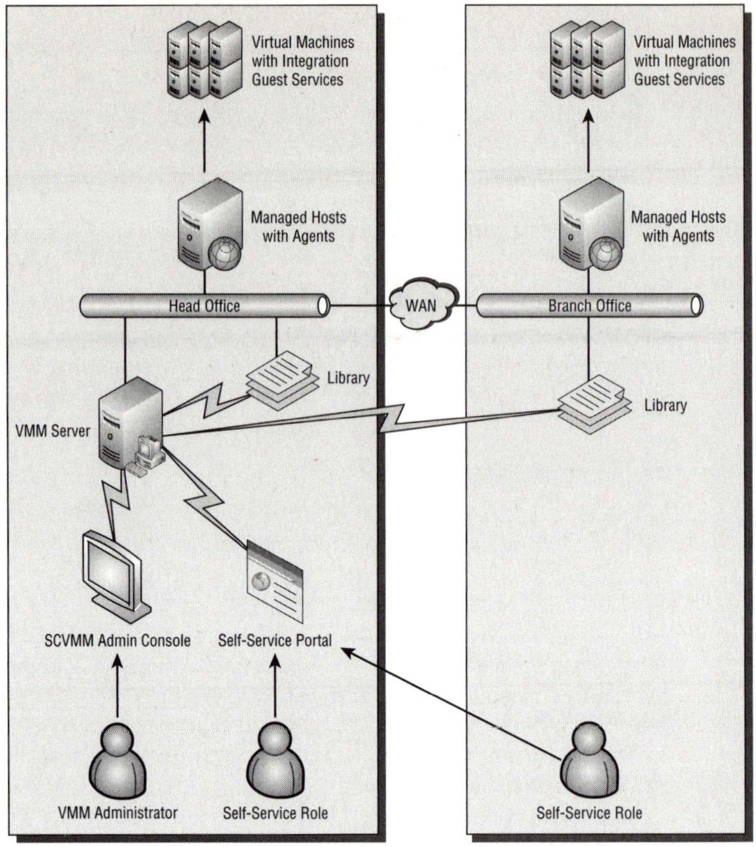

FIGURE 7.2
Branch-office Hyper-V hosts and a VMM library

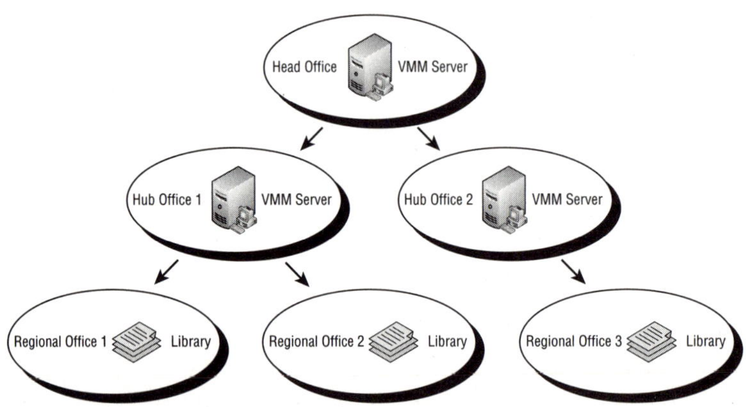

FIGURE 7.3
A hybrid deployment of VMM and library servers

FAULT TOLERANCE FOR VMM 2008 R2

The VMM server should not be installed on a cluster, so it does not really have a built-in method for making its service fault tolerant.

You could install VMM in a highly available virtual machine. There are two considerations for this:

Support Microsoft does not support using VMM to perform a Live Migration of the VMM virtual machine.

Complexity You need to be wary of creating a chicken-and-egg scenario where you might need to use VMM to manage a failed host server and that machine is hosting the VMM virtual machine.

The file share can be created as a highly available file share in a Windows Server 2008 or Windows Server 2008 R2 failover cluster. Windows 2003 clustering is not supported.

You can install the database in a SQL Server failover cluster. The SQL Server installation can run on a Windows Server 2003 or later cluster. The cluster must reside in a domain with a two-way trust with the domain that the VMM server is in. A service principal name (SPN) for the clustered SQL instance must be registered in Active Directory with the account of the SQL server.

VMM 2008 R2 System Requirements

The requirements for your installation will depend on your architecture. A single-server installation will have one set of requirements. And logically, installations with multiple servers will have different requirements.

The list of software requirements is pretty lengthy and spans multiple web pages. You can find the complete set here:

`http://technet.microsoft.com/en-us/library/cc764289.aspx`

The highlights are as follows:

Operating System The VMM server must be installed on Windows Server 2008 R2 or Windows Server 2008 64-bit.

Database You can use either SQL Server 2005 Express, SQL Server 2008 Express, SQL Server 2005, or SQL Server 2008. You should note that the free SQL Server Express edition has a maximum database size of 4 GB. The Express editions do not support VMM reporting. The Express edition is also not supported for integrating with Operations Manager 2007/2007 R2.

Windows Automated Installation Kit (WAIK) Much of the work done in VMM is operating system deployment. Like the rest of the Microsoft solutions in this space, VMM uses WAIK, mainly for the offline conversion method for physical machines. This allows you to customize and tweak the deployment of templates from the VMM library. VMM 2008 R2 will install WAIK for Windows 7 and Windows Server 2008 R2. This includes support for Windows Vista and Windows Server 2008.

We'll describe the specifications for each of the different architectures next. You should note that there is no recommendation for the size of the library. That is because no two organizations will have the same library contents. Some organizations may choose to keep a few dynamic VHDs and ISO images in the library. Some may keep many large fixed-size VHDs and ISO images in the library. The sizes of the VHDs will all be determined by the local VMM and Hyper-V administrators. You will need to add the required space to the following storage requirements. The best advice for sizing the library is as follows:

- Determine the type of VHD that you are going to use in your Hyper-V network. It is likely that you will choose fixed-size VHDs for maintenance and performance reasons (see Chapter 6).

- Use data from your previous testing to determine how many VHDs will be stored in the library and what size they will be.

If you are managing 5–10 hosts, then you can use the server specification shown in Table 7.1. This server will host the VMM server, the database, and the library.

TABLE 7.1: Single server with 5–10 hosts

Hardware	Minimum	Recommended
Processor	X64 Pentium 4, 2.8 GHz	X64 Dual Core Pentium 4, 2.8 GHz
Memory	2 GB	2 GB
Storage	10 GB	40 GB

If you are managing 11–20 hosts, then you can use the server specification shown in Table 7.2. This server will host the VMM server, the database, and the library.

TABLE 7.2: Single server with 11–20 hosts

Hardware	Minimum	Recommended
Processor	X64 Pentium 4, 2.8 GHz	X64 Dual Core Pentium 4, 2.8 GHz
Memory	2 GB	4 GB
Storage	10 GB	50 GB

If you are managing between 21 and 150 hosts, then the server specification shown in Table 7.3 should be used. This server will host the VMM server and the database. The library will be located on another server.

TABLE 7.3: VMM server with 21–150 hosts

Hardware	Minimum	Recommended
Processor	X64 Pentium 4, 2.8 GHz	X64 Dual CPU, Dual Core, 2.8 GHz
Memory	2 GB	4 GB
Storage (without a local VMM database)	10 GB	40 GB
Storage (with a local SQL Server Express database)	10 GB	50 GB
Storage (with a local SQL Server database)	80 GB	150 GB

If you are in the rare territory of managing more than 150 hosts, then you need to use the specifications in Table 7.4. SQL Server will not be installed on the VMM server in this type of architecture. The library will also be installed on another server.

TABLE 7.4: VMM server with more than 150 hosts

HARDWARE	MINIMUM	RECOMMENDED
Processor	X64 Pentium 4, 2.8 GHz	X64 Dual CPU, Dual Core, 2.8 GHz
Memory	4 GB	8 GB
Storage	10 GB	50 GB

Note that a single Virtual Machine Manager can manage up to 400 hosts and 8,000 virtual machines.

Supported Host Servers

Virtual Machine Manager 2008 R2 supports the following Windows platforms as manageable hosts:

- Windows Server 2008 R2
- Windows Server 2008 with Hyper-V
- Windows Server 2003/2003 R2 with Virtual Server 2005 R2 SP1
- Hyper-V Server 2008 R2

The free Hyper-V Server product, currently Hyper-V Server 2008 R2, was not listed as a supported host at the time of writing. However, we did confirm with Microsoft that it is indeed a tested and supported platform for VMM 2008 R2 to manage.

Virtual Machine Manager can also manage VMware's ESX and ESXi products using their management product as an intermediary. These are as follows:

- VMware vCenter 2.5
- VMware VirtualCenter 2.0.1

With one of those management solutions in place, you can manage the following VMware hosts with VMM 2008 R2:

- VMware ESX Server 3.5
- VMware ESX Server 3.0.2
- VMware ESX Server 3i

The release of VMM 2008 R2 did add support for vSphere 4.0, but only the VI3 features are supported. This does make one wonder if anyone would really use VMM 2008 R2 as the main console for managing vSphere 4.0 hosts.

VMM 2008 R2 Licensing

There are a number of ways to license VMM 2008 R2. As usual, the Microsoft licensing methods and pricing are subject to change. The methods of prices shown here were correct at the time of writing. You should check with a licensing specialist to see whether they are still valid. You may find that your licensing scheme offers a discount.

WHICH VERSION OF VMM?

Administrators and engineers who have been using Windows Server 2008 R2 Hyper-V and Virtual Machine Manager 2008 may have a question in mind. Can they still use VMM 2008 if they deploy or upgrade to Windows Server 2008 R2 Hyper-V or Hyper-V Server 2008 R2? The quick answer is no. VMM 2008 R2 introduces support for the newer features of the most recent versions of Hyper-V. VMM 2008 cannot support features such as Cluster Shared Volumes and Live Migration. You will need to purchase a new version of VMM for the server and managed hosts if you have not covered your licensing with Software Assurance (for upgrade rights).

You can use the traditional server installation and agent approach. With this approach, you purchase a Virtual Machine Manager 2008 R2 Enterprise edition license for the VMM server, which costs $869. Each managed host will require a client license, which costs $40.

Smaller organizations with fewer than five hosts can purchase Virtual Machine Manager 2008 R2 Workgroup edition. Five hosts can actually be quite a lot. There can be up to 384 virtual machines on a single Hyper-V host server. If you have an Hyper-V cluster, that could potentially be up to 1,000 virtual machines. It's difficult to call that small or even a workgroup! But those figures may be achievable with the new 8- and even 12-core density processors and extremely scalable servers that have recently been announced by hardware manufacturers. The Workgroup edition costs $505 and requires no additional host licenses.

Small to medium-sized organizations may want to use System Center Essentials 2010 for managing their server and desktop network. It includes VMM 2008 R2 as part of the bundle, as well as core components of Operations Manager 2007 R2 and Configuration Manager 2007 R2. There is a limitation of up to 50 servers (physical or virtual) that can be managed. You can learn more about this suite in Chapter 10.

Enterprise deployments of Hyper-V that will use two or more of the System Center products for management will probably be using System Center Management Suite licensing. An Enterprise version of this license ($1,198 per physical server or host) that is assigned to a host includes the rights to use all the System Center products (which includes VMM) to manage the parent partition and up to four virtual machines on that host. A Datacenter version of this license ($749 per CPU with a minimum two CPUs) includes the rights to manage the physical host and all virtual machines on that host with all the System Center products. This method of licensing not only can minimize the cost of deploying Hyper-V but can drastically reduce the costs of managing an existing server infrastructure once it is virtualized.

Using VMM 2008 R2

Installing Virtual Machine Manager 2008 R2 is quite simple. We are not going to cover the process here, but you can learn more about it by reading *Mastering Virtual Machine Manager 2008 R2* (Sybex, 2009).

Real World Scenario

THE DEFAULT LIBRARY

By default, VMM will place a library on the VMM server. As previously mentioned, larger deployments of VMM should use a library that is located elsewhere. Think of this in advance because you cannot change the default library location. A redundant library on the VMM server may be used accidentally and lead to a drop in performance. You can prevent this during the setup of VMM by telling it to use a shared folder on another server.

One thing we will discuss about the installation is the VMM service account. When you install VMM, you are presented with the choice of running the service as Local System or using a domain user account. You should use the domain user account option. Create a domain-based user account that will only ever be used for your VMM installation. If there are multiple VMM servers, then you will need multiple VMM service accounts. In this example, the VMM service will be running as `demo\vmmsvc`. This will enable contents in the library to be accessed across the network by Hyper-V hosts, and it will tidy up the integration with OpsMgr.

We are going to focus on using the core functionality of VMM 2008 R2. In this section, we will be looking at managing Hyper-V hosts. We will start managing Hyper-V hosts, use host groups, add content to the library, build a virtual machine, create a template from it, and then deploy virtual machines from that template.

The lab in this chapter will use a number of machines in the `demo.local` Active Directory domain, as shown in Table 7.5.

TABLE 7.5: The lab

MACHINE NAME	ROLE	SPECIFICATION
DC1	Domain Controller	Windows Server 2008 R2 1 GB RAM 1 CPU C: drive
VMM	Virtual Machine Manager	Windows Server 2008 R2 1 GB RAM (2 GB recommended) 1 CPU C: drive (OS) D: drive (VMM Library)
Host1	Hyper-V Server	Windows Server 2008 R2 8 GB RAM 1 CPU C: drive (parent partition) E: drive (virtual machines)

TABLE 7.5: The lab *(CONTINUED)*

MACHINE NAME	ROLE	SPECIFICATION
VServer	Virtual Server 2005 R2 SP1	Windows Server 2003 R2 SP2 4 GB RAM 1 CPU C: drive (OS) D: drive (virtual machines)
vCenter	VMware vCenter 4.*x*	Windows Server 2003 R2 SP2 2 GB RAM 1 CPU C: drive
ESX	VMware ESX 4.*x*	VMware ESX 4.*x* 4 GB RAM 1 CPU 1 disk
Server3	Physical SharePoint Server	Windows Server 2008 R2 1 GB RAM 1 CPU C: drive
Server4	File Server VM on ESX	Windows Server 2003 R2 SP2 1 GB RAM 1 CPU C: drive
Server5	SQL Server 2005 VM on ESX	Windows Server 2003 R2 SP2 1 GB RAM 1 CPU C: drive
Server6	SQL Server 2005 VM on VServer	Windows Server 2003 R2 SP2 512 MB RAM 1 CPU C: drive

To be economic with hardware, you can run a number of the machines as virtual machines. To write this book, the DC1, VMM, vCenter, and Server3 machines all ran as virtual machines on Host1.

Additional space will be required on Host1 to create a few virtual machines for the exercises in this chapter.

Adding and Configuring Hosts

VMM will manage Windows-based hosts using an agent that is installed on them. You will use VMM to discover those hosts and deploy an agent.

If you plan to manage a new Hyper-V installation with VMM, then you should delay any virtual machine installations until VMM is in place. This is because VMM maintains a few extra settings per virtual machine. VMM will also be a major time-saver once you have configured the library with just a little content.

Discovering Host Servers

Figure 7.4 shows the VMM admin console of a new and nonconfigured VMM installation. This is how it will appear the very first time you run the tool. For the sake of your own convenience, you will probably want to install the VMM admin console on your own computer and manage the VMM server from there.

FIGURE 7.4
A new VMM installation

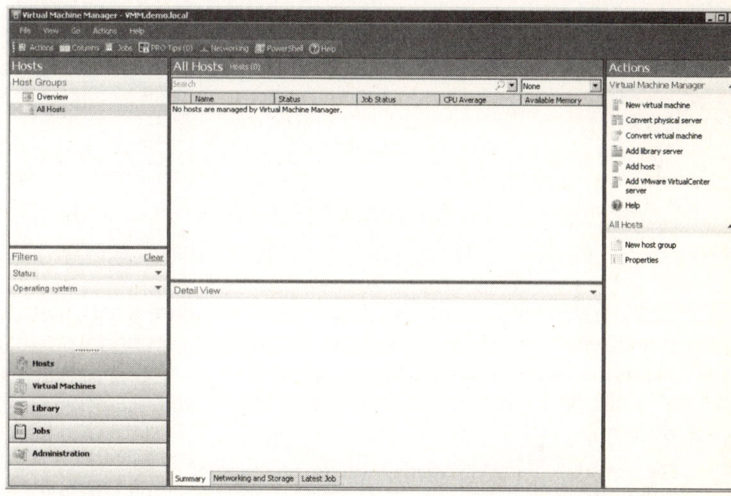

You can start the discovery process for a new Hyper-V (or any supported) host by clicking the Add Host link in the Actions pane on the right side. Figure 7.5 shows the wizard.

By default this wizard (as shown) will attempt to discover and add a Windows-based host that is a member of a trusted Active Directory domain. With this method, VMM will automatically deploy the VMM agent on the host. If the host is running Windows Server 2003, then VMM will automatically install Virtual Server 2005 R2 SP1 if it is not already present. If the host is running Windows Server 2008 or Windows Server 2008 R2, then VMM will automatically enable the Hyper-V if it is not already enabled. VMM will warn you before it installs the virtualization software on the host.

VMM will also automatically enable Hyper-V on each member machine if you enter the name of a cluster. You might consider this to be a time-saver, but you really should take a more considered approach to setting up a Hyper-V cluster. Set up Hyper-V and Failover Clustering before you set up VMM. This will allow you to take control of absolutely everything and test the cluster before you bring it under the control of VMM. Once you are ready, you can add the cluster.

To find a host server that is an Active Directory member, you can search Active Directory for currently unmanaged hosts. You will need to enter your administrative domain-based credentials for the host. The Host Is In A Trusted Domain check box allows you to let VMM know either if the host is in a domain in the same forest as the VMM server or if it is in a domain where there is a two-way trust in place.

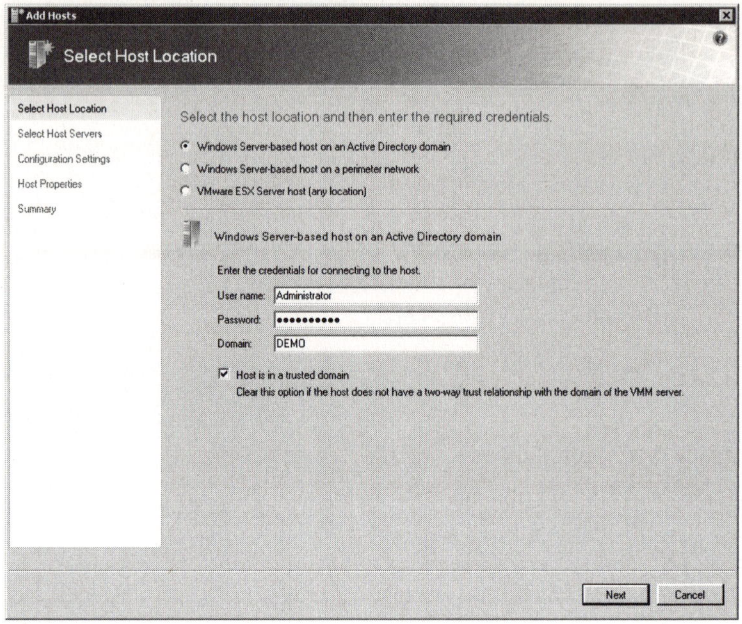

FIGURE 7.5 Adding an AD member Windows host

Note that Hyper-V clusters must be in a domain where there is a two-way trust with the domain that the VMM server is in. VMM does not support managing Hyper-V clusters that are in a nontrusted domain.

If the host is not in a trusted domain, for example, a workgroup, then the procedure will be different.

To start the process, you will need to manually install the agent on the desired host. The Agent Setup Wizard (the setup routine will guide you through the creation of an encryption key pair and a security file). You will copy this security file to the VMM server and then start the Add Hosts Wizard. You will select the Windows Server-Based Host On A Perimeter Network option, shown in Figure 7.6. You will then provide the security file when prompted. This will allow VMM and the host's VMM agent to communicate in a secure and trusted manner in the absence of a domain two-way trust or Active Directory authentication.

The host server in this lab, Host1, is a member of the `demo.local` domain, so we will use the Windows Server-Based Host On An Active Directory Domain option.

Figure 7.7 shows the Select Host Servers screen in the Add Hosts Wizard. Here is where you will specify the names of any hosts you want to control with VMM or search for any available hosts.

Enter the fully qualified domain name, such as **demo.local**, in the Domain field. You can enter the computer name of the host in the Computer Name field.

The Skip Active Directory Name Verification option will be used if the host server is in a different tree in the forest, that is, if there is a disjointed namespace. The computer name of the host server must be a registered SPN in Active Directory.

FIGURE 7.6
Adding a host on a perimeter network

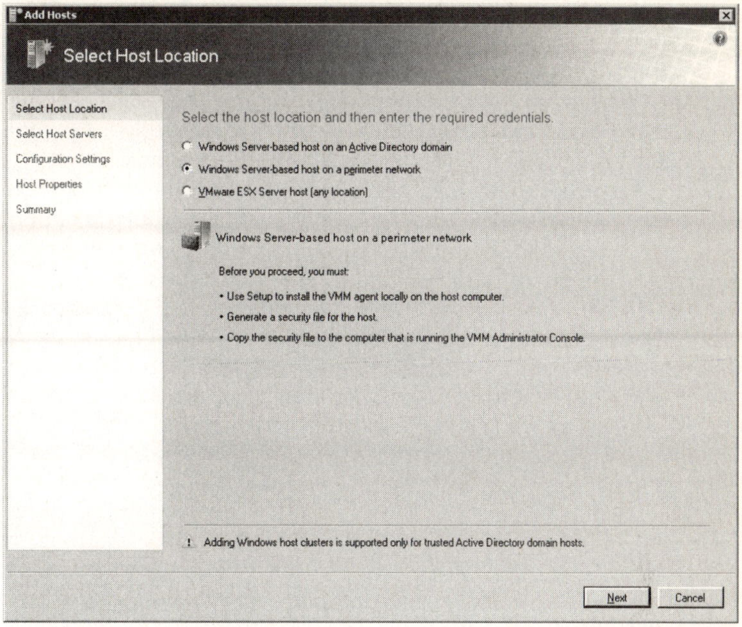

FIGURE 7.7
Selecting host servers

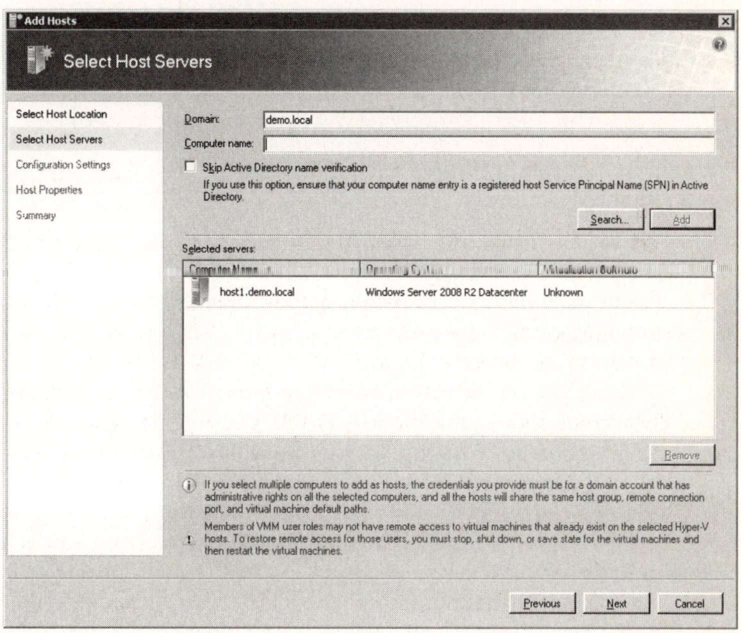

In this case, Host1 is a member of the same DNS namespace as the VMM server, so you can simply enter **host1** in Computer Name and click the Add button. In the case of a cluster, you will enter the name of the cluster account object here.

When you click the Next button, you will be warned that the host server might have to be rebooted if virtualization must be installed or enabled. That will not be required if you have already enabled Hyper-V on the host or the cluster.

Figure 7.8 shows the Configuration Settings screen. Here you will specify the host group that the new host will be added to. We'll cover host groups in a little while. Without any host groups, you will add the new host or cluster to the All Hosts group.

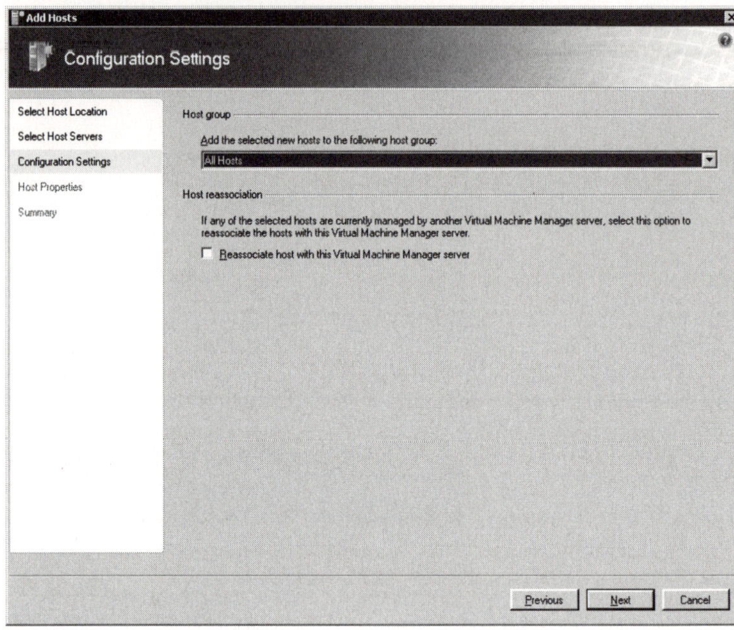

FIGURE 7.8
Configuration Settings screen

The Reassociate Host With This Virtual Machine Server check box is used when the host is currently being managed by a different VMM server.

Figure 7.9 shows the Host Properties screen. This is where you can specify the storage locations on the host where virtual machines can be created. This is simple enough with a standalone host, as shown in Figure 7.9.

Things are a little different with Hyper-V clusters. In the case of a Windows Server 2008 R2 cluster, you should add the paths to the Cluster Shared Volumes (CSVs) that are present in the cluster. Actually, in reality, you will probably only enter the paths to the currently active (for new VM placement) CSVs. You should return to Chapter 6 to learn more about CSV.

In the case of a Windows Server 2008 cluster, you cannot really add any entry. That is because you will be using the one VM per SAN LUN approach, so there is no repeatable storage location.

The last screen is Summary. The View Script button is where you can see some of the magic happening. This will open a Notepad document containing the PowerShell script that will be used to add your Hyper-V host.

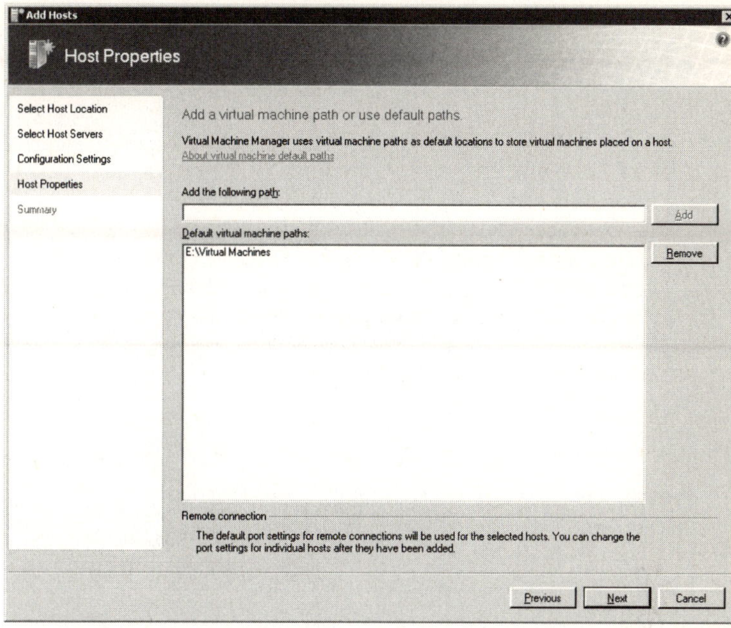

FIGURE 7.9
Host Properties screen

Imagine that you are adding Host1 and Host2, all the way up to Host20 into VMM. Would you really want to go through all of that work? If you view this script, you can save it into the library for later reuse. The library in this case is a share (`\\vmm\msscvmmlibrary`) that is located in `D:\MSSCVMMLibrary` on the VMM server. You could save the script into `D:\MSSCVMMLibrary\Scripts` as `Add Hosts.PS1`. You then could edit it and copy the `Add-VMHost` cmdlet (pronounced as "command-let") for the other 19 hosts that you need to add. You then just run that script, and your hosts will be added in exactly the same way as Host1 was.

With more experience, you'll soon learn how you can take advantage of this feature to automate many operations and responses to situations that may occur. For example, you could run a script to deploy a new virtual machine from a VMM library template whenever Operations Manager notices some drop in performance in a monitored n-tier application.

You can monitor the progress of any job that is running in VMM. Figure 7.10 shows how you can track the progress of a managed host or virtual machine. You navigate to the object you want to check on and click the Latest Job in the lower pane. Here you can see the progress and status of each step in the job.

This is actually a great place to learn how VMM works. You can see each step that is performed. More complex operations such as creating a virtual machine or running a Quick Storage Migration job contain many steps. Monitoring their progress gives you a peek under the hood to see some of the mechanisms in action.

You can see the progress and status of currently running and past jobs by clicking the Jobs wunderbar in the bottom left, as shown in Figure 7.11. The Summary tab will show the progress and status of the steps if the job is still running. The Details tab will show information about when each step started and ended. The Change Tracking tab shows previous and new values for the object that was managed. You can consider this to be like a high-level event viewer for VMM.

FIGURE 7.10
Monitoring the latest job

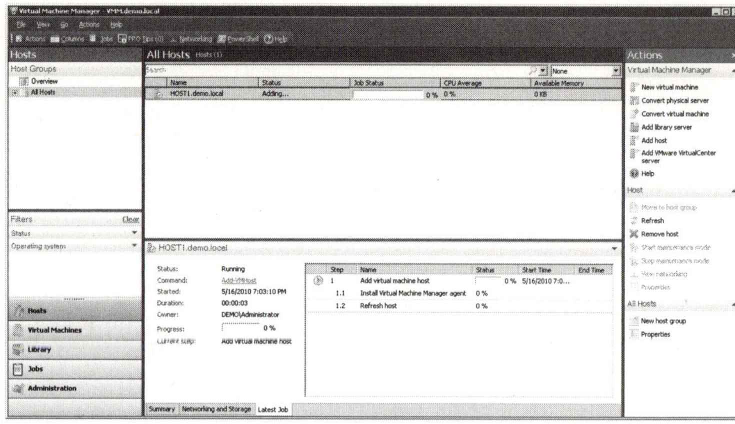

FIGURE 7.11
Job progress

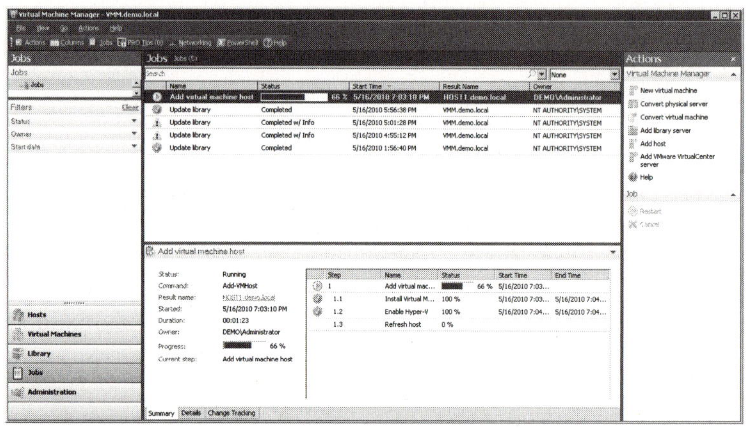

When the job has completed, a new host object will appear in the console. Click the Hosts wunderbar in the bottom left to see it. It will appear in the Host Groups pane and in the center details pane. Any added cluster will also appear. You can expand the cluster to see the member Hyper-V hosts that are automatically added by VMM.

VMM is not wired into any objects that it manages. This means that it is not aware of the exact progress of any running job, nor is it aware of any changes that may happen outside of its control. For example, a change to a virtual machine on a managed host won't necessarily appear in VMM straightaway. Instead, VMM uses a series of scheduled refresh jobs to detect changes. The host refresher runs every 30 minutes, by default. You can force a host or a cluster refresh by right-clicking it and selecting Refresh or by using the `Refresh-Host` cmdlet. This will cause a refresh job to run. Like any job, you can monitor its progress. Any changes to the host will be detected.

CONFIGURING A HOST

You can start troubleshooting and configure a host by right-clicking it and selecting Properties. The Summary tab gives you a quick view of the configuration of the host in question.

The Status tab, shown in Figure 7.12, shows the status of the various components on the host. This is where you will go if the host status (in the Host views when you click the Hosts wunderbar) is set to Needs Attention. Ideally it will only indicate the need to upgrade a VMM agent after a VMM patch has been deployed.

FIGURE 7.12
Host status

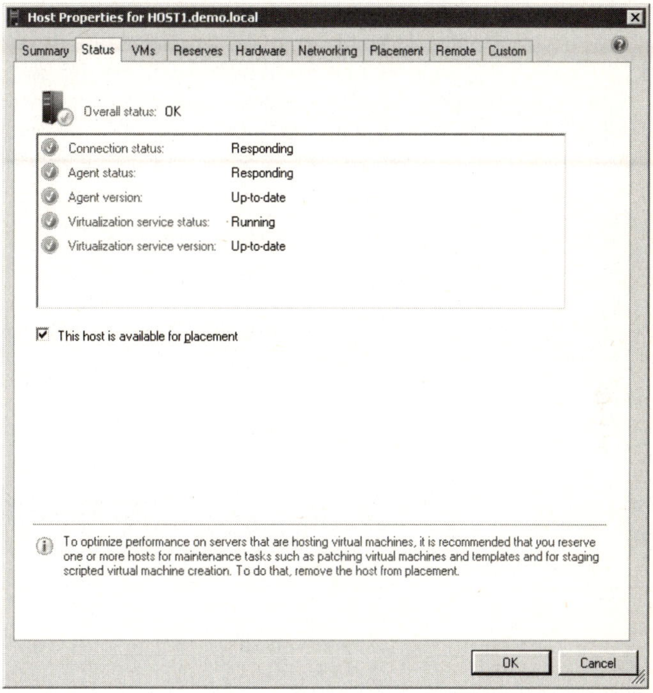

VIRTUAL MACHINE MANAGER PATCHING

Microsoft has released patches for VMM 2008 R2 since it was released. Some of these appear in Windows Updates. You can control these via System Center Configuration Manager (WSUS). Make sure that the VMM product is enabled in the catalog synchronization. Then make sure that the updates are approved.

An update to VMM may require any deployed VMM agents to be updated. You can do this by selecting a host and clicking Update Agent. This can be a labor-intensive task if you have lots of hosts to update. In this case, you can use the `Update-VMMManagedComputer` PowerShell cmdlet to script the job. Write the script, save it in your library, and run it whenever a VMM update requires an agent update. You will know of this requirement with a little bit of research on your updates. This means you can schedule the execution of the script immediately after the update is deployed to the VMM server, assuming that all of your change control processes are completed and signed off.

The This Host Is Available For Placement check box is enabled by default. This is pretty self-explanatory; VMM will consider this host when trying to migrate or create a virtual machine. You can clear this when you prevent a host from having new virtual machines. For example, you could use this when you consider the host to be fully utilized and VMM occasionally tries to place virtual machines on it.

The VMs tab gives you a glimpse at what virtual machines are currently running on the host. The Browse button allows you to add virtual machines to this host. The registration process requires that you browse to the folder containing the virtual machine's files. In the case of Virtual Server, you browse to the folder containing the `.vmc` file.

Figure 7.13 shows the Reserves tab in the Host Properties dialog box (right-click a host and select Properties). This is where you can configure how much spare capacity must be kept on a host when VMM is trying to decide whether a virtual machine can fit on the host. A number of criteria are configurable:

- CPU percentage: Set to 20 percent by default
- Memory (in MB): Set to 512 MB by default
- Disk space (in MB): Set to 100 MB by default
- Maximum disk I/O per second (IOPS): Set to 10,000 by default
- Network capacity percentage: Set to 10 percent by default

FIGURE 7.13
Host reserves

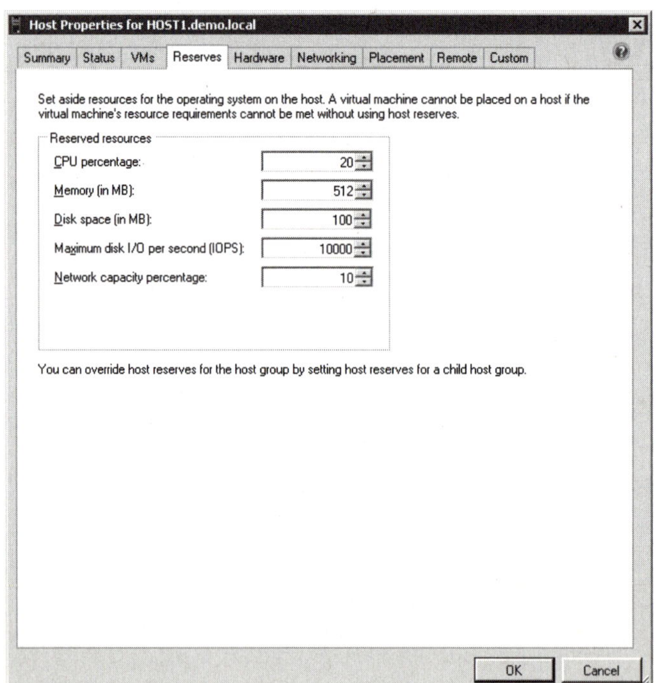

The concept of a reserve can be misunderstood at first. Take memory, for example. You might immediately think that VMM is keeping 512 MB for the parent partition. In a host with 48 GB of RAM, would this mean that there is 47.5 GB available for virtual machine usage? No; what this setting will do is keep an additional 512 MB (or whatever you configure) of RAM spare in addition to whatever is currently being used by the parent partition (often around 2 GB). Typically this means that VMM is allowing for 2.5 GB of RAM (if the actual parent partition usage is 2 GB) to be used by the parent partition. In the case of the 48 GB RAM host, there would be around 45.5 GB RAM available to virtual machines on the host.

The Hardware tab is where you can see and control the status of the hardware in the host.

The Networking tab allows you to manage virtual networks (switches) on the host without having to use the Hyper-V console.

The Placement tab allows you to alter the folder locations where virtual machines will be created or placed.

The remote connection port on the Remote tab allows you to modify the TCP port that is used for connecting to a virtual machine on that host.

The Host Properties dialog box allows you to configure one host at a time. That might be OK in a small environment, but it will be an ordeal for the poor engineer, administrator, or consultant who has to do it in a larger environment. Instead of using this method, you can use a host group instead.

Host Groups

A host group is like a folder in the Hosts view in the SCVMM admin console. However, it does more than just organize your hosts and clusters. A host group is a mechanism that allows you to configure all hosts within it through a single interface.

A default host group called All Hosts is present in VMM. This will suffice if you have just a few hosts to manage with identical settings. These settings include host reserves and PRO configuration. You will need to create more host groups in larger environments where hosts may require different settings. You can also use host groups as part of your delegation of VMM administration.

You can create a host group in the Hosts view by right-clicking an existing host group (such as All Hosts) and selecting New Host Group. This creates what appears like a folder under the selected host group.

The interface provides a drag-and-drop mechanism. You can drag one host group into another. The following are the potential host group inheritance scenarios:

Create a Child Host Group This is when you create a host group within another host group. The host reserve settings configured in the parent will automatically be inherited by the child host group. The PRO settings will be inherited from the parent.

Drag a Child Host Group to a Parent The host reserve settings are not inherited. The child host group will inherit the PRO settings from the parent host group if the Inherit PRO Setting From Parent Host Group option is enabled in the child host group.

Change the Parent Host Group Settings You are given the choice to force inheritance of new host reserve settings from the parent to all child host groups when you change them in the parent host group. This will cause all settings in the parent to be applied to the contained host groups. The children host groups will inherit the PRO settings from the parent host group if the Inherit PRO Setting From Parent Host Group option is enabled in the children host groups.

You can also drag a managed host or cluster into a host group. This will force the hosts to take the settings from the host group that contains them. Once your host groups are set up, you can do the following:

- Organize your hosts and clusters.
- Quickly apply reserve settings and PRO settings to many hosts at once.
- Use them for delegation of VMM administration.

We've already covered the subject of host reserves, so we'll move onto the PRO properties of a host group.

As you can see in Figure 7.14, PRO can be enabled only when VMM has been integrated with an Operations Manager server. This makes sense — Operations Manager uses PRO management packs to detect issues with virtual machines or hosts and then instructs VMM to respond to the situation.

FIGURE 7.14
Host group PRO settings

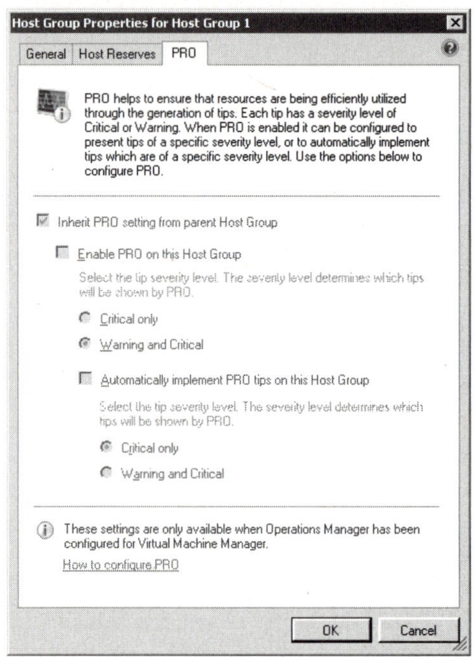

When you enable PRO, you can force the settings in the current host group to be applied to all children host groups by selecting the Inherit PRO Settings From Parent Host Group check box.

PRO can be enabled for a host group by selecting Enable PRO On This Host Group. With this enabled, you can specify whether PRO should react to critical or warning and critical events. Choosing Critical Only will cause there to be responses to only the most severe issues detected by OpsMgr.

By default, PRO does not do anything automatically. Most organizations will want to get the most out of the integration of VMM and OpsMgr by enabling automated implementation of PRO tips (the responses to detected issues). You can do this by selecting the Automatically Implement

PRO Tips On This Host Group check box. You can then choose whether PRO tips should be implemented automatically for critical or warning and critical events.

What will happen if you do not enable automated PRO tips implementation? VMM will open a window with the PRO tip. It will wait for an administrator to choose how to respond to the situation. Imagine if the PRO tip detected a performance or a hardware fault issue on a host that affected the virtual machines. Would you really want to wait for an administrator to see the window on their desktop (assuming they have the VMM console open) and respond to it? It is likely that most who integrate VMM with OpsMgr will enable some form of automated PRO tips implementation.

Hyper-V hosts and clusters are now controlled by VMM. You will want to create some virtual machines on the hosts. To do that, you will need to start managing the library.

Library Management

The library is where you will store reusable resources such as scripts, templates, virtual machines, and ISO images. You will need to be able to add resources to the library and maybe even create additional VMM libraries that are located close to remote host servers. Large Hyper-V installations will require one or more libraries in the one site to be created on servers other than the VMM server.

Creating a Library

The requirements for a library server are as follows:

Operating System The library server must be running Windows Server 2008 R2, Windows Server 2008, or Windows Server 2003 with Service Pack 1 or newer.

Active Directory The library server must be a member of a domain that has a two-way trust with the VMM server's domain.

Filesystem The filesystem cannot be case sensitive.

The process of creating an additional library starts with creating a file share on the server that will be the library server. In this example, a folder called MSSCVMMLibrary has been created and shared on Server3.

The share should grant the read permissions to the VMM server computer account. You will probably want to grant access to the Hyper-V hosts to contents in the library share. This will allow them to mount an ISO image without copying it locally. The process of setting this up will be discussed later. It will require that each Hyper-V host will have read access to the share as well. You should probably create a Hyper-V hosts Active Directory–based security group and add the computer objects for the hosts into it. You can then grant read access to that group. The Hyper-V hosts will require a reboot afterward.

Multiple Library Servers

VMM does not have a method to synchronize the contents of multiple library servers. Distributed File System Replication (DFSR) or a third party can be used to replicate files between libraries, but it is not supported. This is because VMM is not DFSR aware. Some library contents exist only in SQL. Every file that is added to the library is assigned a GUID. Some SQL objects, such as templates, will link to files (such as VHDs) based on their GUID. Use of DFS namespace is not supported.

You can navigate to the Library wunderbar in the SCVMM admin console and click Add Library Server to create the new library. The first screen in the Add Library Server Wizard asks for you to enter domain-based credentials that will have administrative rights on the new library server.

The Select Library Servers screen asks for you to enter the name or search for the new server that will be configured as a library server.

Figure 7.15 shows the Add Library Shares screen. Here you can select the shared folder on the server that you want to use as the library folder. You should select the Show Hidden Shares check box if the shared folder is hidden.

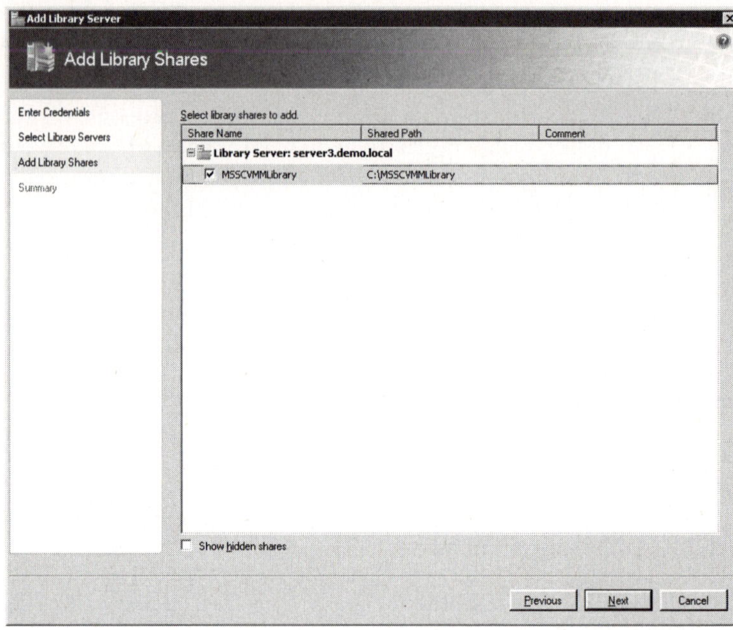

FIGURE 7.15
Add Library Shares screen

You can remove the library server from VMM by selecting it and clicking the Remove task in the Actions pane.

ADD CONTENT TO THE LIBRARY

This is one of the simpler tasks you'll do. Adding files to the library is just a matter of file copying in Windows Explorer. The trick to this is to keep things organized. Imagine all the different types of ISO images you might download and use in Hyper-V. You could have dozens of ISO images to support the various versions, editions, and architectures of Windows Server alone. Add in SQL Server, SharePoint, Windows desktop operating systems, Microsoft Office, Exchange, and all of their service packs, and that's a pretty big set of files. You should try to use a folder structure that keeps the files organized and easy to find. You might have folders called ISO, VHDs, and Scripts in the library folder. ISO might be further broken down by vendor and then by product group, such as SQL, Windows Server, and Windows Desktop.

Another useful tip is to rename any ISO files that you download. `Windows Server 2008 R2.ISO` means a lot more to people than `en_windows_server_2008_r2_standard_enterprise_datacenter_and_web_x64_dvd_x15-59754.ISO`, especially since we know that the ISO always contains all editions of the operating system and that it is x64 only.

Many downloads are not provided as ISO files. You should find a good utility for creating ISO images and install it on your workstation. This will save you quite a bit of time; you can simply provide access for the ISO to the virtual machine just by mounting the ISO instead of repeatedly copying or downloading the file.

You will rush back to view the library in the SCVMM admin console the first time that you add a file to a library server. And you will likely wonder why your file isn't there. You'll double-check everything and think something is broken.

Remember that VMM isn't wired into everything to get always-current status updates. It uses scheduled refreshers. The library refresher runs every hour by default. You can force a refresh by selecting the library server and clicking the Refresh task in the Actions pane. You can also use the `Refresh-LibraryShare` cmdlet in PowerShell. You can change the default refresh interval by clicking Library Settings in the Actions pane while viewing the library.

Figure 7.16 shows the refreshed library. The Resource pane in the top left allows you to select a library server and drill down through the folders within the library share. The Filters pane allows you to control what content will be shown. By default, all content is visible. The central pane shows the content that is present within the location that is selected and that is allowed by the filter.

FIGURE 7.16
The library contents

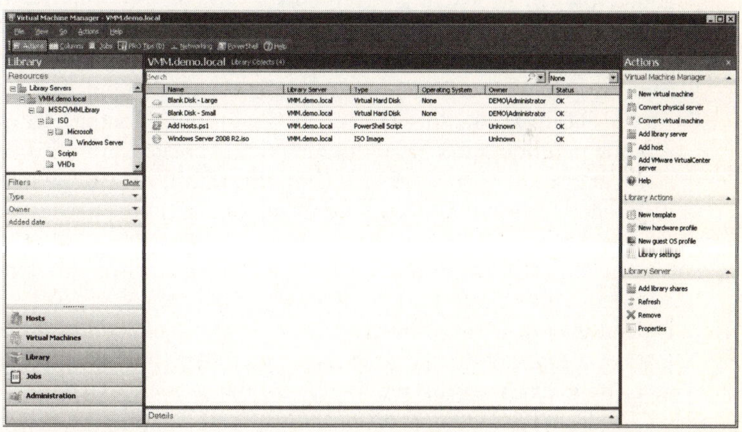

When you refresh the library, you will be able to see the PowerShell script that was created and any other content that you might have added to the library. You should add at least one ISO image for a Windows Server operating system. You can see in Figure 7.16 that the ISO for installing Windows Server 2008 R2 has been added.

Real World Scenario

OPERATING SYSTEM DEPLOYMENT

Once you create your templates, you will likely never need to install a Windows operating system from an ISO image until a new version is released by Microsoft. You might not want to even deal with ISO images. You might already have a build process in place.

You can use network-based operating system deployment solutions such as Windows Deployment Services or the operating system deployment feature of Configuration Manager 2007. Remember that you cannot boot from the network using a synthetic network adapter in Hyper-V; you must use the legacy network adapter.

You then have a choice to make. You can create a template from your new virtual machine. The advantage is that you can use self-service, delegation, and PowerShell to quickly deploy new virtual machines with operating systems. You can also choose to only ever use your existing operating system mechanisms. The advantage is that this will service both physical and virtual machines. However, it will require delegated roles to deploy virtual machines with blank disks and legacy network adapters, deploy an operating system, and then change the network adapter to a synthetic one (for performance reasons).

CREATE HARDWARE PROFILES

A hardware profile is a virtual machine specification. It describes the virtual devices that will be added to a virtual machine that is created based on this hardware profile.

You can create a hardware profile in the library. Browse to Profiles in the Resources pane, and click New Hardware Profile in the Actions pane to start the New Hardware Profile dialog box, shown in Figure 7.17. The General tab allows you to name and describe the profile.

The Hardware Settings tab allows you to configure the hardware. This will be used as a starting point for any virtual machine that is created from this hardware profile.

Most of this will be identical to anything you have done in the Hyper-V console. The one difference is the configuration of the virtual machine processor, which is illustrated in Figure 7.18.

You still need to specify how many virtual processors the virtual machine will have. But VMM also uses a rather vague processor model approach. This doesn't actually restrict or expand the processor resources that are made available to the virtual machine. It is actually used by VMM to estimate what resources will be required by the virtual machine when VMM is trying to place it on a suitable Hyper-V host server.

A few changes were made in this example. The processor was configured to match the requirements of this type of virtual machine. The legacy network adapter was deleted and replaced with a synthetic network adapter. A SCSI controller was also added; this will allow the hot-addition of VHDs while the virtual machine is running.

The hardware profile is saved into the library. It is not visible as a file. It resides in the SQL Server database and is independent of the physical library servers and not linked to any files. This means that you do not need to re-create this hardware profile on other library servers. It will need to be re-created on any other VMM servers that you may have.

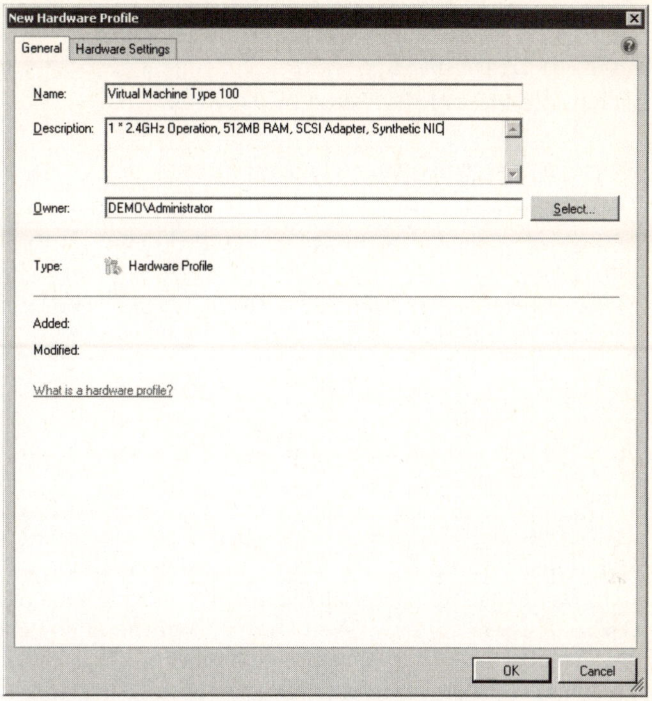

FIGURE 7.17
New Hardware Profile Wizard

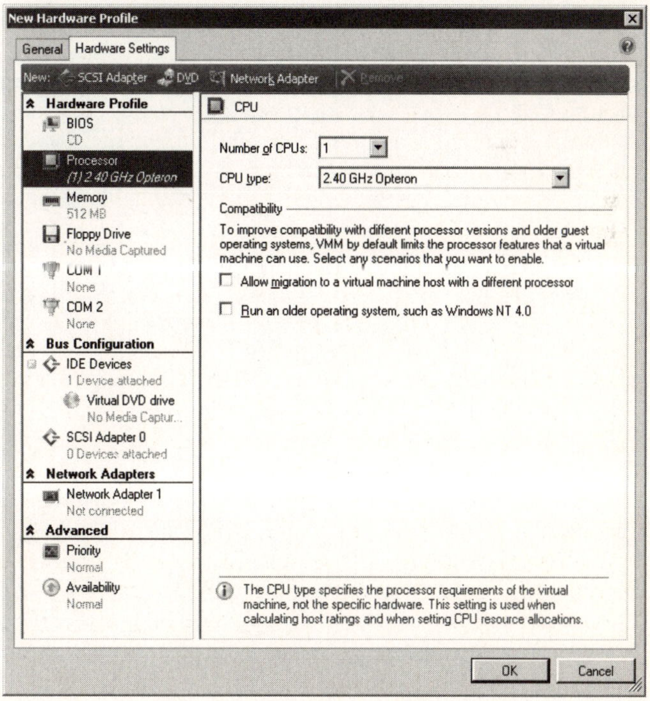

FIGURE 7.18
Hardware settings and processor settings

You may have many hardware profiles. You can copy this hardware profile to create new ones, which can then be customized. This will speed up the process of creating custom hardware profiles. This technique was used in this exercise to create an additional hardware profile with two virtual processors and 1 GB of RAM.

Enable Network Access to Library Files

There are two ways to mount an ISO image in a virtual machine using VMM. One method will copy the file to the virtual machine's storage location. This is slow (a 4 GB ISO takes time to copy) and consumes disk space. Sometimes the ISO gets left behind. This not only can consume storage but also can prevent the ISO being mounted again using the same technique. If this happens, you need to either delete the file or mount it manually using the Hyper-V console.

The other technique is to mount the ISO image over the network without copying it from the library. This is where one of the more common questions arises; this option is often tried without the required preparation, and it ends up as a support call or a post to a forum. This operation will fail with a confusing lack of privileges error if you don't do the required Active Directory preparatory work.

This process will require you to modify permissions on the Hyper-V computer objects in Active Directory. You will need to launch Active Directory Users and Computers, navigate to each Hyper-V host computer object, and edit the properties.

Browse to the Delegation tab (Figure 7.19), and select the Trust This Computer For Delegation To Specified Services Only. Select Use Any Authentication Protocol. Click the Add button. This will open another dialog box called Add Services. Click the Users Or Computers button, and enter the name of the library server (VMM). You should then select the cifs protocol. You would repeat this for every library server that this host will access. You can click OK to return to the host properties and close that dialog box. You will then repeat this process with each Hyper-V host object.

Figure 7.19
Configuring CIFS delegation

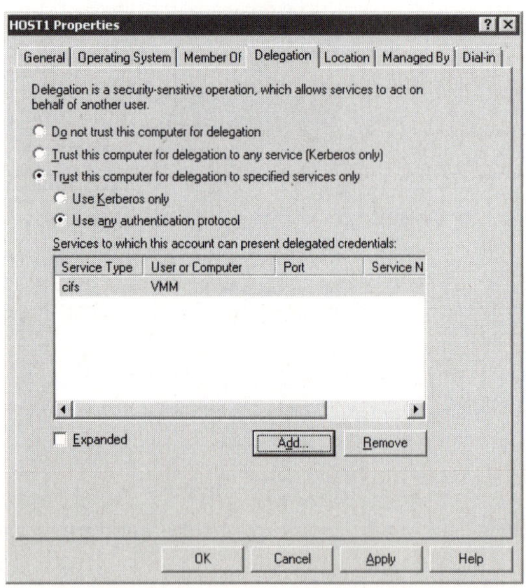

At this point, you have an active VMM library with content that can be shared with virtual machines. You are now able to create a virtual machine.

Creating Virtual Machines

The most valuable parts of VMM center on the creation of virtual machines from templates that are stored in the library. The process is similar to what you might do in the physical world of operating system deployment:

1. A workgroup member machine is built.
2. The computer is set up with service packs, patches, and configured as required.
3. Sysprep is run, and an image is captured.
4. New machines are deployed from the template.

The difference is that the tools you use are different. There is no need to create boot images, create installation images, or deal with drivers. You don't even have to run sysprep. The VMM job will take care of that for you, as well as doing all of the file copying. It even makes the unattended parts of the setup quite easy.

In this section, you are going to do the following:

1. Prepare a workgroup member virtual machine by building it manually.
2. Convert that machine into a template.
3. Deploy a virtual machine from the template.

We will also discuss some of the ways you can customize deployments based on this single template.

Manually Build a Virtual Machine

Without any templates in the library, the only way to build a virtual machine is the old-fashioned way; you need to create a virtual machine with an empty VHD and install the operating system. You can use unattended techniques such as Windows Deployment Services, Configuration Manager, or even an unattended answer file supplied in a second mounted ISO (remember to remove the second virtual CD/DVD drive afterward). We will create the virtual machine and deploy the operating system from the Windows Server 2008 R2 ISO installation media that is in the library.

You can create and manage virtual machines by clicking the Virtual Machines wunderbar in the bottom left of the SCVMM admin console. Click New Virtual Machines in the Actions pane to start the process.

Figure 7.20 shows the New Virtual Machine Wizard. You have two choices. You can create a machine from an existing virtual machine, template, or VHD that is present in a VMM library. Otherwise, you can create a virtual machine with an empty virtual hard disk. The latter is your only choice at this point.

The Virtual Machine Identity screen, shown in Figure 7.21, is where the virtual machine is named and described. The Owner field is used to specify which user or group will have access to or manage the virtual machine (operating system access rights still work as normal). The user or group must be specified as a role in VMM.

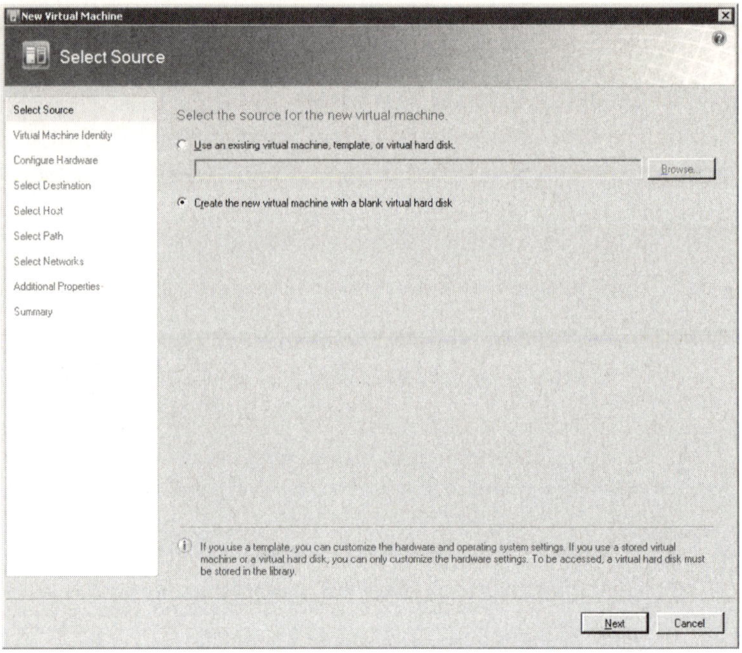

FIGURE 7.20
The New Virtual Machine Wizard

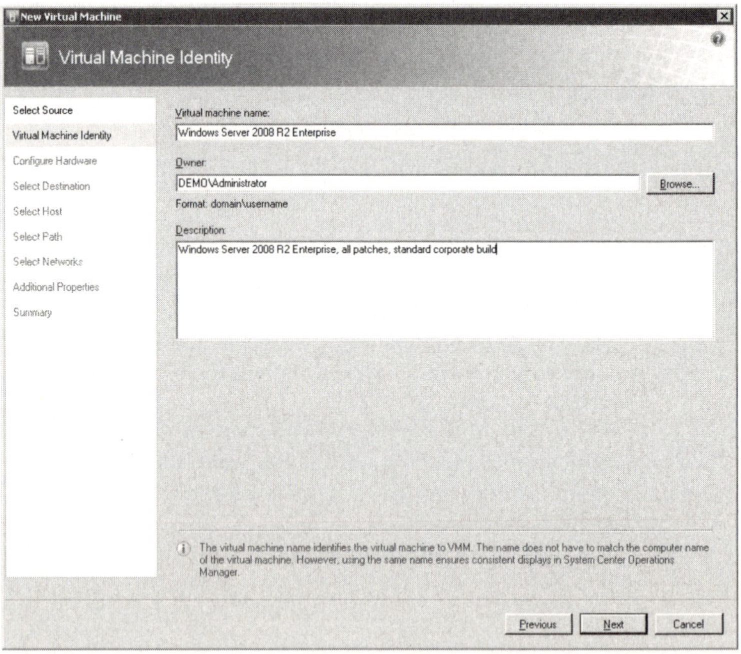

FIGURE 7.21
Virtual Machine Identity screen

Try to use appropriate names and useful descriptions. One approach to running virtual machines might be to name the virtual machine after the computer name of the operating system that runs in it. For example, the operating system computer name might be `server3.demo.local`. The virtual machine could be called `server3`, or maybe you would use the name `server3.demo.local` in a multidomain environment. This makes it easy to find the virtual machine for any computer account.

This virtual machine is being named after the operating system that will be installed into it. That is because it will be converted into a template, and you will want that template to describe its contents.

Figure 7.22 shows the next screen where you can configure the hardware for the virtual machine. There are a few ways you can use this screen.

FIGURE 7.22
Configure Hardware screen

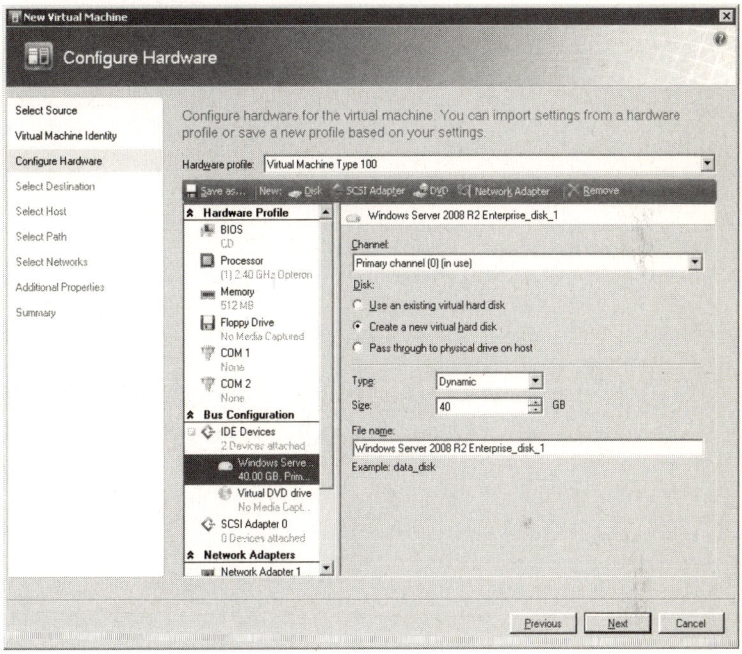

Use an Existing Hardware Profile You can expand the Hardware Profile drop-down list box and select one of the hardware profiles that you created earlier. This will configure the new virtual machine with the hardware specification contained within that hardware profile.

Customize an Existing Hardware Profile You can choose a hardware profile and make changes to it. It is fair to assume that not all virtual machines will fit into some predefined specification and that customizations will be required. You might find that one or some of these customizations become quite common. If you like, you can click the Save As button to save the customized specification as a new hardware profile in the library.

Use a Custom Hardware Specification You can alter the default virtual hardware specification instead of loading a preexisting hardware profile. You can choose to save the resulting specification as a new hardware profile by clicking Save As.

You will be able to return to the properties of the virtual machine to make changes to the virtual machine. But be aware that most of the settings are locked if the virtual machine is not shut down.

You can mount an operating system installation ISO image (or even a boot image) before you skip ahead to the next screen. Figure 7.23 shows that the Windows Server 2008 R2 ISO image is going to be shared with the virtual machine over the network. This takes advantage of the constrained delegation configuration and allows the ISO image to be used via the library file share instead of the costly copy to the storage location of the virtual machine.

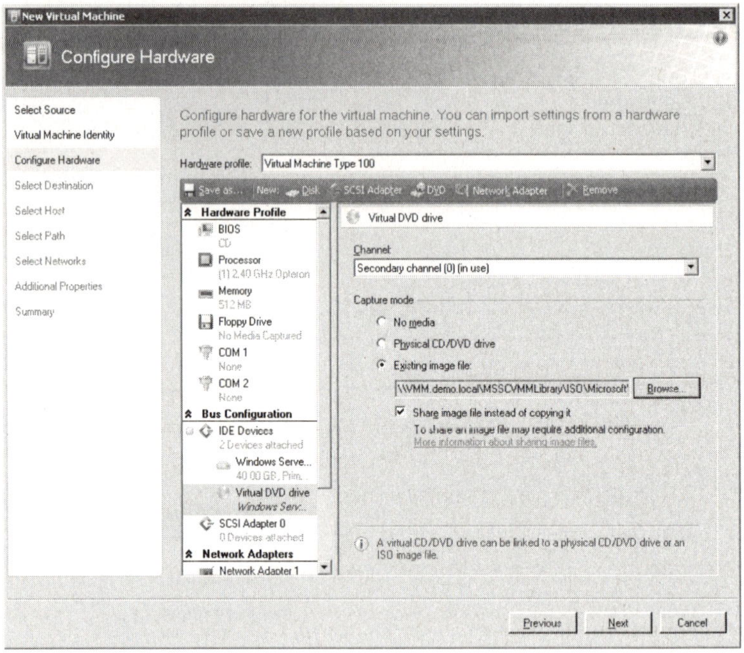

FIGURE 7.23
Mounting an ISO image in the New Virtual Machine Wizard

FIXED VS. DYNAMIC VHDS AND THE LIBRARY

When you create a template from a virtual machine, the operating system is generalized, and the virtual hard disk is moved into the library. The type of the virtual hard disk is not changed. For example, if you prepare a virtual machine with an 80 GB fixed-sized VHD, then that 80 GB VHD will be added to the library and consume the entire 80 GB, even if it is mostly empty. There is no clever fix to the dynamic conversion process.

A dynamic VHD will be more space efficient in the library, but dynamic VHDs are looked down upon in a production environment even with the performance gains they achieved with the release of Windows Server 2008 R2.

If library space is a worry, then you could prepare your template virtual machine with a dynamic VHD. New virtual machines could be deployed using this dynamic VHD. Then you can convert the dynamic VHD into a fixed size VHD using the Convert To Fixed Type Virtual Hard Disk check box in the disk properties. This is located in the virtual machine's properties. This task can be run when the virtual machine is powered down. Unlike the Hyper-V console, VMM will take care of converting the disk into a new fixed-sized VHD, swapping the files, and replacing the original dynamic VHD file.

The result is that you have optimized library disk usage, but you have added an extra step to the virtual machine deployment. You could probably script the deployment of your virtual machine (by saving a script) and add the `Convert-VirtualDiskDrive` cmdlet to convert the disk at the end of the script.

The next screen allows you to select a destination for the virtual machine. You can choose to store the virtual machine in a library. It won't execute, and it won't be able to install an operating system. It will simply be stored there until it is placed on a host.

The other option, and the one you will use in this chapter, is to place the virtual machine on a host server. That brings up an interesting and very important feature of Virtual Machine Manager: Intelligent Placement.

Intelligent Placement

VMM uses Intelligent Placement to decide which managed host server is the most suitable for running a virtual machine that is either being migrated or being created. You can control the algorithm that is used by clicking the Administration wunderbar in the SCVMM admin console and navigating into General. Here you can open the placement settings.

There are two placement goals that you can choose from. VMM will use them to decide how to place virtual machines on host servers.

Load Balancing The objective of this goal is to spread the load of virtual machines as evenly as possible across all VMM-managed host servers.

Resource Maximization The objective of this goal is to fill each host server as much as possible before adding virtual machines to another host. VMM will ensure that the requirements of the virtual machine will fit into the host server.

Intelligent Placement uses four criteria for considering the placement of virtual machines. Each of them has a slide control to allow you to specify how important they should be in the algorithm.

- CPU usage
- Memory free
- Disk I/O
- Network utilization

VMM will run a refresh job every nine minutes to gather performance information from the managed host servers. This refresh job will also run when VMM detects a change in workloads, for example, when a virtual machine is moved from one host to another. This data allows VMM to assign a rating that can be used for the Intelligent Placement routine.

You will see the Intelligent Placement rating when you move or create a virtual machine. It is displayed as a zero- to five-star rating with half-star increments.

VMM will also use Intelligent Placement when it automatically moves virtual machines, for example, when a host is put into maintenance mode or when VMM implements a PRO tip.

The Select Host screen (Figure 7.24) leverages the star ratings that are created for Intelligent Placement. The host with the most stars is calculated as being the most appropriate host server to run the new virtual machine. This takes into account current physical resource utilization, the host reserves that are configured in the host's properties in VMM, and the requirements of the new virtual machine.

FIGURE 7.24
Selecting a host for the new virtual machine

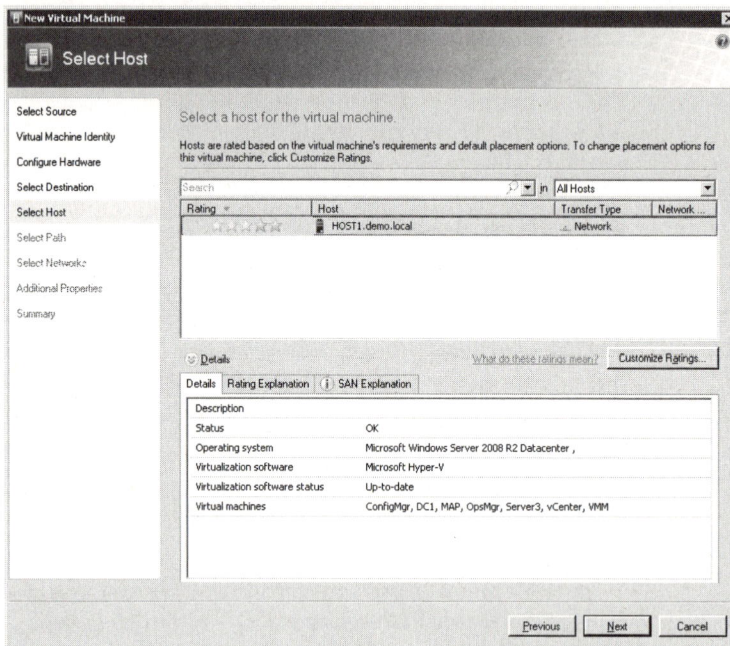

Clicking the Customize Ratings button allows you to alter the VMM-wide placement options. VMM will track the resource utilization of virtual machines. It can associate this history with the template that was used to build the virtual machine. Any new virtual machines based on this template will use this history to estimate their future requirements for Intelligent Placement. You can click the VM Load tab to set the expected requirements for the virtual machine. This includes metrics for CPU utilization, disk space, storage IOPS, and network utilization.

Back on the Select Host screen, you can click the Rating Explanation tab to see why some host is included. Some hosts may have a zero-star rating. This could be because of some incompatibility (usually a virtual machine configuration), or it could be because of the lack of available resources on the host.

VMM is capable of leveraging some advanced SAN techniques to optimize the movement of files between the library and host servers. This will use functionality that must be present in the

SAN. You should consult with your hardware manufacturer or service provider for assistance with this topic.

When you select a host, you are brought to the Select Path screen, which is shown in Figure 7.25. VMM will choose a suitable storage location. You can see in Figure 7.25 that the virtual machine path was taken from the list of default virtual machine paths that was defined for the Host1 server. You can click Browse to choose an alternative location on the selected host server. You can then choose to save that new path in the host server's properties by selecting Add This Path To The List Of Default Virtual Machine Paths On The Host.

FIGURE 7.25
Selecting a virtual machine path

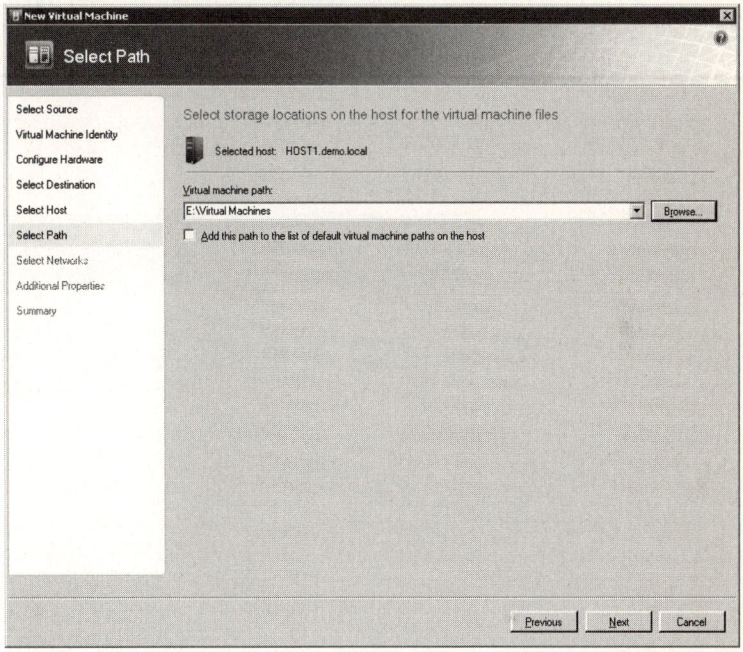

The Select Networks screen allows you to connect each network adapter in the virtual machine to a virtual network that is configured in the host. If you configured a network location for the network adapter in the hardware profile, then the virtual network on this screen will automatically detect a suitable virtual network on the host server. This can be a bit of a time-saver, but you should double-check the automated setting to ensure that it is appropriate. You can see that this mechanism was used in Figure 7.26.

Figure 7.27 shows the Additional Properties screen. Here you can configure a few useful settings:

Action When Physical Server Starts This is the action that Hyper-V will initiate when the host server boots up and the virtual machine is located on that host. You can choose Never Automatically Turn On The Virtual Machine. This is the default option. It is very unlikely you will want this option with a production virtual machine. You could boot up your host after some maintenance, and the virtual machine would stay powered off. Of course, in a clustered environment, you will ideally have migrated the virtual machine to another host.

You can choose Always Automatically Turn On The Virtual Machine. This is another option that you might not like to use in production. The host will power up the virtual machine after booting up, whether the virtual machine was running or not when the host was shut down. This could cause problems when a virtual machine is deliberately powered down to avoid conflicts, save resources, or other similar situations.

The most likely option you will use is Automatically Turn On The Virtual Machine If It Was Running When The Physical Server Stopped. That is pretty self-explanatory. You get an option to delay the start-up. By default, the virtual machine will start up as soon as the hypervisor starts up, which could cause problems. You might want to prevent any virtual machine from starting up for a few minutes so that the parent partition and any agents installed on it have a chance to start up cleanly. You might also need to start up some virtual machines before others. For example, a SQL Server instance might need to be started before an application server. Many administrators are choosing to delay the start of virtual machines by 120 seconds, as you can see in Figure 7.27.

FIGURE 7.26
Automated virtual network placement

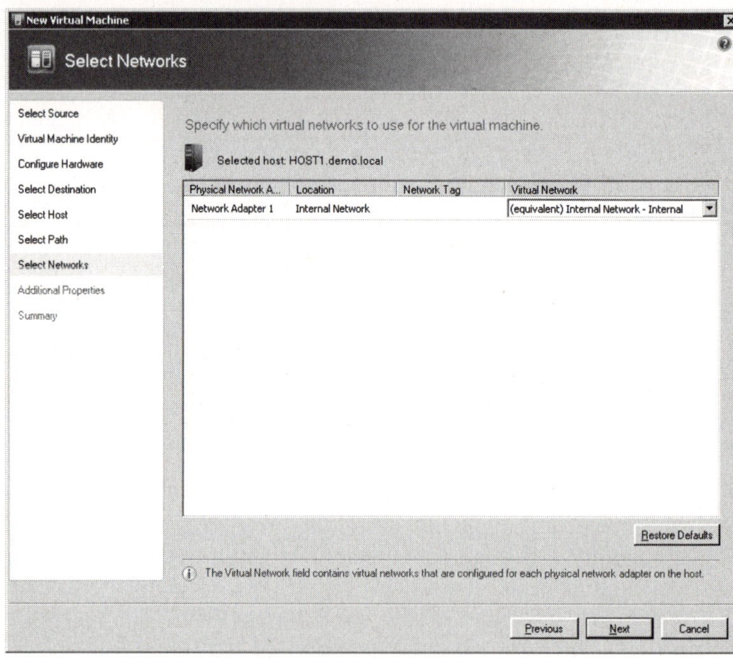

Action When Physical Server Stops This instructs the host server how to deal with a virtual machine that is running on a host when the host server powers down. On clustered hosts, you will use Live Migration (maybe the Maintenance Mode action) to flush virtual machines off of a host server before it powers down. But this is not always an option. You have a few options.

You can select Save State. The virtual machine will be hibernated. Its running state will be saved in the virtual machine's configured location for saved states. This is normally in the same location as the virtual machine. The benefit is that the virtual machine will return to its exact state when it is restarted after the host powers back up. This is usually combined with the Automatically Turn On The Virtual Machine If It Was Running When The Physical Server Stopped option.

The Turn Off Virtual Machine option is a pretty harsh action. It will effectively hit the power button of the virtual machine, stopping it without cleanly shutting down the operating system and any running applications. There are risks to this option including filesystem and data corruption.

The Shut Down Guest OS option will leverage any installed integration services (part of the Hyper-V integration components) in the virtual machine to initiate a clean operating system shutdown. This is usually the alternative to the Save State option. Note that integration services (including the ability to initiate a shutdown) exist only for selected operating systems. Prior to the version 3.0 Linux integration components, there was no clean way to shut down a Hyper-V hosted Linux virtual machine. This required shutting down the guests manually, which proved to be rather unpopular with Linux administrators.

FIGURE 7.27
Virtual machine additional properties

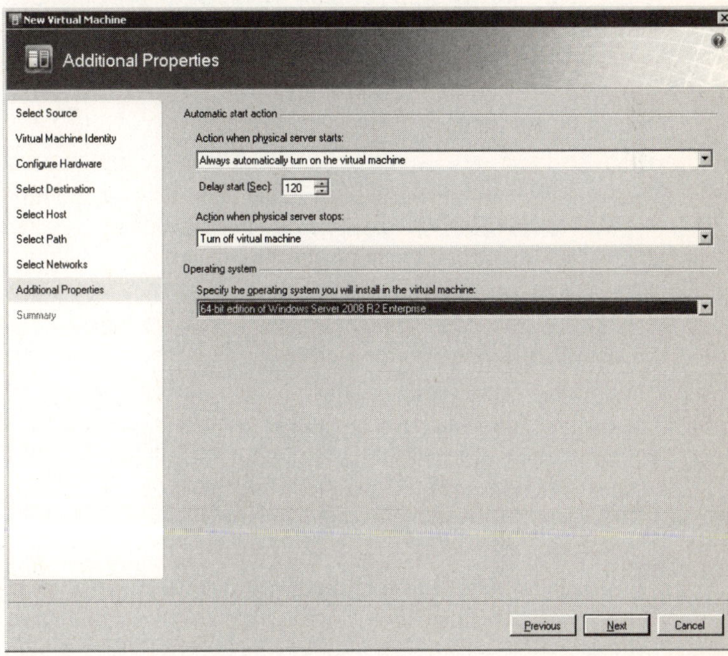

Specify The Operating System You Will Install In The Virtual Machine This drop-down list box presents a list of operating systems that VMM is aware of. You can select the one that will be installed in the virtual machine that you are creating. This isn't required, but it is a form of built-in documentation that will prove to be helpful in the future if you do configure it.

The final screen summarizes the actions that will be performed by the PowerShell script (which you can save to the library, tweak, and reuse) on your behalf. There is also a check box to start the virtual machine once it is created. This is handy because the operating system installation will kick off for you.

You will see a new entry for the virtual machine when you return to virtual machines in the SCVMM admin console. You can track the progress of the Create Virtual Machine job by clicking the Latest Job tab and then sit back until the job is completed. At this point, you can click the Connect To Virtual Machine task in the Actions pane to initiate a connection to the virtual machine using the VMM Virtual Machine Viewer. This tool pales in comparison to the Hyper-V console's Virtual Machine Connection tool. It has less functionality and can connect only to a running virtual machine. You might find yourself using the Hyper-V console when you need to hit F12 to initiate a network boot using a legacy network adapter in a virtual machine.

You can use whatever connection tool you prefer to get access to the virtual machine's console and install, patch, and configure the operating system (and maybe the applications too). You should install the Hyper-V integration components. You can do this from VMM by powering down the virtual machine and running the Install Virtual Guest Services task in the Actions pane. Note that Windows 7 and Windows Server 2008 R2 have integration components built in. However, these may not be up-to-date because Hyper-V and VMM continue to be improved by Microsoft using patches and service packs. Do not join the machine to a domain; leave it in a workgroup. Use the normal golden or template image preparation techniques that you would use in operating system deployment. But there is one difference: do not run sysprep. VMM will take care of that for you when you convert the virtual machine into a template.

CREATE A TEMPLATE

With traditional physical operating system deployment, the word *template* is associated with an operating system or disk image that is kept on a server and deployed to computers.

VMM uses slightly different terminology. Two items are created in the library when you convert an existing virtual machine into a template:

Virtual Hard Disk The virtual hard disk of the virtual machine is generalized using sysprep and moved (not copied) into the library. The virtual machine is removed from the host as part of this operation.

Template This, rather confusingly to be honest, refers not to the virtual hard disk but to a collection of settings that are linked to the virtual hard disk of the source virtual machine. The template is stored in the VMM SQL Server database. It contains information about the hardware profile used to create virtual machines from the template. It also contains information that will be used to perform a silent deployment and customization of the operating system contained within the linked VHD.

It should be noted that you can create a new template in the library that will be linked to an existing VHD. This allows you to create many customized deployments based on a single image.

You will normally choose to deploy new virtual machines from this template (or others that you create) rather than go through the previously described manual process. You will also learn later about how this template will be used for self-service provisioning.

The process we are going to describe now will run sysprep (automatically), move the virtual machine's VHD into the library, and create the first template linked to this VHD.

Without running sysprep, you should shut down the virtual machine that has been prepared. Make sure you unmount any ISO images. Now you can select the virtual machine and run the New Template task in the Actions pane.

You can see in Figure 7.28 that there is a warning. It is an important one to be aware of. The virtual machine that you have worked on will be destroyed. The remaining VHD will be moved into the library. No trace of the virtual machine will be left on the host.

FIGURE 7.28
Create template warning

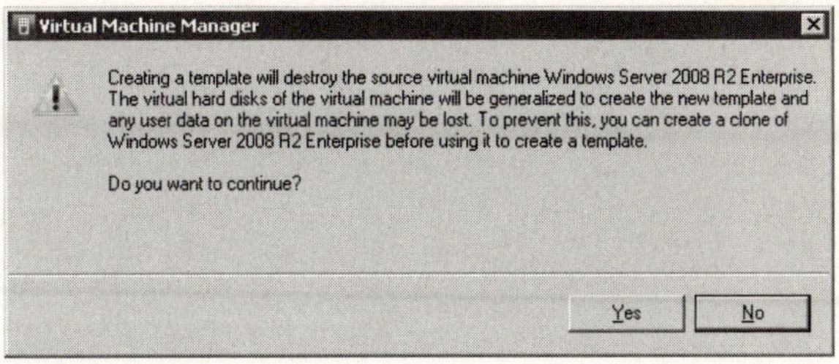

Once you accept this, you can move onto the New Template Wizard, which is shown in Figure 7.29. You start by naming and describing the template. The Owner field allows you to list the user or group (preferred option) that will have the rights to access this template. We will return to this when we deal with roles and self-service provisioning.

FIGURE 7.29
The New Template Wizard

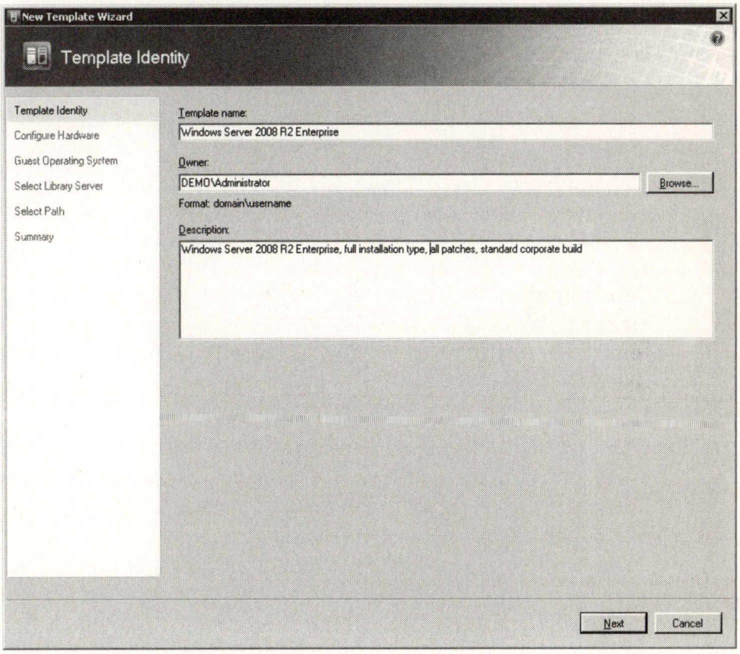

Next up is the Hardware Profile screen. The configuration of the source virtual machine is loaded. Don't bother making any changes now; this isn't supported. Any changes you make will be ignored and cause the resulting job to end with a warning status. You can always cancel the wizard to modify the virtual machine and then restart the wizard.

Figure 7.30 shows you where you can edit the Guest Operating System profile of the template. The generalized image will be configured using the information you enter here when it is deployed. For example, you can enter a password that can be used by all virtual machines deployed from this template. You can do the same thing with the product key (a real time-saver!).

FIGURE 7.30
Guest Operating System profile's information

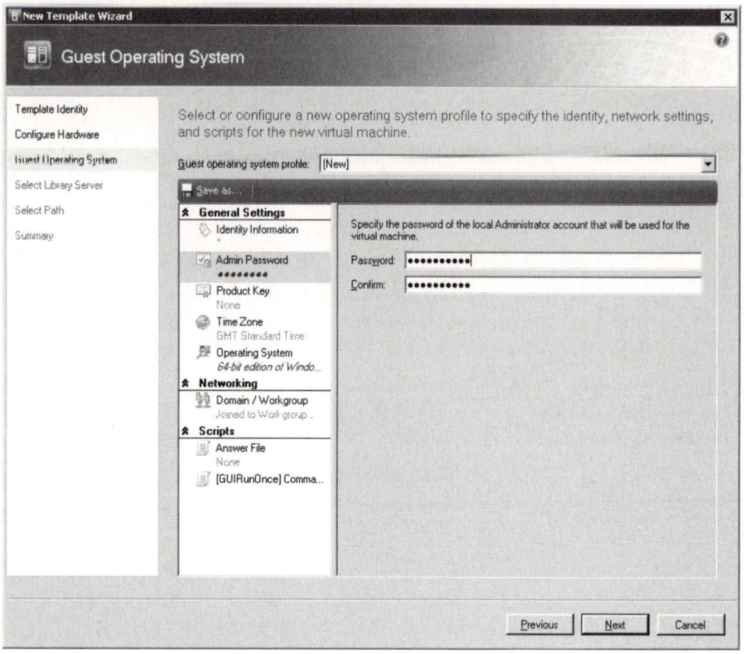

You might want to leave the Identity Information screen blank with the default entry of *. This can be replaced by the New Virtual Machine Wizard when you deploy a virtual machine from this template. It will be used to name the computer account of the contained Windows operating system.

The Scripts option is pretty interesting. You can provide an answer file that would be generated using Setup Manager (Windows Server 2003 R2 and earlier) or Windows System Image Manager (WSIM for Windows 7 or Windows Server 2008 R2 as well as Windows Vista and Windows Server 2008). This can be used to perform very advanced configurations during the VHD deployment.

You can also use the GUIRunOnce Commands option to run commands or scripts, which can be very powerful. You can have a file share with a series of scripts that could be automatically run when the new virtual machine is deployed. For example, these could be Setup Manager scripts to install roles and features on a Windows Server 2008 (or newer) virtual machine. Or it could be a script to perform a silent slipstreamed installation of SQL Server. You can create many templates (with these settings) in the library and combine them with a single VHD. That could allow you to deploy many types of virtual machine with different configurations from a single image.

After this, you select the library server to store the new template and the VHD on. You should choose a library that is both close to the current Hyper-V host and close to the hosts that this template will be used with.

You will be asked to select a location in the library share for the VHD (Figure 7.31). As we talked about earlier, you should try to keep things well named and organized. This image will be stored in `\\VMM.demo.local\MSSCVMMLibrary\VHDs\Windows Server 2008 R2`.

FIGURE 7.31
Selecting a library location for the VHD

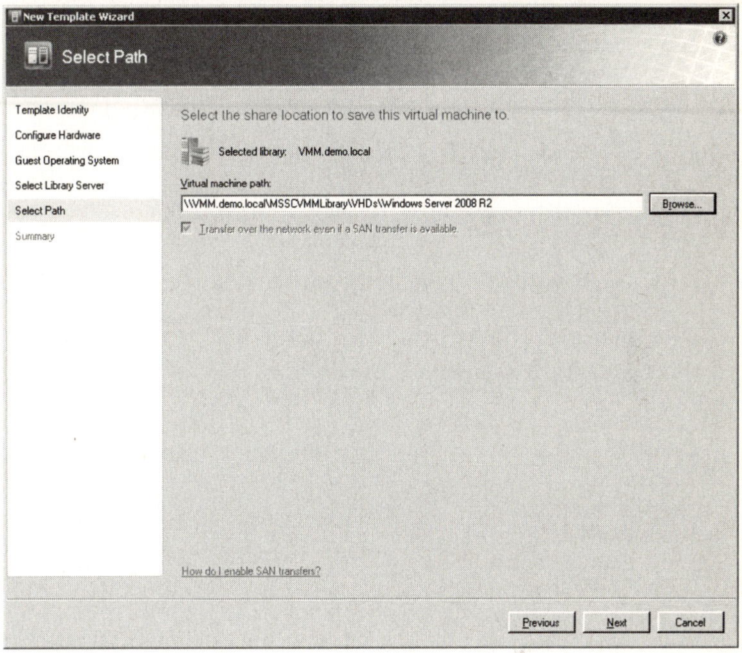

There are a lot of clicks involved in this. You could script this with the PowerShell, but you should be creating templates only once in a while so the GUI approach won't be too time-consuming.

The following job will run sysprep to generalize the operating system in the virtual machine's VHD, move the VHD to the library, create the template, and remove all traces of the virtual machine from the host. You will then have a template and VHD that can be used for operating system deployment. If you want, you can even create more templates in the library that are linked with this VHD.

CREATE A VIRTUAL MACHINE FROM A TEMPLATE

Those of you who are used to physical machine operating system deployment must be wondering, is this whole process really this easy? The answer is yes. Deploying virtual machines from your image is just a few clicks with no need to mess with drivers. In fact, VMM will even make sure that the latest version of the integration (components) guest services is installed on the

Windows virtual machines every time it creates a virtual machine or changes its physical storage location.

You can start the deployment of a new virtual machine from your library contents from a few places:

Virtual Machines ➤ New Virtual Machine This will give you the choice of using a template or virtual hard disk in the library as the source. Using the template will deploy the virtual machine but will also use the data in the template to get a silent operating system configuration with the data you entered.

Library ➤ Select Template ➤ New Virtual Machine With this approach, the New Virtual Machine Wizard will load the defaults from the template and use the linked VHD. You can customize the template information as required during this deployment.

Library ➤ Select VHD ➤ New Virtual Machine This method will start the New Virtual Machine Wizard without loading any template. The generalized VHD will be deployed, and the operating system will start up in the normal manner you would expect after running sysprep.

For this example, select the template, right-click, and select New Virtual Machine. The New Virtual Machine Wizard starts up (Figure 7.32). Enter the name of the virtual machine. This one will be called Server7. You will see that this name will be used automatically on the Guest Operating System screen to name the computer account.

FIGURE 7.32
New virtual machine from template

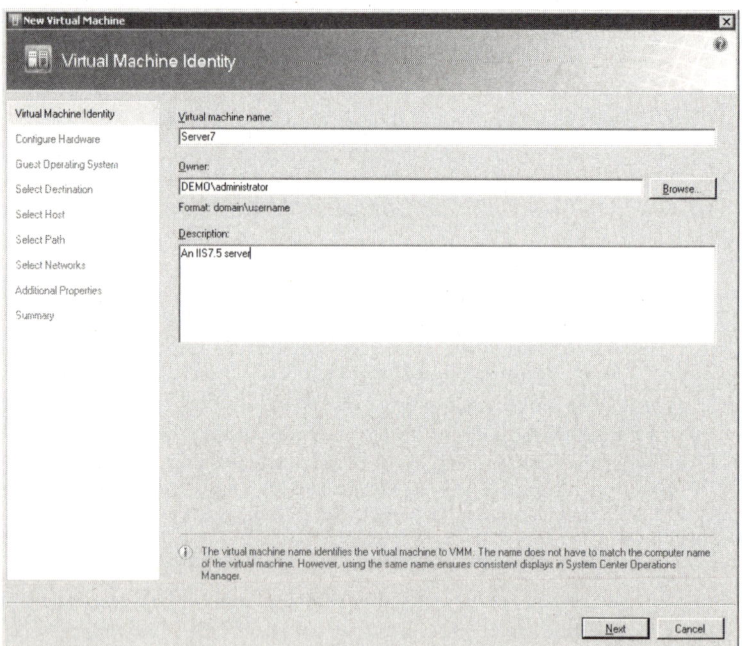

The Configure Hardware screen appears. This is where you can customize the virtual machine deployment. For example, this virtual machine might require additional VHDs and network adapters, or the processor configuration might need to be altered.

LINUX VIRTUAL MACHINE NETWORKING

Some Linux distributions bind the TCP/IP configuration of a NIC to the Ethernet (MAC) address of that NIC. By default, VMM and Hyper-V will assign dynamic Ethernet addresses to virtual machines. The Ethernet address will change every time the virtual machine is moved. This will happen when a Live Migration is performed, when a Quick Storage Migration is performed, or when a virtual machine is moved by using an export and an import. Each of these moves will cause the TCP/IP configuration to become invalid, and the Linux virtual machine will lose network connectivity.

The solution is to always configure Linux virtual machines with a static Ethernet address. You can do this in the network configuration, as shown here. You can select the Static option and click the Generate button to select an Ethernet address from the VMM-managed pool of addresses.

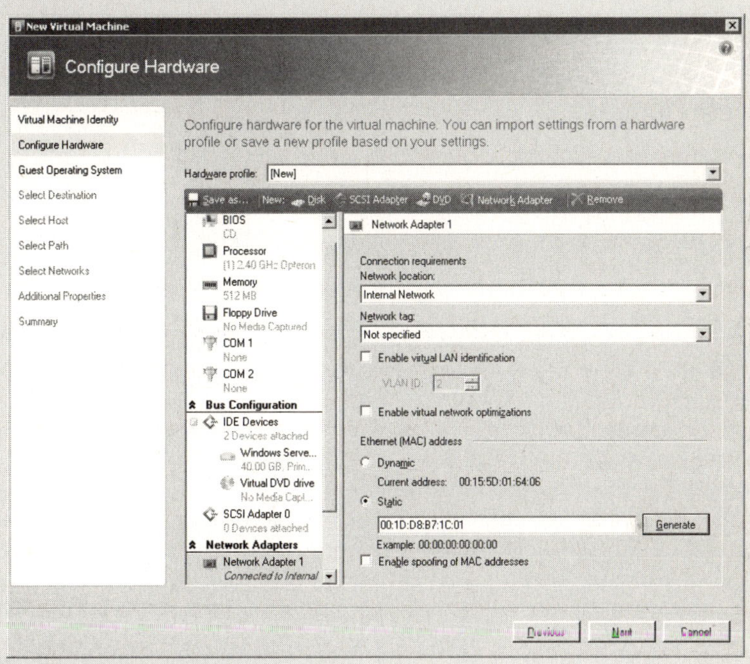

You can configure the available set of Ethernet addresses by clicking the Administration wunderbar and modifying Global Static MAC Address Range.

Configuring a Linux virtual machine with a static Ethernet (MAC) address will prevent this issue from occurring when the virtual machine is moved.

You can see in Figure 7.33 that the Identity Information Computer Name field inherits its contents from the virtual machine name. You can change this if required. For example, the virtual machine could be called `server7.demo.local`, and the computer name could be set to `Server7`.

You can alter the other information provided by the template as required. You could enter some information to automatically join this computer to the `demo.local` domain. All that is required is that the virtual machine is created on a network with DHCP, and you can enter the domain name and some credentials with the rights to join the server to the domain.

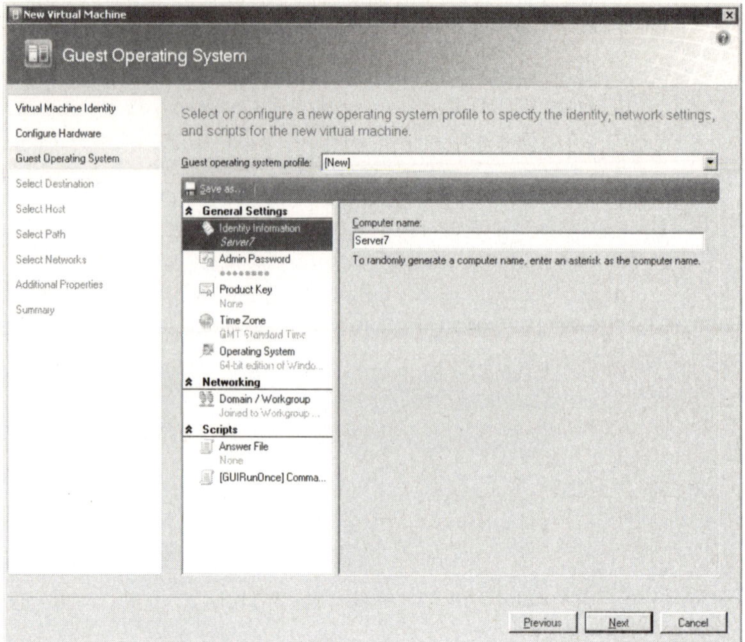

FIGURE 7.33
New Virtual Machine Operating System Information

The Select Host screen will present you with your Intelligent Placement ratings for the available hosts. If a host is not appearing, then check its properties to see whether it is available for placement.

You normally should choose to place the virtual machine on the host with the highest rating (the most stars). However, would you place two load-balanced servers on the same host? Would you place two members of a virtualized cluster (using iSCSI for shared storage) on the same host? The answer should be no. You would want to protect your web farm or cluster from a host failure. In this scenario, you might find yourself ignoring the host rating if it wants you to put all of your eggs in one basket. Instead, you might choose the second-highest-rated host. Unfortunately, VMM does not have an affinity or avoidance setting to force groups of virtual machines either to be on the same host or to not be on the same host. This means that you will have to do this work either manually, by writing a custom solution (maybe authoring a PRO management pack for OpsMgr), or using a clustering technique via AntiAffinityClassName (discussed in Chapter 8).

The rest of the wizard has been described before when we showed how to deploy the original template virtual machine. You will choose the location on the selected host for the virtual machine, configure the networks, and set up the behavior of the virtual machine during host shutdown and start-up.

Now you can sit back as the new virtual machine is deployed, starts up, and is configured. VMM will even install the integration services (components) if required.

By the way, you should remember to check out the job status of this task. It does quite a bit of work, and you can learn a good deal about the deployment process by following its progress a few times. For example, you will see that the Guest Operating System information is provided to the starting virtual machine by using a virtual floppy disk.

> **INTEGRATION GUEST SERVICES INSTALLATION FAILURE**
>
> VMM will always try to install the integration guest services after a VM creation or move. Sometimes this isn't appropriate. For example, a Windows operating system might be unsupported because it is too old or because it doesn't have the right level of service pack installed.
>
> Linux virtual machines will also fail. VMM installs the integration guest services by mounting the VHD and injecting them into an NTFS filesystem. Linux does not use NTFS. This means that you will have to perform manual installations and upgrades of the Linux integration components.

You can very easily deploy many more virtual machines from the same template and virtual hard disk in the library. You could do this even quicker by using a PowerShell script. You can use the Show Script at the end of the New Virtual Machine Wizard to get a template script.

Once you know what you are doing, you can get through this wizard in just a matter of seconds. That's very little work. It's a lot quicker than the process of deploying an operating system to a physical server, even with automated tools.

The process we have described will be fine for VMM administrators. They will be able to deploy virtual machines and manage them as required. The power of VMM is that it can allow delegated administrators and empowered end users to deploy virtual machines as required. We have laid down the foundations for this, but now we need to set up the delegation model.

Delegation of Administration

Virtual Machine Manager uses profiles and user roles to enable delegation of administration. There are three types of profile. They have different functions and offer different kinds of access.

Administrator This is the built-in user role and grants access to all administrative functionality in the SCVMM admin console.

Delegated Administrator A delegated administrator is granted complete control over selected items in the virtualization infrastructure. They can use the SCVMM admin console to manage those items.

Self-Service User A member of this role has the right to access the Self-Service Portal. Being an administrator or delegated administrator does not grant this right. A user can see items in the Self-Service Portal only if they have been granted ownership rights to them.

A user role is created in one of the three profile types. Active Directory users or groups (preferred) can be made members of the user role, and rights can be granted or filtered. Members of the user role will be able to perform the allowed actions on the specified set of hosts with the allowed library resources.

By using user roles, VMM administrators can empower delegated administrators to take more control of VMM and/or the virtual machines that are managed by Hyper-V. They can even let people who would not normally be considered to be administrators have self-service virtual machine provisioning and management functionality via the VMM Self-Service Portal.

ACCESS THE SCVMM ADMIN CONSOLE

Only VMM administrators and delegated administrators can log into the SCVMM admin console. Members of all user roles can log into the Self-Service Portal.

CREATING USER ROLES

You can create and manage user roles in Administration ➤ User Roles in the SCVMM admin console. In this exercise, we are going to be working with two groups of people who require some form of rights to manage virtual machines.

Server Management The members of this team or department are mid-level administrators who are responsible for the day-to-day operations of the server network. Much like with membership of the Domain Admins group, you will want to limit full administrator rights to your virtualization infrastructure. You will grant the Server Management team limited access to VMM and selected Hyper-V hosts via the SCVMM admin console. They will be delegated administrators. You have created a domain-based security group called Server Management to aggregate all of their user accounts.

The Delegated Administrators user role profile allows you to grant access to hosts in specified host groups and library servers. The members of this role type will have access to all functions on servers in those host groups and all resources in those libraries.

Application Development It often feels like IT administrators and application developers teams are in an eternal conflict. Administrators can feel like developers don't know what they want and are always asking for something new. Developers feel like they never get what they asked for and that administrators are always slowing them down. The members of this team are aggregated into a domain-based group called Application Development. They will be granted self-service provisioning rights.

Members of the Self-Service user role profile will be granted access to very limited actions, which you have granular control over. You can restrict access to resources in the library. You can also control access to host servers by granting access to host groups.

You can create a new user role by clicking the New User Role task in the Actions pane on the right side. This will open the Create User Role Wizard, which is shown in Figure 7.34.

You can see that we have named the user role Demo\Server Management. This is to make it clear that the user role is associated with the group from the `demo.local` domain.

We also entered a good description. We have mentioned how important this is when performing virtual machine management. It is even more important when you are doing work that is related to security. A good description will be a form of documentation that will explain what the role is for. You might log into the SCVMM admin console in a year or two and be wondering why the role was created. A description will answer your question in a couple of seconds.

The User Role Profile drop-down list box allows you to specify whether this user role will be a delegated administrator or a self-service user.

You can specify who will be a member of the group on the Add Members screen, which is shown in Figure 7.35. You can add one or more users or groups on this screen. We have added the Server Management group.

FIGURE 7.34
Creating a new delegated administrator

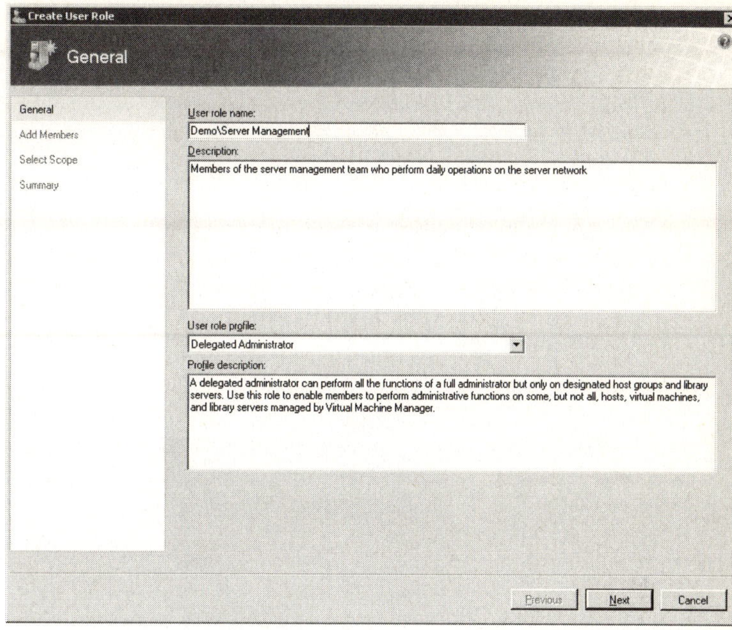

FIGURE 7.35
Adding members to the User role

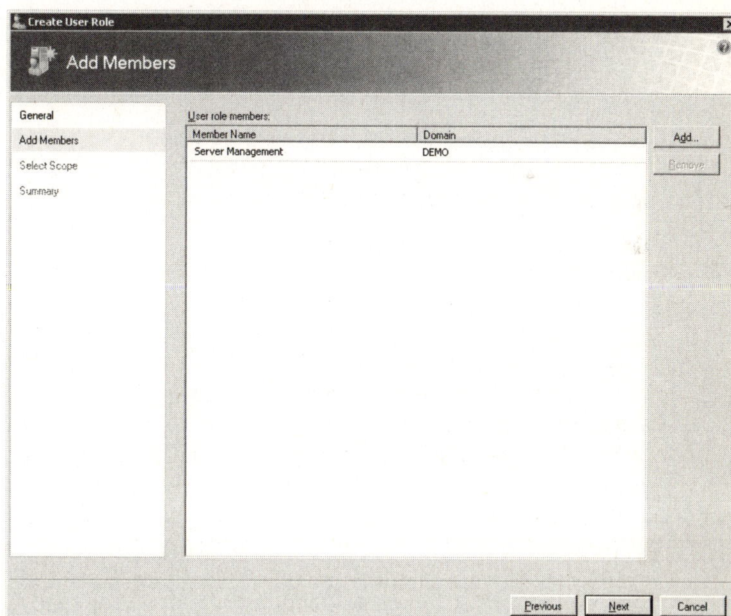

It is strongly recommended that you do not add user accounts directly into a user role. Over time, there will be many users, and this will make managing your delegation model extremely complicated and near impossible to track and control.

You should adopt the same approach that is recommended with file server security management. This means that you will add users into a domain-based security group and then grant permissions to the user group. This is why we have added the Server Management security group as a member of the new user role.

The next screen defines what libraries and host groups the user role will be able to access. There are two host groups in our example, which you can see in Figure 7.36. These were created in the SCVMM admin console under the Hosts wunderbar. The Server Management group will have access to Host Group 1 and the library on the VMM server. Selecting the boxes beside those items will grant them access. Deselecting the check boxes (which is done by default) will deny or revoke access to the server resources.

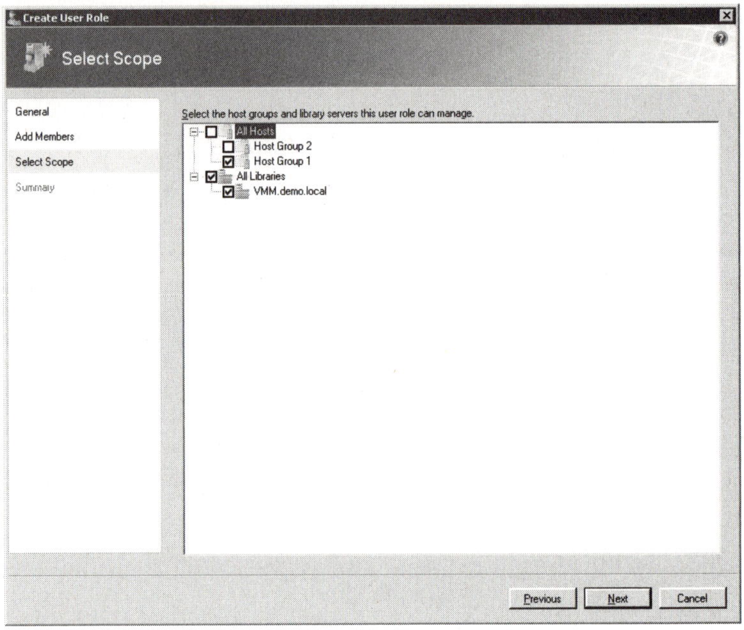

FIGURE 7.36
Selecting the scope of the User role

That's all you need to do to grant Server Management administrative access to the SCVMM admin console, the library, and the Hyper-V hosts via VMM. Any member of the Server Management security group can now log into the SCVMM admin console to manage hosts in the delegated host group. They can do anything they want to those hosts and the virtual machines on those hosts. They can also access any resource in the library.

Now it is the turn of the Application Development team. Start the Create User Role Wizard again by clicking New User Role. You can see in Figure 7.37 that this is will use the Self-Service user role profile. We do not want developers to be using the SCVMM admin console because it will give them too much access to the infrastructure.

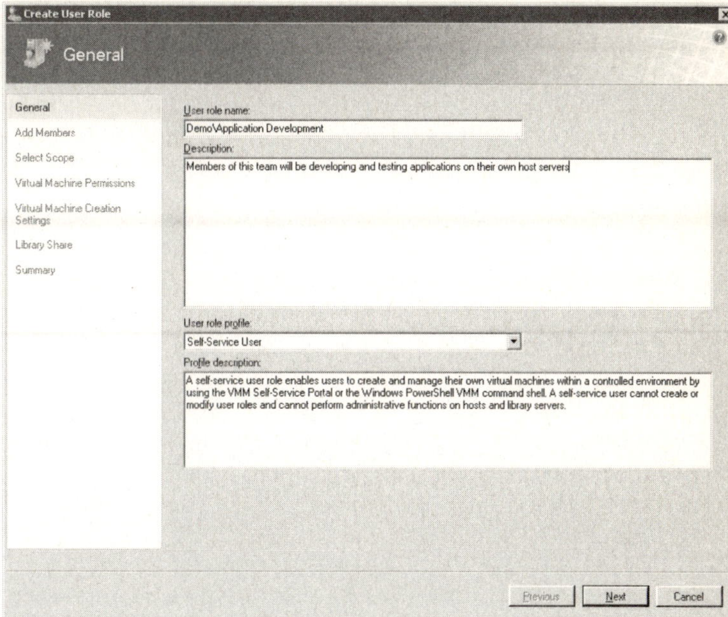

FIGURE 7.37
Creating the User role

You can add the Application Development security group as a member of the user role in the Add Members screen.

The Application Development team will require access to Hyper-V host servers that they will purchase from their budget. The servers are located in Host Group 2 in the SCVMM admin console. You can see how the members of this role will be granted rights to place virtual machines on these hosts in Figure 7.38. Only Host Group 2 is selected, which will limit Application Development members' access.

Figure 7.39 shows the Virtual Machine Permissions screen. This allows VMM administrators to have granular control over the virtual machine management actions that members of this user role will be permitted to use.

By default all actions will be permitted. You can choose to select a subset of the available actions:

- Start: Power up a virtual machine.
- Stop: Power off a virtual machine.
- Pause and Resume: Freeze a virtual machine without saving its state to disk.
- Checkpoint: Create a snapshot.
- Remove: Delete virtual machines.
- Local Administrator: Set the local administrator password during the creation of virtual machines.
- Remote Connection: Access the console of the virtual machine.
- Shut down: Shut down the virtual machine via the Self-Service Portal.

FIGURE 7.38
Granting host group access to application development

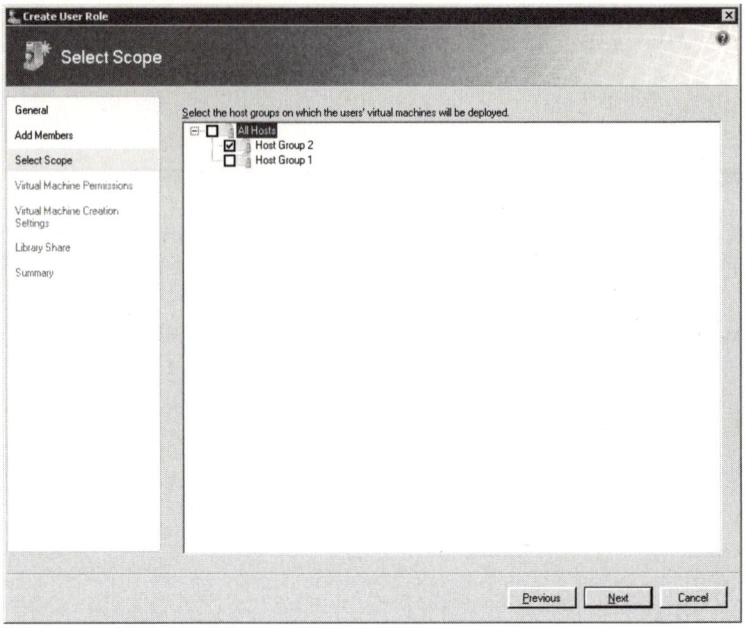

FIGURE 7.39
Self-service virtual machine permissions

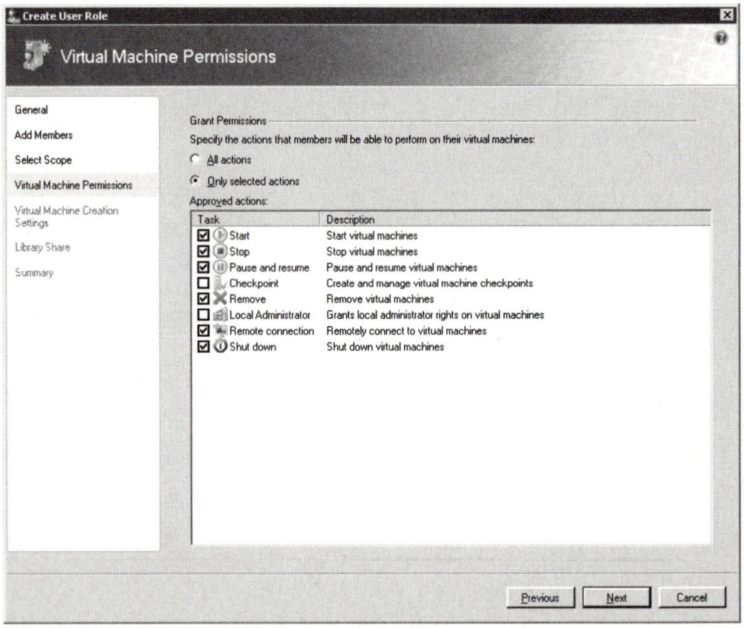

It is up to you to decide which actions a user role should have access to. Some users may be less educated about server management and shouldn't have access to settings such as Stop or Local Administrator. Some organizations may have a policy to prevent the usage of snapshots or checkpoints because of the performance issues that they can cause. This would mean that user roles should not have access to this action.

The Virtual Machine Creation Settings screen (in Figure 7.40) is where you will grant access to virtual machine templates.

FIGURE 7.40
Self-service virtual machine creation settings

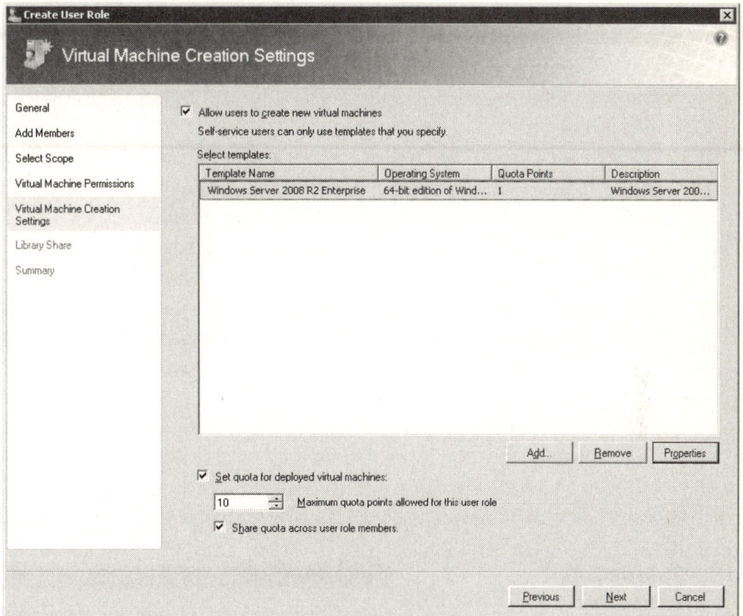

When you create self-service roles, you have two basic decisions to make. Are you creating this role just to give console access to the virtual machine? The answer would be yes if they have very limited IT knowledge but still require access to virtual machines. If so, VMM administrators will have to create the virtual machines on behalf of members of this role. You can deselect the Allow Users To Create New Virtual Machines check box on this screen.

You will select this box if you want to allow them to create virtual machines. They will need to have access to templates, which will be used to perform a silent creation of the virtual machine with very limited input from the self-service user.

You can click the Add button to browse the library for preexisting templates. You can add more than one template. You can click Remove to delete access to a template for this user role.

Virtual machine sprawl is a syndrome where virtual machines are created without any control. Often a surprisingly high number of these virtual machines are a waste of host, storage, and licensing resources. Eventually additional hardware needs to be purchased to host required virtual machines. Granting an uncontrolled ability to deploy virtual machines to those outside of IT is almost guaranteed to lead to this problem.

VMM provides a quota mechanism to control this. Every template is assigned a quota points value. The default is 1. You can set this according to the calculated cost of ownership for the virtual machine. For example, a virtual machine with 1 GB of RAM, 40 GB of disk, and one CPU could have a quota point value of 1. A virtual machine with 2 GB of RAM, 40 GB of disk, and one CPU could have a quota point value of 2.

A self-service user role can be configured with a quota. The default is 10 points. If you used this score, then the user role could deploy 10 virtual machines with a 1-point score or 5 virtual machines with a 2-point score. The quota points would be released back to the user role for reuse if the userdeleted virtual machines.

This mechanism allows you to grant the ability to create virtual machines in a controlled manner while averting the risk of virtual machine sprawl. It also raises the prospect of being able to cross-charge for virtual machine resource usage. You could calculate a cost for each point. For example, there could be a cost of $200/month for each quota point. The user role with 10 points would be charged $2,000 per month for the resources that are made available to them for hosting virtual machines. It would be up to that user role to actually consume those resources.

The Set Quota For Deployed Virtual Machines check box allows you to enable quotas for a user role. If you do enable it, then you can set the maximum quota by entering a value (the default is 10) in the Maximum Quota Points Allowed For This User Role control.

The last check box, Share Quota Across User Role Members, allows you to decide how the maximum quota will be used. If you enable this, then all users in the user role must share the points. So if there are 10 maximum quota points, then only 10 of the 1-point virtual machines can be deployed. If you do not share the quota points, then all users will be granted an individual allotment of the maximum quota points. If there were 10 users in the role, then each user would get 10 points to use.

You can set the quota point value for a template by editing its properties and browsing to the Settings tab. You don't need to leave this wizard to do that. You can select the template on the Virtual Machine Creation Settings screen and click the Properties button. You can see how you can check and change the quota point value of a template in Figure 7.41.

FIGURE 7.41
Managing a templates quota point value

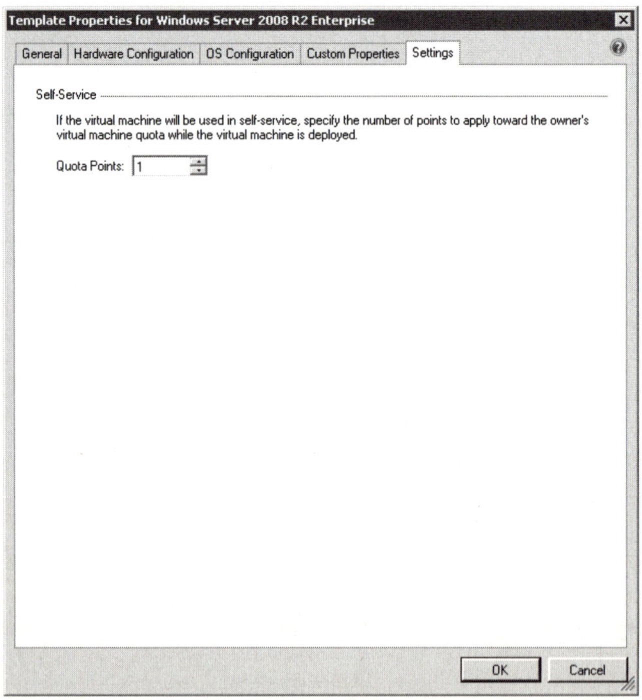

The library is a very powerful resource, and you can grant self-service roles access to it. This is controlled in the Library Share screen (Figure 7.42).

FIGURE 7.42
Self-service library share access

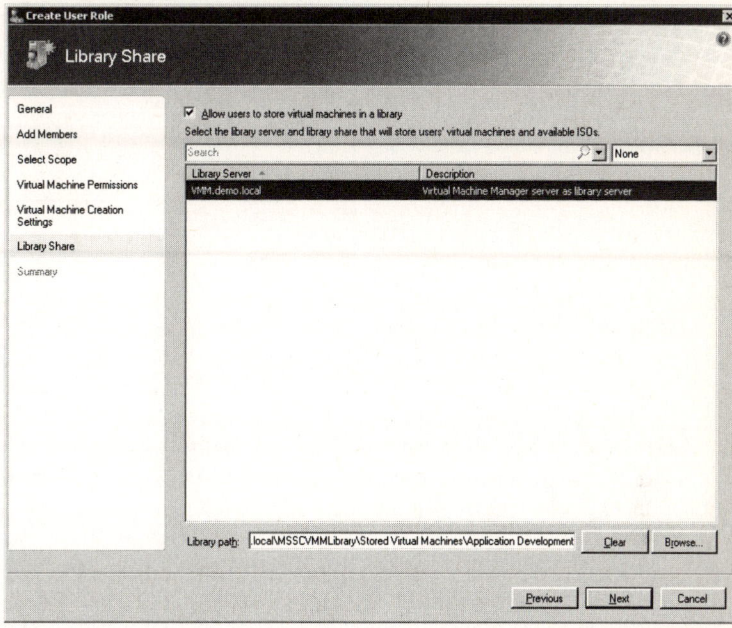

One of the possible actions for a self-service role member is to move a virtual machine from a host (where it is consuming quota points) to a library (where it is not consuming quota points). You can allow access to the library (and this action) by selecting Allow Users To Store Virtual Machines In A Library.

This is a rather confusingly named control. This is because this control also controls access to ISO images in the library. You cannot grant permission to self-service users to mount a library ISO image without allowing them to move virtual machines into the library.

This brings up an architectural issue. Imagine you have a production library that is located on your SAN. That is an expensive type of storage. Now imagine that you need to create a self service user role that can store virtual machines in a library. The self-service user role has the potential to totally consume all of your library storage without any ability to control or measure it using quota points.

The solution is to create a library share for each self-service user role that requires access to the library. You can simply cross-charge them for the disk that is allocated. They can have their own ISO images in this folder, and they can store their virtual machines in it as well. This dedicated library approach might be a great way to provide controlled access to MSDN and development media for testers and developers.

When you select a library share, you can specify the subfolder within the library share that the self-service user role will have access to. All of their content will be stored in here, including ISO images and stored virtual machines. The actual location remains hidden to the members of the user role; VMM accesses the location on their behalf. In our example, the self-service user role will be granted access to this location:

```
\\VMM.demo.local\MSSCVMMLibrary\Stored Virtual Machines\Application Development
```

You can see the two new user roles in Figure 7.43.

FIGURE 7.43
The created User roles

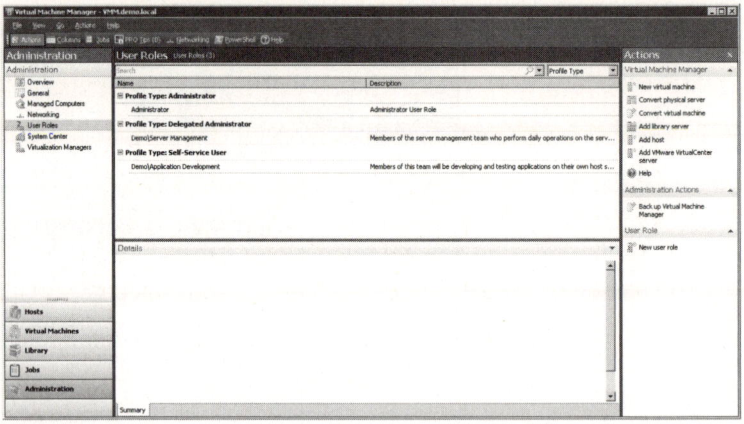

You can copy an ISO file into the self-service role's folder in the library. You can also change the owner value of a virtual machine to grant the self-service role access to it (assuming that the virtual machine is running on a host in the host group that the role has rights to use).

USING THE SELF-SERVICE CONSOLE

Say the user Lisa Garcia (Demo\LGarcia) is a member of the Application Development Active Directory security group. This makes her a member of the Demo\Application Development self-service user role in VMM. She has the right to log into the Self-Service Portal and to deploy new virtual machines. Any virtual machines that have Demo\LGarcia or Demo\Application Development as the owner will be visible to Lisa when she uses the Self-Service Portal.

SELF-SERVICE ADMINISTRATIVE CONTACT

Users of the Self-Service Portal are likely going to be less technically capable than the typical administrator in the IT department. This means they'll need a little help from time to time. There is a Contact Administrator hyperlink at the top of the page to allow members of the user role to get some help. This will open a new email with the preconfigured email address already entered.

You can configure this email address (which is blank by default) in the SCVMM admin console under Administration and by clicking Self-Service Administrative Contact. This will open the screen shown here.

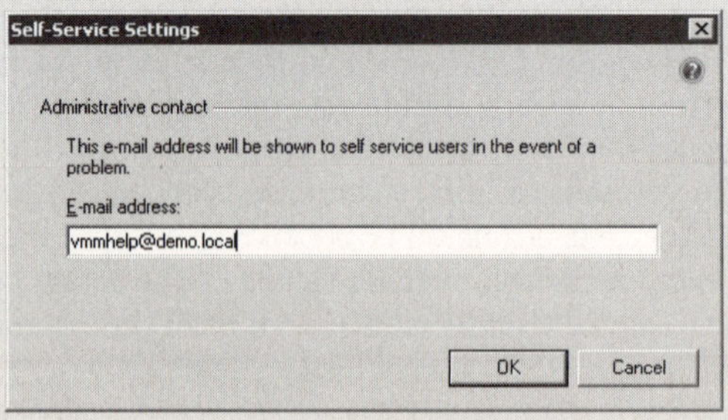

You can open the Self-Service Portal using your browser. The default URL is the name of the server. It is recommended that you configure this site to use SSL so that all username and password details are encrypted. Figure 7.44 shows the logon page with this warning.

FIGURE 7.44
The Self-Service Portal logon page

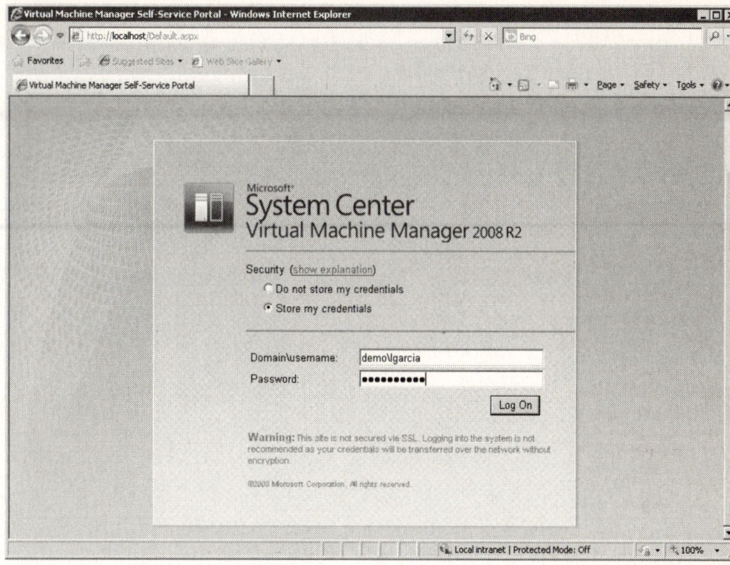

The user, Lisa Garcia, can log into the portal using the username of Demo\LGarcia.

The Computers view of the portal appears after a second or two, as shown in Figure 7.45. This shows all the virtual machines that the user will have access to. All of the permitted actions are on the right side. They are context sensitive, so actions that are inappropriate for the current state of the selected virtual machine will be grayed out.

FIGURE 7.45
The Computers view in the Self-Service Portal

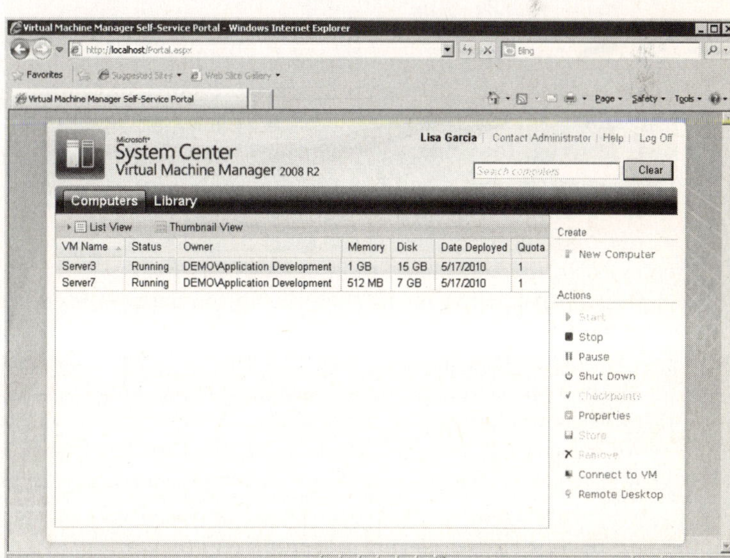

You can get an alternative view by clicking the Thumbnail view (Figure 7.46). Not only will this reveal a little bit more information about the currently selected virtual machine, but you can also get a console screenshot of the virtual machines. This can be manually refreshed as long as no one else is connected to the console of the virtual machine.

FIGURE 7.46
The Self-Service Portal's Thumbnail view

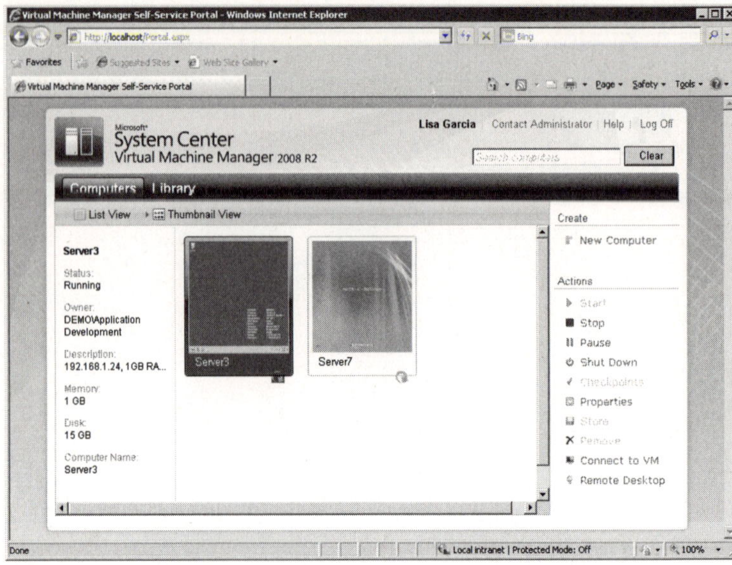

The library view will reveal any virtual machines that have been stored there. You can move a running virtual machine into the library by powering it down and running the Store action.

Now we'll move on to what you really want to know about: the ability to create virtual machines using the Self-Service Portal. You can do this by clicking the New Computer action, which opens the page shown in Figure 7.47.

You'll notice that a lot of information is already provided and cannot be edited. This information is extracted from the template in the library, saving the self-service user from having to know it. You can see that the product key is hidden, protecting the organization from piracy. You could leave this field blank in the template, forcing the end user to find the budget for their own licensing. You could also have many templates, each with a product key for different budget/license owners in the organization.

In this example, all the user has to do is select a template (only one is available here), enter the virtual machine name, enter a computer name (or a random one can be created), and optionally enter a description (which is recommended).

It is possible that a user will be a member of many self-service user roles via different Active Directory security group memberships. If this is so, then they can select a different self-service role at the top of the page to reveal different sets of available templates.

The bottom of the page shows the available set of quota points for virtual machine deployment. The available templates show how many points they will consume if deployed.

All the user will have to do now is click the Create button to create the virtual machine. That's pretty easy; in fact, it's easier than booking an online flight or hotel. There's no excuse for an end user such as a developer, tester, or administrator not being able to provision their required virtual machines without any help from the VMM administrators.

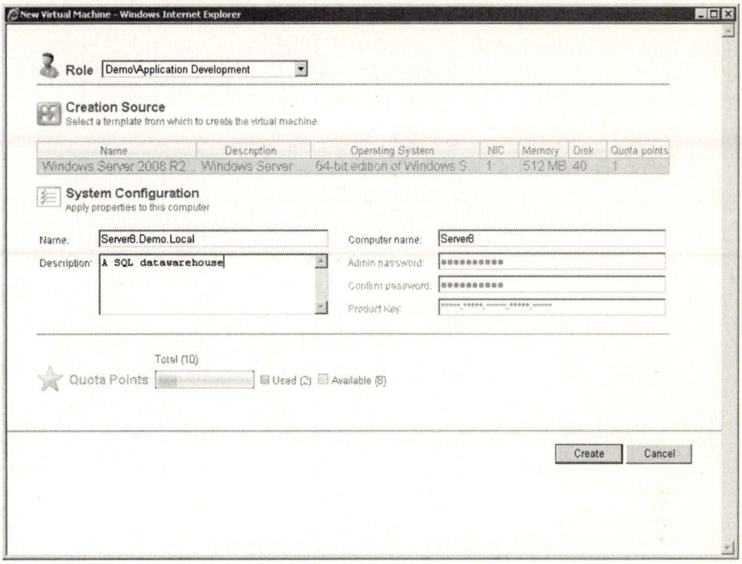

FIGURE 7.47 Creating a self-service virtual machine

Back in the portal, you will see that there is a very limited number of changes that a self-service user can make to a virtual machine's properties. Select a virtual machine, and click Properties. This will open the page shown in Figure 7.48.

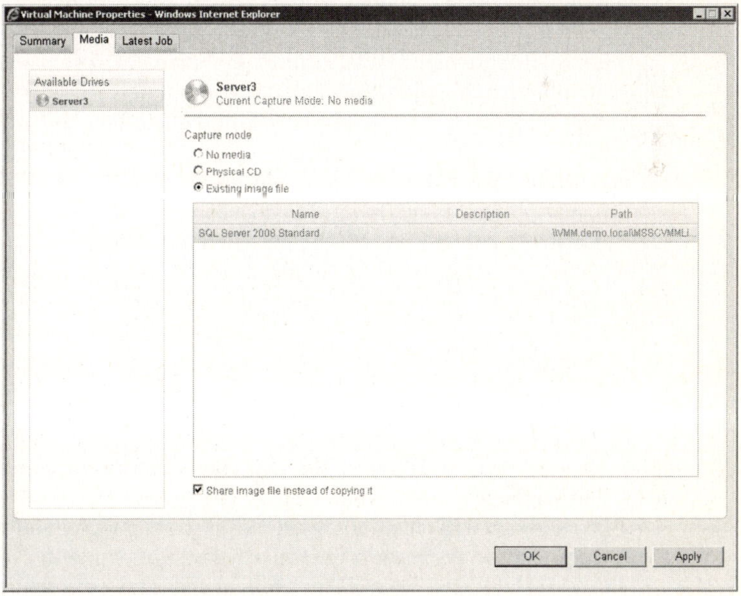

FIGURE 7.48 The media properties of a virtual machine

The Summary tab allows you to change the description of a virtual machine. It also allows the owner of the virtual machine to be configured for a specific scenario.

When the user, Lisa Garcia, creates a virtual machine, it will have her (Demo\LGarcia) as the owner, not the self-service user role (Demo\Application Development). That's a bit of an issue because other members of the user role will not be able to see the virtual machine until this is changed.

The Summary tab also allows the user to select the self-service user role as the owner. This will fix the problem. Unfortunately, this is probably going to be one of those issues that will cause a few help-desk tickets to be opened.

The Media tab allows the self-service user to connect the virtual machine either to an ISO image or to physical media that is loaded in the host server. Remember that this feature requires the ability to store virtual machines in the library. The ISO image must be in a folder that the self-service user role is configured to use. There is no need to configure an owner for the ISO image.

The Latest Job tab will allow the self-service user to track the progress and success/failure of the last job to run against this virtual machine.

At this point, you have learned how to populate the library with content, deploy administrator-managed virtual machines, delegate administrator access, and enable self-service provisioning of virtual machines in a controlled manner. That is a lot of VMM functionality. But we are not finished yet. We still need to look at how we are going to deal with preexisting physical and virtual servers on the network.

Converting Physical Servers

Most organizations that install Hyper-V will have an existing physical server network. It is likely that many of these servers (some PC operating systems are supported in physical to virtual [P2V] conversions as well) have been identified as machines that should be converted into virtual machines. Virtual Machine Manager provides Microsoft's supported mechanism for converting physical servers into virtual machines. This physical to virtual conversion is often referred to as a P2V conversion or just P2V.

There is an argument that P2V conversions are not always the right way to move a server network into virtualization. Some would say that new machines should be built as replacements to the original physical machines. This would encourage the introduction of up-to-date or 64-bit operating systems. It would also prevent some of the instabilities of the physical servers from being brought over to the new virtual infrastructure. There are merits to this approach, but would an organization really want to do a complete rebuild of its entire server infrastructure instead of a P2V conversion? Maybe they will use P2V conversions and migrations for the majority of servers. And maybe some servers that have become unstable or are running unsupported or near-end-of-life operating systems will be rebuilt.

We're going to assume that the organization will choose to convert the physical servers into virtual machines. We'll start off by comparing the two techniques that are included with Virtual Machine Manager 2008 R2. Then we will cover the requirements. We will then show how to prepare the physical servers for conversion and show each of the 2 P2V techniques in action.

P2V Techniques

A P2V conversion will create a near-identical copy of a physical machine that will run as a virtual machine on your Hyper-V hosts. Each physical disk will be copied as a virtual hard disk.

Microsoft states (see `http://technet.microsoft.com/en-us/library/cc764232.aspx`) that VMM will perform P2V conversions on a "best-effort basis."

This is because there are countless variables that Microsoft cannot test and account for. This makes the process sound a bit daunting, but you will find that one of the two provided methods will usually give you the results you want.

Online P2V This is the first and preferred method of P2V that VMM supports. With this approach, a VMM agent is temporarily deployed (not requiring a license) to the physical machine that will be converted. VMM will use the Volume Shadow Copy Service (VSS) to create a copy of all NTFS volumes in a consistent manner. The resulting snapshot is used to create the VHDs on a Hyper-V host. Online P2V will probably be used in most conversions. The major drawback of this approach is that it will convert files in a sequential basis. Files might change as the conversion is running. This means that the resulting VHDs may not be up-to-date. The operating system and all running applications on the server will also require VSS support or a VSS writer.

Offline P2V This approach will be the one that is used when an online P2V fails or when you identify that it is not supported (lack of VSS support) or not appropriate (because there is a lot of change of file content on the server while it runs). With this process, a Windows PE boot image is deployed to the machine that will be converted. The machine is configured to boot from the boot image, and the server will be rebooted. The P2V conversion will start when the server is restarted. It is important to understand that the boot image will require drivers for the mass storage controller and the network card (that will be used to talk to the VMM server) on the server. These will be provided on the VMM server.

P2V TO PASSTHROUGH DISKS

It is not possible to use VMM 2008 R2 to perform a P2V conversion where a virtual machine will be created with passthrough disks instead of VHDs. If you do need to do this, then you should consider either rebuilding the server as a virtual machine or using a technique such as cloning or bare-metal recovery from backup.

Supported Configurations for P2V

The following operating systems are supported on physical servers that will be converted into virtual machines:

- Microsoft Windows 2000 Server with Service Pack 4 or newer (offline P2V only)
- Microsoft Windows 2000 Advanced Server SP4 or newer (offline P2V only)
- Windows XP Professional x86 SP2 or newer
- Windows XP Professional x64 SP2 or newer
- Windows Server 2003 x86 Standard SP2 or newer
- Windows Server 2003 x86 Enterprise SP2 or newer
- Windows Server 2003 x86 Datacenter SP2 or newer
- Windows Server 2003 x64 Standard SP2 or newer

- Windows Server 2003 x64 Enterprise SP2 or newer
- Windows Server 2003 x64 Datacenter SP2 or newer
- Windows Server 2003 Web edition
- Windows Small Business Server 2003
- Windows Vista x86 with Service Pack 1
- Windows Vista x64 with Service Pack 1
- Windows Server 2008 x86 Standard
- Windows Server 2008 x86 Enterprise
- Windows Server 2008 x86 Datacenter
- Windows Server 2008 x64 Standard
- Windows Server 2008 x64 Enterprise
- Windows Server 2008 x64 Datacenter
- Windows Web Server 2008
- Windows 7 x86
- Windows 7 x64
- Windows Server 2008 R2 Standard
- Windows Server 2008 R2 Enterprise
- Windows Server 2008 R2 Datacenter
- Windows Web Server 2008 R2

You can see that Windows NT 4.0 is not listed. It is not unusual to encounter the occasional server that still runs this legacy operating system because of application requirements. It makes sense to try to convert these servers into virtual machines because hardware support is very difficult to find for Windows NT 4.0, and it is quite a challenge to find spare parts for old hardware. You might be able to use a bare-metal backup/recovery solution or a disk-cloning solution to clone this machine's disks into a virtual machine's VHDs.

P2V of Linux Servers

Microsoft does not provide a method to convert Linux servers into Hyper-V virtual machines. You can find a variety of techniques on the Internet. Each technique appears to be specific to the Linux distribution in question. Oddly enough, one suggested solution is to use VMware vCenter Converter to perform a P2V conversion with an ESX server as the temporary destination. The resulting VMDK files can then be converted into VHDs using a free tool called VMDK2VHD (`http://vmtoolkit.com/files/9/default.aspx`). The VHDs can then be added to a new virtual machine.

The requirements of the physical server to be converted are as follows:

- It must have at least 512 MB of RAM.
- None of the volumes can be larger than 2040 GB in size. This is because this is the maximum size of a VHD.
- You must have an Advanced Configuration and Power Interface (ACPI) BIOS for an offline conversion because Windows PE cannot boot from a non-ACPI BIOS.
- The server must be in the same domain as the VMM server or in a domain with a two-way trust with the VMM server's domain.
- Itanium architectures are not supported for P2V conversions.
- The boot volume of the server should not be encrypted if an offline migration is to be performed. This is because the resulting virtual machine will not be able to read the new VHD.

The requirements for the destination server that will host the new virtual machine are as follows:

- The host must be running Windows Server 2008 R2 Hyper-V, Windows Server 2008 Hyper-V, or Virtual Server 2005 R2 SP1.
- The host must not be in a perimeter network.
- The host must have sufficient RAM and storage capacity for the new virtual machine (remember to account for the hosts that are configured in VMM, which we discussed earlier in this chapter when dealing with hosts and host groups).

You now understand the requirements for converting physical machines into virtual machines. Have you decided how you will prioritize the physical machines to be P2V converted?

Schedule Server Conversions

Ideally, you have already tried this process during the test and development phase of this project. Unfortunately, it is likely that you were doing those tests with machines that were pretty clean and without complications.

It is important to decide on an order for performing your P2V conversions. Here is a possible order you could use:

Test Machine You should work with a few test machines if you have not tested both P2V techniques during the test and development phase of the project. This will allow you to document and become comfortable with the process. You will be working with nervous server and application administrators. Any sign of uncertainty on your part might cause them to obstruct your plans.

Low-Priority, Low-Risk Pilot Servers You should identify a few servers that are not critical and that are managed by cooperative administrators. You should try to work with a variety of hardware and operating systems. This will give you a chance to pilot your process with production hardware and generate organizational confidence in your solution.

At-Risk Servers You are free to work with other servers now that you have completely tested the solution. Any servers with older or troublesome hardware should be next. The conversion to Hyper-V virtual machines will make them more reliable.

Business-Prioritized Servers The objectives of your project will dictate which direction the P2V process will take next. If disaster recovery is your priority, then you will convert high-importance servers into virtual machines. If power consumption reduction is your priority, then you will prioritize those servers that are estimated to consume the most power.

All Remaining Servers Any remaining servers should be converted. This is the part of the task that is likely to not go according to schedule. All of the high-importance machines have been converted, and other engineering tasks may start to interfere with this part of the project. Define a schedule, and be sure to stick with it. Communicate with management, your team, and your colleagues the importance of completing the project on schedule so that all of the project's objectives can be reached.

In your schedule, you should also record whether you are going to use an online or an offline P2V conversion method. This will affect your server preparations. One of these preparations will be to estimate the time it will take to perform a P2V conversion. There isn't really an accurate way to calculate this because it depends on server activity and network congestion. You will be able to record metrics during tests and use these as the basis of estimates for future conversions. Try to be conservative with the estimates to avoid upsetting people if the process takes longer than otherwise communicated.

With your schedule set, you can now start to work with the physical servers.

Prepare Physical Servers for Conversion

If you are planning an offline migration, then you need to think about NIC and mass storage controller drivers. Virtual Machine Manager uses a Windows PE boot image. It will require access to the disks to read the source content and network access to create the new virtual machine. The boot image will have a number of drivers that it can use following a PNP detection. It is not uncommon to find that Microsoft media may not contain drivers for your hardware.

There are two approaches to this. If you have been working with your servers for a while, then you might know which drivers you have had to supply when you installed Windows Server 2008 or Windows Server 2008 R2. You can use the driver data that can be collected during an assessment or that might be residing in a Configuration Manager database to figure out which drivers you will need to download and supply to VMM.

You can also just try an offline migration. The wizard will scan the physical machine and check whether the required drivers are present. You will be warned if there are any issues. If there are, then you will need to add extracted drivers into the driver cache, which is located here:

```
C:\Program Files\Microsoft System Center Virtual Machine Manager 2008 R2\Driver
Import
```

You should try to keep a very organized folder structure that separates the manufacturer, server model, and device. The drivers must be 32-bit drivers that will load on Windows Vista or Windows Server 2008 R2. This is because the Windows PE image is similar to a stripped-down version of Windows Vista x86.

Any content on the disk that is stored in a bad sector will not be copied by VMM. It is recommended that you prepare the filesystem by running a `chkdsk` job.

You can minimize the time required for a P2V conversion by using a disk defragmentation tool to clean up the filesystem. It might not be a bad idea to schedule this task. If you don't have a third-party product for this, then you can use `defrag`. For example, you can run `defrag c:` to defrag the C: drive.

If you are using an online migration, then make sure that all applications that do not have a VSS writer are shut down.

The last step is to deal with any hardware-integrated software. An example of this will be the manufacturer's management software. This software will cause a newly converted virtual machine to blue screen when it starts up. You should disable any drivers or services related to this software. If you forget to do this, then your virtual machine will probably fail to start up correctly. You can get the virtual machine to boot up into safe mode and then uninstall the software.

You can uninstall the hardware integrated software and services from the virtual machine if the conversion completes successfully. You can reenable the hardware integrated software and services on the physical server if the conversion does not complete successfully and you need to bring it back into production without delay.

The physical server should now be ready for your selected conversion.

Convert the Physical Server

We will now walk you through the process of converting a physical server into a virtual machine using both the online and offline P2V methods.

Online P2V

Start the P2V by clicking the Convert Physical Server task in the Actions pane. The Convert Physical Server (P2V) Wizard, shown in Figure 7.49, will start.

Enter the fully qualified domain name of the physical server that you want to convert and administrator credentials for that machine.

Figure 7.50 shows the next screen, Virtual Machine Identity. This is where you define the name, owner, and description of the virtual machine that will be created.

The next step, System Information, which is shown in Figure 7.51, will install a temporary VMM agent on the physical server and gather some information about it. Click the Scan System button to gather this information.

FIGURE 7.49
The Convert Physical Server (P2V) Wizard

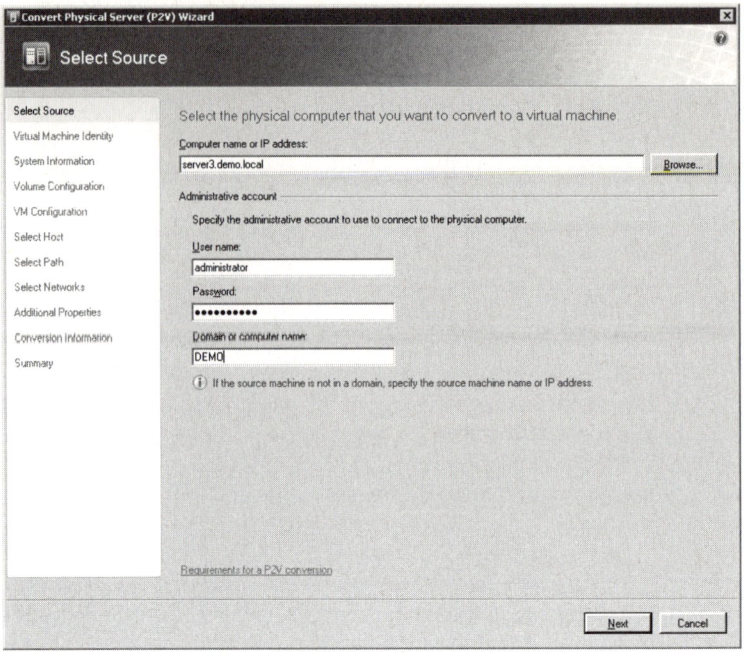

FIGURE 7.50
The Virtual Machine Identity screen

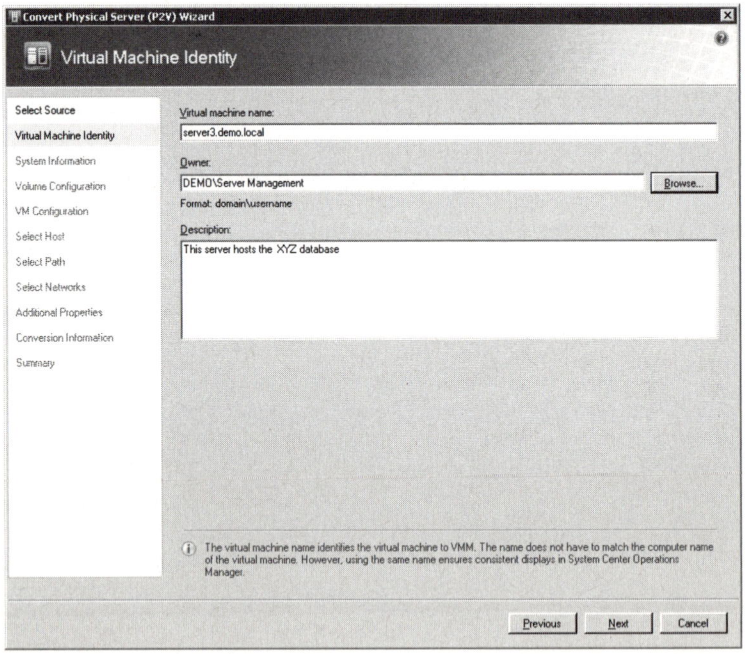

FIGURE 7.51
System Information screen

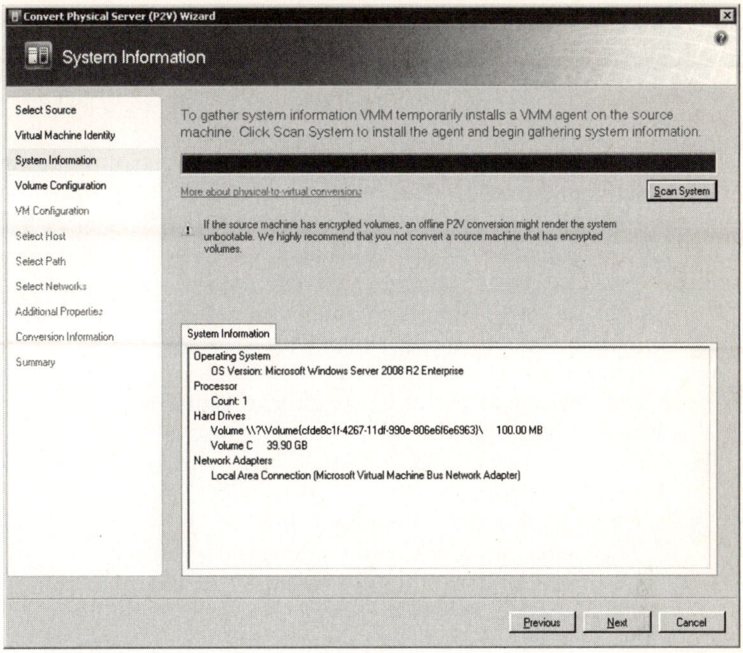

The Volume Configuration screen (Figure 7.52) is badly named because it can be used to do more than just define volume details.

FIGURE 7.52
Configuring the P2V conversion

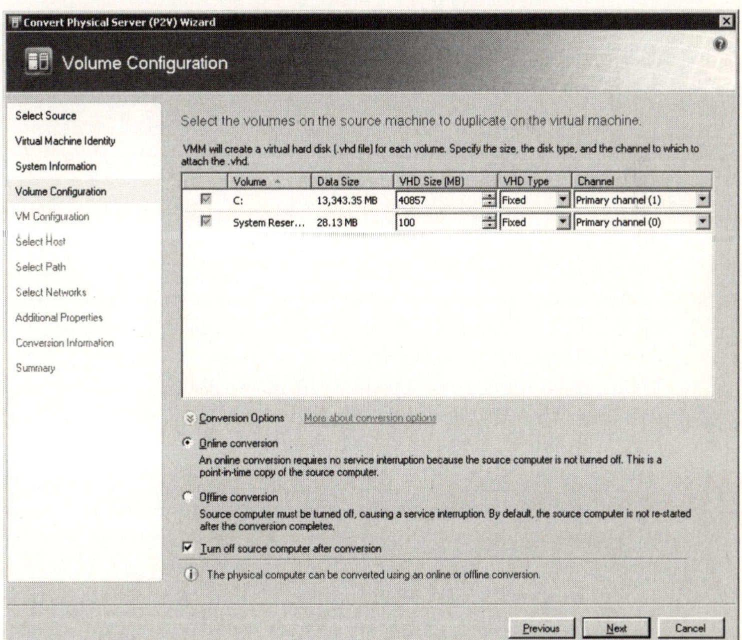

The volumes that were found in the source physical machine will be presented in the upper part of the screen. Each one will be converted into a VHD file.

By default, the size will match the original volume. You can increase the size of each volume if you so choose, up to the maximum of 2040 GB for a VHD file.

VHD Type is set to Dynamic by default. You will usually leave this to speed up the conversion process. You can then edit the properties of the resulting virtual machine to convert the VHDs into the fixed VHD type if your postconversion tests are successful.

You can also change the channel of the VHDs. Remember that boot VHDs must be on the IDE controller. It might not be a bad idea to move data VHDs onto a virtual SCSI controller.

The lower part of the shown screen, Configuration Options, is minimized by default. Here you can choose to perform an online or an offline P2V conversion. We have chosen the Online Conversion option.

You can also choose to shut down the source physical machine once the conversion is completed. You should do this if the new virtual machine is going straight into production or if there is a risk of data changing on it after the conversion. The physical server should not be shut down if you are going to run tests and you need to leave some service up and running — you need to be sure that data will not change on it. If it does, then you will need to figure out how to copy the changes to the virtual machine.

The Virtual Machine Configuration screen will allow you to configure the number of virtual CPUs and the amount of RAM to assign to the virtual machine.

This is an opportunity to correct mistakes that may have been made with the sizing of the source physical server. It is reported that many are finding in their assessments that physical servers were over-assigned with RAM and CPU resources. It is perfectly possible that your assessment also identified that the physical server did not have enough RAM resources. You can configure the virtual machine with the correct resources to suit its workload. You can quickly change these settings if they prove to be incorrect.

The Select Host screen will present your options for a possible host for the new virtual machine. It uses the Intelligent Placement star ratings.

You will follow this up by selecting a path on the host to locate the virtual machine's files and then by configuring a virtual network connection for each of the virtual network adapters. The second-to-last screen configures the host start-up and shutdown settings for the virtual machine.

The Conversion Information screen presents any issues that VMM has detected with this conversion job.

The Summary screen presents information about the job that will be run. You can click Show Script to view the lengthy script that will be run. If you save this script, then you can customize it and rerun it for other online P2V conversions. You could even schedule them if you were confident enough that nothing would go wrong.

The Start The Virtual Machine After Deploying It On The Host check box should be treated with care. The virtual machine should not be started if it will be on the production network and if the source physical machine will be left powered on. You do not want two identical machines running on the network at the same time. It will be OK to start the virtual machine if it is on an isolated network, if the original physical machine will be automatically powered down by the P2V conversion job, or if the virtual machine's virtual network adapters are not connected to a physical network.

The Online P2V job will run once you complete the wizard. If you check out the running steps of the conversion job, you will see that there is a step to install the integration guest services. A new virtual machine will (ideally) be created without any issues.

There is always a risk that something interferes with the VSS snapshot or the transmission of the data. You might need to rerun the job (saving the script will be useful for this). You might need to turn off some service or task that is running on the physical machine. You might even need to attempt an offline P2V conversion.

UNINSTALL THE VMM AGENT

Remember to check whether the VMM agent is still installed on the physical server if you leave it running. It will interfere with future P2V conversion attempts. It is also meant to be a temporary installation. This is why it doesn't require a license.

OFFLINE P2V

You will choose to perform an offline P2V in the following cases:

- You are converting Windows 2000 with SP4.
- The physical server has constantly changing data (like a database, and this includes domain controllers).
- There are applications or services without VSS writers (if you cannot shut them down).
- An online P2V was unsuccessful.

The method starts off similarly to an online P2V. Things change when you get to the Volume Configuration screen. You will select the Offline Conversion option, as depicted in Figure 7.53.

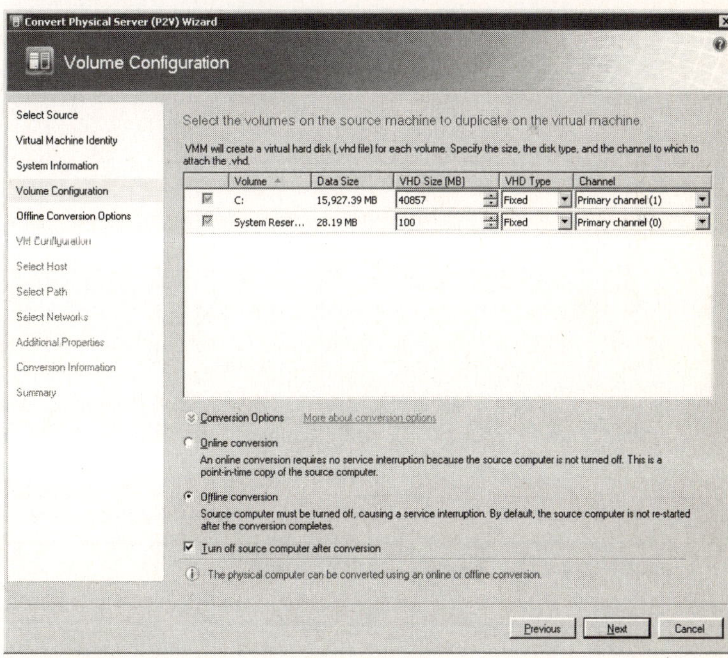

FIGURE 7.53
Choosing the Offline Conversion option

Things change a little now. Figure 7.54 shows the subsequent Offline Conversion Options screen. You are going to have to set up the networking configuration that the boot image will use. You can choose from three TCP/IP options:

Obtain An IP Address Automatically This will retrieve an address from a DHCP server.

Use The Following IPv6 Address The IPv6 address configuration of the server will be extracted from the server by the previous scan and will be available in the lower part of the screen. You can alter this if required.

Use The Following IPv4 Address The IPv4 address configuration of the server will be extracted from the server by the previous scan and will be available in the lower part of the screen. You can alter this if required.

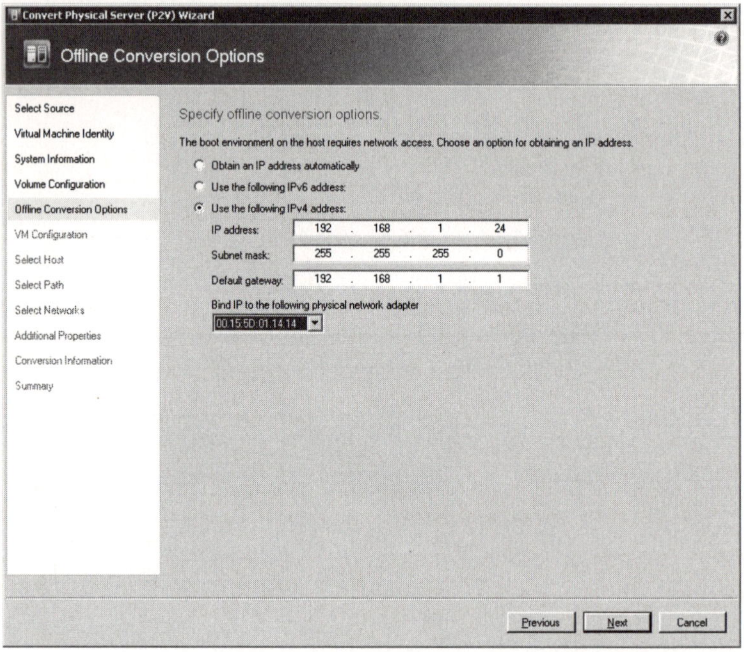

FIGURE 7.54
Offline conversion options

You should set the boot image to use the IP configuration that is normally used by the physical server when it is running normally if there are any firewall rules or routing/switching configurations that might affect communications from this server if its IP address were to change.

The Bind IP To The Following Physical Adapter drop-down list box will present the Ethernet (MAC) addresses of each NIC that was detected in the physical server. You can choose which NIC to bind the previous IP configuration with. This is the NIC that the boot image will then use to communicate with. This is also the NIC that you will need to provide a driver for if it is not already in the boot image.

CAN'T FIND A WORKING NIC DRIVER?

Sometimes you will not be able to get a NIC driver that will work in the offline P2V boot image. If this is the case, then you can insert an additional NIC into the server that you do have a working driver for. You can get the Ethernet (MAC) address of the NIC and configure the Offline P2V job to use this NIC.

The rest of the wizard will run as with the online P2V conversion. You will finally reach the Conversion Information screen where any issues are detected. Figure 7.55 shows VMM has determined that we do not have a suitable driver for the boot image to access the physical server's network card.

FIGURE 7.55
Conversion information warning

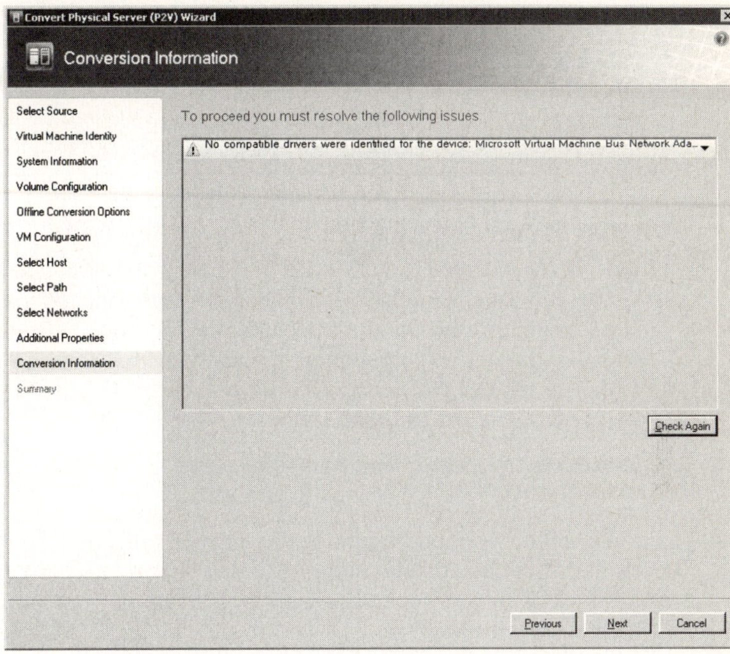

We will have to find a suitable 32-bit Windows Vista or Windows Server 2008 driver, extract it so the `.inf` and `.sys` files are visible, and place them into the driver cache:

```
C:\Program Files\Microsoft System Center Virtual Machine Manager 2008 R2\Driver
Import
```

Once you add a driver into the driver cache, you can click Check Again to see whether it has resolved the issue. You can continue with the job if there are no remaining warnings or errors.

The boot image will be deployed to the physical server, and it will be rebooted. The boot image will start up, and the virtual machine will be created from the source server.

That wraps up the section on P2V conversions. Now we will cover how to deal with any existing virtualization infrastructure that you want to control with VMM. You might even want to move the virtual machines to Hyper-V.

Manage Other Virtualization Solutions

The primary purpose of Virtual Machine Manager is to manage Hyper-V. It can also manage Virtual Server 2005 R2 SP1 and VMware's ESXi. In this section, we will look at how to take control of those other virtualization solutions. You will also see how you can perform virtual to virtual (V2V) conversions so that virtual machines can be moved from those solutions to Hyper-V.

SUPPORTED V2V OPERATING SYSTEMS

Not all operating systems are supported for V2V operations. Microsoft has listed all the supported operating systems here:

```
http://technet.microsoft.com/en-us/library/cc793147.aspx
```

Microsoft does say that it should be possible, in theory, to perform V2V conversions of unsupported operating systems. The main problem is that VMM cannot perform any fix-up operations to make the converted virtual machine bootable. You may need to know how to fix any boot issues for those unsupported operating systems once they are converted.

Virtual Server 2005 R2 SP1

Virtual Server 2005 R2 SP1 (or Virtual Server) was the second iteration of Microsoft's first server-based virtualization product. For a short time, the 2005 version was sold as a licensed product. Not long after, it was released as a free add-on to Windows Server 2003. An R2 release was issued, and this was subsequently updated with a Service Pack 1 release and then with an update to support Windows Server 2008, Windows Vista SP1, and Windows XP SP3 as host operating systems. You can find it here:

```
http://www.microsoft.com/downloads/details.aspx?FamilyId=A79BCF9B-59F7-480B-A4B8-
FB56F42E3348
```

Microsoft does not develop this product anymore. The current server-based virtualization technology from Microsoft is Hyper-V. If you do want to use Windows Server 2003 or Windows Server 2003 R2 as a host operating system, then you can use Virtual Server 2005 R2 SP1.

Virtual Machine Manager 2007 was the first of the VMM releases, and it was intended to manage Virtual Server. VMM 2008 and VMM 2008 R2 both continue to support the management of Virtual Server. You can even perform an automated installation of Virtual Server by adding a Windows 2003 server as a managed host in the SCVMM admin console if that server is not already running it.

A number of organizations deployed Virtual Server to some extent. Some used it just for limited workloads. Some used it as their main platform for test and development. Some even used it as their primary production virtualization system, in anticipation of Hyper-V. With VMM 2008 R2, you can continue to manage Virtual Server from your central console. You can manage almost all aspects of Virtual Server from VMM. We're not going to cover this topic too much. Instead, we're going to cover how to take control of the Virtual Server hosts and move the virtual machines to Hyper-V. This will bring better performance and higher availability (using host failover clustering) and allow the virtual machines to run on a virtualization system that Microsoft continues to develop and improve.

CONTROLLING VIRTUAL SERVER HOSTS

Before you take control of a Virtual Server host, you should know that a few things are not supported by VMM. The really important ones relate to virtual machine storage:

Multiple Versions of the Same VHD Attached to a Virtual Machine Data can be lost if you are using differencing disks and you attach different versions of the same VHD file to a virtual machine.

Undo Disks These are not supported by VMM at all. You will need to disable any undo disks on your Virtual Server hosts. You can find directions here: `http://go.microsoft.com/fwlink/?LinkId=98841`.

The process for deploying a VMM agent to and taking control of a Virtual Server host is identical to what you have already seen for a Hyper-V host.

You must install WS-Management 1.1 on any Windows 2003 host servers before they can be managed by VMM. You can download WS-Management 1.1 here:

```
http://wwwwww.microsoft.com/downloads/details.aspx?FamilyID=845289ca-16cc-4c73-8934-dd46b5ed1d33
```

Our host, `vserver.demo.local`, is being added in the Add Hosts Wizard in Figure 7.56.

FIGURE 7.56
Adding a virtual server host

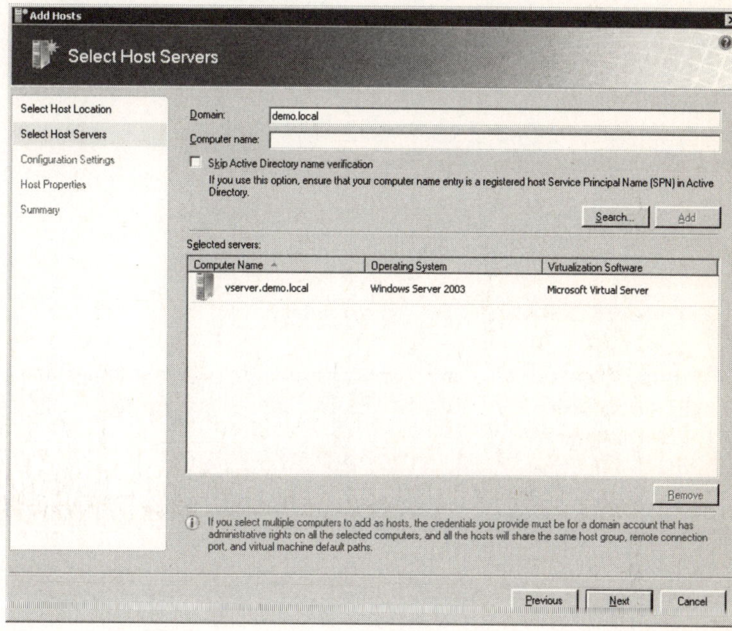

We will add the host into All Hosts\Host Group 2. As you progress through the wizard, you will see that the remote connection port (for console access to virtual machines) is set to 5900 rather than 2179 for Hyper-V hosts.

When the host is added, you need to decide whether you want to secure the communications between the VMM server and the Virtual Server host. Communications are unencrypted by default. You can use an X.509 certificate to secure communications. This can be configured in the properties of the host server in the SCVMM admin console. You can see the Secure Remote Connection With This Host option in Figure 7.57. You will be warned about this potential security issue if you do not secure the agent communications.

After an agent is installed onto the Virtual Server host, a refresh job will run, and the virtual machines will appear in the SCVMM admin console, as shown in Figure 7.58.

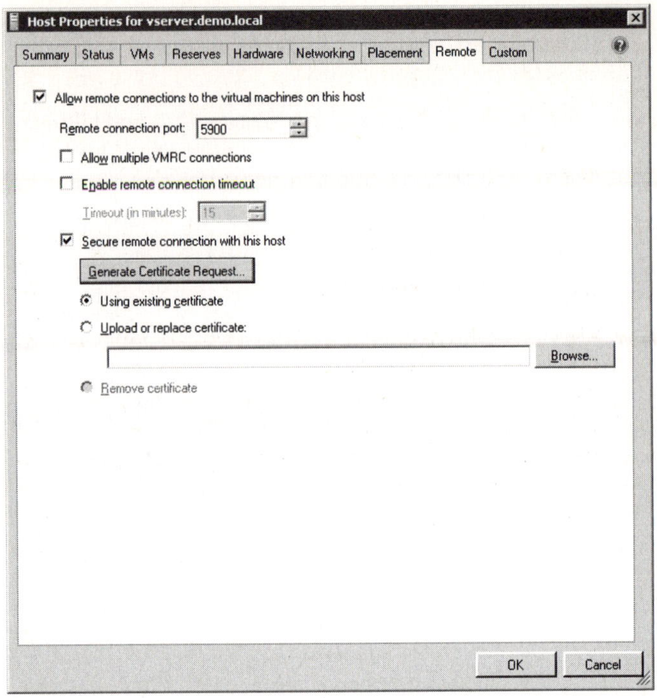

FIGURE 7.57
Securing Virtual Server management

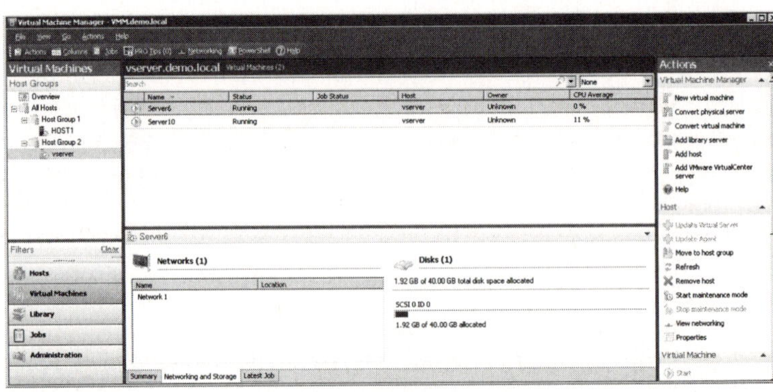

FIGURE 7.58
The Virtual Server virtual machines

Your next step should be to ensure that the latest integration guest services are installed into each of the Virtual Server virtual machines. This requires shutting down the virtual machine. The latest version will allow VMM to manage the virtual machines correctly and will allow a V2V migration of the virtual machines from Virtual Server to Hyper-V.

Take a look at the storage properties of the Server6 virtual machine. It is booting up using a VHD on a virtual SCSI controller. Hyper-V cannot boot from SCSI. This is going to be a typical issue that organizations will face when they move from Virtual Server to Hyper-V, but you'll soon see how to deal with it.

You can continue to use your Virtual Server hosts. You can use VMM to manage almost every feature of them and create and manage virtual machines on them (see `http://technet.microsoft.com/library/bb963754.aspx`). But eventually, you will want to migrate the virtual machines to your Hyper-V hosts.

Migrate from Virtual Server to Hyper-V

The move from Virtual Server to Hyper-V without VMM is a very manual task with a lot of steps, which you can find here:

`http://technet.microsoft.com/library/dd296684(WS.10).aspx`

VMM specializes in simplifying complex tasks, so it makes this operation a simple one for the VMM administrator.

We are going to move the Server6 virtual machine from Virtual Server to Hyper-V to illustrate how simple this operation will be.

Microsoft does not recommend doing a V2V migration of virtual machines that are running an operating system that does not have integration guest services or integration components support. If you are running a Windows operating system, then you should try to apply the latest service pack and Windows updates before proceeding.

It certainly will not do any harm to ensure that the virtual machine is backed up. If something does go wrong, though that is unlikely, then you must have a fallback plan to recover.

The first step for the V2V conversion is to shut down the virtual machine. It cannot be moved from Virtual Server to Hyper-V if it is running.

If your virtual machine is configured to boot using a SCSI controller, then you will have an additional step to do during the conversion. Hyper-V cannot boot from a VHD on a SCSI controller. The migration job that you are about to run cannot do this for you. You will need to edit the properties of the virtual machine while it is powered down and still located on the Virtual Server. There you can move the VHD from a virtual SCSI controller to a virtual IDE controller.

Now you are ready to start the migration. Browse to the virtual machine that you want to move to Hyper-V, select it, and click the Migrate task in the Actions pane. Do not select the Convert Virtual Machine action, which you might see in your view. This is intended to be used with VMware virtual machines. A move from Virtual Server isn't really a conversion because you are still dealing with the same basic VHD files (even if some changes have been made over time) that will be moved and attached to a Hyper-V machine (along with a few other steps such as uninstalling the Virtual Server machine additions, upgrading the HAL, and installing Hyper-V integration components).

Figure 7.59 shows the Migrate Virtual Machine Wizard. You can use the search and the drop-down list at the top to find a particular VMM-managed host server in a VMM host group. The Intelligent Placement host ratings will guide you to the best-suited Hyper-V host. We're selecting Host1, the Hyper-V host server in this lab. As usual, any information about the ratings or usage of SAN features for the migration will be explained in the lower part of the screen.

The subsequent Select Path screen will allow you to choose where on the selected host the virtual machine will be moved to. You can then map each of the virtual machine's network adapters to virtual networks on the Hyper-V host server.

You can choose whether to start the virtual machine automatically when it is migrated. Do you want to do that? It depends, but it is recommended that you don't. Here's why: when the new virtual machine is created on the Hyper-V host, it will have an emulated (legacy) network adapter. This offers less performance than a synthetic network adapter and requires more resources from the host server. If your virtual machine is enlightened (the integration components are installed), then it should use a synthetic network adapter. You will need to swap out the virtual machine's network adapters. Be aware that you will probably have to reconfigure the IP settings of the operating system in the virtual machine.

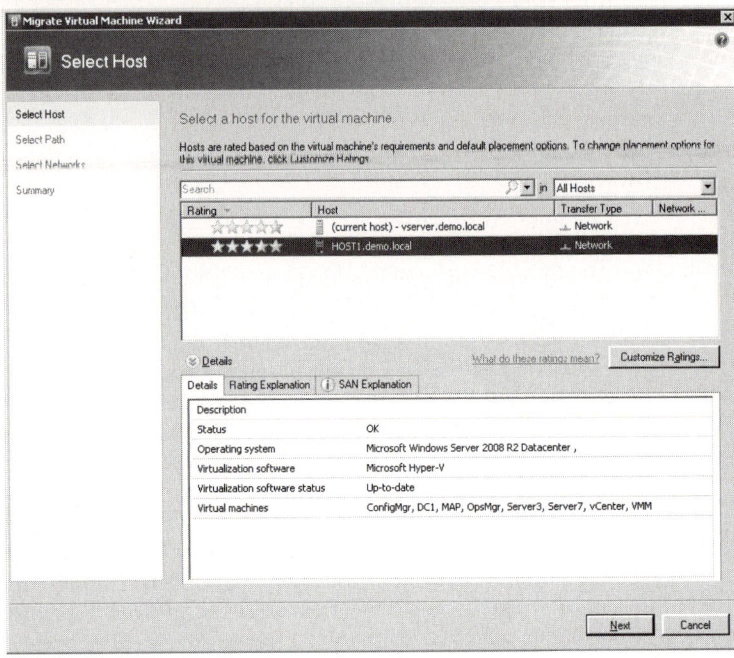

FIGURE 7.59
Migrate Virtual Machine Wizard

The virtual machine will now undergo a migration from Virtual Server to Hyper-V. All of the files will be removed from the Virtual Server host. The time taken for this operation will depend on the size of the VHDs to be moved (using BITS, which makes the process pretty reliable) and the network connectivity between the Virtual Server and Hyper-V host servers. The virtual machine reconfiguration steps will also take a few minutes.

If you do not autostart the virtual machine after the migration, then you can take the opportunity to review the virtual machine properties. You might alter the CPU configuration to change how Intelligent Placement views the virtual machine, change the virtual network adapters as previously discussed, or want to add or remove other resources.

You can then power up the virtual machine and check it out before putting it back into production.

This really should be a pretty smooth process. One of the reasons to adopt virtualization is that it makes migrating from older hardware to newer hardware easier. You are just dealing with files — unless you implement passthrough disks or raw device mapping in the VMware world.

Now we will move on to look at how to take control of VMware hosts and how to migrate virtual machines from them to Hyper-V.

VMware Hosts

There have been, and there will continue to be, many heated exchanges in the Microsoft vs. VMware virtualization war of words. We're not going to get into that. We accept that each solution has its own merits. We accept that VMware does have a very large share of the market. It is also very clear that Microsoft's share of the virtualization market is growing very quickly. Virtualization is like hardware; you pick the right one for the job. It wouldn't be surprising to see a mix of VMware, Microsoft, Citrix, and other virtualization platforms in a medium to large enterprise. Those organizations will want to be able to move between platforms to ensure that virtual machines run on the most suitable host solutions. And just like in the hardware world, organizations will choose to switch vendors.

Microsoft has made it possible for you to manage VMware ESXi hosts and to convert VMware ESX virtual machines into Hyper-V virtual machines.

The management functionality is made possible by the APIs that are provided in VirtualCenter or vCenter. These are the products that VMware sells to allow you to manage many ESX or ESXi host servers, much in the same way that you use VMM to manage VMM host servers. You cannot manage ESX or ESXi without a VirtualCenter or vCenter management server to act as an intermediary.

ONE CONSOLE TO RULE THEM ALL

Virtual Machine Manager has been jokingly nicknamed the "One Console to Rule Them All." This is because you can use a VMM server to manage many vCenter or Virtual Center servers, which in turn can manage hundreds of ESX or ESXi hosts each.

Be aware that VMM 2008 R2 can only manage the VI3 features of vSphere 4.0. Some features such as vNetwork Distributed Switches are not supported. That one seems to appear quite a bit on support forums as the root cause of failures.

CONTROLLING VMWARE HOSTS

VMM 2008 R2 will be deploying one agent to each VMware infrastructure. The agent will be installed on the management server. This will allow VMM to use the VMware APIs to control the hosts through the native VMware system.

You can see the lab VMware environment in Figure 7.60. A vCenter 2.5 server called `vcenter.demo.local` manages the VMware systems. A data center called Demo HQ contains the ESX server, which is running ESX 4.0. Two resource pools have been created, and two virtual machines, Server4 and Server5, are running in them.

Start by adding the vCenter server to VMM using the Add VMware VirtualCenter Wizard, which you can start from the Actions pane. This opens the window shown in Figure 7.61.

You will enter the name of the host server in Computer Name and the communications port for the VMware API in TCP/IP Port.

You then have to enter the credentials for authenticating against VirtualCenter or vCenter.

The Communicate With ESX Hosts In Secure Mode check box at the bottom allows you to specify whether you should communicate with the VirtualCenter-managed ESX hosts using secure mode. This will require an extra step to be carried out when adding the ESX hosts to VMM.

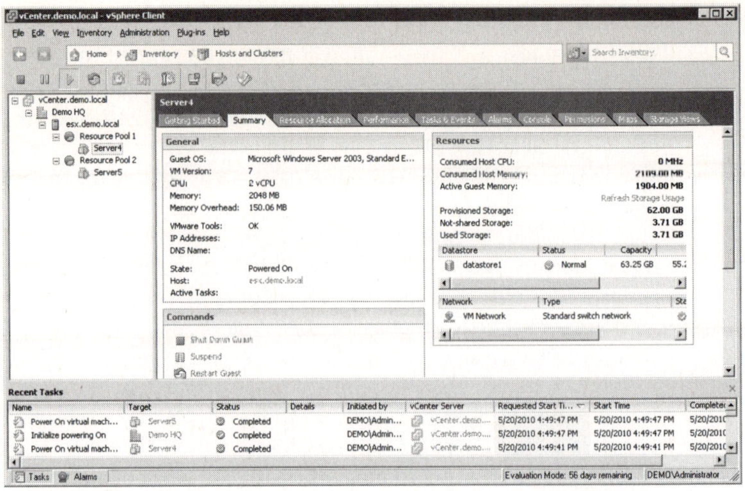

FIGURE 7.60
The VMware environment

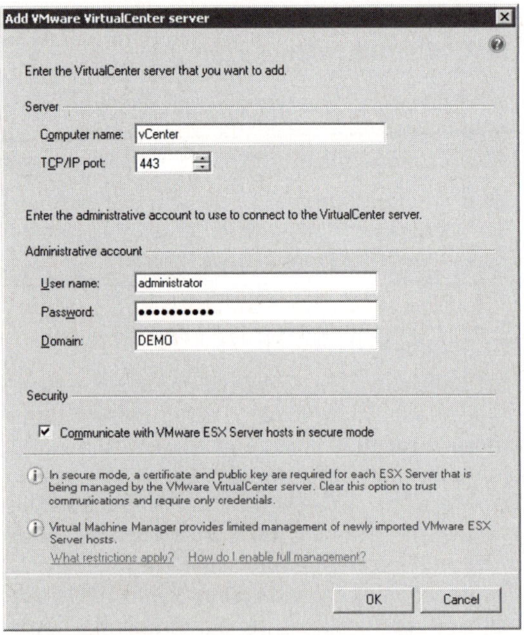

FIGURE 7.61
The Add VMware VirtualCenter Wizard

VMM will start to communicate with the VMware management server. A warning will appear to let you know that this could take several minutes. A new window will then appear, as shown in Figure 7.62.

SSL is used to communicate with the VirtualCenter server. The root CA that issued the certificate to this VirtualCenter is not trusted, so you must initiate a trust by this VMM server. You can do this by clicking Import to import the issuing CA's certificate into the VMM server's certificate store.

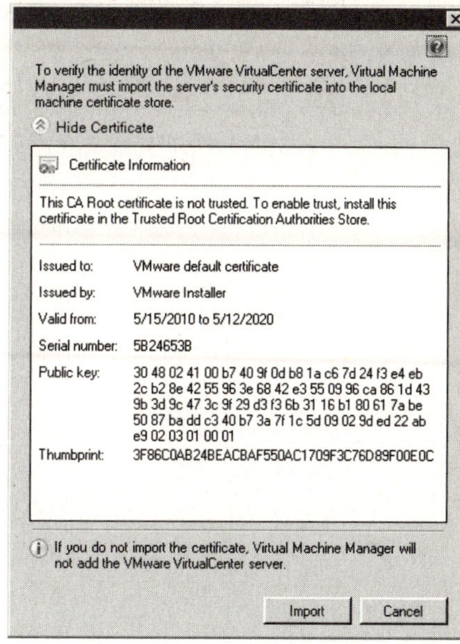

FIGURE 7.62
VirtualCenter certificate information

Things happen behind the scenes now. A job will run to add the VirtualCenter to VMM. You can track its progress by clicking the Jobs wunderbar and looking for an Add Virtualization Manager job.

When that has succeeded, you can click the Administration wunderbar and navigate into Virtualization Managers. The newly added VirtualCenter server will be visible there. You can, if you need to, edit the properties of the server here to change your security and communications configuration with the VirtualCenter.

You should click the Hosts wunderbar. The datacenters that are managed by the VirtualCenter server appear as host groups. Any hosts that were managed by the VirtualCenter server at the time it was added to VMM will appear in that host group. You can see this in Figure 7.63. You will also find that the virtual machines controlled by the VirtualCenter will start to appear in the Virtual Machines view.

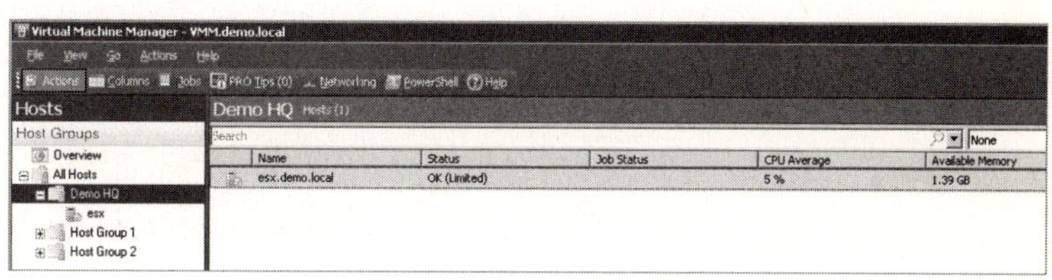

FIGURE 7.63
ESX host with an OK (Limited) status

The ESX host has a status of OK (Limited). This means that you haven't set up the security configuration (required by the earlier secure mode) for communicating with it and the management functionality is limited.

You need to add some security information to allow VMM to manage the ESX host. You can do this by opening the properties of the ESX host and going to the Security tab. Alternatively, you can select the host and start the Configure Security task from the Actions pane.

As you can see in Figure 7.64, you need to enter administrator credentials for logging into the ESX host server. The SSL authentication mechanism also requires that you click Retrieve to get the certificates from the ESX host so that they can be trusted by the VMM server.

FIGURE 7.64
Configuring ESX host security

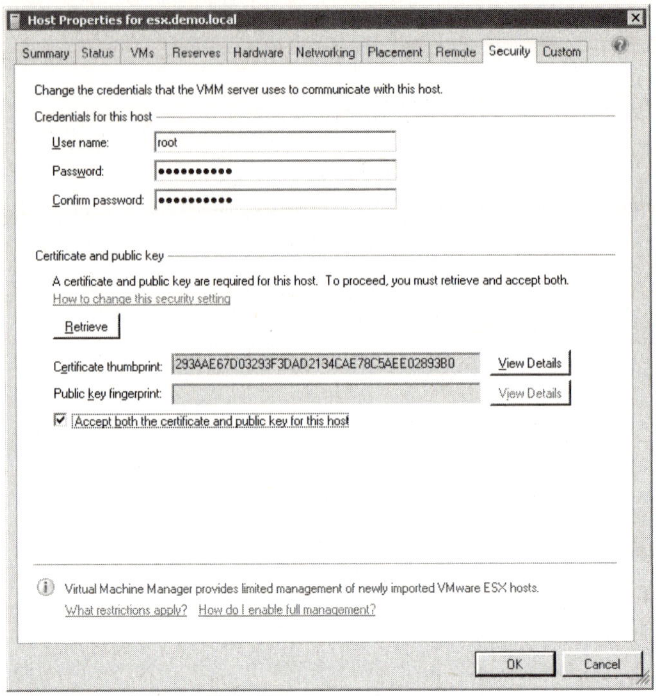

When you click the OK button, the status of the host will change from OK (Limited) to OK, assuming that everything is actually OK. If you return to the host properties, you can check out any problems that might be indicated on the Status tab.

You might be wondering where the resource pools are. They're visible on the VMs tab, shown in Figure 7.65. The Placement tab will show the ESX data stores.

You might very well want to take advantage of the ability to manage most of the VMware functionality from VMM. This includes being able to use the VMM Self-Service Portal. You can import the templates from a VMware library into VMM. You would do this in the Administration view. Select the VirtualCenter server, and start the Import Templates action. This opens the screen shown in Figure 7.66.

You can select any of the available libraries and specify a location in your VMM library to place it.

You must be aware that this will remove the imported objects from the VMware library. Only import them into the VMM library if you do not want to use the VMware library again.

Now you are in a position to start converting VMware virtual machines into Hyper-V virtual machines.

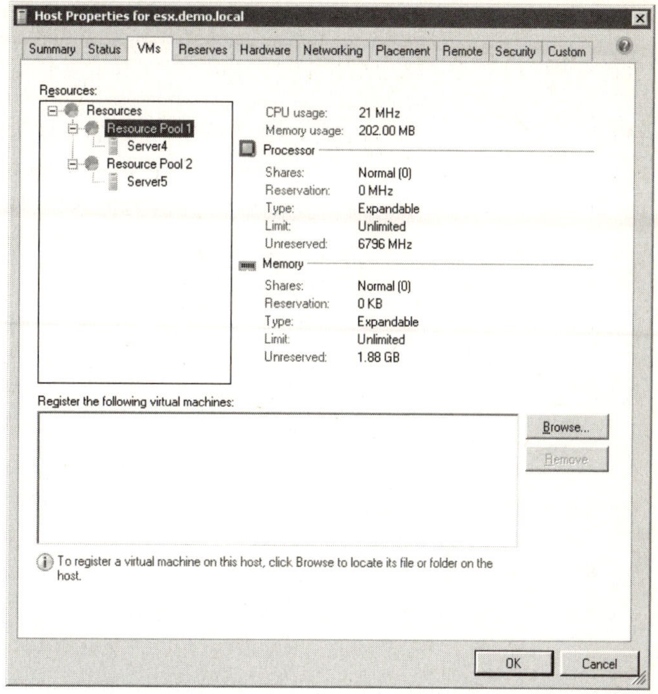

FIGURE 7.65
The resource pools in VMM

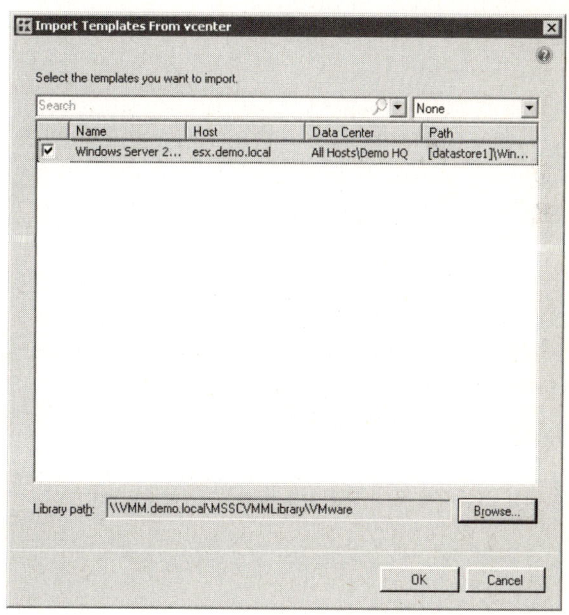

FIGURE 7.66
Importing the VMware library

Migrate from VMware to Hyper-V

There are three ways to perform a V2V conversion from VMware to Hyper-V. The first way is an on offline conversion. The virtual machine files (`.vmx` and `.vmdk`) are placed in a VMM library, and the library is refreshed. VMM reads the files and converts them into a virtual machine.

The second method connects to the VMware infrastructure and converts the machine into a Hyper-V virtual machine.

The third method uses the `New-v2v` PowerShell cmdlet and can convert a virtual machine from a Windows or an NFS share. We won't cover that method here.

Make sure you have a backup of the virtual machine. Then you must uninstall the VMware Tools from the virtual machine. When you are ready, power the virtual machine down, and return to the SCVMM admin console.

You can initiate a V2V conversion of a VMware virtual machine by starting the Convert Virtual Machine action. This opens the Convert Virtual Machine Wizard, which is shown in Figure 7.67.

Figure 7.67
Selecting a VMware virtual machine to convert

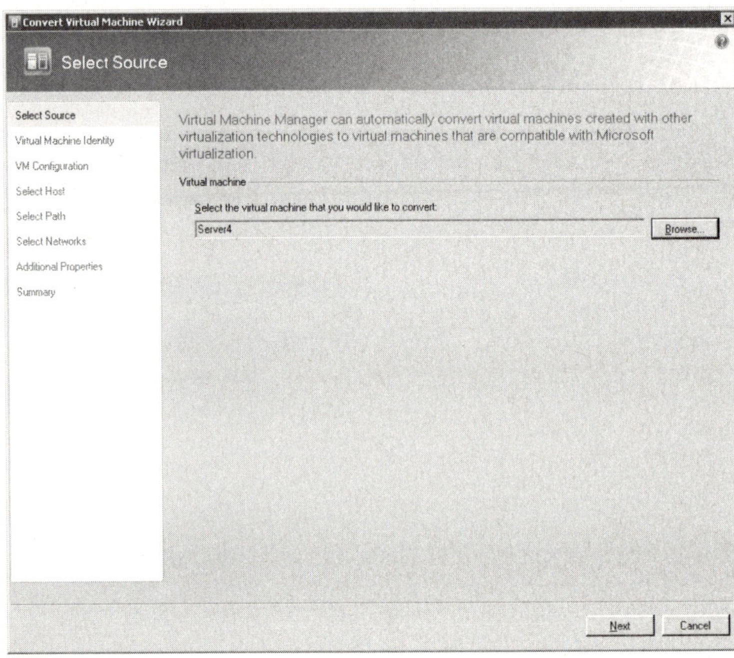

Doesn't ESX Usually Boot from SCSI?

An ESX virtual machine will usually have a SCSI-configured boot VMDK disk. You cannot just convert this to a VHD and leave it as a SCSI device. The V2V conversion process will know to switch the disk to an IDE controller in the virtual machine.

Here you can browse to select a VMware-hosted virtual machine that is managed by VMM and is powered off. You can also place the `.vmx` and `.vmdk` files of an ESX virtual machine into the VMM library and browse for them. This allows ESX-formatted virtual machines from VMware Workstation to be converted into Hyper-V virtual machines.

The remaining screens in the wizard have already been covered. You can alter the number of virtual processors and memory configuration. The destination host and storage location are selected, and virtual networks are mapped to virtual machine network cards. You can optionally automatically start the virtual machine on its new host, but it is recommended that you check its configuration once the machine is built. You may need to alter the CPU configuration.

The conversion process may take some time. The VMDK file is converted into a VHD over the network. You might need to plan the timing of this conversion. You can track the progress of the conversion operation in the Jobs view.

The virtual machine is moved to the Hyper-V host. The VMDKs are converted into VHDs by VMM. Any SCSI-based boot disk is moved to the virtual machine's IDE controller. The integration guest services are installed automatically if the virtual machine's operating system supports them.

From now on, the virtual machine will live in Hyper-V. VMM does not support a reverse migration to VMware. That will require using another solution. But ideally that will never be an issue.

What about Citrix XenServer Hosts?

The current version of Virtual Machine Manager (2008 R2) does not provide a mechanism to manage Citrix XenServer hosts or to migrate virtual machines from them. It is rumored that the next version of VMM, which will be released some time in 2011, will include this functionality.

In the meantime, Citrix has a developmental product called Project Kensho that uses the Distributed Management Task Force's (DMTF) Open Virtual Machine Format (OVF) to allow you to migrate virtual machines from XenServer to Hyper-V. You can learn about this project at `http://community.citrix.com/display/xs/Kensho`.

You now are armed with the knowledge to use VMM to take control of your host servers, manage security, convert your physical servers into virtual machines, control existing virtualization systems on your network, and even move virtual machines from them to Hyper-V. We'll now look at some of the new features that were introduced with Virtual Machine Manager 2008 R2 that can make administration easier.

New Features in VMM 2008 R2

Virtual Machine Manager 2008 R2 introduced a number of new features, most of which added support for the new features in Windows Server 2008 R2 Hyper-V. Some additional features were added. Knowing about what they do and how they work will make your job easier.

Maintenance Mode

This new feature is an action that can be performed on a host machine when you are planning to do some maintenance work on it such as rebooting, patching, or repairing. Enabling maintenance mode on a server will have the following effects:

Intelligent Placement You would not want Intelligent Placement to automatically place a virtual machine onto a host that was having some work being done on it.

Virtual Machine Creation You will not be able to create virtual machines on a host in maintenance mode.

Clustered Hosts When you put a clustered host into maintenance mode, you will be given a choice about what to do with all the running virtual machines on that host. You can choose to put all of them into a saved state. That will leave them in a safe and reliable condition. You can also choose to perform a Live Migration of the virtual machines to another host. Intelligent Placement will figure out on which of the other hosts to move each of the virtual machines.

VMM maintenance mode does not have any integration with Operations Manager's maintenance mode. If you enable maintenance mode on a host in VMM and do some disruptive work to it, an OpsMgr installation will create alerts, which will cause a bit of a fuss.

The VMM team at Microsoft wrote a blog post that contains an OpsMgr PRO management pack to integrate with VMM 2008 R2. You can view this post here:

```
http://blogs.technet.com/scvmm/archive/2009/06/08/integrating-vmm-and-opsmgr-
maintenance-mode.aspx.
```

Quick Storage Migration

You might want to change the physical storage location of a virtual machine for a number of reasons, including the following:

- You want to optimize the deployment of virtual machines on your CSVs.
- You are moving virtual machines between Hyper-V clusters.
- You have to move virtual machines between nonclustered hosts or even from nonclustered hosts and clusters, or vice versa.
- You have run out of resources on a host and need to relocate virtual machines.
- You want to change the storage location of a virtual machine on a single host server.

Normally this would mean shutting down a virtual machine and using a normal offline migration process to move the files using the migrate action in VMM. This process could take a very long time. Fixed-size VHDs are the recommended type in a production environment. They could be anything up to 2 TB in size. A file of many gigabytes in size will take a very long time to copy, even over a 10 Gb network. This will have a negative impact on business operations that depend on that virtual machine. Actually, the business won't be impacted, but your free time at night or on the weekend will be when you have to log into the office network to do the move outside of business hours.

VMM 2008 R2 has a solution called Quick Storage Migration (QSM) where you can move a running virtual machine between clustered or nonclustered Windows Server 2008 R2 hosts with very little down time. Here's how QSM works:

Migrate Action You initiate a migrate action of a running virtual machine on a Windows Server 2008 R2 host. You select another Windows Server 2008 R2 host (clustered or not clustered) as the destination, and VMM will run a job that is made up of a number of tasks. This is an example of how the VMM team takes advantage of PowerShell to automate complex tasks that might otherwise be possible with a lot of manual effort and might otherwise be prone to error.

Checkpoint The VHD(s) are write-locked because the virtual machine is reading and writing to them. That means that the VHDs cannot be copied. VMM takes a checkpoint (known as a *snapshot* in Hyper-V) of the virtual machine. A checkpoint creates an AVHD file for each VHD in the virtual machine. From that point until the checkpoint is removed and merged, the virtual machine will always read precheckpoint data from the VHD and read/write post-checkpoint data from/to the AVHD file(s). The original VHD is no longer write-locked, and it can be copied.

VHD Copy VMM will use BITS to reliably move the VHD files of the virtual machine to the desired Hyper-V host and storage location.

Checkpoint Copy Start your clock. The virtual machine is put into a saved state. This is when the downtime for the virtual machine starts. VMM uses BITS to move the AVHD files of the virtual machine's checkpoint to the destination server and storage location.

Virtual Machine Move The virtual machine configuration is exported and imported into the destination host and storage location.

Merge The checkpoint is removed, and the AVHD files are merged back into the VHD files. It's almost as if the checkpoint never happened.

Virtual Machine Restart Stop the clock; the downtime has ended. The virtual machine is woken up from its saved state in its new location. It continues to use the VHD files that the process started out with, only with the post-checkpoint data merged in.

Microsoft says that the expected downtime with this process will be around two minutes. That really is just an educated guess, and it will depend on a number of factors:

Disk Write Activity The bulk of the downtime is taken to move the AVHD file from the source to the destination. The AVHD file will be bigger if there is a lot of write activity.

Network Speed and Congestion The AVHD will take longer if the network connection between the source and destination hosts is slower or congested.

There is a cautionary warning that you need to be aware of. AVHDs or checkpoints come with some complications that you should account for:

AVHD Speed The performance of your virtualization storage will drop after you create a checkpoint. This won't be too much of an issue if the entire QSM process will happen quickly. It normally takes quite a bit of AVHD growth before you might see an issue.

Checkpoint Location By default, the AVHD files for a virtual machine are stored in the same location as the virtual machine. This is controlled in the virtual machine's properties, available in the Hyper-V console. If there is going to be a lot of write activity or if the QSM will take a significant time, then you need to be sure that the storage location will have enough space for the AVHD to grow. The virtual machine will be forced into a paused state to protect it if the volume fills up. This will also impact other virtual machines that are stored on the same volume.

The Bottom Line

Plan the installation of Virtual Machine Manager 2008 R2 It is important to understand the requirements of VMM 2008 R2 so that you can plan an architecture that suits the technology and business needs of the organization.

Master It You have been asked to design a management solution for a business. The business has a head office in Dublin, Ireland, and a branch office in San Francisco, United States. Hyper-V clusters will be placed in both sites. All administration will be done in Dublin. Software developers and testers in San Francisco also need the ability to deploy virtual machines without waiting for the IT department in Dublin. How will you design this VMM infrastructure?

Use the library for automation and self-service features VMM 2008 R2 includes the ability to delegate administration functions and allow non-IT staff to deploy and manage virtual machines.

Master It Ownership of the new Hyper-V infrastructure will be centrally controlled in a university. All new servers that will be virtual machines will run on this infrastructure. Each faculty has an IT staff that is responsible for their own services and budget. You must design a virtualization administration model that limits administration access to the underlying virtualization layer but also allows for faculty IT staff to deploy their own virtual machines. You must also be able to control and cross-charge for resources used.

Manage and convert existing physical and virtual machines VMM 2008 R2 is able to manage virtual machines on Hyper-V, Virtual Server 2005 R2 SP1, and VMware's ESX. You can convert virtual machines from those non-Hyper-V platforms to Hyper-V. You can also convert physical machines into virtual machines using VMM.

Master It The assessment phase of the project has identified two servers that must be virtualized in an office. One server is a web server with static content. The other server is relatively new and is running a number of very heavily used databases that are used by offices from around the world. How will you convert these servers into virtual machines using VMM 2008 R2?

Chapter 8

Virtualization Scenarios

No matter how well any self-service or management systems are implemented, the success or failure of the Hyper-V project will depend on how well the organization's applications perform in their virtual machines.

You need to be able to understand how components of your hardware and Hyper-V design and implementation will affect the performance of your virtual machines. The subjects of hardware and Hyper-V have been dealt with at this point. We need to cover the often forgotten part of the discussion.

All too often, virtualization engineers will forget to consider the individual needs of virtual machines and applications. Applications will have support statements and supported configurations. Hardware designs for physical server implementations will need to be converted into applicable virtual machine implementations. There is no one standard that you can apply. There are guidelines that will generally steer you, but there are often application-specific rules that will be dictated by the software vendors.

In this chapter, we are going to look at some general guidelines on how to approach the design of individual virtual machines. We will then move on to look at a number of common scenarios that will be found in almost every Microsoft-based server and application network. Here you will see some of the general guidelines in practice alongside some application-specific requirements. We will wrap up the chapter by showing how you can implement some virtualized fault-tolerance solutions that are independent of failover cluster–enabled Hyper-V host servers.

In this chapter, you will learn to

- Understand virtual machine design guidelines
- Deploy common roles in Hyper-V virtual machines
- Configure fault tolerance in virtual machines

Designing Virtual Machines

There are many variations of the anecdote where some organization that deployed a line-of-business application on some hardware virtualization solution noticed unacceptable performance. Depending on the story, either they reversed the decision to convert/deploy the servers as virtual machines or they hired an expensive consultant to investigate. The consultant would identify a few issues, make some changes, and suddenly everything would perform as expected.

The goal of this chapter is to put you in a position to understand what opportunities and pitfalls may lay ahead in a Hyper-V project when it comes to the specifications and configurations of individual virtual machines. Some of these have been discussed already, particularly in Chapter 5 when we showed how to convert your assessment data into a set of hardware requirements. Those were low-level requirements that dealt with the hardware. How you implement each virtual machine will impact not just the performance of the operating system and applications in that virtual machine but will also impact the support for them.

Application Support

Your first port of call during the assessment phase of the project, before you even consider deploying a virtual machine, is to check with the vendor of your application for its support for hardware virtualization and for Hyper-V.

Unfortunately, the vendor will sometimes claim that running the application in a Hyper-V virtual machine will be unsupported. It may be that this is not written in stone; some crafty negotiations based on your future purchase plans (or lack thereof) for its products may alter its support statements. Over the years, we have seen how some companies' lack of support for virtualization is based purely on marketing rather than on technical matters. A quick comment about the need to fully implement virtualization, even if that means switching to a rival company's database or business intelligence applications, can sometimes get the results you require to proceed with your plans with little interruption to business operations.

Unfortunately, there will be those occasions where you cannot get the support that you require. You'll then have three options:

Continue with Virtualization without Support This option happens more often than one would like to think, simply because the organization wants the least disruptive option where the physical server footprint and costs are minimized. The organization will accept the risks and deploy the application in a virtual machine. No mention of virtualization will be made if a support call is opened for the application. If hardware specifications are requested, then the organization will hope that the support agent will be flexible and accommodate the customer's need for assistance. There is a major risk that the support team will reject any requests for support for this application.

Deploy the Application on Physical Servers This is a scenario where there is no alternative to the application. The organization might already be running the application on physical servers. In this case, they will not be converted into virtual machines. The application might be a new purchase. If so, it will be deployed on physical servers. This is unfortunate because it will mean that the costs associated with physical servers will not be as low as they could have otherwise been.

Migrate to Alternative Applications This option is clearly the most disruptive option. For example, an organization that might be invested in some other company's database and business intelligence products would have to undergo great difficulty to switch to a Microsoft platform. Not only would there be downtime and large consulting costs, but the end user experience would be sure to change, requiring a great amount of retraining. However, the result would be that the organization would now have fewer physical servers and a fully supported solution running on its Hyper-V servers. You might be interested to know that as of July 15, 2009, all software being tested for official Microsoft Windows Server certification must include testing in a Hyper-V environment (`www.microsoft.com/windowsserver2008/en/us/isv.aspx`).

MICROSOFT VIRTUALIZATION SUPPORT STATEMENTS

Even Microsoft has some support statements for its applications on Hyper-V. You can find the Server Virtualization Validation Program here:

```
http://windowsservercatalog.com/svvp.aspx?svvppage=svvpwizard.htm
```

Using this site, you can pick a server application, a virtual machine operating system, and CPU architecture. A brief support statement will be produced. However, the best and most detailed results will be found if you search for your product's system requirements on TechNet.

Once you have ascertained the supportability of your application in a Hyper-V virtual machine, you can progress to finding out how the vendor requires the virtual machine to be configured. Much like with hardware design, the configuration of a virtual machine will impact on how it will perform and behave in different circumstances.

Virtual Machine Configurations

Consider how you would deploy a physical SQL Server machine. You will usually have a certain amount of memory that will be sized according to the requirements of the databases and applications that are hosted on or using the server. You will choose certain types of storage connections, disk types/systems, and RAID levels for the operating system, log files, and database files. You might have certain configurations of network cards, and there will be a backup solution. Each of these must comply with the recommendations and support statements from Microsoft. And each of these will have an impact on how well that SQL Server instance will perform its role for the organization.

The same applies to the design and implementation of a virtual machine. How many virtual machines you put on a host, what type of physical storage disk and configuration you use, the setup of physical network cards, the setup of the virtual networks and virtual network adapters, and the configuration of the virtual machine storage all impact how SQL Server will perform in a virtual machine. We will now spend a bit of time considering how various aspects of the design will impact performance. It is easy to say that we must throw resources at the solution, but we must also be realistic and justify the costs.

INTEGRATION COMPONENTS

A virtual machine is considered enlightened when the integration components are installed. These integration components will optimize the performance of a virtual machine. This applies to Windows and Linux operating systems. You should always install the integration components when you can. VMM will automatically take care of that for you with supported Windows guest operating systems.

PHYSICAL STORAGE

This is a pretty complex topic, and the exact solution you will need will depend on the storage system you are using. You should include an expert on your storage system in your design. It is highly recommended that members of the engineering team attend basic and advanced training courses to completely understand their system.

How will you deploy your storage for your virtual machines? Some have taken the approach of using all RAID-5 storage. This may produce the most usable storage, but it comes at a performance cost; the disk may have a write speed of only 25 percent of its potential. Most have taken the approach of using all RAID-10 storage. This provides the best read and write performance, but it comes at a cost; 50 percent of the storage space is lost to fault tolerance. Maybe the best approach is to strike a balance between the two, just as we have always done with physical servers.

A useful guide is that if a physical server required RAID-5 or RAID-10, then the virtual machine should be stored on similarly set up storage.

How could you approach this if using a Hyper-V cluster with Cluster Shared Volumes (CSVs)? You could use one CSV that is based on RAID-10 storage and another that is based on RAID-5 storage. If a VM requires a RAID-10 VHD and a RAID-5 VHD, then you can place the VHDs on the appropriate storage by using the appropriate CSV.

You may see some guidance from software vendors that either might be out-of-date or does not consider enterprise storage systems. For example, one application's virtualization best practices may advise that each VHD used for the application should be implemented on disk spindles that are not shared with any other VHD. This would be impractical and unadvisable when using something like an HP EVA SAN. When using traditional storage systems, you select a number of disks and create a LUN of some RAID level. This LUN is presented to the server, which then formats it with NTFS. In a storage system like the HP EVA SAN, you will add many (minimum of eight) disks, probably 450 GB or more each, to a disk group. This group may span many disk trays for fault tolerance. The more disks that are added to the group, the better the performance. A virtual disk is created from the disk group of a selected RAID level. This virtual disk is spanned across all the disks in the disk group; this offers extreme performance for the virtual disk. The virtual disk is presented to the server, which sees it as any ordinary disk or LUN, and it is formatted with NTFS. In this example, it appears inappropriate to dedicate an entire disk group of at least eight disks to a single VHD that might be only a couple of hundred gigabytes in size. It also won't have the same potential performance of a VHD that spans possibly half or even all the disks in the SAN.

Virtual Machine Storage

The question of the physical storage has been dealt with. You might have optimized your performance by using RAID-10 storage for your virtual machine. But that might be all for nothing if you do not use a suitable type of virtual storage.

Each virtual machine will have disks. Typically these are files that simulate a virtual hard disk (VHD). The VHD files are stored on the physical storage that is presented to the host server. Virtual machines can also use physical storage that is presented directly to the storage. You have a lot of options when it comes to choosing how to store the operating system and data in the virtual machine.

Passthrough Disk This is when you connect an unformatted partition to a virtual machine. The virtual machine will be responsible for formatting and managing the file system. This type of storage offers the best performance you can get in Hyper-V. However, it does not offer the mobility and management options that will come with the VHD options. For example, you cannot use the Quick Storage Migration feature of VMM 2008 R2 to relocate a virtual machine. Because this solution is not a file-based solution, like VHD's, this storage type is not constrained to a maximum size of 2040 GB. Instead, it can grow the largest volume size supported by both your storage solution and your virtual machine's operating system.

Fixed-Size VHD A fixed-size VHD is a file that is created to be the full size of the disk that it simulates. For example, if you create a 40 GB VHD, then the file will be 40 GB. The creation process can take a little while. This is because Hyper-V will zero out the contents of the VHD. This is a security measure to ensure that the virtual machine cannot scan the contents of the VHD and thus gain access to data that may have been on the physical storage where the VHD file is located. There are tools that will allow you to create VHD files in a rapid manner, but they do not take this security measure. They should not be used in a production environment where security, regulatory compliance, or data protection are a concern. Fixed-size VHDs have the best performance of all the VHD types. The performance of a fixed-size VHD is almost identical to that of the underlying physical storage.

Dynamic VHD A dynamic VHD is created as a very small file. It will grow as data is stored in it. This growth will continue until the VHD has reached the defined maximum size. For example, you might create a 40 GB dynamic VHD. It will start out as a very small file. It might grow to around 10 GB when you install Windows Server 2008 R2. It will continue to grow up to 40 GB in size as you install software and add data to it. An audit of storage usage vs. storage allocation can reveal massive wastage. Dynamic VHDs can be attractive because they consume only the physical storage that is required. Dynamic VHDs came with a significant hit on performance in Windows Server 2008. Windows Server 2008 R2 improved this somewhat by increasing the amount of free space that was allocated during a growth of the file. Microsoft claims that the performance is almost identical to that of a fixed-size VHD. However, experience has shown that over time, dynamic VHDs can become fragmented and have a negative impact on performance and management. Defragging and/or compacting your dynamic VHDs is not recommended by Microsoft.

Differencing VHD A differencing VHD or disk is a VHD that starts out as an empty file, just as a dynamic VHD would. However, it is linked to another existing and populated VHD. The virtual machine mounts the differencing disk. All data that is created before the differencing disk was created is read from the linked parent VHD. All data that is created after the differencing disk was created is written to and read from the differencing disk. Many differencing disks can be linked to a single VHD. This can be useful in a lab environment. For example, a VHD could be prepared with a `sysprep` generalized operating system. Many virtual machines could be instantly deployed with minimal storage requirements by using differencing disks that link to this VHD. All of their original operating system files are stored only once — in the linked VHD. Only the machine-specific files are stored in the differencing disks. Differencing disks come at a great performance cost. Although they may be supported by Microsoft virtualization teams, some of the Microsoft products do not support being installed in differencing disks. It is strongly recommended that you do not use differencing disks in a production environment. However, they are great in a lab where disk space is scarce.

Which one of these will you use in your production environment? Differencing disks are not appropriate because of their complexity and performance. Dynamic VHDs do save on disk space, but they come at a cost in performance (lesser than that of differencing) and at the risk of fragmentation issues. Fixed-size VHDs are the ideal VHD to use in a production system, allowing you to use all the mobility and management features of VHDs with performance that almost matches the underlying storage. Passthrough disks should be used when extreme disk performance and scalability beyond 2040 GB per disk is required.

A virtual machine can have a mixture of disk types. You could use dynamic VHDs for the operating system disk. This will be convenient if using a library to rapidly provision virtual machines. Other disks in the virtual machine could be fixed or pass-through disks, depending on the requirements of the workload.

Microsoft VHD Performance White Paper

Microsoft released a white paper on Windows Server 2008 and Windows Server 2008 R2 VHD performance in March 2010. You can download it from here:

`http://download.microsoft.com/download/0/7/7/0778C0BB-5281-4390-92CD-EC138A18F2F9/WS08_R2_VHD_Performance_WhitePaper.docx`

In this paper, Microsoft compares all the options and essentially recommends using either passthrough or fixed-size virtual hard disks in a production environment.

Virtual Processors

Depending on the operating system installed in it, a virtual machine can have up to four virtual processors. Adding processors adds computing power to the virtual machine as it gains a greater potential share of the underlying physical processors. You can further control the reserve and maximum percentages as well as a weighting for virtual processors in the properties of a virtual machine in the Hyper-V console.

Physical Network Adapters

There are three approaches to connecting virtual machines to the physical network:

Many Virtual Network Adapters per NIC With this approach, a single physical NIC is used to connect many or all virtual machines on the host to the physical network. A single virtual network is created and linked to the NIC. All virtual machines network adapters are connected to the same virtual network. The benefit to this is that the hardware costs for switches and network cards are minimized. The downside is that the network link could become congested. This should be considered when you are designing your hardware solution based on your assessment data.

Many Virtual Network Adapter and Many NICs Using your assessment data, you might include many physical NICs for virtual machine connectivity in a single host server. There could be four physical NICs and four virtual networks. The virtual machines would be balanced across each of the virtual networks.

One Virtual Network Adapter per NIC This is the approach that would be taken when virtualized network must be maximized. In this approach, each virtual network adapter is bound to its own physical network card via a virtual network. Hardware features such as jumbo frames, and Chimney Offload might be used in scenarios where this method is used. There would a much greater hardware cost to this approach because of the required switch ports and physical NICs. This approach will also greatly limit the number of virtual machines that can be placed on a host server.

Most of the time it is likely that you will use one NIC (or a teamed pair) to connect all of a host's virtual machines to the physical network. Usage of 10 Gbps networking will increase the capacity of this solution. Hosts that are capable of a huge virtual machine density may need to use multiple network cards. There are specific scenarios where you will need to provide a full 1 Gbps or 10 Gbps pipe to a virtual network card, and that's when you will use the one virtual network adapter per NIC method.

Virtual Network Adapters

There are two types of virtual network adapter. The legacy network adapter is used in a couple of situations. The first is when you need to use PXE for booting from the network. This is often used in network-based machine diagnostics and operating system deployment solutions. The second reason to use a legacy network adapter is if you are using an operating system where you cannot install integration components. The emulated legacy network adapter does not offer the best possible performance and requires more processing resources from the host server.

The synthetic network adapter (also often referred to as a *network adapter* in the administrative tools) offers the best possible performance for virtual machine networking. This virtual device requires that the integration components are installed in the guest's operating system. This is done by default in Windows 7 and Windows Server 2008 R2. You cannot boot using PXE from a synthetic network adapter. You should mount an ISO with a network-enabled boot image (Windows PE, for example) if you need to do operating system deployment with virtual machines that have a synthetic network adapter.

> **Windows 2003 Networking Won't Work?**
>
> A common issue on support forums is that a virtual machine with Windows Server 2003 cannot access the network. The usual cause for this is that Service Pack 2 and the integration components are not installed. This means that the (synthetic) network adapter cannot work, and you will be restricted to the (emulated) legacy network adapter.

Memory

We saved the most complicated one for last. How you size the memory of a virtual machine can affect how well the underlying physical memory will be used.

Non-Uniform Memory Access (NUMA) is a mechanism where multiple processors can share memory in a physical server. A NUMA node boundary divides the total memory in a physical server into performance optimized chunks. You can size a NUMA node boundary by dividing the total amount of RAM in the physical server by the total number of physical processor cores. If a four-core (a single quad-core processor) server has 32 GB of RAM, then the NUMA boundary size is 8 GB.

A process that uses more RAM than in the NUMA node boundary will have inefficient physical memory processing. In our example, a virtual machine with 16 GB of RAM will not perform as you would expect. This is because its memory spans two NUMA nodes. It would be more efficient to use two virtual machines to perform the same role.

This may impact on how you will deploy some applications or application roles. You may decide to run a few load-balanced virtual machines instead of one big one. Not only will this offer fault tolerance, but it will also optimize how the physical memory of their Hyper-V hosts will be used.

Virtual Machine Placement

There are several aspects to virtual machine placement. They may have an influence on how well virtual machines perform, how fault tolerant your virtualized applications may be, and whether your applications will be supported or not by the vendor.

Placement and Performance

The needs for performance and virtual machine placement were discussed in Chapter 5 when we talked about hardware design, but a reminder will not hurt. If a physical machine requires a certain amount of resources to provide adequate performance, then its virtual equivalent will require at least the same amount of resources. If we ignore some of the marketing materials, some tests (from Microsoft on Exchange and domain controllers) have shown that there might be up to a 10 percent drop in the capabilities of the virtualized alternative. Most of the time that reduction isn't even noticed because the average resource utilization rate for physical servers is a mere 12 percent.

There is also this to consider. Your current physical server or vendor guidance is probably based on dual- or quad-core processors. The new generation of 6-core, 8-core, and 12-core processors offers more computing power per core. During hardware and virtual machine design, we would typically allow a virtual machine to have 90 percent of two host cores if the physical equivalent required 90 percent of a dual-core processor. Maybe we could allow for 50 percent utilization of a modern six-core CPU host instead? This would require doing some investigations on how the different processors compare.

Some application vendors will have very specific guidance on virtual machine placement. Microsoft says that a Hyper-V host will support up to 384 virtual machines. An application vendor might override that guidance by saying that only four virtual machines should run on the host. Unfortunately, this may be based on the hardware that was available to them at the time of their testing, rather than the new generation of much more capable hardware that was available one year after the release of Windows Server 2008 R2 Hyper-V. You will need to balance the risk of an application vendor not supporting your deployment if you decide to ignore their guidance in order to use fewer resources in a virtual machine configuration.

You must consider how the placement of virtual machines on your host servers will affect their mutual performance. If virtual machine A requires massive connectivity to SAN storage, then it either will be affected by or will affect other virtual machines on the same host thanks to a congested iSCSI or Fibre Channel connection. This sort of resource congestion can happen with any of the resources used and shared by the virtual machines on a single host. You have to plan for this and allow for periodic spikes in resource requirements.

Using Virtual Machine Manager 2008 R2 and Operations Manager 2007 (or 2007 R2) with Performance and Resource Optimization (PRO) management packs can automate this. The Microsoft-provided management packs will handle operating system–detected issues such as CPU utilization at the parent partition and virtual machine levels. Hardware manufacturer PRO management packs may handle issues that are detected by the hardware, for example, the iSCSI network card or Fibre Channel HBA. VMM will then be able to relocate virtual machines in a clustered environment using Live Migration to rebalance the virtual machine workloads across the cluster.

PLACEMENT AND FAULT TOLERANCE

Many applications will require some level of fault tolerance. A Hyper-V cluster does provide hardware fault tolerance, but it cannot provide zero-downtime application fault tolerance. An unplanned host failure will cause its virtual machines to fail, migrate to another host, and reboot. There may be a minute or two until the application restarts.

You can implement application fault tolerance at the virtual machine level. This may be in the form of clustered virtual machines (independent of the clustering provided by Hyper-V integrated host failover clustering) or application-level load balancing between virtual machines. The application will stay running at full capacity, albeit with a very short outage as disk ownership is swapped, if one virtual machine fails or is put into some form of maintenance.

It will be of no use if fault-tolerant virtual machines are located on the same host. Figure 8.1 shows a scenario where there is a pair of virtual machines. They host a fault-tolerant application. You'll notice that both virtual machines are on the same host. This is probably a bad idea.

FIGURE 8.1
Fault-tolerant application on the same clustered host

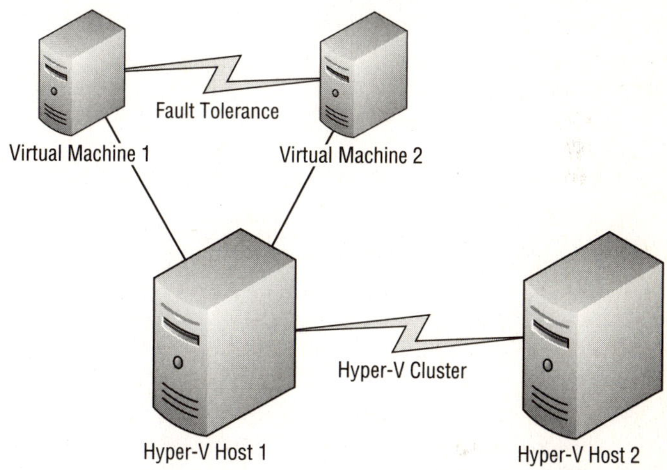

Figure 8.2 shows what will happen if the host fails suddenly. Both virtual machines will have a sudden failure, as if they were powered down rather than shut down. Failover clustering in the host will move the virtual machines to a redundant node and restart the virtual machines. The application will be back after a few minutes.

Think about this for a moment. Why did you make this application fault tolerant? You did it to avoid a scenario where the application would be offline for a few minutes because a virtual machine might go offline (planned or unplanned). The result we have just seen would be viewed as a failure of the design.

Before you look at a solution, you should see what will happen if your host was not clustered, as shown in Figure 8.3. If you placed both virtual machines of the fault-tolerant application, then they both will fail when the host fails. This is more drastic than the clustered host scenario because you have no automated recovery. If you are lucky, you might be able to restore the virtual machines to another host with an hour or two of work. Even with this heroic action, your boss and the application owners will be quite unhappy. That is because building fault tolerance into the application was a waste of time because of the dependence on a single host server.

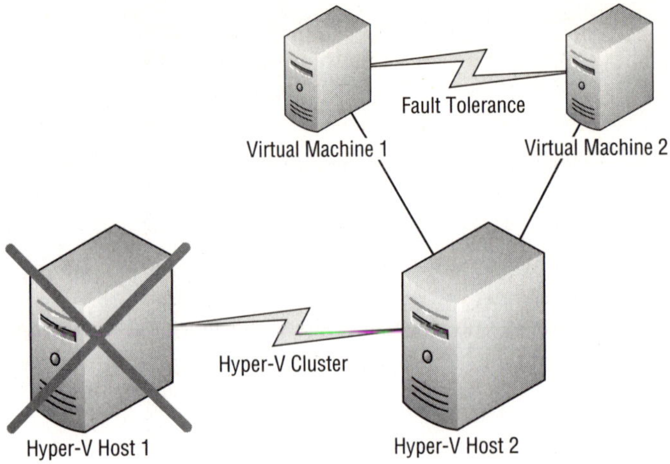

FIGURE 8.2
Fault-tolerance application fails over

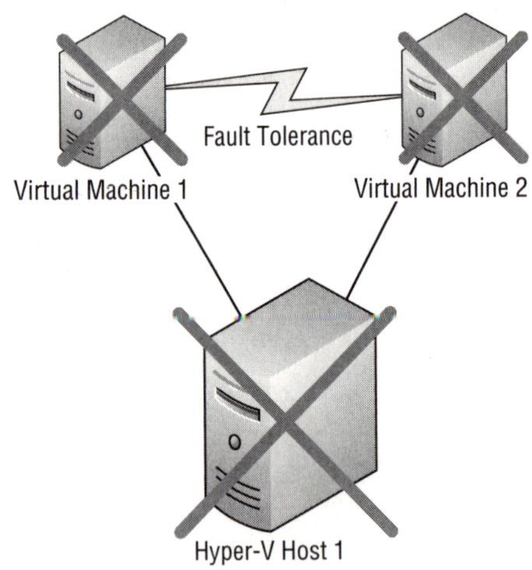

FIGURE 8.3
Fault-tolerant application on a single host

You need to apply some form of control to ensure that virtual machines that are running a fault-tolerant application are not running on the same host. In a clustered environment, you would place the virtual machines on different hosts in the cluster, as shown in Figure 8.4. If Hyper-V Host 1 fails, then only the first virtual machine in the fault-tolerant application will be affected. The second virtual machine in the fault-tolerant application will continue to run, making the application truly fault tolerant. In fact, the first virtual machine will relocate to another host in the cluster. If you control this, it could even move to a third host in the host cluster.

You can reduce the risk of both virtual machines in the guest cluster from being on the same host as a result of a failover by the host cluster. This can be done using the `cluster.exe` command and the `AntiAffinityClassName` property. You will edit the properties of both virtual machine cluster groups and specify a label:

```
cluster.exe group "VirtualMachine1" /prop AntiAffinityClassNames="SQLCluster1"
cluster.exe group "VirtualMachine2" /prop AntiAffinityClassNames="SQLCluster1"
```

FIGURE 8.4
Fault-tolerant application across a host cluster

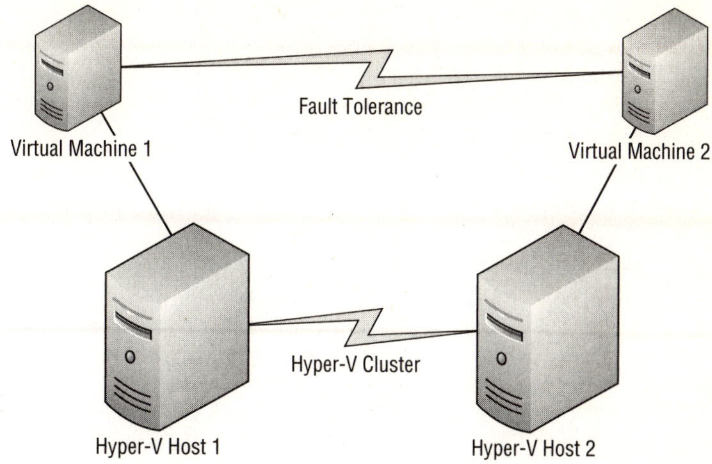

You can review the assigned `AntiAffinityClassName` property by running this:

```
cluster.exe group "VirtualMachine1" /prop
```

Now, Windows Failover Clustering will do its best to prevent VirtualMachine1 and VirtualMachine2 from being on the same clustered Hyper-V host servers. However, there will be circumstances where placement will be unavoidable such as when there aren't enough free hosts or when available host resources are constrained.

Figure 8.5 shows how to create a virtualized fault-tolerant application when host failover clustering is not being used. The first virtual machine is on Hyper-V Host 1. The second virtual machine is on Hyper-V Host 2. Any unplanned or planned outage for either host will have no impact on the availability of the application.

FIGURE 8.5
Guest cluster on nonclustered hosts

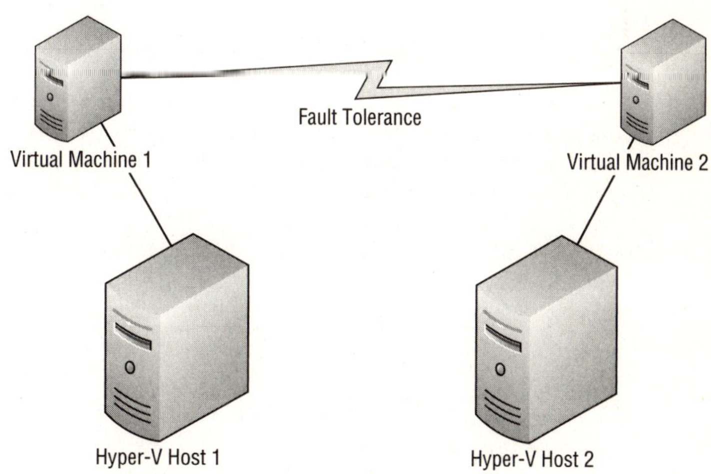

When creating these virtual machines, you should be careful that you place them on different Hyper-V hosts. It would be pointless to place them on the same nonclustered host and risk having the entire cluster being put out of service if the host were to experience an outage.

Placement and Application Support

It is rare, but some application virtualization support guidelines may dictate your placement options for that application in a virtual machine. They may dictate the usage of nonclustered Hyper-V hosts. They may even state that only certain numbers of virtual machines can run on a host. This information should have been gathered during the assessment and will have steered your hardware design.

The complication comes when you are using clustered hosts. You might suddenly have nonclustered hosts to manage too. This will impact any custom automated solutions that you might have implemented. On clustered hosts, you will also need to control the placement of virtual machines by Failover Clustering and VMM's Intelligent Placement.

There is quite a lot to think about there. At first it might feel quite overwhelming. After a little while, it becomes second nature, just like the design of physical servers and storage may have previously become for you. We'll now leave the theory behind and show how to deploy some of the more common applications in Hyper-V.

Application Virtualization Guidance

The vendors of your application can sometimes provide you with information on how to configure your virtual machines and how to get the very best performance. This is also true of Microsoft. We're going to look at some of the Microsoft applications that will be commonly found or deployed on Hyper-V servers.

Real World Scenario

Microsoft and the Fortune 1,000

Sometimes it appears like Microsoft only considers the IT needs of huge corporations with hundreds of thousands of users. You will definitely think this when you start to research Microsoft's guidance for deploying its server products on hardware virtualization platforms.

For example, your organization might be quite happily running Exchange on a couple of low- to medium-specification physical servers. However, the guidance for running Exchange on Hyper-V (or XenServer or ESX) looks like you need a lot of high-spec virtual machines.

You may even see that passthrough disks seem to be recommended in almost every instance. There is very little difference between passthrough disks and fixed-size VHD. A fixed-size VHD will have 95 percent or more of the performance of the underlying physical storage's performance.

Remember that Microsoft has biased the guidance toward larger organizations. This is true of most of the Microsoft guidance. The only way to determine the best solution for your application and your organization is to test, measure, and analyze.

SQL Server 2005, 2008, and 2008 R2

SQL Server consolidation can take two paths. One is to run many databases on fewer high-specification physical servers. This brings up the risk of depending too much on a few pieces of hardware. There are also complications about ownership and access rights; never underestimate the power of company politics when it comes to databases.

> **SQL SERVER SUPPORT POLICY**
>
> You can read the full text of the support policy for running SQL Server in virtual machines at `http://support.microsoft.com/kb/956893`.

An alternative is to use the more common one database per server deployment and to use virtualization to deploy those servers. This makes it easier to handle ownership, delegated access, security, updates, and server customization. It also makes better use of the Hyper-V infrastructure and simplifies future upgrades to business applications.

One of the myths that used to exist was that you could never run a production Microsoft SQL Server in a virtual machine. Microsoft went to great lengths to dispel that myth soon after the release of the original Windows Server 2008 Hyper-V. Their argument was that a virtual machine could run SQL Server very effectively if the virtual machine was appropriately configured.

Microsoft ran a number of tests to compare the performance of SQL Server running on Hyper-V virtual machines and on physical hardware. Microsoft found the performance to be quite similar when sized equally and when the appropriate virtual machine design was used. Application throughput was practically identical thanks to the addition of Second Level Address Translation (SLAT), which leverages RVI in newer AMD processors and EPT in newer Intel processors. Database and workload scalability was only affected by storage I/O, but we'll come back to that in a moment. The only discrepancy between the physical and virtual alternatives was a slightly higher CPU (about 11 percent to 13 percent) overhead when SQL Server was run in a virtual machine.

The main consideration when it comes to SQL Server planning is storage. An operating system will typically be on RAID-1 storage. The paging file may be on a dedicated RAID-1 disk. A database log file will be on a RAID-1 disk, and a database file is usually found on a slower (for writes) RAID-5 disk. The same guidance will apply to a virtual machine, just like it did for a physical machine.

If you are setting up a low to midrange SQL Server virtual machine, then you can use fixed-size VHDs. Dynamic VHDs are not appropriate because of the fragmentation concern and the latency that they can introduce when writes to disk occur.

A host with dedicated storage may require multiple LUNs to be created of the suitable size and RAID level for each VHD to be stored on. For example, LUNs for the operating system VHD (RAID-1), log file VHD (RAID-1), and database file (RAID-5) would be created. If you are using a Hyper-V cluster, then you may create a RAID-1 CSV and a RAID-5 CSV to place the VHDs on.

A SQL virtual machine with extreme storage performance requirements will require passthrough disks. Microsoft found that passthrough disks gave approximately 5 percent better performance than fixed-size VHDs when testing SQL Server on Hyper-V. You can approach the usage of passthrough disks in a couple of ways. The operating system could be stored on a fixed-size VHD. The log file and the database file would be placed on passthrough disks. This approach assumes that the only disks requiring extreme performance are the database-related files. Alternatively, all the virtual machine's storage would be on passthrough disks.

As usual with virtual machine sizing, the host server should be sized appropriately for the CPU requirements of the virtual machine. That means that the machine should have the same access to virtual processor resources that it would have had as a physical server. Newer physical processors are capable of taking advantage of the SLAT feature in Windows Server 2008 R2 to reduce processor overhead for virtual machine memory mapping to physical memory. This was found by Microsoft to significantly reduce the overhead of running SQL as a virtual machine. The advice here is to implement SQL virtual machines on hardware that can support the SLAT feature.

Your memory should be sized as usually required. As an IT pro, you have probably have had the "what size do you think?" conversation with your application management colleagues many, many times. Dynamic memory will allow for some variability when exact sizing cannot be predicted. Note that a Hyper-V virtual machine can have a maximum allocation of 64 GB of RAM.

Live Migration of a SQL Server 2005 or newer virtual machine is supported. Guest failover clustering (by SQL Server virtual machines) is supported by Microsoft as long as the virtual machine is running Windows Server 2008 or later.

You should also note that using snapshots or checkpoints with SQL Server virtual machines is not supported. This does not affect VSS-enabled host or storage backup solutions such as Data Protection Manager 2010.

A common practice with some SQL Server administrators is to use the CPU affinity feature to associate the SQL service with a physical processor. Microsoft states that this is not of any use with a virtual machine. That is because the virtual CPU is not dedicated to a physical processor or core in the host.

Any backup solution that will be implemented at the host level must have support for the Hyper-V VSS writer. This will be able to put the virtual machine, the contained file system, and the SQL services into a quiescent state, suitable for a consistent backup.

You might wonder if Live Migration of a SQL Server virtual machine is supported. The quick answer is: yes it is. That means you can have a basic form of hardware fault tolerance for your SQL virtual machines without having to cluster your SQL installations. SQL replications such as mirroring are supported in highly available virtual machines.

Server Virtualization Validation Program

All implementations of Microsoft software on Hyper-V, or any other virtualization platform for that matter, should start with a trip to the Server Virtualization Validation Program website at `http://windowsservercatalog.com/svvp.aspx?svvppage=svvpwizard.htm`.

You then can further search for pages that might be on TechNet to provide additional guidance on updated best practices. Much of this information is very fluid. That is because Microsoft can only support scenarios and sizes that it has tested. The variations on supported scenarios will expand over time, so you should be sure to check more than one source for best practices. You can then check the web page's date stamp to see whether it is the most current advice.

Exchange 2007 SP1 and 2010

Just like with SQL, there are arguments for running Exchange either as a virtual machine or as a physical machine. The arguments for virtualization are the same as with any server application. You do have to be careful; Exchange has some special considerations and support policies that you might not have considered.

Exchange 2007 with Service Pack 1 (or later) and Exchange 2010 (or later) are supported to run in virtual machines. Exchange 2003 (with SP2 or later) is supported only on virtual machines that are running in Virtual Server 2005 R2 or Virtual Server 2005 R2 SP1.

> **THE EXCHANGE SUPPORT POLICY**
>
> You can find the full text of the support policy for running Exchange in virtual machines here:
>
> `http://technet.microsoft.com/library/cc794548(EXCHG.80).aspx`

Exchange comprises many roles that can be deployed on multiple servers when fault tolerance is required. This can get a little complicated with Exchange 2010. The database availability group (DAG) feature allows databases on a Mailbox server to be replicated to up to 15 other Exchange 2010 Mailbox servers for high availability. It is not supported to use Live Migration on a DAG member (and Exchange 2010 server that participates in this replication). In fact, between all the variations on support, an Exchange 2010 DAG member virtual machine cannot run on a clustered Hyper-V server. You could attempt to set up a virtual machine on a Hyper-V cluster that has dedicated disk and that is marked as not being highly available. But that is unsupported too, and Virtual Machine Manager is sure to warn you about this with an unsupported cluster configuration error.

An Exchange 2010 Mailbox server that is not a member of a DAG can be placed on a clustered Hyper-V host and moved using Live Migration.

Exchange 2007 SP1 uses Cluster Continuous Replication (CCR) to attain high levels of fault tolerance for Mailbox servers. Although Microsoft does not explicitly deny support for this on a Hyper-V cluster, the company does not recommend it. Their text on this only refers to the Windows 2008 Quick Migration feature, which did have downtime when a virtual machine moved from one host to another. Microsoft recommends enabling an Exchange feature called *transport dumpster* to avoid data loss during the brief outage of a CCR member server during Quick Migration.

The no support (for Exchange 2010 DAG) or not recommended (for Exchange 2007 SP1 CCR) policy for Hyper-V clusters and Live Migration complicates things. Enterprises that run a Hyper-V cluster will value application high availability. Email is considered as a mission-critical application for business communications. You will probably want to run Exchange 2010 DAG. If you do want to run a DAG and you do want to run Exchange in virtual machines, then you must run those virtual machines on nonclustered Hyper-V host servers. This might sound like it might be a waste of hardware. Don't worry because the hardware will have plenty to do; there are more Exchange roles to deal with. If you do run Exchange in Hyper-V, then you will probably have dedicated Hyper-V hosts to run your Exchange roles.

The other roles are Client Access Server, Hub Transport, Edge, and Unified Messaging. The Unified Messaging role server must not be virtualized; the support policy states that it must run on a physical machine. Each of the other roles can be virtualized, but there are considerations.

An Edge or Hub Transport server should be configured with up to four virtual processors. 1 GB of RAM should be allocated to the virtual machine for each virtual processor. This would mean that an Edge or Hub Transport server running in a virtual machine with four virtual processors would be allocated 4 GB of RAM. There should be one Hub Transport for every five Mailbox servers.

A Client Access Server (CAS) virtual machine should be given up to four virtual processors. For each virtual processor in the virtual, there should be 2 GB of RAM. A CAS virtual machine with four virtual processors would have 8 GB of RAM. There should be three CAS virtual machines for every four Mailbox server virtual machines.

A smaller or midrange organization might want to combine the CAS and Hub Transport roles into a single virtual machine. You can do this. The virtual machine would be sized identically as with a CAS virtual machine. There should be one Hub Transport/CAS virtual machine for every Mailbox server virtual machine.

Let's think about the placement of these virtual machines for a moment. Normally we have support from Microsoft to run very large numbers of virtual CPUs in a host server; it works out as eight virtual processors per physical processor core. That's an impressive 8:1 ratio. The Exchange team supports a 2:1 ratio on hosts that are running Exchange virtual machines. You should also deduct at least one core for the parent partition. The Exchange team actually wants you to deduct two cores for the parent partition. If you had a server with 2 × 6 core processors, then you would have 12 cores. Ten of those cores would be available for Exchange virtual machines. You could allocate up to 20 virtual CPUs on this host. That would be enough for five virtual machines, each with four virtual processors.

If you want fault tolerance, then you would have two of these hosts. The two Mailbox servers would be part of a DAG so they can replicate databases. Network load balancing could be used to provide fault tolerance for the other roles.

On the storage side, the Exchange team states that database and log files should be installed on dedicated spindles. This means that they want the log file on a dedicated group of physical disks and the database file on a dedicated group of physical disks. This may be achievable with internal, direct attached and lower-end SAN storage, but it probably won't be with enterprise-level SAN systems that use forms of storage virtualization. In those cases, you can probably create a dedicated virtual disk (or whatever it is called by the manufacturer) for each file to be stored on.

Exchange supports the use of fixed-sized VHD and passthrough disks. Passthrough disks are recommended for the best possible performance. However, there is only a minimal overhead to using the more manageable fixed-size VHDs. Large databases will require passthrough disks if they grow to more than 2040 GB.

Initiating iSCSI by the virtual machine's guest operating system is supported with Windows Server 2008 and newer. However, the best performance will be obtained by initiating iSCSI connections from the host server and using passthrough disks to allow the virtual machine to access the LUN. Using MPIO is strongly recommended.

Dynamic VHDs are explicitly not supported. The usage of snapshots and checkpoints is also not supported.

Realistically, a backup solution will be implemented within the virtual machine, as if it were a physical server. This will facilitate more granular backup of the Exchange database contents. A host-level backup can provide rapid recovery from total disaster for the virtual machine. Any host-level backup solution that is being used must have support for the Hyper-V VSS writer. This will put the virtual machine, the contained file system, and the Exchange services into a quiescent state, suitable for a safe and consistent data backup.

SharePoint 2007 and 2010

Windows SharePoint Services 3.0, SharePoint Server 2007, and SharePoint Server 2010 all have support to be run in virtual machines. Microsoft prescribes only a small amount of guidance and restrictions for running SharePoint in virtual machines on their websites. However, there is some other information that is of use when designing a virtualized SharePoint installation. Most of what you will need will actually apply to the SQL machines that store the SharePoint data.

SharePoint Support Policy

You can find guidance for deploying SharePoint 2010 here:

```
http://technet.microsoft.com/library/ff621103.aspx
```

You can find guidance for Windows SharePoint Services 3.0 and SharePoint Server 2007 here:

```
http://technet.microsoft.com/library/cc816955(office.12).aspx
```

Once again, you will find that the snapshot or checkpoint feature is not supported with virtual machines that run these products. In general, snapshots are supported in production by the Hyper-V product group, but many of the other product groups have chosen to not support it for virtual machines that run their software. This is because a poorly managed or long-running snapshot can lead to some unusual performance issues that may produce unexpected symptoms. The merge of a long-running snapshot will require significant downtime for a virtual machine while the AVHD(s) merges back into the original VHD(s).

SharePoint virtual machines should be sized just as you would size a physical machine alternative. The guidance for SharePoint states that there should be a 1:1 ratio between processor cores in the Hyper-V host server and virtual processors that it will use in hosted SharePoint virtual machines. You will need to allow one or two cores for the parent partition. That means a physical host with 12 cores could run just 10 virtual processors in SharePoint virtual machines.

This was easier to manage when we dealt with Exchange. More often than not, a business will want a fault-tolerant, multimachine installation of Exchange, which will require nonclustered hosts. You will manually control the placement of virtual machines and the ratio between physical and virtual processors. SharePoint virtual machines can run on a Hyper-V cluster. You will be able to control placement in a network where there is no System Center. But you will find that OpsMgr and VMM will take control over VM placement if you do have System Center. It will be totally automated. That might mean that SharePoint virtual machines will be on hosts with greater virtual CPU densities than are recommended. However, the Microsoft PRO management packs will ensure that the virtual machines will have adequate resources by using Live Migration and Intelligent Placement.

The guidance for storage is actually quite flexible. It simply advises you to choose the storage that is most suitable for your environment. Our advice will be that you use either fixed-size VHDs or passthrough disks. Fixed-size VHDs offer superior manageability and portability. Passthrough disks offer approximately a further 5 percent in performance and can support disks that are larger than 2040 GB.

A number of roles may exist in a SharePoint deployment. They can be deployed on different machines, and each will have its own requirements.

The web servers or presentation layer of SharePoint are memory intensive rather than storage I/O intensive. Running these VMs on hosts with SLAT functionality will optimize their performance. Passthrough disks probably won't offer much benefit. Web server virtual machines should be distributed across two or more hosts for zero downtime fault tolerance.

Query servers are I/O intensive. Larger environments should use passthrough disks to get the very best performance. You can improve storage I/O performance if you separate the index and query disks. This is also a memory-intensive role and can benefit from SLAT. Once again, you can have zero downtime fault tolerance by running this role on virtual machines that are placed on two or more host servers.

The application servers usually are not memory or disk intensive. Fixed-sized VHDs will probably be OK in all but a few implementations. These exceptions are where you configure the application role to consume storage or caching, and so on.

Index servers are pretty highly loaded machines, using lots of CPU, memory, and storage I/O. They can be network intensive if they are crawling external data sources (self-crawl topologies can minimize this). It is recommended that passthrough disks be used for index servers. The query and index content should be placed on separate disks to prevent I/O contention.

The SQL Server instance can be a virtual machine, as you have already seen. If you use passthrough disks for the other roles, then you will use passthrough disks for the SQL Server instance. You can create a guest failover cluster to make the SQL Server installation more fault-tolerant. This is where failover clustering is enabled in the virtual machines so that a service they run can become highly available, independent of Hyper-V.

There is one other recommendation when you deploy SharePoint 2010 in virtual machines. The time synchronization integration service should be disabled. The SharePoint virtual machine's operating system will probably be part of a domain and can automatically synchronize its clock from a domain controller. The time synchronization integration service may introduce complications, and this will interfere with scheduled SharePoint 2010 functionality.

System Center

You can run your System Center management suite as virtual machines. But you would have to ask yourself why. Remember, System Center is your management system that will alert you if major systems have failed, will back them up and recover them, and so on. How do you do that if the major system in question is the Hyper-V host that they are running on? Maybe you would have dedicated System Center Hyper-V hosts or clusters. Maybe you would use it for select roles such as just System Center Configuration Manager. You need to consider the implications of running System Center as virtual machines and determine whether the potential negatives outweigh the positives of greater physical server density.

All of the System Center products use SQL Server to store data and configurations. You should take the guidance for SQL Server into consideration when planning a virtual machine implementation of a System Center product. The use of snapshots or checkpoints is explicitly not supported for SQL and therefore will not be supported with any of the System Center products.

Data Protection Manager

Data Protection Manager 2007 and newer can be run as a virtual machine. The only support requirement is that you cannot use VHDs for the storage pools in a supported production environment. This means you will use iSCSI disks that are initiated by the virtual machine or passthrough disks. You also won't be able to use physically attached tape libraries. Emulated tape libraries may prove useful.

Configuration Manager

Configuration Manager 2007 SP1 or newer server and agents are supported in virtual machines with no apparent restrictions.

Configuration Manager usually doesn't have significant hardware requirements. But that entirely depends on the site role and the size of the site being supported. You may find that some roles, such as a distribution point, may require a passthrough disk to meet the demands of managed clients.

Features such as Operating System Deployment (OSD) and Software Distribution can place a rather large load on the network card. This may require setting up a network adapter in the host server especially for the ConfigMgr virtual machine.

Operations Manger

Operations Manager 2007 and newer supports all roles being installed in virtual machines. If you are running a multimanagement server deployment, then Microsoft recommends against using a virtual machine for the Root Management Server (RMS).

> **Operations Manager Support Policy**
>
> You can read the support policy for running Operations Manager in a virtual machine here:
>
> `http://technet.microsoft.com/library/bb309428.aspx.`

Microsoft also recommends against running the OperationsManager and OperationsDW (data warehouse or reporting) databases in virtual machines. They can have large resource consumption requirements, which makes them inappropriate for a virtualized deployment. If you do run these roles in virtual machines, then we recommend that you use passthrough disks. These databases are heavily used even in smaller implementations.

Virtual Machine Manager

Virtual Machine Manager 2008 and newer can be run in a virtual machine. It is probably best that it is not. Should a virtualization management system really be running on the virtualization platform that it manages? It has the potential to create complications. For example, VMM cannot implement PRO-initiated actions if the host that it is on is out of action and is the cause of the PRO alert. This could lead to extensive and unneeded downtime for other virtual machines on that host server. Microsoft makes one important support statement about running VMM in a highly available virtual machine. Initiating a Live Migration from VMM of the virtual machine that it is running in is not supported. You may consider placing a VMM virtual machine onto a nonclustered Hyper-V host server, possibly with other systems management virtual machines.

Service Manager

At the time of writing, there was no guidance available for the newest member of the System Center family, namely, Service Manager 2010. It is probably safe to assume that it has some form of support for running in a virtualized environment. It is a database-dependent product, so much of the SQL Server support and guidance policies will apply.

System Center Essentials (SCE)

SCE 2007 and newer are supported as virtual machines. If you are deploying SCE, then it will likely be the 2010 version, which contains some of the functionality of OpsMgr, ConfigMgr, WSUS, and VMM 2008 R2. This is quite a lot of management functionality. It also includes virtualization management. Running this in a virtual machine might be supported, but we strongly recommend against it. We would suggest you run it in a suitably specified physical server (which actually is quite modest) so that it can independently manage the Hyper-V host servers and their virtual machines.

Domain Controllers

The domain controller is the heart of the Microsoft-based network. If your Active Directory breaks or becomes unreliable, then everything else in your network is soon to follow. Everything that is done with domain controllers should be carefully planned and managed. It should come as no surprise that Microsoft has had a support policy for domain controllers for quite a while, actually since the release of Virtual Server 2005.

> **Domain Controllers Support Policy**
>
> You can read the very important guidance on deploying domain controllers as virtual machines at `http://support.microsoft.com/kb/888794`.

The two big concerns with domain controllers are clock synchronization and USN rollback:

`http://technet.microsoft.com/library/dd348479(WS.10).aspx`

USN rollback is caused when a domain controller with a badly recovered database is started up and it introduces inconsistencies across the network.

Most of the guidance from Microsoft about running a virtual domain controller can be boiled down to a simple statement: you should treat it like a physical domain controller. Do not use any clever techniques to try back it up, restore it, freeze it, or undo changes. You should almost pretend that the virtualization layer does not exist when it comes to managing the domain controller.

Normal domain controllers and Flexible Single Master Operations (FSMO) role holders will normally not have significant requirements. Global catalogs in larger, more complex organizations may have greater loads and should be treated accordingly. You can use sizing guidance to determine the specification of virtual machines, if virtualization should even be considered at all.

For the storage, Microsoft demands that caching of the Hyper-V host's storage controller be disabled. This actually isn't a bad idea anyway. Microsoft also recommend the use of passthrough disks. This is one of those recommendations that might be useful for the very large government agencies or corporations. Most organizations will probably be OK with fixed-size VHDs.

The pause feature of Hyper-V should be used only for very brief amounts of time. Snapshots or checkpoints should never be used. Rolling back a virtual machine can potentially cause an update sequence number (USN) rollback.

System-state backups should be retained for only a certain amount of time. For Windows Server 2008 and earlier, that will be the length of the tombstone retention period. For Windows Server 2008 R2 with the AD Recycle Bin enabled, it will be the length of the tombstone retention period plus the length of the AD Recycle Bin retention period.

A restoration of a system state should follow the normal backup and recovery practices. Do not do something like restoring a VHD or rolling back a snapshot/checkpoint.

The time synchronization integration service should be disabled for all domain controller virtual machines. Domain controllers have their own clock synchronization method, and this should not be interfered with because of its criticality to Kerberos authentication and authorization.

With all that dealt with, you have to ask yourself whether you even want to run your domain controllers as virtual machines.

If you have a smaller organization, then you might only have two domain controllers in the site. We recommend that you leave them as physical servers. Why? Your Hyper-V servers are probably members of the domain. They are probably clustered. Your management systems are members of the domain. You application servers are members of the domain. Your communication systems probably have a domain dependency. Do you want to risk having a chicken-and-egg scenario where a host server has a fault, and it just so happened to be hosting your only domain controllers at the time? Let your domain controllers, which are probably not heavy-duty machines anyway, be physical machines. They should always be the first to be powered up, making services like Active Directory and DNS available so that everything else can start up cleanly. In fact, your Windows Failover Cluster requires physical domain controllers!

Larger organizations that need more than two domain controllers can obviously benefit from running them as virtual machines. Just be sure to specify them appropriately and allow them to have suitable processor resources to meet client demand.

Even smaller organizations can have some benefit. A third domain controller can run as a virtual machine. A backup of that virtual machine can be done at the host level. Remember that it should never be restored as a VHD — but that is only if all other domain controllers are offline. In the event of a catastrophic site disaster, you could recall your off-site backup storage and restore your Active Directory by restoring that virtual machine. But you would have to be sure that no other domain controllers in the domain exist in any other site before doing this. It is a very fine line to walk, so you would have to be very careful and tightly control this process.

Fault Tolerance for Virtualized Applications

We previously discussed the need to provide fault tolerance to applications that are running in your virtual machines. You might have wondered how this was accomplished, so we're going to take some time to look at possible solutions.

Network Load Balancing

This is probably one of the easiest application fault-tolerant solutions to understand in a Hyper-V context because it isn't that different from deploying network load balancing in the physical server world.

Network load balancing is used when applications or services that are hosted on a server either have static data or have no data at all. A number of identical servers can be deployed, and a load-balancing mechanism can be used to spread the load of user or application connections across each of the servers. This allows the application to scale out and to have fault tolerance. If one server fails, then the others in the cluster will share the increased load.

The most basic of these solutions can use the Network Load Balancing (NLB) feature of Windows Server. This might be used in a smaller or economic deployment. In Figure 8.6 you can see a possible implementation of this solution. Three virtual web servers are created and placed on a number of Hyper-V host servers. Each virtual machine has been configured with two virtual network adapters. The first network adapter is connected to a network (probably by using the VLAN ID) where the web servers are accessible to clients. The second network adapter is connected to a network that is used only for the NLB heartbeat or pulse. This heartbeat network may be referred to as a *private network* because it is used only by members of the NLB cluster. Do not confuse this with a private or internal virtual network in Hyper-V. An internal network cannot span Hyper-V hosts. You will need to use a Hyper-V external network for the heartbeat because the virtual machines should be spread across more than one host, ideally with each virtual machine on a different host.

FIGURE 8.6
Windows Network Load Balancing

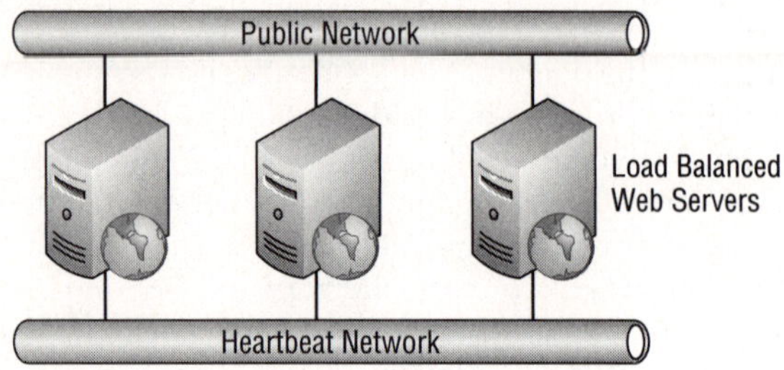

A higher-end load-balancing solution will use a third-party appliance or software solution to perform the load balancing. This means there is no need to use NLB on the application servers. The NLB solution may also offer features such as reverse proxy, SSL offloading, and session affinity.

Figure 8.7 shows a possible implementation where a pair of virtual machines have been installed with a software-based load-balancing solution. Both load-balancing virtual machines run on different Hyper-V host servers. Web server clients will connect to these load balancers. The load balancers have an internal service to balance their own workload. They will optimize traffic and data and forward client connections to the web servers. The web servers are three virtual machines that are running on three Hyper-V host servers. In this solution, the five virtual machines can be running on three Hyper-V hosts.

FIGURE 8.7
Using dedicated virtualized load balancers

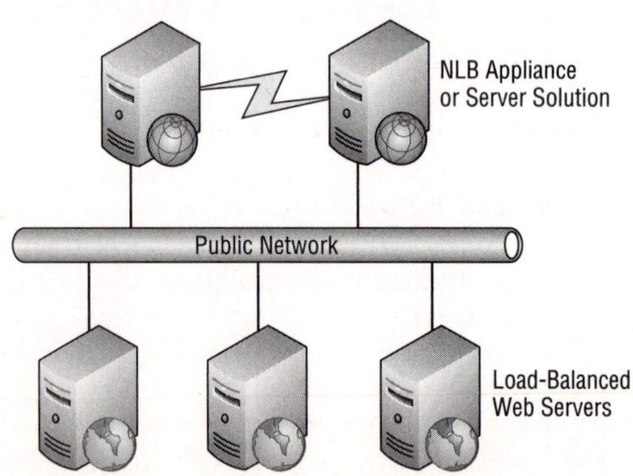

NLB clustering is pretty simple. More often than not, it is a third server or appliance that is doing the work. This makes it a very suitable form of fault tolerance to implement on Hyper-V.

A handy tip will be to take advantage of a new feature in Windows Server 2008 R2 Hyper-V. You can enable MAC (Ethernet) address spoofing of the virtual machine's virtual network adapter. This will mean that the virtual network adapter can adopt the spoofed MAC address of the NLB team.

NLB clustering isn't always appropriate, so you should also look at the alternative form of fault tolerance, failover clustering.

Guest Failover Clustering

Some services, such as databases, have a constantly changing set of data. This makes them inappropriate for NLB clustering. A single operational copy of the data must exist on some form of shared storage. The service that accesses, modifies, and secures this data will run on a single server at once. This service can be failed over from one host to another. We've just described *failover clustering*.

Usually when we talk about failover clustering, it is a physical server implementation, such as with a Hyper-V cluster. But it is possible to implement guest failover clustering with virtual machines. The complication is the storage. The shared storage for data can be connected directly to physical servers using a Fibre Channel SAN. You cannot do that with virtual machines because you do not have the appropriate virtual devices. The other storage connectivity option that can be used is iSCSI. That is something that you can do with virtual machines. All it requires is a 1 Gbps network connection (provided by a virtual network adapter) and an iSCSI target (provided by the storage).

Figure 8.8 shows a possible implementation of failover clustering using virtual machines. The virtual machine will have at least two virtual network adapters. The first one will be for general network and client-server access. The second virtual network adapter is intended purely for iSCSI. This has certain requirements. The virtual network adapter should be associated with a dedicated virtual network on the host. This virtual network should be associated with a dedicated physical network adapter in the host. Features such as jumbo frames and TOE should be enabled on this network adapter to improve the performance of iSCSI between the virtual machine and the host.

FIGURE 8.8
Virtual machine failover clustering

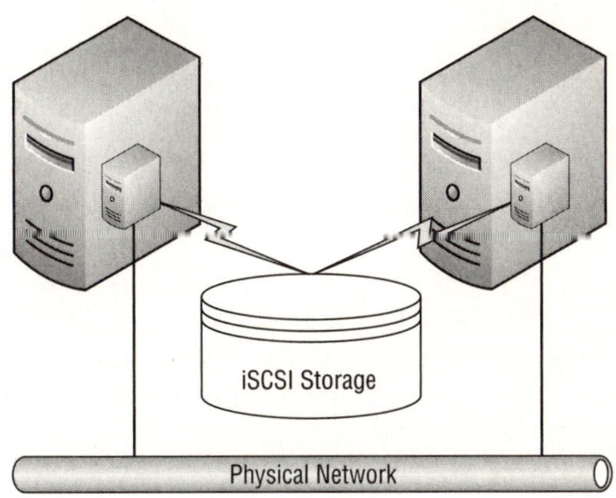

A mission-critical server will usually have more than one link to a storage device. You could add a third virtual network adapter to the virtual machine. This would also be used for iSCSI, and it would also require a dedicated physical network adapter on the host. The MPIO functionality of Windows Server 2008 R2 could be enabled to provide automated storage connectivity fault tolerance across the two virtual network adapters.

Your cluster's shared storage for this solution could be Windows Storage Server 2008 R2, or maybe even the same SAN that your Hyper-V servers are using (assuming that it has iSCSI functionality).

You might wonder whether this kind of solution is fit for a production environment. You may have some lightweight services that are required to be both virtualized and completely fault tolerant. They might be appropriate for this type of solution. However, your critical SQL Server cluster may not be suitable for this.

There are some complications with this design. You can see there is at least one physical network adapter in the host that is dedicated to providing iSCSI connectivity to a single virtual machine. This could be very complicated in a Hyper-V cluster. Each host in the cluster (and that could be up to 16 servers) would require this configuration. Unfortunately, the hosts already have high network card and switch connectivity requirements, possibly already fully populating the expansion slots in the hardware. You'll also have a limit on how many virtual clustered machines you could run per host. If you were going to do this, it would probably have to be done on nonclustered Hyper-V hosts.

The Bottom Line

Understand virtual machine design guidelines With so many design variations available for a virtual machine, it is a necessity to understand the features and how they will affect the performance of a virtual machine.

Master It The MIS department, which is responsible for applications in the corporation, has been assigned a number of Hyper-V host servers and storage that will be placed under your supervision. With a tight budget, they want to make the very most out of their new host servers. A critical new database-based application is to be deployed using a number of virtual machines. You have been asked to give advice on how to best design the storage. What kind of virtual machine storage would you recommend?

Deploy common roles in Hyper-V virtual machines Microsoft has provided recommendations and support policies for virtual machine configurations for many of their server applications.

Master It You are a consultant who is visiting with a new customer. You have been asked to review the Hyper-V installation and the deployment of applications as virtual machines. End users are complaining that a critical line-of-business application is too slow. You investigate the issue and find that the performance of storage for the SQL Server does not meet demand. The customer is using dynamic VHDs. How will you explain the issue, and what will you advise the customer to do to fix the issue?

Configure fault tolerance in virtual machines Hyper-V clustering can provide hardware fault tolerance for virtual machines. A sudden and unplanned host failure can cause an application to be unavailable while its virtual machine fails over to another host and boots up. Fault tolerance can be provided at the application level to avoid any downtime.

Master It You are working as a consultant for a company that has successfully deployed Hyper-V. You are tasked with deploying a new two-tier web application. Performance and uptime are critical. The first tier is a web application that will run an e-commerce application. This must be capable of quickly scaling out with a minimal hardware footprint. A fault-tolerant database is required. It will be running queries and reports on a frequent basis and will have significant storage requirements. How will you design this solution?

Part 4

Advanced Management

- Chapter 9: Operations Manager 2007
- Chapter 10: Data Protection and Recovery
- Chapter 11: The Small and Medium Business

Chapter 9

Operations Manager 2007

At this point, you will already have a good insight into how important System Center is for managing Hyper-V. Virtual Machine Manager (VMM) provides you with an engine to control the virtualization layer of your infrastructure. Operations Manager (OpsMgr) 2007 gives you the ability to monitor the health and performance of your entire IT infrastructure. It will detect issues in the hardware, virtualization layer, operating system, and applications. This complete oversight means it is much more than just a virtualization management solution. Like most of System Center, OpsMgr will change and optimize how you work with your servers, bringing you closer to the ideal world of a highly automated IT infrastructure. Most organizations that will deploy Hyper-V have never seen OpsMgr before. We will introduce the product to you, discuss how it works, and even go through some management functions.

OpsMgr can be integrated with VMM. With additional expertise, in the form of management packs, you get another management feature called Performance and Resource Optimization (PRO). This allows OpsMgr to detect an issue in the virtualization infrastructure and for VMM to respond to it. Microsoft provides a good deal of functionality for Windows, but third parties have extended this to include hardware, application, and even VMware expertise. Everything can potentially be brought under the control of System Center. Now you can see what Microsoft's marketing people are talking about when they discuss a single management solution. In this chapter, we will cover the integration of VMM and OpsMgr. We will also look at how PRO works and how to use third-party management packs.

We previously discussed how OpsMgr's data warehouse could be used for reporting for assessing a physical infrastructure. We will be looking at the reports that will be available to you to manage your Hyper-V infrastructure.

In this chapter, you will learn to

- Understand the functionality of Operations Manager
- Integrate Operations Manager with Virtual Machine Manager
- Understand and configure PRO

Introducing Operations Manager 2007

The first System Center product we covered was Virtual Machine Manager (VMM) 2008 R2. VMM gives you the ability to manage the configuration of your hardware virtualization layer, that is, Hyper-V, as well as Virtual Server and VMware ESXi. The next piece of functionality most organizations will want is something to monitor the health and performance of the infrastructure. That's where System Center Operations Manager, also known as SCOM or OpsMgr, comes into play.

Organizations that are deploying Hyper-V for the first time will probably have never used OpsMgr and may have no idea what it is or how it works. We will start by describing the typical monitoring solutions that are available and then look at how OpsMgr is different. We will then talk about how OpsMgr works and how you can use some of its features.

MASTERING SYSTEM CENTER OPERATIONS MANAGER 2007

OpsMgr is a very large product. We will be covering the essentials of using OpsMgr 2007, but there is a lot more to designing, implementing, and maintaining this monitoring solution. We recommend that you read *Mastering System Center Operations Manager 2007*, published by Sybex, to learn more.

Traditional Monitoring Solutions

Typically, a monitoring solution falls into one of a few categories:

Sneaker Net This is the term that IT pros use for manual labor. Almost every IT pro has experienced a request from a manager for someone to do a daily or weekly check on something. For example, can someone log into every server on a daily basis to ensure that there is enough disk space? This is a total waste of potential engineering time. It also becomes a dreaded operation for the responsible administrator. As you should know, any manual operation such as this will be prone to mistakes, even when performed by the most diligent of people. Such operations should be automated and should alert the responsible administrators on a by-exception basis.

The Free or Inexpensive Solution A lot of IT decision makers loathe spending any of their budget on a monitoring solution. There is a belief that these solutions are simple mechanisms to check whether a few things are responding. Is the web server service running? Does the server respond to a ping? IT is just not that simple. Minor things that we do not normally even consider can fail and lead to a chain of events that can cause major outages.

The free or inexpensive solution will do very basic monitoring out of the box. Anything beyond this will require extensive learning and engineering. Even then, it requires that the engineer know in advance what might fail. All too often, something that was not considered in the design will fail and require more engineering to extend the monitoring functionality, just in case that event should reoccur. There is false economy in adopting a cheap or economic monitoring solution for anything but the smallest and simplest IT infrastructure.

The Traditional Enterprise Solution Selling this type of a solution is a consultant's dream. The license costs alone can be hundreds of thousands of dollars for just a couple hundred servers. These solutions promise to be all things to all people. Stories of how they are used by the military or Formula 1 racing teams will tempt even the most cynical potential purchaser. It is usually true that the product has the potential to be extremely powerful and to manage absolutely everything in the organization. It is also true that it will probably be a very basic solution out of the box. In fact, it will probably require a team of consultants to even get the out-of-the-box product to install. This is the main problem; these are consultancy-led products, requiring massive amounts of niche product expertise, effort, and project funds to get anything close to what the salesperson promised and demonstrated in their lab environment. In reality, what you get is often just a more expensive version of the free or economic product, just with the backing of a major software/consultancy hybrid company. You will also find that some of these products tend to be biased toward the other products (such as server or storage hardware) that they offer, thus preventing you from considering products from rival companies.

So, what makes Operations Manager different? You'll need to understand how Operations Manager works to see how it is differentiated in the market. Once you do understand it, you'll see why many consultants and engineers, who have worked with the traditional solutions in the past, now consider OpsMgr to be best of breed.

Understanding Operations Manager

From a high level, the components and functionality of OpsMgr are pretty simple. You can break down the components, shown in Figure 9.1, as follows:

Root Management Server There is always at least one management server where the OpsMgr services will run. The first management server is referred to as the *root management server* (RMS). All monitoring data is passed to management servers, and all administration interaction will be done through the management server.

Operations Console The Operations Console is the tool that administrators, operators, and delegated users will use to interact with the OpsMgr management servers. The tool that will be used by the OpsMgr administrators is a traditional System Center MMC utility. A web console is also available with most of the functionality of the MMC utility. This is normally used for remote and delegated administration.

Additional Management Servers An OpsMgr server can monitor a certain number of agents and devices. Once it approaches this maximum, you must add additional management servers. The additional management servers are subservient to the root management server. Additional management servers can also be added for fault tolerance. This will allow agents to report to an alternative management server should their primary management server go offline. This will allow the business to continue to ensure that business applications are continuing to run efficiently. A hierarchy of management servers is referred to as a *management group.*

Agent Computers that will be managed by OpsMgr will normally have an agent installed on them. This agent will use secured communications to report to its assigned management server. The management server can use basic heartbeat monitoring to ensure that the agent, and thus the monitored computer, is available. The agent will also offer other management functions on the computer to perform more advanced monitoring operations.

It is not always possible to install an agent onto a device that will be monitored. For example, network or storage appliances usually do not allow for this. It is possible to perform agentless monitoring. Basic agentless monitoring provided natively by OpsMgr offers less functionality. However, some solutions will use an intermediary service. OpsMgr will integrate with that service, and that service will manage appliances via agentless monitoring. These intermediary services are usually provided by the manufacturer or a manufacturer partner of the appliance in question and can offer extensive functionality that Microsoft could not offer in OpsMgr. Manufacturer-supplied solutions are usually free downloads that, once installed, integrate seamlessly into the Operations Console.

Gateway There are a number of reasons that an organization may have a number of individual Active Directory forests including recent acquisitions, company politics, and IT security. An OpsMgr agent secures its communications with a management server using Kerberos by default. You will have multiple Kerberos domains if there is more than one Active Directory forest. This will prevent the default secure communications from working and prevent OpsMgr from being able to span forests.

The OpsMgr Gateway can resolve this issue. It will be located in the forest that will be monitored. It will create a trust with an OpsMgr server using X.509 certificates that are created on a mutually trusted certificate authority (CA) using a custom OpsMgr certificate template (requiring the CA to run on the Enterprise edition of Windows Server). Agents will communicate with the Gateway in their domain or forest using Kerberos for security. The traffic will be relayed to the OpsMgr by the Gateway using the X.509 certificates for security.

AGENTS IN A WORKGROUP

You cannot use the OpsMgr Gateway to secure communications with agents that are installed on workgroup computers. This is because they are not in a Kerberos domain. In this instance, you will use the `MOMCERTIMPORT` utility from the OpsMgr media to install a certificate on each agent-managed workgroup member machine. The certificate must be published by a CA that is trusted by the workgroup member.

All this talk of certificates may sound a little daunting at first. Once you configure a couple of machines, you might come to the conclusion that the Microsoft OpsMgr team has implemented a pretty powerful and usable solution for handling cross-forest and workgroup trust issues, and maybe it is a method that other product groups should look into.

Management Packs By itself, OpsMgr will only perform basic heartbeat awareness of managed computers and devices. Management packs contain the expertise to understand how to monitor hardware, operating systems, and applications. Microsoft's policy is that no server product can be released without an accompanying management pack. Sometimes it can be several months before the management pack is available. There is a very good reason for this. The group that develops the product to be monitored will be responsible for authoring the management pack to manage it. This means that the monitoring for Hyper-V is written by the people who wrote Hyper-V. The group that wrote Virtual Machine Manager is responsible for the development of the management pack for it too. This is what makes OpsMgr the very best solution for managing a Microsoft-centric server network. The developers of the managed products best understand what to monitor and how to monitor it. You will get more out-of-the-box expertise in a Microsoft management pack for Windows Server, SQL, Active Directory, and so on, than you possibly ever could from any third-party solution. You effectively have Microsoft developers sitting in your network, keeping an eye on your systems and applications!

Microsoft's management packs and those from many third-party providers are free downloads and continue to be developed and improved based on customer feedback. Some third-party providers will author and sell management packs for products where the manufacturers do not offer a solution. It is also possible to author your own management packs using the free-to-download Authoring Console or using the Operations Console. Authoring a management pack is a difficult process, requiring a great deal of knowledge of how OpsMgr internals work. Fortunately, there are a number of templates in the Operations Console that make it easier to create customized monitoring for common applications.

Unlike many legacy monitoring solutions, OpsMgr will use an automated discovery process to deploy management packs. The management pack contains instructions for discovery. This allows an agent to check whether the management pack should be downloaded and activated. No manual operations are usually required. This means that your Hyper-V and VMM management packs will automatically discover the appropriate servers and start monitoring those roles with no effort by you — after you have imported the management packs into OpsMgr.

Management packs contain rules and monitors to manage an application, operating system, or device. They will have predefined thresholds and automated responses to detected conditions. More often than not, these will be appropriate. However, there will be times when you will want to customize, enable, or disable them. You can do this on a global basis or for a particular monitored object.

Available Management Packs

There is a large collection of free Microsoft-provided management packs and third-party management packs, both free and requiring purchase that you can use. They cover a wide variety of software and hardware technologies. Microsoft maintains a catalog of these management packs on the Microsoft Pinpoint site here:

```
http://pinpoint.microsoft.com/systemcenter/managementpackcatalog
```

Always be careful to ensure that you have the prerequisites in place and that you read the documentation before importing any management pack. Some management packs require manual configuration to enable monitoring rules, to integrate with the items being monitored, and to control noise (unnecessary alerts).

Administrators and Users The administrative model of OpsMgr allows for incredibly powerful granularity. This allows OpsMgr administrators to reveal selected parts of the monitored server infrastructure and applications to delegated OpsMgr users. The administrators can also allow certain rights, such as administrator, operator, and read-only operator privileges. An example might be that an OpsMgr administrator might delegate rights to Hyper-V administrators to see all parts of the Hyper-V infrastructure. When a Hyper-V administrator logs into the Operations Console, they will only be able to see the resources that they manage. They will also only receive alerts for the resources they have access to in the Operations Console. This will be useful in larger organizations where responsibility for OpsMgr and Hyper-V will be split into different teams.

Data Warehouse OpsMgr will maintain an operations database containing current data. This data is exported to an optional data warehouse so that it can be kept for a much longer time. This allows administrators or users of OpsMgr to run reports on performance, faults, and uptime using data that can span over a year. Each imported management pack will contain reports that can be easily accessed and used in the Operations Console. With a bit of SQL knowledge, you can create custom reports to pull data from the data warehouse.

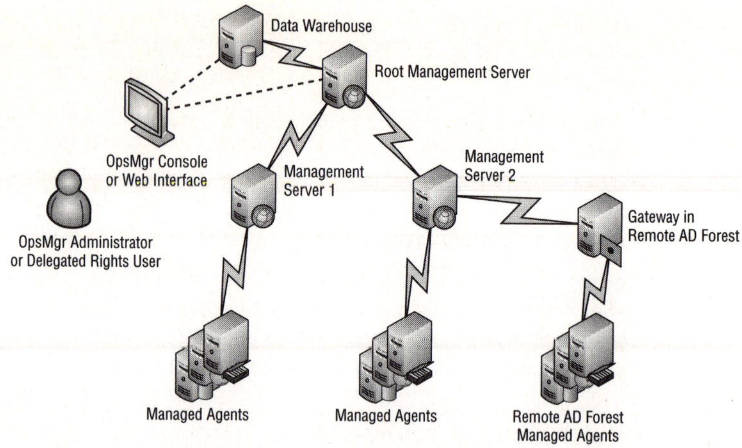

FIGURE 9.1
The components of Operations Manager 2007

There are a few other pieces in OpsMgr 2007 for gathering and centralizing information. We're concentrating on Hyper-V, so we won't cover them here.

SOME USEFUL OPERATIONS MANAGER FEATURES

A couple of features might prove useful in an enterprise deployment of Hyper-V:

Audit Collection Services (ACS) The security of Hyper-V host servers is critical. Any person who can access the filesystem of a Hyper-V server can access the virtual machine VHDs and their contained data.

ACS is a feature where an Operations Manager agent can gather the events of a Windows security log and store them in a dedicated and secured SQL database. This means you can enable auditing on the Hyper-V hosts and centrally store all security events where the security events can be secured and audited.

Agentless Exception Monitoring (AEM) Anyone who has implemented a change, such as hardware, operating system, or service pack, knows what is in their future when a plan to deploy a virtualized environment is announced. Some owners of business applications are going to protest. It is a safe bet that some of those owners will blame Hyper-V for every fault once the implementation and any conversions are completed, even if it is an application-supported configuration.

AEM allows you to centrally gather application crash data (also known as Dr. Watson). This can be later used for crash analysis and maybe even allow you to fix the problem.

HOW SYSTEM CENTER CHANGES IT

A lot of service companies do not sell Hyper-V as a virtualization solution. They sell it as part of a package, which is a package that will change how IT works. The package comprises Hyper-V, System Center Virtual Machine Manager 2008 R2, and the rest of the System Center family.

OpsMgr is a perfect example of how the package extends beyond just virtualization. With OpsMgr, you get a monitoring solution to detect issues with all aspects of IT, not just the virtualization layer and not just with Windows, but the entire computing stack.

OK, that's the Microsoft marketing message. But the truth is that OpsMgr, when it is correctly designed and deployed, makes running an IT infrastructure much easier. Third-party add-ons allow you to monitor network appliances such as firewalls, routers, and switches; detect issues in server and storage hardware; and gain an insight into how non-Microsoft applications such as MySQL and Apache Tomcat are behaving.

This means you can potentially become Big Brother to every aspect of the network, detect issues as they happen, and resolve them possibly before your users are affected. Ask those engineers and administrators who have that experience, and they will tell you that OpsMgr is the first systems management product that they will want on their network.

Combine OpsMgr, Data Protection Manager 2010, and VMM with the tight integration into Hyper-V, and you can start to see why this sales approach of changing IT is so attractive. And bear this in mind; we haven't even talked about System Center Configuration Manager or System Center Service Manager.

Those are the various pieces you can find in OpsMgr 2007. Let's take a look at the versions of OpsMgr that you might encounter in a Hyper-V deployment.

Versions of Operations Manager

Microsoft released Microsoft Operations Manager (MOM) 2000 soon after it acquired the product. To be honest, it was not met with a great reception.

MOM 2005 was released after a great deal of development. This proved to be a technically excellent solution but wasn't that widely adopted. It did prove a few things. Microsoft was serious about entering and being successful in the world of enterprise monitoring. It also provided a best-of-breed system for managing Microsoft-centric server networks that was easy to deploy and easy to customize. Partners started to work with Microsoft to include monitoring of non-Microsoft products.

It was around this time that Microsoft launched the System Center family, including MOM 2005 and System Management Server (SMS) 2003 (the predecessor to Configuration Manager 2007). Microsoft wanted to produce an integrated family of systems management solutions that would change how IT would work. Instead of fighting fires as they popped up, administrators could build automation and expertise into the network by installing System Center products. This would identify potential issues earlier than before, possibly fix them automatically, and simplify deployment of servers and applications. This would go on to become the backbone of the sales pitch for Hyper-V from Microsoft and its partners.

System Center Operations Manager 2007 followed MOM 2005. Many still refer to it as MOM. Some call it SCOM, but it is often referred to just as OpsMgr. This makes using a search engine for help a little more work, but *Operations Manager* works well with Microsoft sites, and *OpsMgr* works well with third-party sites.

OpsMgr changed how Microsoft did monitoring. It truly did become an enterprise solution. Monitoring became state-aware, allowing management pack developers to specify what a healthy and unhealthy state (warning and critical) were and allowing the management pack to transition between them automatically. The console was changed to make it more user friendly. The product was radically changed, and it took a huge leap in functionality. Because of these changes, the product was adopted more widely by medium and large organizations. This was the version that saw a very large number of partners add support for monitoring their own or third-party products.

For Hyper-V administrators, OpsMgr 2007 is the oldest release that supports an enterprise deployment. You can integrate VMM 2008 R2 with OpsMgr 2007.

System Center Operations Manager 2007 R2 is the most recent release of OpsMgr, and it supports integration with VMM 2008 R2 for managing Hyper-V. The big change with it was the introduction of Cross Platform Extensions. This is a set of Microsoft-written agents and management packs for Linux and Unix. This makes OpsMgr truly ready for the enterprise. It also makes a marketing feature of Hyper-V a reality. Now you can truly monitor everything from the hardware (using manufacturer management packs), the hypervisor (Hyper-V), the virtual machines, the operating system (Linux and Windows), through to the applications running on those guests. OpsMgr 2007 R2 (with the latest updates) is the ideal version of OpsMgr to use in a Hyper-V deployment.

Real World Scenario

CHOOSING A LINUX DISTRIBUTION FOR HYPER-V VIRTUAL MACHINES

Microsoft is split into many different product groups and teams, each working with different schedules. This can mean that they sometimes have a slightly disjointed solution. This is apparent when you look at the supported Linux operating system distributions for OpsMgr and for Hyper-V. Hyper-V with Linux Integration Components 2.1 supports the following:

- SUSE Linux Enterprise Server 11 (x86 and x64)
- Red Hat Enterprise Server 5 (x86 and x64)
- SUSE Linux Enterprise Server 10 SP3 (x86 and x64)

Operations Manager 2007 R2 with Cumulative Update 1 can support the following Linux distributions:

- SUSE Linux Enterprise Server 11 (x86 and x64)
- Red Hat Enterprise Server 5 (x86 and x64)
- SUSE Linux Enterprise Server 10 SP1 (x86 and x64)
- SUSE Linux Enterprise Server 9 (x86)
- Red Hat Enterprise Server 4 (x86 and x64)

You might notice that the only common denominators are as follows:

- SUSE Linux Enterprise Server 11 (x86 and x64)
- Red Hat Enterprise Server 5 (x86 and x64)

It makes sense then to choose from one of those two Linux distributions if you want to monitor Hyper-V hosted Linux virtual machines using OpsMgr.

You should note that there are some notes with Red Hat Enterprise Server 5 x64. The Pluggable Time Source integration service (integration components) does not support that distribution. The Project Satori (`http://www.xen.org/download/satori.html`) mouse driver also does not support it. The latter usually won't matter much because few server installations of Linux include a GUI where the mouse would be required.

Requirements and Architecture

There are a huge variety of options for architecture and installation of the OpsMgr components. You can read about them here:

`http://technet.microsoft.com/library/bb309428.aspx`

`http://technet.microsoft.com/library/dd789005.aspx`

`http://technet.microsoft.com/library/bb419281.aspx`

It is important that you understand OpsMgr design before implementing the product.

At the very least, you should install OpsMgr on two servers. The first server will be the root management server. The second server will host the operations and data warehouse databases. Both servers should have at least two quad-core processors and 4 GB of RAM. This will support up to 200 managed servers.

Sizing of the databases is quite tricky because no two environments will be the same. Some will produce less information to be stored in the databases. Some environments will have lots of issues and generate lots of data to be stored. A rule of thumb for the data warehouse is to allow 3 MB of data per managed server per day, with a year of retained data. The operations database will require 5 MB of data per managed server per day, and this will be retained for seven days.

Windows Server 2003, Windows Server 2008, and Windows Server 2008 R2 are all supported. SQL Server 2005 with SP1, SP2, or SP3 and SQL Server 2008 with SP1 are also supported for the database roles.

You should really aim to use 64-bit versions, and it will make sense to use Windows Server 2008 R2 and SQL Server 2008 with SP1.

RUN OPSMGR ON A VIRTUAL MACHINE?

We discussed this option in Chapter 8, "Virtualization Scenarios." It is possible to run OpsMgr in a virtual machine, but it really is not recommended in a production environment because of the resource requirements.

A Quick Tour of OpsMgr

It is not our intention to teach you everything there is to know about OpsMgr. It's a pretty big product, and our focus is on Hyper-V deployment. However, we will give you a quick look around so you can either get a refresher or have a quick introduction.

The Operations Console is where most users of OpsMgr spend their time. You are greeted with a summary of the infrastructure health when you launch the tool, as you can see in Figure 9.2.

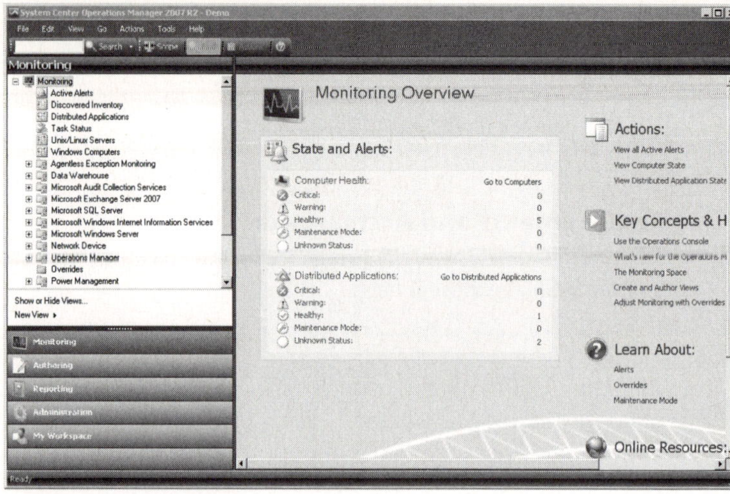

FIGURE 9.2
Launching the Operations Console

Most of the time will be spent in the Monitoring view of the Operations Console, as shown in Figure 9.3. In fact, you might spend a good deal of your time in the Alerts view where all open alerts are displayed. You'll notice that one of the two alerts has been selected. Details about the alert are shown below it, including the responsible monitor and possible cause and resolution information. On the right, in the Actions pane, different context-sensitive tasks will be available depending on what is selected in the center pane.

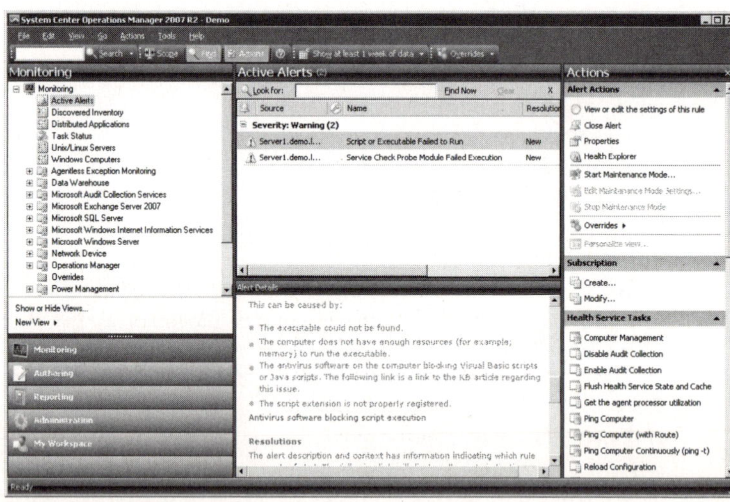

FIGURE 9.3
Operations Console Monitoring view

The navigation tree on the left allows you to browse through different built-in features, management pack data, state views, alert views, and performance views.

Figure 9.4 shows the Authoring view. This is where an OpsMgr administrator will customize and create management pack content. The management pack templates allow administrators to quickly enable monitoring of complex systems. For example, client perspective monitoring of websites can be set up in a matter of minutes. You can even enable monitoring of services on Windows and Linux machines that might not be monitored by any vendor-provided management packs.

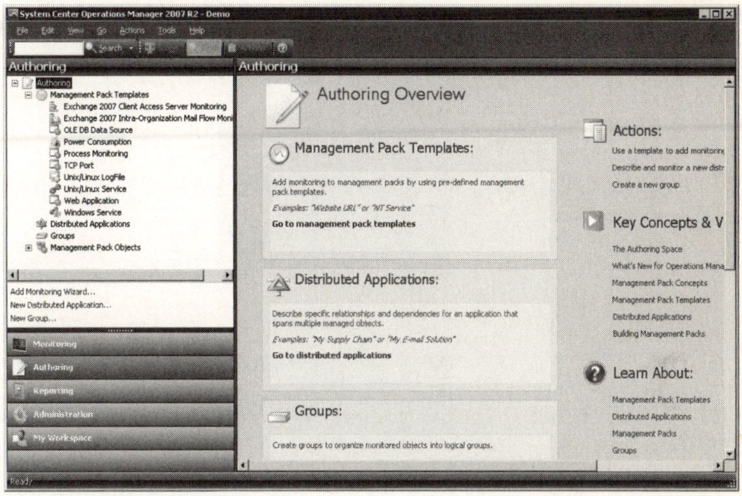

FIGURE 9.4
Operations Console Authoring view

Distributed applications allow you to build up a model of an application from the components that make it up, such as websites and databases. This allows nonadministrators to understand how well their application is performing, without needing to understand its construction and browsing around the Operations Console. This can be made use of for SLA reporting using the free Service Level Management Dashboard download here:

```
http://www.microsoft.com/downloads/details.aspx?FamilyId=67EF9823-631B-49B7-9D7F-
9F125BDF27AE
```

You will use groups to create buckets for grouping your monitored servers, appliances, and applications. This allows you to create granular delegations. The Management Pack Objects view contains all the currently imported and used rules and monitors for monitoring your infrastructure.

Figure 9.5 shows the Reporting view. This is where you will interact with the data warehouse and produce reports about the performance and health history of the OpsMgr-managed infrastructure.

The Administration view, in Figure 9.6, is where the less frequent administration work is done by the OpsMgr administrators. Delegated rights, alert notifications, OpsMgr configuration, and agent/appliance management are handled here. This is also where management packs are imported into OpsMgr.

The final view is My Workspace. This is where you can configure a summary view of the important aspects of the monitoring system. You can aggregate numerous views of data into one screen and jump from there to other parts of the console when you need to do so.

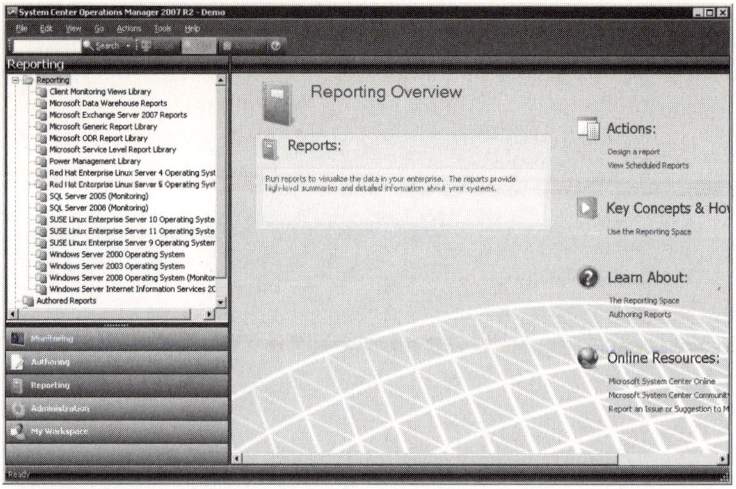

FIGURE 9.5
Operations Console Reporting view

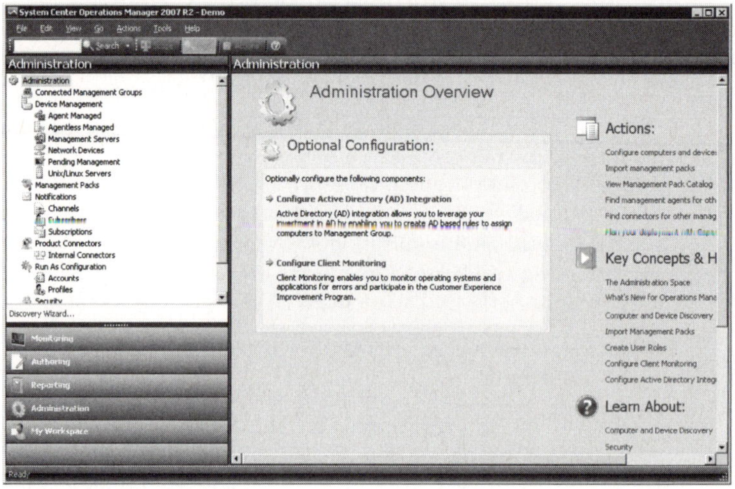

FIGURE 9.6
Operations Console Administration view

Integration with Virtual Machine Manager 2008 R2

The PRO feature was introduced in Chapter 8 when we talked about Virtual Machine Manager 2008 R2. PRO is a mechanism where OpsMgr can detect an issue and VMM can respond to it. You must have both products and implement an integration to be able to use PRO. We are going to look at this procedure and then look at how you can implement and test PRO in a lab or production environment.

You should note that all the integration work will be done on the root management server of your OpsMgr management group.

Prerequisites

You must manually prepare a number of prerequisites to have a successful integration of VMM 2008 R2 and OpsMgr 2007.

Supported Version

You must be running System Center Operations Manager 2007 with Service Pack 1 or System Center Operations Manager 2007 R2.

Domain Membership

The OpsMgr management servers must be either in the same domain as the VMM server or in a domain where there is a two-way trust with the VMM server's domain. Kerberos authentication will be used for communications between the two products.

SPN Registration

The OpsMgr SDK service must be able to register service principal names (SPNs) in Active Directory.

VMM Service Account

We mentioned in Chapter 7 that you should use a domain-based user account for the VMM service. That user account will be used for the integration. Don't worry too much if you did configure the VMM service to use Local System for authentication. You can set up a domain-based account and set up the Virtual Machine Manager service to use this account to log on. But make sure you add this domain-based user account to the local Administrators group on the VMM server. Then you can restart the VMM service and proceed.

The VMM service account must be an OpsMgr administrator. The setup routine you will run later will do this for you. However, this could be undone by Group Policy's Restricted Groups if not configured correctly. You could grant the VMM service account administrator rights via any applied policy to prevent issues later.

Alternatively, you can grant the right directly in OpsMgr. You will use the Administration view to do this. Navigate into User Roles under Security, and edit the properties of Operations Manager Administrators, as shown in Figure 9.7. We have added the user account into an Active Directory group and granted rights to that group.

OpsMgr Management Packs

Three sets of management packs and their prerequisites must be imported:

- Windows Server
- IIS
- SQL Server

The versions that are downloaded and imported should match the versions being used by VMM. This should not be a big deal. There is a good chance that they will be either already imported or planned for a later import. They are some of the key management packs for Windows server management by OpsMgr.

FIGURE 9.7
Adding VMM to Operations Manager Administrators

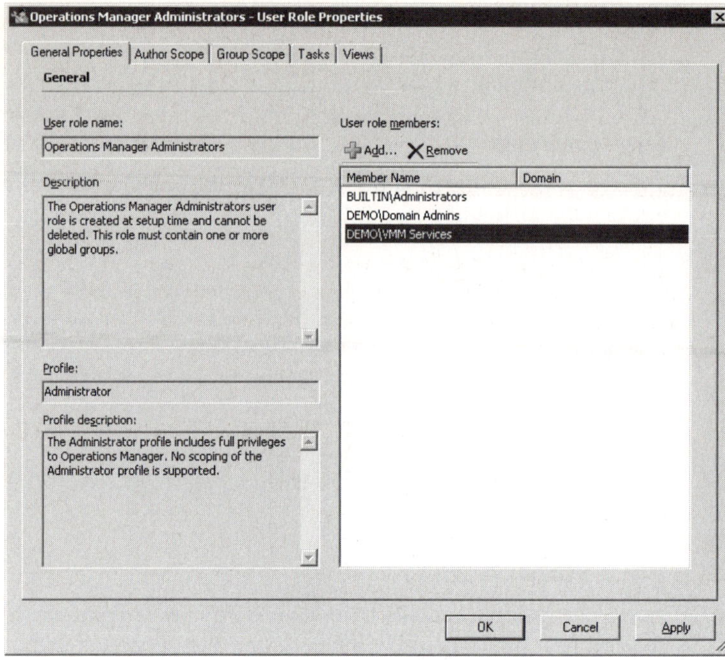

OTHER USEFUL MANAGEMENT PACKS

You should consider importing management packs for each of your required products. Two other management packs that you will find of use are the Hyper-V and the Windows Server Cluster management pack. The Hyper-V management pack makes sense; you will be running Hyper-V. There is a good chance that you will run a Hyper-V cluster so you will want to monitor Windows Failover Clustering.

It's a little ironic, but hardware plays a big role in virtualization. You are using fewer servers to run many operating system environments and probably a shared storage solution such as a SAN. You need to know of any hardware issues so that you can deal with them quickly and effectively. You should aim to purchase server and storage hardware for a manufacturer that has made a significant investment in System Center (VMM, OpsMgr, as well as Data Protection Manager 2010 and Configuration Manager 2007) if you are basing your management processes on Microsoft System Center. Do your research to make a well-informed purchasing decision.

Don't get carried away with importing management packs. Each should be considered as a mini-project to be planned and tested.

You can import management packs by using the Administration view in the Operations Console. Right-click Management Packs, and select Import Management Packs. This opens the Import Management Packs screen. Click the Add button, and select Add From Catalog if you want to download the management packs directly from the Microsoft website. Alternatively, you can import management packs from disk if you have already downloaded them.

READ THE MANAGEMENT PACK DOCUMENTATION

Every management pack comes with accompanying documentation. Sometimes this can include additional instructions for enabling features of the management pack or controlling noise that might be generated by the management pack. You won't necessarily get any clue that this documentation exists if you download the management packs directly from Microsoft in the Operations Console.

We chose to download management packs from the catalog, and this caused the Select Management Packs From Catalog screen (Figure 9.8) to appear. Here we searched the entire catalog, selected the required management packs, and clicked Add to mark them for download and import.

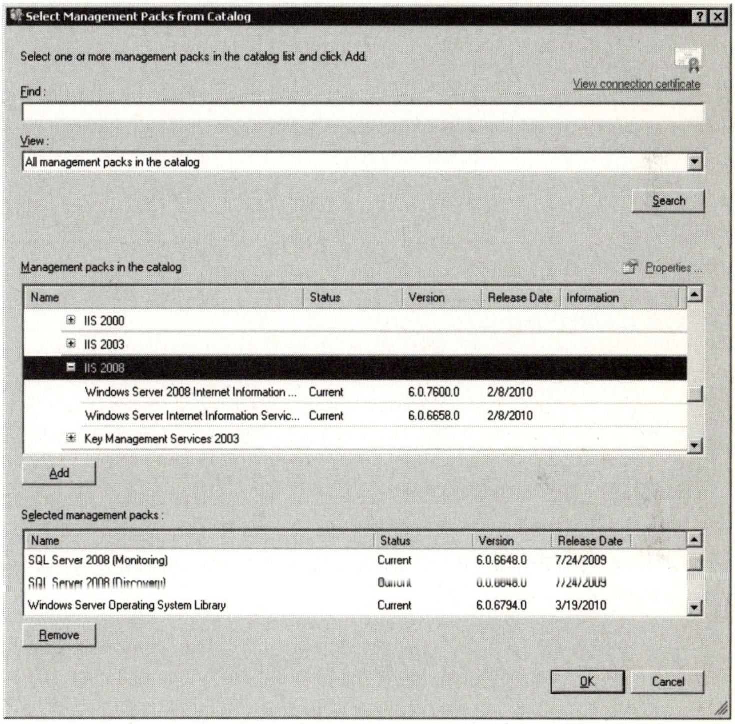

FIGURE 9.8
Selecting the required management packs

You can then complete the wizard, which will download and import the management packs for you.

OPSMGR AGENTS

OpsMgr will need to be able to monitor your Hyper-V host servers, your virtual machines, and your VMM server. Make sure that an OpsMgr agent is installed on each of machine to be managed.

Real World Scenario

WHERE DO YOU DEPLOY OPSMGR AGENTS?

Assuming you have the correct licensing, you can and should try to deploy an agent onto every manageable operating system. An agent that is deployed to the parent partition of a Hyper-V host server will be able to monitor that operating system, the hardware, and Hyper-V on that computer. It won't know about the inner workings of the virtual machines.

If you install OpsMgr agents into each possible virtual machine, then you will be able to monitor their health, their resource utilization, and that of their installed applications.

Consider the System Center Management Suite licensing for your host servers if you plan to use OpsMgr to monitor all of your virtual machines. This economic licensing option can save your organization a lot of money. This is because it includes licensing for the virtual machines that are running on the host server.

You should give some consideration about installing agents onto machines that are used for test and development purposes. These are the sorts of machines that have short life spans and go through large amounts of uncontrolled change and reboots. A monitoring system will raise a lot of alerts for those sorts of virtual machines. In fact, you may even want to decide what you will do with host servers that are dedicated to hosting test and development virtual machines. Their owners are likely to have local administrative rights and may cause a lot of false alarms.

ADMINISTRATION CONSOLES

The final prerequisites are for the VMM server. You must install the Operations Console and the VMM administrator console onto the VMM server. The VMM console should not be installed onto any OpsMgr management servers; this will be done during the integration.

Installing VMM 2008 R2 Integration

This process is actually pretty easy. We will be installing the integration on the root management server and then installing the VMM administrator console onto every other management server in the OpsMgr management group.

Mount the VMM 2008 R2 media in your OpsMgr root management server. If autoplay is enabled, then a splash screen will appear. If not, then you should run `setup.exe` from the VMM 2008 R2 media. Click Configure Operations Manager to start the installation. You will have to click through the usual EULA screen, assuming you agree to Microsoft's licensing terms. The following screen will configure Microsoft Update. Then the installer will check the hardware and software prerequisites. Next up is the screen where you will configure the installation path. The default location is usually OK.

Figure 9.9 shows the Port Assignment screen. Here you will specify the name of the VMM server that you want to integrate OpsMgr with. This will be in the form of *`<domain>\<computer NetBIOS name>`*. We have entered **`demo\computer`**. You will then enter the port for VMM server communications. The default port of 8100 is entered. You can leave this as is unless you have altered the default port in the VMM administrator console.

The last screen will present a summary. After that, the installation is complete.

You're not finished yet. The integration may be installed, but there is some configuration work required to allow it to function completely. Before we go there, let's look at some troubleshooting tips for the OpsMgr integration setup.

FIGURE 9.9
VMM integration port assignment

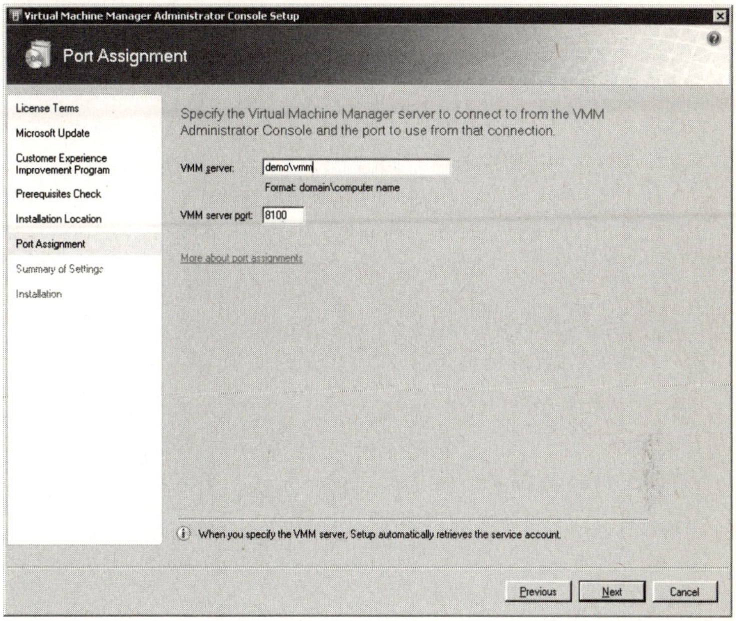

TROUBLESHOOTING THE OPSMGR CONFIGURATION

It is possible that something can go wrong at this point. You may be informed that "Setup was not able to retrieve the service account from the specified Virtual Machine Manager server." There are a few possible reasons for this.

The first things to check are the prerequisites. Is every single one of them configured correctly? Are you logged in as domain user with administrative rights?

A log file for the failed OpsMgr integration will be created in a hidden folder on your OpsMgr. You will need to set up Windows Explorer to allow you to view hidden folders. Then browse to `C:\ProgramData\VMMLogs`, and open `ClientSetup.Log`. To be honest, it is unlikely that you will find anything of help in here, but the contents will be useful if you do need to engage Microsoft's support services.

Next you need to check the SPNs of your VMM service account. Assuming that your account is `demo\VMMSvc`, then you should run this command at the command prompt while logged into the domain:

```
Setspn -L VMMSvc
```

It should return something like this:

```
Registered ServicePrincipalNames for CN=vmmsvc,OU=Services,OU=Demo,DC=demo,DC=lo
cal:
  HOST/vmmsvc
  HOST/vmmsvc.demo.local
```

If it doesn't, then you will need to add those SPN records. Open ADSIedit (with domain administrator rights), browse to the VMM service account, and open its properties. Scroll down through the contents of the Attribute Editor tab, find `servicePrincipalName`, and double-click it. You should edit it so that it is something like what is shown in Figure 9.10.

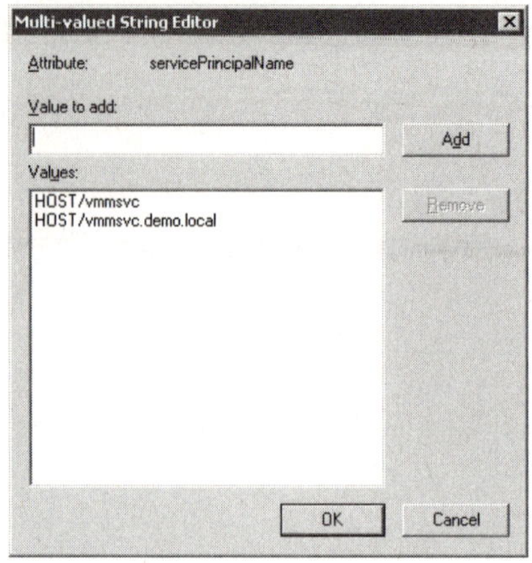

FIGURE 9.10
The VMM SPNs

The next thing to look for is the service connection point (SCP) for the VMM service. Using ADSIEdit, browse back to your VMM service account, and try to expand it, like a folder in Windows Explorer. You should find an SCP object. It will appear like a folder and be called CN=MSVMM.

You can manually create the SCP using a tool on the VMM 2008 R2 installation media. Browse into `<architecture>\Setup` in the media using the command prompt, and find a tool called `configurescptool.exe`. Run it as follows:

```
configurescptool -install
```

Your SCP should now be created, and you should retry the installation. If that doesn't fix the problem, then you can find more information at `http://technet.microsoft.com/library/cc764223.aspx`.

It is easy to jump into the OpsMgr Operations Console and start looking to see what will happen. You will be disappointed. We have not finished the integration yet. The real fun won't happen until we do.

Non-RMS Management Servers

Every other OpsMgr management server in the management group will need to be able to work with VMM 2008 R2. The connector is in place thanks to the previous step. Now you need to install the VMM 2008 R2 administrator console on every other management server in the OpsMgr management group.

Configuring the VMM-OpsMgr Integration

You will need to complete a number of steps before the integration is completed.

PowerShell Execution Policy

You will now have an appreciation for the importance of PowerShell in VMM. PowerShell extends far beyond VMM. It is not just integrated into all management solutions, but many of the newer ones are built on PowerShell. OpsMgr and VMM work closely together using PowerShell. This requires that you make a quick change to the remote execution policy for PowerShell on every OpsMgr management server and VMM server. The command you will run is as follows:

```
Set-ExecutionPolicy RemoteSigned
```

You may want to consider using Group Policy to control this setting. This may be required if you have a number of machines to configure or if Group Policy is already used to lock down this setting.

Using Windows Server 2008 R2 Group Policy, you can find the Turn On Script Execution policy setting in Computer Configuration ➢ Policies ➢ Administrative Templates ➢ Windows Components ➢ Windows PowerShell.

Default Action Accounts

Operations Manager uses a number of service accounts to perform specific actions. One of them is called an *action account*. In particular, we're interested in the default action account. There will be one of these accounts configured on an OpsMgr server. The default action account can be used to access and manipulate local resources on computer on behalf of OpsMgr. This allows it to monitor secure resources and to perform tasks that are initiated manually by administrators from the OpsMgr console or that are initiated automatically as responses to detected conditions on the computer or network.

We need to grant administrative rights to VMM to the Default Action Account of every OpsMgr management server. This will allow OpsMgr to integrate with VMM.

You can identify the OpsMgr Default Action Account in the OpsMgr console. Browse into the Administration view, and then navigate into Run As Configuration ➢ Profiles. Find the Default Action Account in the center details pane, and open its properties. Figure 9.11 shows the Run As Accounts for the Default Action Account role. The highlighted `Demo\OpsMgrAction` account is the Default Action Account. You can ignore the other entries in this case. Those are instructions to OpsMgr to use System as the action account for those managed computers.

With the identified Default Action Accounts from each of your OpsMgr management servers, you are ready to configure VMM. Launch the VMM admin console, open the Administration view, navigate into User Roles, and add the Default Action Accounts into the Administrator user role. You can see an example of this in Figure 9.12.

Configure VMM

By now, you will be glad to hear that you are at the last step in the process of the integration. You will now specify the name of the OpsMgr RMS in VMM. What you have done up to now is make OpsMgr aware of VMM. Now you need to make VMM aware of OpsMgr.

Open the VMM admin console, go into the Administration view, and navigate into System Center. Here you will see two entries:

- Operations Manager Server
- Operations Manager Reporting URL

FIGURE 9.11
Identifying the OpsMgr Default Action Account

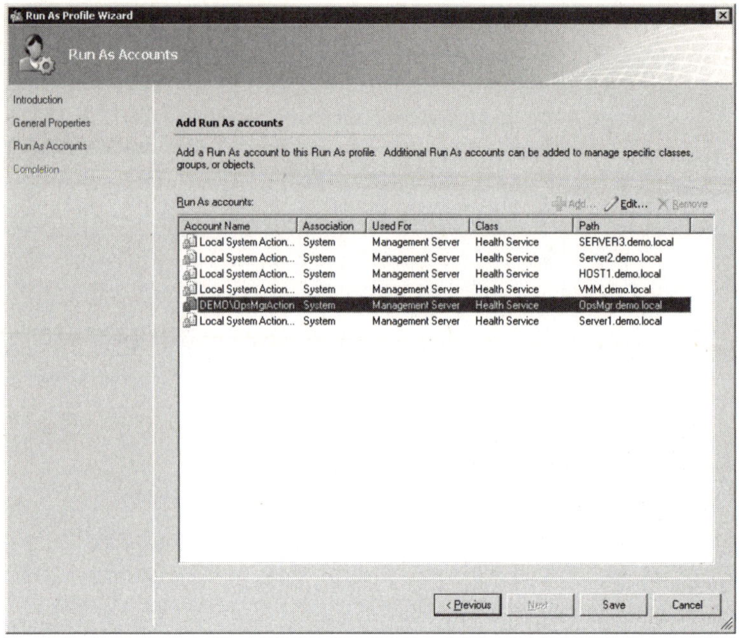

FIGURE 9.12
Granting VMM admin rights to Default Action Accounts

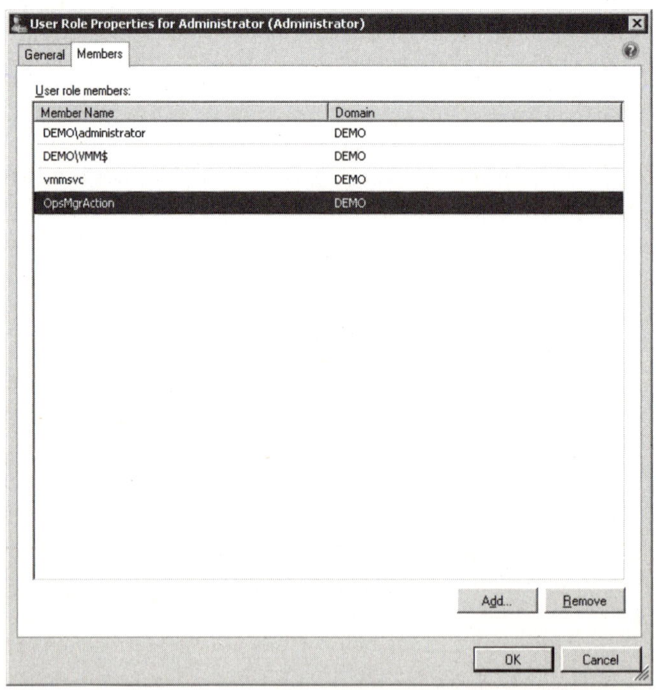

Double-click Operations Manager Server, and the window shown in Figure 9.13 will appear. Here you can enter the NetBIOS or fully qualified domain name (FQDN) of the root management server.

FIGURE 9.13
Specifying the OpsMgr RMS

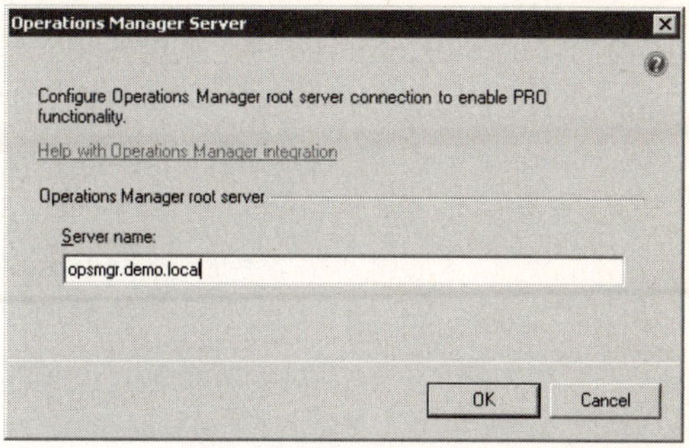

Now the fun starts to happen. This will start to close the loop on the integration, making VMM aware that there is an OpsMgr RMS to integrate with. A dialog box appears to let you know that something is being done. It should process and complete. There is a chance that there will be an error, stating that the integration failed because of the lack of a suitable VMM management pack. Ensure that a VMM management pack is installed in OpsMgr, with a version of 2.0.4071.0 or newer.

Now is the time to return to the OpsMgr console. Go into Monitoring view. A navigation pane on the left side contains all the management packs that have been imported. Browse into the Virtual Machine Manager 2008 R2 folders, and you will find that lots of objects will start to appear within a few minutes. A rather handy diagram will also be visible, as you can see in Figure 9.14.

FIGURE 9.14
VMM data appearing in the OpsMgr console

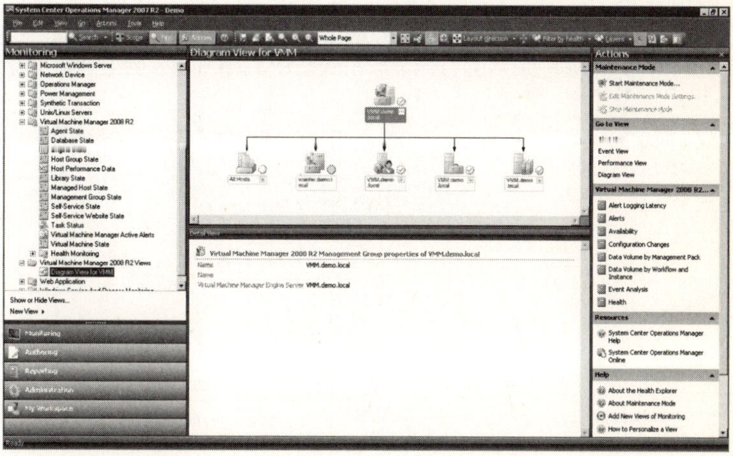

The last piece in the puzzle is to integrate the reporting services. This will allow the VMM-related reports that OpsMgr is responsible for to appear in the VMM administrator console.

This is handy for VMM administrators who might not necessarily have OpsMgr rights, something that is a realistic possibility in large organizations.

You may notice something very cool. If your VMM server is managing a VMware infrastructure, then OpsMgr will have some very basic awareness of your vCenter infrastructure. It doesn't have VMware agents, but you can obtain them from third-party providers.

Double-click Operations Manager Reporting URL, and the window in Figure 9.15 will open. You can enter the URL for the OpsMgr reporting server here. It will take the following format:

```
http(s)://<name of OpsMgr reporting server>/ReportServer
```

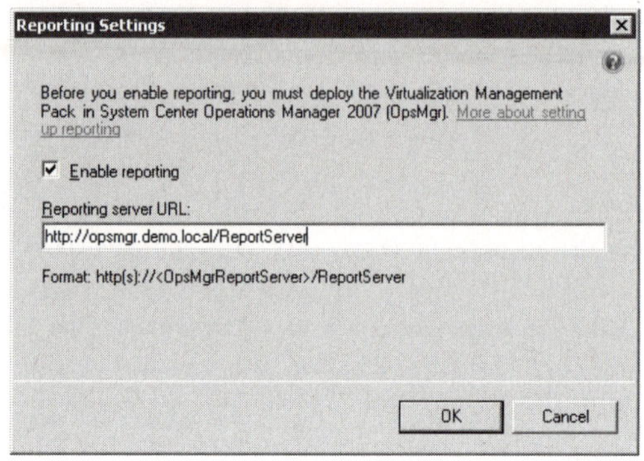

FIGURE 9.15
Specifying the OpsMgr reporting server URL

In our example, it will be as follows:

```
http://opsmgr.demo.local/ReportServer
```

You can get the URL from your OpsMgr administrators and test it using a browser. It is possible that the site is SSL protected. If so, you will have to use `https://` instead of `http://`.

The results of this configuration will be immediately visible. A Reporting wunderbar will appear in the VMM administrator console in the bottom left. You can open this view and see the OpsMgr reports for Hyper-V and VMM managed virtualization. This is shown in Figure 9.16.

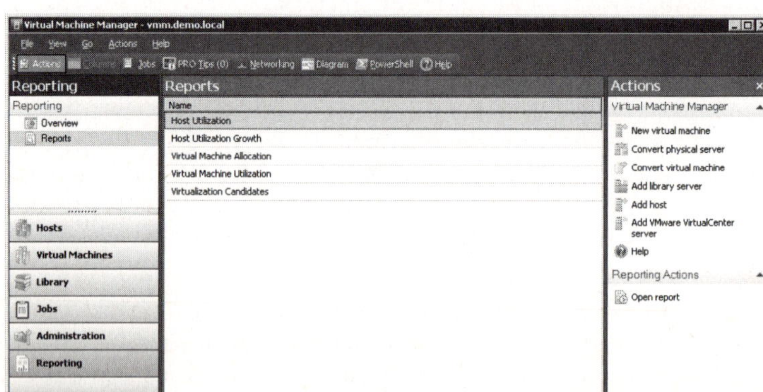

FIGURE 9.16
OpsMgr reports in VMM 2008 R2

The good news is that we have reached the finish line. We will take a look around OpsMgr to show you what we have now.

Managing Hyper-V and VMM in OpsMgr

What will happen soon after your new Hyper-V infrastructure goes into production? It is likely that the occasional hard disk might fail or an ECC memory board might degrade. What tool will alert you of these problems? That's right: OpsMgr.

An owner of an application that is running on a recently converted virtual machine (from a physical machine) could complain of reduced response times. How will you be able to diagnose that issue? You guessed it: OpsMgr will be collecting performance information for the operating system, SQL Server, website, Exchange server, and possibly many more.

OpsMgr is a very powerful tool. A VMM administrator should learn how to use the information and functionality that is provided. Administrators and engineers in smaller or medium-sized organizations should take the time to become experts in managing and engineering OpsMgr. Consultants and administrators in larger organizations may only have delegated operator rights in the OpsMgr management group. They may not have the opportunity to do any OpsMgr engineering, but they should understand how the product works and take advantage of the great intelligence it can provide.

We will now cover what you can do in OpsMgr to manage Windows Server 2008 R2 Hyper-V and VMM 2008 R2.

Monitoring VMM

Hyper-V administrators will actually spend most of their time using VMM. So, we will start by looking at how to manage VMM using OpsMgr.

Diagram View for VMM

We previously saw the Diagram view for VMM in Figure 9.14. This presented you with a high-level view of the VMM-managed virtualization infrastructure. There is another way to view this diagram. Navigate into Distributed Applications in the monitoring view, and find the VMM server. A distributed application in OpsMgr is an application that can be made up of lots of monitored components from various servers or applications. Sometimes these are provided automatically by a management pack. This is done in our case for VMM. But you can also engineer your own distributed applications in the Authoring view. In our example, we want to work with the `vmm.demo.local` distributed application that was created by the VMM management pack using discovered resources. You can right click it and select Open ➢ Diagram View.

Diagram view can be useful in a few ways:

Understanding the Virtualization Architecture The Diagram view does something that we would struggle to do in Microsoft Visio or other similar visualization tools. It draws a diagram of your exact hardware virtualization architecture, assuming that OpsMgr is monitoring every component. This can include the VMM management components, Hyper-V, Virtual Server 2005 R2 SP1, and VMware servers.

The diagram starts at a very high level. If an icon has a plus button on it, then you can click that to expand the level beneath that icon. This allows you to drill down quite deep into the system and even into each monitored virtual machine to see the components of it. This can be useful when explaining your infrastructure to someone. It can also be useful for copying and reusing in documentation.

Troubleshooting It can be difficult to find the root cause of an issue if it generates a large number of alerts. That is a real possibility if you are dealing with a virtualized environment with lots of resources in a dense computing environment such as Hyper-V. A problem with a single host server could potentially lead to alerts about lots of virtual machines. How would you identify the real cause of the problem in a sea of notification emails and alerts in the OpsMgr Operations Console?

The Diagram view has a useful root-cause analysis feature. You can see this in Figure 9.17. A small button at the top called Problem Path allows the diagram to highlight the root cause. All other objects in the application are grayed out. A red line also appears, leading you to the root cause of the problem. You can follow this by expanding any icons until you reach the end of the red line.

FIGURE 9.17
Problem analysis using Diagram view

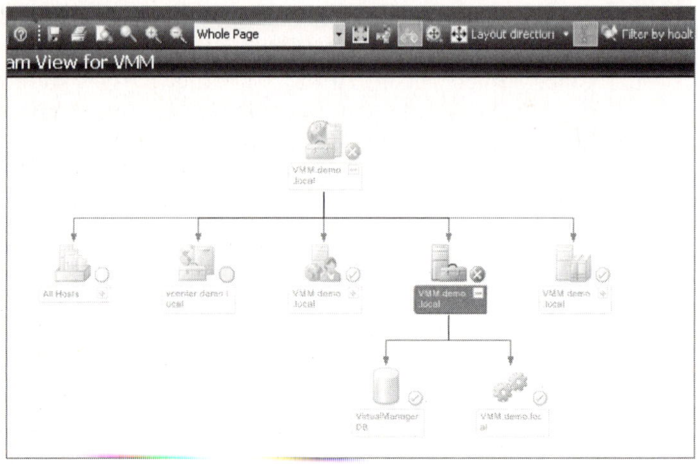

You can right-click the object that has caused the issue and select Open ➤ Alert View. This opens a new window, which you can see in Figure 9.18, containing all the open alerts for this object. Now you can see what has caused all of your alerts.

FIGURE 9.18
Root-cause Alert view

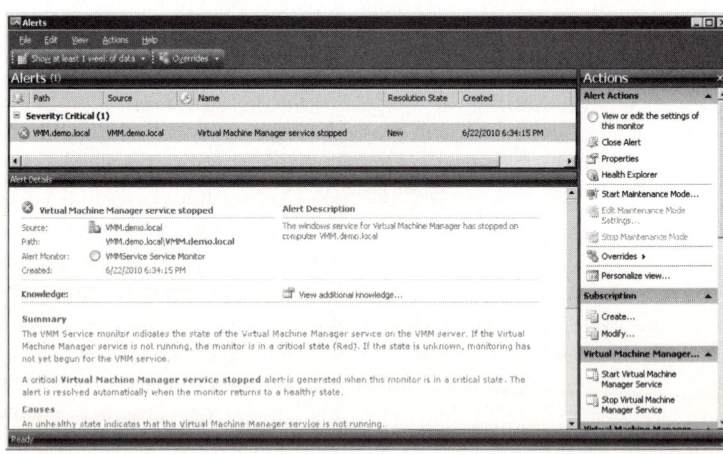

You'll see at the bottom that there is a description for each selected alert. This may also include a cause. In this example, the Virtual Machine Manager service has been stopped on the VMM server. The solution is to start it. You could log into that server, launch Services from the Control Panel, and start the service. Or you could just launch the task on the context-sensitive Actions pane on the right side, which will do that work for you.

A new window will appear to confirm the action. Then a new window will appear (which you can close) to allow you to track the progress of the task. If all goes well, the Virtual Machine Manager service will start up again, OpsMgr will automatically close the alerts, and you can refresh the view to see a healthy VMM infrastructure.

Visio and SharePoint Integration It is possible to integrate an OpsMgr diagram view not only into Visio but also into a SharePoint site. This is possible with the To Visio button in the top-right corner of the window when a Diagram view is open. This is not your ordinary static diagram. This is a living diagram that accurately reflects everything that is going on in OpsMgr. Health changes will be reflected. This could be very useful when you want to share the health of a virtualized infrastructure via a web presence such as Microsoft SharePoint. You can learn how to do this with Visio 2010 and SharePoint 2010 at `http://technet.microsoft.com/library/ff630871.aspx`.

State Views A state view gives a quick way to see the health of a collection of related objects. A number of them are provided for VMM. You can see the health of your host groups or the VMM agents. There are state views for components of VMM such as the VMM server, the Self-Service Portal, and the library. Figure 9.19 shows the health state of the virtual machines that are placed on host servers that are managed by VMM.

FIGURE 9.19
VMM-managed virtual machine State view

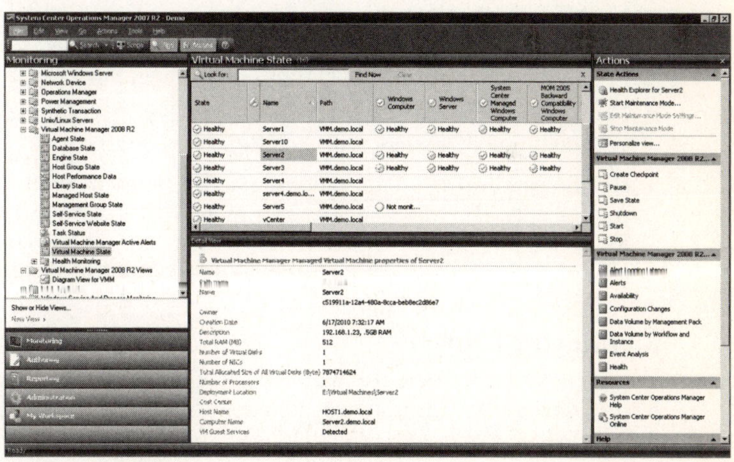

Host Performance Data These views will let you quickly access performance information from a time frame of the last desired number of minutes, hours, or days. This gives you a very quick way to see what it currently happening in terms of performance and what the trend is. Your alternative is to run a report that can take a little longer, but it can produce data from a long and more precise time frame. Figure 9.20 shows the Host Performance Data view. The purpose of this view is to give you a glimpse of the gathered performance metrics of the virtualization host servers that are managed by VMM.

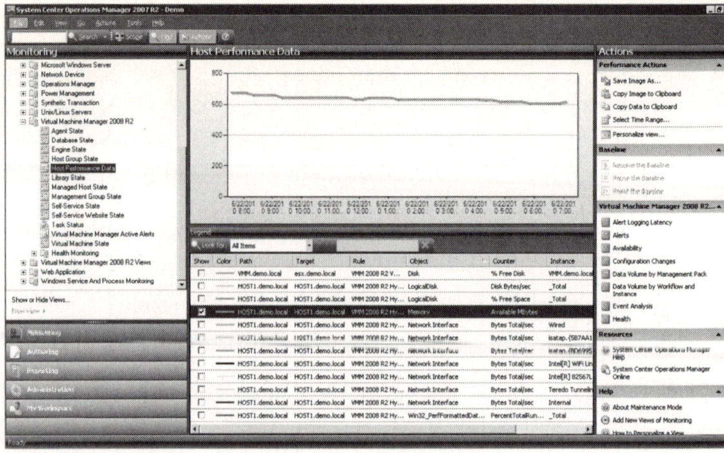

FIGURE 9.20
Host Performance Data view

You can select a metric for a particular host at the bottom, and it will be drawn at the top. You can find yourself in a situation where you need to write an email in response to a performance issue. You might be trying to explain the cause of some complaints. Or you might be trying to request more host or storage resources. Performance diagrams such as these can be useful. There is a handy set of actions at the top left that allow you to copy the image to the clipboard, save it to a file, or even copy the data that was used to create the diagram.

Task Status This view will show the status of any VMM-related tasks that you start from OpsMgr. For example, the earlier request to start the Virtual Machine Manager service will create a task in OpsMgr. The progress of that task can be tracked here. The lower, detail part of the screen will reveal more information about the task, its execution, and its results.

Virtual Machine Manager Active Alerts The title of this view is pretty self-explanatory, and ideally alerts in here will be few and far between.

Health Monitoring This folder contains a series of health views, one for each of the VMM components. The views are a merger of the Alerts view and the State view. The top screen shows the state for the type of component in VMM. The lower part of the screen shows any related open alerts.

Monitoring Hyper-V

You might find it strange, but the VMM integration with OpsMgr does not import the Hyper-V management pack. This is an essential management pack to import because this is not a VMM project you are working on; it is a Hyper-V project. We'll cover how to import the Hyper-V management pack, and then we will cover the features of the management pack.

IMPORT THE HYPER-V MANAGEMENT PACK

OpsMgr will be able to monitor your Hyper-V host servers' virtualization functionality once you have imported the Hyper-V management pack. Make sure you have read the documentation for the latest version of this management pack before you proceed.

Open the OpsMgr Operations Console, and click the Administration wunderbar when you are ready. Right-click Management Packs in the navigation window on the left side, and select Import Management Packs. The Import Management Packs Wizard will launch. Click the Add button on the Select Management Packs screen. You can select Add From Catalog to download the latest management pack from Microsoft. Alternatively, you can download the management pack from the Microsoft Pinpoint site, extract it, read any documentation, and choose the Add From Disk option in this screen. We're going to use the Add From Catalog option.

That opens the Select Management Packs From Catalog window, which is displayed in Figure 9.21. We searched for *Hyper-V*, and that returned all management packs that contained that word. You'll soon see that there are prerequisites for these management packs that we have not installed yet.

FIGURE 9.21
Select Management Packs From Catalog window

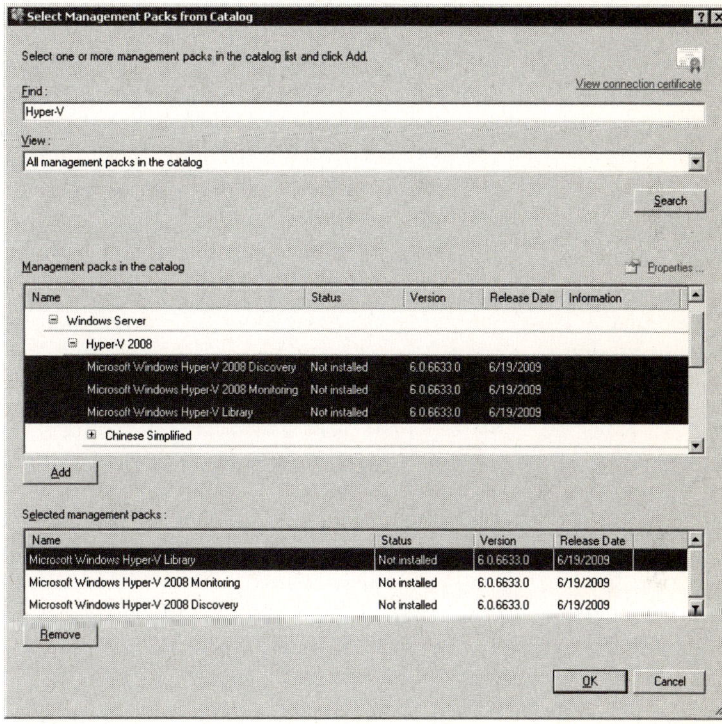

You may notice that localizations of the management packs are also available for download. You can choose to download any languages that are used in your organization. Select the management packs, and click Add.

The next screen, Select Management Packs, is shown in Figure 9.22. You'll notice a warning symbol is beside each of the selected Hyper-V management packs. We're missing one or more management packs that are required to enable these management packs to work. The fix is easy; just click the Resolve hyperlink. OpsMgr will identify the prerequisite management pack(s) and add it to the selected list.

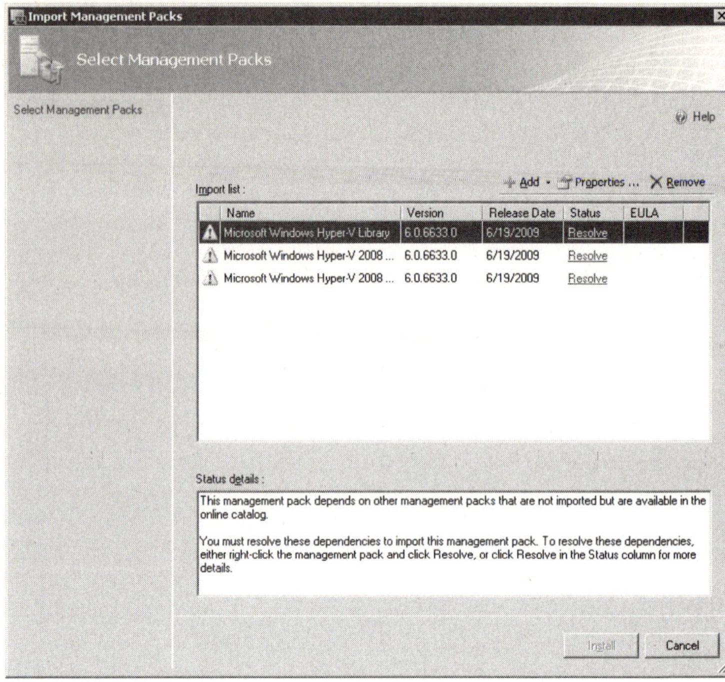

FIGURE 9.22 Selected management packs and warning

You can click Install, assuming that all required change control processes have approved the new management packs.

The Import Management Packs screen appears and displays the download and import progress of your management packs (Figure 9.23). After a few minutes, the management packs will be active in Operations Manager.

What do you need to do now? You would be assigning management packs to agents, creating monitoring rules, and so on, with a traditional monitoring system. It would feel like you were writing the monitoring. You won't be doing that with OpsMgr. The management pack contains monitors and rules for all of your monitoring functionality. They also contain discovery rules, allowing OpsMgr to automatically figure out which agents should use the management pack. All you have to do is sit back for a little while until objects start appearing in the Monitoring view of the OpsMgr Operations Console.

NOT ALL MICROSOFT MANAGEMENT PACKS ARE THE SAME

Remember that every team in Microsoft writes the management pack for their product? Each team seems to have different practices. Some will enable most or all functionality by default. Some will disable most or all functionality by default. The Hyper-V and VMM teams enable the management pack functionality. You'll find out what you must do when you read the management pack documentation. You might have noticed that there is a trend in this chapter when it comes to reading recommendations!

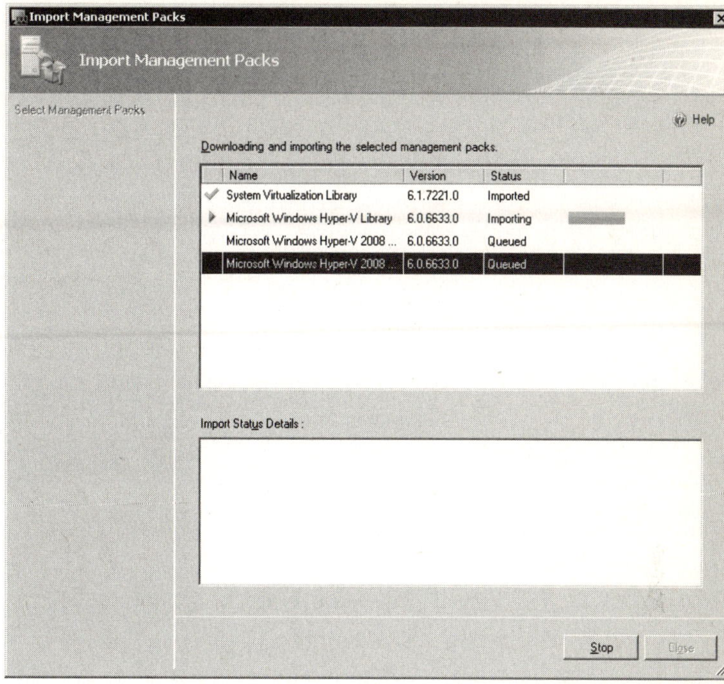

FIGURE 9.23
Hyper-V monitoring is enabled

A few views are created for Hyper-V monitoring. The Alert view will show you all the open alerts that are related to Hyper-V. The Server Role view shows you the health summary for all your agent-monitored Hyper-V host servers. The Virtual Machine view displays all the virtual machines on those host servers. And the Virtual Network view shows the virtual networks that are created on your Hyper-V host servers.

From now on, OpsMgr is using the expertise of the Microsoft VMM and Hyper-V product teams to actively monitor the health and performance of your hardware virtualization infrastructure. Any faults will be displayed as alerts and notifications will be sent to you, assuming that they are configured.

OpsMgr Reporting

OpsMgr reporting is useful for analyzing the performance of physical or virtual machines or the availability of applications. For example, the owner of an application that was recently converted into a virtual machine may log a call to complain about performance. There might be a legitimate complaint. It might be a case of company politics taking advantage of a change. It might even be something other than Hyper-V, such as an increase in user demand. OpsMgr reporting gives you an insight into the long-term trends and a detailed view of what is currently happening.

You can start off by browsing through the performance views in the navigation tree of the Monitoring view in the OpsMgr Operations Console. Alternatively, you can use the Reporting view of the OpsMgr Operations Console to produce more detailed reports. We already covered this functionality in Chapter 4, "Assessing the Existing Infrastructure," when we talked about assessing an existing infrastructure for virtualization.

You can use OpsMgr to produce reports on the availability of an application. You've seen that we have a distributed application for VMM. You might have an SLA on that application and need to be able to report on its uptime. To do this, you start by browsing to Distributed Applications in the Monitoring view and selecting the VMM server. Over in the Actions pane, a series of relevant reports will appear. These include an Events report and a Health report. We're going to run an Availability report, so we will click that.

Figure 9.24 shows the Report window. You can specify the time frame to report on in the top left. You can also configure the aggregation of the data there as well, using Hourly or Daily data.

FIGURE 9.24
Create an Availability report

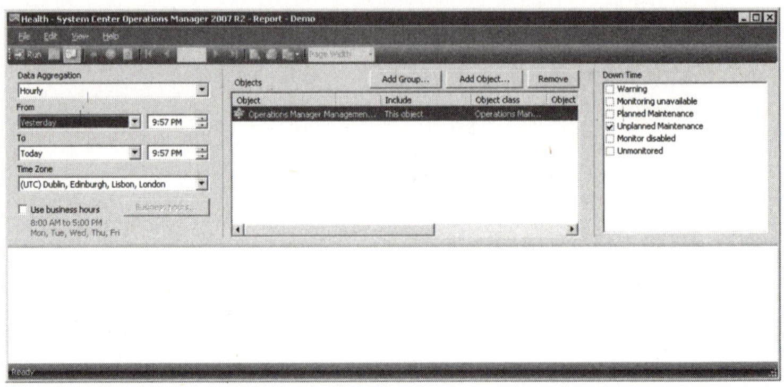

The Downtime box on the top right allows you to specify what your organization considers as downtime. This will be driven by the service-level requirements of your organization. You can click the Run button to generate the report. The time taken will depend on the amount of data to be queried and the abilities of the SQL Server instance that hosts the data warehouse database.

OPSMGR MAINTENANCE MODE

Operations Manager probably will create alerts when you are performing maintenance on machines or applications that are being monitored. You can prevent this from happening by using the OpsMgr maintenance mode feature. This will disable monitoring for selected objects for a defined amount of time. Browse to the object in question, right-click it, and select Maintenance Mode ➤ Start Maintenance Mode. That will open the Maintenance Mode Settings window.

Here you can specify the reason for disabling monitoring. Note the Planned check box. This changes the possible entries in the Category drop-down list box from Unplanned to Planned. This can affect your availability reporting. You can also define that monitoring should be disabled for a number of minutes or until a specific date and time.

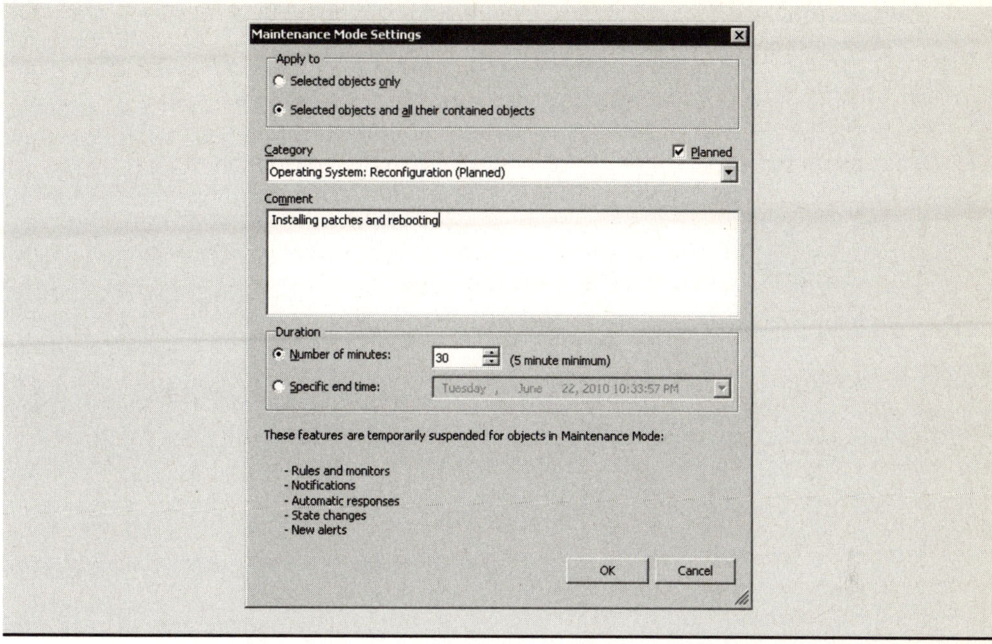

The report is presented once the data is gathered by OpsMgr. You can see that the different kinds of downtime are color-coded. Green means the system was operational and monitored. Red is bad; the system was monitored, and it suffered a critical failure. You can see in the report in Figure 9.25 that users of VMM have enjoyed 99.31 percent uptime in the previous 24 hours.

FIGURE 9.25
The Availability report

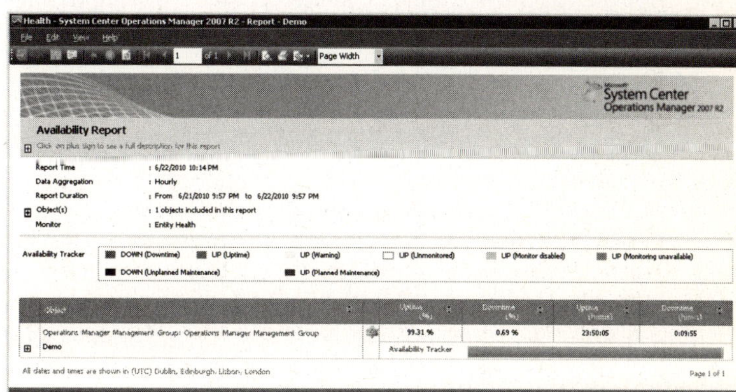

You can get more detailed information by clicking the Availability Tracker hyperlink. This refreshes the report window and produces the report shown in Figure 9.26. This breaks down the time frame in the original report and shows when the downtime occurred.

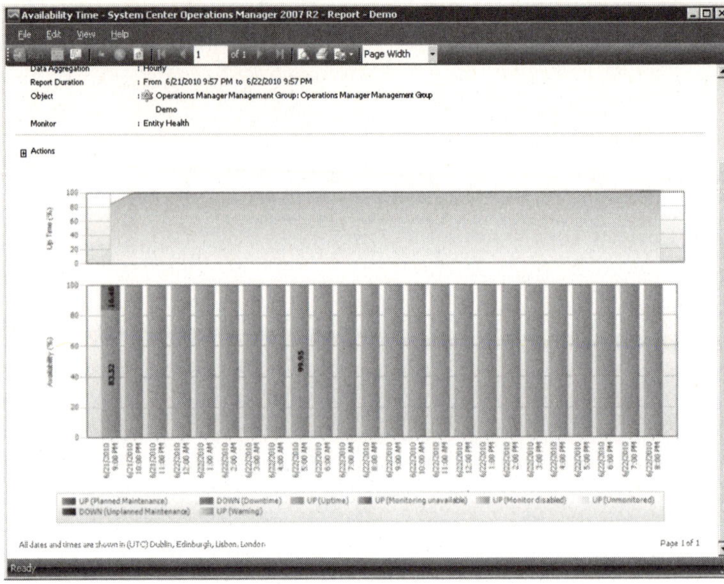

FIGURE 9.26
Availability Time report

That gives you the ability to produce reports from the gathered health and performance information. You'll be able to use these reports to analyze issues. Performance analysis and future sizing can be performed accurately using past and current performance metrics combined with future plans.

VMM Reporting

There is more to managing a virtualization infrastructure than health and performance analysis. The data that OpsMgr gathers, combined with VMM's knowledge of the infrastructure, allows for some reporting of resource utilization by your Hyper-V hosts and virtual machines. Figure 9.27 shows that you can run these System Center Virtualization 2008 R2 reports in the Reporting view.

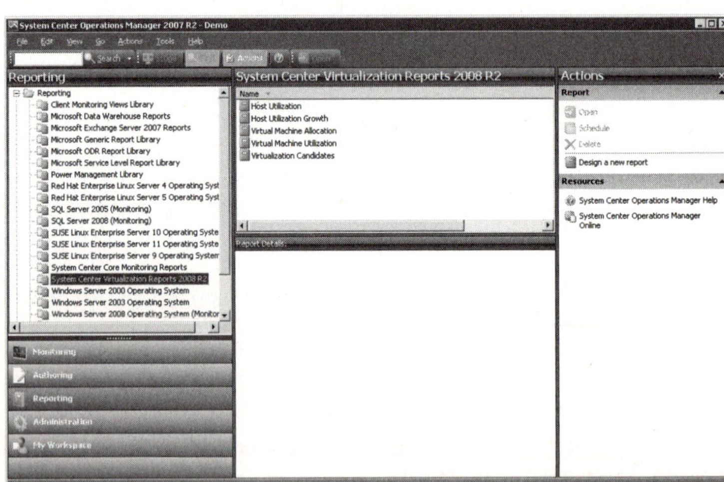

FIGURE 9.27
Virtualization reports in OpsMgr

As a VMM administrator, you might prefer to run these reports in the VMM administrator console. We saw a little earlier how to configure this integration. You can click Open Report from the Actions pane in VMM to launch one of the five reports that are provided.

Host Utilization This report will allow you to view the utilization of selected host server or servers. In Figure 9.28 you can see that you will have to type in the name of the host servers to include in the report. Place each server name, as OpsMgr knows it, on each line.

FIGURE 9.28
Specifying the host servers

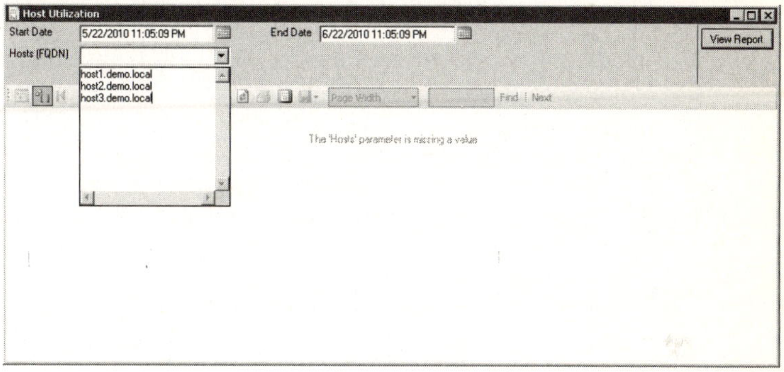

The report, in Figure 9.29, will be generated when you click the View Report button.

FIGURE 9.29
The Host Utilization report

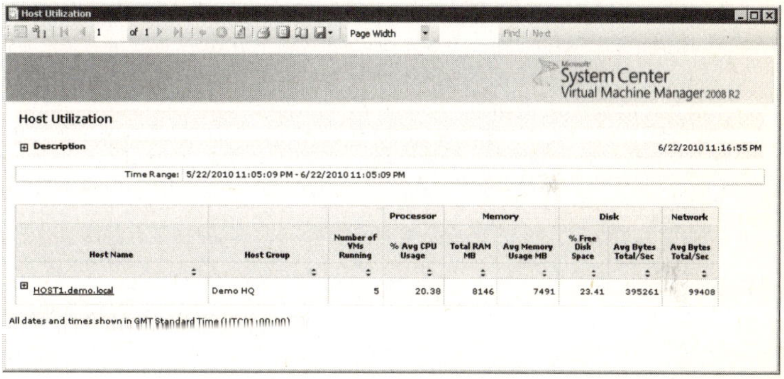

You can click the plus button to the left of the host server's computer name to get some analysis of the resource utilization by the virtual machines on that host server. This will allow you to see how the virtual machines impacted the information in the report.

Host Utilization Growth This report allows you to specify two time frames instead of one. This allows the report to analyze how resource utilization of the host has changed between those time frames.

Virtual Machine Allocation This report will allow you to determine what resources have been reserved for all your VMM managed virtual machines. It is a summary report, providing just the total amounts.

Virtual Machine Utilization This report will allow you to assess how each of your VMM managed virtual machines is using the resources that have been reserved for them. You can use this report to resize virtual machines according to their real needs. The data provided is for each and every virtual machine.

Virtualization Candidates We looked at this report in Chapter 4 when we looked at how to assess a server infrastructure to identify physical machines that would be converted into virtual machines.

Performance and Resource Optimization

The integration of Operations Manager 2007 with Virtual Machine Manager 2008 R2 gives you one of the more powerful features of the Hyper-V virtualization solution. PRO is a solution that allows OpsMgr to detect an issue, which will then lead to actions by VMM to move virtual machines to adjust to that issue.

We're going to look at what PRO is, how it works, how to enable it, and how to extend PRO to include third-party products, and not just the default Microsoft ones.

What Is PRO?

PRO is a mechanism that takes advantage of the abilities of VMM and OpsMgr as stand-alone products and combines them to give a more complete management solution. OpsMgr is a fine solution for detecting health and performance issues. VMM is a fine solution for managing the placement of virtual machines onto the most suitable host servers. PRO allows OpsMgr to use specialist management packs, called PRO management packs, to detect issues that are specific to a virtualized environment. OpsMgr will use the integration with VMM to inform it of the issue. VMM can then respond to this PRO tip by relocating the affected virtual machine(s) to more suitable host servers. This decision-making process will be driven by VMM's Intelligent Placement algorithms.

Microsoft provides a set of default management packs. These are imported into OpsMgr for you when you integrate it with VMM. The management packs that are imported are as follows:

- System Center Virtual Machine Manager 2008 R2 PRO Host Performance
- System Center Virtual Machine Manager 2008 R2 PRO Library
- System Center Virtual Machine Manager 2008 R2 PRO Virtual Machine Right Sizing
- System Center Virtual Machine Manager 2008 R2 PRO VMware Host Performance

You are not hallucinating; you did just read that the VMM OpsMgr integration will bring PRO to VMM-managed VMware host servers. Five classes of object are monitored by default:

- Hyper-V hosts
- Virtual Server hosts
- VMware ESX Server hosts
- Virtual machines
- VMM server

The PRO functionality that is provided by default is actually quite basic. It can be extended using third-party and custom-written solutions. Microsoft decided to focus on virtual machine and host performance.

For host machines, the PRO management packs will monitor host CPU utilization and memory utilization. Table 9.1 shows the monitors that are included.

TABLE 9.1: Host PRO monitors

MONITOR	THRESHOLD	SAMPLING INTERVAL	CALCULATION METHOD
Memory Utilization	Physical memory minus host reserve value	Every 60 seconds	Average of last three samples
CPU Utilization	100 percent minus host reserve value	Every 60 seconds	Average of last three samples

The VMM 2008 PRO management packs used simple thresholds such as 90 percent for the host memory utilization monitor. VMM 2008 R2 uses the administrator-managed host reserve values, which are configured in VMM either at the host level or at the host group level.

The use of host reserves allows you to squeeze more out of a host server in a more intelligent way. With a typical server, we usually don't want to see high utilization rates of memory. However, we do want to see this in well-sized hardware virtualization host servers. If you purchased a host with 144 GB of RAM, then 90 percent utilization would give you just 129.6 GB of utilized memory. That would leave you with 14.4 GB of wasted RAM. OpsMgr would have raise alerts once you passed 90 percent utilization of memory, even though everything was actually OK.

With VMM 2008 R2, you can specify a 512 MB host reserve for the memory. The host might use 2 GB. Between the host utilization and the reserve, you now have 141.5 GB of RAM that is available before OpsMgr becomes concerned. This means OpsMgr will raise an alert only once you reach a point on that host where the host reserve is being encroached upon. In other words, OpsMgr and VMM 2008 R2 will do something only when host or virtual machine performance are at risk, rather than use some rule-of-thumb that doesn't suit hardware virtualization.

There are also two virtual machine monitors for memory and CPU utilization. These are shown in Table 9.2.

TABLE 9.2: Virtual machine PRO monitors

MONITOR	THRESHOLD	SAMPLING INTERVAL	CALCULATION METHOD
Memory Utilization	90 percent	Every 60 seconds	Average of last three samples
CPU Utilization	90 percent	Every 60 seconds	Average of last three samples

You are dealing with a more traditional situation when you gather metrics for individual virtual machine performance. You want to know when there are capacity issues within the assigned resources of a virtual machine. The CPU and RAM utilization metrics are assessed every 60 seconds. An alert is raised when the average of the last three samples exceeds the threshold of 90 percent.

How PRO Works

We'll use a scenario to discuss how PRO works. Figure 9.30 shows a network with a Hyper-V cluster, consisting of four nodes, Host 1 to Host 4. A virtual machine is running on Host 1. OpsMgr agents are deployed to all machines, physical and virtual, in the infrastructure. VMM is managing the Hyper-V cluster, thus meaning that it manages the host servers and the virtual machines.

FIGURE 9.30
A PRO-enabled Hyper-V infrastructure

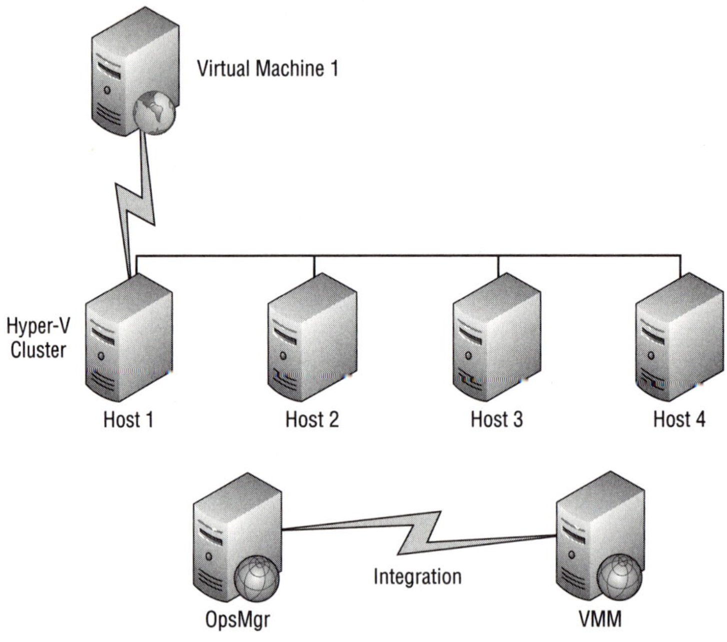

PRO has been enabled and configured in VMM to respond automatically to PRO alerts that are raised by OpsMgr. So far, all is well on the Hyper-V cluster, and there is no need for OpsMgr or VMM to do much.

In Figure 9.31, you can see that a PRO management pack has detected an issue on Host 1. This issue will start to impact the performance or availability of virtual machines on the host, namely, Virtual Machine 1.

VMM is made aware of the issue via the integration with OpsMgr. VMM's response will be to move the affected virtual machine(s). As you can see in Figure 9.32, VMM has issued an instruction to perform a Live Migration of Virtual Machine 1 from Host 1 to Host 3. Intelligent Placement was used to find the most suitable host server. This combines performance metrics of the host and of the virtual machine to find the highest rated host server.

FIGURE 9.31
OpsMgr detects a PRO management pack issue.

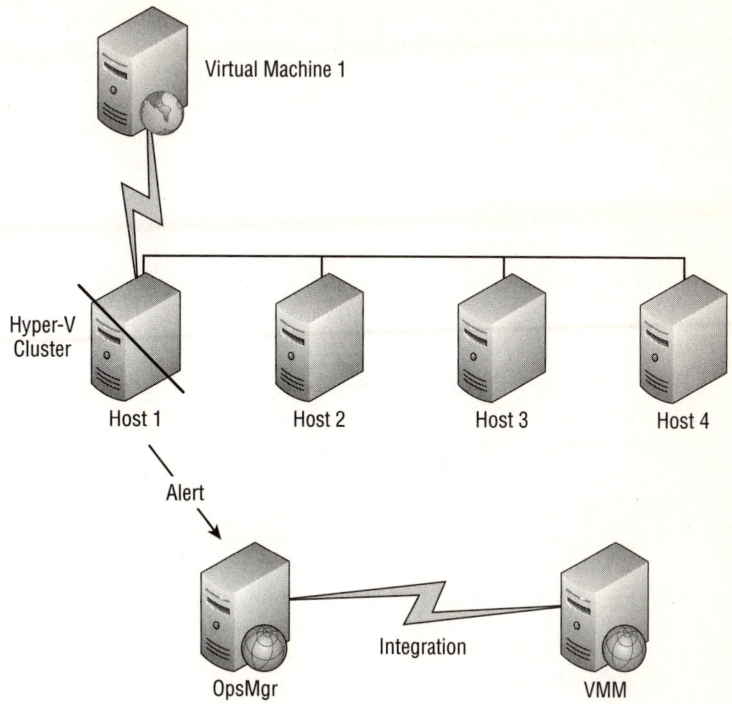

FIGURE 9.32
VMM intelligently relocates the virtual machine.

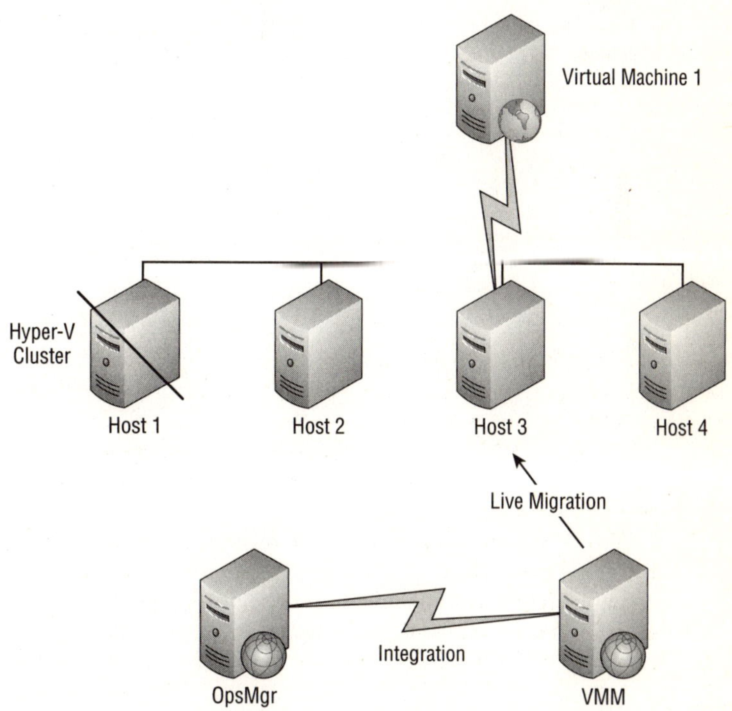

Microsoft started talking about the concept of dynamic IT a number of years ago. The idea that they proposed was that intelligent automation would be built into the network. This would detect issues and respond to them appropriately. This automated response would be much faster than we humans could do.

The scenario we just went through would be completed by VMM in a matter of seconds. What would happen if you had no PRO and this issue occurred at 3 a.m. on a Sunday morning? It could be an hour or more before a human was woken up, connected to the corporate network, analyzed the issue, and resolved it, maybe after trying a few other things.

In our scenario, PRO has dealt with the issue in a matter of seconds by using scientific valuations to identify the issue and for implementing the solution. I think that we can safely say that dynamic IT has arrived.

Enabling and Configuring PRO

The first step to enabling PRO is to install the integration between VMM and OpsMgr. We've already discussed that topic. The next step is to enable it in VMM. That's actually a subject we addressed in Chapter 7, "Virtual Machine Manager 2008 R2," when we covered Virtual Machine Manager 2008 R2, but it is worth returning to because of the value of the subject.

PRO must be enabled in a host group in VMM. You can enable it at the top-level host group (All Hosts), or you can enable it on child host groups. Child host groups can be configured to inherit the PRO settings from parent host groups. This allows you to target your PRO operations appropriately for the host servers in your infrastructure.

Figure 9.33 shows the PRO tab in a host group's properties. There are a series of nested settings.

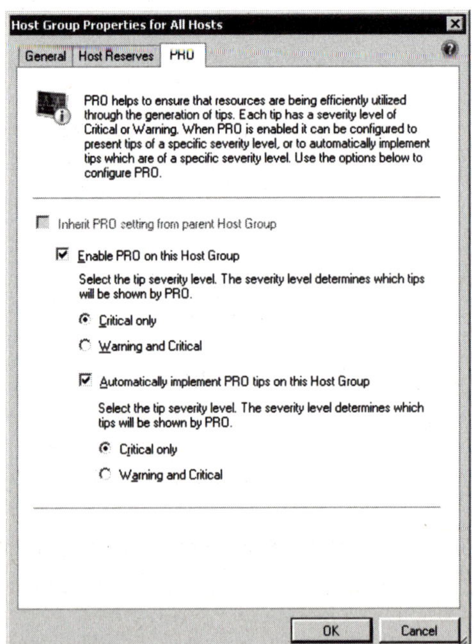

FIGURE 9.33
Configuring PRO settings

Inherit PRO Setting From Parent Host Group This setting when enabled will force the current host group to inherit whatever PRO settings apply to the parent host group. Enabling this check box will gray out the other settings on this tab.

Enable PRO On This Host Group This is pretty self-explanatory. Selecting this box will turn PRO on for all the host servers contained within this host group. With PRO enabled, the other options in the tab become available for configuration.

Enabled For Critical Only Or Warning And Critical OpsMgr will create PRO alerts with either a critical or a lower warning severity level. You can configure PRO to react only to critical events or to react to both warning and critical events. This choice is a balance between achieving optimum performance for the virtual machines and trying to reduce VMM workloads and virtual machine movement across hosts. Remember that virtual machines are being moved using Live Migration so there is no downtime in a normal migration.

Automatically Implement PRO Tips On This Host Group Enabling this feature will allow VMM to automatically remediate any issue detected by a PRO management pack. In other words, will VMM move virtual machines automatically in response to an alert? If you enable PRO and you do not enable this feature, then VMM will require manual intervention to implement a PRO tip. A window will appear if you are logged into the VMM administration console. The PRO tip will be displayed and will await a human response to decide what to do with it.

Almost every organization will implement an automated response to PRO tips if they enable the feature. A human response will typically be too slow. Even the most attentive operator may not notice the notification for several minutes. By then the issue may have already affected business operations and have ended naturally, and any PRO tip implementation will be too late.

Implement for Critical Only Or Warning And Critical You can decide whether VMM automatically responds to critical PRO events only or to both critical and warning events.

You may have scenarios where you need mixed PRO configurations. Some host groups may need PRO enabled, and some may need PRO disabled. Some may need fully automated responses, some may need critical-only automated responses, and some may need manual responses. You can accomplish this by placing host servers into different host groups. You can then apply your PRO policy as required. Just remember that a Hyper-V cluster appears as a single object (with nested servers) in VMM and can reside in only one host group. This may force you to implement multiple clusters if you require different policies for different hosts.

Extending PRO Functionality

The PRO management packs that are provided by Microsoft deal with performance. This is a very important subject, but this is a rather limited implementation of what is possible. It is possible to extend PRO to detect and respond to more issues.

Writing and Customizing PRO Management Packs

A PRO management pack is a type of OpsMgr management pack. Microsoft has provided some documentation on the process of writing management packs. Unfortunately, it isn't great. In fact, many OpsMgr veterans have found that writing a completely bespoke management pack is out of their reach and resort to purchasing third-party solutions or contracting in the required skills.

Microsoft has also provided a document on writing PRO management packs. This is available at `http://go.microsoft.com/fwlink/?LinkId=162654`.

Despite that unfortunate news, it is not too difficult to customize a management pack. This process is known as creating an *override*.

BEST PRACTICES FOR MANAGEMENT PACK OVERRIDES

An override to a management pack must be saved into a management pack. The best practice is to create an override management pack for each imported management pack. This means that you can upgrade your management packs and retain your overrides. It also allows you to easily find overrides at a later point. It's also handy to know that management packs can be exported and imported. This means you can potentially create overrides once and reuse them many times.

There are two ways to initiate an override. One is to wait for an alert to appear in the OpsMgr Operations Console. You can right-click it and override it. The other way is to go into the Authoring view of the OpsMgr Operations Console, find the monitor in question, and override it before an alert is raised.

We're going to preemptively override a monitor in the Authoring view after a request from the virtualization administrators. We have opened up the OpsMgr console in Figure 9.34 and browsed to Management Pack Objects ➢ Monitors.

FIGURE 9.34
All available monitors

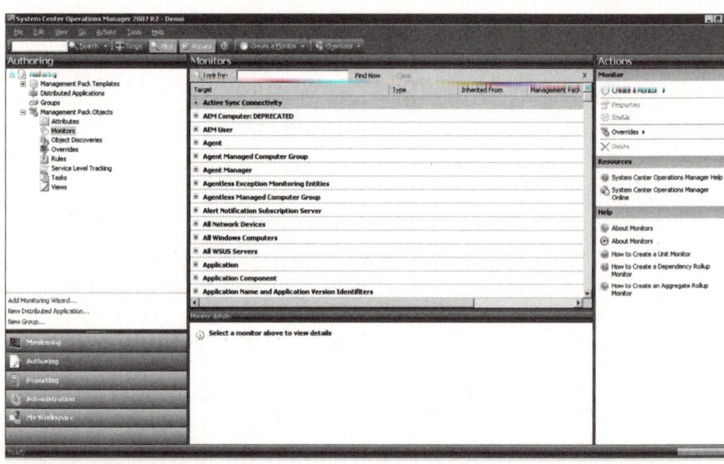

All the monitors from all the management packs are visible. That's a little overwhelming, so we will change the scope of the view to only include the desired PRO management pack monitors.

You can do that by clicking the Scope button, which is located just under the menus. That opens the dialog box that is depicted in Figure 9.35. You can type **PRO** into the Look For text box to reduce the possible number of management packs that are available to select. We will select only the System Center Virtual Machine Manager 2008 R2 management packs with the word *PRO* in the target name.

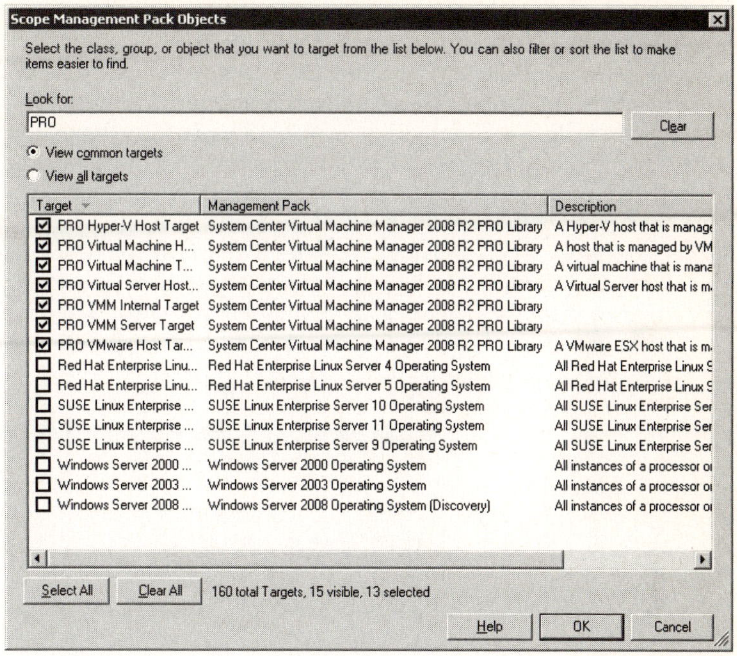

FIGURE 9.35
Changing the scope of the viewed monitors

The OpsMgr Operations Console view is refreshed to show you only the PRO management packs.

We are going to customize the PRO CPU thresholds for virtual machines. We have browsed to PRO Virtual Machine target in Figure 9.36 and expanded it to reveal Entity ➤ Performance. Here you can see a number of individual monitors. Pay careful attention to the Management Pack column. Some of these monitors apply to VMM 2008, and some apply to VMM 2008 R2. We are working with VMM 2008 R2, so we will not touch the VMM 2008 monitors.

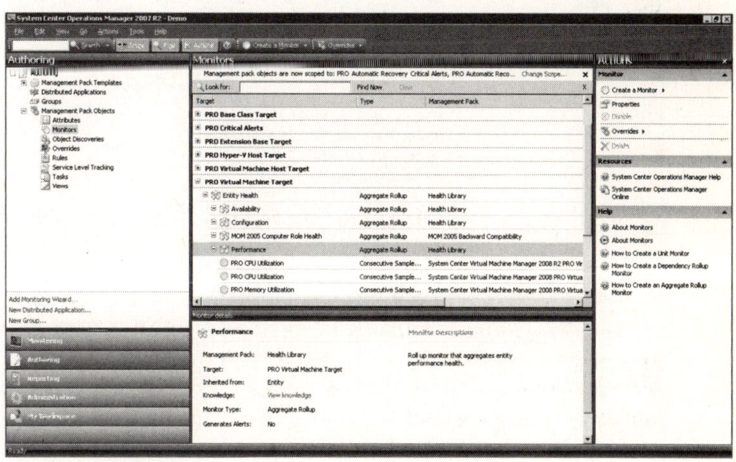

FIGURE 9.36
Browsing through the PRO monitors

Select the PRO CPU Utilization monitor from the System Center Virtual Machine Manager 2008 R2 PRO Virtual Machine Right-Sizing management pack. You can create an override for it by right-clicking and selecting Overrides ➤ Override The Monitor. The menu expands into a number of options. These options are context sensitive and determine the granularity of the override. In other words, do you want the override to apply to all objects of this type, to a specific object, or maybe to a group of objects? You may also notice the option Disable The Monitor. This will turn the monitor off for the selected object or objects. We will override the monitor for all objects of the class.

This opens an Override Properties dialog box. You're not going to override anything yet. The new override will need to be saved into a management pack. You should not use the Default management pack. The best practice is that you create and use an override management pack for this management pack. You can search for one by expanding the drop-down list box at the bottom of the dialog box (Figure 9.37).

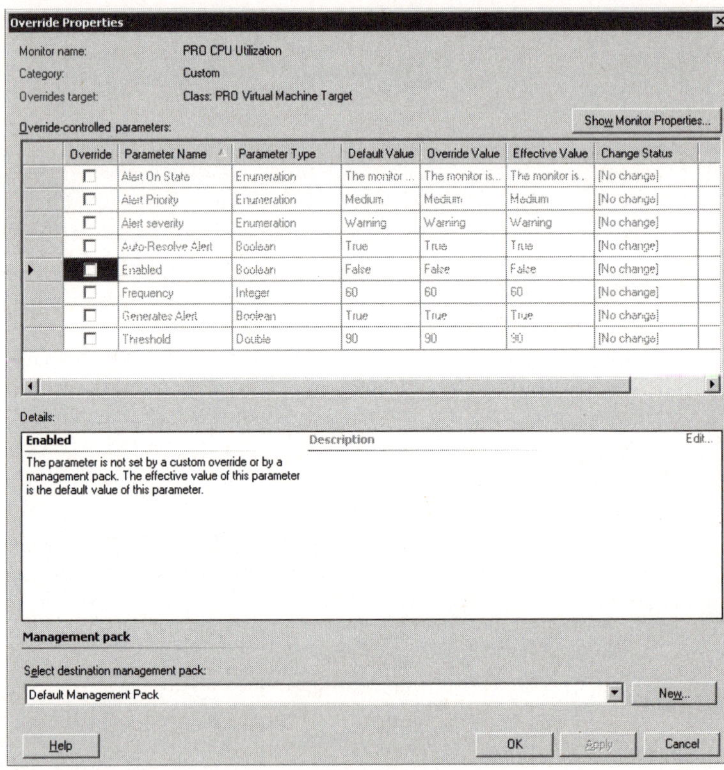

FIGURE 9.37
The unconfigured override properties

Click the New button if you do not find a suitable management pack. You should name the new management pack in a suitable manner so that it is obviously related to the management pack that its contents will override. You can see an example of this in Figure 9.38. Save the new management, and return to the Overrides Properties dialog box where you can select the new management pack as the destination management pack (the place to save the override).

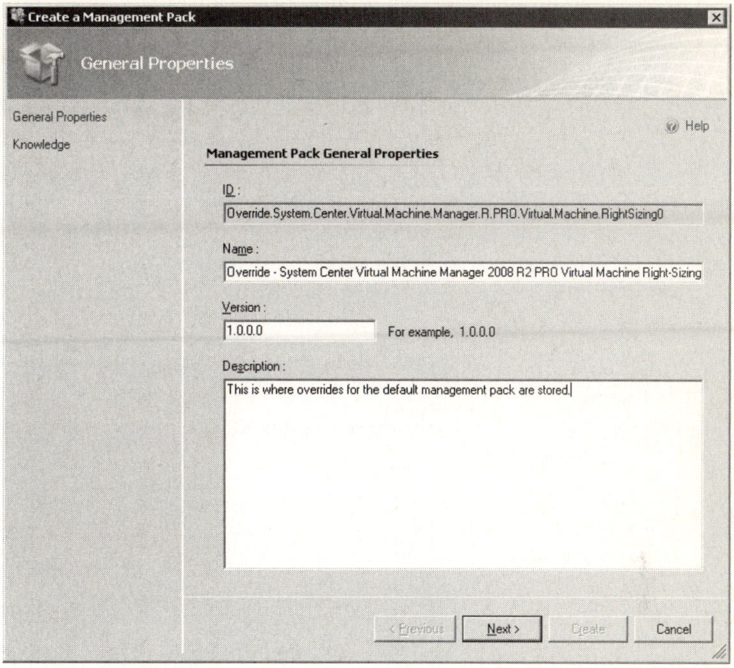

FIGURE 9.38: Creating an override management pack

Now you can override the monitor. You do this by changing the Override Value of the required parameter. The Default Value shows what is normally used. We have reduced the CPU threshold from 90 percent to 85 percent in Figure 9.39.

Save everything by clicking OK, and now your override is implemented. Alerts for virtual machine CPU utilization will be triggered at 85 percent instead of the default 90 percent.

You can view the overrides by right-clicking the monitor (in the Authoring view) and selecting Overrides Summary.

You've done all that hard work to install VMM and OpsMgr, integrate them, configure PRO, and customize it. How do you know that it is working? That's a common question, and we have an answer. We'll look at how you can test PRO in a little while.

THIRD-PARTY FUNCTIONALITY

Microsoft reached out to its partners during the development of VMM 2008 for Windows Server 2008 Hyper-V. A number of software and hardware manufacturers responded by creating third-party PRO management packs. Each of them brings the same core concept to a Hyper-V implementation. OpsMgr will detect an issue, and VMM will perform some action to remediate the issue. Some examples of solutions are as follows:

Hardware PRO Tips Windows Failover Clustering will initiate the failover of a virtual machine from one clustered Hyper-V host server to another only when there is a heartbeat failure between clustered hosts. What if there is a networking issue that affects virtual machines but not the cluster? The virtual machine will go offline and stay offline until an operator sees the alert and initiates a manual Live Migration of the virtual machine.

PRO management packs for hardware can solve this issue. A normal (well-written) hardware management pack will detect degraded memory, high temperatures, and failed network cards. A hardware PRO management pack has this same potential. This means that a failed network that is used for Hyper-V virtual networks can initiate a PRO alert. The virtual machines will be moved from that host to a redundant host in the cluster using Live Migration. The down-time (because of the network card failure) will be limited to a few seconds before OpsMgr and VMM team to resolve the application outage. Administrators can then place the host into VMM maintenance mode and perform a repair.

FIGURE 9.39
Creating the override

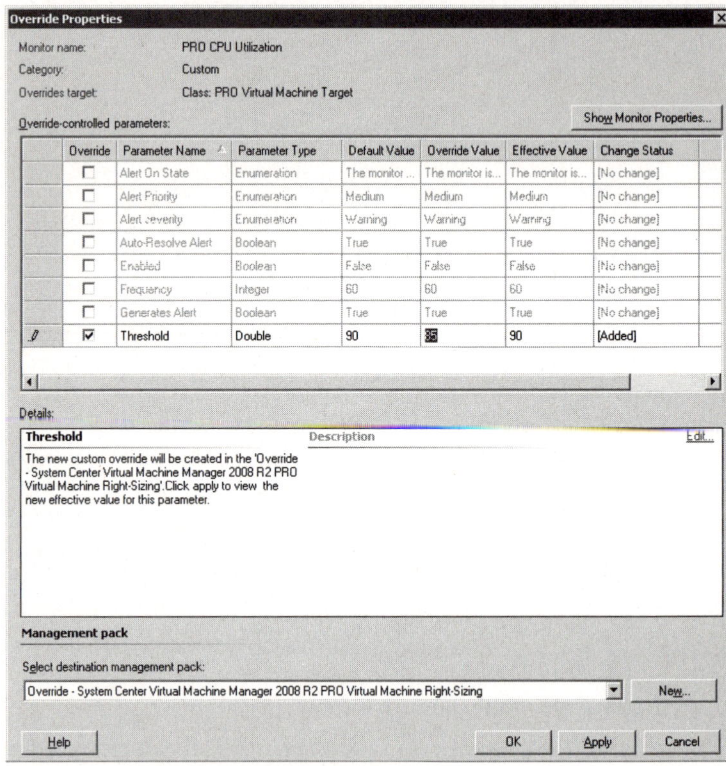

How Important Is System Center to You?

As we've stated, many organizations will be implementing a systems management solution and not a virtualization solution when they deploy Hyper-V. They are making a conscious decision to base their IT systems management on Microsoft's System Center family. For those organizations that want to make the most from System Center, it makes sense to make server and storage purchasing decisions based on the manufacturer's ability to provide management packs. Make sure you choose carefully when OpsMgr and PRO are things that you want to be able to implement fully. Some hardware manufacturers have committed fully to the Microsoft strategy, developing freely available management packs for OpsMgr and for PRO. Unfortunately, some others have not made the same effort, despite their reputation in enterprise computing.

Don't believe the salesperson; ask for the download links for the management packs and to see a working implementation of the solution before you make any purchasing decisions.

Storage PRO Tips This is one of the more clever possibilities. A clustered Hyper-V host server will usually have some form of iSCSI or Fibre Channel host bus adapter (HBA). Some of the Fibre Channel HBA vendors have produced management packs for their hardware. This now allows virtualization performance monitoring and virtual machine placement to take storage connectivity performance and availability into account. For example, virtual machine performance will be reduced on a host if the host server's storage connection is congested. OpsMgr can detect this with the third-party PRO management pack, and VMM can relocate virtual machines using Live Migration to address the issue.

Microsoft maintains a catalog of third-party PRO management packs here:

`http://www.microsoft.com/systemcenter/en/us/virtual-machine-manager/vmm-pro-partners.aspx`

Here you will find a variety of different solutions, some of which are free and some that require an additional purchase.

Testing PRO

Anything new that you implement should be tested before it is put into production. This stuff can be fun to play with as well. Once you do have working tests, it might not be a bad idea to do a quick little presentation with some of your superiors to show them what you've implemented.

These tests will require some software to consume massive amounts of CPU and memory. Find a tool that can do this, and you can start.

Ideally you will have a number of test hosts in an isolated VMM host group. This will allow you to enable PRO on this test host group without turning it on in your production environment. Enable it, and then you can start testing.

Deploy a number of virtual machines to a clustered Hyper-V host server. First you can perform some CPU tests:

- Force up CPU utilization in one virtual machine.
- Force up CPU utilization in all virtual machines on the host.

Then do some memory testing.

- Force up the memory utilization of a virtual machine to 100 percent.
- Force up the memory utilization of a host server so that the host reserve is consumed.

Each of these tests should initiate alerts and PRO tips, causing virtual machines to be relocated.

The Bottom Line

Understand the functionality of Operations Manager Operations Manager (OpsMgr) has a number of components to monitor the health and performance of an infrastructure.

Master It You are working as a consultant. A client has asked for a solution for monitoring their Hyper-V infrastructure. They need to be able to manage Windows and Red Hat Enterprise Linux virtual machines, detect performance issues, detect hardware faults, and produce long-term reports. What can you tell them about how OpsMgr can meet the client's requirements?

Integrate Operations Manager with Virtual Machine Manager It is possible to integrate OpsMgr with VMM. This integrates management and provides additional functionality.

Master It What are the prerequisites for integrating VMM with OpsMgr?

Understand and configure PRO The integration of OpsMgr and VMM allows you to implement Performance and Resource Optimization (PRO). This allows VMM to automatically respond to issues detected by OpsMgr PRO management packs.

Master It Your team leader has asked you to design a Hyper-V infrastructure with VMM and OpsMgr. There will be nine Hyper-V hosts. Three will be for production servers, three will be for software development, and three will be for testing. Your team leader would like it if you could build a single Hyper-V cluster. PRO must be configured with automation for all alerts for production host servers, enabled but with a manual response on the development hosts, and disabled on the testing hosts. How will you respond to the team leader and deploy the infrastructure?

Chapter 10

Data Protection and Recovery

Data protection and recovery is a very specialized skill, which is often carried out by dedicated storage experts. This is even more applicable in a virtualized environment because data protection and recovery adds an additional level of complexity into the mix when you're designing your virtualized infrastructure.

When you are considering how you will ultimately protect your environment, you will need to consider a total protection strategy.

Data protection is now required at potentially two levels. The first is at the host level, and this may be because you are solely responsible for the infrastructure and not the applications that run within those virtual machines. The second is that the application-specific data residing inside that virtual machine may need a level of protection.

The most widely used approach to protecting data in virtualized environments is placing a backup agent inside the virtual machine. This is the standard approach that is used within the physical world today.

The backup agent is often application-aware, communicating to the application being protected that a backup or restore is taking place. But what impact does this have when this backup agent runs within a virtual machine?

The agent consumes system resources just as it did in the physical world. The difference now is that in a virtualized environment all virtual machines residing on that host can be potentially impacted by the backup process. The standard of a consistent workload is broken, and the physical server hosting the virtual machines is also impacted.

In this chapter, we will discuss backing up hosts, backing up clusters, and the forgotten subject of backing up System Center Virtual Machine Manager.

In this chapter, you will learn to

- Use the inbox backup tool, Windows Server Backup
- Understand what the backup options are in a virtualized environment
- Use Data Protection Manager to protect virtual workloads

An Overview of Hyper-V Backup

Windows Server 2008 R2 provides a built-in data protection solution called Windows Server Backup (WSB). Windows Server Backup uses the inbox VSS writers in Windows Server 2008 R2 and can therefore perform a block-level backup and restore.

> **BLOCK-LEVEL BACKUP**
>
> A block-level backup essentially is an entire backup of a disk and is in contrast to a file-level backup. A block-level backup means you get an image of the entire disk!

Windows Server Backup provides some of the normal protection and recovery features of an enterprise backup program. In addition, Windows Server Backup can be extended to support protection and recovery at an application level, if the application provides a VSS-compatible writer.

Hyper-V and the virtual machines running on Hyper-V can be protected and recovered by using System Center Data Protection Manager or a third-party application written to work with the Hyper-V VSS writer. However, Windows Server Backup cannot be used to back up and restore individual virtual machines running on Hyper-V. Windows Server Backup can be used only to protect and recover the host itself.

> **VSS WRITER**
>
> The VSS writer is the component that guarantees a consistent data set to back up. This is typically provided as part of the application that you are protecting. A VSS writer for Hyper-V offers basic protection and is included with Windows Server 2008 R2.

If the virtual machine contains its own protection and recovery application as part of the installed operating system or via a third-party installed component, it can be leveraged to protect the virtual machine. The virtual machine's protected data can be located on another mounted virtual hard disk in the virtual machine or on a network location, provided the virtual machine has access to the physical network.

Protection and Recovery Concepts

In its most basic form, a backup is a copy of a file. You create a backup in case the original file is lost or somehow corrupted. Backing up data is admittedly a routine and very repetitive task, and you might have more critical tasks to carry out, but once you have a backup schedule and proven recovery procedure in place, it really shouldn't take much time to maintain.

One of the first tasks is to determine what the business requirements are for protection and recovery. Next you need to determine exactly what information you need to protect, and finally you need to determine how often you need to carry out a backup. This essentially comes down to deciding what you and your company can afford to lose. There, of course, is no one-size-fits-all answer to this question, so it is impossible to provide a single quantifiable answer.

DEFINING THE BUSINESS REQUIREMENTS

When defining your business requirements, here is a list of some of the things you should consider:

- What is your current data protection policy, and how can this policy be applied to your virtual environment?
- What backup application do you use today, and does it provide full support for Hyper-V R2?
- What production applications do you intend to run inside your virtual machines?
- How many virtual machines do you intend to run on average per physical host?
- How many Hyper-V hosts do you intend to implement as part of this project?
- How many physical locations require data protection, and do you intend to replicate data to an alternative location?
- What data storage medium do you intend to use? Will disk, tape, or the Cloud be used as a target for protecting your data?
- What is your recovery point objective (RPO)? This is the maximum acceptable loss of data measured in time (hours/days).
- What is your recovery time objective (RTO)? This is the time to restore operations for different levels of events, such as after a disruption, incident, or disaster.

You may need to prioritize which systems you protect, in terms of the order in which you back them up and the frequency you back them up. Most of this will be governed by the type of service level you have in place with the business you are supporting.

Finally, you may need to consider any regulatory or legal constraints placed upon you by the type of company you work for, which will impact your requirements for retention and how recovered data is restored and accessed.

There will be various stakeholders to consult with. A good place to start with would be the application owner, who will help you define the business requirements; the application support owner, who will explain any technical requirements; the legal department, who will define any legal requirements that need to be put in place; and the auditor/compliance officer, who will need to review the overall solution for compliance to applicable auditing standards.

Backup Terminology

There are four backup types: full or initial backup, incremental, differential, and selective. Plus there are two backup strategies: host-level or guest-level backups. Each is useful and applicable in its own right. However, the particular kinds of backups available to you will likely depend on the backup software you deploy.

FULL BACKUP

A full backup consists of a copy of your entire system. Typical components include your operating system, which includes components such as the registry, device drivers and settings, the applications you have installed, and all of your data.

Of the four types of backups, this one takes the longest to create, but it has the distinct benefit of restoring your system to its exact state at the time you created it. After you have the full backup, you'll most likely want to switch to another backup type. The choice you make will really come down to how much storage you have at your disposal, as well as how much time you have to back up your system.

Incremental and Differential Backup

Incremental and differential backups are very similar to one another in that both only make copies of the files that have changed since the last time you ran your full backup. The main difference between the two types is that differential backups do not indicate which files have changed. Because incremental and differential backups don't copy each and every file on your system, you'll find that they generally take less time to run and thus less time to recover. For small to medium businesses, differential backups might be the best option. They're much easier to deal with than their incremental counterparts. The advantage to this is the quicker recovery time, requiring only a full backup and the last differential backup to restore the system. The disadvantage is that for each day elapsed since the last full backup, more data needs to be backed up, especially if a significant proportion of the data has changed since your last full backup.

Selective Backup

With a selective backup, you effectively back up the files you'd like to protect at a given point in time. This type of backup gives you more control over what is backed up, at the expense of leaving part of the hard disk unprotected. Selective backups make sense when some files are changing much more rapidly than others or when backup space is limited, although in many cases doing a differential backup is better and easier from a tape management perspective.

Host-Level Backups

A host-level backup is the most flexible type of backup that you can perform in a virtualized environment. This is because a host-based backup will operate regardless of the operating system running in the virtual machine.

It is not possible to carry out a host-level backup either for virtual machines that have passthrough disks assigned to them or where the virtual machine connects directly to remote storage, as is the case with iSCSI, so an alternative strategy will need to be considered for protecting those specific types of virtual machines.

Guest-Level Backup

A guest-level backup is where the backup agent runs within the virtual machine, and you might use this approach to best protect the data that resides in the virtual machine. With a guest-level backup, you can selectively back up and thus selectively restore individual files.

Learning to Back Up on a Budget

Windows Server Backup is a feature in Windows Server 2008 R2, but by default it is not installed. To install Windows Server Backup so that you can configure it to support Hyper-V, you need to do the following:

1. Launch Server Manager, and select the Features node.
2. Click the Add Features option; the Add Features Wizard will launch.
3. Expand the Windows Server Backup Features node (Figure 10.1), and select Windows Server Backup. Optionally select Command-Line Tools. Click Next.

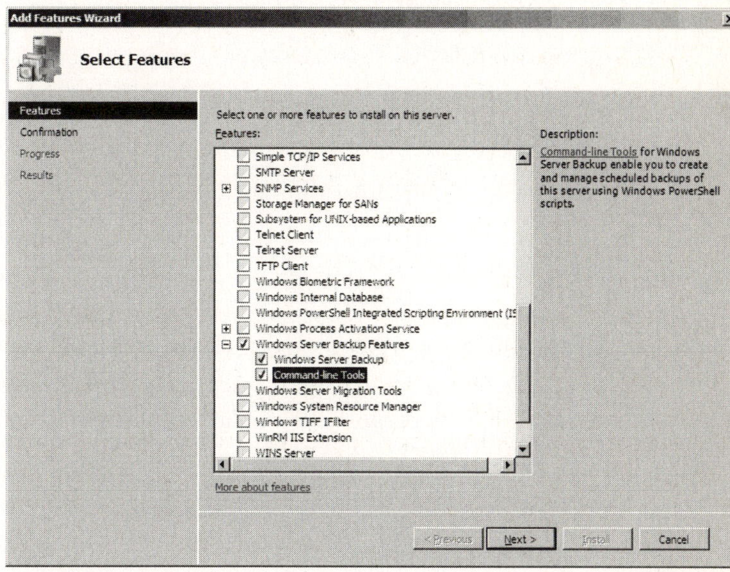

FIGURE 10.1
Add Features Wizard

4. Click Install to begin the installation.
5. Verify the successful installation of Windows Server Backup by monitoring the installation process and reviewing the Installation Results page.

Configuring Windows Server Backup for Hyper-V

Windows Server Backup can support additional VSS writers, but it does not have an ability to import or register those VSS writers; you must do this manually. When you install Windows Server Backup, it has no additional VSS writers registered. To add support for the Hyper-V VSS writer, you must create the Windows Server Backup registry locations and register the GUID for the application's VSS writer.

Registering the Hyper-V VSS Writer

To register the Hyper-V VSS writer with Windows Server Backup, follow these steps:

> **Warning: Modifying the Registry**
>
> This section includes information about modifying the registry. Modifying the registry may cause damage to your system. Proceed with caution, validate any changes in a test environment first, and always perform a backup before you make any changes.

1. Click Start ➤ Run, type **regedit**, and then click OK.
2. Locate the following registry key:

   `HKEY_LOCAL_MACHINE\SOFTWARE\Microsoft\Windows NT\CurrentVersion`
3. Right-click CurrentVersion, choose New, and then click Key.
4. Type **WindowsServerBackup**, and then press Enter.
5. Right-click WindowsServerBackup, choose New, and then click Key. Type **Application Support**, and then press Enter.
6. Right-click Application Support, choose New, and then click Key. Type **{66841CD4-6DED-4F4B-8F17-FD23F8DDC3DE}**, and then press Enter.
7. Right-click {66841CD4-6DED-4F4B-8F17-FD23F8DDC3DE}, choose New, and then click String Value. Type **Application Identifier**, and then press Enter (Figure 10.2).

Figure 10.2
Registry Editor changes

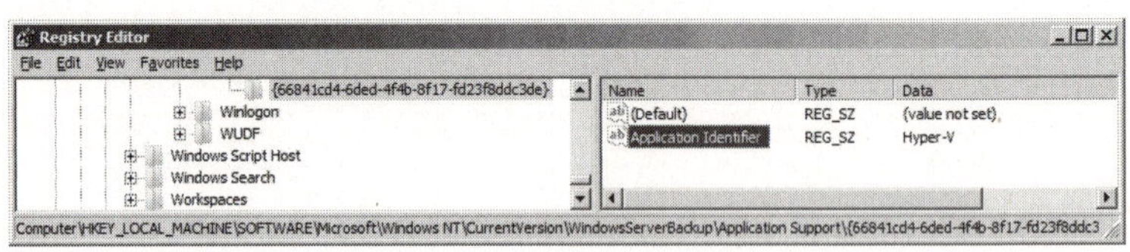

8. Right-click Application Identifier, and then click Modify. In the Value data box, type **Hyper-V**, and then click OK.
9. On the File menu, click Exit.

> **Determining Which VSS Writers Are Present**
>
> To be able to determine which VSS writers are present on your system, you can use the VSSADMIN tool to list all the currently installed writers.
>
> The command syntax is as follows:
>
> ```
> vssadmin list writers
> ```
>
> The added benefit here is that VSSADMIN will list the associated GUIDs, so you can cut and paste this long string into the registry.

Protecting Virtual Machines by Using Windows Server Backup

Before carrying out a backup, you need to identify a storage location for your backup. If you are going to use a local disk, then make sure the disk is either USB 2.0 or IEEE 1394 and is internal or attached to your host. Next you need to decide whether you are going to carry out a one-time backup or a scheduled backup. Finally, decide what you want to include in your backup schedule. To create a manual backup on an attached disk, follow these steps:

1. Click Start ➤ Administrative Tools, and then click Windows Server Backup.
2. From the Actions pane of the snap-in's default page, under Windows Server Backup, click Backup Once (as shown in Figure 10.3). This opens the Backup Once Wizard.

FIGURE 10.3 Windows Server Backup's Actions pane

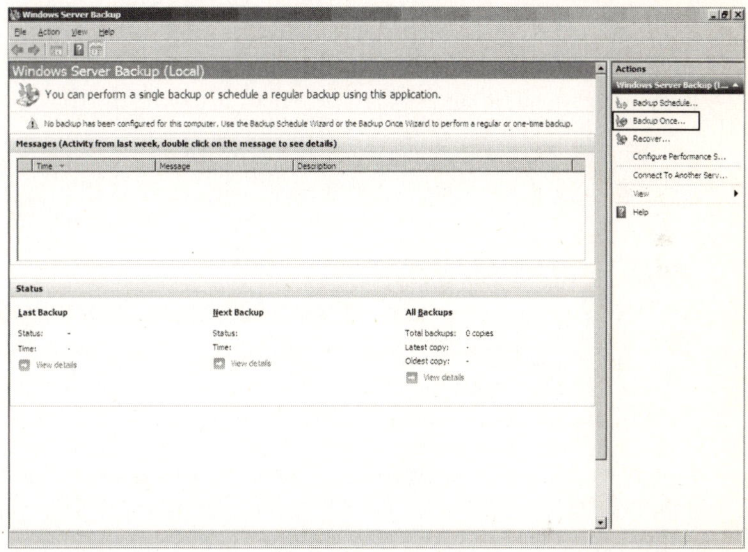

3. On the Backup Options page (Figure 10.4), leave Different Options highlighted, and then click Next.
4. On the Select Backup Configuration page (Figure 10.5), do one of the following, and then click Next:
   - Click Full Server (Recommended) to back up all volumes on the server. This is the recommended option, especially if this is your first full backup.
   - Click Custom to back up just certain items.
5. On the Select Items For Backup page, click Add Items.
6. In the Select Items dialog box (Figure 10.6), select the check boxes for the items that you want to back up. Click OK.
7. On the Select Items For Backup page (Figure 10.7), click Advanced Settings.
8. Click the Exclusions tab, click Add Exclusions, and then expand the folder tree and select any items that you want to exclude.

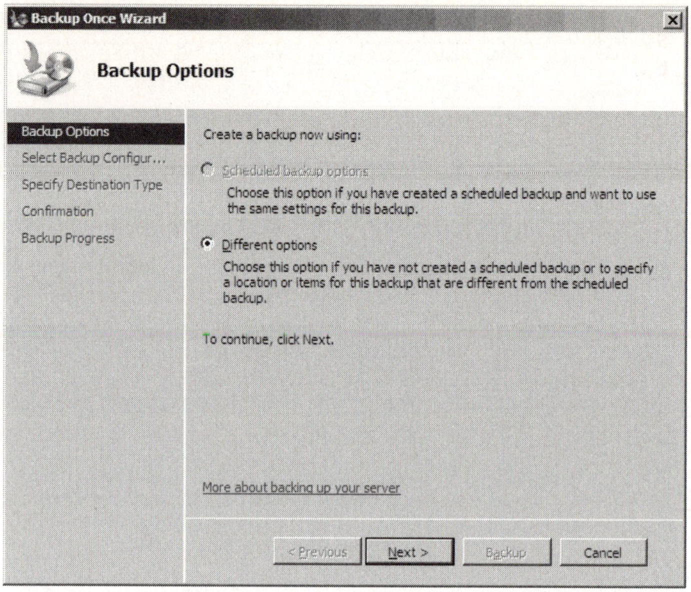

FIGURE 10.4
Backup Options page

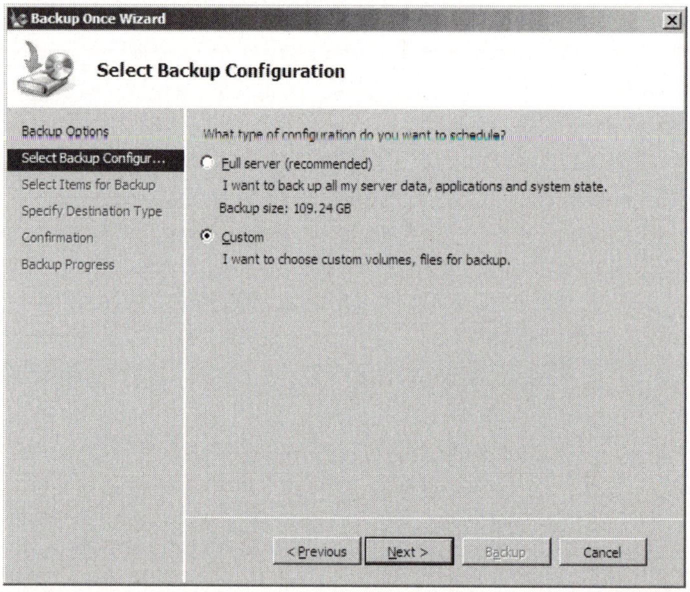

FIGURE 10.5
Select Backup Configuration page

9. On the VSS Settings tab (Figure 10.8), select either VSS Full Backup or VSS Copy Backup. Click OK, and then click Next.

FIGURE 10.6
Select Items dialog box

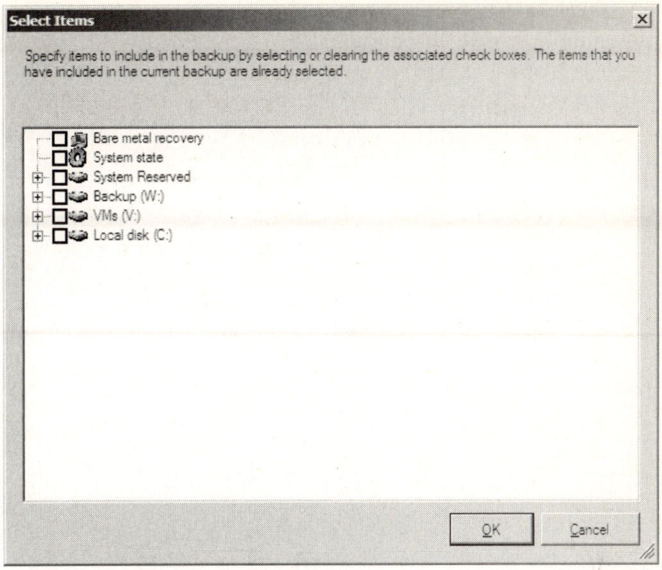

FIGURE 10.7
Select Items For Backup page

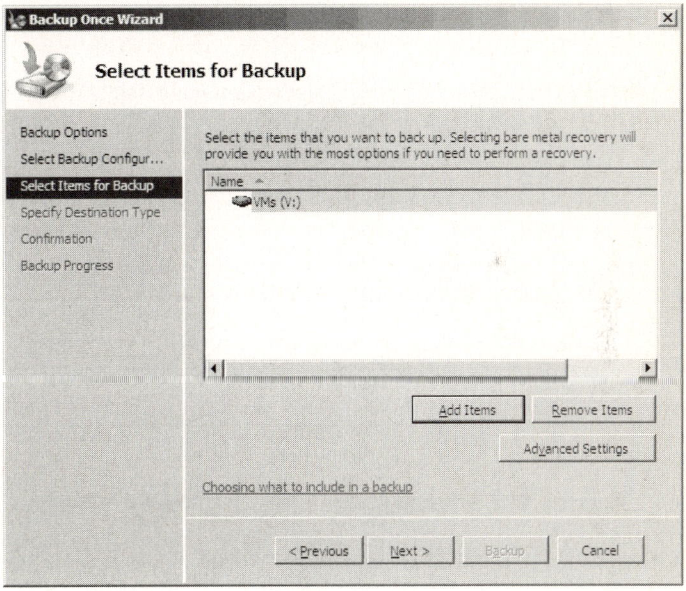

10. On the Specify Destination Type page, click Local Drives (the other option is Remote Shared Folder), and then click Next.

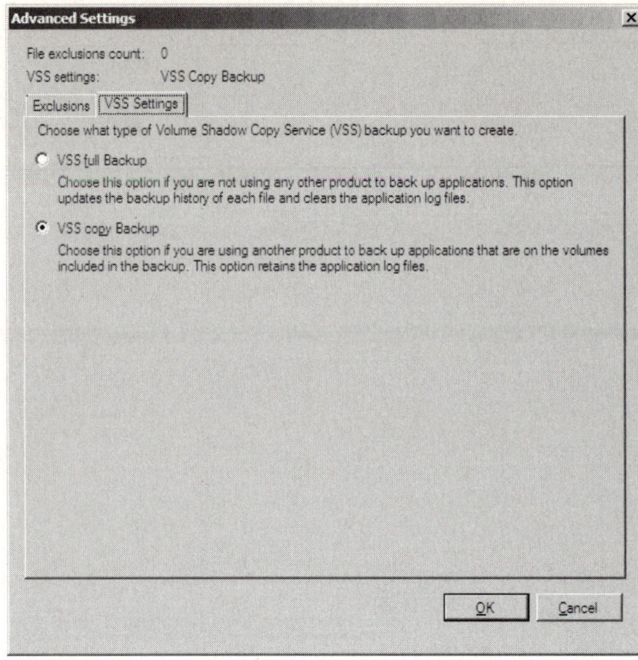

FIGURE 10.8 Advanced Settings — VSS Settings tab

11. On the Select Backup Destination page, select the destination that you want to use to store the backup from the drop-down list. If you choose a hard disk, confirm that there is enough free space on the disk before you execute the backup.
12. On the Confirmation page, review the details, and then click Backup.

> **REMOTELY MANAGING YOUR BACKUP**
>
> These tasks do not have to be carried out at the local console and can be performed remotely. To create a backup using Windows Server Backup, you must be a member of the Backup Operators or Administrators group.

Recovering Virtual Machines by Using Windows Server Backup

To recover virtual machines by using Windows Server Backup, follow these steps:

1. Start Windows Server Backup in Administrative Tools. On the Actions menu, click Recover (refer to Figure 10.3 if necessary).
2. Select the server that you want to recover data from — either This Server or A Backup Stored On Another Location — and then click Next.
3. Select the date and time that you want to restore from (Figure 10.9), and then click Next.
4. Select the application's recovery type (Figure 10.10), and then click Next.

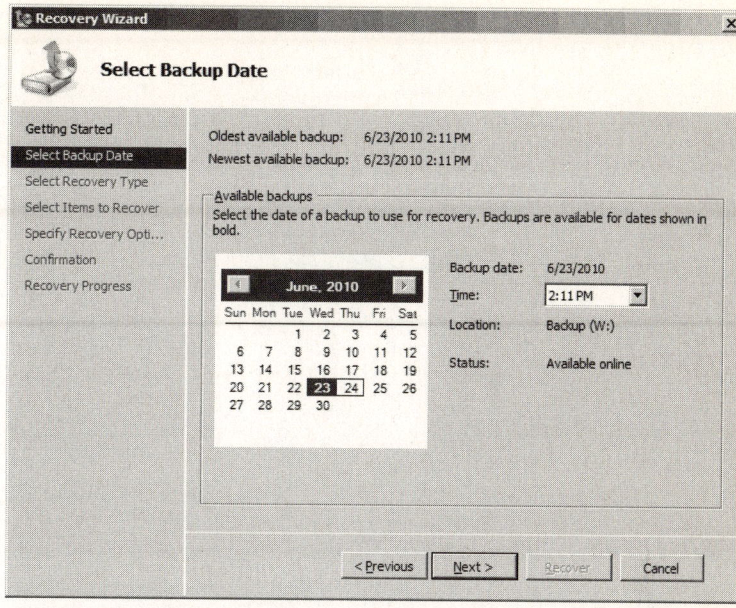

FIGURE 10.9
Select Backup Date page

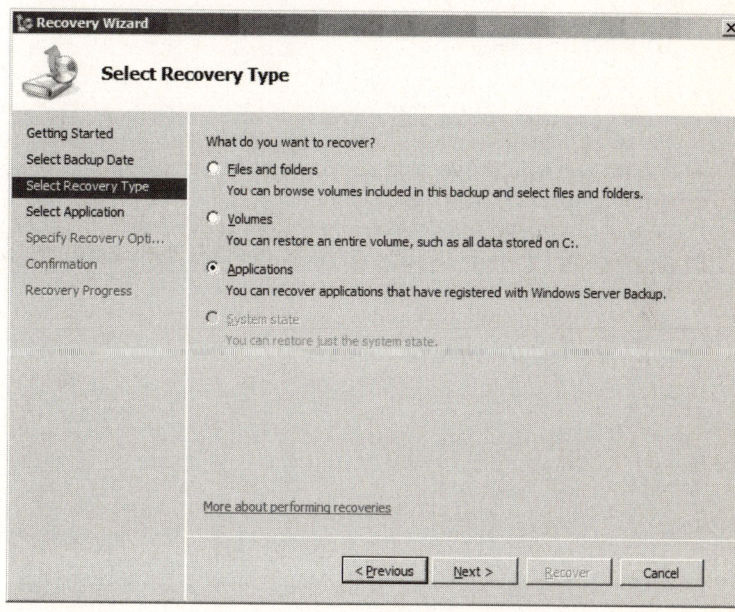

FIGURE 10.10
Selecting a recovery type

5. On the Select Application page, select Hyper-V, and then click Next.
6. Select the restore location — either Recover To Original Location or Recover To Another Location — and then click Next.
7. On the Confirmation page (Figure 10.11), click Recover to start the restore process.

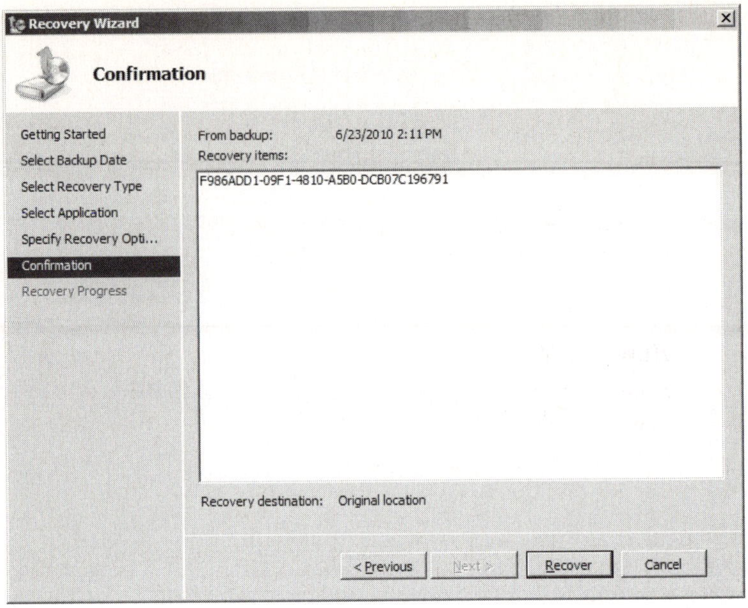

FIGURE 10.11
Confirmation page

Understanding VSS

Volume Shadow Copy Service (VSS) is a Microsoft framework that provides a backup infrastructure that was first introduced in Windows Server 2003. It produces consistent point-in-time copies of data, known as *shadow copies*, by coordinating with server-based applications, file-system services, the backup application orchestrating the backup process, and potentially the storage hardware you have deployed.

You can use VSS to back up open files and application data as well as create transportable shadow copies via the hardware provider, which can be leveraged to speed up both backup and recovery times.

The Components of VSS

Four basic components of a VSS solution need to be in place for a complete system to work:

- The VSS coordination service
- The VSS requester
- The VSS writer
- The VSS provider

The VSS coordination service is part of the operating system, and its job is to make sure that all the components can communicate with each other properly and work together.

The VSS requester is the software that orchestrates the actual creation of shadow copies. Typically, this is the backup application itself. The inbox backup tool in Windows Server 2008 R2, Windows Server Backup, is a VSS requester and so is the Data Protection Manager 2010. Third-party VSS requesters include a number of backup applications that run on Windows Server 2008 R2.

The VSS writer is the component that guarantees a consistent data set to back up. This is typically provided as part of your application software. A VSS writer for Hyper-V is included with Windows Server. Third-party VSS writers are included with many applications for Windows Server and guarantee data consistency at the time of a backup.

The VSS provider is the component that creates and maintains the shadow copies on demand. This can be done either in software or in hardware. Windows Server includes a VSS software provider that uses "copy on write" functionality. If you use a SAN, you probably want to make sure you install a supported vendor's VSS hardware provider so you can have a more efficient way to split your shadow copies without putting an extra load on the host Hyper-V server itself.

How VSS Works

Now that you understand what each component does, here is an oversimplified explanation of how VSS works:

1. Using the backup software (VSS requester), you orchestrate the start of the virtual machine backup.
2. The Hyper-V VSS writer freezes the virtual machine, making sure that it is in a consistent state.
3. The VSS provider creates a snapshot of the data.
4. The Hyper-V VSS writer is notified that the shadow copy is done and thaws the virtual machine for reuse.
5. The backup software (VSS requester) tells you that the shadow copy was successfully created.

The critical part of this operation is when the VSS writer is told to hold all writes, because this can take only a few seconds. During this period of time, all I/O operations are simply queued. Because of this, creating a shadow copy does not significantly impact the performance of the production Hyper-V host. If the system is unable to queue the I/O requests during this period or if it takes longer than 10 seconds, the shadow copy creation process will just fail and the backup will be unsuccessful.

So, how does VSS copy large files in such a short space of time, that is, under 10 seconds? The VSS provider marks all the data blocks currently in use so that it can keep a copy of the "pre-backup state" if the data needs to be overwritten after the shadow copy is completed.

SAN arrays have built-in abilities to create snapshots, which implement this behavior. Some SAN arrays actually start a background copy of the data to another volume and will eventually put the volume back in a regular state, with no need for extra tracking.

Hyper-V Backup and Recovery Considerations

Now that you have Windows Server Backup configured to support Hyper-V, there are some key considerations you need to know when creating backups of the Hyper-V host and virtual machines:

- Windows Server Backup no longer supports tape as a media.
- When backing up the host, you must back up the boot volume as a minimum to get the host configuration information.

- You cannot back up specific virtual machines; you can only back up volumes with Windows Server Backup.
- If you want to ensure that you have backed up a specific virtual machine, you must back up each volume that contains components of that virtual machine. For example, if you keep configuration files associated with the virtual machine in a different location than the virtual machine's virtual hard disk or disks, you must back up both volumes to be able to restore the entire virtual machine.
- Virtual machines that do not have Integration Services installed will be put in a saved state while the VSS snapshot is created.
- Virtual machines that are running operating systems that do not support VSS will be put in a saved state while the VSS snapshot is created.
- Virtual machines that contain dynamic disks must be backed up offline.
- When you carry out a restore, you must select the application-based recovery option.
- When restoring a virtual machine, you cannot restore files within a virtual machine, just the entire virtual machine. Once the virtual machine is restored to an alternative location, you can mount it and copy files out as needed.
- Windows Server Backup does not provide support for Cluster Shared Volumes and so is not enterprise-ready.

Using Data Protection Manager 2010

System Center Data Protection Manager 2010 (SCDPM 2010) is a member of the System Center family suite of products that provides protection and recovery for a number of Microsoft applications, including support for Microsoft Hyper-V including Cluster Shared Volumes.

SCDPM 2010 is a server-based application that enables both disk-based and tape-based protection and recovery. SCDPM 2010 performs replication, synchronization, and recovery point creation and is designed to run on Windows 2008 x64 or Windows 2008 R2 x64 Standard or Enterprise edition.

SCDPM 2010 uses replication and the VSS infrastructure to provide business of all sizes with nearly continuous protection and reliable recovery.

Planning for Data Protection Manager 2010

When planning for SCDPM 2010, it is important to understand what the system, software, security, network, SQL Server, and hardware requirements are.

System Requirements

Before you install SCDPM 2010, you need to ensure that the computer used as your server and that all the computers and applications you want to protect meet or exceed the minimum hardware, software, and network requirements. SCDPM 2010 is designed to run on a dedicated, single-purpose server. The SCDPM 2010 server should *not* be installed on any of the following:

- A computer on which the Application Server role is installed

- A computer that is a System Center Operations Manager Management Server
- A computer on which Exchange Server is running
- A computer with Windows Failover Cluster Services enabled

Software Requirements

SCDPM 2010 can be installed only on Windows 2008 x64 or Windows 2008 R2 x64 Standard or Enterprise edition. SCDPM 2010 will also guide you through the installation of the following components if they are not present during the installation:

- PowerShell 2.0
- .NET 3.5 Service Pack 1
- Windows Installer 4.5
- Windows Single Instance Store

PowerShell

If an installation of PowerShell version 1.0 already exists before you install SCDPM 2010, then you must uninstall PowerShell version 1.0 prior to installing SCDPM 2010.

Optionally consider installing the Hyper-V role on your SCDPM 2010 server. Although this idea might seem a little odd at first, this is how Data Protection Manager is able to do item-level recovery.

Item-Level Recovery

SCDPM 2010 supports item-level recovery, which allows you to do granular recovery of files, folders, volumes, and virtual hard disks from a host-level backup of Hyper-V to a network share or a volume on an SCDPM 2010 protected server.

You must have the Hyper-V role enabled on the SCDPM 2010 server to perform item-level recoveries. During item-level recovery, SCDPM 2010 has to mount the virtual hard disks of the protected virtual machines.

Security and Network Requirements

SCDPM 2010 has the following security and network requirements:

- Before you install SCDPM 2010 as a Server or Agent role, you must log in to the computer with an account that is a member of the local Administrators group.
- After installing SCDPM 2010, you must log in to the computer with an account that has administrative access to the SCDPM 2010 administrator console.

- The SCDPM 2010 server must be deployed within a Windows 2003 or Windows 2008 Active Directory domain.
- The domain controllers can be running either the Windows 2003, Windows 2003 R2, Windows 2008 or Windows 2008 R2 operating system.
- If you are protecting data over a wide area network, there is a minimum network bandwidth requirement of 512 kilobits per second (Kbps) connection in order to protect a remote computer.

SQL Server Requirements

The SCDPM 2010 database requires a dedicated instance of either the x86 or x64 version of SQL Server 2008 Service Pack 1 using either Standard or Enterprise edition of SQL Server.

> **SQL Server Licensing**
>
> The instance of SQL Server that is installed by SCDPM 2010 Setup is included with the SCDPM software and does not require a separate SQL Server license. However, this is licensed for SCDPM use only, and it is against the licensing agreement to use that SQL Server instance for anything other than hosting the SCDPM 2010 database.

The hardware and software requirements for a remote instance of SQL Server are the same as those that are specified to install and run SQL Server itself. Note the following:

- A remote instance of SQL Server on a domain controller is not supported except when installing onto a read-only domain controller.
- The computer running a remote instance of SQL Server must be located in the same domain as the SCDPM 2010 server.

Server Hardware Requirements

SCDPM 2010 has a number of server hardware requirements, which are shown in Table 10.1.

Table 10.1: Hardware requirements

Components	Minimum requirements	Recommended requirements
Processor	1 GHz x64.	2.33 GHz quad-core x64.
Memory	4 GB.	8 GB.
Pagefile settings	0.2 percent of the combined size of all recovery point volumes, in addition to the recommended pagefile size (generally, 1.5 times the amount of RAM on the computer).	Not applicable.

TABLE 10.1: Hardware requirements *(CONTINUED)*

Components	Minimum Requirements	Recommended Requirements
Disk space for Data Protection Manager 2010	System Volume: 1 GB. SCDPM 2010 installation location: 3 GB. Database file drive: 900 MB. The system volume space requirement is necessary if you choose to install the dedicated instance of SQL Server. If you use a remote instance of SQL Server, these disk space requirements are considerably less.	SCDPM 2010 requires a minimum of 300 MB of free space on each protected volume for the change journal. Additionally, before archiving data to tape, SCDPM 2010 copies the file catalog to a temporary installation location; therefore, we recommend that the volume on which SCDPM 2010 is installed contains 2–3 GB of free space.
Disk space for the storage pool	1.5 times the size of the protected data. The storage pool does not support Universal Serial Bus (USB) disks.	2-3 times the size of the protected data.
Logical unit number maximization	Not applicable.	Maximum of 17 TB for GUID partition table (GPT) dynamic disks. 2 TB for master boot record (MBR) disks.

Installing Data Protection Manager 2010

Installing SCDPM 2010 is like installing many of the other products in the System Center suite. Once you have completed all your planning and you have met all the requirements for SCDPM 2010, you are ready to start your installation.

To install SCDPM 2010, log into the server using a domain account that is a member of the local Administrators group on your Data Protection Manager server, and follow these steps:

1. Insert the SCDPM 2010 installation media into the server, and run `SETUP.EXE`.
2. On the splash page (Figure 10.12), click Install Data Protection Manager.
3. On the Microsoft Software License Terms page, review the license agreement, and if you accept the terms, click I Accept The License Terms And Conditions. Then click OK.

> **Installation of Prerequisite Components**
>
> After you click OK, SCDPM 2010 installs the Visual C++ Redistributable 2008 package on your server, if it isn't already installed.

4. On the Welcome page, click Next. SCDPM 2010 begins its prerequisite checks for all the required hardware and software components. The prerequisite checks allow Data

Protection Manager to check the system and verify that it meets the necessary hardware and software requirements.

5. On the Prerequisites Check page (Figure 10.13), click Next to install any necessary required components, such as Single Instance Store Filter (as shown in Figure 10.14).

FIGURE 10.12 Installation start screen

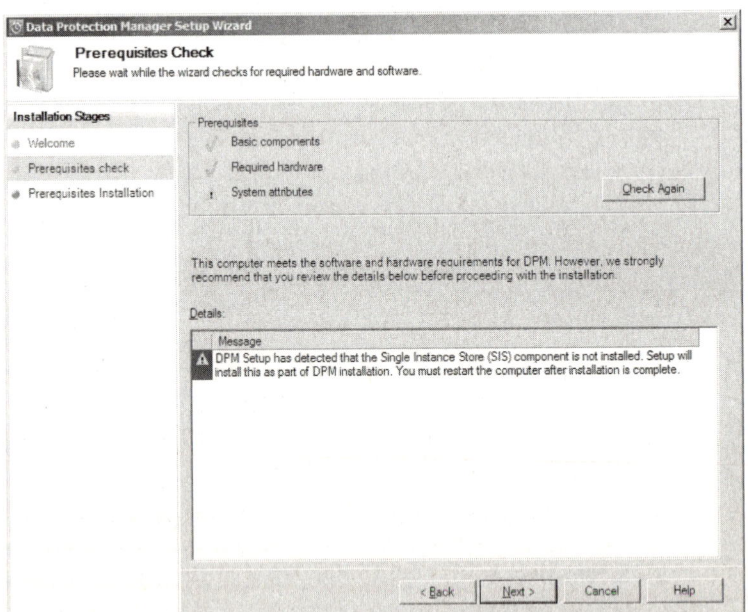

FIGURE 10.13 Prerequisites check

FIGURE 10.14
Prerequisites installation

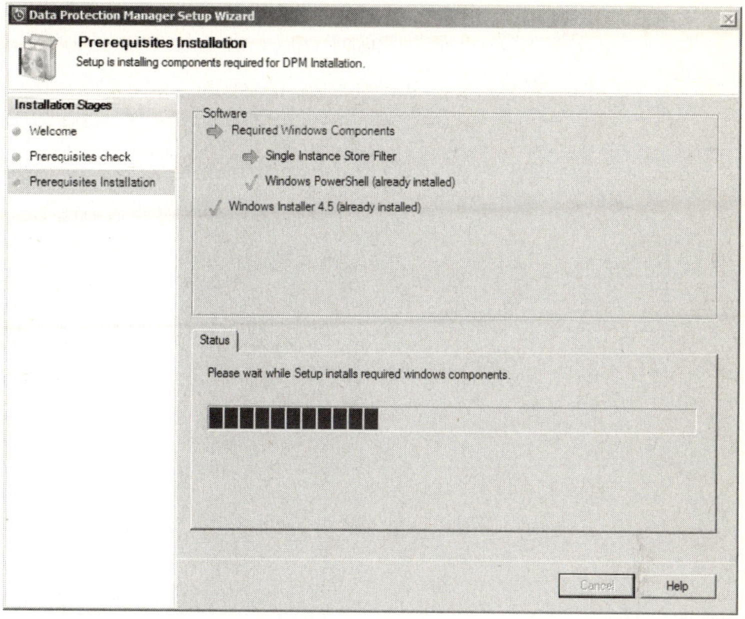

SINGLE INSTANCE STORE FILTER

SCDPM 2010 requires that Single Instance Store Filter component be installed on the server. SCDPM 2010 will install this as part of the installation process, but it will require a reboot, forcing you to reinitiate the installation after reboot.

6. On the Prerequisites Installation page (Figure 10.15), click Restart, and then click Yes to restart now. Although the installation will not carry on from where it left off, you can follow the previous steps to return you to the Prerequisites Check page successfully.
7. On the Product Registration page, enter your registration information, and click Next.
8. On the Installation Settings page (Figure 10.16), specify the Data Protection Manager and SQL Server settings.
   - In the DPM Program Files section, either accept the default installation path `C:\Program Files\Microsoft DPM` or click Change and browse to the folder where you want to install.

DEFAULT INSTALLATION PATH

You can install SCDPM 2010 only on a local drive. You can't install SCDPM 2010 to the following folder types: read-only, hidden, or directly to a local Windows folder, such as Program Files (although SCDPM 2010 can be installed in a subfolder of Program Files). The installation partition must be formatted NTFS.

FIGURE 10.15
Prerequisites installation — complete

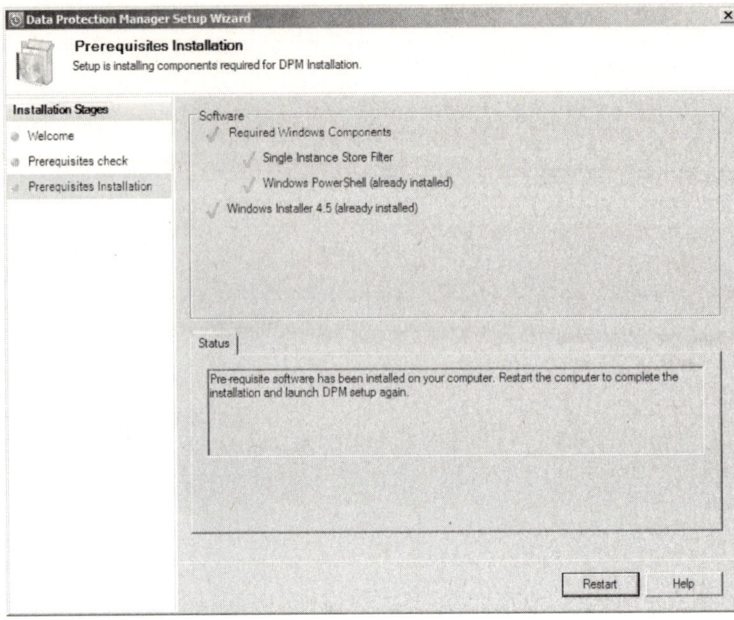

FIGURE 10.16
Installation settings

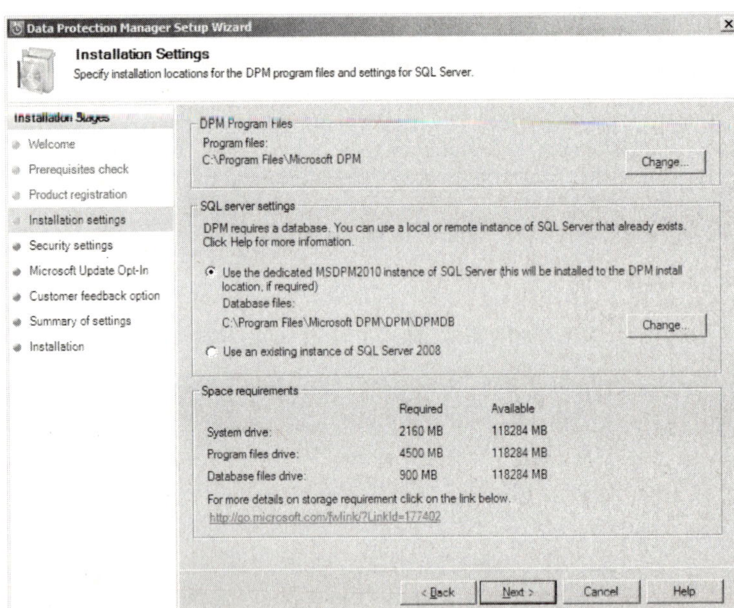

- On the SQL Server Settings page, specify whether you want to install the dedicated SCDPM2010 instance of SQL Server or an existing instance of SQL Server 2008. If you choose to install a local instance of SQL Server, you can accept the default location for the database by clicking Change to select a different location.

SQL Server Prerequisites

DPM setup creates the DPMDBReaders$*<DPM server name>* and DPMDBAdministrators*<DPM server name>* local groups on the remote instance of SQL Server. The account you plan to use to administer Data Protection Manager must be added to these groups to use the remote instance of SQL Server.

---

9. On the Security Settings page, specify and confirm a strong password for the restricted MICROSOFTDPMACCT local account, which is used for a local installation of SQL Server and the DPMR$DPM local account used for secure report generation, and click Next.

Strong Password

The password that you specify for both these accounts does not expire. A strong password is typically defined as a password that is at least six characters long, does not contain all or part of the user's account name, and contains at least three of the following four categories of characters: uppercase, lowercase characters, base 10 digits, and symbols.

---

10. On the Microsoft Update Opt-in page, select whether you want to use Microsoft Update to obtain updates for Data Protection Manager 2010, and click Next. On the Customer Experience Improvement Program page, choose whether you want to participate in or opt out of the program, and click Next.
11. On the Summary Settings page, review the summary installation settings, and click Install.

After the installation is complete, the Installation page displays its installation status. Click Close to finish the installation.

Performing Basic Configuration Tasks

Before you can start protecting data using SCDPM 2010, you need to complete a number of basic configuration tasks:

- Allocate storage to Data Protection Manager by adding one or more disks to the storage pool.
- Install protection agents on each Hyper-V server you want to protect.
- Create one or more protection groups.

ADDING DISKS TO THE STORAGE POOL

Following installation, SCDPM 2010 uses a dedicated storage pool. The storage pool is a set of disks on which the SCDPM 2010 server stores replicas and recovery points for protected data. Before you can start protecting data, you need to add at least one disk to the storage pool. Post-configuration, you can add more disks to the storage pool as desired.

> **WHAT HAPPENS WHEN YOU ADD DISKS TO THE STORAGE POOL**
>
> When you add a disk to the storage pool, SCDPM 2010 will convert this disk from a basic disk to a dynamic disk but will not format the disk. If the disk is greater than 2 TB, then you must convert the disk from MBR to GPT before adding it to the storage pool.

To add a local disk to the storage pool, you need to do the following:

1. In the DPM 2010 Administrator Console (Figure 10.17), click Management on the navigation bar, and then click the Disk tab.

FIGURE 10.17 DPM 2010 Administrator Console

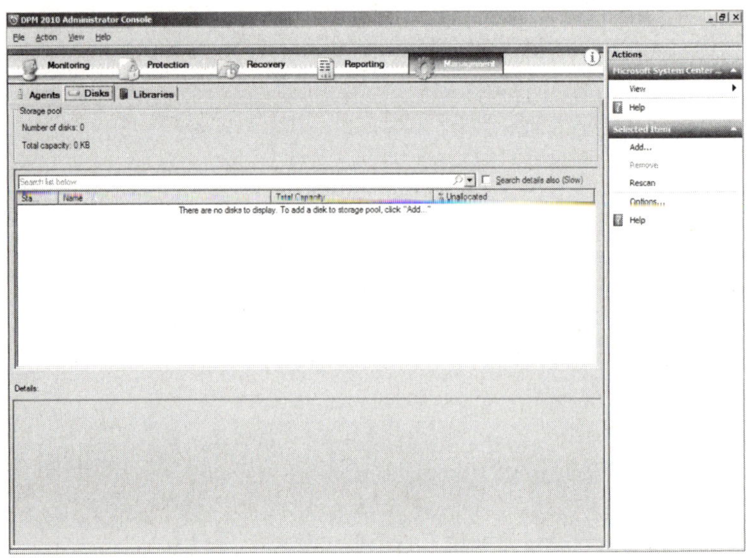

2. In the Actions pane, click Add. The Add Disks To Storage Pool dialog box appears (Figure 10.18). The Available Disks section lists the disks that you can add to the storage pool.

3. Select one or more of the disks, click Add, and click OK. In the DPM 2010 Administrator Console, you will now see the added disks, as shown in Figure 10.19.

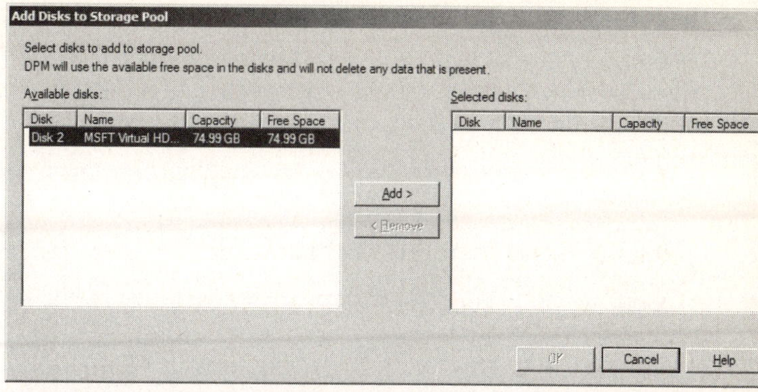

FIGURE 10.18
Adding disks to the storage pool

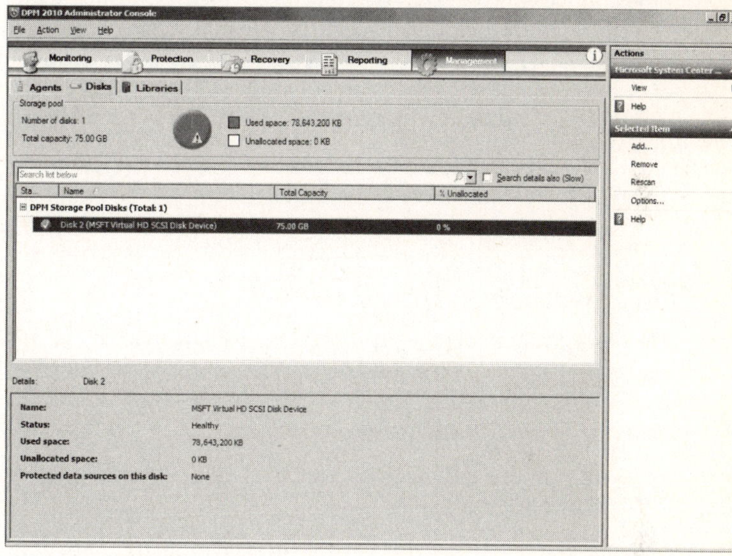

FIGURE 10.19
Added disks in the storage pool

Real World Scenario

STORAGE POOL SIZING

Microsoft has released a series of draft storage calculators to aid SCDPM 2010 administrators in sizing the SCDPM storage pools. The calculators are based on the workload being protected, and there are three different spreadsheets available, including one for Hyper-V.

They are very simple to use and can be downloaded here:

```
http://www.microsoft.com/downloads/details.aspx?FamilyID=c136c66c-bd4a-4fb1-8088-f610cd02dc51&displaylang=en
```

Installing Protection Agents

Before you can start to protect your Hyper-V host or cluster, you must install a protection agent on each computer and potentially each virtual machine that contains data that you want to protect. Protection agent software performs the following tasks:

- Identifies data on a computer or virtual machine that Data Protection Manager can protect and recover
- Tracks changes to protected data
- Transfers changes from the protected computer or virtual machine to your Data Protection Manager server

There are various ways to install protection agents; you may decide to manually install the protection agents on your Hyper-V hosts, you may decide to push install protection agents from your Data Protection Manager server, you may decide to incorporate the protection agents into your corporate build, or you may deploy the agents by using some form of electronic software distribution solution such as System Center Configuration Manager.

There are two steps to getting a protection agent up and running with your SCDPM 2010:

1. The agent software needs to be installed on the computer to be protected, and the SCDPM 2010 server is specified.
2. SCDPM 2010 attaches to the protection agent.

Deploying Protection Agents

The easiest way to deploy protection agents is to use the Protection Agent Wizard to install agents on Hyper-V hosts that are members of the same domain, on Hyper-V hosts that reside in trusted domains, and on Hyper-V hosts that are stand-alone in a workgroup or on a perimeter network. To push install a protection agent on a Hyper-V hosts, follow these steps:

1. In the DPM 2010 Administrator Console, click Management on the navigation bar, and then click the Agents tab.
2. In the Actions pane, click Install. The Protection Agent Installation Wizard starts (as shown in Figure 10.20) and prompts you to install an agent or attach the Data Protection Manager server to an agent that has already been installed.
3. To install an agent, select Install Agent, and click Next.
4. A list of available servers in the DPM domain will appear (Figure 10.21). On the Select Computers page, select one or more servers (50 maximum) from the server list, click Add, and then click Next.

   If you know the name of an individual Hyper-V host on which you want to install the protection agent, you can quickly find and select that host by typing the name of the server in the Computer Name box and clicking Add. SCDPM 2010 will query Active Directory for the name and then add it to the selected computer list.

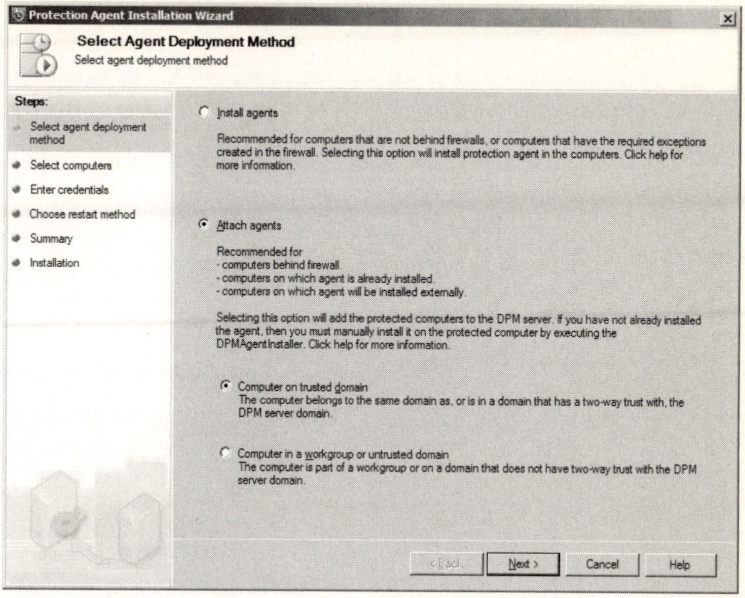

FIGURE 10.20
Selecting the agent deployment method

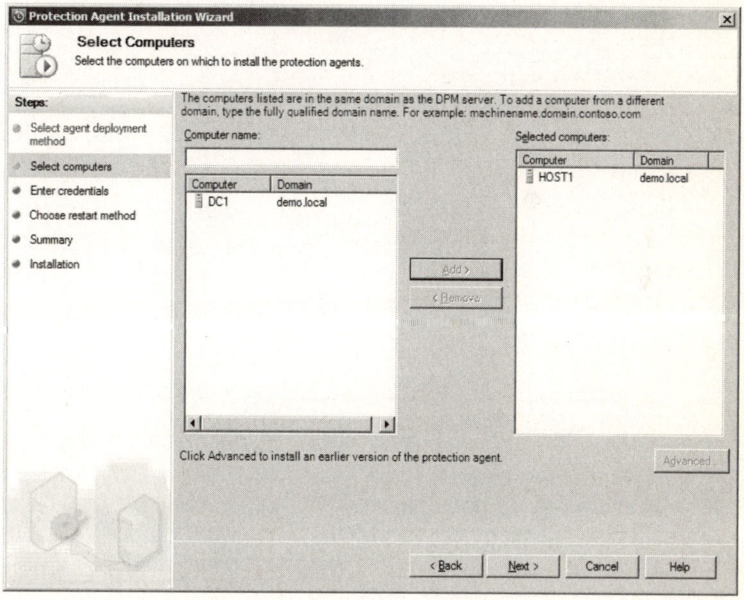

FIGURE 10.21
Select Computers page

Finding Hyper-V Hosts across Trusted Domains

To find a Hyper-V host across a trusted domain, you must type the fully qualified domain name of the server you want to protect.

5. On the Enter Credentials page (Figure 10.22), type the username and password for a domain account that is a member of the local Administrators group on all selected servers, and click Next.

Figure 10.22 Enter Credentials page

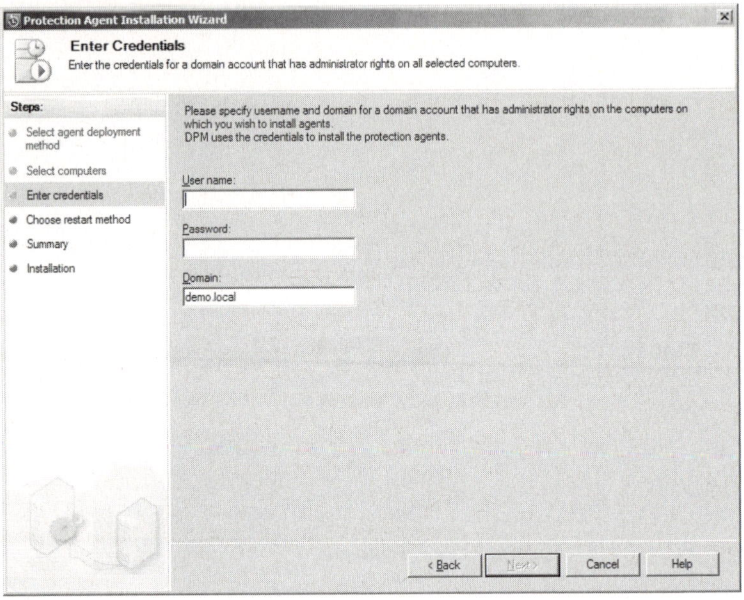

6. On the Choose Restart Method page (Figure 10.23), select the method you will use to restart the servers after the protection agent is installed, and click Next.

Microsoft Windows Failover Clustering

SCDPM 2010 will not restart a server that belongs to a Microsoft cluster. You must manually restart a server in a Microsoft cluster.

7. On the Installation Summary page, click Install to begin the push installation. On the Installation page, the results appear on the status tab to indicate whether the installation is successful. Clicking Close before the wizard has finished performing its task allows you to monitor the installation from the DPM 2010 Administrator Console (as shown in Figure 10.24).

FIGURE 10.23
Choose Restart Method page

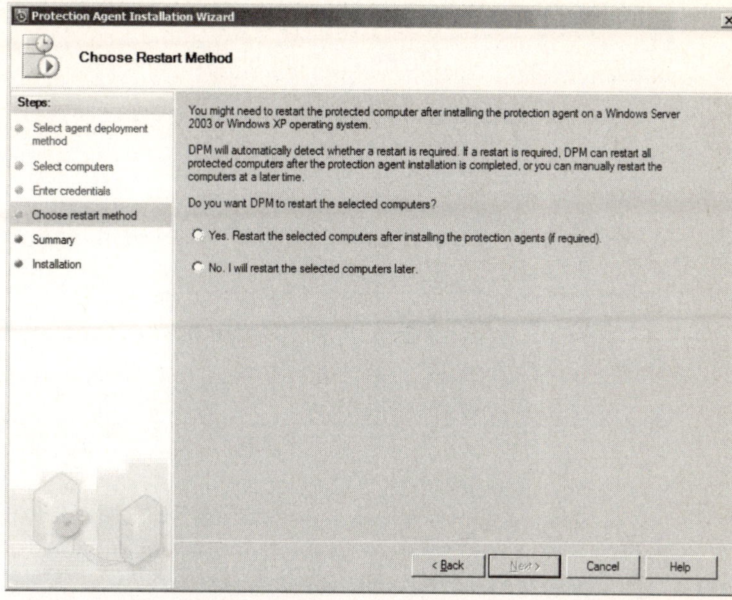

FIGURE 10.24
Monitoring the installation

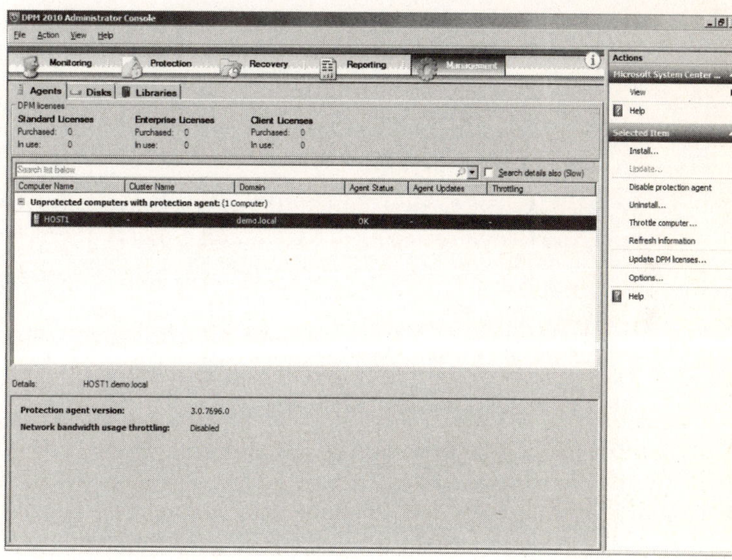

INSTALLING PROTECTION AGENTS BEHIND A FIREWALL

It is probably inevitable that you will need to deploy protection agents on a Hyper-V server that is running some kind of firewall, such as Windows Firewall, or is behind a dedicated firewall within a perimeter network. To that end, it is important to know how to deploy protection agents in this scenario.

On the Hyper-V server on which you want to install the protection agents, it is recommended that you map a network drive to the SCDPM 2010 server. Once you have mapped a drive, then from a command prompt, navigate to the following location:

```
<mapped drive letter>\Program Files\Microsoft DPM\DPM\ProtectionAgents\
RA\3.0.<build number>.0\amd64
```

and run the following:

```
DPMAGENTINSTALLER_x64.EXE <FQDN of your DPM server>
```

SPECIFYING THE FQDN

If you use the SCDPM 2010 server name in the command-line syntax, SCDPM 2010 installs the protection agents and configures the security permissions for the SCDPM 2010 server.

If you run `DPMAGENTINSTALLER_x64.EXE` but do not specify the FQDN of your SCDPM 2010 server, then you will need to complete the protection agent configuration for the appropriate SCDPM 2010 server as well as configure the firewall settings.

With the agent now installed on the Hyper-V server, you now need to add this protected computer to the SCDPM 2010. Follow these steps:

1. In the DPM 2010 Administrator Console, from the navigation bar, click Management, and then click the Agent tab.
2. In the Actions pane, click Install. The Protection Agent Installation Wizard starts and prompts you to install an agent or attach the SCDPM 2010 server to an agent that has already been installed.
3. Select Attach Agent (Figure 10.25), and then designate whether the computer is part of the Active Directory domain or is in a workgroup or perimeter network.
4. You will then be prompted for credentials on the computer you are protecting. You will need to provide an account that has administrative rights on the Hyper-V server you are protecting.

CREATING A PROTECTION GROUP FOR HYPER-V

So, what is a protection group? A protection group is a collection of data sources, in this case Hyper-V servers, that share the same protection configuration. Before you can start protecting your Hyper-V servers, you must create at least one protection group. You will find that there are a number of decisions that need to be made up front about how you want to configure this protection group. These decisions include the following aspects:

- Selecting the data you actually want to protect
- Selecting the type of protection method you want to leverage
- Specifying what your recovery goals are for the data you are protecting
- Allocating space on the storage pool for replicas and recovery points

- Specifying what your long-term media details are
- Specifying when you want replica creation to occur
- Specifying performance improvements methods you want to leverage

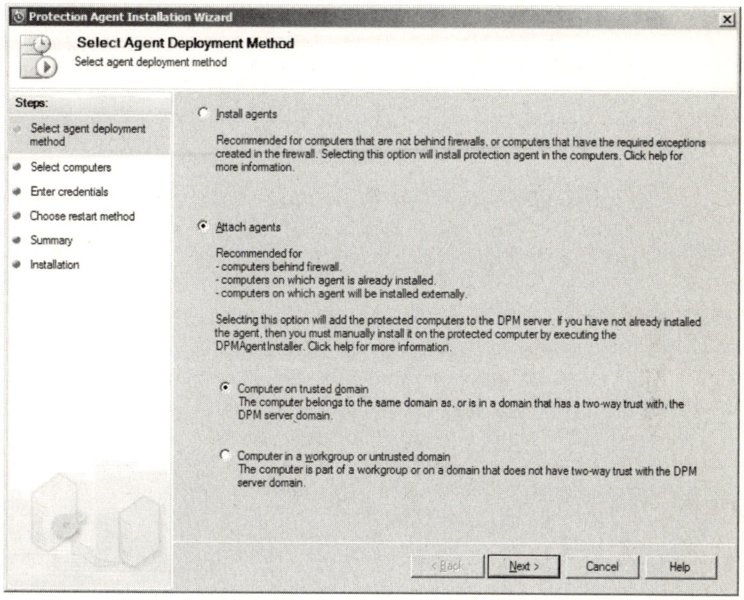

FIGURE 10.25
Selecting an agent deployment method

CREATING YOUR FIRST PROTECTION GROUP

You can use the Create New Protection Group Wizard to guide you through the process of creating your first protection group. To start the Create New Protection Group Wizard, follow these steps:

1. In the DPM 2010 Administrator Console, on the navigation bar, click Protection.
2. In the Actions pane, click Create Protection Group to display the Welcome To The New Protection Group Wizard page.
3. Review the Welcome To The New Protection Group Wizard page, and then click Next.
4. On the Select Protection Group Type page (Figure 10.26), you need to determine what kind of protection group you are going to create. Since you are protecting Hyper-V servers here, you will select Servers and click Next.

> **SERVER PROTECTION GROUP**
>
> The option is used to protect file servers and application servers. Protection agents must already be installed on the Hyper-V servers you want to protect. In addition, these Hyper-V servers need to be online when you configure protection.

FIGURE 10.26
Select Protection Group Type page

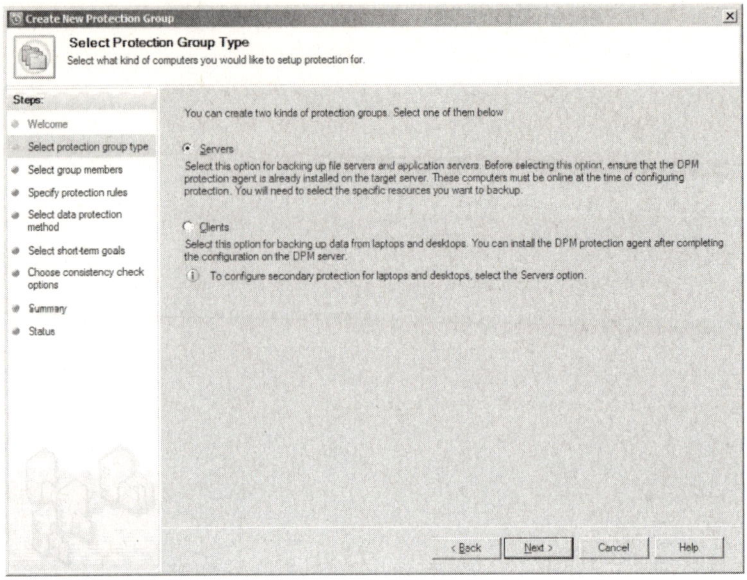

5. In the Create New Protection Group Wizard, you use the Select Group Members page (Figure 10.27) to select the data source you want to protect.

FIGURE 10.27
Select Group Members page

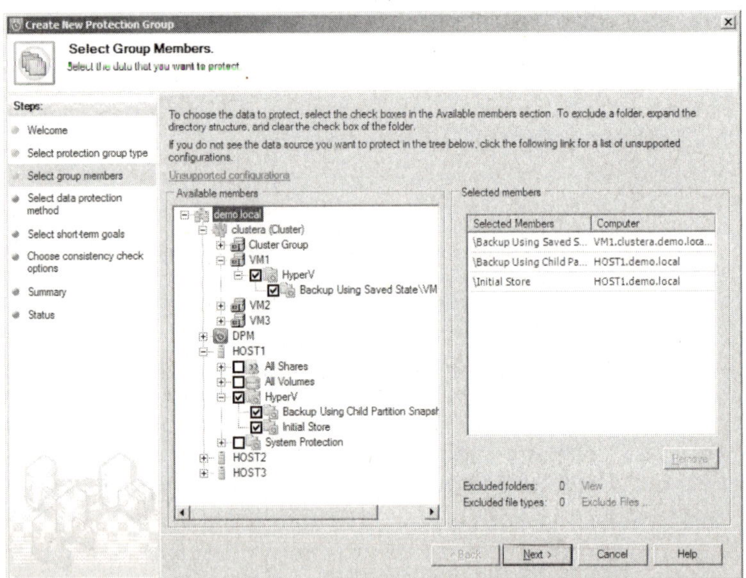

If you are protecting a cluster, expand your cluster node, which will show you which virtual machines reside on your cluster. If you are protecting a nonclustered Hyper-V server, then simply expand the Hyper-V server in question, and select the data source you want to include in your protection group.

6. As a selected data source, your selections appear in the Selected Members box. After you have selected protection group members, click Next.

Virtual machines will be listed as either Backup Using Child Partition or Backup Using Saved State. This determination is based on the operating system running within the virtual machine. If a virtual machine is capable of performing a VSS snapshot, then SCDPM 2010 can capture the virtual machine without shutting the virtual machine down. This is backing up using the child partition. If for some reason the Hyper-V writer determines that the virtual machine can't perform online backups, then it will put the virtual machine into a saved state, and SCDPM 2010 will do a backup using saved state.

SCDPM 2010 can't back up a Hyper-V virtual machine in an online state if one or more of the following conditions are true:

- The backup (volume snapshot) Integration Service is disabled or not installed.
- The virtual machine has one or more dynamic disks.
- The virtual machine has one or more non-NTFS volumes.
- The virtual machine cluster resource group in a cluster is offline.
- The virtual machine is not in a running state.
- All NTFS volume must be greater than 1 GB and have more than 300 MB of free space.

Disabling Saved State Backups

There can be cases where an administrator will want to avoid saved state (offline) backups because a disruption of service can occur. To disable save state backups, create the following registry key on each Hyper-V server:

Key equals: HKLM\Software\Microsoft\Microsoft Data Protection Manager\Agent

Type equals: DWORD

Value equals: AllowOffline

Data equals: 0

After you have selected the data you want to protect, use the Select Data Protection Method page to select short-term protection, which can be either disk or tape, or long-term protection, which is limited to tape.

7. On the Selected Data Protection Method page, in the Protection Group Name box (Figure 10.28), either accept the default name or type a more meaningful name for the protection group.

FIGURE 10.28
Data Protection Method page

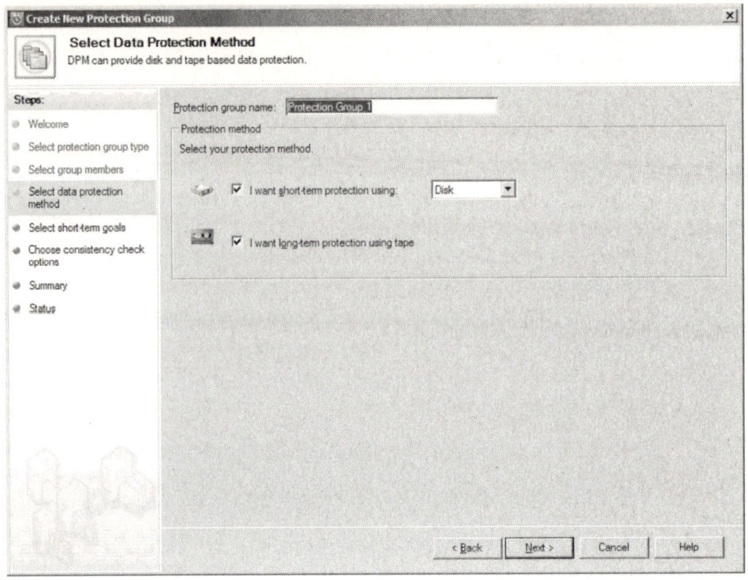

8. In the Protection Method section, you can specify your short-term and long-term protection options as follows:

   - For short-term protection, select I Want Short Term Protection Using, and select the media you want to use from the drop-down list.
   - For long-term protection, select I Want Long Term Protection Using Tape.

If you do not have a tape library attached to your Data Protection Manager 2010 server, only Disk is available for short-term protection. The I Want Long Term Protection Using Tape option will be unavailable.

9. After selecting your protection method options, click Next.

USING TAPE FOR BOTH SHORT- AND LONG-TERM PROTECTION

If you are using tape for both your short-term and long-term protection methods, SCDPM 2010 creates copies of the latest short-term tape/full backup to generate your long-term tape backup. Therefore, it is recommended that you schedule your short-term protection/full backup to run a day prior to your long-term protection method.

SCDPM 2010 generates a protection plan based on the short-term recovery goals you specify in the Create New Protection Group Wizard. You define your short-term recovery goals by selecting the retention range for you data.

10. On the Specify Short-Term Goals page (Figure 10.29), select the duration of time in the Retention Range box that you want the data to be available for recovery.

FIGURE 10.29
Specify Short-Term Goals page

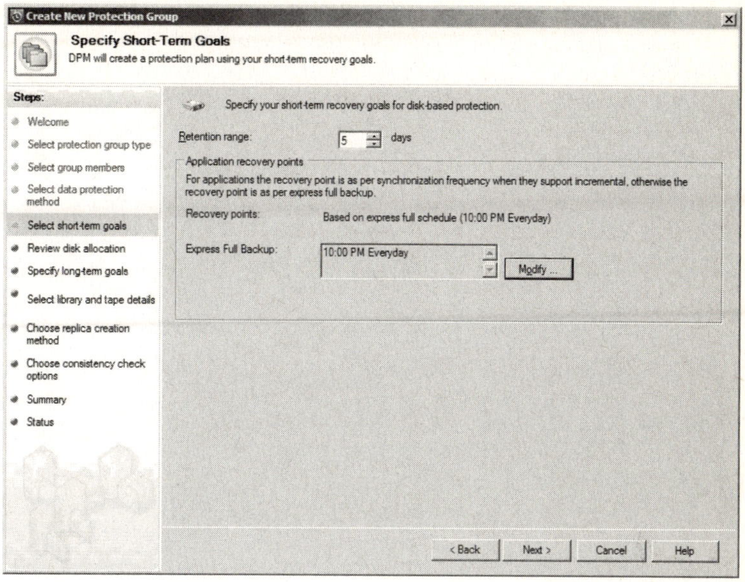

RETENTION RANGE

The retention range is the duration of time for which the data should be available for recovery. SCDPM 2010 retains recovery points for the duration of time specified in the retention range.

---

11. In the Application Recovery Point section, click Modify, specify the days and times that you want to create a recovery point, and then click OK.
12. After specifying your short-term protection goals, click Next.

RECOVERY POINT SCHEDULE

The recovery point schedule for data protection of applications such as Hyper-V, which do not support incremental backups, is defined and based on the express full backup schedule, and this schedule defines the recovery points available.

When creating a protection group, SCDPM 2010 recommends and allocates raw disk space, from the storage pool, for your protection group, based on the size of the data you are attempting to protect.

13. On the Review Disk Allocation page (Figure 10.30), you can either accept the recommended storage allocations or change the recommended allocations by clicking Modify.

You can also opt to additionally enable both Co-Locate Data In The DPM Storage Pool and Automatically Grow The Volumes.

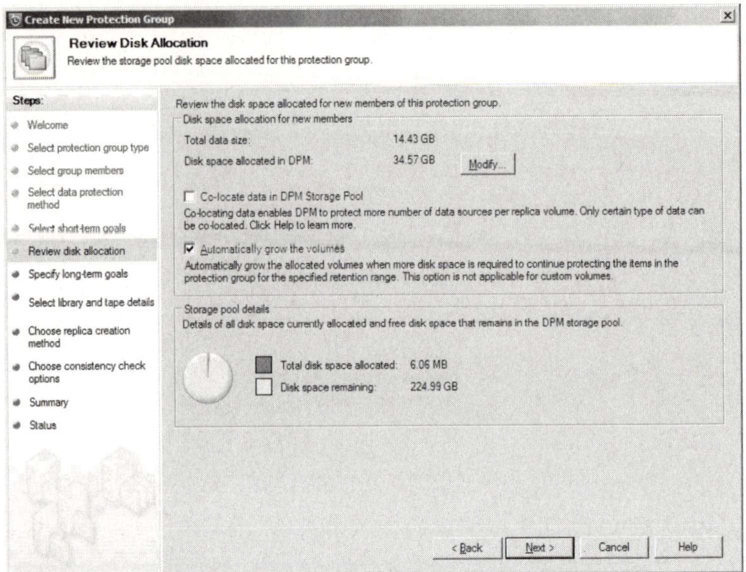

FIGURE 10.30
Review Disk Allocation page

14. When you have finished selecting your disk allocation options, click Next.

ADVANCED VOLUME OPTIONS

SCDPM 2010 supports the concept of co-location of data. Co-locating data enables SCDPM 2010 to protect a number of data sources on the same storage volume. However, only certain types of data can be co-located. SCDPM 2010 supports the co-location of the following data sources:

- Hyper-V virtual machines
- Desktop and laptop computers (client protection)
- SQL Server 2005 and 2008 databases

You can enable co-location through the Create New Protection Group Wizard at the time you define the protection group. Because Data Protection Manager 2010 supports co-location for Hyper-V virtual machines, the Review Disk Allocation page shows you a check box that allows you to select co-location as an option.

The automatic grow feature in SCDPM 2010, if enabled, will automatically grow the storage volume size by 25 percent or by 10 GB (whichever is greater) as your storage protection needs increase. This option is enabled by default but can be configured at the time you define the protection group.

SCDPM 2010 creates a protection plan using a set of default long-term recovery goals. You can accept the SCDPM 2010 defaults or define your own long-term protection goals by selecting a retention range for your data set and a long-term backup schedule. To select long-term protection goals, follow these steps:

15. On the Select Long-Term Goals page (Figure 10.31), in the Retention Range boxes, select the duration of time for which you want the data to be available for recovery.

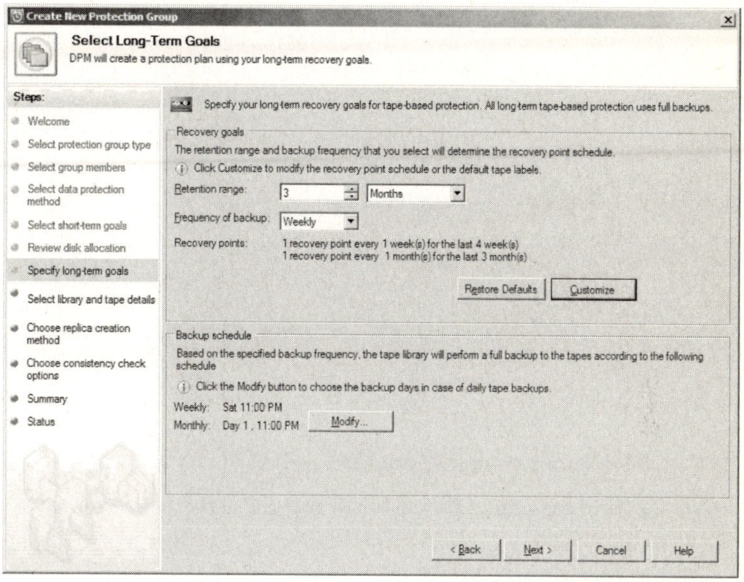

FIGURE 10.31
Specifying long-term goals

16. In the Frequency Of Backup box, select the backup frequency that you want from the drop-down list:

   - You can click Restore Defaults to restore the defaults to a retention range of three months with a weekly backup frequency.
   - You can click Customize to change the tape label and customize the schedule of the backup jobs in the Customize Recovery Goals dialog box.

In the Backup Schedule section, Data Protection Manager will display a recommended schedule for creating a full backup to tape based on the frequency you specified.

17. To change the backup schedule, click Modify to display a Modify Long-Term Backup Schedule dialog box.

18. When you have finished specifying your long-term recovery goals, click Next.

When you are protecting data based on your long-term goal, you must specify the number of copies that you need and how many tapes you want to allocate for your long-term protection needs. You also need to specify whether you want SCDPM 2010 to check backup integrity and encrypt or compress the data.

19. On the Select Library And Tape Details page (Figure 10.32), in the Library Details section, in the Library box, select the tape device that you want to use for your tape backup.

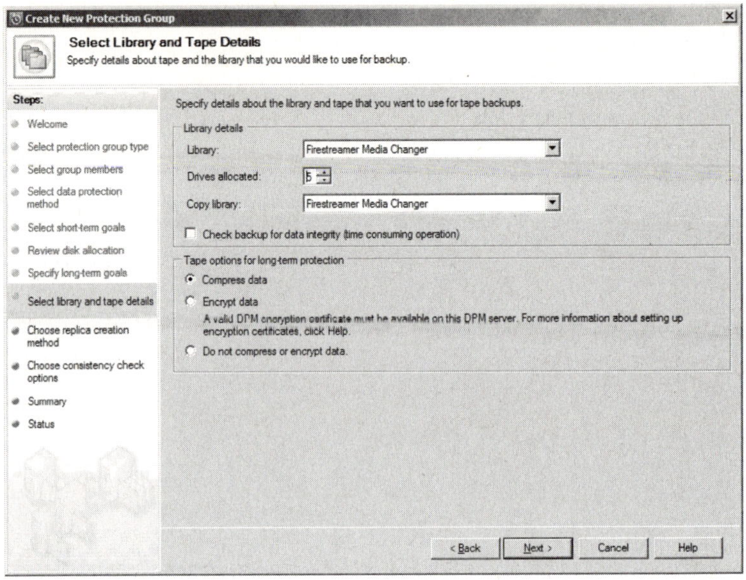

FIGURE 10.32
Select Library And Tape Details page

20. In the Drives Allocated box, select how many drives you want to allocate.

21. In the Copy Library box, select the tape device you want to use for multiple backup copies.

22. Optionally, select the Check Backup For Data Integrity check box to verify tape data against disk replica data after copying to tape. In the Tape Options For Long Term Protection section, you can select any one of the following options:
    - Compress Data
    - Encrypt Data
    - Do Not Compress Or Encrypt Data

23. When you have finished selecting your library and tape options, click Next.

When you create a protection group, a replica is created for each protected volume in the protection group. In SCDPM 2010, a replica is a complete copy of the protected data from a single volume, database, or storage group.

24. Select Automatically Over The Network (as shown in Figure 10.33) for Data Protection Manager to create a replica by copying data across the network.

25. Select Now to have SCDPM 2010 immediately begin copying the data from the protection group members, or select Later plus the date and time to schedule data replication at a later time (typically after business hours).

26. Select Manually to use tape, USB storage, or some other portable media to transfer the baseline data to the SCDPM 2010 server (this is a preferred option when having to synchronize large amounts of data across a slow WAN for the first time).

FIGURE 10.33
Replica creation method

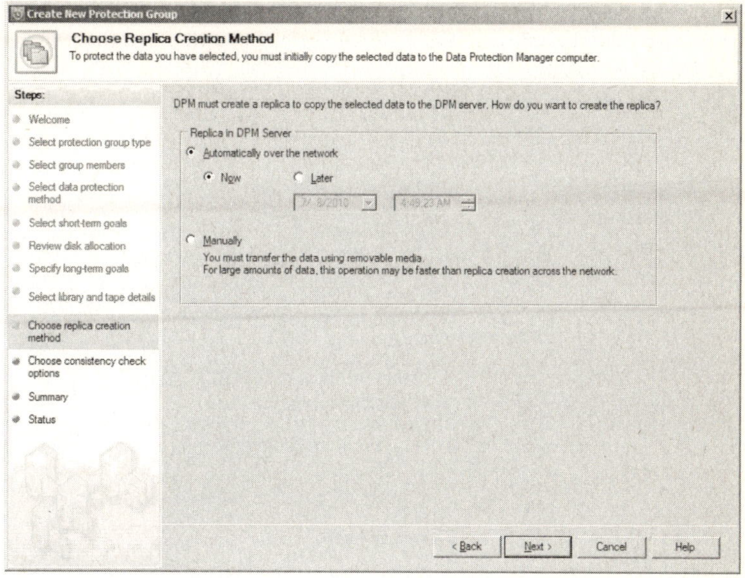

When you create a protection group, you will need to choose how you want to run consistency checks on inconsistent replicas. This allows you to have a consistency check run automatically either based on the condition of the replica or based on a defined frequency no matter what the status of the replica.

27. If you do not want SCDPM 2010 to automatically run consistency checks on the protection group, unselect both options.

28. Select Run A Consistency Check If A Replica Becomes Inconsistent (as shown in Figure 10.34) if you want SCDPM 2010 to perform this action automatically, when data is found to be in an inconsistent state.

29. If you are dealing with large workloads or a poor connection to the SCDPM 2010 server, you may want to run a daily consistency check. If this is the case, then select Run A Daily Consistency Check According To The Following Schedule.

30. After selecting the consistency check options, click Next.

Before SCDPM 2010 begins to create the protection group, you will be presented with a summary screen (as shown in Figure 10.35) that lists all the selections you have made for this particular protection group. At this point, you have an option to optimize the performance of this protection group by clicking the Optimize Performance link. Click Create Group to have SCDPM 2010 create the protection group.

Monitor the status progress for any errors (as shown in Figure 10.36). The process should complete successfully, and the new protection group should appear in the DPM 2010 Administrator Console.

If you elected to have SCDPM 2010 create a replica immediately, you can monitor the status of the replica creation by selecting the Monitoring tab and locating the running job within the administration console (as shown in Figure 10.37). Upon completion, if you select the Protection tab, you should see the newly created protection group as well as the replicas that were created. If you elected not to create a replica at that point in time, you will not see the protection group until the replica is actually created according to the schedule you specified, when you set up the protection group.

FIGURE 10.34
Consistency check options

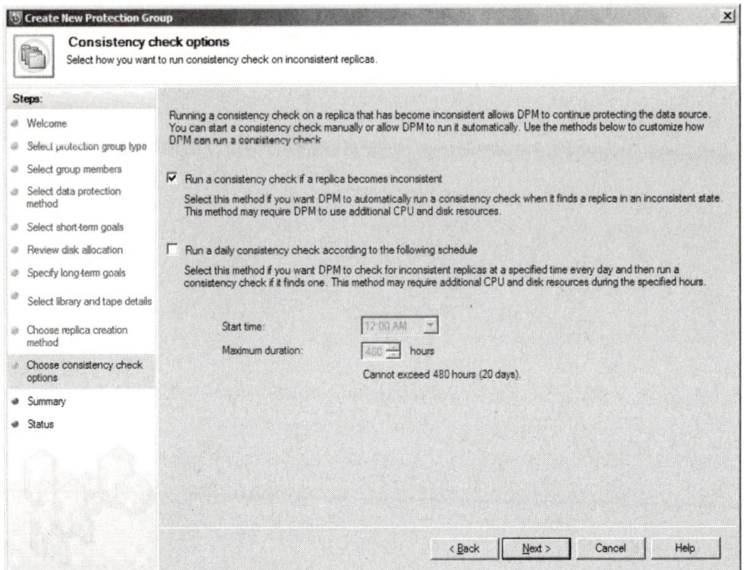

FIGURE 10.35
Protection group summary

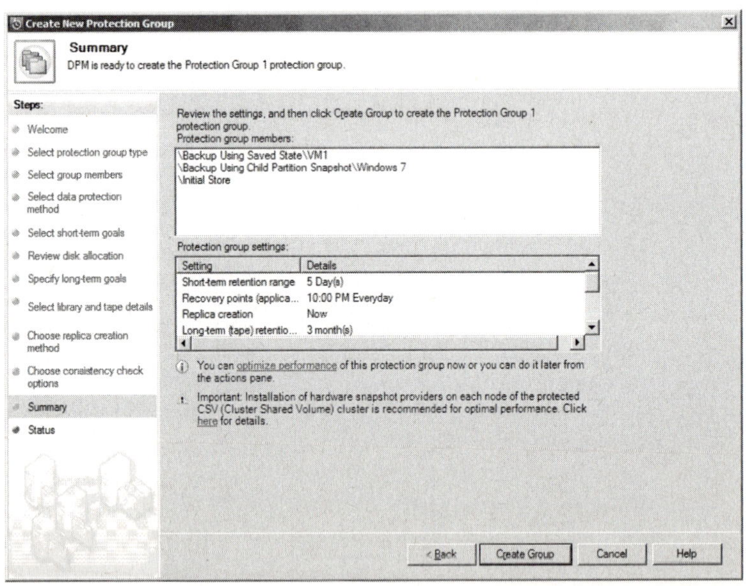

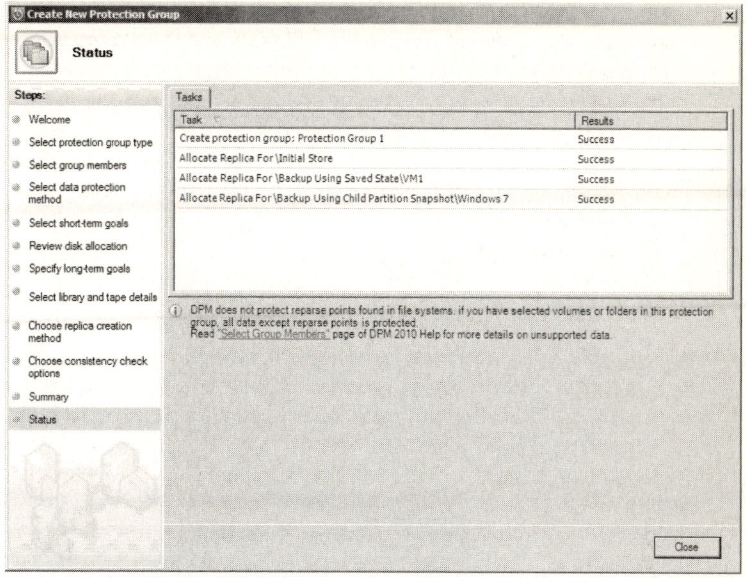

FIGURE 10.36
Monitoring the status of the protection group

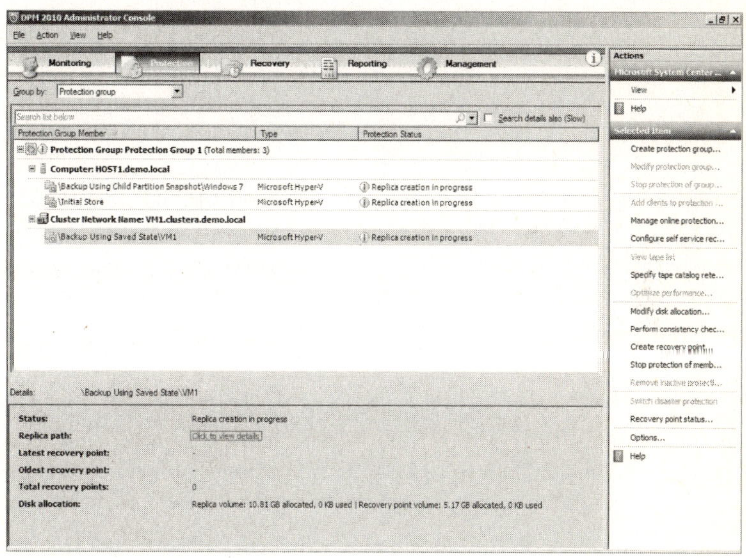

FIGURE 10.37
Protection tab

Recovering Hyper-V Virtual Machines

Restoring a virtual machine consists of a number of steps. For instance, you can restore an entire virtual machine, which would include the configuration files and its associated virtual hard disk files. This restore could be to its original location. In this scenario, the original virtual machine is deleted. SCDPM 2010 will recover the configuration files and the virtual machines associated virtual hard disks by using the Hyper-V VSS writer. You can restore a virtual machine as a series of flat files and manipulate those files as needed. SCDPM 2010 supports the recovery of a virtual machine to an alternative location. Virtual machines recovered in this way to a cluster node will not be marked highly available.

Or you can even restore and enumerate a virtual hard disk so that you can restore specific files or folders that reside within that virtual hard disk. SCDPM 2010 supports item-level recovery, which allows a granular recovery of files and folders from a host-level backup of a virtual machine to either a network share or a volume on an SCDPM 2010 protected server.

To restore a virtual machine because it has simply become corrupt or deleted and thus needs to be restored to its original location, you can follow these steps:

1. In the DPM 2010 Administrator Console, go to the Recovery tab (as shown in Figure 10.38), and find the virtual machine listed under the recoverable data. Expand this and select All Protected Hyper-V Data. If you choose the second option, that is, Backup Using Child Partition Snapshot or Backup Using Saved State, then the recovery will be of the virtual hard disk only.

FIGURE 10.38
DPM 2010 Administrator Console — Recovery tab

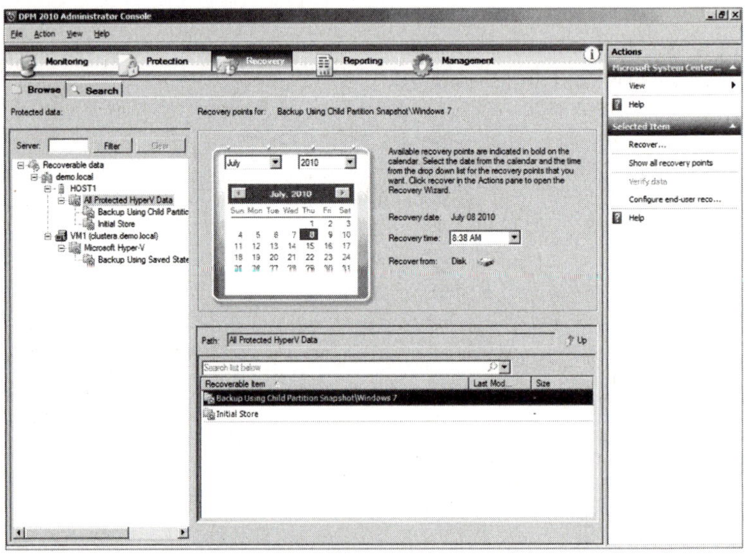

2. Available recovery points are indicated in bold on the calendar in the Recovery Points For section. Select the bold date for the recovery point you want to recover.

3. In the Recoverable Item section, click to select the recoverable item you want to recover. In the Actions pane, click Recover.

4. Data Protection Manager starts the Recovery Wizard (Figure 10.39). Review the recovery selection options, and click Next.

5. On the Select Recovery Type page (Figure 10.40), select Recover To Original Instance, and click Next.

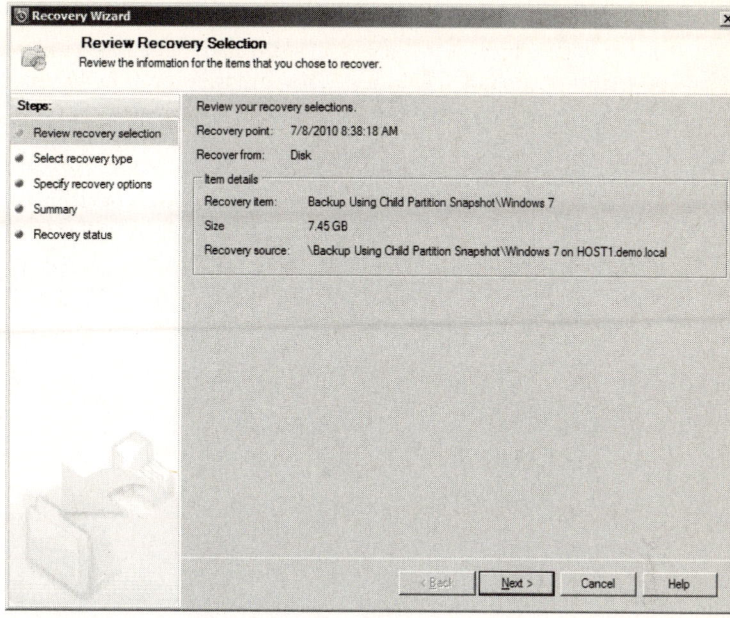

FIGURE 10.39
Recovery Wizard

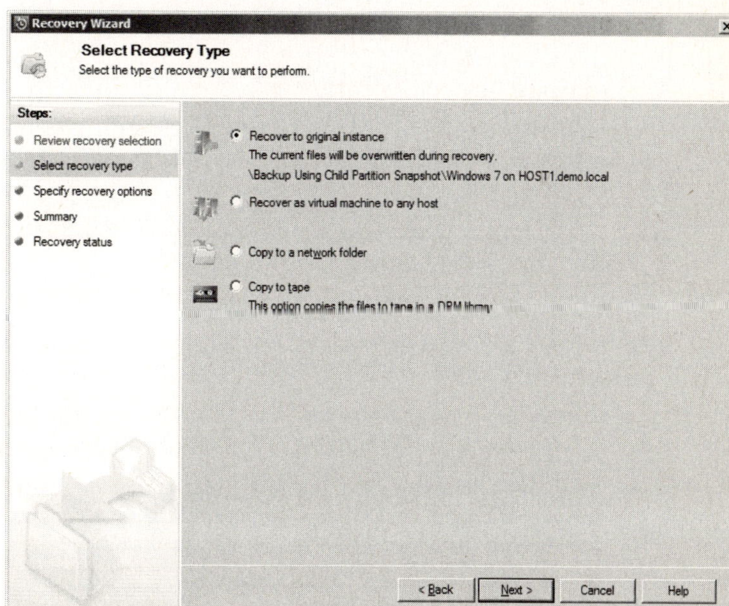

FIGURE 10.40
Select Recovery Type page

6. On the Specify Recovery Options page, click Next.

7. On the Summary page (Figure 10.41), verify the items selected for recovery, and click Recover.

FIGURE 10.41
Summary page

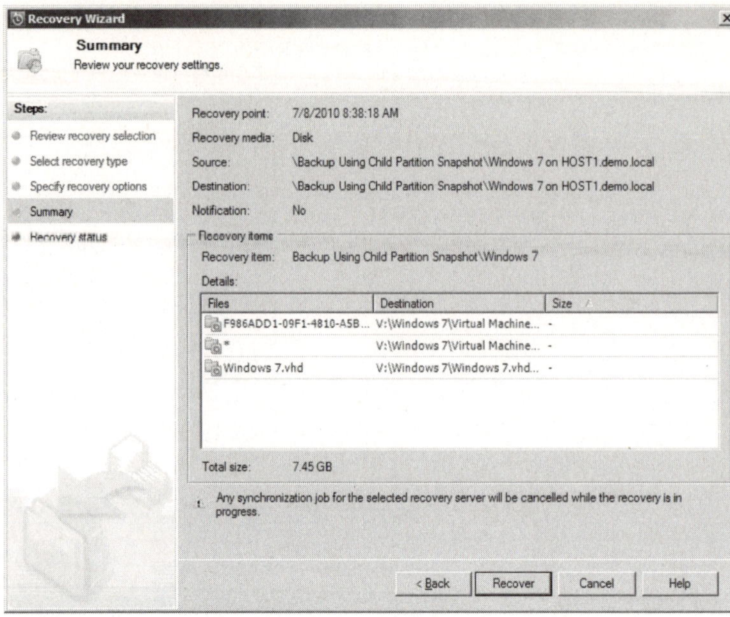

RECOVERING TO ORIGINAL LOCATION

This option restores the virtual machine to its original Hyper-V host and will overwrite any existing files. So, if there is a virtual machine still there and in use, this will be overwritten with the restored version.

> **RECOVERING A CLUSTERED VIRTUAL MACHINE**
>
> If you attempt to recover a clustered virtual machine that has been deleted, the recovery will fail. In the case of a disaster where the entire virtual machine cluster resource has been deleted or lost, you have two options:
>
> - Restore the virtual machine to an alternative location, and then once restored, make the virtual machine highly available, using Failover Cluster Manager.
> - Re-create a dummy virtual machine using the same name and CSV (without mounting any virtual hard disks). Make the virtual machine highly available, using Failover Cluster Manager, and then use Data Protection Manager to restore to the original location.

RECOVERING A VIRTUAL MACHINE TO ANY HOST

This will restore the virtual machine to another Hyper-V server so that it can run on the new host. If you are restoring the virtual machine to a Cluster Shared Volume, the space available shown will be that of the `C:\` drive and not the free space on the underlying CSV volume. This can often lead to some confusion, especially when the available space is less than actually required space or is less than you expect to be available. Despite these inconsistencies, you will not be prevented from proceeding. However, if the underlying CSV volume really does not have enough space, then the recovery will fail.

Recovery of a Virtual Machine to an Alternative Host

Using this option, you will be prompted for a location on your target Hyper-V server to restore to. This location will be where the virtual machine is homed and is not a temporary location. The target Hyper-V server in this instance must have an agent installed on it from the SCDPM 2010 server conducting the restore.

Copying to a Network Folder

This will export the configuration files and the virtual hard disk for you and will allow you to manipulate these files as appropriate.

Copying to a Network Share

Using this option, you will be prompted to browse for a folder where the files can be restored to. This can be any file location on a server that has an agent installed from the SCDPM 2010 server conducting the restore.

Copying to Tape

This puts the configuration files and the virtual machines hard disks on a tape so that it can be moved offsite or to another Data Protection Manager 2010 server for recovery at an alternative location.

Understanding Data Protection and Recovery for Cluster Shared Volumes

First, to serve as a reminder, what is a Cluster Shared Volume? A Cluster Shared Volume is a distributed access filesystem feature optimized only for Hyper-V, allowing virtual machines and their disk resources to reside on any Hyper-V node within the cluster. CSV enables multiple nodes to concurrently access a single shared volume, providing complete transparency in respect to cluster node ownership of virtual machines and client access during failover, using Live Migration.

However, CSV has an impact on how you back up your virtual machines. CSV has huge implications for VSS, because VSS assumes that the node you are backing up completely owns the storage. So, what does this mean?

When you carry out a backup of a virtual machine that resides on a Hyper-V server that is not the coordination node, the Hyper-V server running that virtual machine takes temporary ownership of the CSV LUN. The impact of this is that other Hyper-V servers housing virtual machines from that same CSV LUN go into Redirected I/O mode for the period that the backup executes.

If you take a look at a two-node cluster running a couple of virtual machines (as shown in Figure 10.42), what does this actually look like in reality? Node A is the coordinator node and owns the CSV LUN, and VM1 has direct I/O for both NTFS metadata operations and actual data reads and writes. However, VM2 has Redirected I/O for NTFS metadata operations but direct I/O for actual data reads and writes.

FIGURE 10.42
CSV access prior to backup

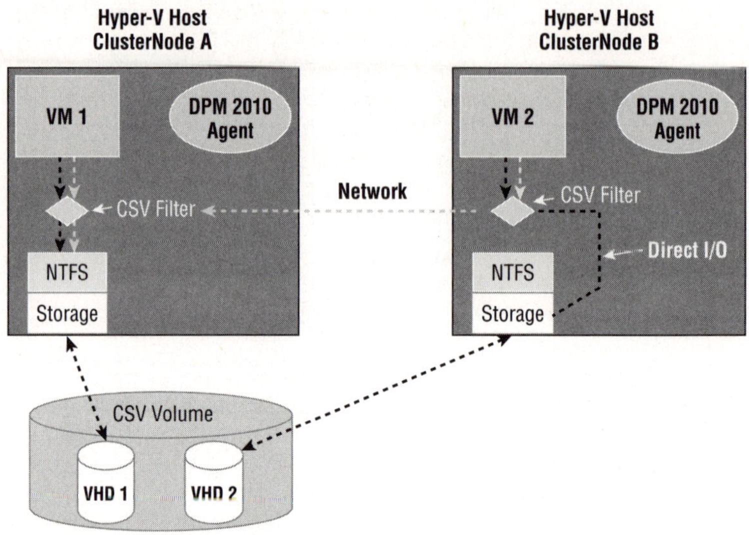

So, what happens when you want to back up VM2 on node B? Well, in this example, node B will take temporary ownership of the CSV LUN, and this will force all I/O for VM1 over the network through the CSV filter driver (as shown in Figure 10.43). This will affect the performance of VM1, and VM1 will remain in this degraded state until the backup completes.

To reduce the impact on Redirected I/O, Microsoft recommends using hardware snapshot-based backups (as shown in Figure 10.44). These types of backups allow normal I/O operation to resume — that is, direct I/O for both VM1 and VM2 in our previous example — for actual data reads and writes, as soon as the hardware snapshot has been taken.

Hardware snapshots leverage VSS and the underlying backup technology to create an instantaneous copy of the data. The instantaneous copying is typically accomplished by creating a mirrored volume or by temporarily creating a copy of a disk block, both of which are removed by the SCDPM 2010 agent after a successful backup of this temporary volume occurs.

VSS Hardware Provider Considerations

If you plan to use a VSS hardware provider, you can back up multiple virtual machines from the same CSV LUN/node. To specify the number of concurrent backups that can run from that node, you need to set the following registry key:

Key equals: HKLM\Software\Microsoft\Microsoft Data Protection Manager\2.0\Configuration\MaxAllowedParallelBackups

Type equals: DWORD

Value equals: Microsoft Hyper-V

Data equals: 3

FIGURE 10.43
CSV access during a backup operation

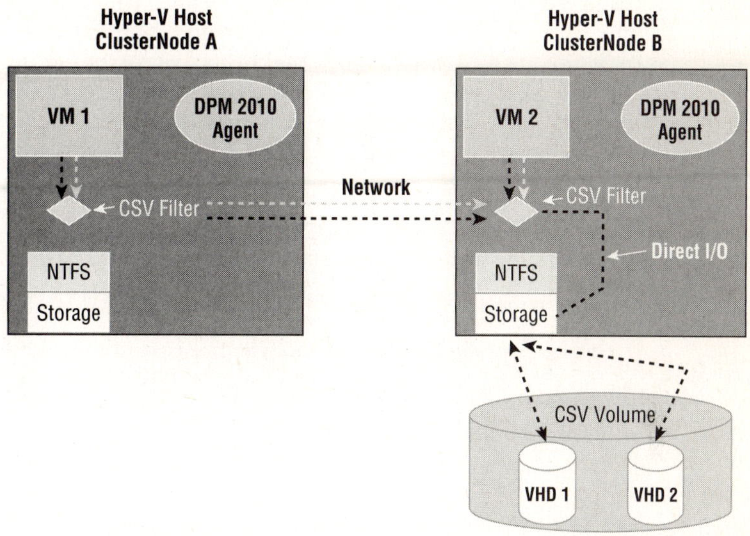

FIGURE 10.44
CSV hardware snapshot

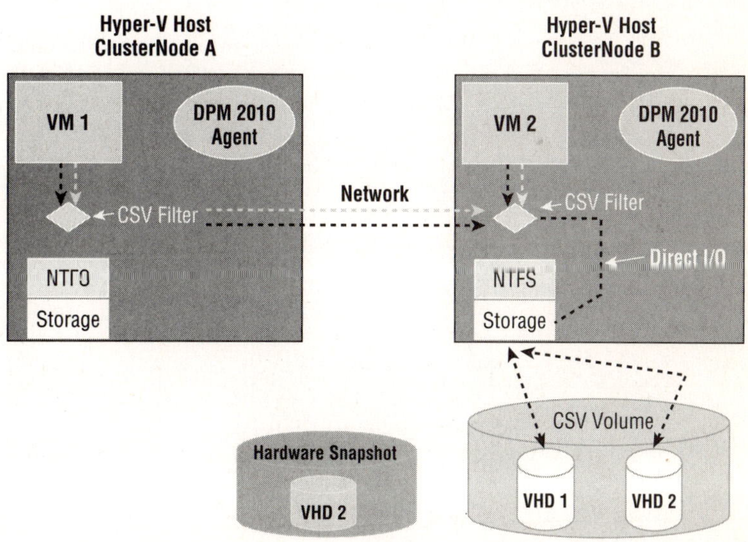

This allows a maximum of three backups to run concurrently on each node, and Microsoft recommends that you don't use a value greater than three for optimal performance. If possible, work with your storage vendor, because they will also have some experiences here to share in relation to optimally configuring SCDPM 2010 when used in combination with hardware snapshots and your SAN array.

Software VSS Provider Considerations

If your SAN vendor does not have VSS hardware providers, then you will need to use software snapshots to back up your virtual machines. If this is the case, then Microsoft recommends that virtual machines deployed on a CSV LUN be backed up serially. The reason behind this is because exclusive ownership of the CSV LUN must be maintained throughout the period of the backup. For instance, if another backup were to take place for a virtual machine that was homed on another Hyper-V server in the same cluster, before the backup of the original virtual machine had completed, the CSV LUN would be moved, and the partial snapshot for the original virtual machine would be deleted, which would result in a failed backup. Likewise, if the CSV LUN were to be manually moved to another node while the backup was in progress, the backup would fail for the same reason. There are two aspects to serialization of backup jobs in a CSV environment:

- Serializing virtual machine backups on a per-node basis
- Serializing virtual machine backups on a per CSV LUN basis

To configure per node serialization, you need to set the following registry key:

Key equals: HKLM\Software\Microsoft\Microsoft Data Protection Manager\2.0\Configuration\MaxAllowedParallelBackups

Type equals: DWORD

Value equals: Microsoft Hyper-V

Data equals: 1

To enable per-CSV serialization and to minimize the number of backups that can occur on a single CSV LUN, you need to generate a XML file (`DataSourceGroups.xml`) and place this file on the DPM server at `%ProgramFiles%\Microsoft DPM\DPM\Config`. This file provides DPM with information about the virtual machine deployment configuration and distribution across your CSV LUNs so as to serialize the backups.

Microsoft has produced a script (`DSCconfig.ps1`), available here:

`http://technet.microsoft.com/en-us/library/ff634192.aspx`

which creates the `DataSourceGroups.xml` by listing all the virtual machines hosted on one CSV LUN. Only one backup from each group is permitted at a time by DPM.

Creating DataSourceGroups.xml and Serializing the Backup Jobs

Follow these steps:

1. Generate `DataSourceGroups.xml` by running `DSCconfig.ps1` on any node in the cluster.
2. Repeat this process for each cluster that you want to protect with SCDPM 2010.
3. Merge all `DataSourceGroups.xml` files into a single file on the SCDPM 2010 server. You can skip this step if you are protecting only one cluster.
4. If a protection group has already been created for the virtual machines you want to protect, run through the Modify Protection Group Wizard.

The `DataSourceGroups.xml` file needs to be updated only when you add, delete, or modify virtual machines within the cluster and protection is already configured for them.

Merging the DataSourceGroups.xml Files from All CSV Clusters

Follow these steps:

1. Copy one of the `DataSourceGroups.xml` files that was generated to the SCDPM 2010 server under the location `%ProgramFiles%\Microsoft DPM\DPM\Config`, and open the file to edit it.
2. Copy the `<Group>` tag from all the `DataSourceGroups.xml` files generated, and add the text between the `<DataSourceGroup>` tags. The `DataSourceGroups.xml` file will now contain only one `<header>` tag, one `<dataSourceGroup>` tag, and one `<Group>` tag from all CSV clusters.
3. Close the `DataSourceGroups.xml` file on the DPM server.

Protecting System Center Virtual Machine Manager

Before you can understand the best way to protect and recover System Center Virtual Machine Manager (SCVMM), you need to understand the architecture of SCVMM. Knowing this architecture will help you determine your protection strategy going forward.

Understanding SCVMM Roles

SCVMM has a number of core roles that need to be backed up, and each role will have differing requirements. SCVMM's core roles are as follows:

- SCVMM Server
- Database Server
- Library Server
- Self-Service Portal

SCVMM Server

The Virtual Machine Manager Server is the core component that communicates with the virtual machine hosts and maintains its system information in a Microsoft SQL Server database. The VMM Server runs on the x64 bit version of Windows Server 2008 or Windows Server 2008 R2 and can be accessed through the SCVMM administrator console, through Windows PowerShell, or through the Self-Service Portal.

Database Server

SCVMM uses a SQL Server to store SCVMM's database. This database is used to store some configuration options, such as details on the managed hosts, host configuration settings, virtual machine settings, library resources, and things such as port number, which are used for communication with various subcomponents; one such example of this would be the communication ports used for communication with VMWare's vCenter Server.

The version of SQL Server that is used with SCVMM depends on the requirements and size of the environment. By default, if there is no previously installed version of SQL Server in the environment, SCVMM will install SQL Server Express edition on the local SCVMM server. However, SCVMM can leverage a remote SQL Server/SQL Server instance.

The placement of the SCVMM database can be influenced by not only the size of the environment but by your SQL Server strategy. A dedicated SQL Server or an instance of SQL Server may be provided by a separate team, and in this scenario, you will still want to ensure that regular backups occur. However, you might not have access to the chosen backup application or SQL Server Management Studio.

Library Server

The Library Server is a storage repository (think of it as a semistatic file server) that holds stored virtual machines, virtual hard disks, ISO files (these are CD/DVD software images), post-deployment customizations scripts (files such as `SYSPREP.XML`), hardware configurations, and templates.

Self-Service Portal

In addition to using the SCVMM administrator console or Windows PowerShell, administrator-designated users can access SCVMM by way of a web portal, designed for user self-service. This portal enables test and development users to quickly provision new virtual machines for themselves, according to controls set by SCVMM administrators.

Backing Up SCVMM

You need to make a judgment call about how you want to back up SCVMM. Do you protect the SCVMM server, and if so, what kind of backup strategy do you use?

First it is worth nothing that Microsoft supports running SCVMM as a highly available virtual machine, so if SCVMM is mission critical to you and you can't bear the downtime, then virtualizing SCVMM could be the way to go for you. But if you can, SCVMM has a very fast install, and Microsoft supports a number of ways to recover SCVMM, so you can always keep a recent backup of the VMM database and use it to build up a new VMM server in a matter of minutes.

Backing Up the Library Server

So, how should you protect the Library Server? Your backup strategy for Library Servers should follow the same strategy you use for your file servers. The only difference here is the frequency of the backups. How often you back up the Library Server will really depend on the frequency of change. In some environments, you may find very little is changing once you're at a steady state, so backing up the Library Server weekly (or even monthly perhaps) may be acceptable.

What is important to SCVMM is the library share on the Library Server; essentially, this is a file share. If the server goes down, the library objects will go missing. Once you restore the file server/share, SCVMM should pick those objects back up because SCVMM stamps all object in the SCVMM library.

BACKING UP THE SELF-SERVICE PORTAL

What about the Self-Service Portal? How should you protect the Self-Service Portal? Your backup strategy for the Self-Service Portal should follow the same strategy you use for your web servers. Again, the only difference here is the frequency of the backups. Since the Self-Service Portal is fairly static, backing up the Self-Service Portal monthly may be acceptable.

BACKING UP THE SCVMM DATABASE

It is important to back up the SCVMM database regularly as part of a comprehensive backup plan for protecting all SCVMM data, including data that resides on your hosts, the virtual machines, and the library servers. Besides using the tools provided in SCVMM, you can also use SQL Server Management Studio to back up and restore the SCVMM database as well as SCDPM 2010 or a third-party backup solution that includes support for SQL Server. Be careful, however, not to use more than one method, or a correct recovery of the database may not be possible.

Using SCVMM to Back Up the SCVMM Database

Follow these steps:

1. In Administration view, click General, and then click Back Up Virtual Machine Manager in the Actions pane.
2. In the Virtual Machine Manager Backup dialog box, type the path for a destination folder for the backup file.

Restoring the SCVMM Database onto the Same Computer

Follow these steps:

1. To restore the SCVMM database, run the `SCVMMrecover.exe` tool from the command line. This tool is located on the product DVD at the following path: `%ROOT%\amd64\bin`.
2. On the VMM database computer, open a command prompt window with elevated privileges, and then run the `SCVMMrecover.exe` tool using the following syntax: `SCVMMRecover [-Path <location>] [-Confirm]`, where *location* is the location of the SCVMM database backup.
3. If any hosts had been added or removed since the database backup and the physical computer that you are restoring the SCVMM database on has the same System Identification Number (SID) as the computer it was on before, you must perform the following steps. In the SCVMM administrator console, in Hosts view, do the following:
   - Remove any hosts that may have been removed from VMM since the last backup was created. If a host had been removed from SCVMM after the last backup was created, it will have a status of Needs Attention in Hosts view, and any virtual machines on that host will have a status of Host Not Responding in Virtual Machines view.
   - Add any hosts that may have been added since the last backup.

Third-Party Solutions

We dare say you already have a chosen backup vendor; it may be the product you used in your last successful project, it may be because you have a strategic partnership with that particular vendor, or it may be something you inherited when you took over the infrastructure you are now managing. No matter what product you are using, it is crucial you work with that vendor to determine their support for Hyper-V R2, and more importantly, it is important to understand if they provide support for CSV.

You can go to the Windows Server catalog `www.windowsservercatalog.com/` and search for supported backup vendors. There are a number of categories you can use to narrow down your search such as Windows 2008 R2 and even additional subcategories such as Hyper-V, but this won't help you determine whether that particular product supports CSV.

Would it surprise you to know at the time of writing this chapter Microsoft has no formal published list of third-party vendors that support CSV? So, you need to check with your current vendor (do the due diligence) or shop around.

Although there is no third-party list available, at the time of writing this chapter, a number of third-party vendors support Hyper-V R2 and CSV. Although not a definitive list or a series of recommendations, take a look at the following two vendors if you are considering an alternative approach.

Symantec Backup Exec 2010

Symantec Backup Exec 2010 Agent for Hyper-V provides protection support for the entire Hyper-V host and all its virtual machines. The Symantec Backup Exec 2010 Agent provides support for individual granular file and folder recovery from inside virtual machines. The agent for Microsoft Hyper-V includes the following:

- Protecting the Hyper-V host configuration data
- Protecting both Windows and Linux virtual machines
- Protecting applications such as Exchange, SQL Server, or Active Directory as part of the entire virtual machine

Backup Exec 2010 Agent for Hyper-V includes support for Hyper-V R2, which includes the support of CSV. Backup Exec 2010 Agent for Hyper-V can automatically protect the highly available (HA) configuration of virtual machines on a Hyper-V R2 CSV and can recover the virtual machine with this configuration intact.

Computer Associates ARCserve R15

ARCserve Backup R15 provides protection for Hyper-V. It lets you protect virtual machines located on a CSV volume by using the ARCserve Backup Agent for Virtual Machines. ARCserve Backup R15 has an automatic discovery function for virtual machines to help ensure that all virtual machines are backed up, regardless of how dynamic your environment becomes.

The Bottom Line

Use the inbox backup tool, Windows Server Backup VSS is a framework developed by Microsoft, which provides a backup infrastructure that was first introduced in Windows Server 2003. Knowing the components and how the components work will help you understand how the backup process works.

> **Master It** Name the four basic components of a VSS solution that need to be in place for a complete solution to work. Provide an oversimplified explanation of how VSS works.

Understand what the backup options are in a virtualized environment There are four backup types and two methods to actually carry out a backup within a virtualized environment. Each is useful and applicable in its own way.

> **Master It** Name the four backup types, and list the two methods for carrying out a backup.

Use Data Protection Manager to protect virtual workloads When planning for SCDPM 2010, it is important to understand what the system, software, security, network, and hardware requirements are.

> **Master It** Name the five prerequisite software components that need to be installed prior to installing SCDPM 2010. Define the recommended hardware requirements for SCDPM 2010.

Chapter 11

The Small and Medium Business

You could be forgiven for thinking that Microsoft only thought of huge corporations and government departments when designing Hyper-V. In fact, it's difficult to find mention of small or medium businesses in the marketing material for Hyper-V, and so far in the book, we have talked about Hyper-V clusters with up to 1,000 virtual machines, expensive storage solutions, and Microsoft System Center products that appear to be reserved for large networks.

The truth is that the vast majority of Microsoft's customers are small and medium businesses. These same customers face all of the same challenges that international corporations do. You could say that they feel the pain even more because downtime and high costs are the difference between people having a job and the business going under.

We're going to start this chapter by focusing on how Hyper-V can be used with Small Business Server (SBS), Microsoft's packaged solution for the smaller organization. SBS has been a huge success for Microsoft. Its implementers have to be experts in many technologies and in ways to implement them on a shoestring budget. We're going to show you how you can use Hyper-V virtualization in smaller organizations to reduce costs, increase flexibility, and allow for easier management in the future.

We won't forget the medium-sized business either. These are the organizations that need some form of systems management solution but find the usual System Center products to be too expensive or require too much work. System Center Essentials (SCE) 2010 is a new version of the systems management package aimed at this market. Microsoft knew that these were likely to be the organizations that would quickly adopt Hyper-V, so it has included much of the functionality of VMM 2008 R2 in SCE 2010. We will take a look at what this product brings to the table and how it can be used.

In this chapter, you will learn to

- Deploy Small Business Server 2008 on Hyper-V
- Understand System Center Essentials 2010
- Understand licensing for small and medium businesses

The Small and Medium Business

Microsoft considers a small business to be one with just a few servers (maybe even just one) and less than 75 users. There is a bit of overlap with the medium-sized business, which has between 50 and 500 users and up to 50 servers. You don't hear or read about these organizations very much. There aren't many press releases or case studies about them. You could be forgiven for thinking that they are a bit of an irrelevancy if you work in a large organization, but you would be badly mistaken.

Maybe the majority of Microsoft's revenue does come from larger corporations and government departments, but the majority of its customers fall into the small and medium business (SMB) category. Most IT professionals either work in SMBs or provide services to them as part of services companies that specialize in the SMB market.

There are unique challenges in this market. IT is often considered a huge cost. It's a bit of an evil necessity. The role that IT can play is often undervalued. That makes the IT professional's job more difficult. They have little or no time for training, let alone the budget for it. They often work with old technology. Too often they have to be rather inventive by engineering solutions from duct tape and wire.

SMBs also face the same challenges as the multinational companies, but they sometimes don't realize it, nor do they realize that the same solutions can save them effort and precious budget. Here are some specific areas to look at:

Power Electricity is an expensive resource, and it is not getting any cheaper. In fact, many countries have already started to introduce carbon taxes. Small and medium businesses are the most sensitive to these cost increases. They cannot be absorbed, and they must be passed onto their customers, putting the business at increased risk.

Flexibility An organization with little budget will not have any spare hardware. Upgrades to Small Business Server usually require additional hardware to perform what is referred to as a *swing migration*. This is an unwanted expense, so it leads to the upgrade not taking place. As a result, small businesses often cling to older versions of software. That denies them access to new business solutions, denies their staff access to new skills, and makes it harder for services companies to support a broader base of products.

Backup and Recovery It is challenging enough to guarantee the recovery of systems and data if you have a huge budget. Imagine what it is like when your budget is small or is almost nonexistent. Traditional servers are difficult to back up and recover. Advanced solutions that simplify backup and recovery can be very expensive. When faced with the question of budget vs. recovery, the small and medium business often makes the unfortunate decision to gamble on the future of their business.

Business Continuity SMBs face the same requirements to implement disaster recovery or business continuity plans. Some industries are regulated and mandate some form of offsite recovery within a defined time frame. Others face the prospect of closing down if they lose access to their IT infrastructure, business applications, and data. Even larger organizations find implementing these offsite solutions to be a technical and financial challenge. Many businesses simply decide to ignore the necessity to implement a business continuity plan because it is too expensive.

Test and Development SMBs have business applications that need to be upgraded and tested. Hardware for doing this is expensive. Testing for upgrades cannot happen. The business faces a nasty decision as a result of this. Do they upgrade the applications without testing? Or do they stick with the currently working version, even if the vendor is threatening to end support for it?

Most software development companies are actually pretty small. They have restricted budgets for hardware to test and develop on. With tight deadlines, they have little time to spend on rebuilding hardware for clean environments.

These are all the same problems that the larger organization faces. These problems are just more extreme in SMBs because of the impact that they have on a smaller environment. A solution can therefore have a bigger impact on the success or survivability of a SMB than it might for a multinational corporation.

What is that solution? You've guessed it: Hyper-V. Virtualization gives an SMB an affordable way to reduce power and hardware costs. Flexibility is increased because their critical servers are converted into files (virtual machines) that can be easily moved. Those same virtual machine files are easy to back up and easy to replicate, possibly to economic public Cloud environments.

In this chapter, we will cover how Hyper-V can be deployed in the SMB. We will start by looking at how Small Business Server 2008 can be hosted on Hyper-V. There is some flexibility in Microsoft licensing that can be very advantageous. We will also look at the role of Hyper-V in the medium-sized business and how System Center Essentials 2010 can be used to provide an economic solution for enterprise management.

THE THIRD-PARTY SOFTWARE VENDOR

Third-party software vendors play a huge role in adding features and functionality in the SMB market. Don't be afraid to do some searching and ask some questions if you find a problem that you cannot solve with Microsoft's native tool set.

Small Business Server 2008

We will start off by briefly introducing you to SBS 2008, just in case you have never worked with it before. We will then look at how it can be implemented with Hyper-V.

Introducing SBS 2008

SBS has been one of Microsoft's most successful products and has gone through a number of versions. The current release is SBS 2008. This solution provides a single-server solution that includes the following:

- A Windows Server 2008 machine with Active Directory
- All the usual Windows Server 2008 Standard edition features, such as file sharing
- Exchange 2007 Standard edition
- Windows SharePoint Services 3.0

- Windows Server Update Services (WSUS)
- Supports up to 75 users

The setup is a packaged routine, installing and configuring each of the components through a wizard. Day-to-day administration is made possible through a single administrative utility. Here you have a checklist for the final configuration steps and the ability to provision users (with mailboxes), set up groups with permissions, and manage the overall health of the entire company network.

There are two licenses for SBS:

Standard Edition This provides you with licensing for the domain controller with all of the previously mentioned functionality. It costs approximately $1,089, including client access licenses (CALs) for five users or devices.

Premium Edition This includes an additional license to run Windows Server 2008 Standard edition and SQL Server 2008 Standard edition. You can decide how you want to use this licensing. It is recommended that SQL Server is not installed on the SBS machine; you can install it on the included server license. Alternatively, you can use this included Standard license as a terminal server (it is Windows Server 2008, so the old term still applies). It can even be used as an additional domain controller in the SBS domain, although the SBS server will retain the Flexible Single Master Operation (FSMO) roles for normal operations. The Premium edition costs about $1,899 and includes CALs for five users or devices.

Users or devices require SBS CALs and Terminal Services CALs to access the services provided by SBS; SBS controls that access very tightly. CALs can be purchased individually, or they can be acquired in packs of 5 or 20. A Standard CAL will cost about $77, and a Premium CAL will cost about $189. (These are the U.S. prices, and they will be different in each region.)

Most small businesses don't employ IT experts. Typically they will engage some type of managed services company to install and support their infrastructure on an annual basis. The engineers who work for those services companies will vary wildly in quality. A few will be highly qualified and have an amazingly huge breadth of experience. Many will be quite junior and just getting their feet onto the career ladder. Unfortunately, a few have no place in our industry and do their clients no favors with the quality of their work.

THE CLOUD

You might have thought that you walked into a cult's brainwashing camp if you have been to a Microsoft event or tuned into a Microsoft keynote lately. All Microsoft wants to talk about is *the Cloud*. The Cloud is a new perspective on hosted solutions where some infrastructure, application platform, storage, or service is provided on a subscription basis. All you need to use the service is an appliance with Internet access and a credit card. There is no need to install a server, deal with infrastructure, or deal what can feel like endless delays to get on-premises installations up and running. One Microsoft executive was clocked at saying *the Cloud* more than 80 times in a single presentation. Why is that? Microsoft has invested a huge amount of money building datacenters around the world to host a number of public Cloud services.

One of these services is Business Productivity Online Suite (BPOS). BPOS provides online file storage and collaboration in the form of SharePoint. Email is possible with Exchange Online. Internet messaging and communications are possible with Office Live Meeting and Office Communications Online. BPOS can provide most of the features of SBS with no server purchase or maintenance. Getting the service up and running takes only a few minutes, and it provides a configuration program to configure your computer and Microsoft Outlook. Your entire small business can be up and running in minutes. Microsoft is pushing hard on services such as BPOS. The company completed a process to reinvent itself as a Cloud company in 2010, and it now starts every sales and marketing effort with its Cloud offerings.

Competitors to Microsoft offer alternative solutions. Some provide a shared computing experience. Others provide you with your own hosted Small Business Server with some method for accessing it.

The point is that many traditional SBS customers will not be renewing the traditional maintenance contract with a field engineering company. They have alternatives where they don't need to have servers in their office or pay for people to install and maintain SBS.

There will be those companies who will continue to use SBS. Some might have Internet connectivity issues. Others might have regulatory or trust issues with data being in a datacenter. And some might have more practical concerns where they must have a local domain and server presence. These are the people you will want to focus on for your Hyper-V and SBS efforts.

Using SBS on Hyper-V

You can install SBS 2008 as a virtual machine on a Hyper-V host server. This is a supported solution. This will solve many of the problems faced in a small business. Hyper-V abstracts the hardware from the machine. The virtual machine files are easy to move, easy to replicate, and easy to back up. A valuable feature of this solution is that the SBS engineer or administrator is using a virtualization platform that is pretty familiar. Hyper-V runs on Windows, so there is less for the responsible person to learn, and there is a good chance that existing utilities will be useful for managing the host server. The host server can run the SBS 2008 virtual machine, as well as other virtual machines, including the server that is included in the Premium edition.

Working with Licensing and Architecture

There are a number of possible ways to use Windows licensing to implement a Hyper-V architecture for SBS. Some of these solutions take advantage of Windows Server licensing to give a free license. *Free* is a word that SBS customers love! We will look at a few different scenarios and see how SBS 2008 can be effectively deployed.

SBS 2008 Standard

This is the most basic scenario that you will deal with. The company has a very small network, and its only server will run SBS 2008. Normally you would purchase a small server and install SBS 2008 onto that. Even with Hyper-V, that is probably the option you are most likely to continue to use.

However, there are a few reasons why you might want to deploy SBS 2008 as a virtual machine on a Hyper-V host server.

Installing SBS 2008 as a virtual machine will abstract it from the hardware. The host server may experience a complete hardware failure. You will be able to quickly move the virtual machine VHDs to another host, create a new virtual machine, attach the VHDs, and get the company back up and running with very little downtime.

This mobility will also be useful when the host server ages and must be replaced. A small amount of work can be done to prepare the new host server. The virtual machine can be exported from the original host server and imported on the newer host server.

With any luck, the company will grow. You can choose and specify your hardware carefully. For example, don't populate all the memory and disk slots with very low-end units. This will allow the Hyper-V host server to host additional virtual machines as the company grows.

There is no upgrade process for Small Business Server. There is a side-by-side migration process that you can do to move data and users to a newer version of SBS. This normally requires an additional physical machine to complete the process. Having a Hyper-V host will allow additional virtual machines to be deployed to complete the migration project.

At first glimpse, it might seem like overkill to run SBS on a Hyper-V host in a single-server company. The flexibility, mobility, and agility that virtualization brings can reduce the long-term costs, minimize complexity, and simplify administrative operations.

There is no need to purchase a copy of Windows Server 2008 for the parent partition. This sort of deployment will be able to take advantage of the free Hyper-V Server 2008 R2. The lack of a GUI might require a little bit more work. But on the bright side, it will probably scare away people who should not be going anywhere near the parent partition.

SBS Premium

Think about how Microsoft licenses Hyper-V. Hyper-V Server 2008 R2 gives a lot of value, but it lacks a GUI. That can be a problem for services companies that often must employ many junior field engineers. Time is money, and struggling with a command prompt when a GUI would allow a quick solution sometimes just won't do. The Datacenter edition of Windows Server provides free licensing for all guest operating systems on the licensed host server. The Enterprise edition provides free licensing for up to four guest operating systems on the licensed host server. And the Standard edition includes one free license.

Hey, SBS Premium includes a copy of Windows Server Standard edition. And it just so happens that you can install that on physical machine, enable the Hyper-V role, and still get one free copy of Window Server Standard edition to run as a virtual machine. You've lost nothing by doing this. You are doing the following:

- Installing the bundled copy of Windows Server Standard edition as the Hyper-V host server
- Installing SBS 2008 as the first virtual machine
- Using the free Windows Server Standard guest operating system license for the second virtual machine, which will run as your application server

The advantage of this is that you can enable the GUI on the Hyper-V host server, and you will quickly be able to manage it with existing skills in the company. Hardware will be easy to manage, and management products will work as usual.

Make sure that you use the 64-bit edition of Windows Server Standard. You cannot use the 32-bit edition to create a Hyper-V host server.

If you are planning four or more Windows Server virtual machines in addition to the SBS virtual machine, then you should consider a more economic option.

Enterprise or Datacenter Editions

It might seem inconceivable at first, but companies that use SBS can grow to require a number of servers. Over time, a database, maybe a web server, a Remote Desktop Services session host, an accounting system, a small CRM system, and so on, might appear. They may be small, but they have the same needs as a bigger company.

In Chapter 5, "Planning the Hardware Deployment," we discussed why it could be more cost effective to purchase the Enterprise edition or even the Datacenter edition of Windows Server instead of licensing each individual virtual machine with the Standard edition. The savings are because of the free guest operating system licensing that is included with those editions. A small business can take advantage of this savings too.

An Enterprise edition of Windows Server 2008 R2 could be installed as the parent partition if four copies of Windows Server are required in addition to SBS 2008 as guest operating systems. This will be cheaper than buying individual copies of Windows Server Standard edition for the four virtual machines. If many virtual machines are required, then a Datacenter edition of Windows Server 2008 R2 could be installed as the parent partition.

There is a lot to digest and consider. Here are some of the questions that usually arise at this point:

Can I Install SBS as the Parent Partition and Enable Hyper-V? This one is simple: no. This would be a really bad idea. Remember that a parent partition should have no other roles installed. The only things you should install on a parent partition are server management agents.

What Are the Network Requirements? You should have at least two network cards on the Hyper-V host server, as normal for a nonclustered Hyper-V host. One will be used for the parent partition. The other will be used for the virtual machines. You can double that number if you need to use NIC teaming for network path fault tolerance.

Should I Add the Parent Partition to the SBS Domain? The parent partition should not be a member of the SBS domain. Rebooting the Hyper-V host server would create a chicken and-egg scenario. The parent partition will probably be a workgroup member. You can use HVRemote (`http://code.msdn.microsoft.com/HVRemote`) to configure remote administration of the parent partition.

Can I Create a Snapshot of the SBS Virtual Machine? Microsoft recommends that you never pause, save the state of, or create a snapshot of a domain controller virtual machine. This includes SBS.

What Do I Back Up? Microsoft recommends that you back up the parent partition and the virtual machines using a product that supports your version of Hyper-V. You can use a backup product that has support for Hyper-V to back up the parent partition and the virtual machines at the storage level using the Volume Shadow Copy Service (VSS). The SBS virtual machine can be backed up using its native backup mechanism.

Knowing the System Requirements

The system requirements for SBS are as follows:

SBS Server (Standard and Premium Editions) The server will require the following:

- CPU: 2 GHz x64 processor or faster.
- Memory: Between 4 and 32 GB RAM.
- Disk space: Minimum of 60 GB.
- Fax modem: This is required for the SBS Fax Services feature.

Additional Server

- CPU: 2 GHz x86 or x64 (recommended) processor or faster.
- Memory: Between 2 GB and 4 GB for 32-bit and 2 GB and 32 GB for 64-bit.
- Disk space: Supported minimum of 10 GB. The recommended minimum is 40 GB.

Both Servers

- Network connectivity.
- Internet connectivity.

Those who are new to Small Business Server might guess that some lightweight piece of hardware will do the work. That is certainly not the case. Look at the features that are included in SBS. Exchange 2007 requires significant resources to run even just a few mailboxes. It also needs a 64-bit operating system. Windows SharePoint Services will use the Windows Internal Database, and that will require processor and memory. The minimum supported amount of memory is 4 GB, but many SBS veterans will start with 8 GB of RAM, knowing that they will have to do the upgrade eventually. 60 GB of disk space will not suffice; that does not include space for data in the SharePoint database, in the Exchange mailboxes, or in any file shares. 60 GB is just enough space to install SBS 2008.

Designing the SBS Virtual Machine

The design principles discussed in Chapter 8, "Virtualization Scenarios," will be applied to the design of the SBS virtual machine.

Let's start with the processor. The parent partition will require at least one physical processor core. Exchange is probably the big consumer of processor resources in the SBS virtual machine. If you refer to Chapter 8, you'll find that you can have a 2:1 virtual processor to physical processor with Exchange. You would need to allow at least two physical cores on the host server if your SBS virtual machine is configured with four virtual CPUs. That would total three physical cores including the parent partition. You might use a 1:1 ratio if you are conservative. That's because the SBS virtual machine is also running domain services, file services, WSUS, and SharePoint. That will require five physical cores including the parent partition. Add another virtual machine, and you are probably looking at a Hyper-V host server with at least a six-core processor, an eight-core processor, or a pair of quad-core processors.

If we assume that the SBS virtual machine will be assigned 8 GB of RAM, then we can calculate the total required physical RAM as follows:

```
RAM Required = (1024 + 32) + ((1024 + 8) × (GBRAM − 1))
```

If GBRAM is 8, then we have this:

```
RAM Required = (1024 + 32) + ((1024 + 8) × (8 − 1)) = 8,280MB
```

That means the virtual machine requires just over 8 GB of physical RAM. The parent partition will require 2 GB of RAM. This adds up to just over 10 GB of RAM, not including any additional virtual machines.

The parent partition will require 40 GB of disk space. We might assume that SBS will require 500 GB of disk space. For performance reasons, a fixed-size VHD should be used. Anything SBS that approaches 2040 GB of disk should use a passthrough disk instead.

The virtual machine can have one synthetic network adapter. The `C:` drive will boot from an IDE-attached VHD. You should use the virtual SCSI controller to attach any additional disks. Remember to install the latest version of the Hyper-V integration components once the operating system is running in the SBS virtual machine. The setup of the additional components in SBS will fail if they cannot detect devices such as an operating network adapter.

MICROSOFT GUIDANCE FOR SBS WITH HYPER-V

You can find the best practices for running SBS in a Hyper-V virtual machine here:

`http://technet.microsoft.com/library/dd239199(WS.10).aspx`

You can find information about known issues here:

`http://technet.microsoft.com/library/dd239204(WS.10).aspx`

LOOKING AT THE TRICKY BITS WITH SBS

Let's look at the challenges of running SBS as a virtual machine on a Hyper-V host server.

The fax modem is where you hit the first hitch. You will not be able to pass through that device natively in Hyper-V. It is because of this that Microsoft does not support the Fax Services role in a virtualized SBS machine.

Some companies may have invested in a tape backup device. There is not a Microsoft-supported way to connect a virtual machine to a SCSI-attached tape device. Don't try to take a shortcut; do not install the backup management application on the parent partition.

Speaking of backup, SBS 2008 has a native backup mechanism that assumes you are going to attach a USB hard disk as the backup media. You cannot plug a USB device to a Hyper-V virtual machine. One option is to present a SCSI-attached VHD to the virtual machine and use this as the backup media. Another one is to plug a USB drive into the host server and present it as a SCSI-attached passthrough disk in the SBS virtual machine. Just be sure that the VHD is detached from the virtual machine before you unplug the USB hard disk. We recommend using the virtual SCSI controller because it supports Plug and Play on Windows Server 2008 R2 Hyper-V host servers.

There are a few things to overcome when considering running SBS as a Hyper-V virtual machine. It might not be a solution for every small business, but Hyper-V will solve problems and reduce costs for many SBS customers.

Real World Scenario

COMMON SMALL BUSINESS SERVER ISSUES

The typical SBS customer may have several service providers working on their site, each of various skill levels, with some of those being of a less than desirable level. You will have to account for the lowest common denominator when implementing and documenting SBS on a Hyper-V host server.

You might have deliberately decided not to put any antivirus software on your Hyper-V host server. You might have secured it appropriately (workgroup member and local firewall policy), but someone might have come along afterward and decided that your parent partition should have antivirus software and that it should scan everything. You should do your best to prevent this by documenting why antivirus software should not be installed or why it is configured a certain way. See Chapter 12, "Security," to learn more about that subject.

Some service providers might try to install the newest version of the accounting system or some multifunction printer software on the parent partition. This is an absolutely horrendous idea. You should try to communicate, again with documentation, that this too is a bad idea.

Leaving the parent partition in a workgroup (as recommended by Microsoft) will discourage anyone from trying to use it as a service provider to the domain.

Nothing works like an in-your-face reminder. You might be able to use wallpaper or a document/web page that autostarts when you log in to communicate the importance of the parent partition and how it should be treated differently than other servers.

System Center Essentials (SCE) 2010

The medium-sized business is defined by Microsoft as having between 50 and 500 personal computers and up to 50 servers. The companies that were in this market were forgotten about for quite some time. They looked at their smaller neighbors who had the excellent Small Business Server. They looked at their larger neighbors who had access to bulk licensing deals and expensive systems management products.

Medium-sized businesses are caught in a catch-22 situation. They have a requirement to provide a larger IT infrastructure to enable the business, but their budget is small. The medium-sized business faces all the same challenges as the small and large business. They have had two choices:

- Spend more on IT to acquire and implement the products aimed at the larger enterprise.
- Use cheaper, non-Microsoft products that might not integrate very well.

Very often they have chosen the latter option. Those management products can be a false economy. They may have the potential to provide an amazing service, but they will require huge amounts of skill development and engineering to ever provide a service that could match even some of what is offered by Microsoft System Center.

The other difficulty lies in the skill base that medium-sized businesses can afford to hire. Limited budget means either hiring a few overworked people or hiring more people of a junior to mid-level grade. They may depend on managed services contracts, often from multiple vendors at once, for different pieces of the infrastructure. The medium-sized business will also use consulting firms quite a lot to implement any changes because of the lack of experience within the firm. The IT staff members in the medium-sized business don't have the time to manage the IT infrastructure. Ironically, they don't have either the time or the funds to implement the systems that can automate much of that management.

Microsoft acknowledged the gap in its product catalog to cater to this market and released two products:

Windows Essential Business Server 2008 This was a three-server package (with an option of four servers) that was intended to be Small Business Server for the medium-sized business. It was an odd offering because it tried to replace much of what the target customer would already have in place. They already had a firewall, antivirus software, email, and so on. This package would really be of use only to those organizations that were starting up or growing beyond the limits of SBS. But even then it was a bit restrictive. Microsoft eventually withdrew this product in 2010.

System Center Essentials (SCE) 2007 This System Center product was intended to provide management features to the medium-sized business. It packaged features from System Center Operations Manager (monitoring), WSUS (patch distribution), and software distribution into one product. The original release supported up to 30 servers and up top 500 desktops or laptops. It also had no virtualization management features. A new, improved version of System Center Essentials was released in 2010.

What Is SCE 2010?

VMware might have an established foothold in the Fortune 1000 companies, but the medium-sized market is an open sales battlefield. The medium-sized business wants virtualization for all of the same reasons as the larger enterprise. However, they cannot afford the more expensive licensing that VMware offers, and they don't see why they should have to use versions without host fault tolerance. Windows Server 2008 R2 Hyper-V has given them an opportunity to implement enterprise-level virtualization that offers excellent performance, high availability, and Live Migration.

Microsoft released SCE 2010 in the summer of 2010. Two major changes were made to the original product in acknowledgment of the importance of Windows Server 2008 R2 Hyper-V to the medium-sized business:

Virtualization Management System Center Virtual Machine Manager (VMM) 2008 R2 is Microsoft's System Center product for managing Windows Server 2008 R2 Hyper-V. Elements of VMM were integrated into the SCE 2010 package. This allows administrators in the medium-sized business to use a single console to manage their entire server infrastructure, including the virtual machines.

Increased Scale Virtualization means that a company may have more servers running on the network. In response to this, Microsoft increased the supported server limit from 30 to 50 in SCE 2010.

Installing SCE 2010

There are a few versions of SCE 2010 that you can purchase. There is the normal single-server package of System Center Essentials 2010, which costs $103. This includes SQL Server Express edition. This will provide enough database capacity for managing up to 150 computers.

System Center Essentials 2010 Management Server Software License with SQL Server Technology costs $870. The included SQL Server 2008 Standard edition will allow SCE 2010 to manage up to its limits of 50 servers and 500 computers.

Each server that is managed by SCE 2010 will require a management license that costs $103. Each client that is managed by SCE 2010 will require a management license that costs $17.

There is also a product called System Center Essentials Plus 2010 Server, which is priced at $412. This includes System Center Data Protection Manager 2010 with server management licenses to protect (back up) up to 50 servers. This license includes only SQL Server Express edition. You will require client management licenses to back up computers. This SCE Plus client management license costs approximately $32 per client.

The recommended minimum hardware requirements for SCE 2010 are as follows:

- 2.8 GHz or faster processor(s)
- 4 GB of RAM
- 20 GB of available hard disk space
- 150 GB or more of available hard disk space if using virtualization management

The Windows Server Catalog indicates that it is supported to install SCE 2010 in a virtual machine. You have to question whether this is a good idea. It seems illogical to manage your virtualization platform with a virtual machine that is running in that infrastructure. You might need to provide four virtual processors in a SCE 2010 virtual machine. You probably should allow for one physical core on the Hyper-V host server for every virtual processor in the SCE 2010 virtual machine. This is because it includes a lot of management features and a SQL Server database.

There are three different deployment scenarios depending on the size of the infrastructure that SCE 2010 will manage (Table 11.1).

TABLE 11.1: SCE 2010 deployment scenarios

Managed computers (clients and servers)	SCE 2010 architecture	Recommended SQL Server edition
Up to 150	Single server with all components	SQL Server 2008 Express edition with Advanced Services
Up to 300	Single server with all components	SQL Server 2008 Standard or Enterprise edition
Up to 550	Database server and SCE 2010 management server	SQL Server 2008 Standard or Enterprise edition

SCE 2010

We're not going to cover SCE 2010 in too much detail in this book. The relevant features of SCE 2010 are present in VMM 2008 R2, which was covered in Chapter 7.

Comparing Products

SCE 2010 will probably have sufficient functionality to meet the needs of many medium-sized businesses. However, 50 servers and 500 user machines are quite a lot to manage. Some medium-sized businesses might require some of the functionality of the individual System Center products:

- System Center Configuration Manager 2007 R3
- System Center Operations Manager 2007 R2
- Virtual Machine Manager 2008 R2

Let's compare the features of each of the individual System Center products with SCE 2010. Table 11.2 shows how SCE 2010 compares with OpsMgr 2007 R2.

TABLE 11.2: SCE 2010 and Operations Manager 2007 R2 feature comparison

FEATURE	OPERATIONS MANAGER 2007 R2	SCE 2010	NOTES
Monitoring of servers, clients, software, and appliances	Yes	Yes	SCE 2010 includes a management pack for network appliance monitoring that is not included with OpsMgr 2007 R2.
Uses management packs	Yes	Yes	
Agentless exception monitoring	Yes	Yes	
Add Monitoring Wizard	Yes	Yes	
Reporting	Yes	Yes	No report authoring available in SCE 2010. SCE 2010 is limited to 40 days of reporting data.
Branch office monitoring	Yes	Yes	SCE 2010 is limited to a single management server and a single domain.
Role-based security	Yes	No	Local server or domain administrator has full SCE 2010 rights.

TABLE 11.2: SCE 2010 and Operations Manager 2007 R2 feature comparison *(CONTINUED)*

FEATURE	OPERATIONS MANAGER 2007 R2	SCE 2010	NOTES
Connector framework	Yes	No	
Audit Collection Services	Yes	No	
Web console	Yes	No	
Cross-platform support	Yes	No	No native support for UNIX or Linux in SCE 2010.

An organization with 500 computers may have up to 10 IT staff. It might be possible that delegated roles would be required. This depends on role-based security. This sort of company may also have a heterogeneous server network, requiring cross-platform support. A connector framework might be required for third-party software integration. And it is also possible that an organization of this size must retain security logs (Audit Collection Services) for regulatory compliance. These are example situations where you might need to use the stand-alone OpsMgr 2007 R2 instead of SCE 2010 to monitor your IT infrastructure and applications.

Table 11.3 shows how SCE 2010 compares with Configuration Manager 2007 R3.

TABLE 11.3: SCE 2010 and Configuration Manager 2007 R3 feature comparison

FEATURE	CONFIGURATION MANAGER 2007 R3	SCE 2010	NOTES
Microsoft and third-party patch management	Yes	Yes	
Software distribution	Yes	Yes	SCE supports only basic .MSI and .EXE installation with no command-line parameters.
Hardware and software inventory	Yes	Yes	SCE 2010 supports included 60+ attributes; ConfigMgr is extensible.
Branch-office support	Yes	Yes	SCE 2010 has BITS 2.0 support. This can support Windows 7 Ultimate/ Enterprise BranchCache.
Operating system deployment	Yes	Yes	Use MDT 2010.
Desired configuration management	Yes	No	

TABLE 11.3: SCE 2010 and Configuration Manager 2007 R3 feature comparison *(CONTINUED)*

FEATURE	CONFIGURATION MANAGER 2007 R3	SCE 2010	NOTES
Wake-on-LAN	Yes	No	
Network Access Protection integration	Yes	No	
Advanced power policy management and reporting	Yes	No	

The differences between Configuration Manager 2007 R3 and SCE 2010 will be felt most by the medium-sized business that is closer to the 500 computer limit of SCE 2010. The desktop administrators in such an organization will desire the complete automation, policy auditing/enforcement, and zero-touch features that are included with the stand-alone ConfigMgr 2007 R3. The power enforcement features of ConfigMgr 2007 R3 might even pay for the licensing!

CONFIGURATION MANAGER V.NEXT

The successor to Configuration Manager 2007 R3 was an early beta release when this book was being written. It is slated for release in 2011 and may already be available by the time you read this. It provides a new, user-centric architecture where users can use a portal to request and initiate automated software installations on their desktop. This sort of feature can improve the relationship between the users and IT as well as reduce the administrative workload.

Finally you get to see the virtualization piece of this story. Table 11.4 shows how SCE 2010 compares with Virtual Machine Manager 2008 R2 and the Hyper-V Console.

TABLE 11.4: Feature comparison of SCE 2010 and Virtual Machine Manager 2008 R2

FEATURE	SCE 2010	VIRTUAL MACHINE MANAGER 2008 R2	HYPER-V CONSOLE
Templates	Yes	Yes	No
Virtualization conversion candidate information	Yes	Yes	No
Physical to virtual (P2V) conversion	Yes	Yes	No
VMware virtual to virtual (V2V) conversion	Yes	Yes	No
Quick and Live Migration	Yes	Yes	No (Use Failover Clustering Console)

TABLE 11.4: Feature comparison of SCE 2010 and Virtual Machine Manager 2008 R2 *(CONTINUED)*

FEATURE	SCE 2010	VIRTUAL MACHINE MANAGER 2008 R2	HYPER-V CONSOLE
Virtualization reports	Yes	Yes	No
Monitoring virtual machines	Yes	No	No
Physical Resource Optimization (PRO)	Yes	Yes	No
Library	Yes	Yes	No
Provisioning	Yes	Yes	Yes
Virtual machine configuration	Yes	Yes	Yes
Virtual machine state	Yes	Yes	Yes
Checkpoints or snapshots	Yes	Yes	Yes
Live thumbnail	Yes	Yes	Yes
Import virtual machine	No	Yes	Yes
Virtual network configuration	No	Yes	Yes
Inspect disk	No	Yes	Yes
Virtual machine cloning	No	Yes	No
VMware management	No	Yes	No
Self-Service Portal	No	Yes	No

The main piece that a medium-sized business might miss is the Self-Service Portal, but that is only if it really needs to allow non-IT staff to deploy virtual machines. Otherwise, SCE 2010 is a pretty feature-rich virtualization management product.

SCE 2010 is an impressive management suite that will be able to manage an entire server and desktop infrastructure as well as Hyper-V in a medium-sized business. It includes many of the features of the individual System Center products at a fraction of the cost.

The Bottom Line

Deploy Small Business Server 2008 on Hyper-V Small Business Server (SBS) 2008 can be deployed as a virtual machine. This can increase flexibility and reduce hardware costs for many small businesses.

Master It You are working as a field engineer for a managed services company. A new client has decided that they want to hire your company to install Small Business Server

2008 Premium Edition. The additional server will run SQL Server Standard edition with a line-of-business application. They require a deployment that offers maximum flexibility with minimum installation and operational costs. Your company requires that the system be easy to manage. How will you design this installation?

Understand System Center Essentials 2010 System Center Essentials provides a management solution for medium-sized businesses to manage their physical and virtual IT infrastructure and applications.

Master It You are working with two medium-sized client companies. Company A requires an economic management solution that will monitor health and performance, will distribute software, and will manage a small number of Hyper-V host servers. Company B is a software development company. They require a Self-Service Portal to allow developers to quickly deploy test and development virtual machines. What solutions will you recommend for both companies?

Understand licensing for small and medium businesses There are a lot of licensing variations for small and medium businesses. You should choose the correct license for the specific scenario because it can provide extra functionality or reduce costs.

Master It Your company has decided to deploy System Center Essentials (SCE) 2010. You need to manage 40 physical and virtual servers as well as 250 computers. It has been decided that Data Protection Manager (DPM) 2010 should also be deployed to back up all the computers and the Hyper-V host servers. What SCE 2010 licenses will you purchase?

Part 5

Additional Operations

Chapter 12

Security

Securing your Hyper-V infrastructure will be an important step to achieving reliability and stability. The steps taken can start with the placement and architecture of the Hyper-V host servers. Some choose the rather extreme step of placing them in secure networks as workgroup members. Others simply choose to place them in the normal server network and just lock down access to them.

One of the first pieces of software we place onto any Windows computer is antivirus software. We will cover the merits and risks of doing this with Hyper-V host servers. If you do choose to install antivirus software onto the parent partitions, then you will need to know exactly how to configure it. Failing to do this correctly can have massive consequences.

Finally, we will cover how you patch your Microsoft infrastructure. Do you need to patch your virtual machines? How will you patch your Hyper-V host servers? How will you keep your Virtual Machine Manager (VMM) library content up-to-date? This will give you an opportunity to look at the newest version of the Virtual Machine Servicing Tool, a free download that will make every Hyper-V administrator's job a little bit easier.

In this chapter, you will learn to

- Place and secure your Hyper-V host servers
- Use antivirus software on your Hyper-V host servers
- Patch your Hyper-V host servers and VMM library content

The Importance of Security

We've said this many times in the book, but it is worth repeating once again: Hyper-V, your hardware virtualization platform, will be the foundation of probably at least 80 percent of your server infrastructure. Like any hardware virtualization product, you need to consider where you will place your Hyper-V hosts on your network, how you will lock down access to them, if and how you will run antivirus on them, and how you will patch your entire infrastructure.

Failing to manage the security and security updates on any hypervisor product will lead to a vulnerable server network. As an IT infrastructure expert, you are probably used to paying attention to the details for server deployments. You need to be extra careful with these servers. Any vulnerabilities in a hardware virtualization infrastructure can lead to a completely insecure server network. Remember, whoever controls a host server will have access to all content that it is hosting.

That being said, security can be taken too far. It has been said that the only 100 percent secure server is one that is powered off, dropped into a hole in the ground, and buried with concrete. IT security is a balancing act. The more secure an IT system is the less usable and manageable it becomes. And the opposite is also true. The more manageable and usable an IT system is, the less secure it becomes. The key to this phase of your deployment is to find that balance where the system meets the security requirements of the organization, the data, and any industry or state regulations, while still being a system that meets the manageability requirements of your IT department and the usability needs of your end users. These end users are probably your IT department colleagues, those who are developing and testing software, and possibly end users accessing a Virtual Desktop Infrastructure (VDI) — where Hyper-V hosted virtual machines run desktop operating systems.

It will probably be true that deployment in larger organizations will lead to some in-depth, and maybe even heated, discussions with an IT security or auditing department. They will probably be using traditional checklists of how IT security should be accomplished. Virtualization changes things, and you may need to do some education about how Hyper-V architecture works. You may find that creating a cooperative workshop type environment (instead of a potentially confrontational meeting), where you start with the Hyper-V architecture and work through the needs of your solution, as described by the goals and objectives you have gathered from the business at the very start of the project, will help. With that and some patience, you will eventually find the security solution that is right for the project that you are working on and that the IT security overseers will sign off on.

We'll now cover how to deal with some of the security issues in a Hyper-V deployment.

Network Architecture

Server security starts with placing the server in the network. There are a few ways you can approach this, depending on how extreme you want your security to be and how usable you need the system to be. You could place your Hyper-V hosts into a totally isolated network, while leaving the virtual machines in their normal VLANs. You need to decide whether your Hyper-V hosts should be in a domain or a workgroup. Should the domain be your normal domain, a new domain in a forest, or a new forest? Maybe you could leave the Hyper-V hosts in your normal production network and treat them as ordinary servers?

Whatever happens, in an enterprise environment a Hyper-V deployment is usually managed by Microsoft System Center. The services that Hyper-V will provide, such as self-service virtual machine deployment or VDI, will require simple user authentication. You'll need to understand how you will manage these Hyper-V hosts and provide authentication for their provided services.

There are a lot of options, with more variations than we can investigate here. We'll look at a number of scenarios and describe the merits and flaws of each one.

Isolated Network with Workgroup Member Hosts

This architecture, shown in Figure 12.1, is probably the most extreme approach that you might take to secure Hyper-V host servers. It allows the Hyper-V hosts to be treated as if they are sacred. Access, whether it is basic network communications or administration, to them can be very restricted.

FIGURE 12.1
Isolated workgroup member Hyper-V hosts

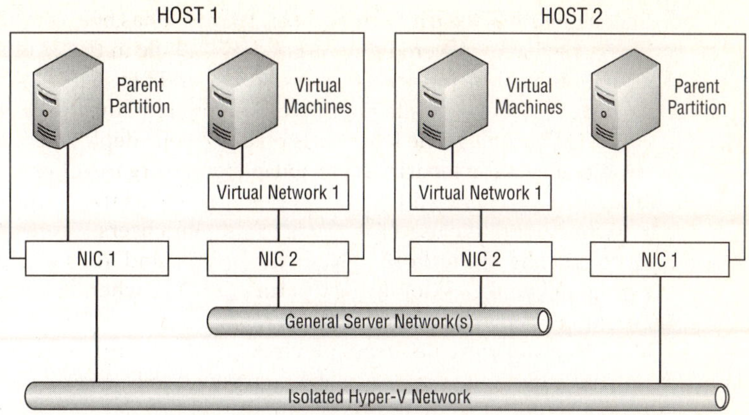

The parent partitions of the hosts will be connected to a network that is completely isolated from the rest of the network. Restricted access through firewalls might be allowed for remote administration by Hyper-V administrators.

The virtual machines on the Hyper-V hosts will be connected to the normal server network or networks. This is made possible by using at least one dedicated physical network card in the Hyper-V hosts for virtual machine traffic (this should be done in a production environment anyway). You can also use the VLAN ID settings of the virtual networks or virtual machine network cards to bind the virtual machines to specific VLANs. This normal network connectivity allows the virtual machines to communicate on the general network as they would have if they were physical machines. It also allows them to participate in Windows domains and forests.

The biggest complication with this approach is that the Hyper-V hosts will be workgroup members. Think back to your early lessons and training on Windows administration. Workgroups are not easy to manage.

This is especially true for Hyper-V host servers. There is a long series of steps that you must complete to allow remote administration of Hyper-V hosts where the parent partition is a member of a workgroup. Microsoft's John Howard has gone through this process in great detail over five blog posts. You can find part one of the series here:

```
http://blogs.technet.com/b/jhoward/archive/2008/03.aspx
```

Manually configuring remote administration for a workgroup member Hyper-V host server requires a lot of work. Luckily, John did write a tool (which is not formally supported by Microsoft) to do all of those steps for you. You can find the tool and its instructions here:

```
http://blogs.technet.com/b/jhoward/archive/2008/11/14/configure
   -hyper-v-remote-management-in-seconds.aspx
```

Workgroup members do have one other flaw, and it is rather obvious: they are not members of a domain. Domain membership is a prerequisite for Failover Clustering. You will not be able to build a Hyper-V cluster or create highly available virtual machines by placing the Hyper-V hosts into a workgroup. The only way you will be able to build fault tolerance will be to create guest failover clusters. That will increase your Hyper-V host utilization. It will also require shared storage such as iSCSI to allow shared storage between virtual machines that is initiated by the virtual machines and not the Hyper-V hosts. Bear in mind that not all applications will support installation on highly available virtual machines (see Chapter 8).

REQUIRED PORTS FOR BASIC HYPER-V MANAGEMENT

The ports required for using the Hyper-V administration console are as follows:

- TCP 135: DCOM endpoint mapper
- TCP 49152-65535: WMI/DCOM
- TCP 2179: Hyper-V Remote Control

This lack of domain membership also complicates management using Microsoft System Center or solutions from other software vendors. Typically these products are optimized for domain membership. Some of the products even require the Hyper-V hosts to have domain membership in a trusted domain.

If you do adopt this approach, then you need to consider that long-term management of the Hyper-V hosts will be difficult and time-consuming. Even patching for bug fixes could be a labor-intensive task. You really need to consider how much additional security you might get from completely isolating your Hyper-V hosts like this.

Isolated Network with Domain Member Hosts

This is a slight variation on the previous architecture. The parent partition of the Hyper-V host servers is still placed in an isolated network with minimized connectivity to the rest of the network. However, to facilitate integration with other services, the host servers are members of a domain. There are a number of ways this could be accomplished:

Dedicated Forest An Active Directory forest with at least two domain controllers is built in the isolated network. The only members of this forest are the parent partitions of the Hyper-V host servers and any other virtualization-specific management systems.

This sort of approach might be taken if there will be an isolated systems management infrastructure for controlling the Hyper-V infrastructure. It will mean that there will be a lot of duplicated administration effort unless there is a dedicated team for looking after Hyper-V and its systems.

It would be possible to create a trust between this forest and the forest(s) of the rest of the network, as shown in Figure 12.2. This would require some firewall rules to be created to facilitate these communications.

This solution gives all the isolation of the dedicated network with workgroup members. However, it provides all of the manageability options of domain membership, not to mention the ability to create Hyper-V clusters with highly available virtual machines. Be aware that some management systems in the general company network still may not like traversing an interforest trust and may need dedicated installations in the isolated network.

FIREWALL RULES AND ACTIVE DIRECTORY TRUSTS

You can learn more about the required ports for Active Directory trusts at `http://support.microsoft.com/kb/179442`.

FIGURE 12.2
Isolated network with dedicated Hyper-V forest

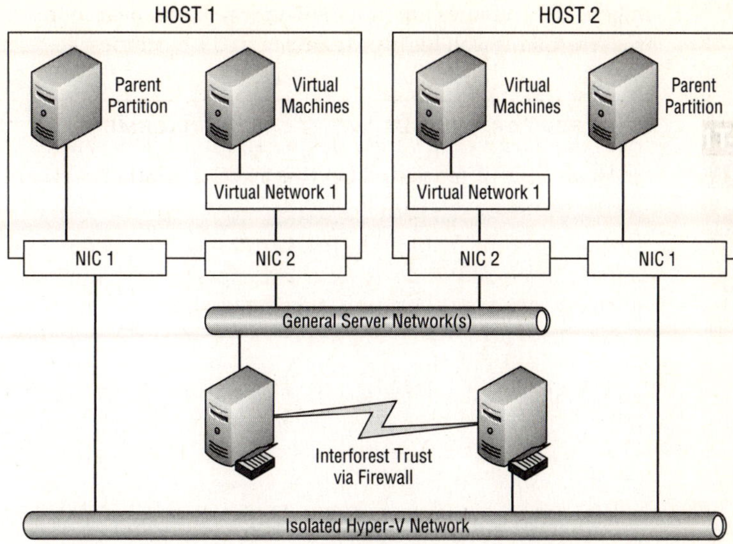

Dedicated Domain With this solution, shown in Figure 12.3, the Hyper-V parent partitions will be members of a domain that is built especially for the task. Unlike the previously discussed architectures, this domain is a member of an Active Directory forest that is used in the general network.

FIGURE 12.3
Isolated network with dedicated domain

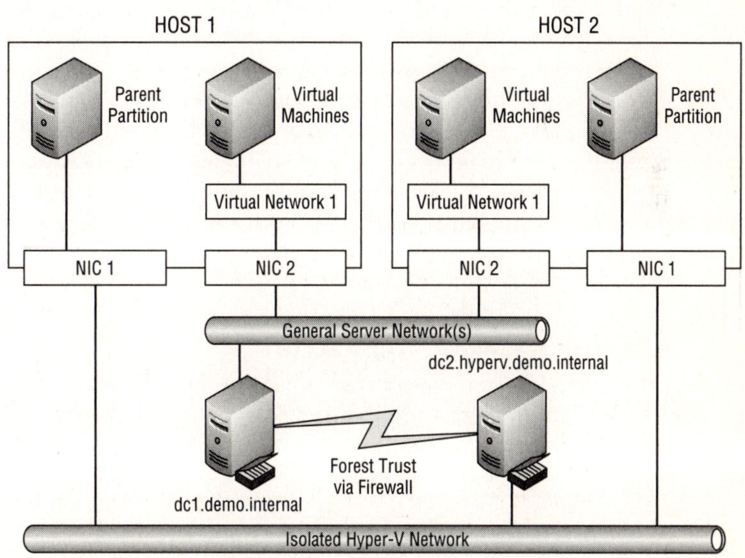

The benefit of this solution is that all of the management systems that reside in the general network can easily be used to manage the Hyper-V infrastructure. There is no duplication of effort to manage these systems. The nicest benefit of all is that now the end users have a highly integrated virtualization platform. They can interact with it seamlessly, without having to navigate firewall rules or remembering alternative user account names and passwords.

There is an important Active Directory security issue to consider here. Microsoft tells us that a Windows domain is not a security boundary. The Active Directory forest is the real security boundary. When you sit down and think about this for a moment, you'll start to wonder about the role of the firewall in this architecture. Is it really doing anything more than what the Windows Firewall on the Hyper-V parent partitions can do? The answer is probably not.

One has to wonder about the real reasons for this sort of implementation. Does it have a place if there is no real Windows security boundary? It might have. Large organizations often have security teams or officers who have legacy opinions on networking and security. They could throw up a road block to a Hyper-V implementation, wanting the domain controllers to be isolated. The engineers and administrators may want integration for management and to allow the business to access the services provided by the infrastructure. In the end, the Windows administrators may have to make a compromise, knowing full well that any firewall appliance sitting between the Hyper-V infrastructure domain and the rest of the forest does nothing that the Windows Firewall would have done. Unfortunately, it comes at the cost of including another layer of administration and change control, namely, the networking team and the change control process of the security officers.

Open Network

This will probably end up being the most common implementation. The Hyper-V host servers will not be isolated using network firewalls. Instead, they will be part of the general network. It is possible that a dedicated VLAN will be configured, just to isolate network traffic. The Windows Firewall on the parent partitions can be configured to control traffic, as required, using Group Policy.

This implementation assumes that the team that is responsible for Hyper-V will be OK with the domain administrators or enterprise administrators having complete access to their systems. Those administrative users have access to anything and everything on a forest member computer. Really, they should be a very small set of highly trusted (and audited) administrators. There is always the chance that there needs to be some segregation to isolate the two groups of administrators and to mitigate risk. Not only do the Active Directory administrators have complete access to data and systems, but the Hyper-V administrators will have access to all data contained in virtual machines that are hosted on their servers and storage.

A Hybrid Network Architecture

Large enterprise and government organizations have complex security, administration, and usability requirements. Although most Hyper-V administrators may never have more than a dozen Hyper-V hosts, a few lucky people will have hundreds of them to manage. It is in these organizations where you may see Hyper-V hosts being placed into farms with different security requirements. Some critical systems may reside in dedicated and isolated forests. This will keep critical data away from prying eyes and limit network traffic. Some low-end farms of Hyper-V hosts may reside in test and development domains. This allows testers and developers to have their own delegated Hyper-V hosts (probably in a VMM host group) that they can easily manage and use. Some clustered hosts may reside in the general network, suitable for normal server operations. And other nonclustered high-performance machines may also be on the general network but are used for virtual desktop infrastructure implementations such as Microsoft's Windows Server 2008 R2 Remote Desktop Services or Citrix's XenDesktop.

Physical Security

Forget Hollywood movies with the latest starlet clicking strange icons on a website; the easiest way to steal your data is to steal your servers or disks. It could be argued that hardware virtualization host servers (such as Hyper-V) require even greater security than normal physical servers because the virtual machines that are stored on them are usually just files. Files can be easily copied by an attacker if they gain physical access to the servers.

The first defense against a physical attack is traditional physical security. The servers and storage should be stored in a physically secure room. Access to this room should be restricted, controlled, and monitored.

Unfortunately, these mechanisms can fail. An example of this is the security guard who wants only to help his employer or customer. An attacker will turn up either very early or very late on the weekend, pretending to be something like an electrician, and claim that they've been called out to fix an urgent issue. The helpful security guard will want to help resolve the issue and may overlook normal authorization procedures by letting the attacker in.

The next step is to use disk encryption. Windows Server 2008 added Microsoft's BitLocker, a disk encryption solution. This can be used to encrypt the physical disks of a nonclustered Hyper-V host. This is the sort of host server that you might find at a branch office where physical security is probably not as strong as you would prefer. Gaining physical access to the encrypted Hyper-V host server will achieve little for the attacker. The downside for the organization is that you have to maintain encryption keys and manually intervene (for BitLocker authentication) whenever the host server is rebooted. Unfortunately, you cannot use BitLocker on the shared drives that would be used to store highly available virtual machines in a Hyper-V cluster.

Active Directory

This section is to help you configure your security in Active Directory. There are a few things you can do to facilitate easier administration and to increase security.

MASTERING WINDOWS SERVER 2008 R2

Most of Windows security is based on Active Directory Group Policy Object management. You can learn more about this by reading Mark Minasi's *Mastering Windows Server 2008 R2*, published by Sybex.

Organizational Units

The basic building block for administration in Active Directory is the organization unit (OU). OUs allow you to group objects together for policy inheritance or for delegating administration.

It is strongly recommended that you create an OU architecture for your Hyper-V host servers. This will allow you to create policies specifically for your Hyper-V hosts and to even create granular policies for different host groups. These granular policy OUs could match the host groups found in Virtual Machine Manager. Figure 12.4 shows an example OU setup.

FIGURE 12.4
A possible Hyper-V OU architecture

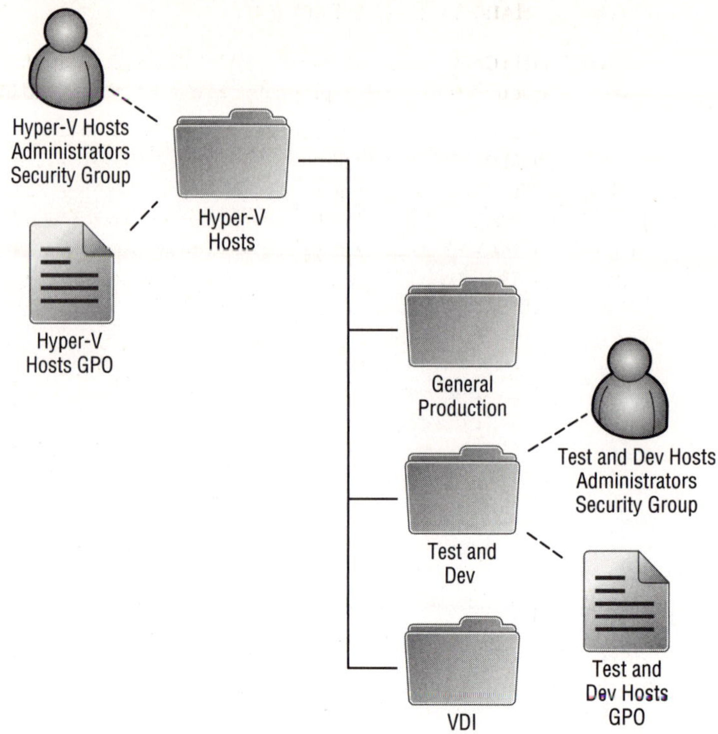

An OU called Hyper-V Hosts is created to contain all Hyper-V host servers. A Group Policy Object (GPO) is created and linked to this OU. Settings that should apply to all Hyper-V hosts, such as Windows Firewall configurations, are defined here. A security group is created here as well. This will contain the few members of the Hyper-V administration team. Restricted Groups in Group Policy can be used to populate the local Administrator group of each Hyper-V host that inherits this policy. That will make it easy to set up service accounts, such as that of VMM and administrative users. New Hyper-V host servers that are added to this OU, or a child OU, will inherit this policy and be automatically configured.

Child OUs can optionally be configured as and when required, such as when you need to create customized policies. The example shown in Figure 12.4 illustrates how this is being done for a team of developers and testers. They might have provided their own Hyper-V host servers and require local administration rights and a few more policy settings. Their user accounts can be added to the domain-based administrators security group for these servers. The Hyper-V Hosts security group can be nested into this group, granting them rights to the servers too. Once again, GPO will populate the local Administrators group of the servers in this child OU, granting the required rights to the group associated with this OU.

This sort of implementation will automate a lot of administration and keep things organized. It almost becomes a form of documentation that is built into the network. It might seem like a lot of work at first, but over time it will pay dividends in the amount of effort required to build and customize new Hyper-V host servers.

Real World Scenario

VIRTUAL HARD DISKS AND SECURITY

As you read in Chapter 8, fixed-size virtual hard disks and passthrough disks are the recommended disk in a production Hyper-V deployment. Fixed-sized disks will be the most commonly used type.

A common complaint is that fixed-sized VHDs take too long to create. The time to create them has improved from Windows Server 2008 to Windows Server 2008 R2, but there is still some time required. This is because the new, fully created file is being secured by Windows. The contents of the VHD are zeroed out. Without this step, a person could log into a virtual machine and scan the contents of the VHD, thus gaining access to data that were previously contained on the physical filesystem. This could be a serious breach of data security. That is why Microsoft decided to be careful and secure the disk space.

Some free utilities have appeared on the Internet to facilitate the rapid creation of VHDs. Although they are superb in a lab environment, you should consider very carefully if these should be used in a production system. They will usually not implement any security measures to protect any data that may have previously been stored on the physical filesystem. It is strongly recommended that you use the native tools provided by Microsoft in Hyper-V and VMM for all VHD operations in a production environment.

Administrators

You have read how critical the Hyper-V infrastructure is. This is similar to the criticality of Active Directory. Both will be the foundation blocks of your server and application infrastructure. The people who are granted Hyper-V administrative rights should be highly qualified and trusted individuals. Just like the with the Domain Admins group, the number of Hyper-V and VMM administrators should be limited to the absolute minimum required.

General production Hyper-V hosts should only have Hyper-V administrators (and any required service accounts) as members of the local Administrators group. There should be no need to grant access to anyone else. No one else should have any need to log into those servers; in fact, there should be limited need for anyone to log into them other than to patch or do some troubleshooting.

Use the features of VMM to delegate administrative rights as required. A few Hyper-V/VMM administrators will be members of the built-in Administrators user role. Host groups and the delegated administrators and self-service profiles will allow you to construct a least privileged required administrative model. This will provide all and only the required rights to each individual user account using Active Directory groups.

Antivirus

During the Windows Server 2008 Hyper-V prerelease test phases, a number of early adopters came into work to find virtual machines were missing. To this day, this problem generates many requests for help on support forums and to Microsoft's support services. The cause is that engineers, consultants, and administrators have assumed that they can install an antivirus product onto the parent partition of a Hyper-V host server as if it were just a typical Windows Server. This is definitely not the case.

Hyper-V must have complete and unhindered access to all files related to virtual machine activity. Any interruption can lead to virtual machines disappearing. It may even cause virtual machine configuration files to become corrupted.

What exactly had been happening with these missing virtual machines? Usually, antivirus software was installed onto a parent partition. For one reason or another, such as patching, the Hyper-V host server was rebooted. The antivirus would start up and start to scan files as they were accessed. Many virtual machines probably didn't start until a few minutes after the parent partition had started. This would cause the antivirus to scan those files. And that would prevent Hyper-V from being able to access the files as it wanted to. The virtual machines would simply disappear from the console.

The solution was often quite simple. The antivirus was either uninstalled or reconfigured not to scan those files. The host was rebooted, and usually everything would return to normal. Unfortunately, this was not always the case. A corrupted virtual machine configuration file (error code 0x800704C8) would cause the virtual machine to be permanently missing. The solution to this is to re-create the virtual machine and mount the previous machine's virtual hard disks so that no data would be lost. Alternatively, a backup of the virtual machine could be restored.

RE-CREATING VIRTUAL MACHINES AND NETWORK ADAPTERS

Re-creating a virtual machine configuration will have an undesired effect. Any virtual network adapters in the virtual machine will be seen as new and completely different network adapters by the guest operating system. The original network configuration, such as IPv4, will not be bound to the new network adapters. They will be configured with DHCP instead. You will have to remove the original network adapters from the guest operating system and configure the new network adapters with the original network configuration. See:

```
http://sqlsolace.blogspot.com/2008/11/hyper-v-vm-removing-hidden-network.html
```

The purpose of this section is to help you avoid that awkward morning when you walk into the office, looking forward to a productive day, and notice everyone watching your boss, who is beckoning you into her office to explain some missing servers.

The Argument over Antivirus

Many Hyper-V veterans recommend that it is best not to install any antivirus product on a Hyper-V host. Their arguments are as follows:

Limited Risk of Infection The Hyper-V host server has a limited attack surface. It has only one Windows role enabled, namely, Hyper-V. The only other pieces of software installed are management agents, such as Microsoft System Center. As long as no other software is installed, the host is patched on a regular basis, the Windows Firewall protects the host, and the number of Hyper-V administrators is limited and controlled, there should be no risk to the Hyper-V host servers. The only data stored on a Hyper-V host are the virtual machines, and their files cannot be scanned safely at the host level. Even if they could be scanned, there would be a serious degradation in overall virtual machine performance by doing so.

Risk of Problems There is the risk that the antivirus package will cause virtual machines to disappear on a host server. This can be avoided by preventing the scanning of Hyper-V, the virtual machine–related files, the process, and the CSV location (`C:\ClusterStorage`).

However, this does not account for operator error or even faulty antivirus software upgrades, something that has unfortunately been known to happen. A simple mistake could put many virtual machines at risk.

Cluster Shared Volume Support CSV is a very specialized filesystem. Antivirus scanning, even if it did support the scanning of files on a CSV, would probably cause the CSV to enter into redirected I/O mode and impact SAN performance for the Hyper-V cluster. In fact, Microsoft does explicitly state that the CSV should not be scanned by antivirus. We'll have more on that later.

So in summary, the Hyper-V host is pretty locked down, and the only data it has are virtual machines, which should not be scanned. Clustered Hyper-V hosts shouldn't even allow scanning of CSVs. What's the point in installing antivirus on the host at all? For those that do, the reason is usually one of the following:

IT Security Officers Legacy technology security officers who cling to their 1990s checklists will demand that antivirus is installed on every Windows Server. Quite often the IT security officer has the ear of very senior management, independent of IT, and can make a lot of trouble if they do not get their way. It is often easier to install antivirus than to fight this battle.

Management Despite all of the arguments and the reasoning, your boss may still demand that antivirus is installed. They are the people who hire and fire people like you, so they always get their way in the end.

A possible solution is to document the risks of installing antivirus on Hyper-V hosts. Include information about limited risks and gains of doing this. Then ask a sign-off from the person responsible for making the demand so that you have documented proof that they understood and are responsible for any problems that may occur.

Scanning Virtual Machines

You should protect your virtual machines as you would normally protect any physical servers. This usually means that an antivirus package will be installed in the virtual machines. Antivirus software on the host does not currently have the ability to scan the ongoing activities of virtual machines from the host's parent partition.

Configuring Antivirus Software

Make sure you are using antivirus software that explicitly states that it will support Windows Server 2008 R2 Hyper-V. Do not take any chances; remember that Hyper-V will be critical to the majority of your servers and business applications. At this time, Microsoft's ForeFront Client Security is possibly the best product for protecting Hyper-V host servers.

Microsoft gives very clear guidance on what should not be scanned by antivirus on a Hyper-V host server. You can find this at `http://support.microsoft.com/kb/961804`.

Each of the following files and paths must be excluded from the antivirus scanner:

- Default virtual machine configuration directory (`C:\ProgramData\Microsoft\Windows\Hyper-V`)
- Any virtual machine configuration directories that you create
- Default virtual hard disk drive directory (`C:\Users\Public\Documents\Hyper-V\Virtual Hard Disks`)

- Any virtual hard disk drive directories that you create
- Snapshot directories
- Cluster shared volumes (`C:\Clusterstorage`)
- `Vmms.exe`
- `Vmwp.exe`

You need to be extremely careful that every one of these paths is excluded. It is easy to browse the default virtual machine configuration directory and make the mistake of thinking that it only contains a bunch of shortcuts. These are symbolic links to help Hyper-V find critical files and must not be scanned.

If your antivirus scans processes, then you may also need to exclude the following processes:

- `Vmms.exe`
- `Vmwp.exe`

There is only one person who will benefit if you get this wrong; that's the Hyper-V consultant who will be able to charge you a lot of money to repair your corrupted or missing virtual machines.

A veteran Windows security expert understands that antivirus software has a limited impact on your ability to protect your business assets. The most important thing you need to do to defend your systems is patch them.

Patching Your Hyper-V Infrastructure

It is important to patch any Windows application or server, Hyper-V is no exception. We have two reasons to patch Hyper-V host servers. The first is to fix bugs in the software or to make feature improvements. These are the sorts of fixes that come out once every few months. The second is to fix security vulnerabilities. Unfortunately, these are the sorts of patches that are released every month and usually require rapid testing and deployment.

HOTFIXES AND INTEGRATION COMPONENTS

You should carefully read about and test any updates that you will be approving for installation on your network, especially for your Hyper-V host servers. Some updates can upgrade the Integration Components on the host server. These upgrades are not automatically applied to the virtual machines or child partitions. You must ensure that, when necessary, the integration components are upgraded in the virtual machines to achieve the desired results.

Patching Strategy

An organization needs to decide what sort of patching strategy they should adopt. There are two basic ways that you can deploy updates for software and operating systems.

The first, and the one that Microsoft recommends, is to deploy updates as soon as you can after their release. Microsoft believes that security fixes should be deployed with no delay. This minimizes not only the risk of infection but also the ability of malware to spread. This approach will minimize your security risks. It also requires the least amount of management because your patching solution can potentially automatically approve updates for deployment as they are downloaded. There is a risk that an update will have a flaw or will interfere with third-party software (which may be depending on a vulnerability or bug in the Microsoft software). This doesn't happen very often, but it does happen.

The second option is to deploy updates to a test or pilot system first. This can be completely automated because these are only test systems. You can keep an eye on support forums, blogs, and RSS feeds for potential issues while the updates and test applications are being assessed for issues. You can approve the updates for production deployment once you are sure that there will be no problems. Stories of infrequent issues can lead some people to distrust automated updates. This approach gives application owners some peace of mind. They are often quite wary of updates that are deployed immediately after their release. With this approach, you take control of the updates instead of abandoning a vital process in IT infrastructure ownership. On the negative side, it does require a little bit more work. However, systems such as the free Windows Server Update Services (WSUS) or System Center Configuration Manager do streamline the process.

Installing Hyper-V Hotfixes

From time to time, Microsoft will discover a bug in Hyper-V or make an improvement to a feature of the software. These updates or hotfixes are sometimes made available on Windows Update. This allows you to easily deploy the hotfixes using automated solutions. Some updates are not supplied by Windows Update. This means that they must be manually downloaded and deployed.

The hardest bit about deploying these hotfixes is knowing what updates are available. Normally, there is no central list of elective updates. It can be annoying when you are dealing with a software issue, only to find out that a hotfix has been around for some time to prevent the issue from happening. Luckily, there is a page on TechNet that lists all of the hotfixes for Windows Server 2008 R2 Hyper-V. You can find this page here:

```
http://technet.microsoft.com/library/bb632895.aspx
```

After a quick scan of the hotfix descriptions, you'll see that important functionality is fixed. You should ensure that these updates are installed on your servers when you deploy them into production.

There aren't all that many updates there. Unfortunately, to install them one at a time could take some time. This would be compounded if you are building many Hyper-V host servers. You have a few options to optimize their deployment:

Deploy Updates Automatically You probably won't want to manually install updates that you have downloaded from Microsoft's website. All is not lost if they are not provided by Windows Update. If you have System Center Configuration Manager, then you can deploy any manually downloaded updates thanks to the System Center Updates Publisher (SCUP). You can learn more about SCUP here:

```
http://technet.microsoft.com/library/bb632895.aspx
```

Deployment and testing work will be required every time that an update is released by Microsoft to ensure that it will be deployed correctly. You may find that you will need to use this approach even if you choose to use one of the others as the primary deployment solution. Hotfixes will be released after the installation of your Hyper-V hosts, so you will need a way to distribute them.

Build the Hotfixes into Your Operating System Images The Windows Image (WIM) format that was introduced with Windows Vista, and Windows Server 2008 adds an interesting feature. The traditional `setup.exe` and file copy installation process has been replaced by an image deployment from the installation media. The default images are contained in a file called `install.wim` on the DVD. It is possible to add hotfixes into the Windows image that will be used to install the parent partition operating system. Using this technique, any operating system installed from this updated media will already have the hotfixes and will require no updates. You can accomplish this using the `dism.exe` tool, which is included with the free Windows Automated Installation Kit for Windows 7 and Windows Server 2008 R2. It is also built into Windows 7 and Windows Server 2008 R2. You can learn about `dism.exe` and the `add-package` command here:

`http://technet.microsoft.com/library/dd744311(WS.10).aspx`

This technique offers the quickest installation of an operating system. It can be used with Windows Deployment Services, the image installation system included with Windows Server. It does require some complicated manual work for each update that is released by Microsoft.

Deploy Updates with the Operating System Larger organizations will usually not perform manual installations of Windows clients or servers. This will include the Windows Server 2008 R2 operating system that will be installed onto Hyper-V host servers as the parent partition. Advanced systems such as the free Microsoft Deployment Toolkit or the Operating System Deployment feature of Configuration Manager employ a technique called *task sequences*. A task sequence is a collection of ordered steps that will be performed to prepare the computer, install the operating system, and then configure the operating system. This can include installing security updates and hotfixes automatically as a step that will be executed after the installation of the operating system. This is a very flexible system that will require little work after the initial implementation.

You now have ways to distribute hotfixes for Hyper-V because Microsoft makes them available for manual download and installation. You now need a way to schedule their deployment to existing Hyper-V host servers. We will look at this as we move on to dealing with the distribution of security updates.

Distributing Security Updates

Security updates for Microsoft products are usually released on the first Tuesday of every month, Pacific Standard Time. Windows Server 2008 R2 is usually included in this. This will impact your Hyper-V infrastructure and will require some techniques to allow for automating the deployment of updates. The potential impact on a Hyper-V and Virtual Machine Manager infrastructure is substantial. Fortunately, this is something that Microsoft has been working on over the past few years, and it finally has a solution.

How Security Updates Impact Hyper-V

Patching of physical servers really does not compare to the potential issues you will face when patching Hyper-V in an enterprise environment. Security updates will impact Hyper-V and Virtual Machine Manager in a number of ways:

Offline Virtual Machines in the VMM Library Virtual machines that are powered off for long periods might be moved into the VMM library to reduce their storage cost. Typically, high-performance and higher-cost storage will be used in the Hyper-V hosts or Hyper-V cluster shared storage. Lower-cost disks can be used in the VMM library. Security updates will be released and approved for installation, while the virtual machine is offline in the library. This virtual machine will not receive those security updates. If it is moved back to a host and powered up, then it will be vulnerable to network threats. The virtual machine may also be noncompliant with company security policies. It will stay this way until it eventually is updated, which may take several days depending on the Windows Update configuration in the operating system.

Offline Virtual Machines Some virtual machines will be powered down or placed into a saved state for short periods of time. Like offline virtual machines in the VMM library, they will not receive security updates and will be vulnerable when they are powered back up.

VMM Library VHDS That Are Associated with Templates You learned in Chapter 7 that a template is a description of a virtual machine that is linked to one or more generalized VHDs that reside in a library. You can quickly deploy virtual machines that will use those VHDs by deploying that template. There is no way for these VHDs to receive security updates because they are not running virtual machines.

VHDs Stored in the VMM Library These are VHD files that are not associated with a template. Just like the template VHDs, they have no running operating system and therefore cannot run the Windows Update service to download security updates.

Clustered Hyper-V Host Servers This is an interesting topic. The reason for deploying a Hyper-V cluster is that you can have highly available virtual machines. The Windows Update client has no integration with Hyper-V, VMM, or Failover Clustering. Virtual machines will suddenly stop (as if they were powered off) and failover to another host (where they will power up again) if the parent partition is patched and rebooted automatically.

Nonclustered Hyper-V Host Servers Controlling this will be up to the Hyper-V administrators. Windows Updates can be configured to be deployed to the parent partition on the Hyper-V host servers. A reboot will usually follow. What will happen to the virtual machines? They cannot live migrate anywhere. The answer depends on how you configured the host shutdown and startup options in each of the virtual machines. The ideal will be that the virtual machines are put into a saved state when the host server powers down and that they are started up again from that saved state when the host has started up again. We won't talk anymore about this scenario in this chapter.

Running Virtual Machines Each running virtual machine is a separate security boundary and a separate operating system environment. Each operating system in each virtual machine will require security updates, just as if it were an operating system that was installed on a physical server. Use Group Policy or registry edits to control the settings of

Windows Update on these virtual machines. Linux virtual machines will also require configuration, using their native patch management solutions. This topic won't be covered anymore in this chapter.

Ideally, we want a solution where whenever we deploy a new virtual machine from a template, deploy an offline VHD, or power up an offline virtual machine, it will be fully patched, secure, and ready for the end user to start using without any patching and rebooting.

Microsoft is aware of each of these issues. It has been working on an evolving solution over the past few years. We're going to cover that solution next.

Virtual Machine Servicing Tool 3.0

Microsoft's solution for deploying updates is to use either ConfigMgr or WSUS servers with the Windows Update client on managed machines. By themselves, those products do not have the ability to deal with the more complex issues we face with patching and securing a Hyper-V and VMM environment. However, Microsoft has been developing and evolving a solution over the years.

The Offline Virtual Machine Servicing Tool gives you the ability to patch virtual machines that are stored in the VMM library. The current version of this tool at the time of writing this book is 2.1. For the majority of organizations using Hyper-V, this ability resolves only a tiny percentage of the patching issues we face. At the time of writing this book, a successor was in the works. A beta version Virtual Machine Servicing Tool (VMST) 3.0 was available for testing. This tool is likely to gain widespread acceptance because it will resolve each of the issues that Hyper-V and VMM administrators face when it comes to patching their environment. We will look at this tool now and see how it works in each of the scenarios.

> **VMST 3.0 Beta**
>
> We really don't like to write about beta products because there is a chance that they will change before they are finalized and released. However, this is a critical tool to include in this book because it does add so much more functionality over the previous versions of the product.

VMST 3.0 gives you the ability to patch the following:

- Offline virtual machines in the VMM library (which all the previous versions could do)
- Offline virtual machines
- VMM library VHDs that are associated with templates
- VHDs stored in the VMM library
- Clustered Hyper-V host servers

Each of those scenarios requires a slightly different approach. We'll come back to that later. First we will cover the basic architecture of VMST 3.0.

VMST 3.0 Architecture

VSMT 3.0 leverages the PowerShell functionality of VMM to do its work. Either WSUS or ConfigMgr is used to deploy the security updates. Figure 12.5 shows the architecture of the whole solution.

Figure 12.5
The VMST 3.0 architecture

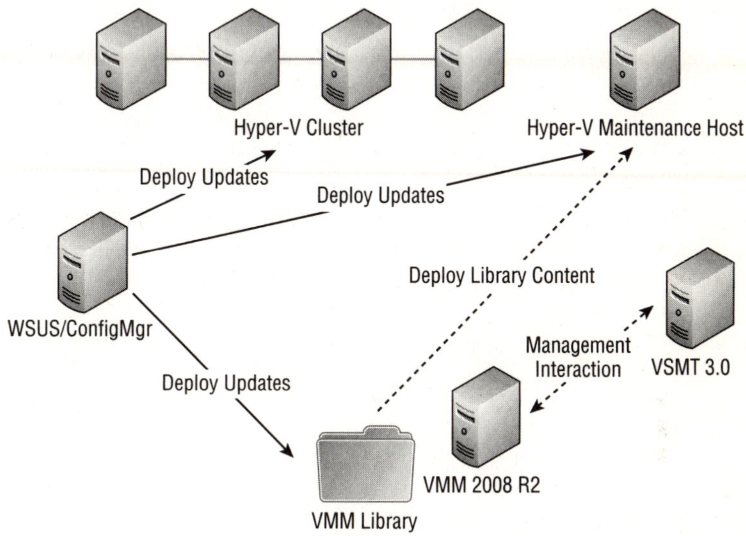

WSUS or ConfigMgr is used as normal to download, test, and approve updates. Any processes that you have been using up to now with physical servers will continue as normal.

VMST 3.0 is installed on a server. The choice of a server for VSMT will really depend on how big your architecture is. You can use the sizing for VMM (Chapter 7) as a guideline. You will probably install VSMT on your VMM server. You may need to install it onto a dedicated machine (or virtual machine) in very large environments.

VMST will leverage the functionality of VMM not only to manage the contents of the VMM library but also to manage offline virtual machines on the host servers and clustered Hyper-V host servers. The actions of VMST will appear as jobs in the VMM console, making it very easy to track and audit VMST activity.

Some content that is stored in the library will need to be deployed and powered up in order to be patched with the security updates. One or more maintenance hosts can be defined. These are Hyper-V host servers that will be in a common host group in VMM. The library resources, such as library-stored offline virtual machines, will be deployed to the maintenance hosts, patched, and returned to the library. The specifics of this change depend on the patching scenario. The maintenance hosts need to be of sufficient capacity to be able to run any virtual machines that will be deployed to them.

Microsoft makes two recommendations for the architecture of the solution:

Secure Network You can set up a VLAN or network for all patching operations. Any virtual machine or template that is powered up or deployed may be out-of-date and be considered a risk. An isolated network might reduce the risk.

If you do regularly update your templates and virtual machines, then they will present no greater risk than any physical or virtual machine in the general network. No gain will be achieved. Instead, there will be additional architecture and network maintenance operations. Also, the virtual machines will require the ability to communicate with critical production systems such as Active Directory domain controllers and the patching systems. There is, in reality, little isolation.

Fibre Channel Storage Connectivity Microsoft recommends using 2GB or greater Fibre Channel connections for virtual machine storage. This will speed up file transfer and storage operations.

It is true that Fibre Channel storage will optimize storage operations. However, patching of offline resources doesn't need to be very fast. It is something that can be done in out-of-business hours. There is no real need to implement a special storage system just for patching. You should continue to purchase a shared storage system based on your primary business and technology objectives and budget.

Next, we will cover the prerequisites for installing Virtual Machine Servicing Tool 3.0.

VMST 3.0 Prerequisites

A lot of components are involved in a VMST 3.0 patching solution for Hyper-V and VMM. We're focusing on the 2008 R2 versions of those products, so that will reduce the size of the list.

Management Products

The supported versions of the management products are as follows:

- System Center Virtual Machine Manager 2008 R2
- System Center Configuration Manager 2007 R2 with SP2
- System Center Configuration Manager 2007 with SP2
- Windows Server Update Services 3.0 SP2

Note that WSUS 3.0 SP2 is required to update Windows Server 2008 R2 and Windows 7 operating systems. ConfigMgr must have Service Pack 2 installed for Windows 7 and Windows Server 2008 R2 client support. The ConfigMgr database must allow remote connections.

The supported operating systems for the management servers are as follows:

- Windows Server 2008 x86 or x64
- Windows Server 2008 R2

Virtual Machines

The supported virtual machine operating systems are as follows:

- Windows Server 2003 R2 SP2 x86 or x64
- Windows Server 2003 SP2 32 x86 or x64
- Windows XP Professional SP2 x64, SP3 x86Windows Server 2008, SP2 x86 or x64
- Windows Vista SP1, SP2 x86 or x64
- Windows Server 2008 R2
- Windows 7 x86 or x64

All offline virtual machines must be able to power up cleanly. The following are the technical requirements:

- They must be domain members.
- They must have network connectivity. Those virtual machines using DHCP will require static MAC (Ethernet) addresses.
- The VMM Integration Services must be installed and working correctly.
- Firewall exceptions for File and Printer Sharing, Windows Management Instrumentation (WMI), Remote Administration, and Incoming Echo Request for ICMP v4/v6 must all be enabled.

If you are using WSUS for your updates, then the virtual machine must have the following configurations:

- The WSUS client must be installed.
- The virtual machine must be configured to use the WSUS server.

If you haven't already done it, then you can configure virtual machines to use a WSUS server either using Group Policy:

`http://technet.microsoft.com/library/cc720539(WS.10).aspx`

or using a registry edit:

`http://technet.microsoft.com/library/cc708449(WS.10).aspx`

Group Policy doesn't usually instantly apply settings to computers. Virtual machines that are in a saved state might not refresh their settings for several hours after they wake up. Powered-down virtual machines might not apply the new settings straightaway. It may be necessary to preconfigure the virtual machines as early as possible by forcing Group Policy to apply to the virtual machines before returning them to their normal powered-down or saved state. You can do this by logging into the virtual machine and running `gpupdate /force`.

If you are using ConfigMgr to update your virtual machines, then you must do the following:

- Install the ConfigMgr client in the virtual machine.
- Make sure the machine is active in the ConfigMgr database. That means it must be appearing in the relevant collections for software updates.

Nothing happens instantly with ConfigMgr. It requires patience. So, like with the alternative WSUS client configuration, if you are only introducing ConfigMgr's Software Update feature to your network now, then you should preconfigure your virtual machines well ahead of the required time to get VMST up and running.

Managed Host Servers

If you are using VMM 2008 R2, then the following virtualization technologies are supported:

- Windows Server 2008 R2 Hyper-V
- Virtual Server 2005 R2 SP1 x86 or x64
- Windows Server 2008 Hyper-V

Maintenance Hosts

VMST will need to start up resources that are stored in the VMM library. This will require Hyper-V host servers. These are referred to as *maintenance hosts*. A small environment can use an already existing Hyper-V host server or servers. However, larger environments with 20 or more virtual machines will require one or more dedicated maintenance hosts.

A maintenance host group will contain all of the currently available maintenance hosts. This is just a host group that you create in VMM. There are no special types of host group for this task. It's just a normal host group where you place your maintenance hosts. VMST can use only one maintenance host group at a time. A maintenance host group can contain nest host groups.

Virtual Machine Servicing Tool (VMM Server)

VMST 3.0 must be installed on a server that already has the VMM Administrator Console installed. The requirements are as follows:

- Windows Server 2008 or Windows Server 2008 R2
- .NET Framework 3.0
- Windows PowerShell 1.0 or 2.0
- VMM Administrator Console
- PsExec Utilities

PowerShell must be configured to have the execution policy set to `remotesigned`. You can query the current execution policy by running the following PowerShell cmdlet:

```
get-executionpolicy
```

You can set the required execution policy by running the following PowerShell cmdlet:

```
set-executionpolicy remotesigned
```

You can download the free PsExec utilities from here:

`http://technet.microsoft.com/sysinternals/bb795533.aspx`

Depending on the operating system you install VMST on, you may need to mark the `psexec.exe` executable and `pdh.dll` to be unblocked. You can do this by opening the properties of the files in Windows Explorer and clicking the Unblock button (see Figure 12.6).

Once VMST is installed, you copy these two files from PsExec to the VMST folder at this location:

```
%ProgramFiles%\Microsoft Offline Virtual Machine Servicing Tool\Bin
```

VMST has the ability to inject updates into offline VHDs that are stored in the VMM library. By default, this requires that you manually download all of the required updates to the VMST server. However, it can directly access the WSUS server and download the updates if you install the WSUS administration console on the VMST server. The updates will be downloaded to this location:

```
C:\Program Files\Microsoft Offline Virtual Machine Servicing Tool\Updates
```

Unfortunately, that is not a great location, often because the `C:` drive does not have much space. This location cannot be changed so you will have to plan for this if you want to update offline VHDs.

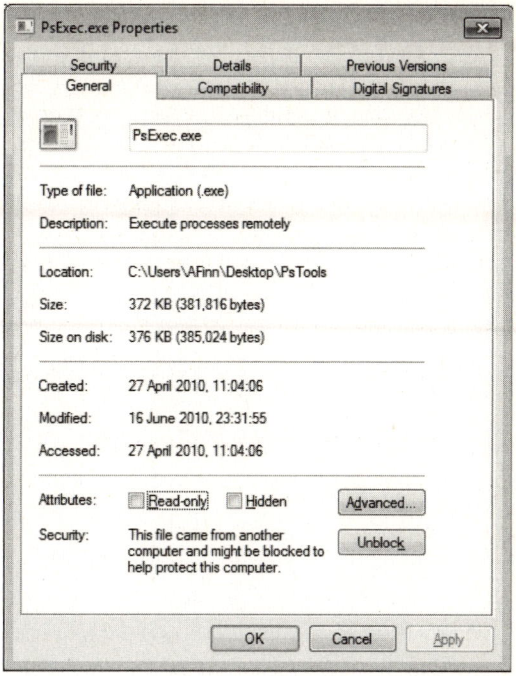

FIGURE 12.6
Unblocking the PsExec utility

Offline Disk Server

It is possible to inject updates into offline VHDs that are stored in the VMM library. This will use `dism` and `diskpart`. The requirements for this machine are as follows:

- It must be running Windows 7 or Windows Server 2008 R2.
- The PowerShell execution policy must be set to `remotesigned`.

There are a lot of prerequisites to get through. Make sure you have each and every one configured before proceeding to the installation of VMST 3.0.

WSUS or Configuration Manager

You will manage these products as normal. Groups or collections may need to be configured for your virtual machines, depending on your architecture. A catalog synchronization with Microsoft should be done to download and approve any required (and tested) updates.

Administrative User Account(s)

VMST will run servicing jobs to update Hyper-V and VMM resources. Each job will require an administrative user who has administrative rights to VMM and the objects to be updated. This may require some clever engineering of delegated administrative rights, possibly working with your Active Directory administrators.

INSTALLING VMST 3.0

You must first uninstall any previous version of the Offline Virtual Machine Servicing Tool that you may have installed. You should make sure that the server is backed up before doing that.

Download the free installer from Microsoft's website. The installation is pretty simple, compared to the prerequisites. There are two installers, one for 32-bit architectures and one for 64-bit architectures. Make sure you choose to run the correct one for the architecture of your server; for example, you'll run the 64-bit install on Windows Server 2008 R2. In our lab, we'll install VMST 3.0 on the VMM server, `vmm.demo.local`.

Start up the installer and proceed through the EULA screen if you agree with Microsoft's terms and conditions. The installation location screen does not give you a choice. The installation will be placed here:

```
C:\Program Files\Microsoft Offline Virtual Machine Servicing Tool
```

The setup doesn't ask any more questions. It just installs when you are ready to proceed.

Don't try to start up the Microsoft Virtual Machine Servicing Tool console just yet. You need to copy the two PsExec files into the installation location. Copy `psexec.exe` and `pdh.dll` into here:

```
C:\Program Files\Microsoft Offline Virtual Machine Servicing Tool\Bin
```

A shortcut to start the console will be added into the Start menu under Microsoft Virtual Machine Servicing Tool. You can launch the tool once the previous files have been copied into place. This will open the VMST Console, as shown in Figure 12.7.

FIGURE 12.7
The unconfigured VMST console

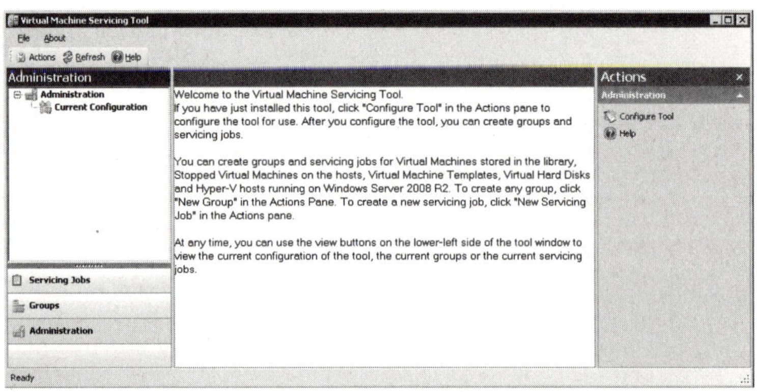

The tool has almost no content at this point. It must be configured, so that is what we will look at next.

CONFIGURING VMST 3.0

You should click the Configure Tool task from the Actions pane to configure VMST for update deployment management. This will launch the Configure Tool Wizard, which is shown in Figure 12.8.

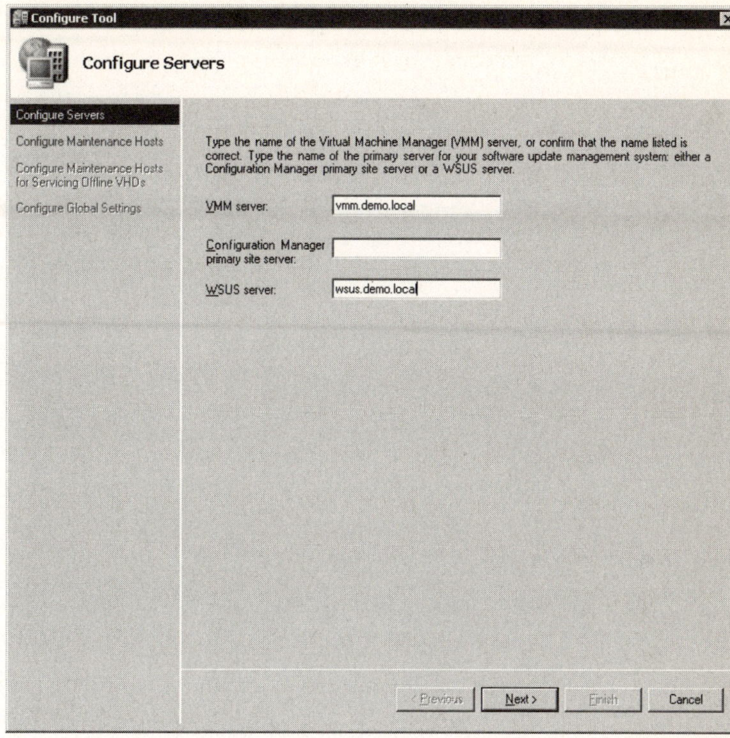

FIGURE 12.8
Configuring VMST servers

The Configure Servers screen requires two pieces of information. Enter the name of the VMM server that VMST will work with to manage the updates of your VMM and Hyper-V infrastructure. You should also enter the name of the ConfigMgr site server or WSUS server that is responsible for deploying updates to this infrastructure.

The Configure Maintenance Hosts screen, as shown in Figure 12.9, allows you to specify the host servers that will be used to host and run VMM library resources so that they can be updated.

You can navigate through the Maintenance Host Group drop-down list to find the maintenance host group that you created in VMM.

All the host servers in that maintenance host group will appear in the Available Hosts list box on the left side. You can use the arrow buttons to move one or all of the available hosts into the Selected Maintenance Hosts list box in the right side. These are the machines that VMST will use to host the VMM library resources.

The next screen, as shown in Figure 12.10, is the Configure Maintenance Hosts For Servicing Offline VHDs screen. These optional settings allow you to specify a Windows 7 or Windows Server 2008 R2 computer that will be used to mount offline VHDs in the VMM library and inject updates from the WSUS or ConfigMgr server. This does not need to be, and really should not be at all, a Hyper-V host server.

FIGURE 12.9
Configuring maintenance hosts

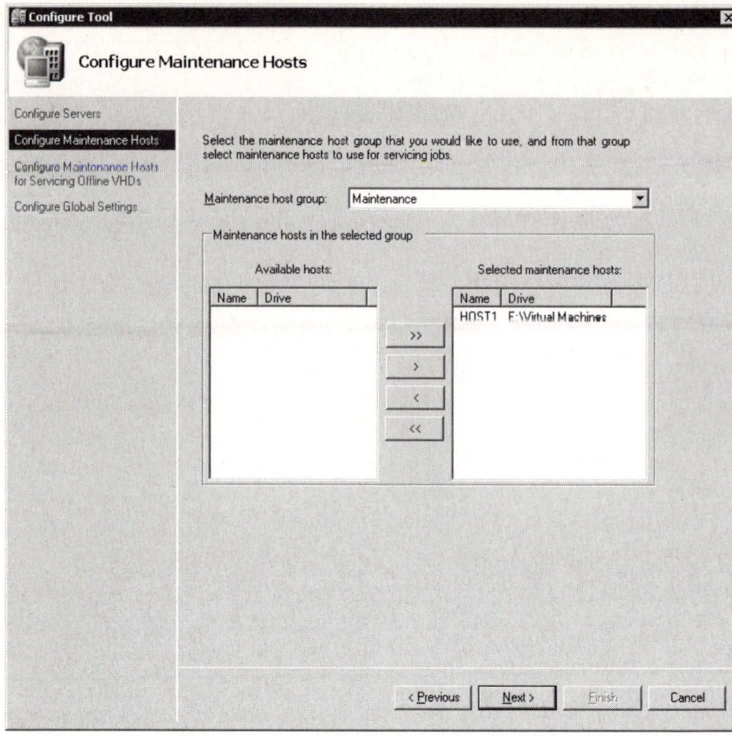

You simply need to provide the administrator credentials, the name of the server, and the storage location to temporarily store the offline VHD files. Remember to click the Add button to add your server before moving to the next screen.

You can add more than one server if you want. You can also delete servers if you change your mind by clicking the Delete button that appears to the right of the added servers.

You can simply skip this screen if you do not want to update offline VHDs that might be stored in the VMM library. There is another mechanism that will be used to update VHDs that are associated with VMM templates.

The Configure Global Settings screen (Figure 12.11) allows you to specify two timeout values. These are the amounts of time, in minutes, that VMST will wait for specific tasks to complete. If the task is not completed within that time, then VMST will cancel the task and report it as failed. The values are set to zero minutes by default. You should set them to realistic values.

Timeout for Moving a Virtual Machine You should know how long it typically takes to move a virtual machine that is stored in the VMM library to a host server. Remember that the bigger it is, the longer it might take to copy if the files are being copied over the network. You should allow some extra time in case the network is congested.

Timeout for Updating a Virtual Machine This one is a tricky one, and it is one that ConfigMgr and SMS administrators may have encountered before when deploying service packs. How long should VMST wait for your security updates to install? Usually this might take only a few minutes, but it really does depend on how many updates there are. There is also another consideration. Service packs can be deployed via Windows Update. They can take quite a long time to install.

Be very careful with this value. Don't be overly aggressive. These are offline resources, so the update does not have to be that quick. Remember that half-installed updates or service packs can lead to an unusable and unrepairable system.

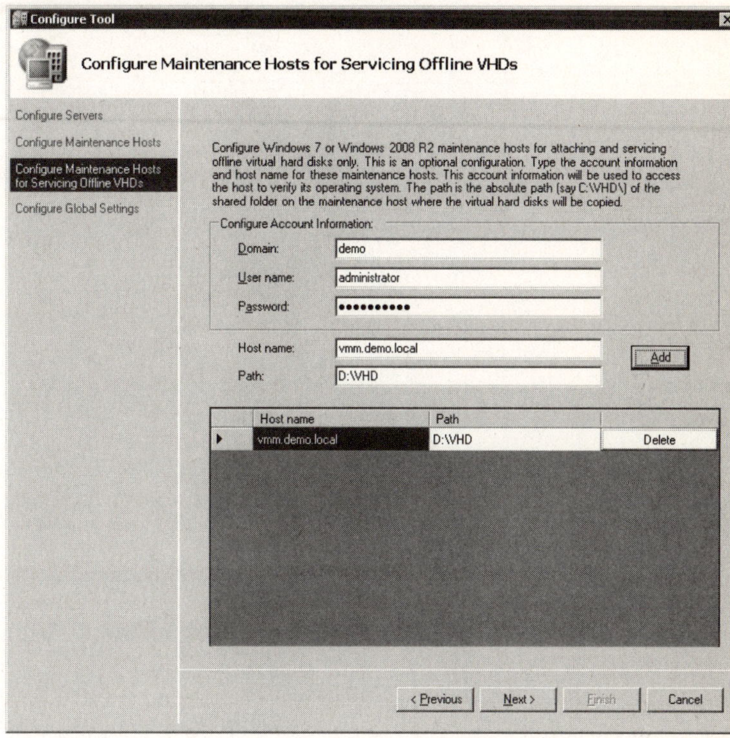

FIGURE 12.10
Configuring servicing offline VHDs

BACK UP EVERYTHING OF VALUE

It takes time to prepare the content in your VMM library. You should probably back it up once a day or once a week. This will protect you if something goes wrong with the update process. The same applies to offline virtual machines on your host servers. If they are of value, then they should be backed up in some way.

You can view the results of the Configure Tool Wizard by viewing the Current Configuration in the Administration view in the VMST console, as shown in Figure 12.12. You can alter the existing values by rerunning the Configure Tool Wizard.

VMST is now ready to work. It's time for us to show how VMST can be used to update your Hyper-V and VMM resources.

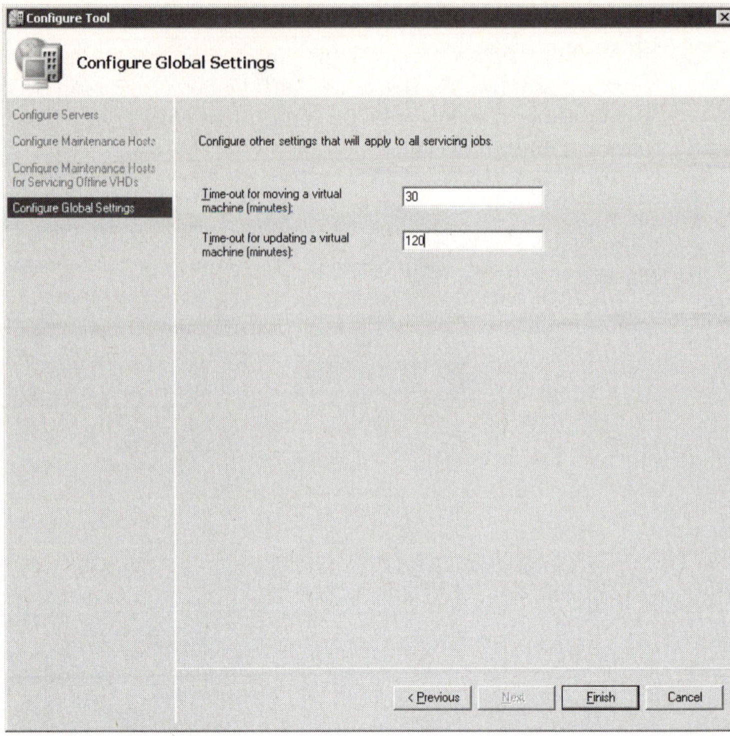

FIGURE 12.11
Configuring global settings

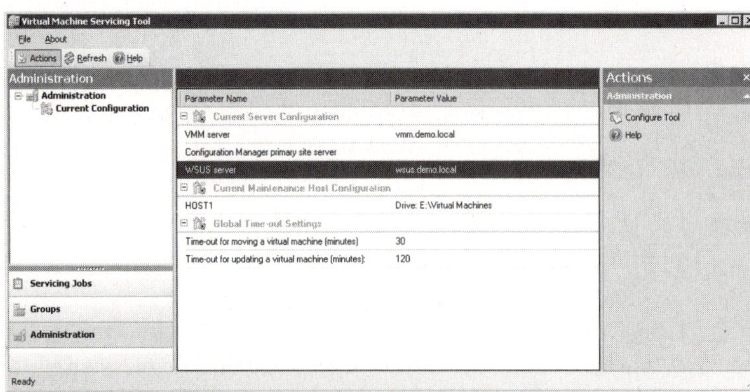

FIGURE 12.12
VMST current configuration

VMST Interfaces Very Tightly with VMM

VMST extracts knowledge of your Hyper-V and VMM infrastructure from VMM. VMM is not always aware of work that is being done using the Hyper-V console. In that scenario, VMM has to wait for a refresher to run and gather the new state of virtual machines that were managed using the Hyper-V console. Therefore, do not expect to see immediate changes in the VMST console if they were made in the Hyper-V console and not the VMM Administrator Console.

Creating Servicing Jobs in VMST

A servicing job is a set of steps that will run to update a Hyper-V or VMM resource. You will be able to track the progress of and troubleshoot the servicing job in the VMM Administrator Console using the Jobs view.

Servicing jobs can use groups as targets. There is a group type for each of the service jobs types, with one exception, which we will look at later. You can create a group and populate it with the objects that you want to manage in a servicing job. Alternatively, you can just select objects to update when you create a servicing job. Using groups will allow you to aggregate resources into meaningful collections.

You can have many servicing jobs, each running at different schedules. You will need to create groups for each job. A servicing job will use a single set of credentials for some remote administration work. Be sure that all managed items in the servicing job can be managed using that single set of credentials. You can create more jobs if you need to divide up the managed resources.

We are now going to look at each of the servicing job types, see what they can do, and see how to configure them to update your Hyper-V and VMM infrastructure.

Offline Virtual Machines in the VMM Library

Patching offline virtual machines in the VMM library was the only solution provided in the Offline Virtual Machine Servicing Tool versions prior to VMST 3.0. You have the ability to patch virtual machines that are stored in the VMM library from WSUS or ConfigMgr. Then they can be moved back out onto a host server and powered up in a completely patched and secure manner.

The Virtual Machines In Library servicing job will do the following:

1. Move the virtual machine to a maintenance host server.
2. Power up and patch the virtual machine.
3. Move the virtual machine back to the library.

You need to create a Virtual Machines In Library group and populate it with the virtual machines that will be patched by the job. You can do this in the Groups view in the VMST console by right-clicking the Virtual Machines In Library group type and selecting New Library Virtual Machine Group.

This opens the New Library Virtual Machine Group dialog box shown in Figure 12.13. Name the group, and give it a useful description. Then you can select a VMM library server; remember that you can have many library servers.

This allows the contents of the Available Offline Virtual Machines list box, on the left side, to be updated with virtual machines that are stored in the selected VMM library.

There is a check box to also allow virtual machines in a saved state to be listed and selected. When you select it, you are given a warning. Any virtual machine with a saved state will lose its saved state as a result of the update. What this means is that VMST cannot return it into the saved state that it was in before the update. That's because processes will have been unfrozen, and patches will have been applied to the operating system and programs.

Select whatever virtual machines you want to include in the new group and click the arrow buttons to move them into the Selected Virtual Machines group on the right side.

A servicing job must be created now. You can do this by going into the Servicing Jobs view, selecting the Virtual Machines In Library Jobs, and clicking the New Servicing Jobs task in the Actions Pane. That will open the New Library Virtual Machine Servicing Job Wizard, which is displayed in Figure 12.14.

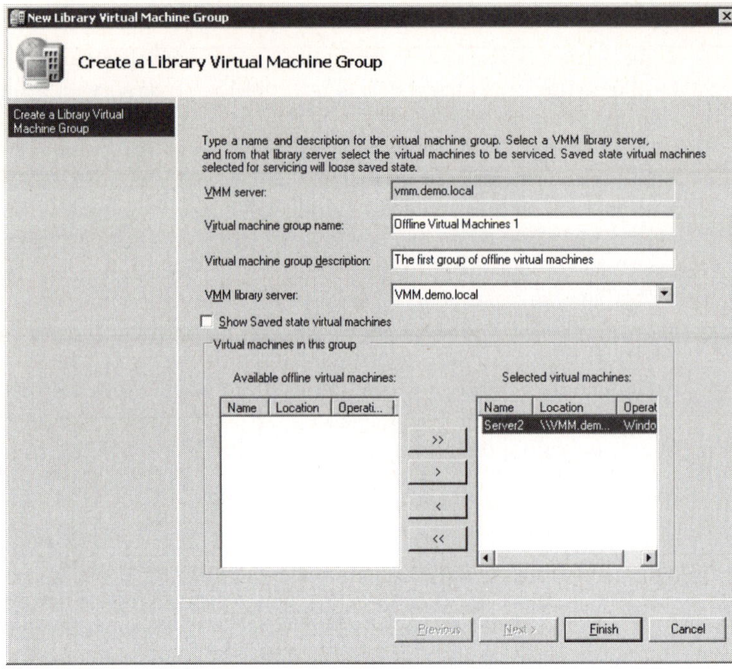

FIGURE 12.13 Creating a New Library Virtual Machine group

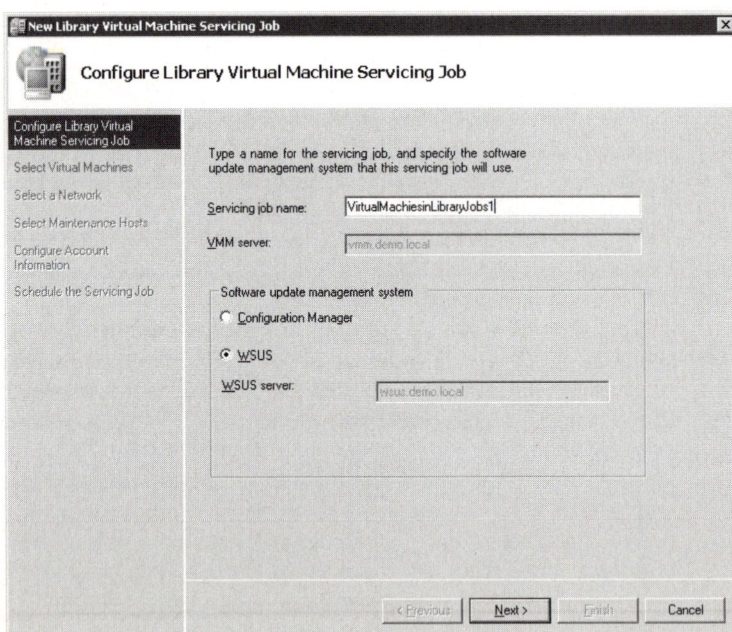

FIGURE 12.14 New Library Virtual Machine Servicing Job Wizard

Here you can name the servicing job. You can use only alphanumeric characters for the name. Spaces and special characters cannot be used. You can also specify whether you want to use ConfigMgr or WSUS as the source of your updates.

Figure 12.15 shows the Select Virtual Machines screen, which allows you to select virtual machines from your group. You may also notice that you can just pick virtual machines from the library without using a group at all. This would be useful if you ever have only a few resources and don't want to bother with the extra administration of groups.

FIGURE 12.15 Selecting offline library virtual machines

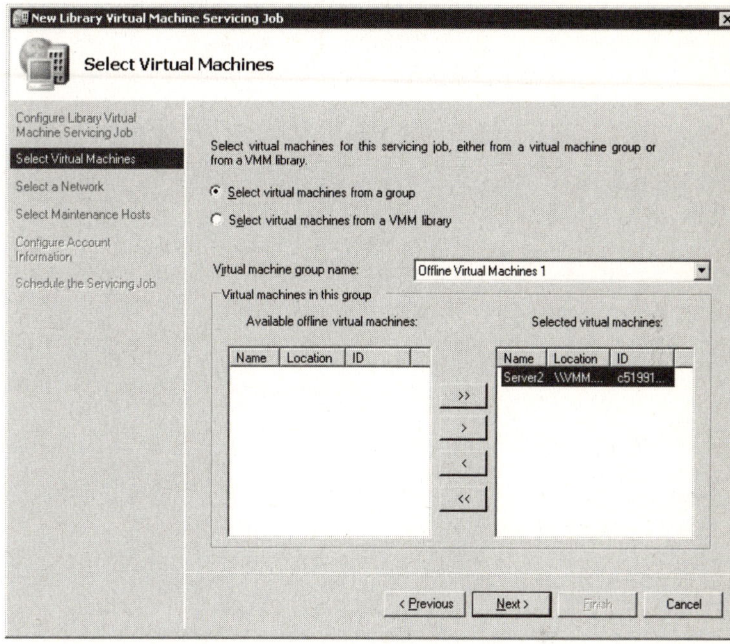

Remember that Microsoft recommends using a dedicated network for patching? The next screen, shown in Figure 12.16, is where you can do it. In Select A Network, you can choose to do either of the following:

Use the Virtual Machine's Configured Network Connection This is probably the simplest solution. The virtual machine will use its normal network connection for administration and patching. The servicing job will require that VMST can manage the virtual machine via PsExec and that the virtual machine can access the patching services.

Use an Isolated Virtual LAN This is the solution that Microsoft recommends. For many, it may seem like overkill. However, it does allow a not up-to-date virtual machine to be powered up on a specific Hyper-V virtual network for patching in a secure manner. This also may simplify firewall rules management so that the virtual machine can access WSUS or ConfigMgr and so that VMST can manage the virtual machine using PsExec. This sort of solution will require a dedicated Hyper-V virtual network that is identically configured on each available maintenance host in the current VMST configuration.

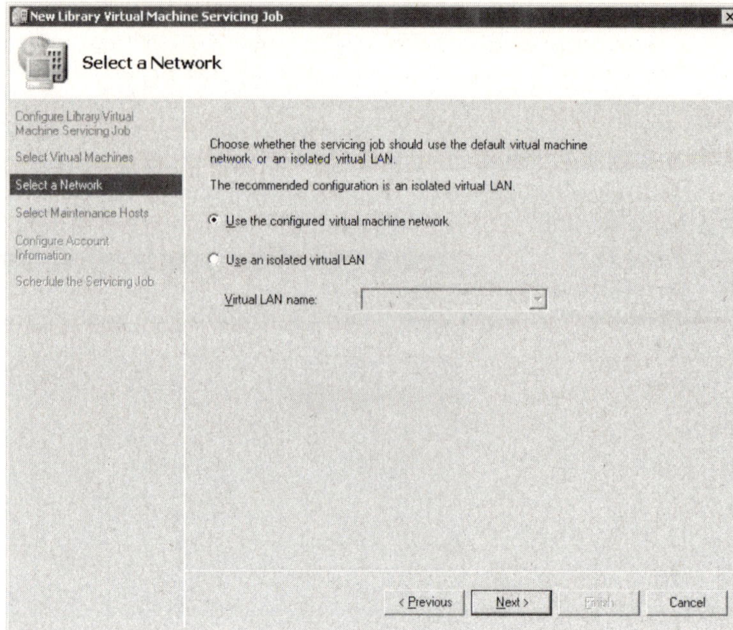

FIGURE 12.16
Selecting a network for the offline virtual machine job

Figure 12.17 shows the Select Maintenance Hosts screen for the servicing job. Here you use the arrow buttons to select which of the available maintenance host servers will be used for this servicing job.

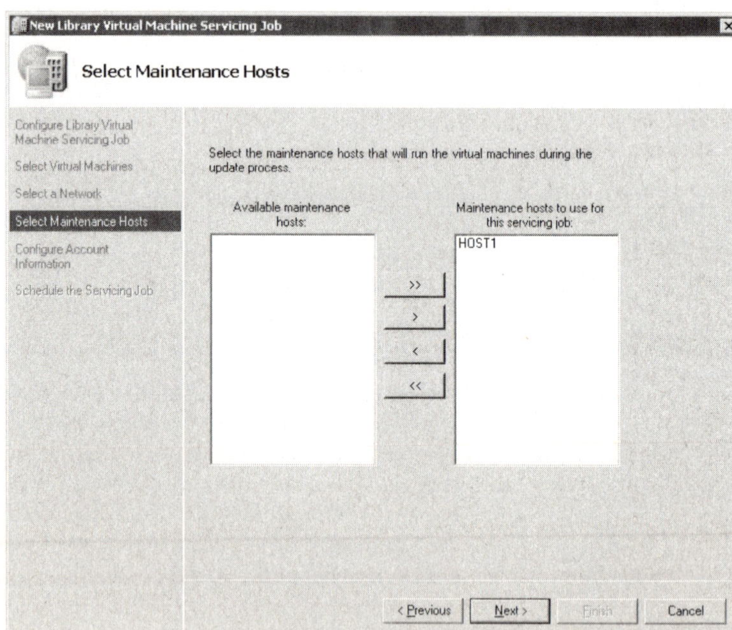

FIGURE 12.17
Selecting maintenance hosts for offline virtual machines

Figure 12.18 shows the second to last screen, Configure Account Information, in Figure 12.18. You need to enter the domain name, username, and password of a user account that will have administrative rights on:

- The virtual machines serviced by this job
- The VMM server
- The WSUS or ConfigMgr server

You really should not be using a domain administrator for this. Create a dedicated VMST service account, and grant it rights using your normal mechanisms, such as Group Policy and the Restricted Groups setting.

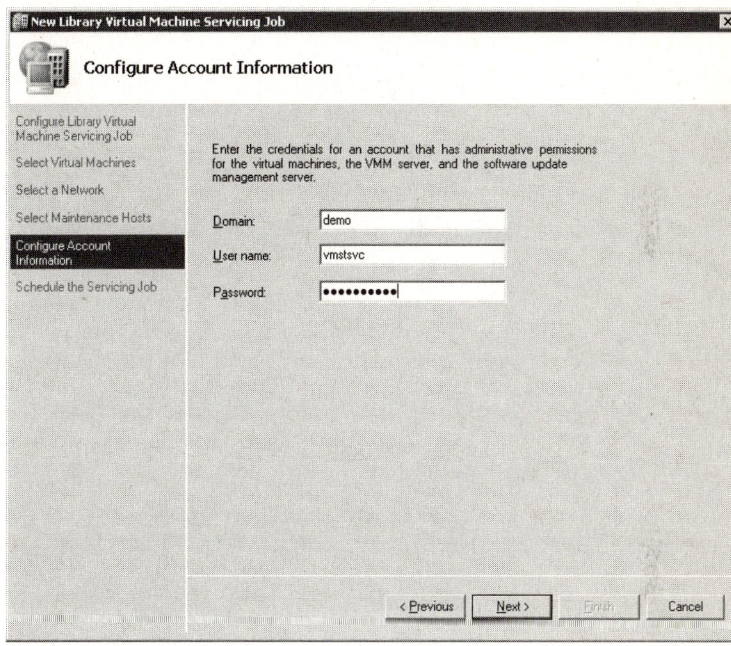

FIGURE 12.18
Configuring offline virtual machine account information

The final screen, Schedule The Servicing Job (Figure 12.19), for this wizard is where you will configure a schedule. Here you can specify when the servicing job should run and whether it should recur on a daily, hourly, weekly, or monthly basis. You must specify an end date for the servicing job if you want it to recur. Set that end date to be a time far into the future if this job will be part of your normal production.

The servicing job will now appear in the VMST console. You can create copies of this job to quickly create new servicing jobs. What has really happened in the background is that a schedule task has been created in Windows. If you open the Task Scheduler in Administrative Tools, you will be able to see a new VMST task there (Figure 12.20).

Now, you can sit back and wait for the servicing job to run. Alternatively, you can just run the task from Task Scheduler. Switch back to VMM, and navigate into the Jobs view. Here you will see each of the actions in the servicing job taking place. Figure 12.21 shows you that the VMST console can also show some basic information about the current status of a job.

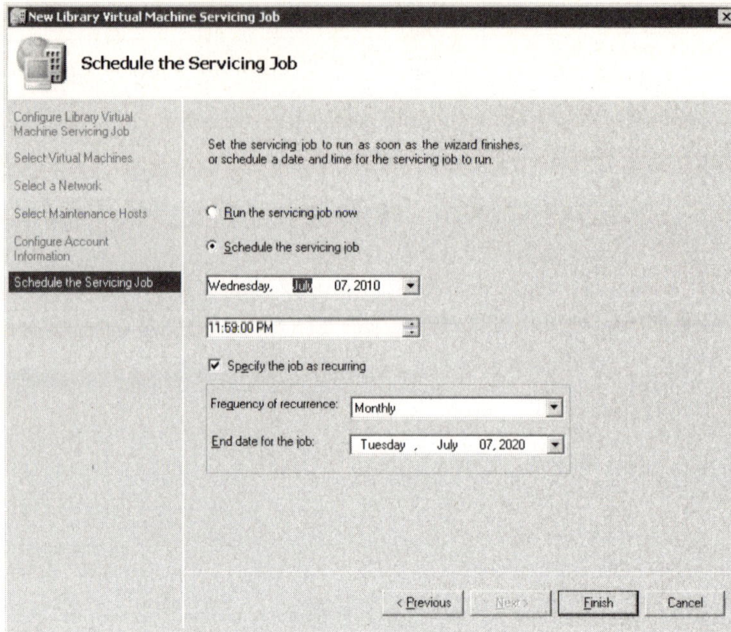

FIGURE 12.19 Scheduling the offline virtual machine servicing job

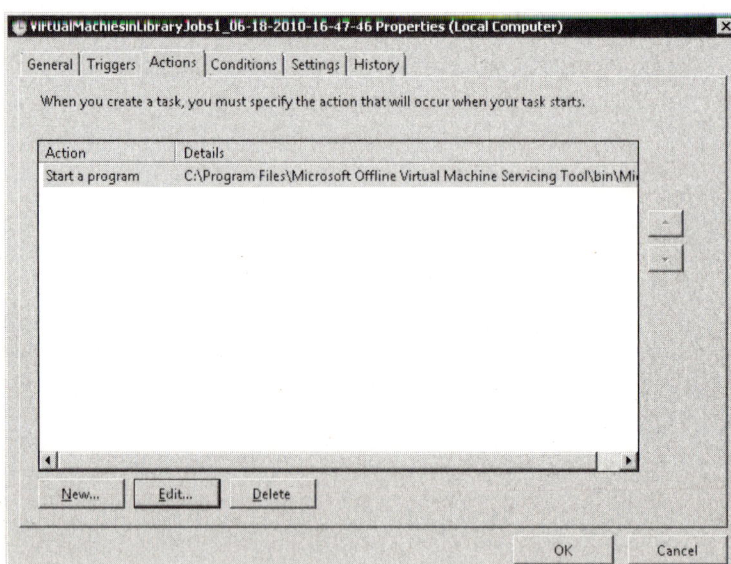

FIGURE 12.20 The servicing job in the Task Scheduler

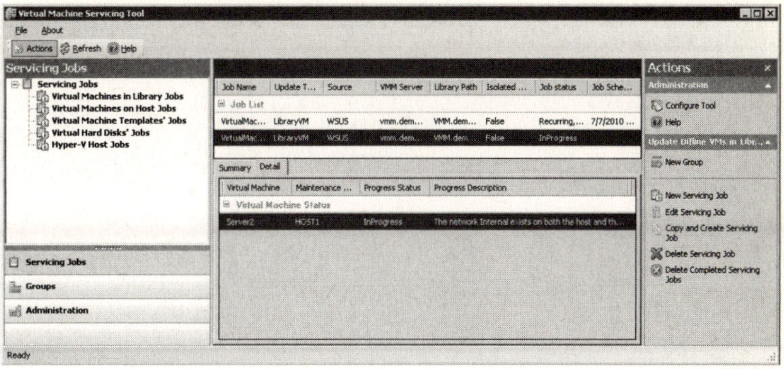

FIGURE 12.21
The servicing job in action in VMST

Once the virtual machine is running, your ability to monitor the progress of the next stage is very limited. There is no recording of the patching activity in VMM or in VMST. If you are using ConfigMgr, then you might be able to use its reporting functionality. You really only can see what's happening once again when the patches are installed and the virtual machine powers down.

VMST does generate logs, but they are a little difficult to follow. You'll find them here:

```
C:\Program Files\Microsoft Offline Virtual Machine Servicing Tool\Log
```

Offline Virtual Machines on the Hosts

Offline virtual machines aren't restricted to the library. In fact, many of them will be sitting on host servers, either powered down or in a saved state. The Virtual Machines On Host Jobs servicing jobs will give you a mechanism where VMST, working with VMM, will do the following:

1. Power up the virtual machine on a maintenance host server.
2. Patch the virtual machine.
3. Power down the virtual machine.

Once again, you can choose to create one or more groups and populate them with virtual machines. Otherwise, you can just create the servicing job and add in virtual machines as required.

Creating the servicing job is not that different from the previous one. You start by selecting virtual machines to patch. This can include saved state virtual machines and powered-down virtual machines, as you can see in Figure 12.22. Serverl is in a saved state, and Server2 is powered down.

After that, you will configure the networking for the servicing job and the credentials, identically to how you did it with the previous job. You finish up the wizard as before, by entering the servicing job schedule information.

As you can see, configuring the servicing jobs is actually pretty easy, and the process is quite similar in each of the different types.

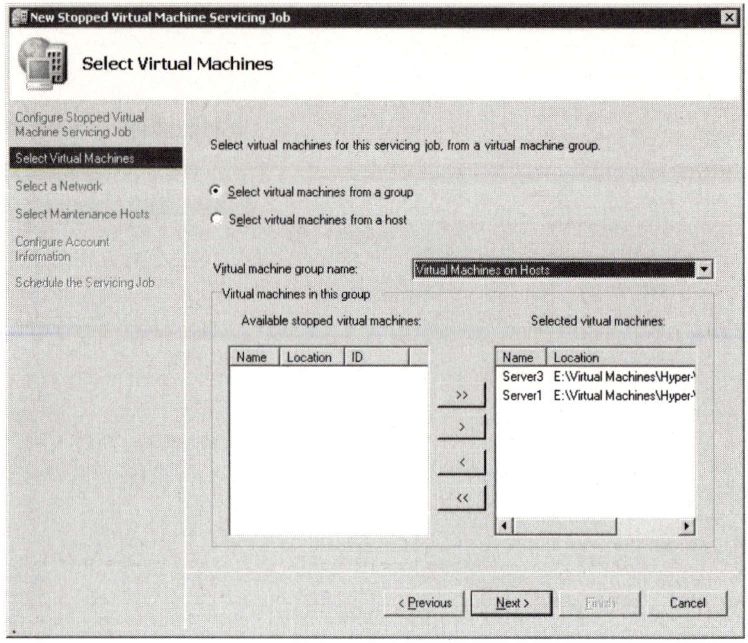

FIGURE 12.22
Selecting virtual machines

VMM Library VHDs That Are Associated with Templates

The most common way to deploy virtual machines in an enterprise environment is to deploy them from a template. This is the method that the VMM Self-Service Portal is based on. End users will expect that new virtual machines should be fully patched. It will be a waste of their time and the organization's time if they are prompted to perform and update and reboot a few minutes after deploying the virtual machine.

VMST has a mechanism for keeping templates fully patched. It is a little complicated. You first have to prepare the environment:

1. You deploy a virtual machine to the VMM Library from the template.
2. You create a group in VMST to link the deployed virtual machine to the template.

A VMST servicing job is configured. It will do the following:

1. It will attach to the deployed virtual machine.
2. It will move the virtual machine from the VMM library to the maintenance host.
3. It will patch the virtual machine.
4. It will clone the updated virtual machine to create an identical copy of the virtual machine.
5. It will optionally back up the original template.
6. It will create a new template from the cloned virtual machine, replacing the original template.
7. It will return the patched virtual machine to the VMM library from the maintenance host.

The process requires permanently consuming space in the VMM library for the deployed virtual machine. This virtual machine serves no other purpose and should not be used in any other way.

Let's look at the step-by-step process of maintaining a VMM library template. First you need to prepare the environment. Use VMM to deploy a virtual machine from the template to the VMM library. Give the template a meaningful virtual machine name (in VMM) and computer name (in the operating system). For example, if the template is called Windows Server 2008 R2 Enterprise, then you can call the deployed virtual machine VMST Windows Server 2008 R2 and call the computer name something similar. This will make them stand out and be self-documenting. Make sure that your virtual machine does not have a saved state or any snapshots.

You must create a group for this type of servicing job. The group will bind or link the deployed (or gold) virtual machine to the template in the VMM library, as far as VMST is concerned. You need to be very careful that no one tries to use that virtual machine for something else because there is no mechanism to stop that.

Figure 12.23 shows the first screen where you select the template that you want to include in this job. Select the templates that you want to maintain. Remember that you must have deployed a gold virtual machine from each selected template.

FIGURE 12.23
Selecting a template to link

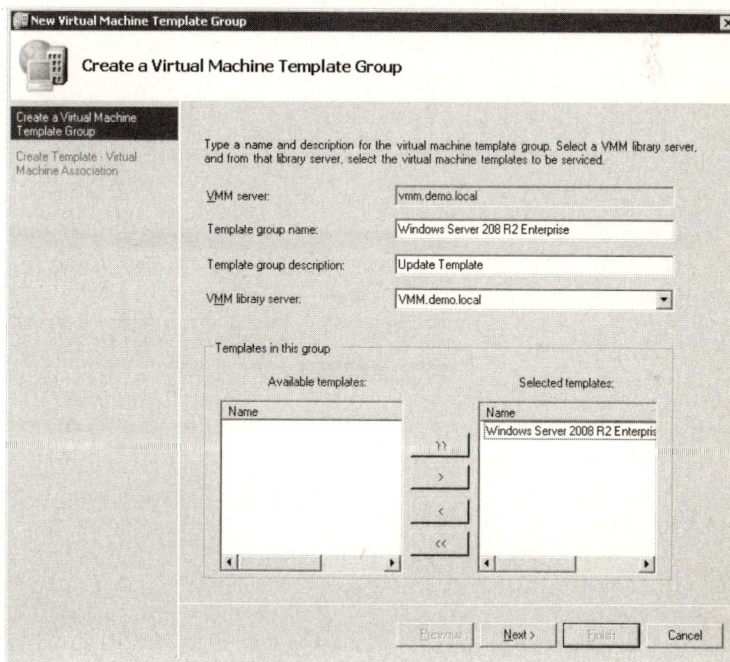

On the following screen, you can select a template, select the gold virtual machine that was created from that image, and click the Add button. Repeat that for each template that you added in the previous screen.

With the group created, you can create the servicing job. The wizard works identically to previous servicing job wizards. The only difference is that you can choose to create a backup of the template in the library. Only one backup will be kept by VMST. This will give you an easy way to restore an original template should the patching process or a patch introduce a problem.

When the servicing job runs, it will move the virtual machine to a maintenance host, patch the gold virtual machine, clone it, create a replacement template from the clone, and return the virtual machine to the VMM library.

VHDs Stored in the VMM Library

It is possible, with VMM, to store VHD files in the library that have nothing to do with a template. You can use them for virtual machine deployment. For this reason, you need to be able to keep them up-to-date.

VMST uses some of the functionality of VHD files to do this. A VHD can be mounted by Windows 7 or Windows Server 2008 R2 as a filesystem. You can do this from the command prompt using `DISKPART.EXE`. This allows you to use a tool called `DISM.EXE` to inject drivers into the VHD file. The VMST servicing job for doing this will do the following:

1. Copy the VHD file from the VMM library to the configured computer for servicing VHD files.
2. Mount the VHD.
3. Inject updates into the VHD.
4. Copy the VHD back to the VMM library.

The servicing job follows the usual template. You will select which VHDs from the VMM library will be updated. You should not do this with the VHDs that are linked to templates. You can see the screen in Figure 12.24.

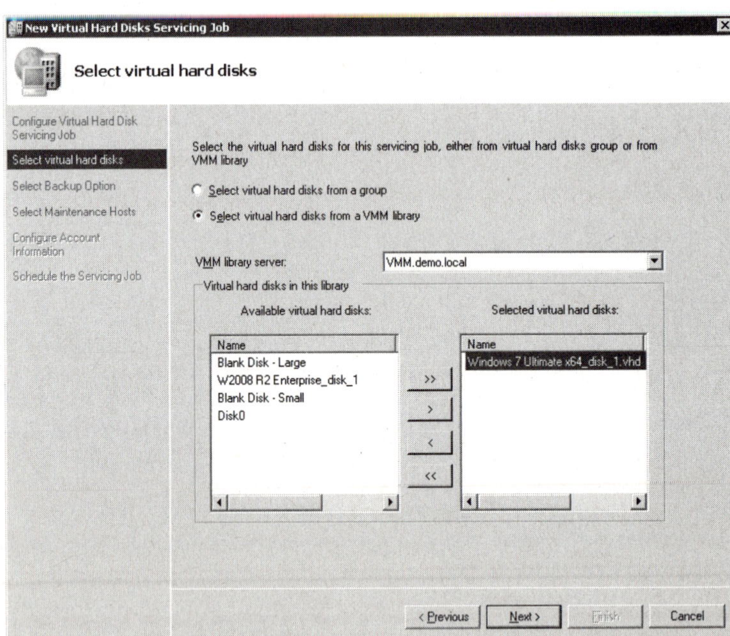

FIGURE 12.24
Selecting VHDs to update

There is a risk that patching may introduce a fault to a virtual machine or VHD. You will probably want an easy way to undo any changes. You can choose to instruct VMST to back up the VHD before it is replaced (Figure 12.25). Only one backup can be kept by VMST.

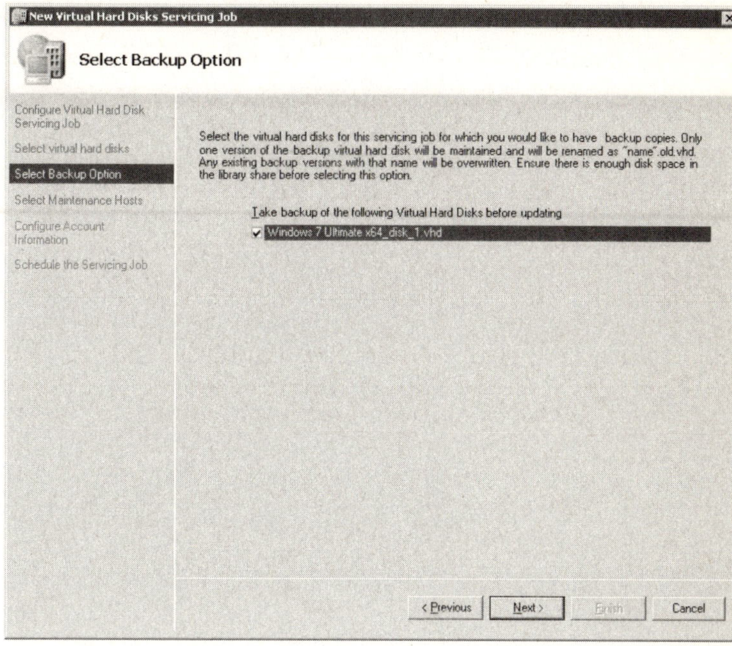

FIGURE 12.25
Selecting a VHD backup option

The maintenance hosts that you are using for this servicing job are usually (and probably should not be) Hyper-V host servers. They are going to be Windows 7 or Windows Server 2008 R2 computers with sufficient disk space to temporarily store VHDs. You can select from the available VHD maintenance hosts (specified when you ran the Configure Tool Wizard) in the screen shown in Figure 12.26.

You will then complete the wizard as normal, entering the required credentials and schedule information.

Clustered Hyper-V Host Servers

This feature is the one reason to install VMST on your network, even if you do not want to patch any of your offline virtual machines or VMM library content.

If you have a Hyper-V cluster, the only way to apply patches to your Hyper-V host servers is to do it manually. You will place a node into maintenance mode, which triggers Live Migration to move the virtual machines onto other nodes in the cluster without downtime. You can then manually apply updates. That is a manual process, consuming a lot of time, especially in very large environment with a 16-node cluster, or even many clusters.

Alternatively, you could schedule PowerShell scripts to start maintenance mode before each host is scheduled to automatically apply updates. That's a bit risky because the two operations are not linked. There isn't a way to automatically prevent patching and reboots (and therefore virtual machine downtime) if the PowerShell maintenance mode script fails for some reason.

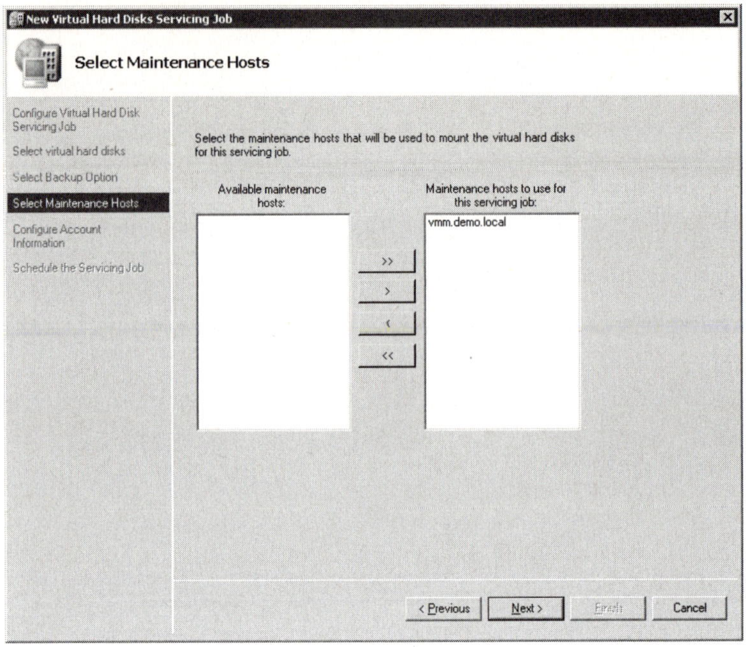

FIGURE 12.26
Selecting VHD maintenance hosts

The Hyper-V Host Jobs servicing job is intended to resolve this situation. It is a simple job to configure the following:

- Provide the usual servicing job information.
- Select a Hyper-V cluster that is managed by VMM.
- Specify whether virtual machines should return to their original host or not after VMM maintenance mode is ended on that host.
- Provide administrator credentials for the Hyper-V host servers that also have rights in VMM and WSUS/ConfigMgr.
- Configure a schedule for the job.

The only real question here is, when would you schedule the job? Would you schedule it like your normal physical or virtual machines, maybe at 3 a.m. on a Saturday morning? You could do that. Maybe you would prefer to do it during the day when administrators and engineers are around and quickly available should something go wrong. We schedule normal servers to patch during out-of-business hours because there is downtime during the reboot. However, with VMM Maintenance Mode and Windows Failover Clustering, there is no downtime for highly available virtual machines when we patch and reboot each Hyper-V host, one at a time. Virtual machines will simply move around with no downtime.

This is what will happen when the job runs:

1. Host1 is placed into VMM maintenance mode.
2. Virtual machines from Host1 will live migrate to other hosts in the cluster with no downtime.
3. Host1 will be patched and rebooted as necessary.
4. VMM maintenance mode on Host1 will be ended.
5. Host2 is placed into VMM maintenance mode.
6. This continues until every host in the cluster is updated.

There is zero human effort to manage this process. The one thing to watch out for with this is Operations Manager creating alerts. You can schedule maintenance mode for VMM and Hyper-V monitored resources, or you can use the Maintenance Mode management pack that was discussed in Chapter 7.

Virtual Machine Servicing Tool 3.0 requires a bit of work to get up and running. Most of that can be simplified with optimal design using solutions such as Group Policy. However, the daily configuration is pretty easy. The benefits are that deployed and powered-up resources are fully secured straightaway and require no patching and reboots. End users can avail themselves of services with no delays. Even just the ability to patch clustered Hyper-V hosts in a completely automated and job-driven manner is worth the effort of installing VSMT.

The Bottom Line

Place and secure your Hyper-V host servers You have a number of options in how you place Hyper-V host servers in your network. Each option will affect your ability to cluster the host servers, manage them, and provide access to services such as VDI and self-service provisioning.

Master It You work in an organization with mission-critical security requirements. The IT security team has demanded that you maximize the security of several applications and the entire infrastructure that they run on. Those virtual machines must be fault tolerant. The remaining applications servers can run at normal network security levels. How will you design the Hyper-V host servers?

Use antivirus software on your Hyper-V host servers There is some debate about installing antivirus scanning software on Hyper-V host servers. It requires special configuration if you do install it.

Master It A security officer has demanded that the corporate security policy is fully applied to the parent partitions of your Hyper-V host servers. They are saying that these are insecure Windows servers and that all content on them, including the virtual machine files on the cluster shared volume, should be configured for real-time scanning and nightly scheduled scanning. You have been brought to a meeting to explain how antivirus can impact Hyper-V. What will you tell them about the potential problems and how the antivirus should be configured to prevent issues?

Patch your Hyper-V host servers and VMM library content The Virtual Machine Servicing Tool 3.0 can be used to automatically patch clustered Hyper-V host servers and VMM library content.

Master It You are working as a virtualization consultant. A client has asked you to discuss potential solutions for patching their Hyper-V infrastructure. The primary requirement is to find a way to reliably and automatically patch their clustered Hyper-V host servers. The secondary requirement is to be able to provide virtual machine templates that are up-to-date with their security updates so that testers and developers have little wasted time and effort when they use the VMM Self-Service Portal.

Chapter 13

Business Continuity

Organizations have had business and regulatory reasons to implement infrastructure for business continuity or disaster recovery for quite some time. Many decision makers considered this to be yet another big IT expense, one for which the cost was greater than the risk. Those organizations that lived with the risk of natural disaster understood how important it was to design an IT infrastructure that could rapidly respond to a site becoming unavailable. September 11, 2001, put many organizations' ability to recover from a disaster to the test. Hurricane Katrina was another test. Some organizations passed, and some failed. Failing this test can cause a business to lose huge amounts of money or even go bankrupt.

Now more decision makers understand that implementing a disaster recovery site and a business continuity plan are worthwhile expenses and efforts.

By now, you understand that implementing a virtualization infrastructure such as Hyper-V will make huge changes to how your IT systems work. You know that virtual machines are highly mobile. We can move them from one physical server to another with a few mouse clicks or by running a small script. We can make virtual machines highly available. We can also back up entire virtual machines with ease. We can leverage these characteristics of hardware virtualization to facilitate a business continuity plan.

We will start this chapter talking about disaster recovery and business continuity planning. After this, we will focus on how Hyper-V can play a role in this infrastructure by providing a more reliable solution that can automatically and rapidly respond to an issue. Some of this functionality will leverage Windows Server Failover Clustering. Some will use third-party software solutions. The high-end solutions will make use of storage area network replication mechanisms. We will wrap up the chapter by looking at a few tips to help you find the right solution for your organization.

In this chapter, you will learn to

- Understand what business continuity is and identify the needs of the business
- Describe some of the many business continuity and disaster recovery solutions that are available
- Choose between the various types of business continuity solutions

Understanding Business Continuity

Most organizations have a requirement to be able to survive the loss of a building or campus. This might be driven by the business. For example, the owner or shareholders are investing in a business and not in a property. They expect that operations are mobile and able to survive an incident such as a fire, chemical leak, act of terrorism, or natural disaster. Some organizations face regulatory requirements that are dictated either by an industrial organization or by the government.

Know the Basics of Business Continuity

IT people refer to any disaster-proof IT infrastructure as *disaster recovery* (DR). That is a pretty loose term. You could get 100 descriptions of disaster recovery if you asked 100 IT professionals to describe disaster recovery. It could mean having a highly available site with a replica of every production system. It could also mean being able to recover a database from a backup. It all depends on what disaster recovery means to you.

Businesspeople use the term *business continuity. Business continuity planning* (BCP) is the process where various key players in the entire organization (not just IT) play a role in describing the required infrastructure and reaction plans to various kinds of disaster that can affect the business.

Typically with a traditional disaster recovery plan, IT makes those systems that they think are critical highly available in another site. IT will have plans to bring them online in the order they believe is important and in time frames that they believe are acceptable. They might test these plans once a quarter or once a year to ensure that they can bring the systems online. There is a problem with all this. Something is missing.

What use are systems without the people who run them? Yes, you're probably thinking what all IT pros think: what use are the people who use the systems? But joking aside, people need to be considered in a plan. The all-encompassing business continuity plan will consider everything the business must do to continue essential operations with minimal impact to revenue, customers, and partners. This includes the following:

- If, when, and under what conditions the BCP will be invoked
- How people will be contacted in the event of a disaster
- What they will be told and where they will go
- Who will be contacted.
- What systems must be in place, how quickly they must be brought online, and in what order they must be brought online
- How the business will communicate with customers and partners

The ability for the organization to communicate after the disaster is absolutely critical. Imagine for a moment that you work for a city government and your office is shut down because of a natural disaster such as a flood. How do you think it will impact the citizens of your city if you cannot communicate with them? How will the customers of a bank react if the bank cannot contact them? How will sales distribution partners of an airline react if they suddenly cannot book flights for their partner? Unfortunately, these are not unrealistic scenarios. Tornadoes, hurricanes, floods, and earthquakes do happen. Fires, chemical leaks, and electricity outages do occur.

Most of business continuity planning does involve the business outside of IT. But you get to stroke your ego a little bit; the IT systems that you provide are essential to everything the business will do in the event of a disaster. There are no communications without email or phone systems. There are few or no Windows-based applications without Active Directory. There is no data without some form of replication that depends on the network. And it's pointless having these systems and applications if users cannot access them. The quality, effectiveness, and rapid recoverability of the highly available systems that you provide in the secondary or disaster recovery site will be central to how well the business recovers from the disaster.

IT needs to bring systems and applications back online while the business is communicating with staff members, customers, and partners. There are two critical questions:

- In what order must systems be brought online?
- How quickly must they be brought online?

The owner of every business application will insist that their system must be prioritized. Isn't that just typical? In reality, if everything is prioritized, then nothing is actually prioritized. What's the point in having a first class if no one sits in second class? Ideally the decision makers in the BCP program will give you some direction about what the business views as critical and how the recovery of systems should be ordered.

Some organizations will allow an outage of IT systems for five working days. They typically have minimal budgets and are relying on a recovery from tapes that are stored offsite. Wouldn't it be awful if the offsite storage location was also affected by the disaster and if you couldn't successfully recover the backups? There is a huge risk with that sort of solution! It is more typical to have a requirement that the BCP invocation be completed within four hours. All critical systems will be replicated to a disaster recovery site, and end users are accessing the applications and data via some interface. There could be a computer room at the facility, or the users could be accessing some remote computing solution such as Remote Desktop Services via the Internet. Some organizations cannot tolerate any downtime at all.

It doesn't matter whether the organization is a small business with a single server or a stock exchange with a huge budget; implementing the IT systems for business continuity is difficult, expensive, and usually not reliable. Every application seems to require a different method to make it highly available. Each system requires lots of handling with kid gloves to bring it online after the disaster. And that can be catastrophic because you can be sure that no administrator or engineer will be able to concentrate when everyone is screaming for attention.

What is needed is a way to easily replicate entire servers as containers, including their applications and data, from one physical location to another. If servers could exist as files, then maybe we could automatically move them from a production site to a secondary site with little effort. There would be no need to worry about the individual point solution clustering mechanisms of each and every application.

Hold on! Hyper-V allows us to run servers as VHD and configuration files. We like this because it makes virtual machines more agile and more mobile than physical machines. The virtual machine files can be easily replicated over a WAN link to a disaster recovery site.

Understand How Virtualization Benefits Disaster Recovery

As IT professionals, we have three great challenges when it comes to deploying an IT infrastructure for business continuity using physical servers:

Replicate Applications and Data Every application seems to have its own set of guidelines to replicate it to a secondary site. All too often they require special licenses or third-party solutions. You can end up exponentially increasing the complexity of the entire IT infrastructure.

Rapid Recovery Imagine you have the typical four hours to recover critical IT systems in the disaster recovery site. Now consider the number of run books that you have to work through for each and every application because they all have their own invocation plans. How realistic will it be to recover the business in four hours? Remember, this will be your worst-ever day at work, and people will be panicking, including some silly director who is upset because his fancy new mobile phone isn't getting a signal and he demands that you look at it.

Complete Testing It's not practical to do a complete invocation test of a business continuity plan. You cannot failover services without impacting normal, daily operations. You might get a few giggles by failing over the accountancy department's applications, but that will backfire when the accountants cannot process this month's salaries on time.

Virtualization helps in a few ways. The virtual machines in question are usually just files. Files are easy to replicate. You can use a number of mechanisms to replicate virtual machine files to an offsite location. There will be some exceptions where you will use passthrough disks. They will impact your offsite replication plans, either by requiring them to be replicated at the storage level or by treating them as physical servers.

Can I Use DFS-R to Replicate Virtual Machine Files?

Distributed File System Replication (DFS-R) is a file replication mechanism that has been around since Windows Server 2003 R2. It replicates files on a block-level basis when the write file handle on the files has been closed. That's where the problem lies. Virtual machine files close only when the Hyper-V host server shuts down, and you can't exactly replicate anything from the server then! DFS-R is not a supported mechanism for replicating virtual machine files from one host storage location to another.

Because you are normally dealing with virtual machine files such as VHD files, you will have a single replication mechanism. That means there is much less to manage.

Replication mechanisms usually implement some form of clustering such as Failover Clustering in Windows Server 2008 R2. This means that the replication mechanism is doing more than just replicating VHD files from a primary site to a secondary site. The virtual machine configurations are being made available on Hyper-V host servers in the secondary site too. Recovery from a disaster is really simple; you just power up the virtual machines in the secondary site! That will take only a few minutes. Depending on your replication solution, this might even be automated. It's rather morbid to think about it, but this covers a scenario where you and your colleagues in IT are caught up in whatever disaster has brought the primary site out of service. There is no dependence on you to bring all services back online in the secondary site. The business will be able to go on without you, and your successors will be able to quickly start their new jobs without any disaster recovery stress.

Virtual machines do offer the possibility to test your disaster recovery plans. It is theoretically possible to bring virtual machines online in the secondary site using Hyper-V virtual networks that are not connected to the rest of the corporate WAN. Unfortunately, this isn't something that is easy to do with the Microsoft native tools (recover virtual machines from backup), but some third-party solutions may help with built-in disaster recovery testing features.

Looking at Ways to Implement Hyper-V Business Continuity

There are a number of ways to implement business continuity for an IT infrastructure. Your decision-making process for choosing one will depend on your budget and the required recovery time from a disaster. Those factors will be driven by the objectives of the virtualization project. Here we are at the tail end of the book, and the objectives of the project are still extremely important!

We're going to look at a number of ways that you can implement business continuity using a virtualized IT infrastructure, starting with the least expensive and working up to some pretty interesting solutions. The recovery time will vary. The bad news is that the faster recovery times require exponentially larger capital investment and operational costs.

One Size Does Not Fit All

There are many ways to implement a disaster recovery or business continuity solution using a Hyper-V infrastructure. Software and hardware manufacturers have developed many solutions, each with advantages and disadvantages. This chapter aims to introduce you to some of the options and show you the variety of approaches. You should engage with a number of specialists who can analyze your needs and help you find the solution that is right for your organization.

Using Offsite Backup

The simplest and cheapest of the solutions is to use a system that many organizations are already using in one form or another for providing business continuity services. Offsite backup is the process where your regular backups are sent offsite. Traditionally, an operator would collect the backup tapes from the tape library (or libraries) and put them in a container or courier pouch. Those businesses that understand the value of those tapes employ the services of a secure vault service provider. One of their couriers calls around to drop off an old set of tapes for reuse and then collect the new set for secure, offsite storage.

The operational expense is pretty low. The only expense is for the vault service provider. Unfortunately, you do get what you pay for when it comes to business continuity. To help understand this, consider what will happen during a disaster.

Imagine that there is an incident nearby, and your building is shut down. There will likely be some sort of panic in the surrounding areas. Your business will issue an alert to staff members to meet at the disaster recovery site. A low-end solution such as tape recovery usually means that there is no hot standby equipment. The solution will vary widely:

- A hardware service provider doing their best to supply you with some spares
- A specialist provider providing a container full of equipment as part of some insurance agreement
- A disaster recovery site with racks full of blank servers that are provided to customers on a first-come, first-served basis

If you and your colleagues survive the disaster at the office, you have to find your way to the disaster recovery site through the panic. You now are hoping that the secure vault service provider has survived and can get the tapes to your disaster recovery site. Let's face it; this is where things start to fall apart. Anyone who experienced September 11, 2001, will remember the lockdowns on transport and the communications congestion.

If the tapes do arrive, you will face the daunting task of recovering everything from tape to blank machines. A bare-metal recovery is a challenging operation with just one server. Imagine trying to accomplish this for every machine at once while directors stand over your shoulder, salespeople annoy you because their mobile phones don't have a signal, managers complain because their email out of office isn't working, laptops won't connect to the network…it's all just one big mess that will have you issuing expletives in a very short amount of time.

The reality is that offsite backup is the only method of business continuity that is affordable to many smaller organizations and branch offices. The key to success is to tailor the solution to minimize the risks. Virtualization assists with this greatly. And so does Microsoft System Center.

DPM2DPM4DR

The first flaw with offsite backup storage is the offsite storage of tapes. Where are they stored? Is that offsite storage site a secure facility or the boss's house? Is it too close to your office and subject to the same disaster risks? How do the tapes get there? Are they transported by a secure courier, the boss, or the receptionist? Are the tapes (which contain sensitive data) password protected and encrypted? Is your backup system compliant with any data protection laws for your industry and state? Are your tapes and tape libraries reliable? These mechanical devices are typically prone to high levels of failure. There is an old phrase that says it never rains; it pours. How bad would it be if your DR site tape library failed during a disaster or a tape containing valuable data were chewed up?

Many organizations made the switch to direct-to-disk (D2D) backup to avoid issues with tapes for normal operational recovery jobs, yet they still depend on offsite tape storage for the worst-case scenario.

Some backup products, including Microsoft System Center Data Protection Manager (DPM) 2010, offer the ability to replicate the backup storage to another location. This is an extension of the offsite backup storage concept. Unlike sending tapes offsite, it uses more reliable disk storage, it is completely automated, and it can be secured by using a WAN and/or VPN connection.

Microsoft refers to this feature as DPM to DPM for DR (DPM2DPM4DR). A possible deployment scenario (Figure 13.1) would be to implement a DPM 2010 server in your primary site. It would be responsible for backing up your server infrastructure, including your virtual machines and their contents, to a disk storage device. This storage device would retain data for short-term or operational recoveries. Thirty days might be considered long enough for this by some organizations. A second DPM 2010 server would be located in a secondary site. This second DPM server could be placed in a rack at a hosting company datacenter. The second DPM server would use DPM2DPM4DR to replicate the storage of the primary site DPM server to storage in the secondary site. During a disaster, you could recover from the secondary site's DPM server. As you learned in Chapter 10, recovering an entire virtual machine from backup is not so difficult. It would be possible to quickly recover the virtual machines to Hyper-V host servers that could be already up and running in the secondary site without any of the worries of bare-metal recovery.

FIGURE 13.1
DPM disaster recovery replication

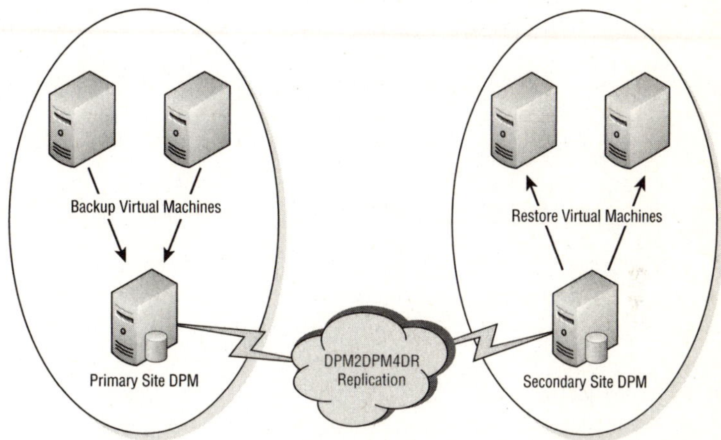

Your ability to restore data from a short time ago, either for normal operations or for a disaster, is possible with this solution. You can still send data to tape for long-term archival. This is possible by adding a tape library to the DPM server in either the primary site or the secondary site.

> **READ ABOUT DATA PROTECTION MANAGER**
>
> Jason Buffington is one of Microsoft's senior product managers for Data Protection Manager, making him one of the leading experts on its usage. Jason wrote a book called *Data Protection for Virtual Data Centers* (Sybex, 2010), which will teach you everything you need to know about Data Protection Manager 2010.

BACK UP TO THE CLOUD

There is a possible variation on the DPM2DPM4DR concept. Some organizations may not be able to afford to maintain a secondary site. They might also decide that the additional usage of tapes for long-term recovery is unsuitable. It is possible to extend your backup solution to send data to a Cloud service provider. For example, you can back up your Hyper-V infrastructure using DPM 2010 and then replicate your store to the Cloud using a service called CloudRecovery, provided by Iron Mountain.

This sort of solution will allow you to restore your data from the Cloud in the event of a disaster and will also provide a long-term archive. It is completely automated, and it is free of unreliable tapes, which require a so-called tape monkey to swap them every day. On the negative side, Cloud services such as this tie you to the service provider, and they are not necessarily very economic. You also must be very careful when considering a Cloud service for online backup functionality. You need to investigate the company, the datacenter locations and physical security, the encryption and communications security, and how they apply to your organization. Some service providers can offer an economic service but are less than reliable, while others such as Iron Mountain have earned a reputation for providing a quality service.

Using Multi-site Clustering

A multi-site cluster is exactly what it says on the tin; it is a cluster that can exist in two or more sites. You may also know multi-site clustering by some of its other names such as *stretch cluster* or *geo-cluster*. You should use *multi-site cluster* as your search criteria if you are searching on the Internet for official guidance from Microsoft.

The basic concept of a multi-site cluster in a Hyper-V context is that you can use Live Migration or Quick Migration (this did not go away in Windows Server 2008 R2), depending on your bandwidth and solution, to move virtual machines between Hyper-V host servers in different sites. The benefits are pretty obvious. You will have a single mechanism that you are already familiar with to control the high availability of your virtual machines between hosts in the same site and hosts in different sites. The downsides are that it does require lots of WAN bandwidth and the storage system (double the requirements and maybe additional licensing) will be expensive.

The design of a multi-site cluster will require some cooperation with your networking colleagues. You need to consider how virtual machines will be made available to each other and to client machines on the network when they failover to the secondary site.

Will the virtual machines retain their existing IP addresses after a failover to the secondary site? If so, then you will need to stretch the VLANs from the primary site to the secondary site, as shown in Figure 13.2. There will be considerable work required, but the benefit is that virtual machines will become instantly available should they failover (after boot-up) or after a Quick/Live Migration. Virtual machines will be instantly available to clients after a migration to the secondary site because their addresses will not change. The initial effort investment will pay dividends in the long term.

Note that you must stretch any VLAN that may be used for Cluster Shared Volume communications.

Maybe your network team doesn't want to or cannot stretch your VLANs between sites. It has not been a requirement to do so for multi-site clustering since Windows Server 2008. The complication with this solution (Figure 13.3) is that a machine that is failed over to the secondary site will need a new IP configuration that is suitable for the secondary site VLAN. A virtual machine that is manually configured with an IP address for a VLAN in the production site will not be able to communicate in the secondary site. It would require manual intervention to modify the IP address, and this would defeat the point of Failover Clustering.

To resolve this, you will have to use DHCP. You can configure the virtual machines with DHCP addresses in the primary and secondary sites. You will want to keep the addresses predictable, so you will need to set reservations for the DHCP addresses on every DHCP server that may respond to the virtual machines' requests. This is based on MAC address, so the virtual machine virtual network adapters will need to be manually configured with static MAC addresses (dynamic is the default) when they are created. Configuring a new virtual machine will require testing in both sites with both IP addresses. And don't forget that you absolutely must back up the DHCP servers now. The DHCP servers probably should be physical servers to avoid a chicken-and-egg scenario where virtual DHCP servers would boot up after other virtual machines search for and fail to find IP configurations.

FIGURE 13.2
Stretched VLAN multi-site cluster

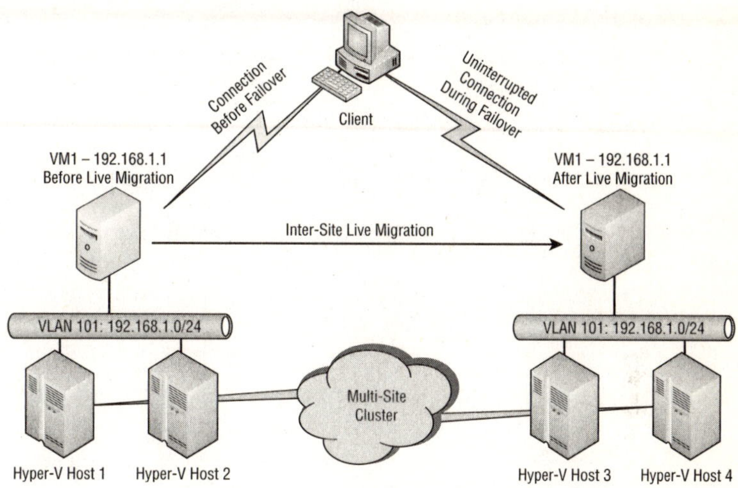

FIGURE 13.3
Multi-site cluster with different VLANs

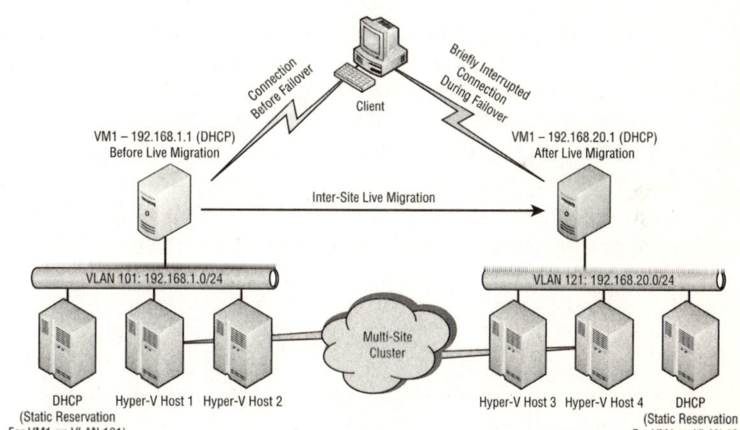

How will clients find the virtual machines with their new IP addresses? They will have cached the results of previous DNS name resolutions. The solution is to edit the properties of the forward lookup records in DNS and to change the Time-To-Live (TTL) properties to something short such as one or five minutes.

The result of this configuration will be that a virtual machine will be able to failover automatically to a secondary site. It will automatically get a new IP configuration from the local DHCP servers after a few seconds of a network outage. Clients will be unable to communicate with the failover virtual machines for a few minutes because they will have cached DNS records with the old name to IP address resolutions. If you do have a disaster, five minutes of an outage for services might normally be considered pretty impressive, especially when you consider that many organizations aim for four hours! However, some organizations need failover to be instant. This might be their required invocation time, or it might be to facilitate disaster recovery testing.

The manual virtual machine configurations to the virtual machines (static MAC address and DHCP reservation) may make the VMM Self-Service Portal a bit pointless for production virtual machines.

Your choice is simple. VLAN stretching might require some extensive network engineering at the start, but the return is automated virtual machine provisioning and instant service availability after virtual machine failover. Choosing not to stretch the VLANs will be easier for the network team, but it will return you to the bad days of manual machine configuration, and it will not be possible to have instant virtual machine availability after a failover.

A failover cluster uses a heartbeat transmission to detect a host failure. A multi-site cluster with member Hyper-V hosts in a remote datacenter will be affected by the latency of the link between the primary and secondary sites. This could cause a heartbeat signal to time out, causing a false alert and unnecessarily triggering the failover of virtual machines. You can avoid this problem by altering the timeout of the heartbeat. You can find details on this operation here:

`http://technet.microsoft.com/library/dd197562(WS.10).aspx`

Real World Scenario

HOST FAULT TOLERANCE IN A MULTI-SITE CLUSTER

You will typically have 1 redundant host in a cluster with up to 8 nodes and 2 redundant hosts in a cluster with 16 nodes. Where do you place a redundant host in a multi-site cluster? In fact, do you have a redundant node at all?

One approach might be to limit the redundancy completely but still allow for a disaster. For example, you might require five hosts to service the needs of your virtual machines in a production environment. Your fault tolerance would be to have five additional hosts in the disaster recovery site. Any host failure or maintenance in the primary site would trigger a failover of virtual machines to the secondary site.

This could cause some issues. Clients will have a brief outage. Administration might become more complicated. What do you do with your backup system when you have some production machines running in the primary site and some running in the secondary site? What direction should the backup system replicate?

It would be advisable to size the number of hosts in the primary site as you normally would. For example, if five hosts are required, then you would have an additional redundant host in the primary site, giving a total of six hosts. An additional six hosts would be placed in the secondary site (assuming that all the hosts are of the same specification). That means there are 12 hosts in the multi-site cluster.

Any maintenance in the primary site will cause virtual machines to be migrated to the redundant host in the primary site. In a disaster, all virtual machines would be migrated to the hosts in the secondary site. You will still be able to handle host machine failure or maintenance during the disaster with the redundant host in the secondary site. This sort of design will provide very high levels of uptime.

You now have redundant hosts in the primary and the secondary sites. Without any configuration, there is nothing to prevent a virtual machine failover (in response to a failure or a PRO migration) to a host in the secondary site instead of the redundant host(s) in the primary site. You can configure a preference for hosts in the primary site by configuring the preferred owners of the virtual machine resource in the Failover Clustering Management console, as described here:

`http://technet.microsoft.com/library/dd197473(WS.10).aspx`

The multi-site cluster is the basis of some of the more advanced design possibilities for engineering a disaster recovery solution for Hyper-V. The precise design of the storage and replication of the storage will be solution specific. You should return to your project objectives and work with possible vendors and service providers to determine the most suitable design for your current and future requirements. Your usual hardware vendor or preferred consultant might not be the best people to help you now. The involved technologies are extremely complex, so make sure you choose to work with companies that have earned a good reputation for working on similar projects. You really should check their references too.

MICROSOFT GUIDANCE FOR MULTI-SITE CLUSTERS

You can find the requirements for a multi-site cluster here:

`http://technet.microsoft.com/library/dd197575(WS.10).aspx`

You can find a checklist for implementing a multi-site cluster here:

`http://technet.microsoft.com/library/dd197546(WS.10).aspx`

Using Host-Based Replication

An organization with nonclustered Hyper-V host servers is not left in the cold. It is possible to make the virtual machines that are placed on these hosts highly available using third-party software products. There are a number of players in this market, each using different approaches. We will discuss two of the more commonly adopted approaches.

FILE REPLICATION

Many system administrators in small and medium businesses have encountered third-party applications that provide business continuity replication solutions for file server, SQL Server, and Exchange Server servers. Many of the vendors in this market have extended their solutions to include support for Hyper-V. You can see how this sort of solution works in Figure 13.4.

FIGURE 13.4: File replication for Hyper-V

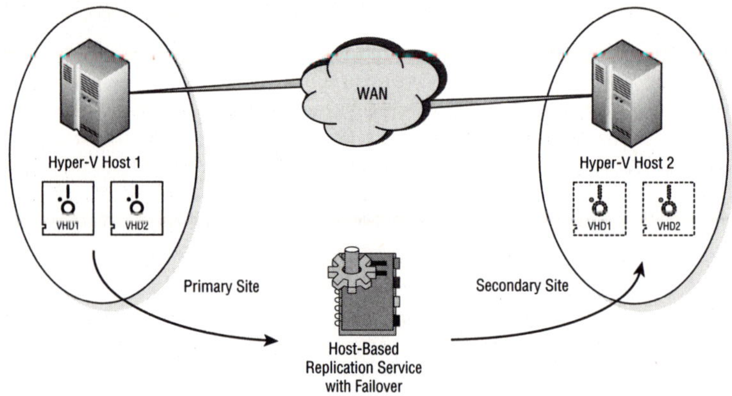

> **SYNCHRONOUS AND ASYNCHRONOUS REPLICATION**
>
> Synchronous replication is when a write operation to a file is not completed until the update is performed on the storage in the primary and secondary sites. This requires high-bandwidth links between the two sites with very low latency. This is because the application or service that is making the change to the file is waiting on the write to be completed in the secondary site.
>
> Asynchronous replication allows you to use links with higher latency and less bandwidth. A change to the file is completed on the storage in the primary site. The replication solution will detect the change and will duplicate it on the storage in the secondary site. The application or service that is making the change to the file does not have to wait for the write to be completed in the secondary site. The price of asynchronous replication is that data that is committed to disk in the primary site may not be committed in the secondary site when a disaster occurs.

A service is installed on Hyper-V host servers in the primary and secondary sites. You create and manage your virtual machines on the primary site host server. The replication solution will replicate the virtual machine configuration and the files to the secondary site, usually using asynchronous replication. This means that changes made to the virtual machine VHDs will be replicated soon afterward to the secondary site.

Many of the file replication solutions will feature their own form of clustering. This will provide a heartbeat between the host servers. This allows the Hyper-V host servers to detect an outage and to initiate an automated failover of the virtual machines.

These software-based products will be useful to small and medium-sized organizations that cannot afford to put in large-bandwidth (1 Gbps or more) WAN links for disaster site replication. Some large organizations may also find these solutions interesting because they will allow replication across higher-latency links where great distance between sites is preventing higher-end solutions from working. An example of this is where a branch-office Hyper-V host server replicates to a central office.

There are a few things to note with these solutions. They are intended for virtual machines with VHDs. That means you will need to find another solution for virtual machines with passthrough disks.

The VHD files that are stored in the secondary site are normally locked. You cannot use them for anything such as backing up. These files will become usable only when the virtual machines are failed over to the secondary site by the replication/clustering mechanism, and then the virtual machines will start using them.

Automated failover can happen by accident if the link between the two sites fails. The heartbeat detection will fail, and the secondary site Hyper-V host server will start up the virtual machines after a brief delay. This is not a Live Migration. The result is similar to a host failure. The virtual machine will stop on one host and start on another, causing a brief delay.

Any system administrator who has managed this form of replication in the past will tell you that this happens, possibly several times a year. This can lead to a nasty situation called *split brain*. Both of the Hyper-V host servers think they are active. What happens now? Which virtual machines are used if you have clients in other locations? What happens when the replication network connection is brought back online? Will both sites try to replicate to each other and corrupt the VHD files? Some solutions will prevent both sites from being active by using a witness in a third site. Some will detect a split-brain scenario when the link comes back online and know to shut down the secondary site without it trying to replicate to the primary site. Some administrators have experienced some nasty situations with these solutions and choose to disable automated failover.

It sounds like we are disregarding file replication products for business continuity. We're not; these products have a place in the market. You just need to understand what that place is and what you need to consider.

Simulated Shared Storage

A variation on the file replication solution is simulated shared storage. These software-based solutions will implement either asynchronous or synchronous replication to replicate the storage where virtual machine VHDs are stored. The big difference is that they don't attempt to provide any clustering solutions. Instead, they simulate the shared storage that you would get with a SAN. The power of this is that you get a replicated SAN-like storage that takes advantage of Windows Failover Clustering. The solution, shown in Figure 13.5, can provide you with Quick Migration or Live Migration.

Wait, Quick Migration in Windows Server 2008 R2? Why would you want to use that? Live Migration requires a 1 Gbps link to copy virtual machine memory between the primary and secondary Hyper-V host servers. Many organizations that are implementing software-based business continuity solutions will not be able to afford a 1 Gbps WAN connection. That is why Quick Migration still has value to move a running virtual machine between sites. There will be several seconds of an outage while the virtual machine's running state is saved to disk, it is replicated to the secondary site, and the virtual machine is restarted. It's hard to criticize Quick Migration too much in this scenario. Even most multinational corporations would be thrilled with a disaster recovery invocation that could be completed in a few minutes.

Windows Failover Clustering is used, but which quorum model will be implemented? The big worry is the split-brain situation. This can be avoided by using Node And File Share Majority Quorum. A file share is placed in a third site. This third site can be a branch office or even a server in the Cloud. A Hyper-V host that detects a heartbeat failure because of a replication link failure can use the file share to determine which host should be active.

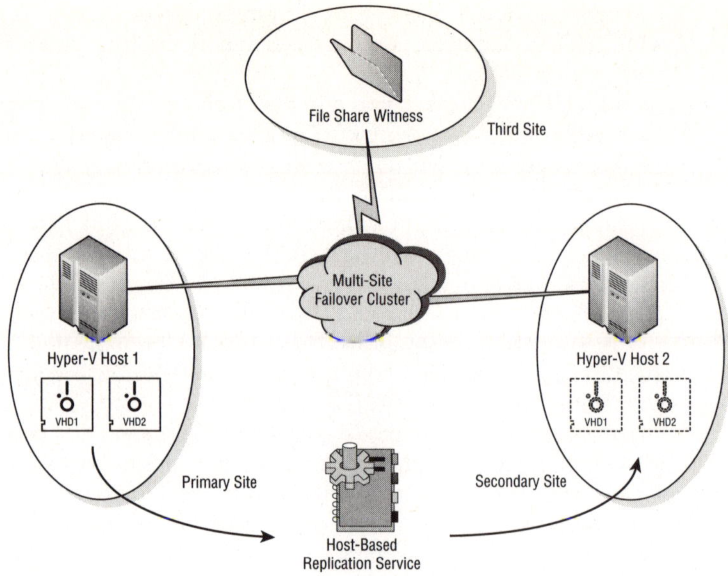

FIGURE 13.5
Simulated shared storage for Hyper-V

Some simulated shared storage solutions are intended for replicating a single Hyper-V host server to another single Hyper-V host server. Some solutions go as far as to provide you with an iSCSI SAN that is made from ordinary storage servers, allowing up to the maximum of 16 Hyper-V host servers that you can have in a cluster. This sort of deployment will even allow you to create Cluster Shared Volumes (CSV). Simulated shared storage solutions offer the flexibility of file replication with the stability, control, and features of Failover Clustering. These solutions are software-based, so there will be limitations on scalability and performance. More extreme deployments will require a hardware-based solution such as SAN replication.

Using SAN Replication

Storage area networks can provide hardware-based replication between identical installations in a primary and secondary site. Every model from every manufacturer may offer something different. Some provide the replication mechanism as a standard feature, and some require additional expensive licensing. You can find the most suitable solution for your organization by working with specialist hardware vendors.

Hardware-based solutions have a number of advantages over software-based solutions, but they do come at a steep (purchase) price. They can replicate VHDs, passthrough disks, and pretty much any LUN you create because they operate at the physical layer rather than at the file system layer. They offer extreme levels of scalability and performance. But these solutions do have tight requirements for bandwidth, latency, and distance between the primary and secondary sites.

INTER-SITE STRIPING

This form of replication is one that is most often associated with iSCSI SANs. It isn't really a form of replication. Instead, data is striped between different SAN installations. Figure 13.6 shows an example. A SAN is placed in the primary site. One or more CSVs are created on the SAN. You can even use passthrough disks or provide storage targets that are initiated directly by virtual machines. The SAN (or SANs) will stripe the storage with another SAN (or SANs) in a secondary site using synchronous replication.

FIGURE 13.6
Inter-site striping for Hyper-V storage

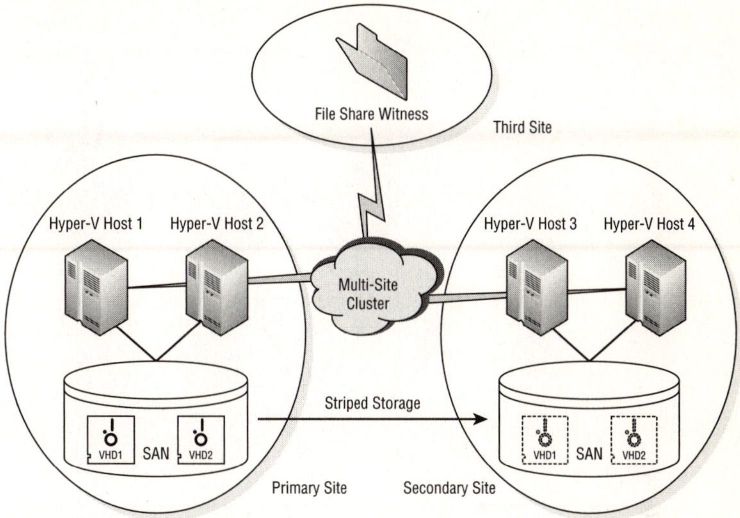

This requires very high-speed connections between the primary and secondary sites. Any modification made to a VHD or physical LUN by a virtual machine must be written to all SANs that participate in the stripe for the write to be completed. Hardware manufacturers will dictate certain requirements such as latency (less than two milliseconds), bandwidth (1 Gbps or more), and even a maximum distance between the sites. Two 1 Gbps links are required. One is for the inter-site striping of the SANs. The second is required for Live Migration.

Windows Failover Clustering with Node and File Share Majority is used for this type of architecture.

This solution provides high performance and scalable storage with support for all the Failover Clustering and Hyper-V features. Cluster Shared Volumes can be present in two sites at once. This is possible because the LUN containing the CSV is striped rather than being replicated. That means that the LUN is active in both sites. Virtual machines can be live migrated, one at a time, between Hyper-V host servers in the two sites. A SAN with this sort of replication mechanism is a very powerful solution.

LUN Replication

At this time, high-end storage solutions such as Fibre Channel SANs use a method of replication that is LUN based. As you would expect with an expensive product, the replication feature usually requires additional licensing. You can see an illustration of LUN replication in Figure 13.7.

The virtual machine and the LUN that it is stored on are active in the primary site. The LUN is replicated to the secondary site. The LUN is not active in the secondary site because it is being replicated to. This means you cannot have granular failover of virtual machines between the two sites if virtual machines are stored on the same LUN. This rules out the usage of CSV and returns you to the days of storing one virtual machine per LUN.

FIGURE 13.7
LUN replication for Hyper-V clusters

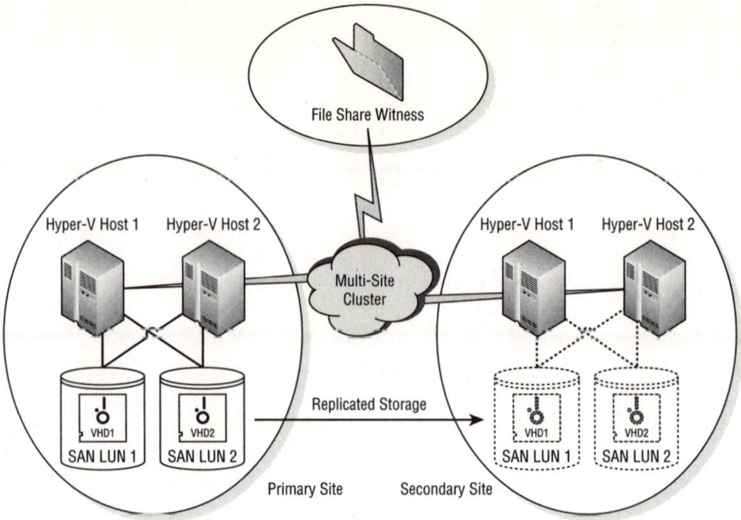

Real World Scenario

ONE VIRTUAL MACHINE PER LUN

Windows Server 2008 did not have the Cluster Shared Volumes feature, so it was normal to deploy one LUN per virtual machine. This complicated storage management required a cooperative relationship between the storage and virtualization teams.

Most deployments of Windows Server 2008 R2 use CSV for storing many virtual machines. The storage team needs to deploy just a single LUN (every now and then) and extend it (every now and then). The Hyper-V team limits their dependency on the storage team and can make better use of some of the automation and self-provisioning tools that are provided.

The one virtual machine per LUN option did not go away with the release of Windows Server 2008 R2. Virtual Machine Manager 2008 R2 has the ability to integrate into a SAN with snap/cloning features. A virtual machine template can be stored on a LUN. This can be replicated to quickly deploy a new virtual machine. Automated solutions such as System Center Virtual Machine Manager Self-Service Portal 2.0 (still in prerelease stages at the time of writing) can use scripts to integrate with a SAN to commission or decommission LUNs as well as clone LUNs with virtual machine templates on them.

These solutions are very dependent on the hardware solution that is in place. You should work with your hardware vendor or manufacturer to develop a solution for your organization if these features are something you want to implement.

This solution will replicate any form of VHD or storage that is created on the SAN. It will be suitable for Hyper-V virtual machines or physical machines, depending on application support for the form of high availability you are implementing.

A virtual machine can be live migrated but usually is quick migrated between the sites one at a time because there is only one virtual machine per LUN. Ownership of the LUN will be transferred by the replicating SANs via an integration with Windows Failover Clustering. This will reverse the direction of the replication, ensuring that changes made by the virtual machine while it is running in the secondary site will be replicated to the primary site SAN.

High-speed (1 Gbps) links, low latency, and distance limitations between the sites are requirements of this sort of solution. Key to the solution is the ability of the SAN replication to support the replication of Hyper-V virtual machines and to integrate with Windows Server 2008 R2 Failover Clustering.

A few organizations require not just a single disaster recovery site but two disaster recovery sites. They need to ensure themselves against a disaster striking their secondary site. It might be a low risk, but these organizations operate in crucial markets and provide critical services that cannot be offline, no matter what happens. These are the sorts of organizations that will deploy the most expensive forms of storage, which also use LUN replication. There will be (at least) one SAN in three sites, and the primary site SAN will replicate to the secondary and tertiary site SANs.

As you can probably tell, this is a very expensive form of replication. Oddly enough, it does not have all the features and flexibility of an inter-site striping solution based on an iSCSI SAN. You cannot use CSV at this time, but the manufacturers are working with Microsoft to resolve this. You cannot use Fibre Channel SANs to provision storage directly to a virtual machine for a virtualized cluster, whereas you can do this with iSCSI storage and the iSCSI initiator in Windows Server.

Choosing a Disaster Recovery Design

We have looked at a number of solutions that allow you to use Hyper-V to provide highly available virtual machines that can survive a disaster by migrating to host servers in another location. Each of the solutions has their advantages and disadvantages. If you have never deployed a disaster recovery site before, choosing the right solution for your organization can be a challenge because of the confusing array of possible solutions. We will now present you with some comparison of the previously discussed solutions to help you decide which is the most appropriate.

As we mentioned before, there are a lot of vendors out there, each with their own unique solutions. We could never hope to include every single one. You should use this chapter and Table 13.1 as a starting point to help you ask the right questions when you start to engage with service provider or reseller presales engineers. It is possible that there will be some products that fall into the following categories and also offer functionality that contradicts this guide.

TABLE 13.1: Comparing the business continuity solutions

DESIRED FEATURE	DPM2DPM4DR	FILE REPLICATION	SIMULATED SHARED STORAGE	INTER-SITE STRIPING	LUN REPLICATION
Off-site disaster recovery	Yes	Yes	Yes	Yes	Yes
Automated failover	No	No	No	No	No
Windows Failover Clustering integration	No	No	Yes	Yes	Yes
Requires Windows Failover Clustering	No	No	Yes	Yes	Yes
Inter-site Live Migration	No	No	Yes	Yes	Yes
Scalable	Yes	No	No	Yes	Yes
Very long distances	Yes	Yes	Yes	No	No
High latency	Yes	Yes	Yes	No	No
Uses third-party Cloud infrastructure	Yes	Yes	Yes	No	No

Remember that Live Migration requires the LUN with the virtual machine to be in both sites and requires a 1 Gbps link for the memory copy operation.

ACCESS TO THE SECONDARY SITE

It is all very well to make the business applications and data available after a disaster but that is all a bit pointless if the users in the business cannot get access to them. The typical approach is to provide a room full of computers that selected key users will use. How are those users going to get to the room if there is a flood, or a travel lockdown?

VPN access to the secondary site might be one solution but this assumes that the home user will have a computer that has all of the business applications installed. The performance will also be pretty poor.

An alternative is to provide SSL gateway access to something such as a Remote Desktop Services session host or a Virtual Desktop Infrastructure. A session host will require considerable maintenance. VDI might come with added financial overheads but it has the ability to automatically deploy virtual machines with ready application installations in the event of a disaster. This can give the business a solution that will respond automatically to user demand without intervention from IT staff. Business users can either use existing laptops or purchase some as required, find a location with Internet access, and start working.

The Bottom Line

Understand what business continuity is and identify the needs of the business Hyper-V can be used to facilitate a disaster recovery site to meet the business continuity requirements of an organization.

Master It You are a senior IT infrastructure engineer in a large organization. You are in the early stages of writing a proposal to implement a hardware virtualization solution based on Windows Server 2008 R2 Hyper-V. Recent news stories about disasters and recent failed disaster recovery site tests have caused the directors to issue an order that the business continuity plans of the organization be revisited. You have been asked to attend a workshop where senior IT staff members will discuss the issue and propose a plan of action. What will you suggest, and why?

Describe some of the many business continuity and disaster recovery solutions that are available There are many hardware-based and software-based solutions for replicating Hyper-V virtual machines from a primary site to a secondary site.

Master It You are working as a consultant. Your client is a medium-sized organization. They have a number of remote branch offices. Each branch office has a pair of nonclustered Hyper-V host servers with a number of virtual machines. Your client desires some level of fault tolerance for the remote branch offices that will replicate data to the head office. Each branch office has a small WAN link, and the client is concerned with data replication affecting operations during business hours. What options will you recommend?

Choose between the various types of business continuity solutions You need to ask a number of questions about the infrastructure and business requirements to determine the ideal business continuity IT architecture for your organization.

Master It You need to find a solution for your organization's business continuity requirements based on Hyper-V. The organization's Hyper-V infrastructure uses a high-end Fibre Channel SAN with many advanced features. A number of local vendors have been invited to consult with you. A few minutes of downtime can be tolerated by your organization during the invocation of the disaster recovery site. Ideally, there will be near zero downtime. What will you ask the vendors about?

Appendix A

The Bottom Line

Each of The Bottom Line sections in the chapters suggest exercises to deepen skills and understanding. Sometimes there is only one possible solution, but often you are encouraged to use your skills and creativity to create something that builds on what you know and lets you explore one of many possible solutions.

Chapter 2: The Architecture of Hyper-V

Understand the architecture of Hyper-V Designing and troubleshooting a Hyper-V infrastructure is much easier if you understand how Hyper-V works.

Master It A virtual machine has been built by a junior Hyper-V administrator on behalf of the business applications department. After a few days, you receive a call from that department. They are reporting that the performance of the virtual machine is unacceptable. The `C:` drive appears to be slow, and network traffic is not as fast as with other virtual machines. What will be the first thing you will check, and why do you suspect that it will be the cause of the problems?

Solution You will check that the current Hyper-V integration components have been installed in the virtual machine. Integration components provide the ability to use synthetic drivers instead of emulated drivers. Emulated drivers are executed in user mode in the VM worker process for the virtual machine in the parent partition. This has a longer data transfer path than synthetic devices and requires context changes. Synthetic drivers use VSCs in the child partition, which will cooperate with VSPs in the parent partition via the VMBus. These operate in kernel mode at Ring 0 on the physical processor and provide the very best performance.

List and describe the features of Hyper-V There are many features in Hyper-V such as the components in the hypervisor or virtual machines, as well as the functions for optimizing or managing those components.

Master It You have been asked to design a Windows Server 2008 R2 with Service Pack 1 Hyper-V cluster that will be used for Remote Desktop Services VDI. The virtual machines will need to run applications with high quality graphics. What hardware features will you need in the Hyper-V hosts for this solution?

Solution The hardware should include processors that have the ability to support Second Level Address Translation. This will provide better memory and CPU performance for the session host virtual machines. The host servers should include GPUs that can be used for RemoteFX. This will enable the usage of graphics-intensive applications.

Understand the management options of Hyper-V Hyper-V can be managed using a suite of solutions from Microsoft.

Master It What products will you use to manage many Windows Server 2008 R2 Hyper-V host servers, monitor the entire server infrastructure including the Linux virtual machines, and quickly back up the virtualization infrastructure?

Solution System Center Virtual Machine Manager 2008 R2 will be used to manage the configuration of the Hyper-V infrastructure. System Center Operations Manager 2007 R2 can manage the entire server infrastructure including Linux virtual or physical machines. System Center Data Protection Manager 2010 can be used to efficiently back up Windows Server 2008 R2 Hyper-V.

Chapter 3: The Project Plan

Understand the need for a virtualization project plan. A project plan will help you organize and schedule the various tasks to be completed during a hardware virtualization project.

Master It You are a consultant, and you have been engaged by a customer to advise on the deployment of Microsoft Windows Server 2008 R2 Hyper-V with various supporting Microsoft System Center products. Upon entering the site, you find that the IT staff is rushing into a deployment. What would you say to them to encourage them to take a more considered approach?

Solution A hardware virtualization project will impact all aspects of the business. How well it runs depends on a structured project plan, gathering requirements from the business, understanding completely the infrastructure to be converted, designing a suitable architecture based on hardware that will meet current and future needs, and using a systems management and administrative model that is suitable to the logical organization. Only by controlling and measuring the process will all required tasks be completed in a satisfactory manner. Failure to take the necessary time for a project of this complexity will lead to a negative impact on the business and on the employment status of those responsible.

Identify the major steps involved in a virtualization project. There are a number of discrete steps in a Microsoft Windows Server 2008 R2 Hyper-V deployment. Some of them should be conducted in every project, and some are conducted only if the associated products are to be deployed.

Master It You are to deploy Windows Server 2008 R2 Hyper-V and Microsoft System Center in an organization with an existing IT infrastructure. This contains a mix of servers including legacy Window NT 4.0 servers and newer Linux and Windows Server computers, all running a wide variety of business-critical applications. You want to design a suitable architecture. How will you start the project?

Solution The first step is to gather the requirements from the business and translate them into objectives for the project. Only by meeting with decision makers and the various owners of the systems employed can you be fully informed. Any design will need to be based on the needs of the existing infrastructure. Use auditing tools such as the Microsoft Assessment and Planning Toolkit, System Center Operations Manager, and

System Center Configuration Manager to gather data about specification and resource utilization. Combine this with data gathered from the various systems owners and near-future needs to size and design your Hyper-V and systems management architecture.

Vary the project plan according to the organization's needs. No one project plan is suitable for all organizations. It will be necessary to vary the project plan according to the directions given by the decision makers and to suit the needs of the organization.

Master It Although it was purchased only as part of the Hyper-V project, your organization will be using Microsoft System Center to manage all IT systems. Various managers have expressed a desire to see immediate results and are providing suitable skills for the project. You will need to schedule tasks in the project accordingly. How will you schedule the implementation of Microsoft System Center?

Solution You can schedule parallel tasks to deploy Microsoft System Center as soon as the objectives for the project are set. It is likely that each deployment will become a project of its own because it expands beyond the scope of the hardware virtualization project. You will need to liaise with each project leader to ensure that everything is in sync and that there are no delays in your project. This early deployment can be taken advantage of for in-depth assessment of the existing IT infrastructure. It also allows for the Virtual Machine Manager library contents to be developed so that they can be made use of earlier.

Chapter 4: Assessing the Existing Infrastructure

Understand the need to assess the existing infrastructure An assessment is a necessary step in any hardware virtualization project where there is an existing physical infrastructure to convert into virtual machines.

Master It You are one of a team of engineers that is designing and deploying a Windows Server 2008 R2 Hyper-V infrastructure in a very large organization. Your objectives from management are to consolidate the infrastructure as much as possible with no negative impact on performance. Overspending on the project will not be tolerated because of economic conditions. One of your colleagues wants to start the installation now without performing an assessment. How will you argue for an assessment?

Solution Management requires that the virtualization project install as many virtual machines as possible onto each Hyper-V host server. You must accurately size the infrastructure so that it is neither overloaded nor underused. An assessment will accomplish several things. It will identify all physical servers and their specifications. Performance metrics will be collected to show their utilization of resources such as processor, memory, and storage. This assessment will allow you to select only those machines that are suitable for virtualization conversion. Using their performance metrics and specifications, you can calculate the required storage and server sizes.

Use the Microsoft Assessment and Planning Toolkit MAP is free to download and can be used to perform an assessment of a physical and virtual server infrastructure.

Master It You are working as a presales technical consultant. A potential customer has asked your company to perform an assessment. The local IT staff will make all the required preparations on your behalf to facilitate the task. They only run Microsoft

Windows on their servers. The goal of the task is to prepare a proposal for the directors of the customer company. They are nontechnical and will be focusing on the cost effectiveness of the project. You do not have budget to purchase software. What will you do to meet the requirements of the potential customer company?

Solution You can bring a virtual machine or laptop that has been preconfigured with the free-to-use Microsoft Assessment and Planning Toolkit. Work with the local IT staff to install this machine on the network. You can run an assessment with this free product of all existing Windows physical and virtual machines. You can produce reports from within MAP for a nontechnical audience. You can then use the Microsoft Integrated Virtualization ROI Calculator website to produce a report and presentation on how a Windows Server 2008 R2 hardware virtualization project will save the company money. All reports and presentations can be easily rebranded and customized before being presented to the potential customer.

Use System Center for assessment System Center is capable of collecting vast amounts of very detailed information from a large and complex network. You can use the System Center reporting features to use this information for an assessment.

Master It You have just joined a large organization as a senior engineer. You have been placed in charge of designing and implementing a Windows Server 2008 R2 Hyper-V infrastructure. The organization is large and complex. It has many servers in branch offices, and there are some Linux servers. Many systems experience demand only once a month or once a quarter. The organization has made a continued investment in Microsoft systems management software and third-party extensions over the years. How will you perform an assessment of the infrastructure to achieve an accurately sized consolidation?

Solution System Center Configuration Manager will identify all Windows servers that are candidates for virtualization. It is possible that the company has purchased an extension for ConfigMgr to allow the same to be done for Linux servers. Using this list, a series of reports can be run on each server in the reporting of Operations Manager 2007 R2. These reports will allow you to select the servers that will be converted into virtual machines based on their performance using over a year of collected metrics. The long period of collecting metrics will account for seasonal-demand peaks and valleys. The specifications of the selected machines can be retrieved from the previously generated Configuration Manager reports to size the Hyper-V hosts and storage.

Chapter 5: Planning the Hardware Deployment

Understand the hardware requirements for Hyper-V Understanding the correct maximum limits of Hyper-V is critical in performing a valid hardware sizing and specification that will be supported by Microsoft and be reliable.

Master It You are working as an engineer in a company that is considering options for deploying Windows Server 2008 R2 Hyper-V. A consultancy company has convinced your manager that they should assist. During your first meeting, the lead technical consultant has started talking about being able to use 2 TB RAM per host on Datacenter edition Hyper-V hosts, with more than 500 running virtual CPUs per host. What is wrong with that statement, and what are the correct maximum limits?

Solution The correct memory limits for Hyper-V running on Datacenter edition is 1 TB RAM. A maximum of 384 running virtual CPUs is supported on a Hyper-V host. A maximum of 1,000 virtual machines is supported on a Hyper-V cluster.

Convert assessment results into a hardware specification When you understand the capabilities of Hyper-V, you can use the assessment data to size your host and storage hardware. Performance and size metrics of existing physical and virtual machines will be used to calculate the specifications and numbers of host servers.

Master It You have been asked to size the amount of RAM that will be required for a number of virtual machines. How do virtual machines consume RAM from a Hyper-V host?

Solution The first 1 GB of RAM in a virtual machine has a potential overhead of 32 MB. That consumes 1 GB + 32 MB. Each additional 1 GB of RAM in the virtual machine has a potential overhead charge of 8 MB. That will consume 1 GB + 8 MB for each additional 1 GB in the virtual machine.

Be able to discuss Hyper-V licensing There are potential savings to be made with the licensing of Hyper-V that also simplify the accounting and administration of licensing the virtualized environment.

Master It You are working as a consultant and are preparing a presentation to give to some potential customers who are deploying a completely new IT infrastructure with no existing servers. You need to discuss the potential cost savings of using Windows Server 2008 R2 Hyper-V. What can you talk about?

Solution When installed as a Hyper-V host, Windows Server Enterprise edition provides up to four free copies of Windows Server (Enterprise edition or lower) that can be installed on virtual machines that run on that host. This can provide for free virtualization. When you install the Datacenter edition per-processors license as a Hyper-V host, you get unlimited Windows Server licenses for the virtual machines running on that host. This can save an organization a lot of money, especially if they can get a high ratio of virtual machines running per host with expected acceptable performance.

Chapter 6: Deploying Hyper-V

Deploy Hyper-V host servers There are a number of ways to build new Hyper-V host servers, depending on the size of your infrastructure and your need to rapidly expand the infrastructure.

Master It You have created an image of a Windows Server 2008 R2 Hyper-V host server. The original machine was configured with a number of external networks. You have deployed the image and found that new virtual machines cannot communicate on the physical network. What is wrong?

Solution Any external networks are converted into internal networks when you generalize a Hyper-V host server to capture an image from it. Change the virtual networks into external networks and the virtual machines will be able to communicate on the physical network.

Configure Hyper-V You can configure Hyper-V to match the requirements of your organization.

Master It You are working as a consultant for a hardware manufacturer. A customer has purchased hardware from your company for a new Hyper-V cluster. They need Live Migration to be as quick as possible. They have purchased the equipment for a 10 Gb network for Live Migration. They are complaining that Live Migration is taking too long. You suspect that it is not operating on the 10 Gb network. What will you do to configure it?

Solution Launch the Failover Clustering Manager, and connect to the Hyper-V cluster. Right-click a virtual machine, and select Properties. Navigate into the Network For Live Migration tab. Reorder the networks so that the 10 Gb network adapter is first.

Manage Linux virtual machines Hyper-V offers support for running Linux as a guest operating system.

Master It You have created a small virtual machine to run Red Hat Enterprise Linux 5. You configured a synthetic network adapter and a disk on a virtual SCSI controller. You have tried to configure the network adapter and the disk, but you cannot find the devices. What will you do?

Solution Download the latest version of the Linux Integration Components from the Microsoft website. Install the integration components in the Linux guest operating system and reboot the virtual machine. Verify that the integration components are running, and attempt to configure the network adapter and disk.

Chapter 7: Virtual Machine Manager 2008 R2

Plan the installation of Virtual Machine Manager 2008 R2 It is important to understand the requirements of VMM 2008 R2 so that you can plan an architecture that suits the technology and business needs of the organization.

Master It You have been asked to design a management solution for a business. The business has a head office in Dublin, Ireland, and a branch office in San Francisco, United States. Hyper-V clusters will be placed in both sites. All administration will be done in Dublin. Software developers and testers in San Francisco also need the ability to deploy virtual machines without waiting for the IT department in Dublin. How will you design this VMM infrastructure?

Solution A VMM server with a library and database will be installed in the Dublin office. Here the administrators can build up a library of content and manage the local Hyper-V host servers.

A VMM library is required to be close to the Hyper-V servers in San Francisco, so one will be set up there. The Dublin administrators can ship or copy the required VHDs from the Dublin library to the San Francisco library. Templates can be prepared in VMM to link to the copies. Other templates and VHDs can be prepared on the Hyper-V hosts in San Francisco and stored in the local library.

Use the library for automation and self-service features VMM 2008 R2 includes the ability to delegate administration functions and allow non-IT staff to deploy and manage virtual machines.

Master It Ownership of the new Hyper-V infrastructure will be centrally controlled in a university. All new servers that will be virtual machines will run on this infrastructure.

Each faculty has an IT staff that is responsible for their own services and budget. You must design a virtualization administration model that limits administration access to the underlying virtualization layer but also allows for faculty IT staff to deploy their own virtual machines. You must also be able to control and cross-charge for resources used.

Solution The solution will center on a VMM library that is populated with templates and VHDs that will suit the needs of the various IT departments in the university. Each template is assigned a quota points score. This score is based on the resources consumed by that template. A Self-Service Portal will be configured. An Active Directory group for each faculty IT department is either used or created. Each group contains the user accounts of those staff in that faculty that will deploy virtual machines for that faculty. A self-service role is created for each faculty and assigned to the group. Each self-service role is assigned a quota. The quota is used to cross-charge the faculties for the resources that they consume. The faculty IT staff will be able to log into the Self-Service Portal and deploy their own virtual machines up to their quota level. They will be billed based on their assigned quota scores. They can negotiate the scores up and down based on their requirements and budget.

Manage and convert existing physical and virtual machines VMM 2008 R2 is able to manage virtual machines on Hyper-V, Virtual Server 2005 R2 SP1, and VMware's ESX. You can convert virtual machines from those non-Hyper-V platforms to Hyper-V. You can also convert physical machines into virtual machines using VMM.

Master It The assessment phase of the project has identified two servers that must be virtualized in an office. One server is a web server with static content. The other server is relatively new and is running a number of very heavily used databases that are used by offices from around the world. How will you convert these servers into virtual machines using VMM 2008 R2?

Solution The web server will have pretty static content. An online migration can be used in VMM to convert this server into a virtual machine. The database server is heavily used, and the files are constantly changing. An online migration is a bit of a risk. An offline migration will be used during a planned and announced maintenance window. The server is relatively new. 32-bit Vista drivers for the storage controller and the network card are added into the driver cache to ensure that the Windows PE boot image will be able to access those devices for the conversion process.

Chapter 8: Virtualization Scenarios

Understand virtual machine design guidelines With so many design variations available for a virtual machine, it is a necessity to understand the features and how they will affect the performance of a virtual machine.

Master It The MIS department, which is responsible for applications in the corporation, has been assigned a number of Hyper-V host servers and storage that will be placed under your supervision. With a tight budget, they want to make the very most out of their new host servers. A critical new database-based application is to be deployed using a number of virtual machines. You have been asked to give advice on how to best design the storage. What kind of virtual machine storage would you recommend?

Solution The MIS department will want to use dynamic VHDs for its storage because they consume only the physical storage that is required to store the data. However, it comes at a slight cost to performance and with a significant amount of management complexity. This makes it unsuitable for a production environment. There are two types of virtual machine storage that are normally recommended in a production environment. A fixed-size VHD offers all the management flexibility of a VHD file, with excellent, near-physical performance. Pass-through disk does not offer any of the features of VHD files, but it is suitable where extreme storage performance is required.

Deploy common roles in Hyper-V virtual machines Microsoft has provided recommendations and support policies for virtual machine configurations for many of their server applications.

Master It You are a consultant who is visiting with a new customer. You have been asked to review the Hyper-V installation and the deployment of applications as virtual machines. End users are complaining that a critical line-of-business application is too slow. You investigate the issue and find that the performance of storage for the SQL Server does not meet demand. The customer is using dynamic VHDs. How will you explain the issue, and what will you advise the customer to do to fix the issue?

Solution You can start by explaining how dynamic VHDs work. They start as small files and grow to meet demand. This growth can slow down write performance of the VHD. Although dynamic VHDs offer much better performance in Windows Server 2008 R2, they still have been found to compare poorly with fixed-size VHDs in real-world deployments.

The Microsoft guidance for SQL Server recommends the usage of fixed-size VHDs or passthrough disks for the log file and database file disks. They should also be placed on appropriately configured physical RAID storage. You can start by placing the database's log file on a fixed-size VHD on a RAID-10 disk. You can then place the database file on a fixed-size VHD on a RAID-5 disk. Use of fixed-size VHDs will offer near physical disk performance.

Alternatively, you can provision RAID-10 (log file) and RAID-5 (database file) passthrough disks to the virtual machine. You can format these disks and move the files onto the disks. Use of the passthrough disk will offer the very best performance.

Configure fault tolerance in virtual machines Hyper-V clustering can provide hardware fault tolerance for virtual machines. A sudden and unplanned host failure can cause an application to be unavailable while its virtual machine fails over to another host and boots up. Fault tolerance can be provided at the application level to avoid any downtime.

Master It You are working as a consultant for a company that has successfully deployed Hyper-V. You are tasked with deploying a new two-tier web application. Performance and uptime are critical. The first tier is a web application that will run an e-commerce application. This must be capable of quickly scaling out with a minimal hardware footprint. A fault-tolerant database is required. It will be running queries and reports on a frequent basis and will have significant storage requirements. How will you design this solution?

Solution The database has significant storage performance requirements, so it will be deployed as a physical server cluster.

The web servers can be implemented as virtual machines. Each virtual machine will be placed on a different Hyper-V host. The company can start with two web servers. A template and VHD can be stored in a VMM library to facilitate rapid deployment to meet client demand. A hardware load balancer or a dedicated application running on virtual machines can provide the load balancing functionality across the virtual machines, as well as providing SSL offloading and reverse proxy services for content delivery optimization.

Chapter 9: Operations Manager 2007

Understand the functionality of Operations Manager Operations Manager (OpsMgr) has a number of components to monitor the health and performance of an infrastructure.

Master It You are working as a consultant. A client has asked for a solution for monitoring their Hyper-V infrastructure. They need to be able to manage Windows and Red Hat Enterprise Linux virtual machines, detect performance issues, detect hardware faults, and produce long-term reports. What can you tell them about how OpsMgr can meet the client's requirements?

Solution Operations Manager will be able to monitor the entire infrastructure using agents and automatically distributed management packs. Operations Manager 2007 R2 includes Cross-Platform Extensions, which include the ability to monitor Unix and Linux using Microsoft written agents and management packs. Microsoft produces management packs for all of their server products, including Windows Server and Hyper-V. OpsMgr will be able to detect performance issues and faults as soon as they happen and notify the responsible administrators or service owners. A data warehouse will store more than a year of data, allowing you to produce reports on availability, performance, and alerts.

Integrate Operations Manager with Virtual Machine Manager It is possible to integrate OpsMgr with VMM. This integrates management and provides additional functionality.

Master It What are the prerequisites for integrating VMM with OpsMgr?

Solution VMM 2008 R2 must be integrated with OpsMgr 2007 SP1 or newer. Both computers must be either in the same domain or in domains with a two-way trust. The OpsMgr SDK service must be able to publish an SPN. The VMM service account should be an administrator on the OpsMgr server or a member of the Operations Manager Administrators user role. This can be done by the integration installation, but that may be undone by Group Policy. The Windows Server, IIS, and SQL Server management packs must be imported into OpsMgr. OpsMgr agents should be deployed to all hosts, virtual machines, and the VMM server. The OpsMgr Operations Console and the VMM administration console should be installed on the VMM server.

Understand and configure PRO The integration of OpsMgr and VMM allows you to implement Performance and Resource Optimization (PRO). This allows VMM to automatically respond to issues detected by OpsMgr PRO management packs.

Master It Your team leader has asked you to design a Hyper-V infrastructure with VMM and OpsMgr. There will be nine Hyper-V hosts. Three will be for production servers, three will be for software development, and three will be for testing. Your team leader would like it if you could build a single Hyper-V cluster. PRO must be configured with automation for all alerts for production host servers, enabled but with a manual response on the development hosts, and disabled on the testing hosts. How will you respond to the team leader and deploy the infrastructure?

Solution PRO is enabled and configured in a host group. A host group can have a single PRO policy. A Hyper-V cluster can reside in only one host group. This means that there can only be one PRO policy for an entire Hyper-V cluster.

You will have to deploy three Hyper-V clusters if there will be three PRO policies. You will install a production cluster, a development cluster, and a testing cluster. Each will be placed into their own host group. Each host group will be configured as required.

Chapter 10: Data Protection and Recovery

Use the inbox backup tool, Windows Server Backup VSS is a framework developed by Microsoft, which provides a backup infrastructure that was first introduced in Windows Server 2003. Knowing the components and how the components work will help you understand how the backup process works.

Master It Name the four basic components of a VSS solution that need to be in place for a complete solution to work. Provide an oversimplified explanation of how VSS works.

Solution VSS has the following four components:

- The VSS coordination service
- The VSS requester
- The VSS writer
- The VSS provider

VSS works in the following way:

1. Using the backup software (VSS requester), you orchestrate the start of the virtual machine backup.
2. The Hyper-V VSS writer freezes the virtual machine, making sure that it is in a consistent state.
3. The VSS provider creates a snapshot of the data.
4. The Hyper-V VSS writer is notified that the shadow copy is done and thaws the virtual machine for reuse.
5. The backup software (VSS requester) tells you that the shadow copy was successfully created.

Understand what the backup options are in a virtualized environment There are four backup types and two methods to actually carry out a backup within a virtualized environment. Each is useful and applicable in its own way.

Master It Name the four backup types, and list the two methods for carrying out a backup.

Solution The four backup types and two methods for carrying out a backup are as follows:

- Full backup
- Incremental backup
- Differential backup
- Selective backup
- Host-level backup
- Guest-level backup

Use Data Protection Manager to protect virtual workloads When planning for SCDPM 2010, it is important to understand what the system, software, security, network, and hardware requirements are.

Master It Name the five prerequisite software components that need to be installed prior to installing SCDPM 2010. Define the recommended hardware requirements for SCDPM 2010.

Solution SCDPM 2010 has the following software prerequisites:

- PowerShell 2.0
- .NET 3.5 Server Pack 1
- Windows Installer 4.5
- Windows Single Instance Store
- Optionally, to support ILR, the Hyper-V role

SCDPM 2010 has the following recommended hardware requirements:

- 2.33 GHz quad-core x64 processor.
- 8 GB of RAM.
- A minimum of 300 MB of free space on each protected volume.
- The volume where SCDPM 2010 is installed should contain 2–3 GB of free space.
- The disk space for the storage pool should be two to three times the size of the protected data.

Chapter 11: The Small and Medium Business

Deploy Small Business Server 2008 on Hyper-V Small Business Server (SBS) 2008 can be deployed as a virtual machine. This can increase flexibility and reduce hardware costs for many small businesses.

Master It You are working as a field engineer for a managed services company. A new client has decided that they want to hire your company to install Small Business Server 2008 Premium Edition. The additional server will run SQL Server Standard edition with a line-of-business application. They require a deployment that offers maximum flexibility with minimum installation and operational costs. Your company requires that the system be easy to manage. How will you design this installation?

Solution SBS 2008 Premium edition includes a copy of Windows Server Standard edition. You can install this as on a host server and enable the Hyper-V role. Windows Server Standard edition includes a free license of Windows Server Standard for a guest operating system. This will be installed in a virtual machine and will be used for the SQL Server and line-of-business application. SBS 2008 will be installed in a virtual machine on the Hyper-V host server.

Understand System Center Essentials 2010 System Center Essentials provides a management solution for medium-sized businesses to manage their physical and virtual IT infrastructure and applications.

Master It You are working with two medium-sized client companies. Company A requires an economic management solution that will monitor health and performance, will distribute software, and will manage a small number of Hyper-V host servers. Company B is a software development company. They require a Self-Service Portal to allow developers to quickly deploy test and development virtual machines. What solutions will you recommend for both companies?

Solution Company A can use System Center Essentials (SCE) 2010. SCE 2010 will provide all the management features that they require. Company B will have to use either the Workgroup or Enterprise edition of System Center Virtual Machine Manager 2008 R2, because they need the Self-Service Portal feature, which is not provided in SCE 2010.

Understand licensing for small and medium businesses There are a lot of licensing variations for small and medium businesses. You should choose the correct license for the specific scenario because it can provide extra functionality or reduce costs.

Master It Your company has decided to deploy System Center Essentials (SCE) 2010. You need to manage 40 physical and virtual servers as well as 250 computers. It has been decided that Data Protection Manager (DPM) 2010 should also be deployed to back up all the computers and the Hyper-V host servers. What SCE 2010 licenses will you purchase?

Solution Purchase a copy of System Center Essentials Plus 2010 Server. This will include the server licenses for SCE 2010 and DPM 2010. Forty SCE server management licenses and 250 SCE Plus client management licenses are required.

Chapter 12: Security

Place and secure your Hyper-V host servers You have a number of options in how you place Hyper-V host servers in your network. Each option will affect your ability to cluster the host servers, manage them, and provide access to services such as VDI and self-service provisioning.

Master It You work in an organization with mission-critical security requirements. The IT security team has demanded that you maximize the security of several applications and the entire infrastructure that they run on. Those virtual machines must be fault tolerant. The remaining applications servers can run at normal network security levels. How will you design the Hyper-V host servers?

Solution The mission-critical applications need to be place in an isolated infrastructure. A Windows domain will be built in a secured network. A Hyper-V host cluster can be built in this network and be members of this domain. All of the mission-critical virtual machines can be placed on this Hyper-V cluster.

The normal virtual machines can be placed on a Hyper-V cluster or nonclustered host servers in the production server network.

Use antivirus software on your Hyper-V host servers There is some debate about installing antivirus scanning software on Hyper-V host servers. It requires special configuration if you do install it.

Master It A security officer has demanded that the corporate security policy is fully applied to the parent partitions of your Hyper-V host servers. They are saying that these are insecure Windows servers and that all content on them, including the virtual machine files on the cluster shared volume, should be configured for real-time scanning and nightly scheduled scanning. You have been brought to a meeting to explain how antivirus can impact Hyper-V. What will you tell them about the potential problems and how the antivirus should be configured to prevent issues?

Solution You can start by discussing the security approaches you will take with the parent partitions. The Windows Firewall will be enabled and configured to lock down access. The parent partitions will be patched and kept up-to-date. Administrative access to the parent partition will be limited to a few people. This information is unlikely to change the mind of someone with such strong opinions about the need to install antivirus software, so you need to discuss how to configure the antivirus.

Antivirus that is configured to scan every possible file, folder, and volume on a Hyper-V host server will break Hyper-V functionality. Virtual machines may disappear (temporarily until the problem is rectified) or virtual machine configuration files may be corrupted.

Antivirus software should be configured not to scan any CSVs or any Hyper-V related files, folders, executables, or processes. The exact details are specified on the Microsoft support site.

Patch your Hyper-V host servers and VMM library content The Virtual Machine Servicing Tool 3.0 can be used to automatically patch clustered Hyper-V host servers and VMM library content.

Master It You are working as a virtualization consultant. A client has asked you to discuss potential solutions for patching their Hyper-V infrastructure. The primary requirement is to find a way to reliably and automatically patch their clustered Hyper-V host servers. The secondary requirement is to be able to provide virtual machine templates that are up-to-date with their security updates so that testers and developers have little wasted time and effort when they use the VMM Self-Service Portal.

Solution The Virtual Machine Servicing Tool (VMST) 3.0 is a free download that will meet the needs of the client. It will provide the ability to patch a Hyper-V host cluster on a scheduled basis. This will integrate with VMM to use maintenance mode and Live Migration to allow host patching with zero virtual machine downtime.

The VMST can also be used to patch offline virtual hard disks and virtual machine templates. This can be scheduled to run every night, applying any updates that are automatically downloaded from Microsoft to Configuration Manager 2007 or WSUS.

Chapter 13: Business Continuity

Understand what business continuity is and identify the needs of the business Hyper-V can be used to facilitate a disaster recovery site to meet the business continuity requirements of an organization.

Master It You are a senior IT infrastructure engineer in a large organization. You are in the early stages of writing a proposal to implement a hardware virtualization solution based on Windows Server 2008 R2 Hyper-V. Recent news stories about disasters and recent failed disaster recovery site tests have caused the directors to issue an order that the business continuity plans of the organization be revisited. You have been asked to attend a workshop where senior IT staff members will discuss the issue and propose a plan of action. What will you suggest, and why?

Solution Disaster recovery invocation with physical servers is subject to a number of technological and manual risks. Many replication and clustering systems must be maintained, and a lot of them require manual intervention. Unfortunately, technology can fail, and operator errors happen.

Hyper-V will make it possible to replicate all systems that are running as virtual machines to the disaster recovery site with a single replication mechanism, no matter what the contained applications are, assuming that there is Hyper-V clustering support. Failover of the virtual machines will be automated. It might even be possible to use Windows Failover Clustering and Live Migration if the WAN links and remote site meet the requirements.

Using virtualization will simplify the replication mechanisms, increase reliability, and reduce the operating costs, physical installation, and carbon footprint of the IT infrastructure in the disaster recovery site.

Describe some of the many business continuity and disaster recovery solutions that are available There are many hardware-based and software-based solutions for replicating Hyper-V virtual machines from a primary site to a secondary site.

Master It You are working as a consultant. Your client is a medium-sized organization. They have a number of remote branch offices. Each branch office has a pair of nonclustered Hyper-V host servers with a number of virtual machines. Your client desires some level of fault tolerance for the remote branch offices that will replicate data to the head office. Each branch office has a small WAN link, and the client is concerned with data replication affecting operations during business hours. What options will you recommend?

Solution The branch-office Hyper-V infrastructure is already in place, and the branch offices are in remote locations with high-latency networks. They also want to schedule data replication to happen outside of core business hours. This rules out any hardware-based replication mechanism.

A Data Protection Manager 2010 solution might be appropriate. A single DPM server could be placed in each site. DPM2DPM4DR or DPM replication could be configured to replicate data to a centralized DPM server in the head office.

Alternatively, a software-based replication solution such as file replication or simulated shared storage could be used to replicate the virtual machine files to redundant Hyper-V host servers in the head office.

A simulated shared storage solution will probably require Windows Failover Clustering to be an option. This requires Hyper-V Server 2008 R2 or the Enterprise/Datacenter editions of Windows Server 2008 R2 to be deployed in all participating Hyper-V host servers.

Choose between the various types of business continuity solutions You need to ask a number of questions about the infrastructure and business requirements to determine the ideal business continuity IT architecture for your organization.

Master It You need to find a solution for your organization's business continuity requirements based on Hyper-V. The organization's Hyper-V infrastructure uses a high-end Fibre Channel SAN with many advanced features. A number of local vendors have been invited to consult with you. A few minutes of downtime can be tolerated by your organization during the invocation of the disaster recovery site. Ideally, there will be near zero downtime. What will you ask the vendors about?

Solution Your infrastructure will require a multi-site cluster with Live Migration support. You need to find out what the network and licensing requirements are for replicating LUNs from your primary site to another SAN in a secondary site. The SAN must have support for a multi-site Hyper-V cluster and have integration with Windows Server 2008 R2 Failover Clustering. Finally, you should ensure that the vendor is qualified to provide skills to implement a multi-site Hyper-V cluster with your SAN, has a support relationship with the SAN manufacturer, and has valid experience in doing this with previous clients.

Appendix B

New and Upcoming Products for Hyper-V

The ideal way to write a book like this would be to take a Volume Shadow Copy Service (VSS) snapshot of Microsoft. This would allow us to write about all of the Hyper-V technologies, including System Center and the accelerators. Unfortunately, we cannot do that, and Microsoft's developers never stop. A number of technologies were acquired, released, and announced during the development of this book. We tried to keep up, but the products kept coming. This appendix will introduce you to some new products and inform you of some technologies that are on the way.

System Center Opalis

Opalis is a technology that Microsoft acquired and added to the System Center family. It is a workflow product that shares data and initiates actions between System Center Operations Manager, System Center Configuration Manager, System Center Service Manager, System Center Virtual Machine Manager, Active Directory, and a number of third-party products. It is intended to automate tasks that would normally be done by a human. This will reduce response times and mistakes.

You can learn more about System Center Opalis here:

```
http://technet.microsoft.com/systemcenter/ff426909.aspx
```

Microsoft Assessment and Planning (MAP) Toolkit 5.0

MAP was introduced in Chapter 4 of this book. MAP 5.0 was released near the end of the development of this book. The big change that is relevant to a Hyper-V deployment project is that it supports the discovery and assessment of Linux computers.

You can learn more about MAP 5.0 and download it here:

```
http://technet.microsoft.com/solutionaccelerators/dd537566.aspx
```

System Center Virtual Machine Manager Self-Service Portal (SCVMM SSP) 2.0

Do Microsoft developers get paid by the letter? SCVMM SSP 2.0 was previously known as the Dynamic Datacenter Toolkit. It was renamed and made available as a release candidate (preproduction) when work on this book completed.

This product extends beyond the native capabilities of the Virtual Machine Manager (VMM) 2008 R2 Self-Service Portal. SCVMM SSP features its own service and database to make use of VMM 2008 R2 for automation. Different business units can be configured with access to VMM library templates and resources (including network, storage, and VMM host groups). Business units can provision their own virtual machines from the VMM library. Automation scripts can be made part of the virtual machine deployment to provision storage and networking resources. This product also allows available and used resources to be charged back to the business unit.

It is the major component in Microsoft's private cloud for Hyper-V solution. You can find the home page for SCVMM SSP 2.0 here:

```
http://www.microsoft.com/virtualization/en/us/private-cloud.aspx
```

System Center Virtual Machine Manager (VMM) v.Next

Microsoft started to announce some details of the System Center products that will probably be launched during 2011. The next version of VMM will see some major changes, some of which have been publicly demonstrated.

This includes the ability to define a model. A model will include a number of virtual machines created from different templates that serve different roles in an application architecture. For example, there might be a number of web servers, application servers, and database servers. A certain amount of elasticity can be defined for each role in the model. That means you can automatically increase or decrease the number of virtual machines used for each part of the model depending on demand. A new application infrastructure can be rapidly created by deploying a model. This will deploy each of the virtual machines defined in the model.

A new concept of service virtualization is planned. This App-V for Servers allows services such as SQL Server to run in a bubble that is isolated from the virtual machine guest operating system that executes it.

A new patching solution for virtual machine guest operating systems has also been demonstrated. This takes advantage of App-V for Servers. Patches can be applied to a virtual machine template in the VMM library. Any deployed virtual machine can be updated by redeploying the virtual machine from the original template. The running application service stays executing in the App-V for Servers bubble. VMM will swap the running virtual machine out for the new one with all the current patches. This could lead to a zero-downtime virtual machine solution.

You should keep an eye on the System Center Virtual Machine Manager website for more information:

```
http://www.microsoft.com/systemcenter/en/us/virtual-machine-manager.aspx
```

Windows Azure Appliance

Microsoft has been pushing the concept of The Cloud for some time. This includes the public cloud, which includes the Azure services. Azure is a Platform-as-a-Service (PaaS) solution that is available on a subscription basis. It allows application developers to build an online application on a Microsoft-hosted infrastructure that can be replicated between their geographically distributed data centers.

Some organizations will not be able to or will choose not to use Microsoft's Azure public cloud services. Microsoft announced in July 2010 that it's going to release a new Azure appliance. This will allow customers to deploy Azure's PaaS in a private cloud. This solution could end up being released within corporations for internal bespoke application deployment and with partner hosting companies for locally located and regulatory compliant public cloud hosting solutions.

The home page for Azure appliance is here:

```
http://www.microsoft.com/windowsazure/appliance/
```

Azure Virtual Machine Hosting

Microsoft has talked about the ability to run full virtual machines on its Azure public cloud infrastructure. One possibility it has discussed is that a future version of VMM (possibly VMM v.Next) would be able to migrate a Hyper-V virtual machine from a private cloud into Microsoft Azure. No further details have been announced since Microsoft executive Bob Muglia discussed it at the PDC conference at the end of 2009.

This is mentioned in a press release by Microsoft that you can find here:

```
http://www.microsoft.com/presspass/press/2009/nov09/11-17pdc1pr.mspx
```

Index

Note to the Reader: Throughout this index **boldfaced** page numbers indicate primary discussions of a topic. *Italicized* page numbers indicate illustrations.

B

C

D

N

Q

T

U

V

W

X

Z